MALISE RUTHVEN

Islam in the World

SECOND EDITION

OXFORD
UNIVERSITY PRESS

OXFORD
UNIVERSITY PRESS

Oxford   New York
Athens   Auckland   Bangkok   Bogotá   Buenos Aires   Calcutta
Cape Town   Chennai   Dar es Salaam   Delhi   Florence   Hong Kong   Istanbul
Karachi   Kuala Lumpur   Madrid   Melbourne   Mexico City   Mumbai
Nairobi   Paris   São Paulo   Shanghai   Singapore   Taipei   Tokyo   Toronto   Warsaw

and associated companies in
Berlin   Ibadan

Copyright © 1984, 2000 by Malise Ruthven

Published by Oxford University Press, Inc.
198 Madison Avenue, New York, New York 10016

First published in the United States in 1984 by Oxford University Press
First issued as an Oxford University Press paperback 1984

Oxford is a registered trademark of Oxford University Press

Library of Congress Cataloging-in-Publication Data
Ruthven, Malise.
    Islam in the world / by Malise Ruthven.—2nd ed.
      p. cm.
    Included bibliographic references and index.
    ISBN 0-19-513841-4
      1. Islam. I. Title

BP161.2 .R87 2000
297—dc21

99-056010

9 8 7 6 5 4 3 2 1
Printed in the United States of America

ISLAM IN THE WORLD

'I found it fascinating ... To have made a thorough examination of intricate and problematic issues and yet to remain completely mindful of the need for understanding of the average lay reader is no mean peformance. I hope, and in fact am confident, that it will satisfy a great need for those among Western English readers who want to understand Islam' Fazlur Rahman, University of Chicago

'An exceptionally insightful and thought-provoking introduction to Islam, explaining its basic religious beliefs, practices and institutions as well as discussing its impact on Muslim life today' John L. Esposito, editor of the *Oxford Encyclopedia of the Modern Islamic World*

'The best and most sophisticated introduction to Islam as a religion and as a culture that is available in succinct form at the moment. Sympathetic, knowledgeable, and critical. Very well balanced' Nur Yalman, Harvard University

'To our knowledge, no book about Islam of a similar quality has appeared in many years, whether written by a Muslim or a non-Muslim' Muhammad Asad, Qur'an translator and author of *The Road to Mecca*

'His exposition of the "Quranic world-view" is the most convincing, and the most appealing, that I have read, and his observations about the development and effects of Islamic law are original and thought-provoking' Edward Mortimer, *The Times*

'An excellent book ... a first class synthesis of the many-sided story of Islam in history, from its origin to the present day ... This is a book which will make many previously mysterious subjects a good deal clearer to the general reader who seeks to come to terms with Islam in the modern world' R. C. Ostle, *Journal of Theological Studies*

Malise Ruthven was born in Dublin. On his father's side he is descended from a family of Scottish soldiers, on his mother's from a line of Irish Protestant clerics and scholars. After leaving school Malise Ruthven spent a year doing relief work in Jordan, where he began learning Arabic and spent several weeks travelling among the Huweitat beduin. He read English literature at Cambridge before returning to the Middle East to study Arabic. After several years as a staff writer and editor with the BBC's External Services in London he became a freelance journalist and writer with a special interest in religion and politics. Prior to its closure in 1999 he was a lecturer at the Centre for the Study of Religions at the University of Aberdeen. He has also taught at the department of religion at Dartmouth Collge, USA and at the University of California, San Diego. His other books include *Torture, The Grand Conspiracy* (1978), *Traveller Through Time: A Photographic Journey with Freya Stark* (1985), *The Divine Supermarket: Shopping for God in America* (1989), *A Satanic Affair: Salman Rushdie and the Wrath of Islam* (1990) and *Islam: A Very Short Introduction* (1997). When not travelling or teaching abroad he lives in London with his wife, the photographer Ianthe Ruthven.

To Tiggy with love

Contents

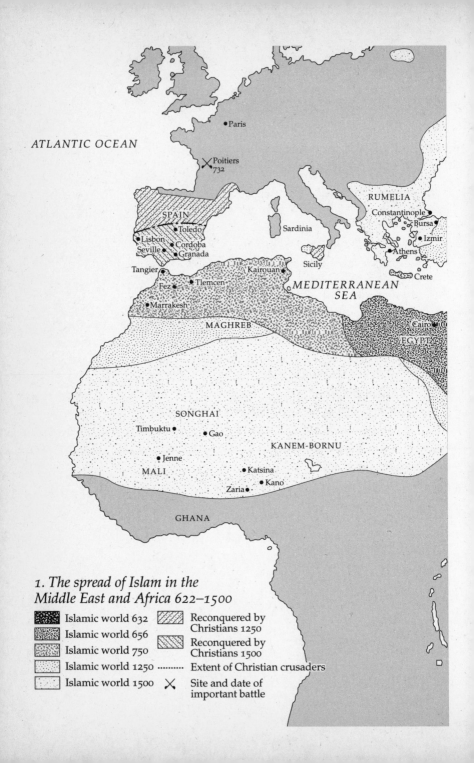

ATLANTIC OCEAN

• Paris

✕ Poitiers
732

SPAIN
• Toledo
Lisbon•
Seville• •Cordoba
•Granada

Tangier• •
Fez• •Tlemcen
•Marrakesh

Kairouan•

MAGHREB

Sardinia

Sicily

MEDITERRANEAN
SEA

RUMELIA
Constantinople•
• Bursa•
• Izmir
Athens•
Crete•

Cairo•
EGYPT

SONGHAI
Timbuktu• • Gao

KANEM-BORNU

•Jenne
MALI

• Katsina
•Kano
Zaria•

GHANA

1. The spread of Islam in the Middle East and Africa 622–1500

Islamic world 632
Islamic world 656
Islamic world 750
Islamic world 1250
Islamic world 1500

Reconquered by Christians 1250
Reconquered by Christians 1500
·········· Extent of Christian crusaders
✕ Site and date of important battle

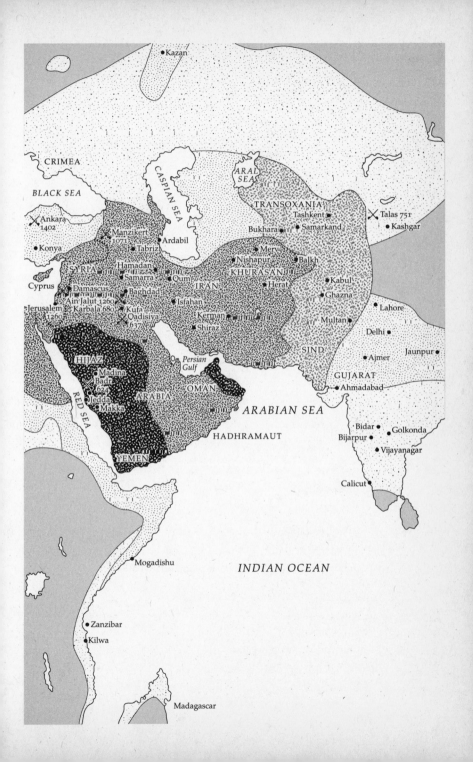

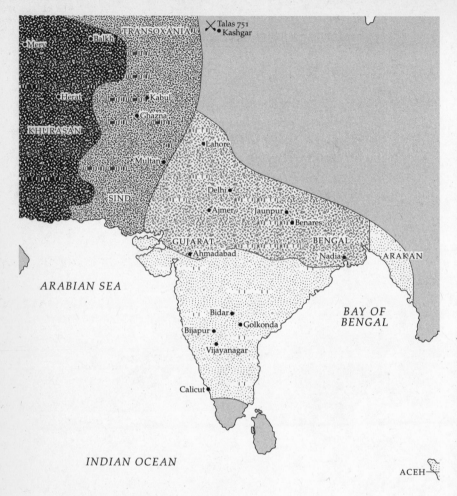

TRANSOXANIA

Merv ○   ○ Balkh   ✕ Talas 751
                           • Kashgar

KHURASAN
Herat ○   ○ Kabul
              • Ghazna

                    • Lahore

Multan •

SIND
                Delhi •

              • Ajmer   Jaunpur •
                                  • Benares

         GUJARAT   BENGAL
         • Ahmadabad   Nadia •   ARAKAN

ARABIAN SEA

                                    BAY OF
              Bidar •   BENGAL
                   • Golkonda
      Bijapur •
         • Vijayanagar

   Calicut •

INDIAN OCEAN   ACEH

2. The spread of Islam in India and the Far East to 1800

Islamic world 656   ✕ Date and site of important battle
Islamic world 750
Islamic world 1250
Islamic world 1500
Islamic world 1800
Muslim concentration in China

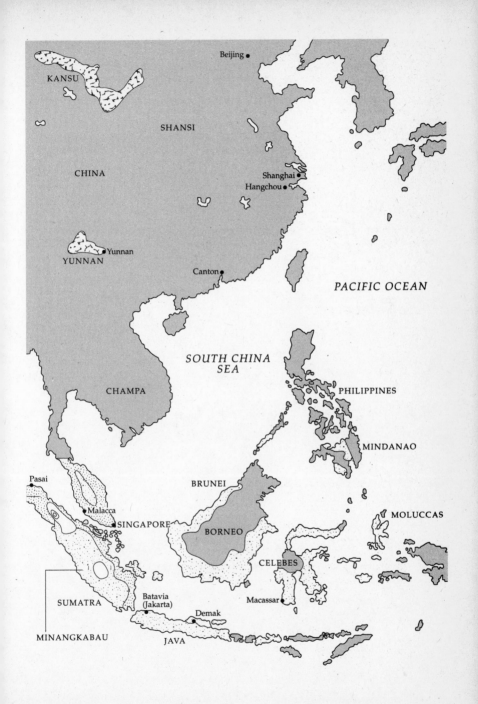

KANSU

Beijing ●

SHANSI

CHINA

YUNNAN
YUNNAN ● Yunnan

Canton ●

Shanghai ●
Hangchou ●

PACIFIC OCEAN

SOUTH CHINA
SEA

CHAMPA

PHILIPPINES

MINDANAO

Pasai ●

Malacca ●
● SINGAPORE

BRUNEI

MOLUCCAS

BORNEO

CELEBES

SUMATRA

MINANGKABAU

Batavia
(Jakarta) ●

Demak ●

JAVA

Macassar ●

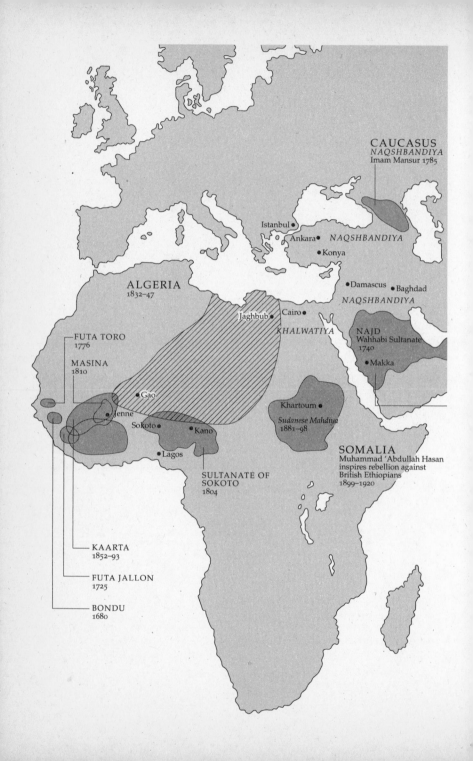

CAUCASUS
NAQSHBANDIYA
Imam Mansur 1785

NAQSHBANDIYA

Istanbul •
Ankara •
Konya •

Damascus • Baghdad •
NAQSHBANDIYA

ALGERIA
1832–47

Jaghbub • Cairo •
KHALWATIYA

NAJD
Wahhabi Sultanate
1740
Makka •

FUTA TORO
1776

MASINA
1810

Gao •

Jenne •

Sokoto •

Kano •

Khartoum •
Sudanese Mahdiya
1881–98

SOMALIA
Muhammad 'Abdullah Hasan
inspires rebellion against
British Ethiopians
1899–1920

Lagos •

SULTANATE OF
SOKOTO
1804

KAARTA
1852–93

FUTA JALLON
1725

BONDU
1680

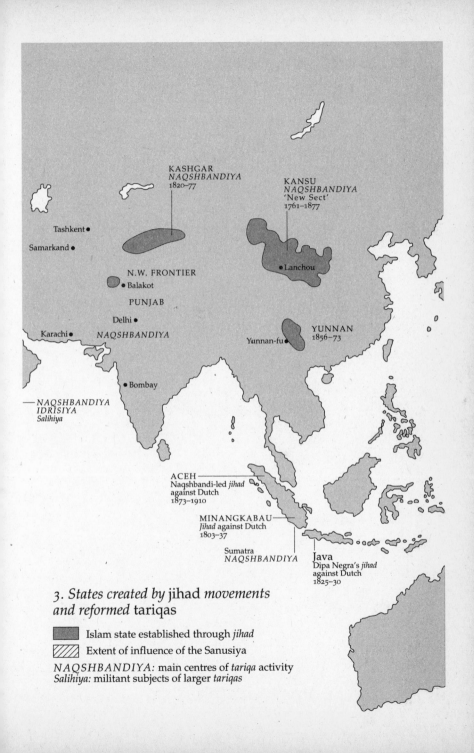

KASHGAR
NAQSHBANDIYA
1820–77

KANSU
NAQSHBANDIYA
'New Sect'
1761–1877

Tashkent •

Samarkand •

• Lanchou

N.W. FRONTIER
• Balakot

PUNJAB

Delhi •

Karachi •   *NAQSHBANDIYA*

YUNNAN
1856–73

Yunnan-fu •

• Bombay

— *NAQSHBANDIYA*
IDRĪSIYA
Salīhiya

ACEH
Naqshbandi-led *jihad*
against Dutch
1873–1910

MINANGKABAU
Jihad against Dutch
1803–37

Sumatra
NAQSHBANDIYA

Java
Dipa Negra's *jihad*
against Dutch
1825–30

3. States created by jihad *movements
and reformed* tariqas

■ Islam state established through *jihad*

▨ Extent of influence of the Sanusiya

NAQSHBANDIYA: main centres of *tariqa* activity
Salihiya: militant subjects of larger *tariqas*

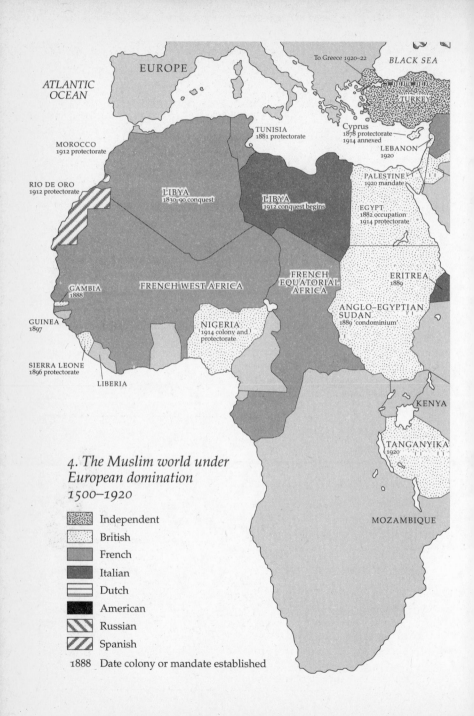

ATLANTIC
OCEAN

EUROPE

To Greece 1920–22   BLACK SEA

TURKEY

TUNISIA
1881 protectorate

Cyprus
1878 protectorate
1914 annexed

MOROCCO
1912 protectorate

LEBANON
1920

RIO DE ORO
1912 protectorate

PALESTINE
1920 mandate

LIBYA
1830–90 conquest

LIBYA
1912 conquest begins

EGYPT
1882 occupation
1914 protectorate

ERITREA
1889

FRENCH
EQUATORIAL
AFRICA

GAMBIA
1888

FRENCH WEST AFRICA

ANGLO-EGYPTIAN
SUDAN
1889 'condominium'

GUINEA
1897

NIGERIA
1914 colony and
protectorate

SIERRA LEONE
1896 protectorate

LIBERIA

KENYA

TANGANYIKA
1920

4. The Muslim world under
European domination
1500–1920

MOZAMBIQUE

Independent

British

French

Italian

Dutch

American

Russian

Spanish

1888   Date colony or mandate established

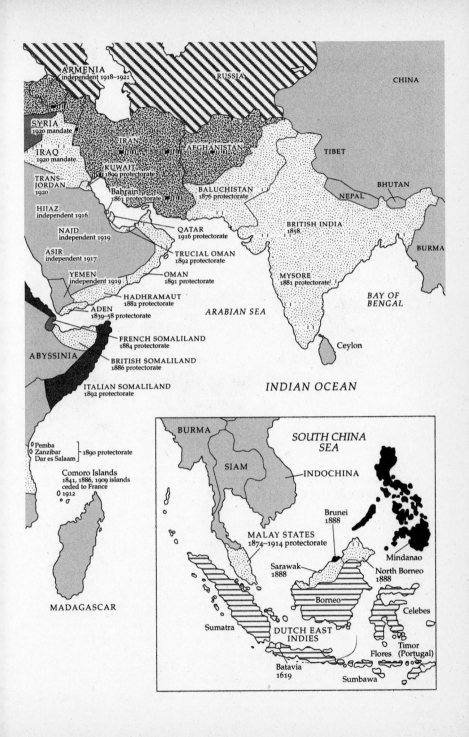

ARMENIA
independent 1918-1921

RUSSIA

CHINA

SYRIA
1920 mandate

IRAN

AFGHANISTAN

IRAQ
1920 mandate

TIBET

KUWAIT
1899 protectorate

BALUCHISTAN
1876 protectorate

BHUTAN

TRANS-
JORDAN
1920

Bahrain
1861 protectorate

NEPAL

HIJAZ
independent 1916

QATAR
1916 protectorate

BRITISH INDIA
1858

BURMA

NAJD
independent 1919

TRUCIAL OMAN
1892 protectorate

ASIR
independent 1917

OMAN
1891 protectorate

MYSORE
1881 protectorate!

BAY OF
BENGAL

YEMEN
independent 1919

HADHRAMAUT
1882 protectorate

ARABIAN SEA

ADEN
1839-58 protectorate

FRENCH SOMALILAND
1884 protectorate

Ceylon

ABYSSINIA

BRITISH SOMALILAND
1886 protectorate

INDIAN OCEAN

ITALIAN SOMALILAND
1892 protectorate

Pemba
Zanzibar   1890 protectorate
Dar es Salaam

Comoro Islands
1841, 1886, 1909 islands
ceded to France
1912

MADAGASCAR

BURMA

SIAM

SOUTH CHINA
SEA

INDOCHINA

Brunei
1888

MALAY STATES
1874-1914 protectorate

Mindanao

Sarawak
1888

North Borneo
1888

Borneo

Celebes

Sumatra

DUTCH EAST
INDIES

Timor
(Portugal)

Flores

Batavia
1619

Sumbawa

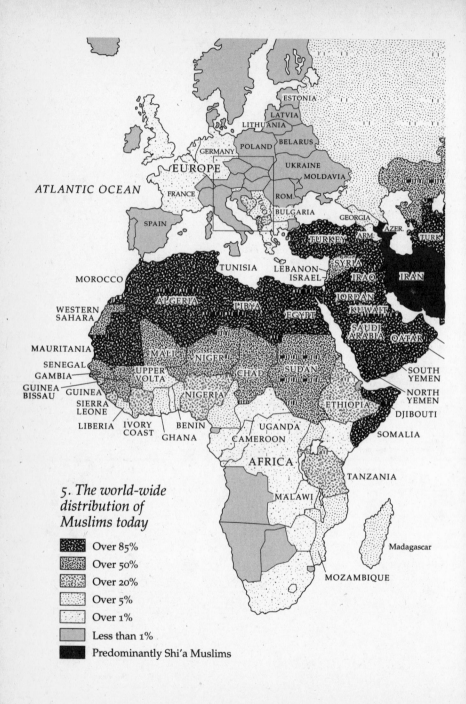

ESTONIA
LATVIA
LITHUANIA
BELARUS
GERMANY
POLAND
UKRAINE
EUROPE
MOLDOVA
ATLANTIC OCEAN
FRANCE
ROM.
BULGARIA
YUGO.
GEORGIA
SPAIN
AZER.
TURK.
ARM.
TURKEY
TUNISIA
LEBANON
SYRIA
MOROCCO
ISRAEL
IRAQ
IRAN
ALGERIA
LIBYA
EGYPT
JORDAN
WESTERN
KUWAIT
SAHARA
SAUDI
ARABIA
QATAR
MAURITANIA
MALI
NIGER
SENEGAL
CHAD
SUDAN
SOUTH
GAMBIA
UPPER
YEMEN
GUINEA
VOLTA
NORTH
BISSAU
GUINEA
NIGERIA
YEMEN
SIERRA
ETHIOPIA
DJIBOUTI
LEONE
BENIN
LIBERIA
IVORY
GHANA
UGANDA
SOMALIA
COAST
CAMEROON
AFRICA
TANZANIA
MALAWI
Madagascar
MOZAMBIQUE

5. The world-wide distribution of Muslims today

Over 85%
Over 50%
Over 20%
Over 5%
Over 1%
Less than 1%
Predominantly Shi'a Muslims

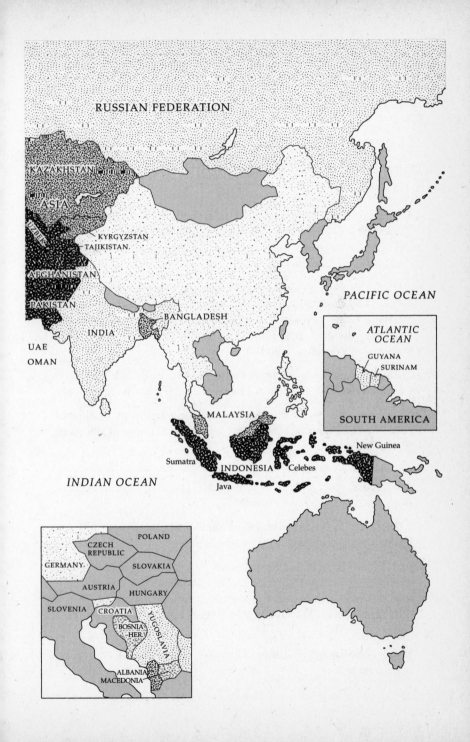

List of Illustrations

Every effort has been made to contact all copyright holders. The publishers will be glad to make good in future editions any errors or omissions brought to their attention. (Photographic acknowledgements are given in brackets.)

1. *Yūsuf Fleeing from Zulaykhā*, illumination from the manuscript of Būstān of Saʿdī, completed by the calligrapher Sultan Muhammad Nur, Bukhara, Uzbek dynasty, *c*.1535. (The Metropolitan Museum of Art, Purchase, Louis V Bell Fund and Astor Foundation Gift, 1974. [1974.294.4] All rights reserved)

2. Double page from a Quran written in Makka or Madina, eighth century or later (© The British Library, London [Or.2165 ff.67v–68])

3. Opening chapter of the Quran and opening passage of *Surat al-Baqara*, in Nashki script, presumably Egypt, *c*.1510 (Private Collection/ET Archive)

4. *Interior of the Mosque of Sultan Hasan, Cairo*, lithograph from 'Egypt and Nubia', vol. 3, by David Roberts (The Stapleton Collection/Bridgeman Art Library, London)

5. *The First Ships Sailing through the Suez Canal*, watercolour, 1869, by Edouard Riou (Compagnie Financière de Suez et de l'Union Parisienne)

6. *A Princely Youth and a Dervish beneath a Tree*, drawing from an album made on behalf of the Sultan of the Poor, Rahemā, by Reza-ye ʿAbbāsī, Iran, Isfahan, Safavid period, second quarter of seventeenth century. (The Metropolitan Museum of Art, Rogers Fund, 1911 [11,84.13]. All rights reserved)

7. Dervishes dancing during Ramadan, Cairo, Egypt (© Abbas/Magnum Photos)

Preface to the Second Edition

Since this book first appeared in 1984, there has been a swelling tide of English books about Islam, many of very high quality. As a student of religion who has also lectured on the subject at universities in Britain and the United States, I have become increasingly aware of my book's shortcomings in trying to address a vastly complex and variegated subject in a relatively short amount of space. The academic in me knows that almost any statement one makes about a topic is open to challenge. At the same time the journalist knows that the reader wants a story with clearly demarcated themes.

When first I wrote this book I tried to find the balance between scholarly fastidiousness and journalistic accessibility. My project was doubtless over-ambitious. The subject area it attempts to cover embraces the beliefs, cultural practices, legal traditions and politics of approximately one thousand million people, about a fifth of humanity. Nevertheless the warm response that greeted the first edition indicated that I had found a small but significant niche. *Islam in the World* partially filled the need for a general book that was introductory in the sense that it did not require a prior knowledge of the subject, without being elementary or simplistic. Lamentably, in a Western world that is home to millions of Muslims, to be without even a basic knowledge of Islam is not yet deemed to imply a lack of sophistication.

In preparing this new edition I have updated sections dealing with current events, and added a section on developments up to 1999. I have also made significant changes to Chapter 4 in the light of recent scholarly research. At the same time I have not attempted to revise everything in the light of the hopefully more refined and detailed knowledge I have acquired in the intervening years. What probably makes this book different from others, whether written by scholars, critics or apologists, is its genesis as an 'outsider's' or non-specialist's encounter with a world that is elemental yet rich in its diversity, strange in its 'otherness' yet familiar in the way in which it draws on so many themes and symbols common to the Abrahamic Tradition. To blunt the sharp edges of the original vision with hypersensitive scholarly nuance would seriously damage its thrust.

In producing this edition I have been guided by the scholarly advice of Professor Gudrun Krämer who subjected the revised manuscript to a critical reading as exhaustive and detailed as that to which my previous expert reader, the late Albert Hourani, subjected the original version. I am extremely grateful to her for the meticulousness with which she performed this task and for her comments, both positive and critical. While some of these comments – particularly on Chapter 4 – sent me back to my books, I did not always agree with them. But in at least one instance they stimulated me to refresh my arguments with materials that would not otherwise have featured in the book. Given that I did not always act on her suggestions, she cannot in any way be held responsible for remaining errors of detail or fact or for my interpretative idiosyncrasies.

I would also like to register my thanks for the support I received from my friend and colleague Professor James Trower at the University of Aberdeen; to James Piscatori who made useful suggestions for improvements in the first edition and to Louise Hosking who assisted with the original research. Others who read parts of the original manuscript, who helped develop my ideas in the course of interviews or discussion or otherwise contributed to the original version of the book include the late Muhammad Asad, Zaki Badawi, James Buchan, Mick Csàky, Omar al-Farouq, 'Abdul Wahid Hamid, Russell Harris, Derek Hopwood, Sayyid Sadiq al-Mahdi, the late Peter Mansfield, Edward Mortimer, Fathi Osman, Terry Povey, Elizabeth Rodenbeck, John Rodenbeck, David Rosser-Owen, Muhammad Salahuddin and Michael Yorke. I wish to thank them all, but would emphasize that none is responsible in any way for matters of fact or interpretation. Finally I would like to thank Caroline Pretty of Penguin for her patience in waiting for these revisions and Pen Campbell for his meticulous copy-editing of the text.

Source material for the maps was drawn from Francis Robinson's *Atlas of the Islamic World since 1500* (Phaidon Press, Oxford, 1982).

London
August 1999

1 Introductory: Pilgrimage to Makka

And proclaim unto all people the [duty of] pilgrimage: they will come unto thee on foot and on every [kind of] fast mount, coming from every far-away point [on earth] so that they might experience much that shall be of benefit to them and that they might extol the name of God on the days appointed [for sacrifice] over whatever heads of cattle He may have provided for them.   Quran 22:27–8

The duty of pilgrimage

Every year during the season of pilgrimage or 'Hajj', about two million people converge on the holy places of Makka, Mina, Muzdalifa and 'Arafat to participate in rites whose origins have been lost in the mists of antiquity. About one million of them come from overseas – 50 per cent from the Arab world, 35 per cent from Asia, 10 per cent from sub-Saharan Africa and 5 per cent from Europe and the Americas. The rest are from Saudi Arabia, most of them foreign workers.

Pilgrimage is one of the five *rukns* or 'pillars' of Islam, a religious obligation which every Muslim must observe at least once in a lifetime if he or she is able. According to most religious scholars, substitutes may be sent by those who for reasons other than poverty cannot make the journey. The very poor are exempted altogether. In the past the hazards of travelling restricted observance to a very small number. The trip to the holy sites took many months and sometimes lasted years: it was not unknown for a man to spend the better part of a lifetime on it, setting out as a youth from one of the distant fringes of the Muslim world and arriving back half a century later, having worked his passage as an itinerant craftsman or labourer. Returning pilgrims have long borne the honoured title Hajji, and were accorded the reverence normally given to religious dignitaries. The coming of cheap air travel, however, which has produced a fifty-fold increase in Hajj attendance since the 1950s, has inevitably devalued the prestige of this title.

The hazardous journey exacted a high cost in human misery. Ibn Jubair, who made the pilgrimage early in the thirteenth century CE, noted the skeletons of those who had died of thirst in the desert. Later, well-organized 'caravan cities' were established, leaving Cairo or Damascus under the command of a specially chosen Amir, a practice originally instituted by the 'Abbasid caliphs. The officials charged with the pilgrims' safety included judges empowered to punish violations of the Shari'a law and to advise pilgrims on their religious duties, medical officials, including doctors, surgeons and oculists, and a public trustee to deal with all the legal problems arising out of a pilgrim's death. Practically speaking, the most important officials were probably the lawyers who scrutinized the contracts made between the Amir and the beduin from whom he hired his camels, and the numerous functionaries in charge of food, water and fodder. Despite these precautions, however, the pilgrims often suffered appalling casualties. Those who survived the extremes of heat and cold, hunger and thirst or attacks by beduin marauders often succumbed to the plague. An Austrian sold into slavery early in the seventeenth century, who accompanied his master from Cairo, recorded that by the time the Egyptian caravan had reached half-way across Sinai, 1,500 men and 900 camels were already dead. In 1824 about one fifth of the 20,000-strong Syrian caravan died from heat or thirst; two years later 12,000 are said to have died from the searing blasts of the hot *khamsin* wind. When the Hajj, which like all Muslim festivals follows the lunar calendar, fell in winter, cold was also a serious hazard. In 1846 500 pilgrims, 1,200 horses and 900 camels died on the return journey from Madina to Damascus.

Cholera also took a fierce toll of pilgrims, especially after steamship navigation had led to a huge increase in numbers from places like India where the disease is endemic. Between 1831 and 1912 some 27 epidemics are thought to have started in Makka, whose insalubrious valley has been described as a 'breathless pit enclosed by a wall of rock'. The dangers of disease were eventually reduced by the adoption of drastic quarantine procedures and fumigation – measures which considerably added to the ordeal of the Hajj. According to a Moroccan who made the journey in 1897, sea-borne pilgrims were made to wait for up to three weeks in the Gulf of Suez with the bare minimum of food and water, for which they were grossly overcharged, before the authorities would let the ships enter the Canal. They were then disembarked and had to wait out the rest of the quarantine period in conditions scarcely better than those of a prison camp. As recently as 1927 Muhammad Asad, a Jewish convert to Islam, described the appalling overcrowding of pilgrim ships as greedy ship-owners sought to make the most of the short but profitable season:

There were only pilgrims on board, so many that the ship could hardly contain them. The shipping company . . . had literally filled it to the brim without caring for the comfort of the passengers. On the decks, in the cabins, in all passageways, on every staircase, in the dining rooms of the first and second class, in the holds which had been emptied for the purpose and equipped with temporary ladders, in every available space and corner human beings were painfully herded together . . . In great humility, with only the goal of the voyage before their eyes, they bore all that unnecessary hardship.[1]

Although the number of pilgrims has always fluctuated with the vagaries of war and other international factors, the age of the charter jet has seen a dramatic increase in numbers. Half a century ago about 30,000 people made the pilgrimage each year – a proportion of roughly one Muslim in 10,000, given an estimated population of 330 million. With the present Muslim population estimated at more than 1,000 million (about one fifth of the human race), the proportion of Hajj attenders has risen to almost two in 1,000 – a symptom not only of improved transport opportunities, but of a general increase in Islamic observance.

In response to this increasing demand, and to reinforce the legitimacy of the Saudi ruling family as guardians of Islam's holy places, the Saudi government invested some $5 billion in developing the new King Abdul Aziz International Airport near Jedda, which occupies an area of some 100 square kilometres (35 square miles) – larger than the international airports of New York, Chicago and Paris. The airport's most spectacular feature is the new Hajj terminal, two vast tented halls making up the world's largest fabric structure enclosing its largest covered space. The tent clusters forming the ceiling, which are suspended from cables and steel pylons high above floor level, resemble the great tented city of 'Arafat where the pilgrims forgather at the high-point of the Hajj ceremonies. The fabric itself, a spin-off from space research, is made from an insulated fibre which reflects back most of the sun's heat and retains enough of its light to make artificial illumination unnecessary during daytime. With a full jumbo jet landing every five minutes, the terminal can 'process' about 5,000 pilgrims each hour, or just under one million during the season. As impressive an example of contemporary design as can be found anywhere in the world, it is an apt symbol of the Saudi rulers' ambition to boost their legitimacy as guardians of the Islamic holy places with the latest technology.

However, neither Saudi money nor the know-how they can afford to buy with it has yet been able to solve the problem of moving such large numbers of human beings within the time-limits specified in the Hajj rituals. With its complicated ceremonies lasting almost a week, in conditions that are often far from comfortable, the Hajj still has the aspect of an ordeal undertaken in the spirit of faith. It has yet to become, like so many Christian festivals or pilgrimages, a mere adjunct to tourism. Indeed, in contrast with that of many European cults, the commercial importance of the Hajj has declined with the advent of air transport and stricter passport controls. Though Makkan rentiers and hoteliers still depend on the Hajj for their livelihood and are often accused of charging exorbitant prices for private accommodation, the Saudi government spends more on servicing the Hajj than it receives back in revenues.

The Hajj and Saudi Arabia

In the history of Islamic ruling dynasties the Saudis are comparative parvenus, descendants of an eighteenth-century desert *shaikh* who formed a military alliance with the Hanbali reformer, Muhammad ibn 'Abd al-Wahhab. Like other reformers throughout Islamic history, 'Abd al-Wahhab sought a return to the 'purity' of the original Islam of the Prophet and his companions. Employing the military power of the Saudis and their tribal allies, he created a state which, following the precedent established by the Prophet of Islam, aimed to reunite the whole Arabian Peninsula. Although this aim was frustrated by the Ottoman governor Muhammad 'Ali, who occupied the Hejaz, opening the way to the replacement of the Saudis by the pro-Turkish Rashids, Saudi fortunes revived under the remarkable leadership of 'Abd al-'Aziz ibn 'Abd al-Rahman al Sa'ud (better known to the world as Ibn Saud). Starting out from Kuwait in 1902 with a band of about 40 followers, he regained the stronghold of Riyadh from the Rashids and proceeded, by war and diplomacy, to recover all the former Saudi dominions and much else besides. By 1913 he controlled the Gulf coast from Kuwait to Qatar, having eliminated the Turks from Hasa, now the Eastern Province, where, in the 1930s, the world's largest oil deposits were discovered. In 1924 his eldest son, Faisal, added Asir on the Yemeni border to the Saudi dominions. By 1926 Ibn Saud had realized his final ambition, the conquest of the Hejaz. The way had unwittingly been smoothed for him by the British, who had helped the local ruler, the Sharif Husain, to remove the Turks.

In creating his dynastic state Ibn Saud had followed the time-honoured pattern, exemplified by his own ancestors, of combining military force with religious enthusiasm. The storm-troopers on whom he relied for his victories, known simply as the Ikhwan ('Brothers'), were former beduin from the Mutair, 'Utaiba and other tribes who had been settled into *hijras* or military cantonments, where, when not actually fighting, the Ikhwan observed a spartan and puritanical regime closely modelled, as they supposed, on the first Islamic community established by the Prophet in Madina. The Ikhwan were extremely rigid and literalistic in their behaviour: they cut their *thaubes* (or gowns) short above the ankles, trimmed their moustaches to a shadow while letting their beards grow freely, and eschewed the black *aghal* or rope-ring which secures the Arab head-dress, all because it was said in certain *hadiths* (traditions) that the Holy Prophet was thus attired or trimmed. Above all, they were utterly fearless in battle, and brutal as well, having defined themselves as the only true Muslims in a world of backsliding heretics. 'I have seen them hurl themselves on their enemies,' wrote an Arab witness, 'utterly fearless of death, not caring how many fall, advancing rank upon rank with only one desire – the defeat and annihilation of the enemy. They normally give no quarter, sparing neither boys nor old men, veritable messengers of death from whose grasp no one escapes.'[2]

Though acknowledging 'Abd al-'Aziz as their leader, the Ikhwan refused to recognize any territorial limits to their power. The Saudi leader's northern and eastern frontiers were controlled by the British, whose officials were invariably impressed by his charm and intelligence. Eventually his international undertakings (not to mention his personal inclinations) obliged him to deal with his over-zealous followers. This was particularly the case after his conquest of the Hejaz.

During the campaign some 300 people had been massacred in the city of Taif, and Muslims throughout the world were alarmed at what the 'Najdi fanatics' might do in the holy places. Their fears were far from groundless: during the previous conquest of the Hejaz in 1802 the Wahhabis had smashed up the Prophet's tomb in Madina and destroyed the remains of most of the saints who had been buried near the holy places. When the pilgrim caravans arrived from Egypt and Syria they were turned away as idolaters. After his family's re-occupation of the sacred territories, 'Abd al-'Aziz did his best to reassure the inhabitants that he was no bloody iconoclast. He had to intervene personally to prevent the Ikhwan from slaughtering the official delegation of Egyptians bearing the *kiswa*, the black silk covering of the Ka'ba, renewed every year at the Hajj season. About forty pilgrims were killed in the incident, after which the Saudis decided to supply the *kiswa* (traditionally a gift from Egypt) themselves. When the Ikhwan attacked the British-held Iraqi territory and two of their leaders revolted, 'Abd al-'Aziz disbanded them. Most of their units became absorbed into the Saudi National Guard. For the moment, the genie was back in the bottle – Islam reverted to its more familiar function, a prop to the social order, not a force to threaten it. 'Abd al-'Aziz, who already held the titles of King of Najd and its Dependencies and King of the Hejaz, gave himself a new one – King of Saudi Arabia (the only state in the world whose citizens are labelled with their ruler's surname). In the eyes of the religious militants, it was a classic case of the ideological 'sell-out': instead of being allowed to restore the Islamic government of their dreams, the Ikhwan, like so many of their predecessors from the time of the early caliphs, had been used to further the ambitions of a worldly dynast.

In a sense the problem, a classic one, had existed from the beginnings of Islam. The Prophet, like Ibn Saud, was a realist who recognized that an accommodation would have to be made with the Quraish, rulers of Makka and once his bitterest enemies, because they were the only power in Arabia strong enough to maintain the tribal alliances upon which the infant Islamic state depended. Before the conquest of Makka, the Prophet and Abu Sufyan, his former enemy, came to an arrangement which guaranteed that Islam would have a brilliant future in this world, but at a price. The generous terms Muhammad granted his former enemies would enable them to rise to the leadership of the new Islamic community, thereby laying down the basis for the

Umayyad caliphate which presided over the first great era of expansion. The first schisms of the community, which have lasted to the present, were caused by a mixture of ideological and personal factors. However, the fact that the 'losers', the party (*shi'a*) of 'Ali and his heirs, the Imams of the Prophet's house, retained their hold over the affections and imaginations of many pious and radical elements, was largely due to the sense of betrayal that accompanies any attempt to translate an ideal into reality. Christians had shelved, not solved, this problem by proclaiming that since Christ's Kingdom was 'not of this world', obedience to secular authority, however corrupt or wicked, could be mitigated or atoned for by an essentially private piety or morality. For Muslims there was no such easy way out: the Prophet had been his own Caesar, a temporal ruler as well as the bearer of a divine message. The Quran had urged the faithful to 'obey God and His Prophet'. The sense of betrayal must always, sooner or later, rouse a significant portion of the faithful to action, in order to restore the purity of an Islam deemed to have been corrupted. If *imitatio Christi* meant renouncing worldly ambition and seeking salvation by deeds of private virtue, *imitatio Muhammadi* meant sooner or later taking up arms against those forces which seemed to threaten Islam from within or without.

The Hajj and politics

The Hajj, the most central event in the Islamic calendar, cannot be described as a purely religious festival. With so many Muslims gathered together from different parts of the world, it contains a political message and the potential for political action. The political ideals of Islam – universal justice and equality, regardless of tribe, nation or race – are implicit in the rituals themselves. They are performed in the the state of *ihram*, ritual purity, in which all men (and most women) wear the white *kaffan* or seamless shroud which they will keep for their burials, a uniform which removes all outward signs of distinction between them. The potentialities for action are in the opportunities presented by Makka as the universal Muslim city, where Muslims from distant parts of the world have the right to congregate at all times, not only in the Hajj season. Many of the revolutionary and revivalist movements which swept through Africa and Asia, creating, albeit temporarily, new 'Islamic' states, originated there in encounters between men of God and men of the sword. At the present time, the role of the pro-Western Saudis as guardians of the holy places and administrators of the Hajj puts them in a very delicate position. Religion is, of course, constantly employed to legitimize their government. As rulers of the Hejaz and major financial contributors to Islamic institutions all over the world, the Al Sa'ud have established themselves as non-titular heads of an increasingly politically conscious pan-Islamic community. This gives them a moral influence within the most important bloc of Third World states which complements their economic weight in the West. But it also makes them increasingly vulnerable to attacks from religious quarters.

After the Iranian revolution of 1978–9 the Hajj became increasingly politicized, with Islamic militants who reject the *de facto* distinction between religion and politics encouraged by most Muslim governments using the Hajj to stage demonstrations which challenged the legitimacy of the Al Sa'ud as guardians of the holy places. The most spectacular of these events occurred in November 1979, a few months after the revolution, when a group of armed extremists occupied the Grand Mosque under the leadership of Juhaiman al-Utaibi. A child of the Ikhwan who grew up in the shadow of its defeat, Juhaiman and his 250 armed followers (who included Yemenis, Sudanese, Kuwaitis, Iraqis and Egyptians as well as Saudis) consciously imitated the style and behaviour of the original Ikhwan, calling themselves by the same name. In pamphlets, and from the mosque's loudspeakers, Juhaiman denounced the worldliness and corruption of the Saudi leaders in the name of a new Messiah or Mahdi, Muhammad Abdullah al-Qahtani. After two weeks of fighting the rebels were successfully subdued and the survivors executed; according to one account, French commandos were called in, who flooded the mosque's voluminous basements where the rebels were hiding, before placing high-voltage cables in the water. ('They floated out like kippers,' a Lebanese witness would later report.) Nevertheless, the desert kingdom was shaken to its foundations. The events in Mecca occurred simultaneously with pro-Khomeini demonstrations among Shi'ites in the oil-bearing district of al-Hasa in the Eastern Province, an area with a history of unrest. Strikes at Aramco (the US-owned company which originally exploited and marketed the bulk of Saudi crude) in 1953 and 1956, as well as purges of Arab nationalist sympathizers in the late fifties and in 1969, were connected to resentments among the Shi'a, who had been ruled since the Saudi conquest in 1913 by the Bin Jaluwis, a cadet branch of the Saudi royal house. Although there were no direct links between the Shi'a in al-Hasa and the rebels in Makka, both drew their inspirations from popular messianic traditions. Institutionalized among the Twelve (Ithna'ashari) Shi'a who predominate in Iran and southern Iraq, the idea of a Messiah or Mahdi who will return at the end of time to bring peace and justice to a world beset by turmoil and corruption appeals strongly – like similar Jewish and Christian millennial ideas – to people who feel threatened by radical economic, social and cultural change. In Iran it proved an essential component in the revolutionary Islamic ideology that brought down the government of Shah Muhammad Reza Pahlavi; in Makka the same chiliastic idea, which is also present in Sunni tradition, was exploited by Juhaiman. Like a previous Mahdi, Muhammad 'Abdullah, who launched the great revolt against the Anglo-Egyptians in the Sudan in 1882 Juhaiman timed his rebellion to coincide with the beginning of the new Islamic century.

Although these Shi'ite disturbances were not directly related to the events in Makka, the Holy City would become a target for political agitation emanating from Tehran. In 1982, for the second successive year, the Saudi authorities accused Iranian pilgrims of disrupting the Hajj by holding political demonstrations. The Iranian representative replied by stating:

Do slogans such as 'Death to Israel' and 'Death to the USA' create disorder? Do such slogans bring discomfort to Muslims? . . . We do not intend to violate security, rather we intend to invite the Muslims to unite against the USA, Israel and the Soviet Union. We are surprised that you oppose this action, as we expect you to lead the way.[3]

Western newspapers reported that Khomeini had been aiming to 'politicize' the Hajj. The Iranians saw things differently: since Islam made no distinction between religious and political activity, the Hajj was inherently political, and those who had tried to make it a purely spiritual occasion had deviated from the true path of the Prophet.

'Revive the great divine political tradition of the Hajj,' Khomeini is reported to have told his representative. 'Acquaint Muslims with what is taking place in dear Lebanon, in crusading Iran, and oppressed Afghanistan. Inform them of their great duties in confronting aggressors and international plunderers.'[4]

The stresses of the First Gulf War (1980–8), in which Saudi Arabia backed Iraq against the Islamic Republic, greatly increased the political tensions of the Hajj. In August 1987, the Saudis reported that 402 people, of whom 275 were Iranians, had been killed in disturbances. What exactly happened is still unclear. Iran claimed that the Saudis opened fire on the Iranian pilgrims; the Saudis, for their part, denied there had been shooting, claiming that the deaths had occurred in the course of a stampede caused by Iranian pilgrims engaged in political demonstrations. The Saudi embassy in Tehran was sacked by Iranian demonstrators. The following year the Saudis introduced a system of national quotas which would have reduced the number of Iranians by more than two-thirds, to 45,000. Refusing to accept the reduction, Iran sent no pilgrims to the Hajj in 1988, which passed off without serious incident. At the next Hajj two explosions in Makka killed a Pakistani pilgrim and wounded several others; 33 Kuwaiti Shi'ites were arrested on terrorism charges; 16 were later publicly beheaded, despite a telephoned plea for clemency by the Emir of Kuwait. Faced with persistent attacks on his Islamic credentials from Tehran, which dismissed his regime as based on a false brand of 'American Islam' designed to serve the interests of the superpowers, King Fahd played down his secular title of King, emphasizing instead the quasi-caliphal office of 'Guardian of the Two Shrines'.

Politics apart, the Hajj has been the occasion of a number of disasters in recent years, leading to mutual recriminations between Saudi Arabia and other Muslim states, including Iran and Indonesia. In 1990 more than 1,400 pilgrims were crushed to death when a pedestrian bridge collapsed at Mina. Most of the dead were Turks or Indonesians, whose governments demanded an official inquiry. Twenty-three of the dead were British citizens. British Muslims contrasted the treatment accorded these deaths by government and media with comparable events involving Britons in Europe such as the Clapham rail or Heysel Stadium disasters. Outrage among Muslims at Saudi maladministration was intensified after a statement by King Fahd, the Saudi ruler, who appeared to shrug off his government's responsibility for the calamity, claiming it to have been 'God's unavoidable will'. At the same time the King also suggested that the pilgrims were partly to blame for not following 'official instructions'. The statement brought predictable response from Iran, whose spiritual leader, Ayatollah Khomenei, accused the Saudi rulers of being callously indifferent to the lives of Muslims. More damaging to Saudi credibility among the rank and file of Sunni Muslims was a statement by the Nahdat ul 'Ulema of Indonesia, a traditionally conservative organization of religious scholars. 'The Saudi government,' said the 'Ulema, 'cannot run away from the responsibility for the disaster by simply saying it was an act of God.'[5] In 1994 a further 270 died on the walkway near Mina where pilgrims line up to stone 3 pillars (*jamaras*) representing different temptations. In 1997 more than 300 pilgrims were burned to death and 1,500 injured when fire swept through the tented city at Mina, 5km from Mecca, where pilgrims stay before and after the Standing (*wuquf*) at Mount 'Arafat. The following year, although the walkways had been widened, more than a hundred died in a stampede at the *jamaras*.

Despite large sums of money spent on improving safety at the sites, it was becoming clear that the Saudis were lacking in the technical or administrative skills required to handle the growing number of pilgrims who arrived each year.[6] These disasters demonstrate how difficult it is to move vast numbers of people who all seek to perform the same rituals at approximately the same time in tightly confined spaces. Nevertheless the Hajj, though unique in its international composition – with pilgrims now coming from more than 100 countries – is very far from being the world's largest religious festival. The Maha Kumbh Mela festival on the Ganges attracts up to 10 million Hindu worshippers without experiencing anything like the casualties regularly sustained by the Hajj.

The pilgrims' progress

On arrival at Jedda, pilgrims who are not already 'packaged' into a travelling group are usually divided into parties on a national or regional basis, each of which is placed in the care of a guide known as the *mutawwif*. Many of the *mutawwifs* are from Makkan families which have been in the business for generations: the success of an individual's Hajj will largely be determined by the honesty, influence and resourcefulness of the *mutawwif*. An efficient *mutawwif* will secure decent food and reasonably priced lodgings, better transport and good camping facilities. A dishonest or incompetent one can make the Hajj a misery.

At some point on the road to Makka the pilgrims will be stopped at a police checkpoint to have their passports examined. For them, this, and not the Saudi entry-point, is the real frontier, for it marks the boundary of the holy territory which no non-Muslim may enter. The

Saudi consulates in their home countries will have issued them with special pilgrim visas, only granted against proof of Muslim birth or conversion. In the past, people suspected of being Christians or members of extremist sects outside the Islamic consensus have been done to death for entering the holy places.

As the pilgrims arrive in the Holy City, the streets will probably be jammed with its characteristically eastern confusion of motors and pedestrians – for despite its dependence on oil, in Saudi Arabia, as in other Middle Eastern countries, the motor vehicle is still treated like the animal it only recently replaced.

As they approach the Haram area, the pilgrims shout the traditional slogan, 'Labbaika, Allahumma, labbaika!' ('Here I am, O God, at Thy command! Here I am!'), also used as a greeting or password during the Hajj. The huge white-clad crowd converges on the Haram like a mighty roaring torrent. Suddenly, as they pass the sign designating the Haram, a hush descends on them: this is the sacred territory, where from the earliest times all fighting, hunting and killing, even the uprooting of plants, have been forbidden. The goal to which the throngs are moving through the vast portals of the Haram is the Ka'ba, the modestly proportioned square building at its centre, the physical and symbolic pole of Islam. The Ka'ba is Islam's holiest shrine, the meeting point, as the mystic Ibn 'Arabi saw it, of the hidden and manifest worlds. During the Hajj the throng is so vast that it takes all of fifteen minutes to pass through the pillared halls, with their chandelier-lit naves and sumptuous carpets, to Islam's devotional epicentre. The colonnades enclose a massive oval floor of marble polished to an ice rink by centuries of pilgrim feet. The oldest columns – more than five hundred of them – stand at the perimeter. Most are carved from local granite, but some have a distinctively classical look. Tradition claims they were brought from Panopolis in Egypt.

Few Muslims, except for the locals who rely on the pilgrimage for their living, can fail to be moved by the sight of the small square shrine, a simple cube of granite covered with a black embroidered veil. Michael Wolfe, an American who made the pilgrimage in 1990, arrived after dark to perform his *tawaf al-qudum*, 'the turning of arrival'.

A doughnut ring of pilgrims ten rows deep circled the shrine, forming a revolving band of several thousand people. We kept to the edge of them, skirting the cube, and faced its eastern corner. Here a black stone in a silver bezel had been set into an angle of the building. We faced the stone and stated our intention:

> Allah, I plan to circle your sacred house,
> Make it easy for me,
> And accept,
> My seven circuits in your name.

Each hadji began at the black stone and circled the Ka'ba counter-clockwise . . . At a distance the wheeling pilgrims obscured its base, so that for a moment the block appeared to be revolving on its axis. As we came nearer the shrine increased dramatically in size . . . The first three circuits of the tawaf were performed at a brisk pace called *ramal*, or 'moving the shoulders as if walking in sand' . . . I had not imagined the hadj would be so athletic . . . It was not the pace or the distance but the crowd that was distracting. On the perimeter of the ring I noticed wooden litters passing, on which pilgrims weakened by age or illness were being borne around.[7]

Later Wolfe observes that some of the litters are actually biers carrying corpses, which jostle oddly under their coverlets. The liminal state in which boundaries separating individuals are temporarily dissolved also weakens the frontier between the living and the dead.[8]

Muslim tradition holds that the Black Stone set in the south-eastern corner of the Ka'ba is a fragment of the original temple built by Abraham (Ibrahim) on the site of Adam's first dwelling upon earth. The Ka'ba was built from the stones of five holy mountains. The Black Stone was restored by the angel Gabriel after the Ka'ba was removed to heaven when Adam died.[9]

Abraham's sacrifice

The 'Abrahamic' origin of Islam is a controversial subject on which there is little agreement between Muslim and non-Muslim scholars. For Muslims it is an article of faith that the patriarch, helped by Isma'il, ancestor of the Arabs, his son by his bondswoman Hagar, built the Ka'ba as the first temple to the one true God on earth; that he also willingly prepared to sacrifice Isma'il until rescued at the last minute by divine intervention in the shape of a ram. The Quranic account of the sacrifice (which in the Bible, of course, is told of Ibrahim and

Isma'il's half-brother Isaac, father of Jacob and ancestor of the Hebrews) does not mention Isma'il by name, which has led some western orientalists to argue that Isaac was understood as the intended victim in the original Quranic story, while the figure of Isma'il only emerged in the course of Muhammad's polemics with the Jews of Madina. References to Ibrahim, however, occur in several Quranic passages accepted as belonging to the period of the Prophet's residence in Makka. It is related that Ibrahim attacked the idol-worship of his father Azar and his people, and advocated belief in the one single God. Others may take the story of Islam's Abrahamic origins symbolically rather than literally. A semi-tribal society, such as Makka's during the time of the Prophet, expresses ideas in terms of tribal formations or lineage groupings. The northern Arabs ('Ishmaelites' to the Hebrews) naturally conceived of all authority in patriarchal terms, and could never have accepted reforms as far-reaching as the Prophet's unless they were seen as a restoration of the religious order instituted by their own patriarchs. Muslims may object to being called Muhammadans because they believe that Muhammad restored an old religion, rather than inaugurating a new one.

According to the Islamic tradition, which continues where the Hebrew tradition recorded in Genesis leaves off, Abraham brought Hagar, who had borne him a son, incurring the wrath of his wife Sara, to the barren rocky valley of Makka, and there abandoned her and their child under a solitary wild *sahra* tree with nothing to sustain them but a waterskin and a bag of dates. (According to Genesis, God is supposed to have reassured him by saying: 'Let it not be grievous in thy sight because of the child and because of thy bondswoman . . . Of her son will I make a nation because he is of thy seed.'[10]) After two nights and a day alone in the valley, Hagar began to despair. The dates were almost finished and there was no more water in the skin. As the child sat on the ground crying vainly for water, Hagar ran to and fro between the hillocks of Safa and Marwa, pleading with God: 'O Thou Bountiful, Thou Full of Grace! Who shall have mercy on us unless Thou hast mercy!' The answer came with the spring the child miraculously uncovered with his hand. 'Zummi, zummi!' he cried, imitating the sound of the water, which duly became the sacred well of Zamzam.[11]

Shortly afterwards a group of beduin from South Arabia passed by the valley and, seeing some birds circling overhead, concluded there must be water. Arriving at the well, they asked Hagar's permission to settle, which she granted on condition that the land should for ever remain the property of Isma'il and his descendants. Isma'il grew to manhood and married a girl from the Banu Jurhum, a South Arabian tribe. Eventually Abraham returned, and with Isma'il's help built the Ka'ba, the first shrine to the One True God. While the work was still half finished, he stood on a small rock and called out to heaven, uttering for the first time the traditional pilgrim cry: 'Labbaika, Allahumma, labbaika!'

The Islamic tradition furnishes several clues about the possible origins of the Ka'ba. Like several other shrines in Arabia, it was part of a *haram*, or sacred area, where inter-tribal fighting was forbidden, facilitating trade. The temple was evidently at the centre of a cult involving idol worship. The presiding deity was Hubal, a large carnelian statue kept inside the temple; 360 other idols were ranged outside. The three goddesses mentioned in the Quran – Lat, 'Uzza and Manat – were also worshipped in the vicinity. By the Prophet's time Christian influences were making themselves felt. When he entered the Ka'ba after the 'opening' of Makka in 8 AH (630 CE), Muhammad is reported to have found two icons depicting Jesus and Mary, which he ordered to be preserved. The rest of the idols he destroyed 'miraculously' by merely pointing his staff at them.

According to the early Muslim authorities, the Quraish, hereditary guardians of the sanctuary, venerated the idol in the Ka'ba and offered sacrifices to it. A number of early monotheists apparently objected to these practices, including the circumambulation of the Black Stone which 'could neither hear, nor see, nor hurt, nor help'. They are described as having believed that their people had 'corrupted the religion of their father Abraham' – the same charge that Muhammad himself was to make not only against the pagan Quraish but against most of the adherents of Judaism and Christianity among his contemporaries. The report cannot be dismissed as legend based on later Muslim piety; its significance is that veneration of the Black Stone is mentioned explicitly in the condemnation of 'idolatry'. However, during the Farewell Pilgrimage in 10 AH (632 CE), when he is said to have laid down the Hajj rituals as they are observed today, the Prophet was recorded as having gone out of his way to venerate the Black Stone. Some of his companions were evidently shocked by his attachment to the old ritual. 'Umar, the second caliph, is said to have once remarked upon greeting the Stone: 'I know you are nothing but a stone, have no power to do either good or evil, and had I not seen the Prophet greet you, I would not do so.'[12]

Another clue to the origins of the cult is the fact that although the Black Stone was venerated as a fetish, it was not directly associated with any particular deity. There seems to have been a general cult of stone-worship in the peninsula. The early Muslim sources suggest that it developed in imitation of the cult of the Ka'ba:

They say that the beginning of stone worship among the sons of Ishmael was when Mecca became too small for them and they wanted more room in the country. Everyone who left the town took with him a stone from the haram area to do honour to it. Wherever they settled they set it up and walked round it as if going round the Ka'ba. This led them to worship whatever stones pleased them or made an impression on them. Thus as generations passed they forgot their primitive faith and adopted another religion instead of that of Abraham and Ishmael.[13]

The inference from this passage is clear: the cult of the Black Stone was intimately connected in the minds of Muhammad's contemporaries with the 'original' cult of Ibrahim and Isma'il.

What was the nature of this original 'Abrahamic' religion? The Quran refers to Ibrahim as a *hanif*, a term used by Muslim writers to indicate a pagan monotheist, Muslim in the religious but not the historical sense. Like Muhammad, he rejected the idols worshipped by his tribe; interestingly, he turned for a time to the worship of the astral bodies – first a star, then the moon, then the sun – and finally to the One God. The Quranic passage (6:74–9) is significant:

And lo! [Thus] spoke Abraham unto his father Azar: 'Takest thou idols for gods? Verily, I see that thou and thy people have obviously gone astray!'
And thus We gave Abraham [his first] insight into [God's] mighty dominion over the heavens and the earth – and [this] to the end that he might become one of those who are inwardly sure.
    Then, when the night overshadowed him with its darkness, he beheld a star; [and] he exclaimed, 'This is my Sustainer!' – but when it went down, he said, 'I love not the things that go down.'
    Then, when he beheld the moon rising, he said, 'This is my Sustainer!' – but when it went down, he said, 'Indeed, if my Sustainer guide me not, I will most certainly become one of the people who go astray!'
    Then, when he beheld the sun rising, he said, 'This is my Sustainer! This one is the greatest [of all]!' – but when it [too] went down, he exclaimed: 'O my

people! Behold, far be it from me to ascribe divinity, as you do, to aught beside God! Behold, unto Him who brought into being the heavens and the earth have I turned my face, having turned away from all that is false; and I am not of those who ascribe divinity to aught beside Him.'

Like Muhammad, Ibrahim regards the idolatry of his fellow-tribesmen not as a sign of backwardness or primitiveness, which would not have been their fault, but as wilfully perverse. He himself arrives at the concept of the One God by a gradual process, highly suggestive in its imagery: the three astral bodies are in turn rejected because they are not dependable, disappearing as they do at certain intervals. But their rejection as suitable objects of worship leads to the perception of the Creator's 'mighty dominion over the heavens and the earth', since their regular motions are evidently part of a process brought into being and sustained by him.

Jewish influences and pagan cults

The association of Ibrahim and Isma'il with the Makkan cult has led some western scholars to suggest that Islam really originated in a Jewish cultural milieu among the partly Judaized Arab tribes of the peninsula, who applied certain Judaic ideas to Arab customs. During pre-Islamic times there appear to have been many *haram* areas in the peninsula where the tribes could enter into trading or other negotiations under a form of truce. Originally these *harams* were cultic centres devoted to a local deity and usually presided over by a hereditary 'holy family'. (Similar functions, up to the present time, have been performed in North Africa by hereditary Muslim 'saints', whose tombs, presided over by the saint's descendants, are often the centres of trucial zones located on the borders of tribal territories.) Thus at ancient Taif there was a shrine devoted to the goddess Lat under the control of the Thaqif clan; there were other, originally pagan shrines at Nakhla, north of Makka, and at Najran and Sana'a in Yemen, which later became centres of Christian worship. Although originally under the aegis of the pagan god Hubal, the Makkan *haram*, which centred round the well of Zamzam, may have become associated with the ancestral figures of Ibrahim and Isma'il as the Arab traders, shedding their parochial backgrounds, sought to locate themselves within the broader reference-frame of Judaeo-Christianity.

After the death of Isma'il, according to the Muslim chroniclers, the shrine and sanctuary fell into the hands of his wife's kin, the Banu Jurhum, with the sons of Isma'il becoming dispersed to the north. The Jurhum were said to have introduced paganism into the sanctuary. According to the chronicler Ibn Ishaq they 'behaved high-handedly in Makka and made lawful that which was taboo. Those who entered the town who were not of their tribe they treated badly and they appropriated gifts which had been made to the Ka'ba so that their authority weakened.'[14] In due course the Jurhum were expelled by a southern tribe, the Kuza'a, who ruled the sanctuary until displaced by Muhammad's people, the Quraish, a sept of the Banu Kinana. The Quraish claimed a superior right to rule since they regarded themselves as 'the noblest and purest of the descendants of Ishmael, son of Abraham'. The Quraishi hero responsible for restoring the Ka'ba to Ishmaelite rule was Qusaiy, who if the later genealogies are to be believed, would have been born around 365 CE. Both Tabari and Ibn Ishaq report that Qusaiy was the first of his tribe to 'assume kingship and to be obeyed by his people as a king'.[15] In Tabari's account Qusaiy 'held privileges of being doorkeeper of the Ka'ba, providing the pilgrims with food and drink, presiding over the assembly, and appointing standard bearers, thus taking all the honours of Makka for himself. He also divided Makka into quarters for his tribe, settling every clan of the Quraish into the dwelling places assigned to them. His authority among his tribe of Quraish, in his lifetime, and after his death, was like a religion which people followed. They always acted in accordance with it, regarding it as filled with good omens and recognizing his superiority and nobility.' We are not told much about the pagan rites performed inside the sanctuary and in the surrounding area.

The earliest Muslim sources suggest that the pre-Islamic cult of the Ka'ba had some astronomical significance. The historian Mas'udi (896–956) stated that certain people had regarded the Ka'ba as a temple dedicated to the Sun, Moon and the five visible planets (making up the mystical figure of seven, the number of circumambulations required for each *tawaf*). The story that there were exactly 360 idols placed round the temple also points to an astronomical significance. Among the votive gifts said to have been offered to the idols were golden suns and moons. Such an astronomical cult may later have been associated with the story of Ibrahim, as is suggested in the Quranic passage already quoted. It is thought that the 'place of Ibrahim', a stone near the Ka'ba, now covered by a gilded cage, where the patriarch is supposed to have stood when completing the building of the temple, was a name originally applied to the whole *haram* area, having been adopted from the Hebrew tradition surrounding the 'place' where Abraham was visited by God. A similar borrowing, it has been suggested, may have occurred in the case of the Black Stone, lodged in the south-east corner of the Ka'ba. In the Hebrew tradition the stone 'pillow' on which Jacob, son of Isaac, had his dream of the heavenly ladder becomes the corner-stone of the Temple, the pivot on which the whole world is balanced. The first ray of light which illuminated the whole world issued from it; it is said to have come down from heaven, being one of the few objects of heavenly origin on earth.

There are very similar traditions about both the Black Stone and the stone known as the 'place of Ibrahim'. One of the commonest traditions about the Black Stone is that it once shone so brightly that if God had not effaced it, it would have illuminated everything between the east and the west. In Muslim tradition the stone's blackness is attributed to its pollution by human sin, or by the various fires which have engulfed the Ka'ba. Whether these are really borrowings from Jewish traditions or parallel traditions from a common source cannot, in the present state of knowledge, be finally determined. Several visitors to Makka, including Richard Burton, who made the pilgrimage in disguise in 1853, have suggested that the Black Stone is really a meteorite. Could this have been the 'Star' originally worshipped by Ibrahim? What more natural object of adoration than a fragment fallen from outer space, which may once have lit up the sky with a trail of blazing particles? Meteorites have been venerated in other cultures, including North American peoples whose serpent mounds, it has been suggested, replicate the passage of meteorites across the sky. The historian of Makka al-Azraqi (d.837) mentions a serpent which guarded the sanctuary and its treasure for 500 years.[16] Such speculation is suggested by the Quranic account of Ibrahim's spiritual progress from the worship of the stars to that of the one Creator. In ritualistically imitating the primal motion of all heavenly bodies, around a temple incorporating an extra-terrestrial object, the Muslim, like Ibrahim, is expressing his allegiance as a subject of a universal cosmic order. For this, in its own distinctive manner, is what Islam demands as the primary religious duty.

The saʿi and standing at ʿArafat

After performing seven circuits of the Kaʿba, the worshippers proceed to the other rituals of the *haram* area. Near the corner of the shrine housing the Black Stone they leave the circling human mass to offer two prostrations at the Place of Ibrahim, now covered by a gilded cage. They may then drink and fill their jars with Zamzam water before proceeding to the *saʿi* – running between the hillocks of Safa and Marwa, in imitation of Hagar's plight. The whole distance, some 460 metres, has to be covered seven times at something between a walk and a jog. The pilgrims start at Safa and end at Marwa. The Iranian writer ʿAli Shariʿati saw the progression as symbolizing the active, purposeful life in the world, as contrasted with the self-immolation of *tawaf*, since Hagar, in her search for water, never lost hope: 'Searching for water symbolizes searching for material life on this earth. It is genuine need which shows the relation of mankind to nature. It is the way of finding heaven in this world and enjoying its fruits on this earth.'[17] The strain of performing the *saʿi*, in which the pilgrim must travel 3.5 kilometres, has been relieved by the architects who have enclosed the whole passage inside a long air-conditioned gallery. The marble-flanked walkway includes a special corridor where the old, infirm or disabled can be pushed along in wheelchairs.

The performance of the *saʿi* after the *tawaf* completes the *ʿumra*, or lesser pilgrimage, which can be performed at any time of the year. The pilgrim who continues to make the Hajj, which only takes place at the appointed season, leaves the *haram* area after performing the *saʿi* and makes for the plain of ʿArafat, a vast natural amphitheatre surrounded by hills about 11 kilometres from Makka. For the Hajj to be valid the pilgrim must reach ʿArafat before sunrise on the ninth day of Dhu al-Hijja – the so-called 'Day of ʿArafat'. Moving some two million people in less than one day through the narrow pass between Makka and ʿArafat is far from easy. Before the Saudis restricted the use of private cars the journey could amount to ten or more hours of nightmarish struggle between traffic and pedestrians. In recent years the Saudis have tried to alleviate the situation by banning vehicles carrying less than nine passengers, but the confusion is still considerable. Nevertheless, despite the distractions of traffic, noise and fumes, the Station at ʿArafat – high point of the Hajj ceremonies – is a most impressive occasion. The sun rises on the Day of ʿArafat revealing a vast tented city which has grown up the previous day in this normally deserted valley (where, according to legend, Adam first met with Eve after their expulsion from Paradise). Each *mutawwif* will have a group of tents assigned to him where his party will spend all the daylight hours in prayer and contemplation. There is room at 'Arafat for everyone, but the crowds are thickest around the rocky prominence known as the Jabal al-Rahma, the Mount of Mercy, and the huge Namira mosque immediately below it. It was here that the Prophet preached his famous last sermon during the Farewell Pilgrimage of 632, a few months before his death, which set the final seal on the teachings of Islam and laid down the sequence of the reformed Hajj rituals, every detail of which has been meticulously followed by the believers since that time.

The most impressive moment arrives with the call to prayer. As the thin nasal voice of the muezzin rises from the loudspeakers in the Namira mosque, echoing across the empty spaces of the valley, the serried masses of people turn towards Makka and with a single movement begin their prostrations – in the streets, in the car parks, under the lee of buses, upon every available surface among the jagged rocks. Prayer in Islam is never an act of purely private mental activity. The sequence of bodily motions – standing, bowing, kneeling, touching the ground with the forehead – are performed with care and precision, like the gymnastic displays beloved of totalitarian states. But unlike these secular rituals which can only be performed to order when the people have been specially drilled together, the movements of Islamic prayer have been fully internalized and assimilated from early childhood. When Muslims who have never met before pray together, their prostrations are usually perfectly timed.

The setting of the sun at 'Arafat is the signal for the *ifada'* or 'Onrush', when the pilgrims make for Muzdalifa, the narrowest point of the pass between Makka and 'Arafat. During the Farewell Pilgrimage the Prophet led the multitude on his camel. For thirteen centuries the pilgrims used to ride their 'finest mounts' at a thundering gallop across the plain, each one of them a 'tiny particle of that roaring, earth-shaking, irresistible wave of galloping dromedaries and men' that once conquered the better part of the known world for Islam. For in that fractious world of Arabian tribalism, where warlike energies were fruitlessly dissipated in internecine strife, the new solidarity brought by the Prophet and welded into a universal brotherhood at 'Arafat was the prelude to the *jihad*, or holy war. Nowadays most people have to make the six-mile journey on foot, or inch their way in the traffic as two million pilgrims and 50,000 vehicles compete for space in the narrow funnel of the hills. At Muzdalifa they are required to 'remember Allah by the sacred monument'. It may once have been a place of pagan worship dedicated to Quzah the thunder-god. Here two evening prayers, the *maghrib* and *'isha*, are performed together: the pilgrims, now cleansed of sin, are expected to purge themselves of all resentments against others. The narrowness of the passage makes it densely crowded.

At Muzdalifa – 'the place where one makes oneself agreeable' – the pilgrims collect the small pebbles, 49 in all, to be used in the most complicated and arcane of the Hajj ceremonies, the ritual stoning of the three pillars, or Jamarat, at Mina. The pebbles, each of which is supposed to be the size of a chick-pea, are thrown in sequences of seven at each of the three pillars situated about 300 metres apart along the road between Mina and Makka, where a huge two-tier walkway has been constructed enabling the people to stone the pillars from either level. It was at this point on the sacred journey that disaster struck in 1990. As the thousands of pilgrims traversed the upper walkway, a railing gave way. Pressed by the crowd, several people fell on to the lower level, eight metres below, causing a massive stampede which spread back along the lower gallery where, oblivious of the obstruction, pilgrims were pressing in. Next, according to survivors (though this was denied by the Saudi authorities), the electricity failed, cutting off light and ventilation, increasing the general panic. About 680 Indonesian pilgrims are believed to have died, and more than 500 Turks.[18]

The stoning ritual is of purely pagan origin, and there is no reference to it in the Quran. The pilgrims perform it because, according to the *hadith* traditions, the Prophet himself did so during his Farewell Pilgrimage. There is no mention in the canonical texts of the popular belief that the ceremonies involve the 'stoning of Satan'. Nevertheless the belief is held universally throughout the Muslim world, and is said to account for the violence with which many pilgrims attack the pillars. 'Ali Shari'ati, the Iranian radical, gives the ceremony an unabashed revolutionary symbolism:

These pebbles will be used as your weapons to kill your enemy . . . What does the pebble represent? It represents a bullet . . . Each soldier in Ibrahim's army has to shoot seventy bullets at the enemies in Mina. They are to be fired at the head, trunk and heart of the enemy. Only those which hit the enemy will be counted. If you are not an expert select more bullets to compensate for your lack of skill . . . If you hit one less than the recommended number, you are not considered a soldier nor is your Hajj valid.[19]

Some Muslim authorities suggest that the three pillars – whatever their symbolic function – mark the route taken by Ibrahim when leading Isma'il to the place of sacrifice. For Mina, as well as being the place of the stoning ceremonies, contains the killing-ground where the animals are sacrificed on the 'Id al-Adha, the final day of the Hajj. All pilgrims will wish to perform it, but it is not obligatory for the very poor, who will benefit from the largesse of the more affluent, since it is stipulated that some of the meat must be given to them. The Feast of Sacrifice is celebrated all over the Muslim world. Even in densely crowded cities, fattening sheep can be tethered in the streets or court-yards in preparation for it. Some agronomists have even suggested that the natural cycle of sheep-production has been interfered with in order to provide sacrificial victims for the 'Id. At Mina the wastage used to be enormous as most of the carcases has to be destroyed in lime-pits to prevent the spread of disease. Nowadays the ritual slaughter is conducted in hygienic abattoirs equipped with canneries and freezer-plants, so the meat can be distributed to the Muslim poor throughout the world. The pilgrims buy 'sheep-certificates', to prove they have make the sacrifice. While this may be more in tune with modern sensitivities than the sacrifice performed in the open, there is inevitably some distancing from the primal drama of Abraham. The animals are counted in 'sheep-units', rating from one for a sheep or goat up to seven for a fully grown cow or camel. In 1981 about one million 'sheep-units' were sacrificed, seventy per cent during the first day of sacrifice, and of these, about half between morning and midday.

The pagan background of all these rites, from the standing at 'Arafat to the Feast of Sacrifice, is still obscure. Muslim authorities are understandably reticent on the subject, while archaeologists are unlikely to be admitted to the area in the foreseeable future. What information there is has to be gleaned from the earliest Muslim writers and measured against comparable data from other parts of the world.

Some anthropologists have seen in the standing at 'Arafat relics of an ancient rain-making cult. Before Muhammad abolished the intercalary month by which the Makkans adjusted their lunar calendar to the solar year, the Hajj probably occurred in autumn, coinciding with the great fair at Ukaz held to celebrate the date harvest. The *'ifada* from 'Arafat to Muzdalifa, which in pre-Islamic times began before nightfall, may have represented the 'persecution' of the dying sun. The stone-throwing at Mina, according to the earliest Muslim sources, only occurred after the sun had passed the meridian, suggesting a ritual pursuit of the sun-demon, whose harsh rule ends with the summer. Similarly the halt at Muzdalifa, home of Quzah the thunder-god, accompanied by shouting and other loud noises, may have been a ritual attempt to call forth the thunder and bring on the rain. Rites such as these are found all over the world at the beginnings of the four seasons.

Muhammad's reforms

The pagan background, however sketchy the evidence, points to the subtle adjustments by which the Prophet accommodated his vision of a single transcendent deity within the prevailing symbolic structure. Just as the Quran did not suddenly appear out of nowhere in a strange and incomprehensible language, but was assembled from existing verbal materials, so the central ritual of Islam, the Hajj, was arranged out of existing cultic practices. The actions themselves were almost unchanged, but their meaning was transformed to fit a new, vastly expanded, cosmic vision. The result was a religious and ideological *tour de force*.

By abolishing the intercalary month, Muhammad freed the rituals from their seasonal connections: from now on the Hajj could fall at any time of the year, for the cosmic deity to whom all the rituals were to be addressed was the same God in autumn and spring, summer and winter. Similarly, the sanctuaries associated with particular localities were not abolished, but included within a set of rituals covering the whole area. 'The whole of 'Arafat is a place for standing, the whole of Muzdalifa is a place for stopping, the whole of Mina is a place for sacrifice,' the Prophet is related to have said on the Farewell Pilgrimage.

Similar effects were achieved by subtly adjusting the timing of the ceremonies. Ancient taboos associated with the rituals were deliber-ately violated to demonstrate the impotence of the pagan gods and the inefficacy of the rituals when dedicated to them. But the forms of the rituals were preserved because the Prophet was fully aware of the importance they held for his people. Beyond that, he knew that the rituals formed part of a universal language composed of bodily movements as well as verbal utterances, by means of which human beings express their deepest needs and apprehensions. The remarkable expansion of Islam, especially in the Far East and tropical Africa, long after its initial political and military impetus had exhausted itself, was in no small measure due to the ease with which it absorbed local cults and then directed them towards the broader social and cosmological purpose of the monotheistic vision.

2 Muhammad the Model

The Prophet's background

Muhammad ibn 'Abdullah of the Banu Hashim of Quraish was born in Mecca in about 570, at a time when the ruling tribe of Quraish were increasing in wealth, power and prosperity. The caravan-city of Makka, probably the 'Makorba' mentioned in the writings of the second-century geographer Ptolemy, had long been a centre of pilgrimage. The shrine from which its name derived, and the surrounding *haram* or sacred area, was a place where the beduin tribes who controlled the traffic in spices and other goods between South Arabia and the Mediterranean could exchange goods without fear of attack. The pilgrimage to the Ka'ba, in addition to its religious functions, encouraged trade, especially during the four sacred months when fighting was forbidden. Other *harams* in the Peninsula similarly combined religious with commercial functions, but Makka seems to have been the most important of these sanctuaries, lying as it did on the strategic road between Yemen, seat of an ancient if declining civilization, and the Mediterranean. In the decades before Muhammad, the volume of trade had increased, partly as a result of the continuing warfare between the Persian and Byzantine empires which disrupted the northern land routes. The tribes who controlled the Hejaz trade were becoming not only more powerful but increasingly civilized as they came into closer contact with the regions of high culture.

Unlike South Arabia, whose higher rainfall and ancient systems of irrigation had led to the development of forms of feudalism in combination with a tradition of divine kingship, the aridity of Northern and Central Arabia was such that society was entirely organized on tribal lines, while anything resembling the state was virtually non-existent. Although the sedentary people outnumbered the nomads, the prevailing ethos was determined by the beduin, whose superior mobility and fighting skills enabled them to subdue the settled pastoralists, semi-nomads, peasants and small merchants, extracting from them payment of taxes similar to the protection money demanded by urban gangsters. Actually, no hard-and-fast distinction can be made between 'nomadic' and 'sedentary' peoples in the Peninsula: there was rather a continuum extending from the camel-herding beduin aristocrats, through the humbler sheep- and goat-herds, to the agriculturalists and date-farmers who lived in permanent settlements (usually in individually fortified households) around the oases. Tribalism was the only mode of social organization. Each individual saw himself as belonging to a kinship group claiming descent from a real or supposed ancestor. Solidarity increased with ancestral proximity: the most immediate loyalty was to the family; then to the clan, a small group of closely related families; beyond that to broader groups of increasingly distant relatives who could sometimes be called upon for support, up to the level of the 'tribe', which can roughly be defined as the largest group capable of providing effective social solidarity.

The beduin camel-breeders were a military aristocracy in the sense that they dominated the more sedentary folk, to whom they felt superior by birth and professional skills. But they were far from wealthy, and in bad years were obliged to prey on the sedentary folk to avoid starvation. Normally, they survived on camel milk and the few staples such as dates that they were able to exchange for their own meagre products, including hides, leather, cloth or livestock. With little surplus to accumulate, every member of the group was directly involved in herding to some degree, so social organization, though hierarchical for military purposes, was relatively egalitarian. Chiefs were usually chosen by their peers as being the fittest in battle and most knowledgeable in the ways of the desert.

In certain cases, however, the mobility of the camel-breeders enabled them to engage in, and ultimately to monopolize, the long-distance trade in such luxury commodities as slaves and spices. The Quraish had gained control of Makka and its shrines some time during the fifth century under their leader Qusaiy. By the time of Muhammad's birth their caravans were converging from the four cardinal points – north and west from Syria and the Mediterranean, south and east from Yemen and the Persian Gulf. In the manner of other beduin leaders the Quraish buttressed their power by forming alliances with neighbouring tribes. In effect, as well as being the leading merchant traders in the Peninsula, they were the rulers of an important military confederation.

A caravan city such as Makka was unusual, even by Arabian standards. Most of the important cities of the region were situated either in mountainous areas such as Taif, south of Makka, or in oases such as Madina or Khaibar. In such cases the city formed the nexus between the nomads and the cultivators, where animal goods were exchanged for agricultural products. Makka was different. Apart from the brackish well of Zamzam, whose output was barely sufficient for the citizens and their stock, it was situated in a waterless valley where cultivation was impossible. Its importance depended exclusively on the shrine (*haram*) protecting the well.

Arabian paganism

It seems probable that, in addition to their possibly astral significance, the 360 idols placed round the Ka'ba represented various tribal totems, signifying adherence to the sanctuary, rather as the flags of member states are ranged in the UN Plaza in New York. The god of Makka, Hubal, represented by a statue of red carnelian, is thought to have been originally a totem of the Khuza'a, rulers of Makka before their displacement by the Quraish. Some accounts state that Qusaiy, who conquered Makka from the Khuza'a, imported the cults of the goddesses 'Uzza and Manat from Syria. There is little evidence that by Muhammad's time the pagan Arabs were particularly attached to idol worship, though in the war which followed Muhammad's proclamation of Islam the pagans carried some of these idols as standards into battle. For most of the Arabs, a vestigial attachment to one's tribal totem would not have seemed incompatible with a general monotheistic belief. There is evidence in the earliest written sources that monotheistic views were widely held. (Indeed, the name 'Abdullah – 'servant of the god or Allah' – was in general use and belonged, among others, to the Prophet's father.) Monotheistic ideas may have been diffused among the Arabs by Christian and Jewish converts, since anyone with a serious interest in religion, as well as a desire to raise his cultural standards, would have drawn close to one or other of the scriptural communities. But it is highly simplistic to suppose that 'monotheism', and the scriptural lore associated with it, was necessarily a 'monopoly' of these two communities. The logic of the prevailing social system – the patrilineal kinship group – led inevitably from monolatry to monotheism once the tribal totem had ceased to be the only available cult object. The presence of a multiplicity of symbols round the inter-tribal forum of the Ka'ba must have focused the attention of the tribes on the things which united rather than divided them – in particular, their supposed common ancestry from 'Adnan, Isma'il and Ibrahim, the original *hanif* or 'pagan' monotheist. By Muhammad's time Allah – meaning simply 'the god' – was certainly understood as a concept. What he lacked was a cult and a ritual, and above all a scripture in a language the Arabs could understand.

The pagan Arabs (the word originally means 'nomad') may have lacked the formal qualifications of a 'people': that is to say, a community owing common cultural and religious allegiance to one of the recognized scriptures. But they had ceased to be mere barbarians. Though without writing, they had developed poetry into a refined and sophisticated art form. Though none of it was written down before about AD 700 – after the earliest recensions of the Quran – much of it had been preserved for hundreds of years by professional *rawis* or reciters, who passed on their knowledge from father to son for generations. Although a certain amount of spurious matter may have found its way into later collections of pre-Islamic poetry, enough of the original corpus has survived to provide a convincing picture of the beduin values which were to be transformed, modified or rejected by the Prophet of Islam.

A key concept in the beduin value system was *muruwa* or 'manliness'. It has been described as meaning 'bravery in battle, patience in misfortune, persistence in revenge, protection of the weak, defiance of the strong'. In the absence of any central authority, tribal solidarity was the only source of individual protection. The 'virtue' of a tribe was conceived of as something inherited: a man would act nobly because of the noble blood that ran through his veins. The extent of individual freedom – defined in terms of choosing between different courses of action – was severely limited. The tribe's honour, and adherence to its norms, were imperatives to be followed at all times. Generosity, a highly praised virtue, was expressed in the lavish hospitality extended to anyone who placed himself under a tribe's protection – less for reasons of pure altruism than for the prestige such lavishness accorded to the tribe and its chiefs. The power of a tribe was due to its wealth and prowess in battle, both of which were commensurate with its size and the number of its dependants. A large and wealthy tribe like the Quraish would have numerous 'clients' or weaker tribes (often previously defeated enemies) dependent upon it. Inter-tribal warfare was endemic – being, as it were, an essential part of the ecology. But it was subject to certain customary limitations. Apart from the ban on fighting during the four sacred months, the beduin warriors deliberately sought to avoid unnecessary risks and casualties. The aim of the traditional *ghazwa* or raid was to detach the enemy tribesmen from their flocks or camels, and to carry the latter off as booty. If the defeated tribe found itself facing starvation, it would have no alternative but to place itself under the protection of a stronger tribe. In such a manner major confederations, such as that led by the Quraish, were built up from smaller units or clans.

The organization of tribal life was aristocratic. The chiefs of the tribe derived their authority from 'noble blood, noble character, wealth, wisdom and experience'. A hereditary principle was acknowledged, but only in so far as it pre-supposed a fitness to lead rather than rule. The leader of a tribal group would, of necessity, belong to its kin. But there was no formal system for electing leaders or for passing the chiefship down from father to son. A chief emerged and retained his leadership by a consensus of his peers – the tribal elders. Success would strengthen this consensus, failure or bad luck would undermine it. The absence of such consensus would lead to bloody internecine disputes; but the elders would always be conscious of the dangers which internal strife would pose to the whole community. Thus the Arabian chief had authority, derived from his superior personal fitness, but little power to give orders or punish his fellow tribesmen. The latter governed themselves according to a moral code developed over generations, based on a highly successful adaptation to the economics of stock-breeding in a desert environment.

Politically, the beduin were conservative and egalitarian. They understood that safety lay in observing the ways of their ancestors. No man could be regarded as inherently better than his fellows, except through his actions and the demonstrable superiority of his blood. This world-view, in which formal religious observance played only a minor part, has been described as 'tribal humanism'. The tribe's survival and growth was a sufficient end in itself, the only standard against which human excellence could be measured. The attitude embodied an element of fatalism: the tribesman depended not, as the peasant-cultivator did, on mastering his environment, but on adapting himself to suit it: in short, he submitted to the laws of nature as he understood them. Fate determined his sustenance, the term of his life and the number of his children: in effect, his happiness or misery. In desert conditions, such matters lay beyond human control. Within these parameters, however, he was bound by the knowledge that prosperity was enhanced by social harmony and cohesion and diminished by strife. Such an austere, and ultimately pessimistic, world-view offered little comfort for the individual. There is scant evidence of a belief in the after-life. Though the Day of Judgement is referred to in at least one pre-Islamic poem, this was probably a borrowing from Christian sources. Belief in individual survival after death was kept in subjection to the practical task of ensuring that the social collectivity of the tribe expanded and prospered in this world.

The relative prosperity of Makka as a centre of trade and pilgrimage attracted a 'floating non-tribal population of individual exiles, refugees, outlaws and foreign merchants'.[1] The older tribal ideas were giving ground to a new sense of individualism, while at the same time the social protection afforded to individuals under the clan system was beginning to break down.

The tensions in Makkan society were reflected in the rivalry between the clans that made up the tribe of Quraish. At the time of Muhammad's birth, the competition for influence and prestige was strongest between the clans of Hashim and 'Abd Shams. Muhammad's grandfather, 'Abd al-Muttalib, was the leader of the Banu Hashim, and a man of considerable importance. He had dug out the well of Zamzam, having inherited from his uncle the responsibility of providing food and water for the pilgrims. He also inherited from his father, Hashim, the franchise of the lucrative Syrian trade. However, by the end of his life he had lost much of the Syrian trade to the rival clans of 'Abd Shams and Nawfal. Muhammad's father 'Abdullah took over what trade was left to the Hashimis, but he died comparatively young on a journey from Gaza. 'Abdullah's wife, Amina bint Wahb, of the clan of Zuhra, was either pregnant at the time, or had just been delivered of her son Muhammad. Her husband's death left her with very little: according to some accounts, one slave, five camels and a few sheep. She herself died when her son was only six.

Birth of the Prophet

We know little about the Prophet's early life that is of historical value, as distinct from mythical or theological significance. The latter category includes stories of impressive encounters with holy men who instantly recognized the young Muhammad's spiritual destiny, and tales about the angelic surgeons who opened his breast and 'cleaned his heart' before replacing it. In accordance with Quraishi custom, Muhammad was farmed out with a wet nurse from one of the beduin tribes: the pure air of the desert was considered to be good for the health of children, while the ties of fosterage (a custom practised by other pastoral peoples, including the Irish), like those of marriage, became a means of strengthening tribal alliances. More importantly in Muhammad's case, his sojourn in the desert at a formative age made him familiar with that special elliptical quality of beduin speech (known as *ïjaz*) which characterizes the style of the Quran.

Many Muslims who accept uncritically the dogma that the Quran is the 'speech of God' are reluctant to admit that literary influences have any part in its formation. The mature Muhammad is supposed to have been illiterate when he received his first 'revelations' at the age of about 40, a tradition enhancing the miraculous character of God's 'messages'. Actually, it is not certain that Muhammad was illiterate, though his knowledge of writing, like that of his contemporaries, was probably rudimentary. The term *ummi* used in the Quran and *hadiths* (reports of the Prophet's deeds and sayings) can mean 'unlettered' rather than illiterate, in the sense that Muhammad was a 'gentile' Arab having no knowledge of the Hebrew or Christian scriptures. The fact of Muhammad's illiteracy, however, would in no way constitute proof of the Quran's miraculous origin. As has already been mentioned, the great pre-Islamic poets were illiterate, and so were the *rawis* who transmitted their verses. Muhammad, who, for reasons to be explained, hated the pagan poets and disclaimed any similarities between their verses and the Quran's, must, consciously or otherwise, have absorbed some of their techniques and facility of expression. Along with the rest of Makka, he must certainly have attended the annual fair at Ukaz, where the poets competed for prizes, as in a Welsh Eisteddfod.

Thus we may reasonably assume that Muhammad, though born

into one of Makka's best families, had experience in the early years of his life both of poverty and of the special intimacy of beduin life, in which human affection acts as a kind of insulating blanket against the harsh realities of the desert. He had learned the pure speech of the Arabs from the beduin and their poets. He was probably familiar with monotheistic ideas, as well as with much of the biblical and talmudic folklore which the pagan Ismaelites shared with the scriptural peoples of the settled regions including the Christians of Najran and the Jews of Yathrib, the oasis-settlement north-east of Mecca.

After his mother's death, the orphaned Muhammad was taken into the household of his paternal uncle, Abu Talib, who became leader of the Hashim clan on the death of 'Abd al-Muttalib, when Muhammad was about eight. According to some accounts, Abu Talib sometimes took his young nephew with him on trips to Syria, where he came into contact with Syrian monks. But there is no evidence from the Quran or the traditions that Muhammad was at all well acquainted with Christian beliefs or practices. Like everyone else, he probably participated in the cults around the Ka'ba. The story that Abu Talib, despite his affection for Muhammad, refused him permission to marry his daughter Umm Hain on account of his poverty, is quite plausible.

Despite the hagiographical tendencies of Muhammad's biographers, a convincing personality emerges from the earliest sources. He was evidently physically well-favoured and mentally astute. He was about average height (which for beduin Arabs is around 5 feet 9 inches) and sturdily built. His forehead was large and prominent, his nose curved, his eyes large and black with a touch of brown. His hair was thick and slightly curly. His skin was lighter than is usual for an Arabian, and a vein could be seen throbbing in his temple when he was angry or otherwise upset. His mouth was large, and he had a pleasant smile. He walked at great speed, and when turning to look round did so with his whole body. He conveyed the impression of great energy, but his contemporaries found him unusually taciturn and self-controlled. When he spoke it was briefly, to the point and without elaboration. He seems to have been a serious-minded introvert in a society where it is usual for men to be excitable, exuberant, boastful and loquacious.

It may have been this quality of seriousness beyond his years that earned Muhammad the nickname al-Amin – the trusty one. His tact and discretion would later show themselves in his political career. Doubtless it was awareness of these qualities, together with an intuitive recognition of his exceptional talents, that persuaded a Quraishi widow of means, Khadija bint Khuwailid, to make him her steward and later her husband.

Khadija is supposed to have been about 40 and already the mother of several children when she married Muhammad, then aged about 25. Since she is subsequently said to have borne him four daughters and several sons (the sons all died in infancy), one finds this hard to believe. At a time when girls were usually married at puberty, 30 was considered more than mature. Perhaps the early biographers exaggerated Khadija's age in order to emphasize the unusual fact that she was older than her husband and that – as a woman of means – she had chosen him for herself.

Muhammad and Khadija seem to have been content together for the 15 years of their marriage, despite the loss of the infant boys. In the patriarchal society of the Arabs, a man's prestige, even his identity, was to some extent dependent on the number of his sons. His *kunya* or nickname came from his first-born male. Muhammad's was Abu Qasim, father of Qasim. The death of his boys must have been a considerable blow. In other respects, however, the outward circumstances of Muhammad's life seem to have been prosperous. The family, if not wealthy, was comfortably off and highly respected. The marriage was evidently happy: Muhammad, who travelled regularly on the Syrian route, appears to have availed himself neither of the slave-girls nor of the temporary marriages permitted by custom. It is conceivable that Khadija, who had been in a position to dictate terms, had insisted that he remain monogamous.

The summons to prophecy

It seems useless to speculate about the psychological causes which inspired Muhammad, when he was about 40, to spend increasing amounts of time in solitary contemplation, in the manner of a Syrian monk or an Arabian soothsayer. Prophets who claim to speak for God or the gods appear in some form or another in virtually all cultures and in all places. In the Middle East and western worlds the critiques they make of the present order and the promise they offer of a better world for the righteous may usually be engendered by the 'destruction of an ancient way of life, with its familiar certainties and safeguards'.[2]

The shaman who visits the invisible world of the spirits and returns with supernatural knowledge is also found in many traditions. There are grounds for suggesting that the experience of the oldest prophet in the traditions of western Asia – Zoroaster – may be rooted in Shamanism.[3]

In Arabia there existed a type of shaman known as *kahin*, or soothsayer. The *kahins* – a word etymologically related to the Hebrew *kohen*, or priest – believed themselves to be inspired by familiar spirits, made repetitious invocations to natural and physical phenomena, such as the morning or evening stars, or certain plants or animals, and were often consulted as oracles in both public and private matters, such as the loss of camels or the interpretation of dreams. When prophesying in this manner the *kahins* would cover their heads with their cloaks and give utterance to their visions in breathless, rhythmic cadences known as *saj*, or rhyming prose. *Saj* was, in fact, the earliest form of Arabic poetry. Its use by the *kahins* suggests that the latter were operating within the most ancient of all oral traditions, in which the rhymes were preserved for purely mnemonic purposes. For a man of Muhammad's more sophisticated background and much broader intellectual outlook, to have become a simple *kahin* would have been unthinkable. But it is significant that the first revelations which he uttered resembled the *saj* of the *kahins* in both form and content. The earliest *suras* (chapters) of the Quran consist, in the main, of shamanistic invocations of natural phenomena in short, ecstatic breaths of rhyming prose. This was the very core of the Quranic message, and it conferred upon the 'speech of God' a demotic and directly inspirational quality which was lacking in the higher style and more finely wrought language of the poets.

Muhammad's favoured retreat was in a cave in the hill of Hira, a few miles from Makka. It was here that, according to the earliest accounts, he received his 'call' to prophethood and the first of the revelations which, assembled into chapters or *suras* (a Hebrew loanword meaning 'row'), make up the Quran (literally the 'discourse', or 'recitation'). According to his widow 'Aisha, to whom the prophet confided his story in later years, 'the beginning of the revelation for the Messenger of God was true vision. It used to come like the breaking of dawn.' For this gifted and intelligent man, these first intimations were enough to set him, temporarily, on the mystic's path. We are told that 'solitude became dear to him', and that he returned to the cave for several days and nights consecutively, taking provisions with him, in order to engage in devotional exercises (which he may or may not have learned from Christian monks). He was evidently expecting something dramatic, and may have felt such despair when nothing happened that he contemplated suicide. At last, unexpectedly, he became aware of a presence (identified, in Muslim tradition, as the angel Gabriel) who told him: 'Muhammad, Thou art the Messenger of God.' Subsequent alternations of certainty and despair may have been repeated several times before divine communication finally came in the form of words.

According to Muslim tradition, the first revelation 'came down' on the night of 26–7 Ramadan, the so-called Night of Power which the Quran says is worth a thousand ordinary nights, and when to be born, or to die, is still seen as a special mark of Allah's favour. The presence was with Muhammad and said to him: 'Read! [Recite!]', to which Muhammad answered: 'What shall I read [recite]?' Variants of this tradition, conforming to the dogma that Muhammad was illiterate, give his answer as 'I cannot read!' The presence then shook him and crushed him until all the strength went out of him. 'Read!' came the command once more. Twice Muhammad refused, twice he was shaken by the presence. But finally the words came to him which would later form the opening of the 96th Sura, regarded by the great majority of scholars as the first of the Quranic revelations (96:1–5):

> Read [recite] in the name of thy Sustainer who has created –
> Created man out of a germ-cell
> Read, for thy Sustainer is the Most Bountiful One
> Who has taught [man] the use of the pen –
> Taught man what he did not know!

Was the presence which spoke to Muhammad something from outside himself, or an irruption from within his unconscious, the result of severe stresses brought on, perhaps, by his religious devotions? Muhammad's experience appears to have been both ocular and auditory: he *saw* the angel, and *heard* the words that were spoken to him. But whether or not the traditional version is accepted, the story of the angelic presence does conform to certain conventional assumptions about the forms of both prophetic and poetic experience.

Within the traditions of prophecy, the encounter on Mount Hira has obvious parallels with that of Moses on Mount Sinai when he received the Torah from the god of the Hebrews. Surprisingly, there are no references to this incident in the Quran, although Moses figures prominently as one of Muhammad's predecessors. The story of the angel seizing Muhammad and shaking him has, however, several precedents among the tales of the Arabian poets. One of them, Hasan ibn Thabit, who later became a Muslim, was assaulted by a female spirit who pressed him to the ground and 'forced' him to utter three verses when previously he had never been able to compose a single line. This and other legends about the supernatural origin of exceptional eloquence embodied the same cultural assumptions as beliefs in the magical powers of poets and soothsayers. With the coming of Islam they were not so much abolished as translated into a broader framework. The language of the Quran, more perspicuous than that of the soothsayers, more eloquent than that of the poets, could not be other than the speech of God himself, transmitted through an angelic intermediary.

The Source of revelation

The belief that God speaks through the mouth of his prophets is central to the Irano-Semitic tradition. Leaving aside the question of whether this claim is 'true' or 'false', it can be said with certainty that the Night of Power represents the moment when Muhammad assimilated this tradition to himself. Henceforth he would see himself as a Prophet charged with a special mission for his people and, through them, for mankind as a whole. He conceptualized this mission in a manner appropriate to the times and circumstances in which he found himself. Convinced that the source of this overpowering sense of purpose, which gave his existence a new meaning and coherence, came from outside himself, he not unnaturally identified it with something with which he and his contemporaries were familiar. The Source could only be the same God who had spoken through the other prophets about whom he had heard. His mission, like that of the prophets who came before him, must be to convey the communications he received from the Source to his fellow human beings, regardless of the cost to himself and to others.

For orthodox Muslims, the externality of the Source must be accepted without question. After the Night of Power Muhammad was the recipient of the revelations which make up the Quran at more or less regular intervals. At first, before he got used to them, the experience of revelation could be agonizing. We are told that he became covered with sweat, was seized with a violent shuddering, and lay unconscious for hours as though in a drunken stupor. At other times, the revelations were accompanied by ocular visions of angels who spoke to him. It is clear that he was unable to summon the revelations at will, and that when they did come, the messages sometimes contradicted his personal judgements or criticized his actions. Sometimes they 'came down' when he was least expecting them, when he was in the middle of a conversation or as he was riding on camelback.

For the non-Muslim, the externality of the revelations may or may not be admitted. Most believers in the existence of God, whether or not they are members of other faiths, would probably find acceptable the distinction that the Quran, taken as a whole, has two messages, one special and the other general. The special revelations were directed at Muhammad's auditors and, by extension, to the whole Muslim community which came after them. The general revelations were applicable to humanity as a whole. If this distinction is accepted, Muhammad can be recognized by members of other faiths as the Muslim Prophet, a man who genuinely received messages from God and conveyed them to his people.

That Muhammad's mental state was abnormal when he experienced visions upon receiving revelations goes without saying. His Marxist biographer, Maxime Rodinson, argues convincingly enough that these visions emerged from within his unconscious:

One has only to dip into psychology text-books to find a hundred perfectly bona fide cases of people in a state of hallucination hearing things and seeing visions which they claim quite genuinely never to have seen or heard before. And yet an objective study of their cases shows that these are simply fresh associations produced by the unconscious working on things which have been seen and heard but forgotten. Facts of this kind we now take for granted. It is therefore conceivable that what Muhammad saw and heard may have been the supernatural beings described to him by the Jews and Christians with whom he talked.[4]

However, only if we regard the unconscious as a discrete entity comparable to the conscious self can this line of reasoning be made to conform with atheistic assumptions. Freud's famous pupil C. G. Jung challenged the idea of a discrete unconscious after analysing the dreams of his patients and finding that many contained the same symbols and archetypes as are to be found in medieval gnostic texts with which the patients could not possibly have been acquainted. From this evidence he inferred the existence of a 'collective unconscious' transcending the boundaries of individual self-hood. He wrote:

I have to admit the fact that the unconscious mind is capable at times of assuming an intelligence and purposiveness which are superior to actual conscious insight ... Since modern research has acquainted us with the fact that an individual consciousness is based upon and surrounded by an indefinitely extended unconscious psyche, we needs must revise our somewhat old-fashioned prejudice that man is his consciousness.[5]

If we take a Jungian, as distinct from a Freudian, view of the unconscious, Rodinson's argument that Muhammad's utterances irrupted from his unconscious need not necessarily support an atheistic version of the origins of Islam.

Perhaps we should say that Muhammad believed that the irruptions from his unconscious mind which he experienced from time to time, and which were subsequently included in the Quran, were the products of an 'intelligence and purposiveness' superior to the conscious insights of which he believed himself capable. Having drawn from this unconscious reservoir, he continued to distinguish the words in which he formulated these perceptions from those of his normal everyday speech. In this respect he was probably conforming to the shamanistic practices of figures with which he was familiar – the *kahins* or soothsayers. But the message he believed himself to have been entrusted with was infinitely grander and more majestic than anything contained in the oracular pronouncements of the soothsayers. It was a message about the unity and purposiveness of the universe, and the special destiny of humanity in relation to it. It was a message which, like the messages of earlier prophets in the Iranian-Semitic tradition, stated that a coherent and rational universe, resulting from a divine act of creation, or 'decree', must needs find its human expression in a harmonious social order, in which extremes of wealth and privilege should be minimized; it was a message, in short, that demanded the creation of the good society, in order to provide men and women with a positive reason for living, to sustain them in times of difficulty, and to moderate their natural urge towards excessive self-indulgence when times seemed good. The message did not, of course, come to him all at once. His mission would be to create for himself an environment suitable for its safe delivery. He knew he would have to make use of all his strength, cunning and ingenuity to achieve this purpose. At times he would be utterly ruthless, resorting to war, assassination, even massacre, to achieve this purpose. Some Muslims shrink from facing up to these actions, many of which run counter to contemporary western ideas about morality. But Muhammad was not a god: at no point did he identify himself with that inner voice prompting him to action. Every pronouncement he made drew attention eloquently and forcefully to the impassable gulf between God and man, between the Creator and his creatures. It was because he never ceased to emphasize the distinction between his own human self-hood and the Source which inspired him that of all the men in history who have wielded political power, he was one of the least corrupted by it.

The first Muslims

Muhammad's first converts were members of his household – his wife, Khadija, 'Ali ibn Abi Talib, his young ward and first cousin, and Zaid ibn Haritha, a freedman from the mainly Christian tribe of Kalb. For three years Muhammad expounded his messages privately, mainly to his family circle and a small group of others who joined them. Centuries later, when the oral traditions were committed to writing, it became a matter of the greatest importance to the political families of the day to have had an ancestor among the earliest converts. The evidence was probably tampered with, so we cannot be absolutely sure who they were. One of them was certainly Abu Bakr, a merchant who succeeded to the Prophet's political authority as caliph in 632. Two other young cousins, Sa'd ibn Abi Waqqas and Zubair ibn al-'Awam, joined early on, as did two younger members of Makka's ruling clans, Khalid ibn al-'As of 'Abd Shams, and 'Uthman ibn 'Affan, the future third caliph, then a somewhat dandyish young man of about 30 who is said to have embraced Islam after falling in love with Muhammad's daughter Ruqaiya. Khalid was eventually joined by his brother 'Amr, future conqueror of Egypt.

Other early supporters included younger men who, like Abu Bakr, came from less aristocratic and influential clans, such as Talha ibn 'Ubaidallah of the Taim, and 'Abd al-Ka'ba (later 'Abd al-Rahman) ibn 'Awf of the Zuhra. The majority of early supporters, however, came from lower down the social scale: some were members of minor clans affiliated to the Quraish, others were artisans, freedmen or actual slaves such as Bilal, the famous Abyssinian whose stentorian voice was to be the first to announce the call to prayer. Most of the first Muslims were young and independent-minded. When they began performing their prayer in public and Muhammad started preaching in the open, the group met with indifference and occasional ridicule from upper-class Makkans because of the lowly status of most of its members. But in the early years they were tolerated, since they were not yet seen as a threat to Quraishi power.

Most of the Quranic passages dating from this period concern the miraculous character of God's creative power, its durability as compared with the transitoriness of mortal existence and the need for human beings to show their gratitude in worship. All references to God, as well as those concerning the Day of Judgement when men and women will be punished or rewarded according to their merits, imply a knowledge of these doctrines on the part of Muhammad's auditors. There is little emphasis on God's unity and the denunciation of idolatrous practices such as occur in the passages of the Quran dating from a later period. The message does, however, have important social implications. The Day of Judgement will be 'a Day when no human being shall be of the least avail to another' (82:19). That is to say, people will be judged on their merits as individuals, not in accordance with their 'inherited' virtue as members of one or another tribe. The accumulation of wealth as an end in itself is attacked: '[Woe unto him] who amasses wealth and counts it a safeguard, thinking that his wealth will make him live forever!' (104:2-3). The rich are denounced as complacent, considering God's bounty as being no more than their just deserts. If they find themselves in straitened circumstances, they think God is being unfair and turn away from him. 'You are not generous towards the orphan,' proclaims the Quran, 'and you do not urge one another to feed the needy, and you devour the inheritance [of others] with devouring greed and you love wealth with boundless love!' (89:17-20). Even the Prophet himself is reproached for frowning and turning away a blind man who approaches him while he is giving his attention to some of the Quraishi chiefs (80:1-2).

The beginnings of opposition

There seem to have been three main reasons for the opposition to Muhammad's teaching that now began to develop among the leaders of the Quraish. His attacks on the private accumulation of wealth almost certainly struck a raw nerve because it was partly couched in terms of traditional tribal values. It is not wealth as such that is condemned, but rather the meanness of tribal leaders who no longer dispense largesse in the manner of the desert.

A second reason may have been that the leaders of the Quraish realized, perhaps before Muhammad himself, that the new allegiance he was beginning to acquire from his followers must eventually represent a threat to themselves. A man who claimed to speak directly for God, and whose followers believed him to be so speaking, was hardly likely to submit to any purely political authority. Makka's 'merchant republic' was governed by a Council on which all the leading clans were represented. Muhammad, though of aristocratic birth, was neither wealthy nor important enough to be part of the city's 'Establishment'. There is evidence that the Quraishi leaders tried to 'co-opt' him, offering money and power if he would stop attacking them.

A third and related reason had a religious dimension. If we accept the chronology of the *suras* as developed by such scholars as Theodor Nöldeke and Richard Bell, none of the earliest Makkan passages contain overt attacks on the pagan idols around the Ka'ba. The real source of religious opposition appears to have had a much more problematic character. The Day of Judgement announced in the early passages of the Quran implied a doctrine of individual resurrection, something which the Quraish, like modern atheists, regarded as self-evidently ridiculous. While it can be accepted rationalistically as a metaphorical way of expressing the notion that man is individually responsible for his actions, the idea that dust and bones can somehow be reassembled after death is not especially convincing. Muhammad's opponents saw this as a weak point in the Quranic message, and made the most of it. The Quran itself deals with their objections in rather general terms. In the miracle of God's creation, it says, all things are possible. If God can create human life out of a 'germ-cell', 'Is not He, then, able to bring the dead back to life?'(75:37–40). This was evidently not enough to satisfy the critics. Those who challenged Muhammad's message were told that they would burn in hell. The implication was that their fathers and grandfathers would burn likewise.

It was probably at this point that the issue of idolatry came to the centre of the argument. The new teaching emphasized *individual* moral virtues in a society where virtue was still thought of as inherent in group lineage. The basic values of honesty, generosity and courage preached by Islam may not have been so very different from the social virtues prized among the beduin. However, from the earliest passages in the Quran it was clear that these values were now to be applied universally, regardless of lineage. Even the disreputable elements surrounding Muhammad would be judged according to these standards; like the beduin aristocrats, they would be expected to live according to them.

Such a doctrine was more than the pride of the Quraishi leaders could be expected to bear. Muhammad was implicitly passing judgement – as they saw it – on their ancestors, and on the deities of their clans. In this they rightly perceived a threat to themselves: for in demanding unqualified recognition of the one true god, Muhammad was now creating around himself an allegiance which superseded the ancient loyalties to the clans of which they were the heads.

The leader of the opposition to Muhammad was 'Amr ibn Hisham of the Banu Makhzum, known to his supporters as Abu al-Hikam ('Father of Wisdom'). The Muslims nicknamed him Abu Jahl, 'Father of Ignorance'. His chief supporter was the prophet's uncle, Abu Lahab, a younger brother of his former guardian and protector, Abu Talib. The persecution to which these men and their followers subjected the Muslims mainly took the form of ridicule and petty harassment. The junior and low-born Muslims suffered most, having no one to protect them. Many who had previously joined the movement were intimidated into renouncing their allegiance. Muhammad was sufficiently alarmed to send about 100 Muslims, including his daughter Ruqaiya and her husband, 'Uthman, to Christian Abyssinia, where they found protection from the Negus.

The 'Satanic Verses'

Attacks on idolatry dating from this period are relatively mild, lending credence to the story of the so-called Satanic Verses preserved by two early traditionists, Tabari and Ibn Sa'd. The story suggests that

Muhammad may have been tempted to compromise with the pagan Quraish by honouring three of their female deities. In Tabari's version, after giving utterance to the revelation preserved in the Quran as part of Surat al-Najm (The Star) 'Have you considered al-Lat, al-'Uzza and Manat, the third, the other' (53:19–20) a reference to three tribal deities, Satan made an interpolation, placing on Muhammad's tongue the flattering words: 'These are the exalted *gharaniq* [swans or cranes, i.e. beautiful ladies] whose intercession is to be hoped for.' On hearing this the Makkan polytheists were delighted, for it seemed to suggest that Muhammad had accepted their goddesses as worthy of worship. The news reached the exiles in Abyssinia, inspiring their premature return. But later the Angel Gabriel came to Muhammad and showed him his error. God replaced the Satanic Verses with the words that are now in the text: 'Why – for yourselves [you would choose only] male offspring, whereas to Him [you assign] female . . .' (53:21), suggesting that since the polytheists were in the habit of killing their female offspring (a practice vigorously condemned in other *suras*) it would be illogical as well as impious of them to ascribe daughters to God and to worship them as divine beings.[6] Despite its presence in Tabari and Ibn Sa'd, the provenance (*isnad*) of the story was considered too weak to be included in any of the six canonical collections of *hadiths* (traditions) assembled in the centuries after Muhammad's death. Three early Quranic commentators, Zamakhshari, al-Qurtubi and al-Baidawi accepted it; al-Razi rejected it as 'a fiction invented by apostates'. While accepted by western biographers of Muhammad including Sir William Muir, Montgomery Watt and Maxime Rodinson, a leading authority on the collection of the Quran and early *hadiths*, John Burton, suggests that the story was invented later to illustrate the legal doctrine of 'abrogation' according to which some Quranic verses are deemed to be superseded by others as sources of law.[7]

The boycott of the Hashimis

During the lifetime of Abu Talib, Muhammad's own position was still fairly secure. Though Abu Talib never embraced Islam, family honour demanded that he continue to protect his nephew. The price of this loyalty, however, was the complete isolation of the whole Hashimi clan. No one was to do business with them, or to form marriage ties with them or their allies. It seems doubtful if this boycott, which lasted two years, was particularly effective, since most of the clans who were persuaded to join it must have realized that it merely served to increase the domination of the Banu Makhzum and 'Abd Shams. The fact was that the split in Makkan society was transcending clan allegiances: Muhammad's uncle Abu Lahab, though a Hashimi, was a keen supporter of the boycotters, and broke off the proposed marriages of two of his sons with two of the Prophet's daughters; while the principal meeting-place of the Muslims during this period – when their numbers had been reduced to about 40 men and 20 women – was the house of Arqan, a member of the Banu Makhzum. A notable convert at this period was 'Umar ibn al-Khattab, the future second caliph and the man who, after Muhammad, probably achieved most for Islam. Like St Paul, he began by being an avid persecutor of the new sect, which his sister Fatima and her husband, Sa'id, had secretly joined. He is said to have been converted after reading a sheet of paper containing the opening verses of Ta Ha – the Quran's 20th *sura*.

During the persecutions of the later Makkan period, Allah's messages became more strident and denunciatory. The Quran alludes frequently to earlier prophets – such as Salih, Hud, Shu'aib, Noah, Lot and Moses – who were sent to warn their peoples, only to be rejected by them. Inevitably those who failed to heed the warnings were punished, like proud Pharaoh and the people of Sodom, 'Ad, Thamud and Korah. Speaking as he was with God's voice, Muhammad identified himself completely with the earlier prophets. The same fate as befell these earlier peoples would overtake the pagan Quraish if they failed to heed God's messages. Sometimes these punishments were administered externally, the forces of nature acting as God's executioners. The people of Madyan and Sodom are destroyed by earthquakes, the people of Noah by the flood which his family alone survives. In other instances the idea of punishment presents itself in an altogether more sophisticated form: those who deny the truth are *wronging themselves* by rejecting God's messengers. Socially and politically, the message reaffirms the teachings of earlier prophets in the traditions of western Asia: abandonment of the traditional morality of the patriarchs leads inexorably to communal disintegration and the suffering associated with it.

Despite the failure of the boycott, in about 619 the Prophet and the small Muslim community suffered a double blow. Within a short period Muhammad lost both his wife, Khadija, and his uncle Abu

Talib. Khadija's death was a heavy personal loss: he had leaned heavily on her during the early days of revelation and despair, and she had been the first of his followers. Soon afterwards Muhammad married Sawda, herself a widow, from among the faithful. About the same time he was betrothed to 'Aisha, the child of Abu Bakr, who evidently wished to strengthen his personal ties with the master.

The death of Abu Talib deprived the Muslims of the protection which, despite the boycott, they had hitherto received from the head of the Hashimi clan. His successor Abu Lahab at first extended his protection to Muhammad, despite his earlier opposition to him: not to have done so would have reflected badly on his prestige as the Hashimi leader. Muhammad's other enemies, however, reminded Abu Lahab that the Prophet's teaching implied that their common ancestor, 'Abd al-Muttalib, must be burning in hell. When Muhammad confirmed that this was indeed the case, Abu Lahab felt free to abandon his nephew without loss of face. The deterioration in Muhammad's position was evident from the insults he was now forced to tolerate, such as having a sheep's womb thrown at him during prayer, or having sand cast in his face.

Up till now Muhammad had probably seen himself as the Prophet of the Quraish – a role which he was to assume again at the end of his career. He may already have realized that any chance of long-term success depended on getting the backing of this, the most powerful of all the Arabian tribes. For the immediate future, however, he realized he would have to look outside Makka for protection. He thought first of Taif, the cool hillside town where some of the wealthier Quraishi merchants had their summer residences (just as Makkan merchants and Saudi princes have today). But a ten-day visit to members of the Thaqif tribe who held their lands from the Quraish produced nothing but ridicule. Muhammad also tried to enlist beduin support; but when the Quraish denounced him they answered back, 'Your family and your clan know you better than we do, and they do not follow you.'

The hijra *(migration)*

Around 620 or thereabouts, Muhammad was approached by some members of the Khazraj, one of two tribal federations controlling the oasis of Madina (then known as Yathrib) about 275 miles north-east of Makka. The previously dominant Khazraj had been in bitter conflict with the rival federation of Aws, who had recently defeated them with the help of three Jewish tribes, the Quraiza, the Nadir and the Qainuqaʿ. Clearly the situation in Madina was tense, for although some kind of equilibrium had been established, it was probable that civil war would soon break out again. The problem of clan rivalries and tribal feuding seems to have been much more acute in Madina even than in Makka, since no one had unchallenged supremacy there, nor managed, like the ruling Quraish, to maintain a precarious consensus among the ruling clans. But the root causes of the malaise in Madina were probably not dissimilar from the ills affecting Makka: the incompatibility of nomadic values with life in a settled community, especially at a time when population growth may have been exercising increasing pressure on food resources.

The Jewish tribes had long been settled in the oasis. Muslim writers traced them back to Abraham through Isaac, ancestor of the Jews. Israeli and European scholars are more likely to consider them Arab tribes converted by Jews who fled from the Romans after the destruction of Jerusalem in 70 CE.

Muhammad was related to the Khazraj through his father's mother. This, together with reports of his persecution at the hands of the Quraish for preaching monotheistic doctrines, may have been enough to recommend him as a possible arbiter by those Madinans who were seeking a way out of the bloody vendettas that had been affecting life in the oasis for decades. In 620, six members of the Khazraj who were visiting Makka for the pilgrimage sought an interview with Muhammad. After hearing an explanation of his teachings and a recitation of the Quran, they accepted Islam. Back in Madina they made some more converts, and the following year they brought along some of the newcomers, including two members of the Aws. Muhammad sent one of his followers back with them, to teach them to pray and recite the Quran. These contacts culminated, in June 622, with a secret meeting at ʿAqaba, close to Makka. Seventy-five Madinese, including two women, were present. Here, in the presence of the Prophet, they pledged themselves to defend any Muslims who should come among them, including, of course, the Messenger of God. Twelve delegates – nine from the Khazraj and three from the Aws – were appointed guarantors of the pact.

The departure of the Muslims from Makka took place gradually over the following three months. For the most part, they met with no opposition from the Quraish, who were generally glad to be rid of the dissenters in their midst. However, some of the leaders, including Abu Jahl, saw that the exodus would sooner or later mean trouble, given that Madina lay on the route to Syria. There seems to have been a plot to assassinate Muhammad before his departure, including the provision that a representative of each clan was to take part in the killing, in order to make it impossible for the Hashimis to take revenge effectively. But the plan probably foundered for lack of agreement. A few Muslims decided to remain in Makka for family reasons. Muhammad and the faithful Abu Bakr were the last to leave their native city. In September 622, they slipped out secretly with a guide, travelling south at first to avoid pursuit. After three days spent hiding in a cave, they decided that the coast was clear and headed north for Madina. A new era in history had begun.

The Madinese polity: germ of the Islamic state

When Muhammad arrived in Madina, he simultaneously had the role of Chief of the Emigrants and umpire of the fractious and divided community which had chosen him as their arbiter. Some of the members of this community – known to the Muslims as the Ansar, or 'Helpers' – had already accepted him as Prophet. But he knew that his position, and that of the Muhajirun ('Emigrants'), was vulnerable. One false move on his part must put an end to the precarious alliance between the Aws and Khazraj, the Jewish tribes and the Muhajirun which had been temporarily stitched together.

Muhammad the Prophet continued to receive God's revelations. If the style of the Quranic verses changed, the passages becoming longer and more sustained, the language more fluent and less breathless, the content more concerned with establishing a positive doctrine with a specific moral and legal content, this was hardly surprising. The Source – like the small but determined community inspired by it – was having to adjust to new conditions. It was no longer enough to fulminate against the Quraish and their iniquities, to proclaim the Day of Judgement and to marvel at the infinite majesty of the Creator and all his works. The new situation demanded a coherent formula for living as well as the will to put this formula into practice. Whether or not

Muhammad became more adept at 'calling up' revelations in order to deal with the demands of the moment, the Quranic passages dating from the Madinese period are mostly of a different character from that of the ecstatic utterances of the early Makkan years. The Quran becomes more conscious of itself as a source of law and as a commentary on current events.

Muhammad's first move on reaching Madina was characteristically astute. Instead of risking offence by accepting the hospitality of one of its many clans, he left the choice to Allah – through the ambulations of his camel. On the spot where the camel settled herself, the Emigrants helped him build the house that would become, after the Ka'ba, the foremost mosque of Islam. It consisted of the simplest of structures, a courtyard overlooked by a number of flat-roofed rooms or huts, surrounded by a sun-baked mudbrick wall. It was here that he received petitioners and visitors and conducted the thrice-daily prayers at which the whole of the Muslim community was present; it was here that he organized and directed the affairs of the infant Islamic state, whenever he was not actually campaigning in the field (which took up most of his time); it was to be in one of these rooms – beneath the floor of that occupied by his favourite wife, 'Aisha – that he would be buried on his death, ten years after arriving in Madina: the ten years of his active career that would transform Arabia and shake the world.

Having established his headquarters, Muhammad set about defining the relationship between the Muslims and the tribes of Madina. According to one tradition, each of the Ansar swore an oath of brotherhood with one of the Emigrants. A detailed agreement governing their relations, however, has been preserved in a written document considered authentic by most western and all Muslim scholars. According to this document, subsequently known as the Constitution of Madina, 'the believers and Muslims of Quraish and Yathrib [Madina] and those who follow and are attached to them and fight alongside them . . . form a single community [Umma] to the exclusion of all [i.e. other] men.' The Jews are specifically included in the Umma: 'To the Jew who follows us belongs help and equality. He shall not be wronged nor shall his enemies be aided. The peace of the believers is indivisible.'[8]

The Umma or community referred to in the agreement – which follows the lines of a *hilf* or tribal pact such as traditionally formed a nomadic confederation – is composed of groups (rather than individuals) consisting of the Muhajirun, the Arab clans of Madina and the Jewish clans attached to them. Each group formed a single unit for the purposes of paying blood-money. Pagan allies are evidently admitted, since they are specifically mentioned. Muhammad must already have been anticipating conflict with the Quraish, so his primary concern was the political one of preventing them from making common cause with the Makkans: 'No pagan is to give protection to any person of Quraish, either his goods or his person.' The Muslims themselves, however, were bound by stronger obligations. They were to help any of their number seriously in debt over blood-money or the payment of ransom; they were never to take the side of an unbeliever against a Muslim; all Muslims, however humble, were to be entitled to aid and protection; in the event of war, no one was to make a separate peace with the enemy. They must maintain internal law and order, punishing the wrongdoers among them.

Muhammad's own role is primarily that of mediator: 'If any dispute or controversy likely to cause trouble should arise it must be referred to God and Muhammad the apostle of God. God accepts what is nearest to piety and goodness in this document . . . God approves of this document.'[9] In other respects, Muhammad appears to be just one tribal chief among many – the Muhajirun constituting, as it were, his own tribe.

Conflict with Makka

The Muhajirun had no means of subsistence: they had little in the way of stock, and could hardly be expected to live on the charity of the Madinese farmers for long without coming into conflict with them. The solution adopted by the Muslims was a traditional beduin one: to prey on the merchant caravans proceeding from Makka. Other tribes, had they been strong enough, would have done the same in similar circumstances. What made for a radical break with custom was that as Quraishis themselves, the Muhajirun would be preying on their own kin. From a superior moral viewpoint they were justified in this, not only because their pagan relatives had treated them badly, but also because they had a legitimate interest in what, after all, constituted Quraishi property.

The earliest raids seem to have been small affairs, without booty or bloodshed. The first blood was spilled during the second year of the *hijra* (in January 624) when a Quraishi was killed in an ambush at Nakhla, south of Makka. The caravan, which must have been a small one since it was attended by only four people, was captured and triumphantly brought back to Madina. Muhammad had misgivings about the raid, which occurred towards the end of the sacred month of Rajab, when, according to custom, bloodshed was forbidden. He withheld distribution of the booty until a revelation came down justifying the raid.

The Nakhla raid greatly helped the Muhajirun, for, in addition to the booty, they received 1,600 dirhams in ransom for the three prisoners. More important, perhaps, was the boost it gave to their prestige in the eyes of the Ansar. The Madinese, who had not taken part in the raiding so far, now became anxious to gain a share of the booty. In March 624, two months after the Nakhla raid, news arrived of a very large caravan returning from Gaza to Makka, with goods estimated at 50,000 dinars. It was accompanied by about fifty merchants, representing all the Quraishi clans under the leadership of Abu Sufyan of 'Abd Shams. Every family in Makka had an interest in its safe return.

Aware of the danger posed by the Muslims, Abu Sufyan called for reinforcements from Makka. A huge force numbering nearly 1,000 men, just about every able-bodied man available, was sent under Abu Jahl to escort the caravan home. The relief force continued to advance on Madina after Abu Sufyan's caravan had passed out of danger by staying close to the sea. Forewarned of Abu Jahl's approach, Muhammad made for the strategic wells of Badr with about 300 men, most of them Ansaris. Muhammad had three of the four wells filled in, forcing the tired and thirsty Makkans to fight for water on ground chosen by their enemies. The Muslims spent the night in prayer. At dawn Abu Jahl's army advanced to be greeted by a hail of arrows from the Muslim archers. After a period of combat, Arab-style, between individual champions, a mêlée ensued which turned into a general rout of the Makkans, 49 of whom, including their leader, were killed. The Prophet watched the action from a palm-fronded booth behind the lines. After the battle he asked one of the Emigrants to see if Abu Jahl's body was among the slain. The man found the Quraishi leader mortally wounded. 'You have climbed high, little shepherd!' he said with his dying breath. The Emigrant cut off Abu Jahl's head and brought it to the Prophet, who gave thanks to Allah.

Aftermath of Badr

The political and ideological implications of Badr, the first major victory for Islam, were more important than the military ones. Like the Cromwellians after Naseby, the Muslims now had proof that their steadfastness had been vindicated. As the Quran proclaimed afterwards, 'It was not you who slew the enemy, but God who slew them' (8:17). Before Badr, Madina had been little more than a place of refuge for a group of persecuted outcasts. After Badr, the feeling that God was on their side would carry the Muslims forward towards those much vaster victories that would culminate in the defeat of Byzantium and the collapse of Persia. Though mostly young and inexperienced in battle, they had shown that unity under the Prophet's leadership and the moral purpose engendered by the sense of absolute justice in their cause could defeat the bigger battalions of their enemies. They had learned that solidarity was the key to success. The Quraish – so the earliest accounts suggest – had been reluctant to kill their own relatives among the Muslims for fear of giving rise to a new round of vendettas. The faithful had had no such inhibitions about dispatching their kin among the polytheists. The new solidarity of faith had triumphed over the older loyalties of kinship.

If Badr vindicated Muhammad the Prophet, it also greatly strengthened his hand as a political leader. Acting on a revelation received after the battle, he established an important precedent by distributing the booty equally among the Muslims. Resisting the demands of 'Umar that the 70 or so prisoners should be put to the sword, he kept all but two of them for ransom. The two he allowed to be executed had incurred his wrath in Makka by comparing passages in the Quran unfavourably to parts of the Persian and Jewish scriptures, casting doubt on the authenticity of the revelation. Muhammad readily forgave his physical enemies, but rarely, if ever, his ideological opponents. It was about this time that he arranged for the assassination of the woman poet and satirist Asma bint Marwan, who had written verses ridiculing the Madinese tribesmen for obeying a leader not of their kin.

With the immediate threat to Madina passed, Muhammad was now faced with the most formidable source of ideological opposition – namely, the Jewish tribes. Although he had a high regard for the Jews as monotheists and had needed their support during the first embattled days in Madina, he must soon have realized that conflict would be inevitable. The Jews could hardly be expected to recognize his claims to prophethood without abandoning their own religious assumptions and their distinctive scriptural heritage and identity as God's chosen people. At some point, possibly before the battle of Badr, the break appears to have been formalized, when the direction of prayer – the *qibla* – was changed from Jerusalem to Makka. The first of the Jewish tribes to be attacked by Muhammad after Badr was the Banu Qainuqa', a clan composed mainly of goldsmiths and other craftsmen. A market-place row involving the wife of a Muslim provided the pretext: a Jew and a Muslim were killed in the fracas and the Banu Qainuqa' withdrew to their quarter. The Muslims laid siege to them till they surrendered unconditionally. Muhammad wanted to massacre the Jews but was dissuaded from doing so by 'Abdullah ibn Ubaiy, chief of the Khazraji clan, of which the Qainuqa' were clients. Instead they were given three days in which to quit the city, leaving their goods behind them. The spoils were enormous, and Muhammad kept one fifth for himself, in accordance with tribal custom. The two most powerful Jewish tribes, however, remained to be dealt with.

At about this time the Makkans, smarting from the defeat at Badr and from further raids upon their caravans, were preparing a new, more powerful expeditionary force. They assembled an army of 3,000 men, including dissident members of the Aws and clansmen from among their tributaries in Taif and among the beduin. They were led by Abu Sufyan, who had succeeded Abu Jahl as leader of the Quraish. As the army of the Quraish advanced on Madina, the Muslims and their allies had no alternative but to withdraw into their fortified dwellings, leaving the horses and camels of the enemy to gorge themselves on their freshly planted crops. The Madinese clan leaders held a council of war and decided at first to sit out a siege behind the defensible stone walls linking the different quarters. However, some of the younger Muslims who had missed the action at Badr urged the Prophet to attack the enemy. For a time Muhammad prevaricated; then he put on his armour and decided to launch an offensive. Of the thousand or so men he had with him only one hundred had armour, and there were only two horses. The Jewish tribes, who had begun the sabbath, remained in their homes.

Half-way towards the hill of Uhud, where the Quraishi army was encamped, Muhammad sent back some of the younger boys whom he felt might prove a liability. At this point 'Abdullah ibn Ubaiy decided to retire with a third of the army, on the dubious pretext that the Muslims did not seriously intend to fight. As a clan leader, he was probably within his rights. He may, however, have hoped that a defeat for Muhammad would strengthen his own position, which had declined considerably since Badr.

The engagement at Uhud proved a major setback for the Muslims. At first things seemed to be going their way until Muhammad's archers, posted on the hillside, abandoned their posts in the expectation of booty and were mown down by the Makkan cavalry under the brilliant command of Khalid ibn al-Walid (later to become the most outstanding of all the Muslim generals). About 70 Muslims were killed, including the Prophet's uncle, Hamza. The Prophet himself was badly wounded and at one time was even reported dead. The Quraish celebrated their triumph in the barbaric manner of the times, the women who accompanied them fashioning necklaces from the ears of their dead enemies.

Despite his victory, Abu Sufyan decided against trying to occupy Madina. The defeat of Badr had been avenged: he was still thinking in terms of traditional beduin warfare. Muhammad, for his part, lost no time in trying to regain his lost prestige. His wounds had scarcely been dressed before he set out in pursuit of the Quraish, a purely symbolic action which nevertheless boosted the morale of his supporters. The lesson of Uhud was not to be lost. If the victory of Badr had constituted proof that Allah was on the side of the Muslims, the defeat of Uhud had been ordained in order to test their faith, and to sort out the steadfast believers from the 'doubters' like 'Abdullah ibn Ubaiy and his followers.

The Battle of the Ditch and defeat of the Jews

The experience of Uhud and the defection of 'Abdullah now made it essential to deal with all possible sources of dissent, especially the remaining Jews. Convinced that the Banu Nadir were plotting against him, he presented them with an ultimatum. They must leave the oasis with their goods and chattels within ten days: otherwise they would be massacred. 'Abdullah ibn Ubaiy urged the Banu Nadir to resist. The Muslims began felling their palm-trees. After about a fortnight, the Jews surrendered. They were allowed to leave with such goods as they could carry on their camels, barring weapons. Most of them went to Khaibar, a mainly Jewish oasis settlement about 70 miles north of Medina.

After his failure to intervene successfully on behalf of the Banu Nadir, 'Abdullah ibn Ubaiy's prestige began to decline. His downfall came with the so-called 'Affair of the Slanderers', an incident in which Muhammad's youngest and favourite wife, 'Aisha, was accused of being unfaithful with one of Muhammad's men on the way home from a military expedition. 'Abdullah and his party, who included those Madinese who had become thoroughly disgruntled at the take-over of their city by the Makkan prophet and his followers, seized on the episode to impugn Muhammad's honour. For an Arab to have an unfaithful wife is a social disgrace. For a prophet, such a thing is unthinkable. Fortunately for Muhammad, after a period of suspense in which he was distinctly cool towards his young wife, there came down a revelation clearing her of all scandal. The faithful sighed with relief, while Allah himself turned on the slanderers. From this episode date the Quranic provisions stipulating that charges of adultery or fornication (punishable by 100 lashes) must be supported by four adult male witnesses, or eight female witnesses, to the act of copulation. About the same time Muhammad received further revelations demanding special protection for his wives.

Although Muhammad's warlike expeditions had led to a signal increase in his prestige among the beduin tribes, Abu Sufyan and the Quraish had not remained idle. A new hostile coalition was in the making, encouraged by the exiled Banu Nadir. Muhammad, on the advice, it is said, of the Persian freedman Salman al-Farisi, decided to reinforce the Madinese defences by digging a ditch along the unprotected northern perimeter of the settlement. The invaders, who had no siege engines and despised manual work too much to build any, swore impotently at the ditch, which they considered some kind of outrage. A few individuals were killed by arrows and stones flung from either side. After a few weeks, the Quraishi army ran out of supplies and decided to withdraw.

Despite the victory of the Battle of the Ditch, Muhammad still did not feel safe. He suspected, with good reason, that during the siege the Jews of the Banu Quraiza had been in contact with the enemy, who were trying to persuade them to attack the Muslims from the rear. The Jews had apparently debated the idea, but little, if anything, was done. Nevertheless Muhammad decided to eliminate them once and for all. After a siege lasting 25 days the Banu Quraiza surrendered. They agreed to accept the arbitration of their leading ally, Sa'd ibn Mu'adh, chief of the Aws, who had been fatally wounded during the siege. He was brought on a donkey, surrounded by his fellow-tribesmen urging clemency. Unmoved, the dying man made everyone present swear that his sentence would be carried out. Only when this had been agreed did he pronounce it: all 600 adult males were to be killed, the women and children sold into slavery and the tribe's property divided among the Muslims.

The truce with Makka

Increasingly, Muhammad's thoughts were turning to Makka. He continued to consolidate his alliances with neighbouring tribes. Still too weak to make submission to Islam a condition of any pact, he concentrated on persuading the beduin to disrupt the Quraishi trade, thereby isolating the Makkans and their allies, the Jews of Khaibar. For their part, the Makkans were becoming thoroughly demoralized. Their continuing ideological poverty was demonstrated at this time by the conversion to Islam of two of their most outstanding soldiers, Khalid ibn al-Walid, future victor of Yarmuk, and 'Amr ibn al-'As, future conqueror of Egypt. No doubt opportunism as well as faith played a part in these conversions. The more far-sighted members of the Quraish were beginning to realize that since there was no beating Muhammad, the next best thing was to join him. This was probably not the first time that the Quraishis had thought of compromise. But they would find in due course that the terms of a compromise would be surprisingly generous – so generous, indeed, that the concluding phase of the Prophet's career and the subsequent period from his death in 632 to the 'Abbasid revolution of 750, could be described as the victory of the Quraish over Islam.

Towards the end of the sixth year of the *hijra* (March 628), the Prophet announced his intention of visiting Makka in order to perform the *'umra* (lesser pilgrimage). He took with him about seven hundred men and four women. The men were armed only with their swords, which they kept sheathed according to custom. The Makkans, however, were alarmed, and deployed their armed men to prevent the Muslims from entering the Holy City. Muhammad headed for Hudaibiya on the edge of the sacred territory, where he received several emissaries from the Quraish, who returned impressed by the discipline and peaceful demeanour of the Muslims.

After discussions, a ten-year truce was signed between Muhammad and the Quraish, according to which the Muslims agreed to forgo the right of pilgrimage until the following year, when the Makkans would evacuate their city for three days, during which the Muslims would be allowed to perform the rituals. Many of the Muslims, including 'Umar, the future second caliph, protested vigorously at what they saw as a 'sell-out'. But Muhammad and Abu Bakr were more far-sighted: the Quraish had recognized the Muslims as equal parties and had given them a free hand to tackle the still pressing problem of the Jews of Khaibar. Muhammad returned to Madina and soon afterwards set off for the oasis with 1,600 men. The Jews were abandoned by their beduin allies and were gradually forced to submit, household by household. Muhammad spared their lives, taking half the date-crop and the better part of their possessions. The men were kept as slaves, the women distributed among the Muslims. Muhammad chose for himself a beautiful girl of 17 named Safiya, whose husband had been killed in the fighting. After the fall of Khaibar, the other Jewish colonies in the region submitted without a fight and were allowed to keep their goods on payment of the *jizya* or poll-tax.

The 'opening' of Makka

The following year Muhammad set out on the pilgrimage, in accordance with the terms of the Hudaibiya treaty. Accompanied by 2,000 Muslims, he entered the empty city, performing the *tawaf* on his camel, as well as the *sa'i* between Safa and Marwa. Bilal, the former Abyssinian slave, made the call to prayer from the Ka'ba roof. While he was in Makka Muhammad is related by some traditions to have married his cousin Maimuna, daughter of his uncle 'Abbas, and to have consummated the marriage in the state of *ihram*.

With the elimination of their last remaining Jewish allies, time was running out for the Quraish. The fickle beduin tribes, always opportunistic, were beginning to flock to Muhammad's standard. The Hudaibiya treaty no longer reflected the true balance of power in the Peninsula. Incidents over blood-money and clashes between beduin clients of Muhammad and the Quraish were making it unworkable. Abu Sufyan decided to confront the coming crisis by visiting Madina and making terms with the Prophet. The true picture of what took place has probably been distorted, since the earliest accounts date from the 'Abbasid period and were written by historians concerned with discrediting Abu Sufyan, ancestor of the Umayyad caliphs. It appears, however, that the Prophet and the Quraishi leader negotiated what followed. In January 630 Muhammad marched towards Makka at the head of an army which eventually swelled to more than 10,000 as his beduin allies joined him on the way. They halted outside the *haram* area, where Abu Sufyan came to the Prophet and formally embraced Islam. The Quraishi leader then returned to Makka, where he delivered Muhammad's terms to the people: there would be no danger so long as the city surrendered peacefully. (A very similar arrangement occurred in 1925, when the city fathers came to 'Abd al-'Aziz al-Sa'ud, who offered almost identical terms.)

On 30 January 630 Muhammad entered the now deserted streets of the Holy City. The event has become known as the 'opening', the same word that is used for the first *sura* of the Quran. Only a few pagans offered resistance in one quarter, where they were soon rounded up by Khalid ibn al-Walid. The Prophet made for the Ka'ba and touched the Black Stone with his stick, proclaiming 'Allahu Akbar' (God is Greater), the traditional war-cry of Islam, in a loud voice. After performing the *tawaf* on his camel, he ordered the idols to be thrown down from their pedestals. Then he called on the pagan Quraish to make their homage to him, which they did by filing past him as he sat on the rock of Safa.

An amnesty was proclaimed for most past offences; only a few individuals were proscribed. Characteristically, they were intellectual enemies. They included the composer of some satirical verses against Muhammad, as well as the woman singer who had chanted them. Another was a former scribe who came to doubt the absolute authenticity of the Quranic revelations, when the Prophet had allowed him to include a statement of his own in the Quranic text. His life was spared, however, after the intervention of his foster-brother, 'Uthman ibn Affan.

Muhammad had not been long in Makka before he was confronted with a new danger. The tribal confederation of the Hawazim, traditional enemies of the Quraish, were amassing against him, in conjunction with some anti-Quraishi elements in Taif. Within a fortnight of the conquest of Makka he had taken to the field once more at the head of an army of 12,000. He defeated the tribesmen at Hunain, but failed to take Taif. The women of the Banu Hawazim were shared out among the Muslims, but returned to their menfolk when the latter embraced Islam. In distributing the spoils, Muhammad infuriated some of the longest-serving Muslims by outrageously favouring the newly converted Quraish. Abu Sufyan and his sons, including Mu'awiya, future founder of the Umayyad dynasty, were each given one hundred camels. Even members of the Quraish who had not yet been converted received some of the spoils. The Madinese became seriously alarmed that Muhammad, now 'King of the Hejaz' in fact as well as in the appellation of his enemies, would settle permanently in Makka. They were greatly relieved when he returned to Madina.

The impact of Islam

The Prophet Muhammad was now approaching the end of his life. He must have been about 60 at the Battle of Hunain, when his personal resolution in the face of the enemy's cavalry converted what might have been another Uhud into a major victory. Among the beduin tribes, the bandwagon effect, already building up before the 'conquest' of Makka, had become a landslide. Delegations from all parts of Arabia came to Muhammad asking to be included in his system. The tribes which made the pact with Madina promised troops and pledged themselves not to attack any other tribes in the alliance. Many, however, embraced Islam only in a nominal sense while remaining attached to pagan practices. Muhammad understood – as his more zealous followers did not – that it would take several generations to 'Islamize' the new adherents. What counted for the present was the protection they could afford the fledgeling state he had succeeded in creating in Madina: the state which must outlive him in order to become the vehicle for Allah's purpose.

The problem to which the Madinese system was primarily addressed was the maintenance of social cohesion. The new solidarity of the Umma, the Islamic community, replaced the old solidarity of the *qawm* or tribe. The doctrine of the Day of Judgement proclaimed in the Quran implied that individuals were primarily responsible for their actions, regardless of birth. This was a reflection on the psychological plane of material changes in Makka itself, where a society of beduin traders was being transformed into one of merchant capitalists. Similar tensions between individualism and group identity had been occurring in Madina, where the clan system of formerly nomadic tribes was proving increasingly ill-adapted to the needs of an agricultural community. A clan system which helps maintain an overall ecological balance under desert conditions breaks down when applied in an environment necessitating a much higher degree of cooperation between different social groups.

The old tribal system had been at the root of Arabia's problems, barring the road to future development. What had once worked well in the desert was becoming unsuited both to the caravan-city and to the oasis. Yet tribalism could not be eliminated overnight, or even abolished altogether. What was required was a new field of loyalty which would smooth the transition to a more individualized society without, however, exposing the individual to a feeling of utter helplessness. The new solidarity provided by Islam was the Umma, a super-tribal entity whose loyalty was to Allah, the super-tribal deity. All other allegiances, symbolized by inferior deities or tribal totems, were either abolished or so subsumed within the new allegiance to the Prophet's community that in due course they could be expected to 'wither away'. None of these changes came about spontaneously. They occurred as a result of a carefully worked-out social and ideological programme.

The Five Pillars

This programme came under five heads. Known to Islam as the 'Five Pillars' of the faith, it is still the basis of belief and practice common to all Muslims. The first pillar is the *shahada*, the profession of faith by which the Muslim acknowledges his allegiance to God and His prophet: 'I testify that there is no god but Allah, and I testify that Muhammad is the Messenger of Allah.' Utterance of the *shahada* before witnesses is sufficient for full conversion to Islam. The second pillar is *salat*, or prayer, a basic duty performed both individually and publicly. In its public or congregational form performed on Fridays and feast-days, prayer is a means of reinforcing group consciousness and expressing social solidarity. Muhammad probably chose Friday as the day for public prayer because this was the time when his Jewish allies were themselves preparing for the sabbath. But the Quran explicitly rejects sabbatarianism. Apart from the congregational prayers usually held at noon, Friday was traditionally a normal work-day in Muslim lands, and indeed one which provided special opportunities for business.

The physical movements of Muslim prayer were, in addition to any spiritual dimension, a means of promoting group solidarity. The old kinship groups of Arab society had been reinforced by all sorts of subtle physical traits: an individual's membership of a particular tribe might be determined by a special gait or gesture. By subjecting itself at regular daily intervals to a series of identical and repeated physical actions, the Umma subsumed the particularisms of tribal or racial identity in a common physical discipline. In the original context of beduin Arabia, and in parallel conditions elsewhere, the Muslim prayer had an effect similar to the discipline of the parade ground: the new recruits were welded into a single uniform body. The psychological impact of prayer was also effective at an individual level: by insisting on the interruption of ordinary mundane activities at least three times each day, it continuously reminded the believer of the superior claims of God and the community.

The social obligations of Islam are made most explicit in *zakat*, third of the five pillars. The word has evolved semantically from its primary meaning – 'purification' – to its current definition of 'obligatory charity'. The implication is clear enough: personal property must be 'purified' by payment of one's dues to the community, for the upkeep of its weaker members. *Zakat* introduced a rationalized form of social security in place of the largesse formerly administered by tribal chiefs. Traditionally it consisted of a two and a half per cent annual levy on income and capital – reflecting, like the Muslim inheritance laws, conditions in a society in which wealth consisted in stock or merchandise rather than land. The distinction between capital (i.e., land) and income (i.e., crops) is much less evident in pastoral than in agricultural conditions, since herds are continuously increasing themselves.

The fourth pillar of Islam is *sawm*, the annual fast of Ramadan, the ninth month in the lunar calendar, during which all food, drink and sexual activity are forbidden between dawn and dusk. The arduousness of the regime varies according to the time of year in which Ramadan falls (as well as the geographical latitude). In general it can be said that the fast confers on the community many of the benefits of asceticism, such as self-discipline and mental control over bodily needs, without falling into the excesses of the eastern churches, where 'spiritual athleticism', by separating the ascetics from ordinary lay believers, tended to undermine group cohesion.

The fifth pillar of Islam, the Hajj, was not instituted in its final form until the Farewell Pilgrimage of 632. While directly connecting the new community with the traditions of Arabian paganism, it also reinforced Islamic cohesion by making the Umma aware of itself as a physical entity.

In addition to the 'five pillars', the community was enjoined to observe certain Quranic injunctions, most of them adapted from existing Arabian customs. Marriage was contractual and polygyny (one man and up to four wives) permitted. The provision was realistic in a warrior society in which women had always been considered part of the booty. In time the practice of marrying non-Muslim women would facilitate the breaking down of ethnic barriers within the community, contributing to Islam's multi-racial character: thus the Hui Muslims of China, descendants of Arab traders, are Chinese by race, just as the Senegalese Muslims are black. The Quran's insistence that every wife should be treated equally should have meant that captive women were accorded the dignity of wives, ruling out concubinage. This law, like the ban on wine-drinking, tended to be honoured in the breach by the Muslim ruling classes. The laws on inheritance, by which the sons shared equally in the property of their parents and the daughters received half the portions of the sons, accorded with the needs of a pastoral community organized on patriarchal lines. Unlike agricultural holdings, livestock can be subdivided without becoming less productive.

The dietary rules of Islam were simple and practical ones for the region, and generally reflected existing Arab practice. The ban on carrion is obviously necessary in a hot climate. Pork contains dangerous bacteria and parasites if not properly cured or cooked, and is not generally economical to produce in non-forested, arid regions. However, its general prohibition by the Hebrews and Arabs may also have reflected the prejudices of pastoralists against the eating habits of peasant cultivators. The insistence that no one must eat meat over which any name other than that of Allah had been pronounced –

usually converted into a positive injunction by adoption of the Halal dietary provisions – was obviously aimed at discouraging idolatry. The progressive prohibition on wine and other intoxicants, while aimed at promoting social decorum, may also have had a religious basis, since wine played an important part in Christian and some pagan rituals.

The Quranic rules were not always clear in themselves, and in later centuries they would receive much elaboration from the scholar-lawyers. There is no way of knowing how strictly they were applied during the Prophet's lifetime. Where they involved a simple adoption or modification of Arab custom it seems reasonable to suppose they were generally adhered to. Some rituals, including prayer, may have been observed more strictly by the pious of later generations: it seems that in the Prophet's time it was considered sufficient to pray three times each day, instead of the five times stipulated later. The Quran hints at certain sexual practices – including temporary marriages – forbidden in later times. Apart from this, however, there can be no question but that the Prophet allowed himself, and was permitted by the Quran, to have wives well in excess of the four permitted under Islamic law.

Muhammad's wives

According to the earliest sources, Muhammad married at least eleven, possibly fourteen, women after Khadija's death. Most of his marriages had a political significance: like any beduin chief, he cemented his alliances within or outside his tribe through marriage. Thus, nine of the Prophet's wives, including Khadija, were from the Quraish or clans allied to them. Three more were captives, two of them from the defeated Jewish tribes: this again accorded with prevailing custom. They included Juwairiya, daughter of the Chief of the Banu Mustaliq, defeated by Muhammad in 626, Raihana, whose husband was a member of the Banu Quraiza massacred in 627, and Safiya, taken captive at Khaibar in 628. In addition, Muhammad had one Christian wife, Mary the Copt, a concubine sent to him by the ruler of Egypt in 628. Mary bore the Prophet a son, Ibrahim, who died in infancy. None of Muhammad's wives came from the Ansar, perhaps because he did not wish to favour any one Madinese clan above the others.

However, although political motives could be found for most of Muhammad's marriages, personal desire definitely played a part, as is made clear by the earliest accounts of his life. A tradition preserved by al-Bukhari states that he satisfied nine of his wives in a single night. While some modern Muslim writers, responding to the charges of lust or sensuality made by western critics, were shocked or embarrassed by such stories, the traditionists who collected them after the Prophet's death do not seem to have regarded sexual prowess as being incompatible with prophecy. Again, there are parallels with that other great Arabian tribal chief, 'Abd al-'Aziz al Sa'ud, who, like the Prophet, declared that he loved nothing better than 'prayer, sweet odours and women'.

The problems caused by Muhammad's multiple marriages are alluded to in the Quran, which offers his wives the choice between the claims of this world and those of God and His Prophet. Having chosen the latter, they are ordered to conduct themselves with the dignity of their position (33:32–3). In the same *sura*, the Prophet is told that he may marry no more women 'even though their beauty should please him greatly'. However, it is also made clear that, because of the purity of his heart, Allah has allowed him sexual privileges denied to other men.

For the ordinary Muslim, the Quran laid down certain norms governing sexual conduct. No sexual relations were to be permitted outside marriage. *Zina*, meaning both adultery and fornication, is punishable by flogging – one hundred strokes for each partner, irrespective of whether they are married.* Marriage itself is a civil contract and may be terminated by either party. If the wife terminates the contract without offence by the husband (*khul'*), she is obliged to give back her marriage portion. If the husband initiates the divorce by declaration (*talaq*), she retains it.[10] Men are allowed up to four wives at one time, women are permitted only one husband. This is consistent with the twofold aim of ensuring that all women from puberty onwards have the option of marriage – which the Quran insists upon as a duty, and of ensuring the paternity of children, essential to the maintenance of the patriarchal structure. Since the husband is responsible for the upkeep of his children, it is absolutely necessary that he should know that they are his.

---

* This was amended in Islamic law, during the reign of the Caliph 'Umar, to death by stoning for offenders who are or have been married.

Modernist writers have argued that the right of polygyny, which is clearly discriminatory, is effectively negated by provisions insisting that all four wives be treated equally – a provision which, in its broadest interpretation, would be impossible to fulfil. However, it is clear, from both the Quranic rules of marriage and the Prophet's own example, that equality of treatment refers strictly to legally enforceable matters such as a woman's right to her own household or to an equal share of her husband's property. The Quranic marriage-laws, as with other provisions, took over and modified existing beduin custom, in this case by strengthening the legal and personal property rights of women. In the context of a mainly pastoral society, polygyny acknowledged an important biological fact: a woman can only be pregnant with one man's child, while a man may father several children in the course of a single pregnancy. It also assumed that the purpose of sex was purely procreative. To allow a surplus of unmarried nubile women meant wasting an important human resource. A tribe's women, like its mares, ewes and she-camels, were an essential part of its capital.

In the long term, Muslim women would suffer a progressive loss of social and sexual rights *vis-à-vis* men. This probably had more to do with the situation prevailing in the conquered Byzantine and Sassanid territories during the period, at least two centuries after Muhammad's death, when the Islamic law was being formalized and consolidated, than with provisions explicitly outlined in the Quran. For example, the verse enjoining the faithful to address the Prophet's wives from 'behind a screen' (*hijab*), originally a matter of protocol, was later invoked to justify such radical forms of sexual segregation as the complete veiling of women. Similarly, in matters of dress generally, the Quran leaves vague the character of the garments considered suitable: it merely enjoins the women believers to 'lower their gaze and be mindful of their chastity, and not to display their charms [in public] beyond what may [decently] be apparent thereof' (24:31).

Attitudes towards wealth

Another aspect of the Madinese Umma which would have important implications for the future was its economic life. The collection of *zakat*, as well as the voluntary donations known as *sadaqa*, provided for the poor and needy. In addition to these funds, the Prophet had at his disposal the fifth share of the booty which, according to tribal custom, was reserved for the chief. In practice this portion, which the Prophet received in his capacity as chief of the Umma, came to be the basis of the Muslim treasury – the *bait al-mal* – from which the Muslim state financed such activities as the purchase of horses and other war material and the subsidies or bribes paid to secure the friendship of allied tribes. In addition to retaining his fifth share of the booty, mainly for military purposes, the Prophet appropriated certain lands for the common pasturing of horses, establishing a precedent for common ownership that would be extensively used by Caliph 'Umar in the conquered Byzantine territories.

Riba or usury, as prohibited in the Quran, is generally equated with the lending of money or goods at interest: 'O you who have attained to faith, do not gorge yourselves on usury [*riba*] doubling and redoubling it, but remain conscious of God so that you might attain to a happy state!' (3:130). Later generations of scholars would interpret the prohibition so strictly as to cover any form of profit or unearned gain, and elaborate tricks (*hiyal*), such as the double contract of sale, were invented to get round the ban. Modern Muslim authorities see the ban as applying to interest rather than profit: where money is earned on money, it is *riba* and therefore forbidden. Where it is earned through trade or productive investment, even if this involves buying cheap and selling dear, *riba* is avoided. Generally, the Quran does not condemn wealth as such, but only its pursuit as an end in itself which can interfere with social concern or spiritual awareness. It is in this spirit that modern Muslim economists have interpreted the prohibition as applying to risk-free interest rather than profit. Where the lender exacts his payment regardless of the borrower's circumstances his action may be exploitative and socially irresponsible. But if he stands to lose as well as to gain by the borrower's enterprise, he becomes not an exploiter but a business partner. Thus modern Islamic banking is based theoretically on equity participation or profit-sharing, rather than on lending at fixed rates of interest.

From the historical viewpoint, the polity created by the Prophet at Madina represented the germ of a system rather than a fully realized ideal. Compared with the flowering of Islamic civilization that would occur in the great riverine valleys, it was a rudimentary and primitive society. It would take several more centuries for this embryonic system to reach maturity. During the Prophet's lifetime the model was incomplete and far from monolithic. Many Muslims look back on the Madinese polity during the time of the Prophet and his immediate successors as a sort of desert utopia, where a state of perfection had been reached which could never be achieved by subsequent generations, like the Garden of Eden before the Fall. Historically this view is problematic. The Madinese polity was born in blood and violence. The decade of the Prophet, its midwife, was a time of almost continuous warfare and armed struggle. What Madina offered was not a final solution to the ills of humankind, but rather a distinctive approach to certain crucial problems in the life of the Arabian peninsula. Because these questions were accurately perceived, the solutions proved generally successful – so successful, in fact, that later generations of Muslims never cease to imitate them.

The Farewell Pilgrimage

In 632 Muhammad the Prophet embarked on his last ('Farewell') pilgrimage and finalized the Hajj and 'Umra ceremonies described in Chapter 1. He returned to Madina stronger than ever. If not actually ruler of a united Arabia, he was now, as the *de facto* head of the Quraish, its virtual master, as well as being a widely acknowledged religious leader. For the first time in its history, Arabia had been unified. This unprecedented political unity was the first fruit of the new religious system, under which allegiance to Allah and his Prophet overrode all prior allegiances based on tribal or family ties. The new solidarity of the Umma opened the way to what would become the most remarkable of Islam's historic achievements – the conquest, almost overnight, of the whole of the Sassanid empire and the southern Byzantine provinces of Syria and Egypt. No doubt the internal weaknesses of the empires, their exhaustion after years of mutual conflict and the religious and class divisions affecting their populations played a part in their defeat, among the most sudden in recorded history. But the decisive factor was the new religion. The greater mobility and superior fighting skills of the Arab warriors was – for the first and last time ever – directed towards a common cause. The energies that had previously wasted themselves in bitter tribal feuding were welded into a new, irresistible power.

The conflict with Rome and Persia was inevitable. Muhammad's system was a dynamic one, depending for its stability on continuous outward expansion. By the time the dwindling stock of Arab pagans remaining outside the *pax islamica* had become absorbed, the only avenue of expansion lay northward and eastward, beyond the Byzantine and Sassanid frontiers. Already, about ten months after the fall of Makka, Muhammad had mounted a great expedition consisting of 20,000 to 30,000 men, which breached the Byzantine frontier at Tabuk, about 250 miles north of Madina. There he received tribute from a number of marcher lords, including the Christian king of Aila (modern 'Aqaba) and Jewish settlers from Jarba and Udra in Transjordan. He had then turned back, partly because his men were exhausted from the heat, partly in order to deal with opposition from a group of Muslims resentful at the privileges accorded to the recently converted Quraish.

Now, on returning from the Farewell Pilgrimage, he was preparing to launch another expedition against Syria when he fell ill and died suddenly on 8 June 632, in the arms of his beloved 'Aisha. He was buried on the spot where he died, in what is now the Prophet's Mosque in Madina.

The problem of succession

The death of Muhammad caused an immediate crisis. The alliance he had created depended largely on his prestige as a great tribal chief who was also the bearer of divine revelation. Now the Message, incomplete or otherwise, had been delivered. Allah had ceased to provide his people with day-to-day guidance. The community must stand on its feet, or disintegrate.

In the half-century following the Prophet's death, disintegration seemed imminent. The infant state was disrupted by internal discord leading to civil war. The divisions have not yet healed, and account for the major sectarian splits in Islam. The survival of the new community was assured, not, as in Christianity, by the religious devotion of its martyrs, but by the military successes of its rulers. Survival on such terms was to prove problematic: whether as a result of Muhammad's foresight in 'coopting' them to lead the new community, or because they themselves 'sold out' on the original message, the first leaders of this new Muslim empire were to be the former pagans of Makka, the Quraish.

The first task after Muhammad's death was to find a leader who could act as his successor (*khalifa* or caliph) in his purely human capacity as military commander and head, both spiritual and temporal, of the Umma. At first, some of the Madinese Ansar proposed that they should choose a leader of their own, leaving the Emigrants under the leadership of the Quraish. But the Ansaris soon realized that their own dissensions made it impossible to agree on a leader, and that the best prospects lay in following a Quraishi, who alone would have the prestige to maintain the fragile tribal alliances. After some deliberations, Abu Bakr emerged as the obvious choice: a Quraishi, one of the first converts to Islam and father of Muhammad's favourite wife 'Aisha, he had been chosen by the Prophet himself to lead the pilgrimage of 631 and to act as Imam (or leader of the congregational prayers) during his final illness. The ablest Muslim general, Khalid ibn al-Walid, was sent to quell the 'apostates' – Arab tribes who had renounced their allegiance to Islam on Muhammad's death and who, in some cases, were rallying round new leaders claiming to be bearers of divine revelation, such as the 'false prophet' Musailima. The defeated tribes were bound more closely into the system and forced to pay *zakat*.

Abu Bakr's death in 634 thus saw the Islamic state ready to embark on the extraordinary expansion which, within less than a century, would bring it from the shores of the Atlantic to the Indus valley. Before he died, Abu Bakr, after consultation with a few of the Quraishi leaders, had designated 'Umar his successor as being 'the best among the Muslims' and therefore the man most fitted to be caliph. During the reign of 'Umar the sporadic raiding of the tribes gave way to a full-scale war of conquest. The governments of the territories surrounding Arabia collapsed like ninepins.

In 635, Hira, in lower Iraq, was occupied and forced to pay tribute. In 636 the Byzantine army in Syria was defeated by Khalid at the Yarmuk, opening the way to the conquest of Jerusalem and the fertile Palestine littoral. In 637 the main army of the Sassanids was defeated at Qadisiya on the Euphrates. After this most of the cities of Mesopotamia, including Ctesiphon, the imperial capital, surrendered to the Muslims. In 641 'Amr ibn al-'As entered Egypt; the following year he occupied Alexandria, the Byzantine capital, having founded a new city on the Nile near the old Persian fortress of Babylon. By the time of 'Umar's death in 644 the Arab raiders were reaching as far as Barqa (Tripolitania) in the west and the central Iranian highlands in the east.

The collapse of the Byzantine and Sassanid armies was hastened by the defection of their Arab auxiliaries who, sensing defeat in the air, went over to the invaders. The morale of the Arabs was, like that of the Muslims after Badr, greatly encouraged by these successes, which proved once again that Allah was on their side. (Even today the rapidity of these early successes is adduced by some Muslim writers as 'proof' of Islam's divine origin.) But the military weakness of the Byzantines and the Persians was also indicative of wider social and religious discontent in the conquered provinces. The Christian peasants of Syria and Egypt were uncertain in their allegiance to the Greek-speaking upper classes. The Aramaean-speaking peasants were closer to the Arabs in blood and language than to their Hellenized overlords, who retreated, with their remaining armies, into the Anatolian highlands. The Copts of Egypt had long been persecuted by the Melkites. They saw no point in making common cause with their persecutors against the Arabs, especially since the latter made no attempt, initially, to convert them to Islam. The loss of Ctesiphon deprived the Sassanids of the political and religious centre from which they might have continued resistance, while the occupation of the well-irrigated and cultivated Iraqi plain deprived them of the revenues with which to finance a counter-offensive. Unlike Syria and Egypt, which were mere provinces of the Byzantine Empire, Mesopotamia was central to the Iranian polity. So, whereas the Graeco-Romans would remain a thorn in the flesh of Islam for eight more centuries, the ancient lands of the Sassanids became the base for much of its later expansion.

The reigns of 'Umar and 'Uthman

During the reign of 'Umar and his successors, the Islamic polity had still to be consolidated. The conquest of Persia, Syria and Egypt had been accomplished by what was still in effect a loose coalition of Arab tribes under Quraishi leadership. 'Umar's problem, like that of his predecessor Abu Bakr and Muhammad himself, was to prevent this coalition from collapsing into a welter of competing tribal interests which would rapidly tear the Islamic polity to shreds. He achieved his task in two ways: by encouraging the expansion of the empire through the continuing *jihad* or holy war; and by systematic indoctrination of his beduin soldiers, aimed at replacing tribal allegiances with loyalty to the new theocracy based on obedience to God and the commandments of His Prophet.

Muhammad and Abu Bakr had realized that the only way to prevent the Madinese polity from collapse was to maintain its outward momentum. The fragile tribal alliances upon which it depended would survive so long as the prospect of fresh gains continued to attract beduin support. But such a policy, pursued in isolation, must ultimately prove self-defeating. Having made themselves rich with plunder and masters of the settled regions of the fertile crescent, the nomads would want to enjoy their new-found luxuries. Like previous invaders of Egypt, Mesopotamia and Palestine, they would end by becoming a new land-owning elite living off the peasants. In due course their descendants would become assimilated into the more advanced cultures of the region, losing their distinctive identities in the process.

'Umar's way of avoiding this danger was to discourage assimilation. Except in Damascus, the regional Byzantine capital in Syria, the Arab soldiers were kept in military compounds outside the main cities of the conquered territories. The distinctive Arab cities of Fustat, near Egyptian Babylon, and Basra and Kufa in Iraq were founded for this purpose. No attempt was made at first to convert members of the scriptural faiths – the Christians, Jews and Zoroastrians – in the occupied territories. On the precedent of Muhammad's treatment of the Jews of Khaibar, they were obliged to pay a special poll-tax – the *jizya*; otherwise they were treated as protected communities in the same manner as the clients (*mawali*) of ruling beduin tribes. The Muslims were thus less likely to face organized opposition from among the conquered peoples, some of whom had in any case welcomed them as liberators.

Most important of all, the Arabs were prevented from settling the conquered lands, which must discourage further military activity. Moveable booty, such as herds and valuables, was divided up among the tribesmen as in Muhammad's time, with a fifth reserved by the caliph for the poor and needy and for military purposes. But the caliph also kept all the land revenues, to be redistributed as part of a central fund in accordance with a register (*diwan*) of the Muslims and their dependants. Seniority in Islam counted for more than military muscle: in effect, the *diwan* enabled the military men to continue campaigning for the faith – and the moveable booty – secure in the knowledge that the state would look after their dependants.

Beduin loyalty to Islam was not, however, to be secured by purely financial measures. The Prophet's religious prestige as the bearer of divine revelation had been instrumental in securing beduin allegiance to him; that this was definitely the case is proved by the fact that, even before his death, several imitators or 'false prophets' appeared on the scene, seeking to supersede older tribal allegiances in a similar manner. The doctrine that Muhammad was the last or 'seal' of the Prophets, only broadly hinted at in the Quran, may well have been fixed during 'Umar's reign, with the aim of finally 'nailing' the false prophets as frauds. In the absence of the Prophet himself, there remained the Quran and the common discipline of prayer. In each of the garrison towns a mosque was built (usually a square enclosure with pillars at one end, a plan derived from the Prophet's home in Madina). Quranic reciters were sent as missionaries to instruct the faithful in prayer and hammer home God's messages to the troops. The Muslim family law, which tended to be laxly observed in the Prophet's time, was tightened up, with a ban imposed on short-contract marriages and tougher penalties for adultery and fornication.

'Umar died in 644, aged 52, murdered by a Persian captive. A great, bearded giant of a man, he inspired fear rather than love. His sternness became proverbial, but he was also respected for his integrity, being as harsh with himself as with others. As he lay dying, he appointed a committee of six – all of them Quraishis – to choose his successor. The leading candidates were 'Uthman ibn 'Affan of the Umayyad clan, husband of the Prophet's daughters Ruqaiya and Umm Kulthum; and 'Ali, the Prophet's first cousin from his own Hashimi clan and husband of his daughter Fatima. 'Uthman was chosen, possibly because it was thought he would continue 'Umar's policies. 'Ali, who had been raised in the Prophet's household and had been closer to him than any other male relative, may already have voiced some opposition to these policies, which he was not convinced accorded with the Quran or the Prophet's own actions. The election of 'Uthman the Umayyad may well have finally confirmed his suspicions that the Quraishis, despite their formal piety, were becoming too worldly and 'selling out' Islam's universal spiritual message. The Umayyads, under their leader Abu Sufyan, had been the most inveterate of Muhammad's enemies and had only embraced Islam opportunistically when there seemed no other way of promoting their clan interests: why should they not now be cornering the best jobs for themselves? Although 'Uthman, an early convert and Companion of the Prophet, was personally devout and above suspicion, he may well have been considered by 'Ali and his supporters too weak to oppose the ambitions of his relatives, led by his exceptionally able young secretary, Marwan.

In fact, with the accession of 'Uthman, the Islamic state was about to face its first major internal crisis, resulting in the sectarian divisions that persist to this day. These will be examined in more detail in a later chapter. Here it need only be said that the seeds of conflict such as occur in all ideological movements were present, and that considerations of interest and religious principle were inextricably bound together. 'Uthman faced opposition from two quarters. First there were the soldiers, especially in Egypt, who felt that the stipend system was depriving them of their just deserts as conquerors, and that too many of the most lucrative posts in the empire were going to Umayyads. Second, there were the wealthy Makkans, whose displeasure 'Uthman incurred for similar reasons. Unlike 'Umar, 'Uthman had been unable to prevent the richer Makkan families from settling in the provinces, especially in Iraq, and conducting business ventures there, to the annoyance of the local Arabs. But he had taken a stand to prevent them from appropriating large tracts of state land in the Sawad, the irrigated region, by forcing them to take land in the oases of the Hejaz instead.

The first civil war

These discontents reached their climax in 656, when a group of Arab soldiers, believing themselves to have been double-crossed in their dealings with the caliph, broke into 'Uthman's house and murdered him. In so doing they unleashed the five-year civil war known as the first *fitna*. The mutineers and most of the Madinese acclaimed 'Ali caliph, as 'First among the Muslims'. But 'Aisha, supported by Zubair and Talha, two of the Prophet's closest companions, called upon 'Ali first to punish 'Uthman's murderers, who had now come out in open support for him. 'Ali withdrew to Kufa, where most of his supporters were ranged, 'Aisha and her followers to Basra. The two armies met near Basra, where 'Ali proved victorious in a battle watched by 'Aisha from the palanquin mounted on the back of a camel (hence its name, the Battle of the Camel). Zubair and Talha were killed, but 'Aisha was sent back to Madina with full honours due to a Prophet's widow.

This, however, proved to be only the beginning of 'Ali's troubles as caliph. Mu'awiya, son of Abu Sufyan (now deceased) and after 'Uthman's death leader of the Umayyads, refused to recognize him. Instead Mu'awiya demanded that 'Uthman's murderers should be handed over to him for punishment, so that vengeance might be done according to the right granted by the Quran to a murder victim's next of kin (17:33). 'Ali marched towards Damascus to enforce Mu'awiya's obedience, and was met by Mu'awiya's army near Siffin, on the Euphrates. After several months of inconclusive skirmishing, the two sides eventually joined battle. Victory seemed to be going to 'Ali's men when the Syrians, on the advice of 'Amr ibn al-'As, fixed sheets from the Quran on their lances and called for arbitration. The Iraqis were so convinced of the justice of their case that they allowed a neutral party, Abu Musa al-Ash'ari, to act as their arbiter. Mu'awiya, on the other hand, used the services of his supporter 'Amr, ruler of Egypt. The arbiters were supposed to decide whether 'Uthman had been unjustly murdered (which would vindicate Mu'awiya's demand for vengeance), or whether he had, through his unjust policies and reprehensible innovations, brought just retribution upon himself (in which case his murderers were really only executioners of God's will). After several months of discussion the verdict evidently went against 'Ali, who repudiated it as being contrary to the Quran and the practice (Sunna) of the Prophet.

The negotiations therefore remained deadlocked, though by now they had acquired the aim of deciding who should be caliph. Mu'awiya was proclaimed by his supporters, but not confirmed by either of the arbitrators. He continued to play for time, with the connivance of 'Amr. The dispute was now acquiring a character familiar to students of twentieth-century Arab politics: Egypt was on one side, Iraq on the other and Syria between them, locked in a struggle for the leadership of the Arabs. In the end Mu'awiya's patience was rewarded. Dissension within his own camp was the cause of 'Ali's downfall. In 661 he was stabbed to death in the mosque at Kufa by a Khariji, one of a group of erstwhile supporters who had turned against his leadership.

The 'Rightly Guided' caliphs

The death of 'Ali brought to an end the Madinese era of Islam, or what has become known as the patriarchal caliphate. Among Muslims it is known as the era of the 'Rightly Guided' caliphs. Non-Muslims may find it astonishing that a period of continuous conquest and almost unremitting violence and civil war should have acquired the after-glow of a golden age. Of the four 'Rightly Guided' successors to Muhammad, only one of them, Abu Bakr, died in his bed. Three were assassinated, two of them by fellow-Muslims. On the historical plane, only 'Umar exhibited outstanding qualities of leadership. Abu Bakr's caliphate was too short to make a lasting impact; 'Uthman, according to his opponents, weakly allowed himself to favour his Umayyad kinsmen, most of whom were late-comers to Islam. 'Ali, for all his well-attested saintliness, lacked one of the essential qualities of a leader, which is to carry one's supporters. Whereas his rival, Mu'awiya, knew well how to gain and retain the loyalty of his Syrian troops, 'Ali alienated his own followers by vacillating between a policy of appeasement (towards Mu'awiya) and harsh brutality (towards the Kharijis).

The historic religions all involve the idealization – or 'theologization' – of events which were originally rooted in the politics of a particular period. The consciousness of the group, like that of the individual, achieves its identity by focusing on certain characters and events which retrospectively acquire an archetypal significance. Just as the child will at a certain stage in its development idealize its parents, being incapable of seeing them as ordinary mortals with an average endowment of virtues and defects, so the founders of charismatic movements acquire a supra-historical aura which raises them above the plane of normal humanity. The immortality conferred upon such figures – the 'giants' of history – may well be a function of the mythopoeic mind; but their potency as archetypes, as bearers of cultural norms and symbols around which individuals or groups can acquire a distinctive image of themselves, cannot be underestimated. The Christians, obsessed with the cruelty of a world which for so long failed to heed the message of the Jewish liberator, focused their consciousness upon the image of his tortured body and convinced themselves that suffering is the price of victory. The Muslims, as heirs to a triumphant period of conquest, could look back to the leaders of this period and find in them the landmarks which gave them their bearings in the new cultural and geographical territory they had won for themselves.

But there may also have been a historic basis to the seemingly idealized picture of the 'Rightly Guided' caliphs. The four patriarchal caliphs were all men who had been close to the Prophet, who had been in daily contact with him and had assimilated something of his remarkable personality. For this reason they were seen by their contemporaries as bearers of a special authority or charisma which distinguished them from the younger men who would now inherit Muslim power. The conflict between two such men of proven virtue and steadfastness as 'Uthman and 'Ali, and their kinsmen Mu'awiya, Yazid and Husain, is not reducible to petty ambition and weakness, however heroic or black their characters may have appeared to their followers or detractors in later generations. The conflicts they fought out, and in some cases paid for with their lives, were conflicts inherent in all ideological movements. They were the conflicts of idealism versus pragmatism, of the universal claims of truth against the practical needs of politics. In this respect they were not dissimilar from the conflicts which developed after the French Revolution, or after the Bolshevik seizure of power in Russia. Could the revolution be launched over the whole world, or should it first be consolidated within the confines of a single country? Could the new solidarity of the Umma, based on the common observance of the Quran and the Prophet's Sunna, be the ideological base for a new Islamic order, or would that order first have to establish itself on the basis of Quraishi – and specifically Umayyad – power? As in the case of socialism in Russia, Islamic history found no conclusive answer to these questions, which represent the boundaries of its dialectic.

The Muhammadan paradigm

The Prophet of Islam created a new dynamic order out of the internecine conflicts of the Arabian tribes. The order was founded primarily on obedience to the commands of God, as revealed through the mouth of His Prophet. God the Creator, who made the world and manifested himself in the natural order, also had a blueprint for the human community which Muhammad, like the previous prophets, was entrusted to communicate to mankind. Belief in the truth of the

Prophet's revelations was antecedent to the results it engendered in the world: the Islamic conquests were the *result* of the new religious faith, 'a remarkable testament to the power of human action mobilized by ideological commitment'.[11]

If the plan was seen as divine, its execution was part of human history. If the blueprint was perfect, the material required to make it real and durable was human and therefore flawed. If the Islamic ideal was universal, and therefore consonant with the natural order of divine creation, Muslim society was subject, like all other human societies, to the conditioning of a particular time and circumstance. The problem of finding a balance between the ideal and the real, the perfection of Islam and the human and material facts of life, became the stuff of Islamic history from the Prophet's time down to the present.

Islam is the least 'other-worldly' of the great religious systems, the one which, above all others, seeks to realize its aims in this world. Though the Day of Judgement is perceived as the ultimate moral reckoning by which the worth of individual action is measured, the good society is generally seen as the necessary precondition to salvation. Since there is no church or form of sacerdotal mediation through which men and women may attain salvation regardless of political circumstance, they must in the last endeavour attempt to realize the ideal of pristine Islam – the Madinese utopia – in order to guarantee their survival in the hereafter. Thus the armed prophet of Madina would remain the perfect exemplar for Muslims of all ages, his career a model of moral and political action that would be consciously imitated by those seeking to create a juster social order in this world.

Time and again throughout Islamic history, pious men would follow the stages of the Prophet's life, withdrawing first from the world to develop their spirituality, then making the *hijra* with a devoted band of disciples to a distant place before launching the *jihad* that would reclaim the backsliding pagans for the true Islam. The pattern was a cyclic one, involving the perennial conflict between the city and the countryside, the townspeople and the pastoralists. In analysing the interaction of the religious and material factors governing this process, the great Arab philosopher of history Ibn Khaldun (1332–1406) developed a theory about state formation in North Africa which is still relevant to the study of most Middle East societies. In the arid zones, where rainfall is sparse, pastoralism must remain the predominant mode of food production. Pastoralists, unlike peasants, are usually organized along tribal lines and are relatively independent of central government. They cannot be taxed or brought under the control of feudal lords who will appropriate a part of their produce. For the tribes, survival depends on maintaining what Ibn Khaldun called 'asabiya, group cohesion. When the tribes decide to unite, their superior cohesion, mobility and fighting skills put the city, the seat of government, at their mercy, for Muslim city life lacks 'asabiya. The reason for the city's lack of 'asabiya will be explained in Chapter 4, but it is due, at least in part, to the character of the Shari'a law, which recognizes few groups outside the family. When the tribesmen conquer the city, they usually end by founding a dynasty there, which lasts for three or four generations until, corrupted by luxury and the loss of 'asabiya, they are replaced by a new dynasty from the pastoralist fringes, repeating the cycle.

Ibn Khaldun's theory applied, in its classic formulation, to the North African milieu he knew and understood best. But it can be modified to suit the conditions of the more sophisticated societies of Egypt and the Ottoman Empire, where the pattern was institutionalized. In Egypt the Mamluks, who ruled from the thirteenth to the eighteenth centuries, maintained themselves against the disintegration of 'asabiya by constantly replenishing their stock with new warriors, bought as boys from Central Asia, whom they trained up in their own households. Similarly, the Ottoman Sultans maintained a form of, as it were, artificial 'asabiya by recruiting from the Christian Balkan provinces janissaries, whom they systematically trained up for war and administration.

In the classic tradition, as we shall see in the following chapters, the banner of militant Islam would be the rallying point around which tribal forces would coalesce and, fired by religious zeal, descend upon the cities. Sometimes they would be fired, like the followers of Ibn Saud, by the zeal for religious reform and revival. In the case of the numerous Shi'i revolts that occur throughout Islamic history, they would be inspired by the eschatological hopes activated by a direct descendant of the Prophet and 'Ali. Sometimes the tribes find allies in the 'ulama, guardians of the legal and scholarly traditions, who would ensure the orthodoxy of the newcomers, or at least guarantee that the urban population would be insulated against heretical excesses introduced by them. Thus the Muhammadan paradigm mediated the conflict between the city and countryside, converting the marauding pastoralists of the 'lands of insolence' beyond government control into the guardians of the orthodox legal tradition: in Ernest Gellner's metaphor, the 'wolves' became 'sheepdogs'. This pattern of Khaldunian 'musical chairs' applied, with regional variations, in most of the central Islamic lands, from Morocco to Chinese Turkestan, until the present century, when motorized transport and air-power enabled central governments, backed by the European powers, to assert themselves effectively and more or less permanently over the marginal regions that had once been the breeding-ground of pastoral revolt. The process is not yet quite complete: there are parts of Kurdish-speaking Iraq, and of Afghanistan outside the cities, that are not yet subject to central government.

Nor has the factor of *'asabiya* ceased to be important. In the absence of corporative institutions, kinship long remained the principal form of social solidarity. In the Middle East and many other Muslim lands tribal and family *'asabiya* have retained their importance as political factors into the age of the computer and the jet aircraft, and in many cases are actively reinforced by these modern inventions. At the same time Islam, paradoxically, condemns such sectional loyalties. The Prophet himself is related to have said, in a *hadith* (tradition) recorded by Abu Dawud: 'He is not of us who proclaims the cause of *'asabiya*; and he is not of us who fights in the cause of *'asabiya*; and he is not of us who dies in the cause of *'asabiya*.'[12] When asked to explain the meaning of *'asabiya*, he is said to have replied: 'It means helping your own people in an unjust cause.' Muhammad's career, as well as the social and ideological programme represented by the 'five pillars', was designed to break down the barriers of *'asabiya* between rival tribes, replacing it with the deeper and more universal loyalty to the Islamic Umma. Just as Islam originally aimed at eroding tribalism, it encouraged the movement of pastoralists into permanent settlements or cities. It was an urban religion conceived in a pastoral milieu, one whose aim was to maintain the supremacy of the former over the latter. It was thus a two-edged sword, upholding the existing political order when this seemed to accord with the commands of God and his Prophet; undermining it, or sanctioning its replacement, when it appeared to deviate too much from the 'boundaries' set by God (*hudud Allah*).

3 *The Quranic World-view*

These are the signs of the Manifest Book
We have sent it down as an Arabic
Koran haply you will understand   *Quran 12:1–2 (tr. Arberry)*

An 'Arabic' Quran

Few things are more indicative of the cultural differences between
Europe and the Arab world than the sounds which emerge from the
radio. In Europe the heavy, stressed rhythms of western rock music,
punctuated by chat from fast-talking disc jockeys, create contrasting
patterns which flash at the ear like so many multi-coloured neon signs.
The aural world of Arab radio seems to operate within a much narrower
range of frequencies. The complex rhythms and quarter-tones of eastern music are considerably more subtle than the strident impulses
which hypnotize western listeners, while the language has a richness
of tone and density of texture that seems to combine the warmth of a
Bukhara carpet with the silken delicacy of Damascus brocade.

If Arabic is the key to this culture, the Quran is the key to Arabic. The
language, if not invented, was specially developed for its transmission.
The art of writing was rudimentary until the necessity for accurate
versions of the Quran produced a dramatic evolution. According to
Muslim tradition, the Prophet's utterances were first written down on
whatever materials came to hand, such as shoulder-blades of camels,
palm leaves, pieces of wood or parchment. These were later collected
into *suras*, or chapters, under the supervision of the Prophet. No 'final'

NOTE: All citations from the Quran in this chapter are from Muhammad Asad, *The Message
of the Qur'ān* (Gibraltar, 1980), an English rendering of the so-called 'Royal Egyptian' edition
published in Cairo in 1337H/1918. *Suras* (chapters) and verses are rendered in accordance
with standard academic practice – e.g. 3:28 signifies *sura* 3 (Āl 'Imrān), verse 28. Where I
have changed Asad's wording I have signalled this with an asterisk *.

version of the text existed during his lifetime, for so long as he continued
to receive revelations, the recension of God's Word was not complete.

The final collection is supposed to have been made during the
caliphate of 'Uthman, based on a text collated by the Prophet's principal
secretary, Zaid ibn Thabit, and passed for safe-keeping to his widow,
Hafsa, 'Uthman's daughter. Because of the manner in which rival
versions of the same passages were being used as propaganda in the
quarrels that had broken out inside the Muslim community, 'Uthman
is supposed to have ordered an authorized version to be collected and
copied, and all other variant texts destroyed. All present editions of
the Quran (in which there are some slight variations, none of them
important) are said to be based upon this so-called 'Uthmanic recension'. Some Western scholars have, however, radically questioned the
Muslim account, using methods adapted from biblical textual analysis.
They argue that the Quran as we know it was assembled at a much
later date out of a fragmentary oral tradition deriving from the Arabian
Prophet, but which also included a large quantity of exegetical or
explanatory matter developed in the course of polemical disputes with
Jews and Christians after the Arab conquest. This revisionist theory
of the Quran has radical consequences for the early history of Islam,
for it would suggest that the religious institutions emerged at least
two centuries after Muhammad's time, to consolidate ideologically,
as it were, the Arab conquest. It would mean that the Arabs, anxious
to avoid becoming absorbed by the more advanced religions and
cultures of the peoples they conquered, cast about for a religion that
would help them to maintain their identity. In so doing they looked
back to the figure of the Arabian Prophet, and attributed to him the
reaffirmation of an ancient Mosaic code of law for the Arabs.

The revisionist theory has several attractions. It fits in with the
available palaeographic evidence, which places the development of
Arabic script much later than the Muslim sources. It provides an
explanation of certain archaeological problems, such as the fact that
the *qiblas* of certain early mosques in Iraq face Jerusalem rather than
Makka. It would account for the absence of any references in Jewish
sources to Madina as a place where the Torah was studied; and it
would account for the repetitious and inconsequential character of the
Quran which so exasperated Thomas Carlyle as well as countless
others who have struggled through translations in various European
languages: 'I must say, it is as toilsome reading as I ever undertook. A

wearisome confused jumble, crude, incondite; endless iterations, long-windedness, entanglement . . . insupportable stupidity, in short! Nothing but a sense of duty could carry any European through the Koran!'[1]

Such words would smack of sacrilege, not just to the devout Muslim, but to almost any Arab Christian, for whom the Quran, whatever religious truth it contains, is the perfection of language. Basically, the historiographical controversy about the Quran's origins, regardless of its scientific merits, reflects the same culture-gap which makes most Europeans dislike the sounds emitted by Arab radio, because their ears, and minds, are ill-tuned to them. An assault upon the Quran's authenticity is an assault upon an identity moulded by these very repetitions and subtle inflexions.

In a special sense, the Arabs are a people moulded by their scripture. The Hebrew and Christian texts were translated into Greek and Latin, and from them diffused into other languages and cultures. European ideologies and political movements no doubt owe much to biblical inspiration. The Mosaic vision of a land promised by God may, consciously or otherwise, have influenced the utopian dreams of protestant settlers and communists, as well as Zionists. But in all such cases many other cultural and political strands have been present. In the West, after the Latin Church had lost its liturgical monopoly, such cultural and ultimately political pluralism was encouraged by the translation of the Bible into different European tongues. Translation, which contributed much to the formation of national identities in the West, was made religiously possible by the pluralistic origins of the Bible itself, which consists of most of the Hebrew scriptures plus an originally oral Aramaic tradition transcribed into Greek. For Christians the Word of God was manifested in Christ's person, not in the language in which he revealed God's speech. Thus in the earliest Christian centuries, national and regional squabbles took the form of conflicts about the nature of this Person. The doctrine that the Quran was the eternal and unalterable Word of God, revealed in Arabic (as the Quran itself states on several occasions), prevented any such diffusion of the Muslim scripture into the surrounding cultural landscape: the very intransigence with which the Arabs defended the integrity of their text was decisive in maintaining a common Arab identity, which would otherwise have disintegrated, like that of other nomadic conquerors both before and after Islam, into a multiplicity of new national groupings, such as occurred after Charlemagne in western Europe.

Structure of the Quran

The most obvious difficulty for those brought up on the chronological sequences of the Bible or Hindu epics is the absence of sustained narrative. The subject matter, including stories of the earlier prophets, punishment stories about those who failed to heed them, psalm-like lyric passages celebrating the manifestation of God's glory in nature, and the Leviticus-like legal prescriptions, appear to be jumbled and diffused throughout the text. For instance, the Sura of Light contains one of the most celebrated passages in all mystical literature:

God is the Light of the heavens and the earth. The parable of His light is, as it were, that of a niche containing a lamp: the lamp is [enclosed] in glass, the glass [shining] like a radiant star: [A lamp lit from] a blessed tree – an olive tree that is neither of the east nor of the west – the oil whereof [is so bright that it] would well-nigh give light [of itself] even though fire had not touched it: light upon light! (24:35)

The same *sura*, however, a few verses earlier, lays down details for the punishment of adulterers (100 lashes) and slanderers (80 lashes), and urges women not to 'swing their legs [in walking] so as to draw attention to their hidden charms'. This mixing of the sublime and the mundane, which Westerners might see as evidence of a 'consistent lack of logical structure', has in the didactic and liturgical context a powerful function. For, despite the proliferation of manuscripts of the Quran, and its extensive use in the highly developed art-form of calligraphic embellishment, it originated as a series of texts designed for oral transmission.

No one who has visited Cairo or any other great Arab Muslim city could fail to notice the position the Quran still occupies in the oral culture of the more traditionally minded sectors of society. Public recitations of the Quran are an important part of such social events as weddings, circumcisions, funerals, wakes and visits to the tombs of dead relatives on feast-days. At Cairo wakes, which are held on the evening of burial and successive Thursdays, male friends and relatives are to be found gathered in brightly lit marquees decorated with arabesques of red and white appliqué work. In the richer, more westernized, parts of the city, they will be seated on gilt salon chairs, of the kind used at concerts or fashion shows. The *muqri*, or professional Quran reciter, may be seated cross-legged on the ground, or loud-speakers may be linked to a microphone in a nearby mosque. Some of the *muqris* become extremely popular – and wealthy. Those who cannot afford to hire a live *muqri* are often to be seen playing their offerings on cassette radios.

Popular piety is still very much alive in Egypt and other Arab countries whose poverty has prevented them from succumbing to the blandishments of consumer capitalism. Taxi-drivers of the traditional kind, who would not dream of overcharging their Muslim passengers, will have the name of Allah on electric-coloured stickers on the facia board, or embroidered on pennants which festoon the interior like the tassles of a lampshade. The meandering nasal tones of the *muqri* will often be playing on the cassette machine, if the driver is especially pious. Cairo taxi-drivers include some of the most devout – as well as the most foul-mouthed – people in the world.

The esteem in which Arabs hold the Quran is not just the result of a religious dogma: it is due to the fact that many people find in its sonorous, rhyming prose an aesthetic pleasure of the kind Westerners usually discover in fine music or painting. Its dense elliptical style is a rich fund of aphorisms, its riddles and allegories the source of countless legends. Although there is a discernible variation in style between the short ecstatic passages from the earliest Makkan period and the much longer *suras* of the Madinese period, the seemingly chaotic organization of the material ensures that each of the parts in some way represents the whole. Good Muslims, especially those groomed for religious leadership, are required to memorize the whole of the Quran at a very early age. Since it consists of some 120,000 words divided into 114 *suras* and 6,000 verses (*ayas*), this is a considerable feat which, in the nature of things, many people fail to master. Nevertheless, almost any one of the *suras* will contain, in a more or less condensed form, the message of the whole. This is especially true of the chrono-logically later *suras* placed near the beginning, in which most of the legislation is to be found. An only partially memorized Quran will, therefore, contain as much as a conscientious but uneducated Muslim will find it necessary to know.

The illogical organization of the text in fact renders it more accessible, and this is central to the Quran's didactic purpose. The more inaccess-ible the scripture, the greater the distinction between clergy and laity.

While Sunni Islam certainly developed a rabbinical class of 'ulama with a superior knowledge of the text and its interpretation, the fact that a substantial part of it was known to everyone in society militated against the emergence of a spiritual elite comparable to the Catholic or Orthodox priesthoods.

Nevertheless, the need for such a class of interpreters was apparent from an early stage. Many passages are obscure, and cannot be understood without reference to the substantial body of exegetical literature, derived from the oral *hadith*-traditions which came to be selected and written down around the third century of Islam. There are many allusions to events in the Prophet's career which can only be explained from these sources. Thus the punishment stories, composed from Arabian folklore and biblical materials, mostly date from the late Makkan and early Madinese periods, and are clearly intended as threats and warnings to the pagan Quraishis. The Madinese *suras* contain many references to such events as the division of the spoils after Badr, the cowardice of the 'hypocrites' at Uhud, the punishment of the Banu Nadir, Muhammad's marriages, and other events mentioned in the previous chapter.

The allusiveness of the Quran's style is, however, not confined to the circumstances of revelation. It is, in fact, integral to its didactic method, which could be described as a series of 'one-way dialogues' between God and the Prophet and between Muhammad and his auditors. The effect is not unlike listening to a person speaking on the telephone: one only hears half the conversation. The inaudible part of the discourse, Muhammad's unspoken questions, the arguments of his critics, and so forth, have to be reconstructed out of the exegetical literature, which draws on the vast body of *hadith*-tradition.

This exegetical literature became, in due course, a source of law: for only by detailed study of the so-called 'occasions' of revelation could the general prescriptions and prohibitions contained in the Quran be given the force of law. This was especially necessary in the case of apparently contradictory statements, such as the prohibition on wine. Thus *sura* 16:67 clearly allows the drinking of wine:

And [we grant you nourishment] from the fruit of date-palms and vines: from it you derive intoxicants as well as wholesome sustenance . . .

However, this is evidently contradicted by 2:219:

They will ask thee about intoxicants and games of chance. Say: 'In both are great evil and some uses for men. But the sin in them is greater than their usefulness . . .'*

An even stronger prohibition occurs in 5:90–1:

O you who have attained to faith! Wine, and games of chance, and idolatrous practices, and the divining of the future are but a loathsome evil of Satan's doing: shun it then, so that you might attain a happy state! By means of wine and games of chance Satan seeks only to sow enmity and hatred among you, and to turn you away from the remembrance of God and from prayer. Will you not, then, desist?*

Without a chronology of revelation derived from the *hadith* literature, it would be impossible to determine whether wine was a possible benefit, an evil to be tolerated, or one to be prohibited absolutely. Although there was some disagreement about the order of some of the verses, the consensus was that 5:90, representing the strongest prohibition, was revealed after 2:219, and therefore overrules it; while 16:67 dates from the Makkan period, when Muhammad still allowed wine-drinking among his followers. One of the famous Quran commentators, Fakhr al-Din al-Razi, commenting on this passage, cites one of his predecessors:

Al-Qaffal said that the wisdom of issuing the prohibition in these stages lies in the following: God knew that the people had been accustomed to drinking wine and drawing from it its many uses. Thus he also knew that it would be unbearable for them if he had prohibited them all at once [from the use of wine] and thus unquestionably [for this reason] he made use of these stages and kindness in the prohibition . . .[2]

More abstruse legal points occur in commentaries on 2:172, where the flesh of swine is prohibited. Are the pig's bristles, used for sewing leather, included in the ban? This was a subject on which authorities disagreed. There was also disagreement concerning the meat of the hippopotamus, known to the Arabs as *khinzir al-ma*, 'water-swine'. Argument depended on whether the hippo's presumed 'swinishness'

---

* The translation of this Quranic quotation differs from that of Muhammad Asad.

overruled its character as a water-creature, allowed under 5:96: 'Lawful to you is all water-game, and what the sea brings forth . . .'[3]

In order to deal with a host of similar problems, the exegetes developed a doctrine of abrogation, based on 2:106: 'Any verse/message [*aya*] which We annul or consign to oblivion We replace with a better or similar one . . .' According to the great Persian grammarian and exegete, Abu al-Qasim al-Zamakhshari (d. 1144), the verse was revealed in response to a challenge from the unbelievers, who had said: 'Look at Muhammad, now he commands his companions to do something, and then forbids it to them and commands the opposite. He says one thing today and retracts it tomorrow!' Zamakhshari continues:

To abrogate a verse means that God removes it by putting another in its place . . . Every verse is made to vanish whenever the well-being [of the community] requires that it be eliminated – either on the basis of the wording or [by] virtue of what is right, or on the basis of both these reasons together, either with or without a substitute.[4]

Zamakhshari belonged to the rationalistic school of theologians (Mu'tazilis) who believed that the Quran, having been 'created' in time, could be interpreted with considerable allowances made for time-bound changes due to historical and social conditions. The Mu'tazilis were eventually defeated after attempting unsuccessfully to impose their doctrines by force during the caliphate of al-Mamun (813–33), but the doctrine of abrogation survived in a more restricted form. Some modern authorities, including Muhammad Asad, have rejected it absolutely. The word '*aya*', according to Asad, means in this context a 'message' rather than a Quranic verse, and therefore refers to the abrogation, by the whole Quran, of the earlier Hebrew and Christian scriptures.

The activities of the exegetes were very far from being confined to legal problems. Only about 600 of the Quran's 6,000 verses deal with legislative matters. Stories of the earlier prophets and the punishments meted out to those who failed to heed them, ecstatic descriptions of God's power in nature and the eschatological passages about paradise, hell and the Day of Judgement occupy much of the rest. Sometimes the language is explicit and self-explanatory, at other times it is highly allusive and allegorical. The Quran itself is eloquent on this point:

He it is who has bestowed upon thee from on high this divine writ, containing messages [ayas] that are clear in and by themselves, and those are the essence of the divine writ [umm al-kitab], as well as those that are allegorical. (3:7)

In his commentary on this passage Zamakhshari writes: 'If the [meaning of the] entire Quran [were clearly] determined men would come to depend on it since it would be so easily accessible, and would turn away from what they lack – research and meditation through reflection and inference.'[5]

The memorizing and study of the Quran, which occupied such a large part of the traditional Muslim education, has always been regarded as the most meritorious of all religious activities. Assimilated and internalized through constant repetition, the sacred book became part of the Muslim's very being, the filter through which he received the world and its mental images. Just as Islamic philanthropy and the requirements of law gave rise to the splendid monuments of Islamic architecture – mosques, schools, hospitals, convents, public drinking-fountains and other pious foundations – Quranic piety created out of the divine text literary artefacts comparable in many ways to the plastic images created out of medieval Christian piety. Thus Zamakhshari's embellishments to 19:16–22, where the annunciation and birth of Jesus are described, convey a typical medieval literalism. Here is the original text, slightly shortened, taken from Asad's translation:

And . . . Lo! [Mary] withdrew from her family to an eastern place, and kept herself in seclusion from them, whereupon We sent to her Our angel of revelation, who appeared to her in the shape of a well-made human being. She exclaimed: 'Verily! I seek refuge from thee with the Most Gracious! [Approach me not] if thou art conscious of Him. [The angel] answered: 'I am but a messenger of thy Sustainer [who says] "I shall bestow on thee the gift of a son endowed with purity." ' Said she: 'How can I have a son when no man has ever touched me? – for never have I been a loose woman!' [The angel] answered: 'Thus it is: [but] thy Sustainer says: "This is easy for Me; and thou shalt have a son, so that We might make him a symbol unto mankind and an act of grace for Us." ' And it was a thing decreed, and in time she conceived him and then she withdrew with him to a far-off place. (19:16–22)

Zamakhshari's embellishments to this passage are too long to give in full. But here is a condensed version:

Some say that Mary settled in an eastern place when she wanted to purify herself from menstruation, and that she concealed herself behind a wall, or perhaps something else that would keep her out of view. The place where she usually stayed was the mosque. As soon as she had her period, she went to the home of her maternal aunt; then, when she was again in the state of purity, she returned to the mosque. Now when she was at the place at which she customarily purified herself, the angel came to her as a young, smooth-faced man with pure countenance, curly hair, and a well-built body, without exhibiting a single blemish in his human appearance . . . He presented himself to her in the form of a man in order that she might have confidence in what he was to say and not flee from him. Had he appeared to her in the form of an angel, she would have fled from him and would not have been able to hear what he had to say. If Mary now sought refuge with God from this charming, towering, and handsome figure, then this shows that she was modest and pious. Through the appearance of the angel in this manner, Mary had undergone a test and her modesty was made certain . . .

According to Ibn 'Abbas [the Prophet's uncle and founder of the exegetical tradition] Mary found comfort in the words of the angel, and thus the latter approached near to her and breathed under her shift so that the breath reached into her womb and she became pregnant. Some say that the pregnancy lasted for six months . . . Others say that it lasted eight months and that beside Jesus no child capable of living ever came into the world after [only] eight months. Still others say that it lasted three hours. Some maintain that Mary was pregnant with Jesus for [only] one hour, that he was formed in one hour, and that she brought him into the world in one hour at sunset. According to Ibn 'Abbas the pregnancy lasted for [only] one hour. [Also] Mary is said to have brought Jesus into the world as soon as she became pregnant with him.

Some maintain that she became pregnant with him at the age of thirteen. It is also said that this occurred when she was ten years old, after she had had her period for two months previously. [Moreover] some say that every [newborn] infant cries and that Jesus is the only one who did not do this.[6]

Like the Quran itself, which is constructed out of the same body of Arabian, biblical and talmudic folklore, the *tafsirs* (commentaries) incorporated a wide range of popular culture which made it accessible to the masses, and hence intelligible across a broad spectrum of cultural assumptions. In this respect the Quranic commentators fulfilled the function which Christianity reserved for religious painting. The Sunni Muslim ban on representational art drove the imaginative evocation of biblical texts (which forms the material of western painting till after the Renaissance) into the realm of the footnote. As with Christian art, such exegetical expression could acquire an inter-regional character impossible for secular literature. Since the Quran was the 'speech of God' and Arabic was the language through which he chose to communicate his final messages to mankind, to translate it into other languages was tantamount to blasphemy. Non-Arab Muslims could only approach the Quran through Arabic: in this manner the scripture continued to exercise its cultural hegemony, ensuring that Arabic would remain the dominant language of intra-Muslim communication long after Arabic speakers had ceased to be a numerical majority in the Islamic world.

A linguistic analysis

There is a linguistic as well as a religious truth in the dogma that the Quran cannot be translated. (Even today, official Muslim translations always carry the Arabic text and usually refer to themselves as 'interpretations'.) Arabic, more than most other languages, eludes translation, at least into European tongues. According to the travel writer Jonathan Raban:

To live in Arabic is to live in a labyrinth of false turns and double meanings. No sentence means quite what it says. Every word is potentially a talisman, conjuring the ghosts of the entire family of words from which it comes. The devious complexity of Arabic grammar is legendary. It is a language which is perfectly constructed for saying nothing with enormous eloquence; a language of pure manners in which there are hardly any literal meanings at all and in which the symbolic gesture is everything ... Even to peer through a chink in the wall of the language is enough to glimpse the depth and darkness of that forest of ambiguity. No wonder the Koran is so notoriously untranslatable.[7]

In thus graphically describing his efforts to cope with the language, Raban omits, however, to make a crucial point. Arabic is a language built around verbs. Substantives and adjectives are almost always verbal derivatives, usually participles or verbal nouns. A clerk is a writer, a book is a writ. Aeroplanes and birds are things that fly. European languages, with their multiple origins, are much more rooted in substances: most nouns in English are things-in-themselves, not parts of verbs, which are *processes*. It is precisely because Arabic refrains from classifying words into discrete particles, but keeps them instead in a logical and balanced relationship with a central concept – the verbal root – that it becomes an eminently suitable language for religious expression.

Religious language, by definition, attempts to express something which defies expression and to evoke a perception of something which lies beyond the realm of human comprehension. In Arabic the meanings of many words depend absolutely on context: hence the word *ghaib* ('unseen') can apply to a reality outside human sense-perception, or to the intimate parts of a woman – 'that which is [i.e., ought to be] concealed'.* In many instances the words cannot be fixed in their contexts without the activities of the exegetes, whose task it thus is to supply them with concrete meanings. Without such exegetical activity a word can range across a whole spectrum of meaning, whose relationship with other spectra is determined by concepts lying at the centre of each verbal cluster. The exegete may try to concretize the meaning of a word by extracting it from a particular point on the spectrum, ignoring its surroundings. But whatever concrete meaning it may temporarily acquire, it will continue to evoke meanings across the whole spectrum. Arabic, the supreme linguistic achievement of a highly developed oral culture, eludes concretization. It is motion distinct from stasis, energy rather than matter. This very dynamism gives the Quran a complexity of meaning, combined with a vigour of expression, which absolutely defies translation, because the multiple meanings tend to vanish as soon as the translator tries to fix them semantically into a foreign language.

The best way to grasp the Quranic message historically and to try to measure its impact on Muhammad's contemporaries, as well as on subsequent generations of Muslims, is to make a comparison between the Quranic and pre-Islamic use of certain terms and concepts. This has been done in two brilliant studies by the Japanese philologist Toshihiko Izutsu, who examines a number of key terms, both diachronically (i.e., in their historic evolution) and in relation to the semantic fields they establish, in order to elucidate the character of the

---

* See Quran 4:34. Muhammad Asad translates *al-ghaib* in this passage as 'intimacy'; at other times as 'secrets'.

new outlook, or *Weltanschauung*, evoked by them. He points out that none of the key terms around which the Quranic message revolves – Allah, Islam, *iman* ('belief'), *kafir* ('infidel') – was new to Muhammad's auditors: obviously they would not have understood his meaning if they had been. What was revolutionary, from the linguistic point of view, was the entirely new conceptual network, or *gestalt*, into which these were ordered: '. . . it was chiefly . . . this transposition of concepts, and the fundamental displacement and rearrangement of moral and religious values which ensued from it, that so radically revolutionized the Arab conception of the world and human existence'.[8]

The name Allah is a simple contraction of 'al-Ilah' – 'the God'. The Quran itself (39:4) provides evidence that the word was used by the pagans to describe a supreme deity. As an abstract term it was common to all pre-Islamic tribes: each must have referred to its own deity as 'the god'. A more universal application would occur naturally when the tribes were gathered together in the *haram* area around the Ka'ba. Where tribal deities might be represented by separate symbols, the underlying abstract concept of 'the-god' must have transcended such particularism, retaining its singularity; 'the-god' becomes 'The God'. Belief in such a single God presiding over all other tribal deities is indicated by the references to Allah as 'Lord [*rabb*] of the Ka'ba' ('Lord of the House') in both the Quran and Jahili poetry. It is probable that the presiding deity of the Jahili Arabs was assimilated to Jewish and Christian monotheistic ideas. Thus the Christian poet Aid ibn Zaid of Hira refers in one ode to 'the Lord of Makka and the Cross'. Added to this we find the 'Abrahamic' conception of God attested by the *hanifs*. The poet Umayya ibn Abi Salt, one of Muhammad's bitterest enemies, was an uncompromising monotheist whose poems contain such phrases as 'He is the God of the whole world', 'the Creator of Everything', 'the Absolute Sovereign on Earth, the Omnipotent', and so forth.

The Quran does not accuse the pagans of denying the existence of such a deity: rather it accuses them of inconstancy and ingratitude:

. . . if you ask them [i.e., the pagan Arabs], 'Who is it that has created the heavens and the earth and made the sun and moon subservient [to His laws]?', they will surely answer 'Allah!'* (29:61)

* The translation of this Quranic quotation differs from that of Muhammad Asad.

In many passages (e.g., 31:31; 29:65) we are told that people, especially seafarers in danger, will cry to Allah for help, only to return to pagan practices when safely ashore. Their polytheistic practices are identified as *kufr** ('disbelief'), a word whose original connotations include 'ingratitude'. *Shirk* – ascribing partners to the divinity – is both ungrateful and illogical because, as the Quran never ceases to point out, these lesser divinities are powerless, mere figments of the imagination. Only Allah has the power to create, to destroy, to save people's lives or in any other way to control the fate of human beings.

This latter point is the real theological departure of the Quran, and the one which we know excited intense opposition. Allah claims an absolute and uncompromising exclusiveness. The attribution of any magical or supernatural power to lesser deities amounts to fraud, since these are nothing but 'empty names' invented by the Arabs without any warranty from God (53:23). The sin of *shirk* is an intellectual as well as a moral one: in the Quran the word is related to *zann* ('conjecture'), as contrasted unfavourably with *'ilm* ('knowledge') (53:28–9;10:37). All *'ilm* proceeds from Allah and leads back to him:

O verily unto God belongs whoever is in the heavens and whoever is on earth: hence, what is it that they follow, those who invoke beside God [*Shuraka*] beings to whom they ascribe a share of His divinity? They follow but conjectures [*zann*] and themselves do nothing but guess. (10:66)

The Quran's insistence on God's uniqueness challenges Christianity as well as paganism: the *sura* just quoted pours scorn on the idea that God could sire a son. Addressing the Christians it says:

No evidence whatever have you for this [assertion]! Would you ascribe unto God something which you cannot know? Say: 'Verily they who attribute their own lying inventions to God will never attain to a happy state...' (68:9)

---

* For readers not familiar with the structure of Arabic, the root consonants of certain words are printed in bold face in order to demonstrate their etymological relationships.

The nature of God

As is suggested by the inclusion of the definite article in his name, the God of the Quran is rather more abstract than that of the Old and New Testaments. Fatherhood is explicitly rejected, a matter of considerable significance in a society which set such store by kinship and paternity. The pronoun *huwa* ('he') is a grammatical necessity, not an indicator of gender. In the Quran Allah often addresses Muhammad in the first person, both singular and plural, while he orders his auditors to address him in the second person singular: 'They will answer: "Limitless art Thou in Thy glory." It was inconceivable for us to take for us anyone but Thyself' (25:18). It is the overwhelming presence of this deity, unique and unknowable, which makes itself felt in every verse of the Quran. Allah is supra-personal rather than abstractly impersonal. The fact that he addresses the Prophet, or is addressed, employing all three grammatical pronouns, adds to the sense of a complex and pervasive presence completely saturating the text. As Izutsu comments: 'God in the Koranic *Weltanschauung* does not subsist in His glorious self-sufficing solitude and stand aloof from mankind as does the God of Greek philosophy, but deeply involves himself in human affairs.'[9]

This god, both abstract and pervasive, transcendent and immanent, describes himself in the Quran using a number of adjectival epithets, such as 'the Just', 'the Wise', 'the All-Powerful', 'the All-Seeing'. The most frequently employed are the etymologically related pair *al-rahman al-rahim* (usually translated as 'the Merciful', 'the Compassionate'), which appear in the invocatory formula preceding all but one of the Quran's 114 *suras*. (This invocation or *basmallah* is used by Arabs and many other Muslims before eating, embarking on a journey, making love and a host of other daily activities.) A pagan deity possessing the same root, *rhm*, was worshipped in South Arabia. The word has female connotations of nurturing or protection: *rahim*, as a noun, means 'womb'. Thus the attributes most generally applied to God are intended to generate the comforting idea of a friendly, all-pervasive presence at work, as it were, behind the scenes of the visible world, a beneficent force or energy permeating the matter of creation, yet utterly distinct from it. Allah is the womb of all created things, the matrix of the universe in which humans find their being.

A very different aspect of Allah, almost as pervasive, is contained in the phrase *Rabb al-'Alamin* – 'Master of the Worlds' (or universe). The word *rabb* has connotations of leadership or ownership, both masculine and feudal. (It is commonly used, for example, for 'head of the family'.) It is usually translated into English as 'Lord', which gives it biblical and feudal overtones. Muhammad Asad renders it 'Sustainer', since, he says, it not only 'comprises the idea of having a just claim to something, and consequently to authority over it', but also that of 'rearing, sustaining and fostering'.[10]

The 'worlds' or domain over which this all-pervasive 'Sustainer' presides are divided into the 'Unseen' (*al-ghaib*) and visible (*al-shahada*) spheres. Only the latter is accessible to man, though he has knowledge of the existence of the former, derived from revelation:

Say: O Allah! Thou originator of the heavens and the earth! Thou who knowest the Unseen [*al-ghaib*] and the visible [*al-shahada*]! (39:46)

Allah, as the Quran repeatedly and categorically declares, 'encompasses everything in knowledge'. Man's knowledge, by contrast, can only ever be partial. Even the Prophet, a mere human, only possesses such knowledge as Allah has chosen to reveal to him:

People will ask thee about the [Last] Hour. Say: 'Knowledge [*'ilm*] thereof rests with God alone; yet for all thou knowest the [Last] Hour may well be near. (33:63)

God's revelations, leading to knowledge of the unseen, are conveyed to human beings by means of signs (*ayas*) or miracles. The *ayas* fall into two categories: first, there are the evidences of the natural world (*shahada*), which can be known directly. Second, there is the 'miracle' of the Quran itself which provides, as it were, an exegetical commentary on the *shahada*, as well as hints about its ultimate relationship with the *ghaib*. Of these two categories, the *ayas* of the natural world are the most continuously celebrated.

All religions, and indeed most philosophies, address themselves to the ultimate questions concerning the origins and destiny of humanity, its relation to the natural world and to the cosmic order. The Quran, true to the Semitic tradition, locates its origin, as well as all the phenomena of the observable universe, firmly in the will or command (*amr*) of a Divine Creator who both stands apart from and participates in his creation. Allah is the creator and sustainer of everything: the angels and jinns who comprise part of the 'unseen' world, as well as such observable realities as the sun, moon and stars, day and night and the earth with its mountains and rivers, its oceans and continents, its trees, fruits, grains and herbs, its variety of animals 'such as crawl on their bellies; and such as walk on two legs, and such as walk on four' (24:45). At its broadest and most universal, the Quran is a 'grand hymn in honour of Divine Creation', one that is saturated with the idea of creation and a 'feeling of profound admiration for it'.[11] The observable facts of this universe – those facts, that is, that humans can perceive and apprehend – are not so much things-in-themselves as evidence of this unseen creative force: no more nor less than the 'signs' by which Allah reveals himself. Man cannot perceive the deity directly, or acquire knowledge thereof except from behind a veil (*hijab*). Even Moses, who of all the biblical prophets mentioned in the Quran came closest to the Divine Presence, is not permitted to look God in the face.

The miraculous quality of creation, as the Quran points to it, must really be self-evident to all who look about them. Passages extolling the creation often end with the rhetorical exhortations: 'Will you not then use your reason!', 'Will you not then remember!'[12] These expressions imply that the pagans must already be aware of the truth in their hearts, even if they are not yet prepared to admit to it. A similar rhetoric is used to persuade the pagans to recognize the divine origin of the Quran itself: the unbelievers are challenged to 'produce another *sura*' (or 'ten *suras*') of comparable merit, or otherwise remain 'conscious of the fire whose fuel is human beings and stones, which awaits all who deny the truth' (2:23–4).

In contrast to the *ayas* of the natural world, which are plain for all to see, the *ayas* of the Quran are of a special kind. The revelation (*wahy*) is treated as 'something extraordinary, something mysterious, the secrets of which cannot be disclosed to the ordinary human mind'.[13] This revelation which has been 'sent down from on high' is God's speech, delivered in Arabic for transmission by an Arabian prophet. The speech itself is evidently conceived of as separate from the words or expressions which make it up. God's messages have previously been delivered to, among other peoples, the Jews and the Christians, who are accused of having wilfully distorted or neglected them.[14]

The speech of God

The relation between 'God's speech' and the actual words of the Quran is a complex question which has been implicated in the relations between Arab and non-Arab peoples from the ninth century down to the present time. In the early 'Abbasid period there arose a controversy among the scholars as to whether or not the Quran had been 'created'.* For a period, victory in the dispute went to the Mu'tazilis, or 'rationalists', who believed in the 'created' Quran, until, following a populist reaction led by Ahmad ibn Hanbal, the opposite doctrine became the orthodoxy, remaining so among Sunni Muslims until the present century. The issue is perhaps best understood as the Islamic equivalent of the controversy about the nature of Christ's divinity that erupted at the Council of Chalcedon (451). The Quran, as 'God's revelation' to mankind, is as central to Islam as Christ is to Christianity. Just as it became important for Christians, during the formative period of their theology, to define as precisely as possible the exact nature of the incarnation, and to build a consensus of opinion around it, so for the Muslims the exact nature of 'God's speech' became a burning and passionate issue.

That the Quran is in the Arab tongue is a fact to which the divine text itself refers on several occasions:

Behold We have sent this down as a discourse in Arabic [literally, 'an Arabic Quran') that you may understand. (12:2)

If We had made it a discourse in some non-Arabic tongue they would surely have said, 'Why are not its messages made intelligible? Is it non-Arabic and Arab [i.e., a non-Arabic revelation given to an Arabian prophet]?' (41:44)

The revelation had to be made in pure Arabic in order to be comprehensible. The question arises, could it have been made in any other tongue? The Quran itself recounts the stories of other prophets sent to other peoples, not all of them Arabic speakers:

And never have We sent forth any apostle otherwise than with his people's tongue so that he might make [the message] intelligible. (14:4)

* See pp. 192–3

The Jews and Christians, among those to whom God's messages have been sent, are accused of 'corrupting' the texts of the original revelations made to them. Leaving aside the question of religious truth, this doctrine is logically necessary if actual differences between Jewish, Christian and Muslim doctrine are to be harmonized with the claim that Islam represents the final truth, as the Quran and the Prophet constantly insist.

Does this mean, then, that the messages delivered to the Israelites by Moses, or to the Christians by Christ, as well as to numerous other peoples in their respective languages, are all identical? The testimony, to say the least, is ambiguous. On the one hand we have the assertion, already mentioned, that Jews and Christians have 'corrupted' their scriptures, while their refusal (especially on the part of the Jews) to acknowledge Muhammad as God's Messenger relegates them to the category of unbelievers. On the other hand we have the following passage in the fifth *sura*, said to be one of the last to be revealed during the Farewell Pilgrimage:

And unto thee [O Prophet] have We vouchsafed this divine writ [*kitab*], setting forth the truth, confirming the truth of whatever there still remains of earlier revelations [*kitab*] and determining what is true therein. Judge, then, between the followers of earlier revelation in accordance with what God has bestowed from on high, and do not follow their errant views, forsaking the truth that has come unto thee.

Unto every one of you We have appointed a [different] law and way of life [*shir'atan wa minhajan*]. And if God had so willed He could surely have made you all one single community: but [He willed it otherwise] in order to test you by means of what He has vouchsafed unto you. Vie, then, with one another in doing good works! Unto God you all must return; and then He will make you understand all that on which you were wont to differ. (5:48)

This is the clearest of many statements implicitly commanding tolerance towards the Jews and Christians, as other 'people of the Book', and, by extension, towards Zoroastrians, Hindus, Buddhists and adherents of other scriptural religions. The term *shir'a* is a cognate of *shari'a*, literally, 'the way to a watering place', as used in the Quran to denote the system of divinely revealed law. *Minhaj* has a similar meaning, approximating to 'open road'. This clear recognition of a plurality of religious faiths accounts, no doubt, in part for the relative tolerance accorded to other religious communities, with some exceptions, under Islamic governments. At the same time it raises a difficulty about which parts of the scriptures (usually referred to as *al-kitab*, 'book' or 'writ', and sometimes as *umm al-kitab*, 'the mother of scriptures') are true and which are false. Is the *kitab* coextensive with the Quran, a kind of divine Ur-text, from which the Quran, like other recognized scriptures (including the Torah of the Jews and the Christian Gospel) derives? A 'created' Quran, as a divine artefact, would place the Arabic scripture on the same ontological level as the 'uncorrupted' versions of the divine messages delivered to other peoples. In short, there is a distinction between 'God's speech' or 'thought' pre-existing in the *umm al-kitab*, and the actual message as conveyed, in his proper tongue, by the Arabian Prophet. This, broadly speaking, seems to have been the attitude of the Mu'tazilis.

For the advocates of the 'uncreated Quran', by contrast, the 'medium was the message' (to borrow Marshall McLuhan's famous phrase). The Divine Writ was not an artefact of God, one of many created to suit different times and circumstances, but rather a manifestation of the divine in speech, in the distinctive and unique tongue of the Arabs. Although there is no absolute correlation between theological notions and national groupings in Islamic history, it seems far from coincidental that it was an 'Abbasid caliph, al-Ma'mun, who tried to impose the doctrine of the 'created' Quran, for the early 'Abbasids, unlike their Umayyad predecessors, sought to integrate the non-Arab Persians into the Empire. Their opponents, not necessarily all of them Arabs, consisted of people who had come to regard Arabic as a *lingua sacra*. As will be shown in later chapters, the Hanbali doctrine which laid particular stress on literalistic or non-allegorical interpretation of the scriptures became a natural rallying point for Arabs who found their linguistic and cultural hegemony diminishing in a multi-national Islamic society dominated numerically by Turks, Persians, Berbers and other non-Arab peoples.

Both groups, however, could agree that the Quran, like the evidences of the natural world it celebrates, is a 'sign' from Allah, a manifestation of his creative power in the medium of language. As with the postulated existence of the supreme deity to which it testifies, we should not suppose that the Quran's claim to a supernatural origin would in itself have inspired or shocked Muhammad's auditors, who were familiar with the inspired rhymes of the poets and the shamanistic utterances of the *kahins* or soothsayers. What was novel was the Quran's claim, consistent with its doctrine that Allah is the only source of supernatural power, that Muhammad's *dicta* came from Allah rather than from some jinn or other spirit.

The English word 'poet' derives from the Greek word for 'maker'; the Arabic equivalent, *sha'ir*, means 'one who has cognizance of [the unseen world]'. The contrasting origins of these words say much about the differing Greek and Semitic world-views. For the ancient Arabs, both poets and *kahins* were people with magical powers, presumed to derive from a special relationship with or possession by a jinn, or 'familiar friend' (*khalil*). The poet al-A'sha al-Akbar describes this relationship thus:

Between us we are two intimate sincere friends: a jinn and a human being who is naturally fit for him. If he only speaks [i.e., if he inspires me] then I will no longer be incapable of saying anything I would say. He suffices me so long as he is neither a tongue-tied one nor an awkward stupid fellow.[15]

The jinn's inspiration is conceived as 'coming down' to the poet; the word normally used derives from the root *nazala*. The fourth form of this verb (*anzalna* – 'We sent down') is consistently used by Allah in the Quran to describe his transmission of the divine writ to the Prophet. There is, indeed, a parallelism between the changes Muhammad instituted in the Hajj ceremonies and the transposition of pagan concepts of inspiration in the Quran. Just as, after the Farewell Pilgrimage, the rites associated with the local deities of Makka, Mina, Muzdalifa and 'Arafat are subsumed into the new 'cult' of Allah, rather than abolished altogether, so the familiar jinns of the Jahili poets and soothsayers give way to the notion of the Prophet's direct 'possession' by God, or rather, to be more precise, by the being, later identified as the archangel Gabriel, sent by him.

The Quranic style

As with the message, so with the style in which it was delivered. All scholars, Muslims and non-Muslims alike, are agreed that the style of the Quran undergoes some development, if only because the content of the Madinese *suras* addresses itself to many mundane matters, such as questions of law and inheritance, arising out of the needs of the community. In the earliest *suras*, however, Muhammad's utterances resemble the oathing formulas sometimes adopted by the *kahins*, where natural phenomena (or their spirits) are invoked to confirm an oath or statement. One such oath, made by the *kahin* Satih to the King of Yemen, is preserved in Ibn Ishaq's Life of the Prophet:

By the evening twilight	*wa-shafaq*
By the darkness	*wa'l ghashaq*
By the dawn	*wa'l falaq*
When it breaks bright	*idha tasaq*
Verily what I have told you is truth.[16]	*inna ma anbá'tuka bí'l lahaq*

This formula is uttered in *saj*, the metreless rhyming style of the Quran's early *suras*, several of which resemble it. The following is a literal rendering of 79:1–5:

By the rising ones sinkingly	*wa'l-nazí'at gharqan*
By the lively ones actively	*wa'l-nashitat nashtan*
By the floating ones sublimely	*wa'l-sabihat sabhan*
And the racing ones taking precedence	*fa'l-sabiqat sabqan*
And thus the managers commanding	*fa'l-mudabbirat amran*

The above passage is evidently addressed to auditors familiar with the *saj* style, which it echoes. A feature of this style, and of the Quranic style departing from it, is its condensed ellipticism – a characteristic, according to Muhammad Asad, of Arabian beduin speech. It is, so he says,

... the language of people whose mental images, flowing without effort from association to association, succeed one another in rapid progression and often vault elliptically over intermediate – as it were 'self-understood' – sequences of thought towards the idea which they aim to achieve or express.

It is impossible, he concludes, to understand the Quran's method and inner purport without being able to reproduce, to some extent, this characteristic of associative thought within oneself.[17]

The *saj* style of the Quran presupposed a familiarity with the manners and outlook of beduin society – so much so that without it passages such as the one quoted above are virtually incomprehensible. Processes, not things, are described: the missing substantives can only be inferred by projecting oneself back into the beduin environment. Without such imaginative projection, A. J. Arberry's translation (although justifiably acclaimed as the most elegant in modern English) seems utterly meaningless:

> By those that pluck out vehemently
> And those that draw out violently
> By those that swim serenely
> And those that outstrip suddenly
> By those that direct an affair[18]

Some exegetes interpreted these verses as referring to houses. Others, influenced, no doubt, by Persian and gnostic ideas, assumed that the reference here is to angels, whose activities concern the souls of the dying. This is the sense of Dr Yusuf Ali's translation (first published in 1934), officially approved by the Islamic Foundation in Britain:

> By the [angels]
> Who tear out
> [The souls of the wicked]
> With violence
> By those who gently
> Draw out [the souls
> Of the blessed]
> And by those who glide
> Along [on errands of mercy]
> Then press forward
> As in a race
> Then arrange to do
> [The commands of their Lord][19]

Muhammad Asad follows the earliest commentators, including Hasan al-Basri, who considered that the passage refers to celestial bodies. His rendering is not only free from supernatural assumptions about angels, but is also convincingly appropriate to a desert setting, where night skies are unusually brilliant:

Consider those [stars] that rise only to set
and move [in their orbits] with steady motion
and float [through space] with floating serene
and yet overtake [one another] with swift overtaking:
and thus they fulfil the [Creator's] behest! (79:1–5)

This single example of three different translations demonstrates the problems of interpretation raised by the Quran's elliptical style, which is far from being confined to the earliest *suras*. Asad's translation also shows how a formula of conjuration is elevated into a hymn to the miraculous power of the Creator. Free from the chronology which places the act of creation at the beginning of the Bible, this theme runs consistently throughout the Quran, reaffirming the notion of creation as a continuous process, rather than just a single act initiated by the Creator.

The Quranic Weltanschauung

This vision of a creative energy constantly at work is at the core of the Quranic doctrine: by insisting that its auditors observe the phenomena of the natural world, not as things-in-themselves but as 'signs' or symbols (*ayas*) of God's benevolence or power, the Muslim scripture forces them to look beyond the realm of appearances (*al-shahada*) to an unseen world (*al-ghaib*) whose ultimate reality is unknowable. Toshihiko Izutsu has pointed out the similarity, in this respect, between the Quranic *Weltanschauung* and the existentialist philosophy of Karl Jaspers. For Jaspers, the whole universe is a vast cryptogram, a *Chifferschrift* or book of symbols. Reality can never be grasped empirically, but must forever recede towards a horizon of inexhaustible appearances. Jasper's term for God is '*das Umgreifende*', 'the Encompassing', consciousness of which can only be acquired by those who move beyond the stage of commonplace everyday reason (*Verstand*) into what he calls *Existenz*, a state of higher philosophical awareness or existential becoming. Izutsu points out that this state exactly corresponds to the state of 'God-consciousness' urged upon believers in the Quran: the truly symbolic nature of Allah's *ayas* can only be perceived by those prepared to exercise their intellects.

Like everything else in the Quran, this attitude towards the symbolic and transient character of reality is not something that proceeds *ex nihilo* from the Prophet's utterances. It is rooted in the outlook of the Jahili poets who never ceased to proclaim – and to lament – the transitoriness of mortal existence. 'Thou seest a man ever yearn and pine for length of life,' concludes an ode by 'Abid ibn al-Abras which looks back nostalgically upon the pleasures of wine and love, 'but what is long life's sum but a burden of grief and pain.'[20] In the Quran the same assumption of mortal transitoriness is maintained, but the Jahili mood of pessimism is transposed into a major, life-affirming key: the illusory character of worldly existence is proof of ultimate immortality:

Know [O men] that the life of this world is but a play and a passing delight, and a beautiful show, and [the cause of] your boastful vying with one another and [of your] greed for more and more riches and children. Its parable is that of life-giving rain: the herbage which it causes to grow delights the tillers of the soil [*kafirs*]: but then it withers and thou canst see it turn yellow; and in the end it crumbles into dust. But [the abiding truth of man's condition will become fully apparent] in the life to come, [either] suffering severe or God's forgiveness and his goodly acceptance: for the life of this world is nothing but an enjoyment of self-delusion. (57:20)

The same image, of rain reviving the desiccated land, is invoked to justify the doctrine of resurrection – the doctrine, which, as we know, the Jahili Arabs had the greatest difficulty in accepting:

. . . for among His signs is this: thou seest the earth lying desolate – and lo! when We send down water upon it, it stirs and swells [with life]! Verily, He who brings to life can surely give life to the dead . . . for behold He has the power to do anything! (41:39)

Philosophically this argument in favour of resurrection is similar to Pascal's: what is more remarkable, the fact that a living being should appear at all, or that a once living being should be reborn? An atheism which takes as given the existence of life, accepting creation and procreation but rejecting re-creation is not necessarily logically consistent.

Human destiny

Allah is both the creator of the universe and its ruler. The laws instituted by him govern the motion of the stars and the planets, the sun and the moon, the natural processes of animal and vegetable worlds. In this essentially harmonious and beneficial world, all created things, except human beings, submit to their Creator. James Dickie, an English Muslim convert, has expressed this aspect of the Quranic vision succinctly, if somewhat arrestingly, by stating that 'all animals and insects are already Muslims'.[21] Humans alone have a propensity to violate God's laws because, unlike the animals, they have consciousness and therefore freedom of choice. This freedom, though contained within the wider field of Allah's omnipotence and omniscience, is implied in the doctrine of the Day of Judgement, when all men and women will be answerable for their actions.

Man's position in the cosmic system created by Allah is unique. On the one hand he is an earthly being created out of 'dust' and given dominion over the earth and its creatures as God's 'vice-regent' (*khalifa*). At the same time he ranks higher in the hierarchy of creatures than the angels and jinns, though the latter are purely spiritual beings. In the Quranic version of the Fall, Satan or Iblis is punished for refusing God's command to prostrate himself before the newly created Adam.

The devil tempts Adam, not Eve, to eat of the forbidden tree, with the false promise that it will lead to eternal life 'and to a kingdom that will never decay'. We are not told, as in Genesis, that the forbidden fruit comes from the 'Tree of knowledge of Good and Evil', merely that the fruit is forbidden – 'an allegory', according to Asad, 'of the limits which the Creator has set to mankind's desire and actions'.[22] This act of disobedience is, however, not dwelt upon. After eating the fruit Adam and Eve discover their nakedness – to find in sexual activity a pleasurable compensation for their banishment. In the biblical version the couple's expulsion from paradise is accompanied by a strong sense of disgrace, particularly for the woman:

Unto the woman He said, I will greatly multiply thy sorrow and thy conception; in sorrow shalt thou bring forth children; and thy desire shall be to thy husband, and he shall rule over thee. And unto Adam He said: Because thou hast hearkened to the voice of thy wife and hast eaten of the tree . . . cursed is the ground for thy sake; in sorrow shalt thou eat of it all the days of thy life.[23]

In the Quran, by contrast, Adam is forgiven immediately: 'Thereafter [however] his Sustainer elected him [for His guidance] and accepted his repentance, and bestowed His guidance upon him . . .' (20:122). Adam becomes the first of the prophets, God's vice-regent (*khalifa*) upon earth. His place of exile, far from being accursed as in the Old Testament, is to become man's 'dwelling place' and a 'source of profit' to him: 'Yea, indeed [O men] We have given you a [bountiful] place on earth, and appointed thereon a means of livelihood for you' (7:10).

In effect, man's act of disobedience is understood not as the cause of 'original sin', but as the unavoidable consequence of his humanity. In the words of the Indian poet and philosopher Mohammed Iqbal, his 'first act of disobedience was also his first act of free choice', a consequence of his 'rise from a primitive state of instinctive appetite to the conscious possession of a free self capable of doubt and disobedience'.[24]

Allah is omniscient and omnipotent; man is endowed with free will and freedom of choice. This paradox, which cannot be reconciled intellectually, establishes the boundaries of Islam's theological dialectic. In the eighth and ninth centuries the rationalistic Mu'tazilis were so concerned with defending the primacy of free will that they were prepared to limit God's omnipotence: by being subject to the principle of *'adl* (justice), Allah, like the Muslim ruler, is obliged to reward the good and punish the evil. The reaction which led to the overthrow of the Mu'tazilis restored God's omnipotence without resolving the problem of free will. The faithful were merely urged to accept the Quranic portrait of God's power as it is, 'without asking how' (*bi la kaif*). Eventually an uneasy synthesis of the two positions emerged with the teaching of al-Ash'ari (d. 935) and his followers, according to which man does not possess free will in the strictest sense, but does have the capacity to acquire, through an act of acceptance, the actions that God has already created for him.

The Arabic word for 'man', or rather 'human being', of which Adam, of course, is seen as the archetype, is *insan*, from the root *anisa*, meaning 'to be companionable, agreeable or genial' – a concept which recognizes the essentially sociable nature of the human animal. The proper posture of man towards Allah is one of fear – or, to be more precise, self-protection. Though his works are to be marvelled at, celebrated and enjoyed, the God of the Quran is too awe-inspiring and comprehensive to inspire love entirely free from apprehension, though in later times the Sufi mystics would find in the Quranic vision a focus for pure devotion. This idea of religious fear is rooted in Jahili concepts which, like so much else, are transformed and given an entirely new content within the vastly expanded Quranic world-view: 'And give thou the glad tidings [of God's acceptance] unto all who are humble – all whose hearts tremble with awe whenever God is mentioned . . .'[25] (22:35–6). The juxtaposition of two key concepts, *karim* and *taqwa*, in the Quran and Jahili poetry provides a useful insight into this process: 'Verily the noblest among you [*akramakum*] in the sight of God is the one who is most fearful [*atqakum*]' (49:13). The root *krm* and its cognates denoted nobility of lineage as outwardly expressed in the lavish hospitality and spending with which tribal chieftains felt it necessary to maintain their prestige. Such prestige spending was, until recently, still a feature of beduin or near-beduin society. (In the 1920s, before oil was discovered in Saudi Arabia, the late King 'Abd al-'Aziz, then one of the world's most impoverished rulers, would regularly provide food for all-comers, numbering perhaps two or three hundred people.) The word *taqwa* – 'fear', as used by the Jahili poets – referred to the instinctive reflexes with which animals protect themselves. Applied to humans, it could mean protection of oneself against social criticism. Thus the poet 'Amr ibn al-Ahtam announces: 'Every man of noble [*karim*] nature guards himself [*yantaqi*] against blame with hospitality.'[26] For the Jahili Arab, the *taqwa* is directed against his fellow men. A similar combination of words in the Quran reorientates it towards God. Later, in the post-Quranic framework of an all-Muslim society, *taqwa* acquires the secondary meaning of piety, or spiritual self-protection. Muhammad Asad further spiritualizes the term and its cognates by the rendering 'God-consciousness' or some similar expression.

There are many comparable shifts from the Jahili to the Quranic and post-Quranic (i.e., formally Islamic) use of certain words. The case of *taqwa* is, however, especially significant because it indicates a change from 'animal self-protection', via 'protection against social disapproval', to piety or 'self-protection' *vis-à-vis* God in a manner closely reflecting the changes in Arabian society during Muhammad's career. In the anarchic conditions of the Jahiliya, the tribal group protected

itself against attacks (whether unprovoked or vengeance-seeking) from
other tribes. In the absence of centralized state authority, justice was
administered laterally, as vengeance. In the Quran God assumes the
duty of administering justice 'vertically', while the new Umma or
'super-tribe' is expected to act as a unit in exacting retribution for the
attacks of outsiders.

Submission and faith

In the new Quranic world-view, people protect themselves against
God's wrath by humbling themselves before their Creator and under-
taking the duties and responsibilities of Muslims. *Islam* in its original
meaning is the primary act of self-surrender: an act of existential choice
whereby a person places his or her destiny in the hands of Allah and
submits to Allah's 'governance' as revealed through the commands of
the Prophet. It is a voluntary act, as implied by the use of the fourth,
reflexive form of the verb *salima*, 'to be safe, unharmed, secure or
intact'. One cannot undertake *Islam* on behalf of another person – which
is why, in the fullest sense, compulsory conversions are forbidden.[27] In
the pre-Islamic context the word *islam* meant 'giving over' or 'giving
up' something particularly precious; transposed in the Quran, such
an act of surrender embraces any autonomy on behalf of the self or
ego. In the primary sense a Muslim (from the active participle, 'one
who surrenders himself') is a person who has made this voluntary act
of self-surrender or existential commitment to God and his Prophet.
The subjective correlative of *Islam* in this primal sense is *iman* or faith:
just as the Muslim is one who has surrendered his whole being to
God, the *mumin* is one who is characterized by an unwavering faith
in him. Generally the two words are interchangeable; however, where
'Muslim' acquires the secondary meaning of one who is formally or
outwardly a member of the Islamic community, but not necessarily a
believer in terms of inner conviction, *iman* and *mumin* acquire the
added force of committed belief/believer.[28]

The negative values of the Quranic world-view revolve round two
key words: *kufr* ('disbelief') and *jahl* ('ignorance'). In its original
pre-Quranic usage the verb *kafara* meant 'he (or it) covered' something.
Thus, in a passage (57:20) cited on p. 104, the word *kafir* (literally, 'one
who covers') is applied to tillers of the soil – i.e., those who cover the

seeds with earth. In the usual Quranic context, however, the term *kafir* and its cognates are applied to those who cover or conceal something in the moral sense – i.e., those who knowingly deny the truth as revealed to them through Allah's messages. In the first instance this means *ingratitude* for the *ayas* as revealed in the natural order. In this sense its antonym is the verb *shakara* – 'to be thankful'. Thus Moses, relating Allah's promise to the Israelites, says:

If you are grateful [*shakartum*] I will surely give you more, but if you are thankless [*kafartum*] verily my chastisement shall be terrible. (14:7)

From mere ingratitude the word acquires the meaning of 'disbelief', in the sense of a refusal to accept or recognize the truths as revealed in the Quran. The most common usages of the term are *kufr* ('disbelief'), *kafir* ('one who denies the truth'), and the more forceful *alladhina kafaru* ('those who [wilfully] deny the truth'). In the broader Quranic context, *kufr* and *kafir* are the exact antonyms of *iman* and *mumin*. Ultimately, in the post-Quranic context where Islam is the prevailing ideology, the word *kafir* is generally applied to unbelievers, including Jews, Christians and pagans. However, it never quite loses its interior meaning of moral ingratitude leading to infidelity. Thus the breakaway Khariji sectarians, like some modern extremists, redefined themselves as the true Muslims in relation to *kafirs* in the rest of the community. They considered all outside their own group to be 'grave sinners' destined for hell who could justifiably be dispatched on their way there. At the intellectual level, the religious scholars, threatened with the challenge to their social power by unauthorized interpreters of scripture, designated as *kafirs* those who deviated from the hermeneutical principles devised by them. Thus Tirmidhi, one of the six universally recognized Sunni canonists, preserves a doubtless spurious *hadith* of the Prophet:

One who interprets the Quran according to his personal opinion, that is, not according to knowledge [*'ilm* – i.e., the recognized methodology] has proved himself by that very fact to be a *kafir*.[29]

The root cause and basis of *kufr* is the state of *jahl*. The term Jahiliya is used universally (as in this book) to describe the 'period of ignorance' before the coming of Islam: as such it stands in direct opposition to *'ilm*, knowledge. However, its primary meaning, both in the Quran and in pre-Islamic poetry, is somewhat different. As Ignaz Goldziher pointed out, *jahl* was originally opposed to *hilm*, a term denoting something like 'the moral reasonableness of the civilized man'. *Jahl* is the typical behaviour of someone who is arrogant, quick-tempered, hot-blooded and impetuous, someone who easily surrenders himself to the control of violent passions. The pre-Islamic poet 'Amr ibn Ahmar al-Bahili (who later embraced Islam) compares the state of *jahl* to the bubbling of a pot:

Many the large black ones [i.e., cooking-pots] which our maid-servants cajole: once their belly [i.e., contents] becomes *jahl* [i.e., boils up] it will never become *halim* [i.e., calm down].[30]

In the Quran the term is employed in the passage where Joseph resists the sexual advances of his Egyptian master's wife:

'O my Lord,' cried he, 'I would sooner be cast into prison than do what these women urge me to do: for unless Thou turn away their guile from me, I might yield to the attraction [I feel for them] and so become one of the *jahil*.' (12:33)

Since Joseph is one who has been granted judgement and knowledge (*hukm* and *'ilm*), in this context the opposite of *jahili* behaviour is indicated by his mastery over his own amorous inclinations, due to his understanding of right moral conduct. (Other factors apart, his yielding to the demands of his host's wife would have entailed a gross violation of the laws of hospitality.) Like other Quranic terms rooted in the material and social conditions of Arabia, the word *jahala* acquires its more far-reaching and universal connotations from being employed in a number of different contexts throughout the scripture. The inability to achieve mastery over one's passions, habitually repeated, distorts the judgement. The habitual *jahil* is thus incapable of forming a judicious opinion, a person who thinks in a shallow, superficial and rash manner. Because of his incapacity to see the truth of God's signs, the *jahil*, like the *kafir*, frequently oversteps the boundaries of behaviour ordained by God.

Quranic ethics

So far, the concepts we have tried to elucidate – *iman* and *kufr*, *islam* (in the original existential sense) and *jahl* – though terms rooted seman-tically in the reality of pre-Islamic Arabia, are capable of universal application. They belong to the category of what one might call Islam's 'universal' message, in so far as their evolution from particular, even morally neutral terms, takes them into the field of universal ethical values. If Muhammad had confined himself to articulating this aspect of the message, Islam would probably have developed, like protestant Christianity, in the direction of a purely ethical religion, capable of a wide variety of different applications according to the circumstances of time and place. This is, of course, far from being the case. The Quran, whatever its origins, arises out of the career of Muhammad the Law-giver. The general ethical principles it endorses are given a positive legal content. Obedience to God and his Prophet demands the observance of certain rituals and rules of social behaviour, as already outlined in the previous chapter. These rules, though only sketched out in the Quran, were elaborated by the scholar-lawyers of the first two or three Islamic centuries to become the basis of the Shari'a law described in the following chapter.

Like most of the terms already examined, the ethical system founded in the Quran also has its roots in the moral and social environment of a desert tribal society. The nearest equivalent to the English word 'good' is *al-ma'ruf* – literally, 'the known'. Its antithesis is *al-munkar*, 'the unknown'. The most celebrated verse employing these two terms is addressed to the Muslim community as a whole:

You are indeed the best community that has ever been brought forth for [the good] of mankind: you enjoin the doing of what is right [*al-ma'ruf*] and forbid the doing of what is wrong [*al-munkar*] and you believe in God. (3:110)

These two concepts, which the Quran integrates into the new Islamic system of ethics, clearly derive from the moral order of a tribal society where the 'known' or familiar way of doing things is socially approved, while the unknown or unfamiliar is disapproved of because it falls outside the framework of established custom.[31]

Several other key terms, all of them reflecting the desert environment, serve to reinforce this essentially conservative social morality. God is the guide (_hadi_ – a term originally applied to the professional guides in the desert); his commands indicate the straight (_mustaqim, rashid_) path (_shari'a, sabil, tariqa, sunna, sirat_, etc.). Those who stray (_dalla, qasata, nahaba_) end by losing their way. In the desert, of course, safety lies in following the well-tried paths of one's ancestors. In post-Quranic usage the _ma'ruf_ applies to the structure of _fiqh_ (jurisprudence) derived from the Quran and the Prophet's Sunna. Unlike Christian ethical concepts, which in many respects represent a radical departure from traditional Jewish morality, the Islamic ethical system continues to represent itself as observance of the _true_ paths of ancestral morality, as contrasted with the 'corruption' or 'straying' of contemporary society. For this reason, among others, Islamic reformers throughout history have invariably been advocates of a _return_ to the Sunna of the Prophet and the first generation of Muslims (_salaf_).

Allah, being omnipotent and omniscient, is the ultimate cause of both man's good and his evil actions.

Whomsoever God wills he lets go astray [_yudlilhu_]; and whomsoever He wills He sets him on a straight path [_siratin mustaqimin_]. (6:39)

Those who are good and follow the path are destined for paradise; those who are evil are destined for hell.

The idea of man's responsibility for his actions is a necessary consequence of the doctrine of free will, however much the latter may be modified by a sense of the unfathomable immensity of God's purpose. The examples of punishment in the Quran imply that groups as well as individuals are answerable for their errors. Three types of punishment are indicated for those who wilfully disbelieve in God's laws, or persist in their disobedience. The historical punishment stories are related of peoples who failed to heed the warnings of earlier prophets. Thus the people of 'Ad rejected their messenger Hud and were destroyed by a great wind which blew for seven days and seven nights and wiped out everything except their buildings. The people of Thamud (mentioned by Ptolemy, Pliny and other classical writers) were destroyed by an earthquake, or 'shout', as were the peoples of Madyan who failed to heed their messenger Shu'aib. The people of Tubba and Saba (biblical Sheba) in South Arabia are similarly punished for their unbelief, in the latter case by a flood which resulted apparently from the bursting of the Ma'rib dam.

In addition to these stories, evidently drawn from Arabian tradition, the Quran has several versions of biblical narratives, including the fate of Noah's people, destroyed by the flood, and of Sodom and Gomorrah, all of whose inhabitants except for Lot and his daughters are wiped out for their homosexuality. (The Quran omits the incestuous sequel to the biblical account of Lot's deliverance, in which the patriarch's daughters, anxious to preserve his line, manage to make themselves pregnant by him without his knowledge.[32] Muslim exegetes cite the story as an example of the 'corruption' of the scriptures by the Hebrews.[33]) The people of Pharaoh are referred to as having been punished for their arrogance in rejecting the prophet Moses, though their destruction while crossing the Red Sea (7:136f.) is recounted in much less detail than in the Old Testament.[34]

The problem of suffering

The ethical doctrine expounded in the punishment stories is problematic. On the one hand there is the clear statement, repeated several times, that 'no one shall be made to bear another's burden' (53:38; 6:164; 17:15; 35:18; 39:7). This is to say that no one shall suffer for another's guilt (as in the Christian doctrine of atonement, in which Christ suffers, and redeems, the sins of mankind) and no one shall be punished unjustly.

However, it is clear from the punishment stories that the just punishments are meted out to groups as well as individuals: whole societies are destroyed for their failure to heed the warnings of the prophets sent to them – and it is made clear that punishment is always preceded by a warning:

We would never chastise [any community for the wrong they may do] ere We have sent an apostle [to them]. But when [this has been done and] it is Our will to destroy a community, We convey our last warning to those of its people who have lost themselves entirely in the pursuit of pleasures and [if] they [continue to act] sinfully, the sentence [of doom] passed on to the community takes effect, and we break it to smithereens. (17:15)

Most of the punishment stories occur in the late Makkan or early Madinese periods, and reflect the Prophet's struggles with the pagan Quraish and the Jews who rejected him as the peoples referred to in the stories rejected those earlier messengers. Clearly they were intended as direct warnings to Muhammad's audiences, and the catastrophes alluded to were almost certainly well known to them. Understood more generally, however, they reflect a communalistic morality, appropriate to a tribal society. As in the Old Testament versions of the destruction of the Temple and the Babylonian exile, political disasters are explained as just punishment for the failure of a whole society to observe the law:

And we made this known to the Children of Israel through revelation: Twice, indeed, will you spread corruption on earth and will indeed become grossly overbearing! Hence when the prediction of the first of these two [periods of iniquity] came true, We sent against you some of Our bondsmen of terrible prowess in war, and they wrought havoc throughout the land: and so the prediction was fulfilled. (17:4–5)

A punishment such as this – military defeat by more powerful neighbours – can be understood, quite rationalistically, as a consequence of social or political failure. In Muhammad Asad's phrase it is 'a metonym for the natural law of cause and effect to which, in the long run, the life of man – and particularly the corporate life of nations and communities – is subject'.[35]

It becomes impossible, however, to reconcile the rationalistic idea of punishment as a consequence of human error, and therefore consistent with divine justice, with the natural catastrophes, such as floods and earthquakes, occurring in many of the punishment stories already referred to. One cannot accept rationally the notion that the innocent victims of such disasters are being punished for their sins, unless one also accepts the notion that all men are at all times irredeemably sinful and that an arbitrary and whimsical deity simply chooses to inflict punishments on some of them wherever and whenever he likes. Natural disasters (such as earthquakes in Algeria and Yemen, which some of the local *mullahs* were reported as having blamed on the sinfulness of their community) may be subject, like political disasters, to rationally discernible laws of cause and effect. The problem in most religions is how to accommodate the seemingly arbitrary and undeserved sufferings of people within a morally coherent universe presided over by a beneficent deity. A personal god who concerns himself with the fate of human beings, as distinct from an abstract deity concerned only with maintaining the cosmic order, must confront the natural human demand for justice. Within the human realm itself reason can explain, and perhaps even remedy, injustice: thus, economic and political theories, for example, will seek to analyse the material causes of poverty or deprivation and try to provide solutions. Within the larger universe, however, whether this is seen as conforming to the laws of 'God' or of 'Nature', reason may be powerless to find causal explanations which are psychologically satisfying to human beings: tectonic plate theory may explain the physical reason for earthquakes without specifying why some people perish in them and others escape.

Ultimately, in Islam, as in Christianity, the gap between the need for a morally coherent and rationally ordered universe and the observable fact that innocence often suffers can only be filled by faith. Faith is an attitude of trust not only that the universe is beneficent in itself, but that the individual has a central part in its ordering and will not be abandoned by his creator. The Quran, like the New Testament, insists that ultimately the demands of faith must supersede those of reason: hence the ethically dubious implication that the victims of natural disasters are somehow deserving of their fate. At the same time the Quran preaches an essentially rationalist morality: those who disobey God's laws are 'sinning against themselves' (34:19) and will suffer accordingly: 'Whatever good happens to thee is from God; and whatever evil befalls thee is from thyself' (4:79).

Only faith, not reason, can reconcile the ethical contradictions. The Quran, like Christianity, cannot accept that God can be other than good: 'verily, God does not wrong [anyone] by as much as an atom's weight' (4:40). Virtue will be rewarded, innocent suffering compensated for in the life to come. In the meantime the victims of injustice must console themselves with the thought that, in the unfathomable depths of God's purposes, not everything man regards as misfortune is really, in its final effects, evil:

. . . it may well be that you hate a thing the while it is good for you, and it may well be that you love a thing the while it is bad for you: and God knows, whereas you do not know. (2:216)

Eschatology

In Islam, as in Christianity, the ultimate reconciliation of faith with reason, morality with history, has to be deferred till the Day of Judgement. The eschatology is not just a consequence of a natural human reluctance to face the finality of death; it is the only context in which the conflicting claims of observable reality and the desire for moral coherence can be fitted together. Muhammad's vision of the Last Hour, a cosmic cataclysm which is simultaneously a moment of judgement, generates some of the most remarkable descriptive passages in the Quran, especially in the earlier Makkan *suras*:

> When the sun is shrouded in darkness,
> and when the stars lose their light,
> and when the mountains are made to vanish,
> and when she-camels big with young, about to give birth, are left
>   untended,
> and when all beasts are gathered together,
> and when the seas boil over,
> and when all human beings are coupled [with their deeds],
> and when the girl-child that was buried alive is made to ask
> for what crime she had been slain,
> and when the scrolls [of men's deeds] are unfolded,
> and when heaven is laid bare,
> and when the blazing fire [of hell] is kindled bright,
> and when paradise is brought into view;
> [on that Day] every human being will come to know what he has
>   prepared for himself. (81:1–14)

The eschatological vision of a Grand Reckoning at the end of time fills in the gaps in the ethical doctrines. The idea, which can be traced back to Pharaonic and Babylonian notions, is the essential prerequisite for a belief in the divine law: if God is the original legislator, he must also be Judge at the Final Court of Appeal. The imagery of judgement is frequently commercial, reflecting the mercantile milieu of Muhammad's Makka:

And as for him whose record shall be placed in his right hand [i.e., whose life has been righteous] he will in time be called to account with an easy accounting and will [be able to] turn joyfully to those of his own kind. But as for him whose record shall be given to him behind his back [i.e., because it is so horrible that he will not wish to look at it] he will in time pray for utter destruction, but he will enter the blazing flame. (84:7–12)

The horrors of hell, though graphically painted, are not given the more extended treatment reserved for the joys of heaven:

Verily for all who sin against themselves [by rejecting Our truth] We have readied a fire whose billowing folds will encompass them from all sides; and if they beg for water, they will be given water [hot] like molten lead which will scald their faces: how dreadful a drink, and how evil a place to rest! (18:29)

But as for those who have persevered in evil . . . [They will find themselves] in the midst of scorching winds and burning despair and the shadows of black smoke – shadows neither cooling nor soothing. (56:41–4)

Heaven, by contrast, is depicted as a place of palpable luxuries and sensuous joys for the righteous:

. . . theirs shall be gardens of perpetual bliss – gardens through which waters flow – wherein they will be adorned with bracelets of gold and will wear green garments of silk and brocade [and] wherein upon couches they will recline: how excellent a recompense and how goodly a place to rest! (18:31)

The joys of paradise find their most graphic description in the earlier *suras*. They were often condemned by medieval Christian writers for their more or less explicit eroticism.

They will be seated on gold-encrusted thrones of happiness, reclining upon them, facing one another [in love]. Immortal youths will wait upon them with goblets and ewers and cups filled with water from unsullied springs by which their minds will not be clouded and which will not make them drunk; and with fruit of any kind that they may choose, and with the flesh of any fowl that they may desire. And [with them will be their] companions [*hur*] pure, most beautiful of eye like unto pearls [still] hidden in their shells . . . [and they will find themselves] amidst fruit-laden lote-trees and acacias flower-clad and shade extended and waters gushing and fruit-abounding, never-failing and never out of reach. And [with them will be their] spouses, raised high, for behold, we shall have brought them into being in a life renewed, having resurrected them as virgins full of love, well-matched with those who have attained to righteousness . . . (56:15–38)

Some Muslim commentators were at pains to point out that these descriptions were purely allegorical. Bukhari, Muslim and others record a *hadith* in which the Prophet is said to have stated of paradise:

God says: 'I have readied for My righteous servants what no eye has ever seen, and what no ear has ever heard, and no heart of man has ever conceived.'[36]

Dr Yusuf Ali, a translator of the Quran recommended by the UK Islamic Foundation, insists that the companions (who have a feminine gender in the Arabic) are purely spiritual beings:

. . . lest grosser ideas of sex should intrude (he writes in his commentary) it is made clear that these companions for heavenly society will be of special creation – of virginal purity, grace and beauty, inspiring and inspired by love, with the question of time and age eliminated.[37]

Some of the medieval Muslim exegetes, however, were in no doubt that the pleasures of paradise were meant to be enjoyed literally rather than allegorically. One of the best-known accounts, that of Shaikh Jalal al-Din al-Suyuti, contains a detailed description of paradise (using the Quran as point of departure) which became immensely popular from the thirteenth century. As well as being a place of abundant rivers and trees of precious stones, of ever-ready horses caparisoned with jewel-studded bridles, it is a place where human beings may enjoy all the carnal pleasures without any of the attendant inconveniences:

The food of paradise is everlasting. When the Elect have eaten or drunk something, they will perspire just a little with sweat as fresh and perfumed as musk. The dwellers in paradise have no anuses: these were made for defecating, and in paradise there is no defecation.[38]

The houris, or female companions, come in a variety of colours, including white, green, yellow and red. Their bodies are made of saffron, musk, amber and camphor, and their hair is of raw silk. Each one of the Elect may have 70 houris in addition to his earthly wives and any other woman he finds attractive. All become more beautiful each day. A man's virility becomes vastly increased. The couples make love as on earth, but each moment of pleasure lasts twenty-four years. Paradise, however, is not just a place of sensuous delights in Suyuti's vision. Its joys will culminate in the ultimate spiritual experience: the vision of God, when the faces of the Elect will 'be bright with happiness looking up to their Sustainer', while the faces of the damned will be 'overcast with despair, knowing that a crushing calamity is about to befall them' (75:22–3). For Suyuti, the 'Beatific Vision' of Allah, seated on a hyacinth throne 'a thousand years high', surrounded by the prophets and the rest of the Elect arranged in order of virtue, is the final goal of paradise and hence the end of life itself:

The Elect then gaze upon the Face of the Everlasting One, resplendent in all His glory. They see him, unveiled, without mediators. As the light of Truth shines upon their faces, they remain transfixed for three hundred years before the Face of Truth, Glory be to His Name, God the One, the Incomparable.[39]

The Muslim vision of paradise – in contrast to the occidental Christian version – represents a steady progression through the senses towards the ultimate ecstasy of the Beatific Vision. Whatever its meaning in religious terms, paradise represents culturally the vision of the Ultimate which society places before itself and before those individuals whom it seeks to persuade to abide by its norms. In the West a celibate Christian Church, infected from early on with Manichaean dualism, taught that the flesh and its joys were essentially evil and that paradise must therefore be a place of purely 'spiritual' pleasures. Just as the political dualism apportioning separate allegiances to God and Caesar upheld the eventual separation of church and state, so the mind– body dualism of Helleno-Christianity forced western consciousness to divide the world into separate categories of spirit and matter. A world thus 'disenchanted' was not only de-sacralized and made secular; it ceased to have any terms in which its own significance could be communicated. Without the sense of an ultimate reality capable of conferring meaning on human existence, ordinary living, with its ecstasies and sorrows, its pleasures and inconveniences, becomes a kind of drudgery in which people are required needlessly and pointlessly to consume their energies.

Conclusion

For all the obvious difficulties it contains as a system of ethics – and therefore as a source of divine law binding human behaviour – the Quranic message militates powerfully against the division of the world into profane and spiritual spheres. The orgiastic vision of paradise may seem naive to a sophisticated modern sensibility, though no less so than the pictures created by European artists. But it is of a piece with the whole of the Quranic vision and its fundamental life-affirming message. It is an integrated vision of ordinary living in which the transcendent is made manifest in every aspect of daily experience. 'Herein is a Message for those who think,' it proclaims incessantly, pointing to the stars, the sky, the trees, the birds and the animals, as well as to the ordinary activities of men and women. The same concern with concrete experience extends to the descriptions of the end of the world, which never so lose touch with sense perception as to become the source of empty theologizing.

In conclusion, it should be emphasized that the positive legal content of the Quran only accounts for a relatively small proportion – about ten per cent – of its overall message. This central message demands an existential commitment to the cause of human freedom, by liberating human consciousness from a fetishistic attachment to limiting objectives. Tribal particularism is replaced by Islamic universalism, the perception of objects as things-in-themselves gives way to a recognition of the contingent character of all existing things. The whole universe is seen as a hugely complex allegory or metaphor of the divinity. Two aspects above all stand out. First, that all dimensions of existence are part of a totality, that every individual object of perception is really a symbol of a much more comprehensive, unifying reality called the divine. Second, that the totality of this reality can never be fully understood by human beings, because of inherent limitations in the structure of their intelligence. There is a portion of totality – the category of *al-ghaib* – whose existence must be taken on trust.

The continuing relevance of the Quran, like that of other great religious works of antiquity, is that it seeks to provide a cosmic context in which to locate humanity and its activities. It places it in a universe that is both beneficent and purposeful, and yet unfathomable. Addressed as it is to Arabic speakers, the Quran also lays down some simple rules – or, rather, guidelines – about the conduct of social and personal life. These rules are specific to geography and period and are addressed to a particular audience whose social and cultural norms are taken as given. The rules of marriage and diet incorporate existing customs: they become increasingly inappropriate the further one is removed from the Arab world, both socially and geographically. The essential message embodied within the rules is the simple one that, since man is a social animal, he needs to accept the social and cultural norms of the society in which he finds himself: social life depends on them. Unfortunately, the undue emphasis on these rules (which have come to acquire a symbolic meaning wherever Muslims experience the social, political or cultural challenges posed by modernity) has created a misleading impression of Islam as a religion of Pharisaic legalism backed by harsh 'medieval' punishments. This emphasis detracts from the main body of the Quranic message, which contains far broader, indeed universal, implications.

The universal message contained in the Quran, and in the example of the Prophet's life to which it is linked historically, has a certain timeless relevance. It is, essentially, that man is not the Lord of the Universe, that he cannot do as he lists regardless of the moral laws that inhere in its very structure – laws which, though he may continue to discover them for himself, are known in their entirety only to the Creator. There are limits to human knowledge, just as there are limits to the permissible range of human behaviour. How these limits can be defined in practical terms is something that different societies and different generations must necessarily decide for themselves. For Muslims – and for non-Muslims who take the trouble to investigate its meanings – the Quran contains the guidelines to such limits: but it cannot define them absolutely, nor does it seek to do so.

4 Law and Disorder

Al-Shafi'i's tomb

Between Cairo's Citadel and the leafy suburb of Ma'adi, much patronized by Egypt's foreign community, there is a fine thirteenth-century mosque and tomb belonging to the Imam al-Shafi'i, the most influential of the early lawyers of Islam and founder of one of the four *madhhabs* or legal schools. The mosque and its tomb stand out from the labyrinthine streets of the Southern Cemetery, known as the City of the Dead, an area which is in fact a good deal livelier than its name suggests. The fine stone tombs in which the Cairenes traditionally bury their dead are really houses built from the same Muqattam limestone as the pyramids, according to the standard Arab pattern consisting of a simple courtyard flanked by rooms and an open loggia. The deceased are buried either in vaults beneath the courtyard, the steps of which are usually covered, except when needed to admit a new occupant, or beneath stone cenotaphs with pillars standing fore and aft, like masts of a ship. In the past the rooms were occupied by the *bawwabs* or doorkeepers employed by the wealthier families to protect the tombs and such valuables as the silver and plate brought out on special occasions – the night after Ramadan, the Prophet's Birthday or the anniversary of someone's death. Despite Islam's discouragement of mortuary cults, many ancient pharaonic practices have survived in Egypt, a fact which is hardly to be marvelled at considering that the pharaonic religion lasted at least three times as long as Islam's fourteen centuries.

Nowadays many of the tombs have been abandoned by their owners and taken over by squatters, who find them considerably more attractive to live in than the crumbling tenements of 'Abbasiya or Bulaq. Many have equipped themselves – legally or otherwise – with electric light and running water, and it is not unusual to see the flicker of a

TV set among the chickens, the bare-legged children and the paraffin stoves that perch on the cenotaphs. The main thoroughfare of this necropolis has developed a lining of cafés, food-stalls and other small shops, most of them of a standard which suggests that the tomb-squatters are far from being the least privileged members of Cairo's teeming social antheap.

At almost any time after sundown, when the people are going about their business, the street leading to the Imam's tomb comes alive with animals and humans, mopeds and handcarts – that special combination of medievalism and modernity that gives the traditional parts of Muslim cities their characteristic flavour. During the second week of Sha'ban, the eighth month of the Muslim calendar, the hubbub reaches its zenith. This is the time when the people celebrate the Imam's *maulid* or anniversary festival. The mosque is festooned with fairy-lights, and antique swings and roundabouts are hauled into the streets to occupy the children. Sufi dervishes dance in remembrance of God (*dhikr*) by the tomb of the saint. A female beduin singer, face tattooed, sings suggestive love songs in praise of the Almighty, whose name – ALLAH – is emblazoned in green neon lighting on the wall of the mosque, bathing the whole carnival in a ghoulish glow. Holy, gaudy, erotic and mystical, the Imam's *maulid*, like other Cairene festivals, promiscuously mingles the sacred and profane in a manner which puritans usually find deeply disturbing.

It is proof of Islam's vigour and catholicity that the saint in whose honour this festival is held is by no means a hero of folklore, renowned for some improbable miracle. The Imam al-Shafi'i was the greatest scholar and systematizer of early Islam, the man who, more than any single figure after Muhammad and 'Umar, left his personal mark on its history. In Christian terms, it would be as if the holy razzmatazz were being held in honour of St Augustine or St Jerome. Even at the most popular level, Islam is still a legalistic faith in which saints are expected to dispense justice as well as miracles.

The Imam al-Shafi'i is a case in point. His mausoleum was built by Salah al-Din's (Saladin's) brother Afdal in 1211, after Egypt had finally been won back to the Sunni fold following the fall of the Shi'ite Fatimids. Saladin's dynasty, the Ayyubids, sought to revive the Imam's memory as the true architect of Sunnism, the mainstream tendency based on observance of the Prophet's Sunna or practice. Their efforts were entirely successful: the Shi'ite tendency, with its 'personality cult' of leaders claiming descent from the Prophet's family, was virtually eliminated, despite almost two centuries of enlightened government by the Fatimid caliphs. The Imam is now the object of a popular cult among peasants who address letters to him seeking redress from injustices unremedied by Egypt's lumbering judicial system.

The letters to the Imam are placed inside the iron grille surrounding his cenotaph. In 1965 a selection of them was published by a criminologist, Sayyid 'Uwais, and they make fascinating reading. Many of the writers seek cures for their sickness or vengeance for injuries, real or imagined: 'I demand that my neighbour 'Abbas be paralysed to the ground, so that he may know that people other than himself have someone to defend them.' (The plaintiff had had his face slapped and his beard pulled by the aforesaid 'Abbas, in public, during the Holy Month of Ramadan.) Other letters contain requests for employment:

I am the breadwinner of a large family but cannot provide the bread for lack of an income. I wrote – O Imam, my master – to the manager of the government factory explaining my situation, but he did not bother about me. So I hope that you will take an interest in my case and see that I obtain a job in one of the government factories so that I may live and guarantee the bread of my children. I have no one to go to but you. So help me for the sake of the grandfather of the believers, our master Muhammad, and for the sake of the Quran![1]

Some of the letters are actually written in the form of legal submissions to the Court of the Bataniya, a kind of celestial Supreme Court presided over by the Imam, Sayyida Zainab and Sayyid Husain (the Prophet's granddaughter and grandson, much venerated in Egypt) and Sayyid Ahmad Badawi (a popular Sufi saint).

Our shaikh attacked and threatened to beat and insult me, in spite of his being the Crown of Islam in our village, whom I respect and venerate . . . And Na'ima Hafiz took my cotton crop in 1952, but denied that she took it . . . I have already submitted a complaint to our master, Husain, and to our virtuous Lady, Umm Hashim al-Sayyida Zainab (may God be satisfied with them). And they accepted my petition and saw to it that the value of my cotton was recorded in the public prosecutor's investigation. But till now the case is still held up in the adviser's office, and has yet to come before the court . . .[2]

Al-Shafi'i's achievement

It is not inappropriate that the Imam al-Shafi'i, though a leading intellectual of early Islam, should be revered as a popular saint by the Egyptian *fallahin*. More than any other figure of his time, he restored a form of unity to an Islamic state undergoing a process of disintegration. He did not succeed in achieving a consolidation at the political level: nor was this his aim. The geopolitical tensions inherent in the vast new territories conquered by the Arabs made an Islamic state with centralized political control an impossible dream. But he developed something which, in the end, would prove much more durable than the Arab imperium. This was the science of *fiqh* (literally, 'understanding') or religious jurisprudence, by which a whole range of customs and practices, derived from the Prophet's teachings, Arabian customs and the customs of the newly conquered peoples, could be merged into an over-arching system of law governing the daily life of the Muslims. It is really from Shafi'i's systematization of *shari'a*, developed according to principles devised by him, that modern Muslims, both Shi'ite and Sunni, derive their common identity and sense of being-in-the-world.

The development of *fiqh* occurred over a period of two centuries against the background of the expansion and threatened disintegration of the Islamic empire. The political conflicts during this, the formative period of an Islamic religious and political culture destined to last for a millennium or more, became the basis of the sectarian divisions to be examined in the next chapter. Here it will be necessary only to sketch in, as briefly as possible, the historical background.

After the first wave of conquest the Arabs became a new ruling class which deliberately avoided integrating itself with the conquered peoples. The soldiers were kept in garrison towns and subject to the rule of *qadis* or judges appointed by the caliph or his governors. The rest of the population, whether Jewish, Christian or Zoroastrian, were accorded protection upon payment of the *jizya*, a poll tax first instituted by the Prophet after the conquest of Khaibar. Conversion to Islam, if not actively discouraged, was scarcely encouraged: the economic privileges of the Arabs depended on the subject peoples retaining their status as *dhimmi* or client communities. Those foreigners who did convert were generally treated as second-class citizens. Many tried to get even with the Arabian rulers by discarding their Greek or Persian names and adopting the names of famous Arab families, buttressing their claims with forged pedigrees. That this was above all an Arab, rather than a Muslim, conquest is best demonstrated by the fact that the Christian Arab tribes which had joined in the conquest were not taxed with the conquered *dhimmi* Christians. Nor was it anomalous that the greatest poet of the Umayyad period, Akhtal (c.640–710), panegyrist of the caliph 'Abd al-Malik, was himself a Christian.

The social distinction between Arabs and non-Arabs, however, became much harder to maintain once a significant number of the latter had converted. Despite the lack of coercion, the financial advantages of becoming a Muslim – quite apart from any religious attractions it may have had for people seeking more enlightened forms of piety – were obvious enough. Conversions among the poorer elements of the subject peoples were facilitated both by the egalitarian character of the Quranic message and the 'levelling' effects of conquest, which greatly reduced the power of the great land-owning Christian and Zoroastrian families. Landless peasants who drifted to the cities in search of work no doubt discovered that there were considerable advantages in becoming Muslims, even though converts were at first given the definitely inferior status as *mawalis*, or clients, of the Arabian tribes. Membership of the Umma ceased to be the badge of a new ruling class: instead it became something of an alliance between the rulers and the least privileged sections of the conquered peoples. A not dissimilar situation occurred after the Muslim conquest of India, when the Moghul rulers succeeded in 'liberating' and converting members of the lowest Hindu castes.

As a result of these conversions and of the growing economic links between the different communities, it became impossible to maintain the dualism of 'Umar's time, with one law for the Muslims and another, autonomously administered, for the subject communities. The customs of the Arabs, based on tribal habits and a few simple rules laid down in the Quran, were beginning to mingle, and sometimes to conflict, with the laws of the majority in the new territories.

Geopolitical tensions were also developing. Under the Umayyad caliphs, Damascus was the capital of a flourishing empire, much of which was administered by the Christian clerical class inherited by the Arabs from their Byzantine predecessors. But increasingly the economic weight of the empire came to be in Iraq and the distant highlands of Khurasan, territories belonging to the former Sassanid empire. Under Walid I (705–15) the Arabs continued to expand, westwards to Spain and eastwards into Transoxania and Sind. But the attempt in 717 by Walid's successor, Sulaiman, to take Constantinople failed, and the Arabs were thrown back behind the Taurus mountains, which still remain their northern frontier.

While Christian Anatolia remained unconquered, the economic – and hence the political – centre of gravity shifted eastwards towards the former Sassanid lands. The powerful Umayyad governor of Iraq, Hajjaj (d. 714) did much to increase that province's prosperity by extending the irrigation works. At the same time he antagonized the Arab garrisons by his ruthless centralizing policies which rode roughshod over older habits of tribal autonomy.

During the third and fourth decades of the eighth century, social and economic tensions began to develop which seriously threatened the unity of the empire. A Syrian-based administration with centralizing tendencies created strong resentments among the garrisons in Iraq and Khurasan. At the same time the new class of non-Arab converts was becoming increasingly resentful of the privileges still enjoyed by the Arabs. The strongest centres of dissent tended to be in Basra and Kufa, one a port of growing importance and both of them garrison towns. It was partly for this reason that, in Kufa especially, factions loyal to the Prophet's family against the 'usurping' Umayyads began to attract support.

The opposition movement was not without an intellectual leadership capable of expressing itself in religio-legal terms. The Umayyad caliphs had from the first found their critics among men and women who accused them of abandoning the pious simplicities of Madina for the new-found luxuries of empire. The movement was compounded of many elements. A traditional Arab element, consonant with the polarities of beduin life – plunder and starvation – expressed itself in terms of an austere puritanism which somehow complemented the excesses of the new, fabulously wealthy, caliphal order. (The same polarities may be observed in modern Saudi Arabia.) A distinctively political element crystallized into support for the extreme Kharijis – who tried to secede from the corrupt Islamic community and recreate the Madinese ideal of a community of saints. A similar trend existed among the people – many of them *mawalis* – who would later be dubbed the Shi'a, or partisans of 'Ali and his house. At a superior cultural level there existed small but influential groups of pious men who spent much of their time in the mosques, reciting the Quran and no doubt asking themselves how, in the vastly expanded world in which they now found themselves, its messages could be properly applied.

A debate, involving moral and philosophical arguments about the right to rebel against unjust rulers, was already in progress when a series of revolts culminated in the downfall of the Umayyad dynasty in 750.

The ʿAbbasids

The new rulers, who took power with the key support of the garrison tribes in Khurasan, enjoyed the backing of the moderate Shiʿite elements and most of the pious intellectuals. Though not of ʿAlid descent, they were descended from the Prophet's uncle ʿAbbas, and were therefore closer to his line than the Umayyads. The ʿAbbasids built a new capital for themselves at Baghdad, hard by Ctesiphon, the Sassanid seat of government. From here they ruled an empire which, though it rapidly lost most of its western territories in the Mediterranean, had a solid agrarian base in Mesopotamia and was free to develop extensive trading contacts across the newly unified Indian Ocean. The ʿAbbasid caliphs became fabulously wealthy: their golden age has been aptly summarized, for both Muslims and Westerners, in the reign of Harun al-Rashid (786–809).

The coming of the ʿAbbasids failed to heal the political divisions that were developing between supporters of ʿAli's line and the rest of the Muslim community. Though allowing Shiʿite expectations of a *mahdi* or messiah to work in their favour, once in power the ʿAbbasids turned against their former Shiʿite supporters, initiating the long history of persecution and martyrdom that came to characterize the tradition. An influential group of intellectuals, however, including the Qadaris and their successors the Muʿtazilis, rallied to the support of the new regime, under whose auspices they laid the foundations of the first truly universal Islamic order.

Intellectuals do not necessarily create history; but at certain times they design institutions through which historical change is effected, which gives them an influence as great as that of rulers or their generals. The formative period of Islamic history was really the first two centuries of the 'Abbasid era. The model of the Madinese polity, elaborated and adjusted to suit contemporary circumstances, was its inspiration. Its architects were the scholar-jurists (*ulama*) of the eighth and ninth centuries, the most outstanding of whom was Shafi'i.

The task facing the pious *ulama* at this time was a formidable one. Under the Umayyads they had become increasingly restive, both about the regime's injustices and about the arbitrary manner in which it took over non-Islamic laws and administrative practices from its Byzantine and Persian predecessors. The 'Abbasid revolution provided the *ulama*, for the first time, with an opportunity to put their criticisms into practice: they must find Islamic solutions to the problems the Umayyads had often solved by recourse to Graeco-Roman precedents. In view of the vastly expanding Muslim community that was coming into being, the task was an urgent one. Since the time of the late Umayyads, the caliphs had been actively encouraging conversions to Islam. After the 'Abbasid revolution, which enjoyed the support of the *mawali*, the stream of conversions became a flood. With peasants flocking to the cities, converting and bringing Islam back into the countryside, the demand for Islamic solutions had a populist character.

The Madinese polity offered little more than a few general guidelines. It had been above all a community with an 'ideal' orientation: Muhammad's aim had been to build a society basing itself on the godly life, and by and large his community had responded. It had been a relatively small community, consisting of, at most, 30,000 persons, many of whom would have been known to each other. Moreover, it had been a culturally homogeneous community, in which common Arab custom had been modified by group allegiance to Muhammad and observance of the relatively few, simple Quranic rules.

Clearly it would have been impossible to have recreated such conditions in the vastly expanded social context of the 'Abbasid empire. The rules governing life in the Madinese community had already been overlaid in many cases by the practices of the Umayyads. This was hardly surprising in view of the amount of time – more than a century – that had elapsed since the death of the Prophet. The Quran itself, as we have seen, contained relatively little legislative material. Only 500 verses out of more than 6,000 deal with legal obligations, and the majority of these are actually concerned with religious matters such as prayer, fasting or pilgrimage. Only 80 or so verses deal with legal topics in the strict sense of the term and the majority of these are about women, marriage and the laws of inheritance. As we have seen, during his lifetime the Prophet had been not only the Quran's transmitter but the ruler of an Islamic state whose authority grew with the progress of his military campaigns. On legal questions, the Prophet himself must have provided detailed guidance. Thus he is said to have clarified ambiguities in the law of inheritance by giving heirs under Quranic law precedence over relatives entitled to legacies under the older Arab customary law. In general the Prophet's practice or *sunna*, in both legal and religious matters, became normative within the community.

Despite the political conflicts in which they became involved, the earliest caliphs inherited something of the Prophet's charismatic power and freedom to legislate. Thus 'Umar appears to have had no scruples about instituting the penalty of stoning for adulterers in place of the milder Quranic punishment of flogging, or increasing the penalty for wine-drinking from 40 to 80 lashes. During the latter years of Umayyad rule, however, the caliph's discretionary power became increasingly unacceptable in the eyes of the pious opposition. The authority of the Prophet was invoked to counter the authority of the caliphs. The intensive study of the Quran itself produced a demand for data about the Prophet's life, for only by establishing the 'occasions' of revelation – the historic context in which a particular verse or group of verses 'came down' – could its meanings be fully elucidated. One school of traditionists, tracing itself from 'Abdullah ibn 'Abbas, son of the Prophet's uncle, tried to give the context of as many of the occasions of revelation as possible in order to clarify the meaning of the divine messages. Other scholars collected narratives about Muhammad's campaigns and his life, based on well-authenticated accounts drawn from oral materials.

In the generations when the actual memory of the Prophet was alive, the law had developed in a more or less *ad hoc* manner around the decisions of individual authorities, such as Malik ibn Anas (d. 796), a lawyer and collector of traditions in Madina. Malik's school could claim, with some justification, to represent a 'living tradition' or *sunna* going back to the Prophet's time. At the same time a certain flexibility had been introduced in interpreting the Quranic rules. The opinion (*rai*) or preferences (*istihsan*) of the jurists were allowed to influence legal doctrines, as was the principle of analogy (*qiyas*) in dealing with new situations unmentioned in the Quran or the *sunna*.

During the later Umayyad period, however, the pious opposition began to adopt an increasingly doctrinaire attitude, rejecting judgements based on anything other than the Prophet's own Sunna. Legal practices that had grown up more or less organically in Madina or Kufa were no longer regarded as acceptable by the pious; nor were *hadiths* attributable to the Prophet's Companions – the 30,000-odd members of the original Madinese community whose statements the earliest lawyers had virtually placed on a par with those of the Prophet himself.

The hadith *literature*

The origins of *hadiths* attributed to the Prophet himself are still the subject of dispute, and some ill-feeling, between Muslims and non-Muslim scholars. The majority of Muslims believed until quite recently that these *hadiths*, which are contained in six canonical collections, genuinely represent the sayings and deeds of the Prophet as preserved in oral tradition and written down in the ninth century. As this literature has become more accessible to people outside the ranks of the traditionally trained 'ulama, a sceptical attitude towards them has been emerging, especially in India and Pakistan. There is no doubt that the *hadith*-collectors, the best-known being Muhammad ibn Isma'il al-Bukhari (810–70) and Muslim ibn al-Hajjaj (d. 875), travelled vast distances to seek out reliable individuals and devoted prodigious amounts of energy to the attempt to distinguish true from false transmitters of the Prophet's alleged sayings and deeds. According to the system they developed, each tradition was equipped with an *isnad*, or chain of authorities, tracing it back to the prophet, rather in the manner that dealers provide rare art objects with provenances tracing them back to their original owners. A doubtless exaggerated story records that Bukhari himself examined 600,000 *hadiths*, 200,000 of which he actually memorized before committing a mere 2,700 of them, which he regarded as unimpeachable, to paper. Another story is told which demonstrates his extreme punctiliousness in rejecting transmitters considered even remotely unreliable. Having traced a particular *hadith* to a pious Iraqi scholar, he eventually, after much travelling, found the source in question, who confirmed the *hadith*, providing it with an impeccable *isnad*. Afterwards the scholar invited Bukhari to inspect a new colt of which he was especially proud. In order to attract the animal the scholar gathered up the folds of his gown as though he were carrying corn in his lap. The colt duly approached him in the expectation of food. Bukhari ruefully rejected the *hadith* which he had heard from the lips of the scholar: a man who would so deceive an animal could not be regarded as a reliable source of the Prophet's Sunna.

The scholars developed an elaborate technical vocabulary defining the degrees of reliability in the chains of transmitters. Their criticisms, however, were mainly confined to the *isnads*: the content of the *hadiths* known as the *matn* was rarely subject to critical examination. Since the pioneering work of the Hungarian Arabist Ignaz Goldziher during the nineteenth century, most western scholars have questioned the authenticity of even the best-attested *hadiths* on the grounds that many are anachronistic in content, contradict each other or are at variance with the spirit or letter of the Quran. Joseph Schacht, following Goldziher, argued that many of the traditions in the classical collections must have been invented shortly before their inclusion, because they were not employed at an earlier date in the course of legal discussions when 'reference to [them] would have been imperative'.[3] Every legal tradition attributed to the Prophet, until the contrary was proved, must be taken not as an authentic expression valid for his time, but as the 'fictitious expression of a legal doctrine formulated at a later date'. Schacht insisted that positive proof of authenticity was lacking in every single *hadith* he examined.

Schacht's scepticism about the authenticity of *hadiths* was shared by some Islamic modernists, including Sir Sayyed Ahmed Khan (d. 1898 – see below, pp. 296–9) and his methodology was accepted by the distinguished Pakistani scholar and reformer Fazlur Rahman (d. 1988). Recent scholarship, however, questions the excessive scepticism of Goldziher, Schacht and their latter-day follower G. H. A. Juynboll. One of the foremost scholars of Islamic law writing in the West, Wael B. Hallaq of McGill University, states that many *hadith* reports can be dated to earlier than had previously been thought, even as early as the Prophet. While the great bulk may have originated many decades after the Hijra, there exists a body of material that can be dated back to Muhammad's lifetime.[4] Another leading authority, the late Norman Calder, argues for a considerably longer period of oral transmission than was previously thought before the *hadiths* took their present form. The word *hadith* originally meant discussion, a precedent or an item of transmitted information, terms that evoke the discussions that took place in mosques, market places or courts in the centuries after the Arab conquest when issues of law became paramount.[5] Originating in a culture of private notebooks kept by students of their masters' *dicta*, works such as the Two Sahihs of Bukhari and Muslim probably did not emerge in their final forms till at least a generation after the dates recorded for the deaths of the putative authors.[6] The same process of retrospective attribution to a widely acknowledged authority applies in the case of eponymous founders of the four legal schools, including Shafi'i. Though considered by Schacht and others the 'master architect' of the Islamic legal theory known as *usul al-fiqh* (the roots of understanding or jurisprudence) recent scholarship has shown that this image of Shafi'i is a later creation. According to Hallaq, there is 'ample evidence to show that even as late as the third/ninth century, legal theory as we now know it, and as we assume it to have issued from Shafi'is work, had not yet come into existence.'[7] In Hallaq's view it was Shafi'i's followers such as Ibn Suraij (d. 918) and his younger contemporaries who raised the Shafi'ite school to prominence, developing the synthesis of revealed sources and rational discourse that became associated with his name. This does not mean, however, that Shafi'i's reputation as the true founder of Islamic legal theory is entirely undeserved. His most celebrated work, the Risala (epistle) may indeed 'represent the first attempt at synthesizing the disciplined exercise of human reasoning and the complete assimilation of revelation as the basis of the law'.[8] Although the arguments dividing the rationalists and their traditionalist opponents persisted for at least a century after his death, the method he pioneered for reconciling rationality and tradition (the products, respectively, of human reason and the divinely revealed knowledge transmitted through the Quran and the Prophet's *sunna*) was eventually adopted by the great majority of scholars and jurists in the Sunni mainstream.

Shafi'i was born in Palestine towards the end of the eighth century. After growing up as an impoverished orphan in Makka, he studied with Malik ibn Anas in Madina and taught in Iraq before going to Egypt, where he finally settled after taking part in an unsuccessful Shi'ite rebellion against the caliph Harun al-Rashid. In Cairo he undertook a systematic revision and harmonization of the existing Muslim law, which, beset by the rising tide of traditions on one side and the increasing divergences between the legal schools on the other, was becoming ever more confused. Shafi'i's main concession to the traditionists was to insist on the primacy of the Prophet's Sunna over the *sunna* of the Companions, their successors or the 'living' traditions of the Kufan and Madinese schools. He employed a formidable argument against those who tried to oppose the traditionists by upholding the supremacy of the Quran over all other sources of law: 'The Quran does not contradict the *hadiths*, but the *hadiths* explain the Quran.'

In effect, the Quran cannot stand alone as a source of law: Shafi'i demonstrated 'by an incisive critique of its language (in which he brought out all the diverse ways in which it called for interpretation) that the Book presupposed Muhammad not only as its deliverer, but as its interpreter'.[9] It followed that it was not the Quran alone, but the Quran plus the Prophet's Sunna, as recorded in *hadiths*, that must guide the Muslims. In Shafi'i's hands the word *sunna* acquired the specific meaning it has today, when the mainstream followers of Islam are known as *ahl al-sunna* – 'People of the Sunna' (Sunnis or Sunnites). In its original pre-Islamic meaning, *sunna* had been applied to ancestral custom: the word has associations with a beaten path in the desert, advancing age, sharpened teeth and well-honed implements. Employed by the legists of the so-called ancient schools, it means the living 'practical' tradition, assumed to be based on the general practice and authority of the Prophet and his companions. By Shafi'i's time a considerable divergence had developed between the 'living' *sunna*, or practical tradition, which varied from one geographical region to another, and the rising tide of *hadiths* attributed to the Prophet. From contemporary writings it is clear that defenders of the living *sunna* regarded the latter as an unacceptable innovation.

The confusing arguments surrounding the question eventually crystallized into a debate between two groups: the 'rationalists' (*ahl al-kalam*), who defended the supremacy of the Quran, and the 'traditionists' (*ahl al-hadith*), for whom the Prophet's example was supreme, even as against the specific injunctions of the Quran. During the early years of the 'Abbasid caliphate, the rationalists won the day: part of their case was that many so-called *hadiths* contained anthropomorphisms which were theologically unacceptable. In this they were certainly closer than their opponents to the Quranic doctrine of God. The problem, however, was that the all-encompassing deity of the Quran was bound to be less attractive to popular piety than the more accessible figure of the Prophet, repository of every local proverb and hero of countless anecdotes. The essential achievement of Shafi'i and his successors was to accommodate these diverging attitudes within a single system which took on board the popular figure of the Prophet while actually maintaining the orthodoxy of the rationalists. By insisting on rigorous *isnad*-criticism before any *hadith* could be accepted, Shafi'i and his successors among the *hadith*-collectors ensured that newly minted *hadiths* would be rejected.

Formation of the Shari'a

The system of which Shafi'i was considered the chief designer matured into the Shari'a, or Divine Law of Islam. The word *shari'a*, like *sunna*, has essentially conservative associations. In non-religious terms, it means the road or way to a watering-place, the well-trodden path which must always be followed. For the beduin, safety lay in following the paths of one's ancestors. Innovation – *bid'a* – was hazardous: *bid'a* was to acquire pejorative connotations – equivalent almost to heresy – in the religious vocabulary.

By common consent the Shari'a or holy law represents the greatest historic achievement of Islam as a religious cultural system, providing Muslim societies with a degree of order and authority under the 'rule of God' that counterbalanced the instability that often prevailed at the political level. Indeed, it is arguable that modern Islamic societies have become victims of this very historic success: because the system worked so well, the legal structure remained intact for more than twelve centuries. As Hallaq comments, 'law has been so successfully developed in Islam that it would not be an exaggeration to characterize Islamic culture as a legal culture. But this very blessing of the pre-modern culture turned out to be an obstacle in the face of modern-ization. The system that had served Muslims so well in the past now stood in the way of change – a change that proved to be so needed in a twentieth-century culture vulnerable to an endless variety of western influences and pressures.'[10] The Shari'a looms large in the social memory (or 'social imaginary') of Muslims from Morocco to Indonesia, from Stockholm to Capetown. In consequence it remains the focus for the most problematic issues in the evolving relationships between inherited traditions and modernity. Until modern times the shared identity of Muslims (an identity, of course, which would become apparent in encounters with non-Muslim *kafirs*, or infidels) was based not just on a common faith but on cultural patterns reinforced by common behavioural conditioning. This is not to say that Muslim social life was everywhere uniform. Inevitably the effects of Islamization might diminish in accordance with a particular Muslim population's cultural or geographical distance from the West Asian epicentre. Berber tribesmen, Egyptian fallahin, Pathan warriors, Gujerati traders and Javanese smallholders – all of these and many more heterogeneous groups adapted themselves to the Islamic patterning to suit a way of life and view of the world that had been moulded by previous cultural, religious and social institutions. The Islamic model proved flexible enough to suit the legal and social requirements of most of the peoples of Asia and Africa who came under Muslim rule or came into contact with Islam through trade and migration. Only in centres of vigorous high culture such as China and India, where ancient traditions of kingship were underpinned by alternative religious ideologies, and among the Christianized nations of Southern Europe (including France, Portugal, Spain and Serbia, all of whose founding epics celebrate anti-Islamic crusading themes) were the cultural, social and military obstacles sufficient to prevent the process of Islamization from taking permanent root.

Shari'a and fiqh

As the legal system came to be elaborated, a distinction emerged between the two key terms, *Shari'a* and *fiqh*. Shari'a, though now used as a generic term, covering Islamic law in all its aspects, has a more specifically religious application referring to what is divine and eternal, the Way commanded by God. Originally the way to a watering place, the source of life and purity, an eighteenth-century dictionary defines it as:

the descent of water which has also been called what God has decreed (*sharr'a*: legislate, decree) for the people in terms of fasting, prayer, pilgrimage, marriage, etc. . . . Some say it has been called *shari'a* by comparison with the *shari'a* of water in that the one who legislates, in truth and in all probability, quenches [his thirst] and purifies himself; and I mean by quenching what some wise men have said: I used to drink and remained thirsty, but when I knew God I quenched my thirst without drinking.[11]

In secular terms Shari'a has been described as the 'utopia' that partially inspires the *fiqh*, the domain of legislation 'in very determinate ways that are various and open to enquiry'.[12] If the Shari'a is eternal and divine, the *fiqh* – meaning understanding – is a purely human construction. Since the Law of God is deemed to have been revealed for all time in the Quran and the Sunna, *fiqh* refers to knowledge of something already presumed to exist, the inquiry into how divine law works out in practical terms rather than the development of a body of jurisprudence based on case law and human legislation. 'All efforts to elaborate details of the law, to state specific norms, to justify them by reference to revelation, to debate them, or to write books or treatises on the law are examples of *fiqh*. The word connotes human and specifically scholarly activity . . . The practitioners of *fiqh* – the *faqihs* – aim to discover and give expression to the Shari'a.' As Norman Calder suggests, the Shari'a evokes loyalty and is a focus of faith; *fiqh*, by contrast 'evokes at best respect for juristic scholarship and for a literary tradition – and amongst some modern thinkers, distaste for dry-as-dust legalism'.[13]

Several modern scholars have suggested that the result of the process initiated by Shafi'i and his successors was to incorporate many of the existing laws, customs and regulations taken over by the Arabs after the conquest within the frame of Quranic revelation. Since many Quranic passages are only explicable by reference to the much more voluminous *hadith* literature, the two came to be seen as interdependent products of revelation (although the Quran was considered superior both in its nature and origins): as an early Syrian jurist, Awza'i (d. 774), put it 'the Book is in greater need of the *sunna* than the *sunna* is of the Book'.[14] Given the relative paucity of Quranic legislation when contrasted with the complexities of the empire, the jurists had an incentive to 'Islamize' local laws and customs, to bring them within the purview of revelation. Calder confirms Schacht's original observation that far from being the primary source of law the Quran was a 'secondary and intrusive' influence on the earliest legal discussions. 'When texts emerge that constitute real evidence for the nature of *fiqh*, they demonstrate . . . that the Quran is not the immediate source of law and that the problem facing the [early] jurists was precisely to find arguments by which scriptural origins for the law could be – in the face of almost insurmountable difficulties – asserted.'[15] Viewed from a secular perspective, the science of *usul al-fiqh* was a process of acculturation by which the variegated oral traditions, narratives and customs of Western Asia were incorporated into a new creative synthesis within the overarching transcendental frame of Islam. While some scholars have suggested that there was a direct impact of Roman or Jewish legal traditions on this process, a more plausible explanation suggests that both traditions are derived from a common origin or matrix in the cultures of Western Asia. Calder, for example, argues that while the *fiqh* defines bodily fluids, excrement and predatory animals such as dogs as being impure, the fact that the Islamic rules are much less exacting than the biblical and Rabbinic rules governing purity is not 'amelioration' or a modified version of the Jewish system but something much closer to the common or basic system prevailing in the region.[16]

The roots of fiqh

The foundations of the science of *fiqh*, attributed to Shafi'i, were based on four roots (*usul*): the Quran, the Prophet's Sunna, the consensus of the community (*ijmá*) and analogical reasoning (*qiyas*). In theory the Quran ranked supreme in the hierarchy of legal roots. In practice, since the divine text required interpretation by reference to *hadith*, the Sunna ranked equally with the Quran and in some cases was superior to it. For Shafi'i the Quran and the Sunna were the final unquestionable authority in matters of law: 'What is based on the Quran,' he wrote in the Risala, 'and on the unanimously recognized Sunna, is true both outwardly and inwardly [*fi al-zahir wa'l-batin*].'[17]

One consequence of this dual sovereignty of God's Word and the Prophet's example was the eventual elevation of Muhammad to a status barely subordinate – in the popular imagination – to that of Allah himself. The Prophet's statements and actions being necessary for the interpretation of the divine text, it followed that the Prophet himself must have been operating continuously under divine inspiration. Certain of his statements came to be regarded as 'sacred' *hadiths*: though not included in the Quran, they were represented as having been revealed by Allah (though not, as in the Quran, in 'Allah's Words'). A logical consequence of the development of *hadith* and its sanctification in the Shari'a was the doctrine of Muhammad's 'sinlessness' held by some, though not all Sunni scholars (e.g. Ibn Qutayba):[18] whatever decisions or pronouncements had been authoritative during his lifetime became *infallible* after his death. Hardly surprisingly, Europeans who came into contact with Muslims saw them as 'Muhammadans' whose veneration of their prophet was no less than that which they themselves accorded to Christ.

The remaining roots of the religious law, *ijma'* (consensus) and *qiyas* (analogical reasoning), though theoretically subordinate to the Quran and the Sunna were structurally part of the system. *Ijma'* as a principle was enshrined in a *hadith* according to which the Prophet is said to have declared: 'Never will God make my community agree upon a wrong course.'[19] Shafi'i's opponents, the *ahl al-kalam* and the legists of the ancient schools, had upheld the principle of scholarly *ijma'* to defend their positions. By a dexterous piece of legerdemain, Shafi'i substituted for the *ijma'* of the religious intellectuals the *ijma'* of the people, who demanded that the traditions of the Prophet, and no other, should be, with the Quran, the source of law. *Ijma'* determined that only those *hadiths* with 'impeccable' *isnads* should be part of the Sunna Shafi'i identified as 'unanimously recognized'. In later generations the *ijma'* of the people was once again replaced by the *ijma'* of the religious scholars or *'ulama*. The principle of *ijma'* did not imply democracy in any modern application of the term. But it did introduce a certain social and intellectual flexibility into the system. The concept of consensus existed among the pre-Islamic tribes. In the early schools of law it expressed the average doctrine on which the scholars and the community were agreed. A distinction was made between consensus on technical points of the law, over which scholars had a monopoly, and on matters related to general practice, in which all Muslims were deemed to participate. As later generations of Muslims would come to understand it, *ijma'* in the broader sense was active during the early phase of Islam's development, when the memory of the Prophet was still alive and the community sufficiently small and culturally homogeneous to engage in common practice, as it were by instinct. The broader less technical use of the term was given Prophetic endorsement by reference to a *hadith* cited by the jurist Muhammad bin al-Hasan Shaybani (d. 805): 'Whatever the Muslims see as good is good in the eyes of God, and whatever the Muslims see as bad is bad in the eyes of God.'[20]

Qiyas, the technique of systematic analogical reasoning, was the method by which the legal experts sought to incorporate new situations within the system of divine law while maintaining the primacy of the Quran and the Sunna. *Qiyas* allowed a role for individual opinion on the part of the judges, although it was generally subject to the dictates of *ijma'*, expressed as the consensus of the *'ulama* or as the consensus of the community in opposition to the rulers and the *'ulama*. If *ijma'* represented in general a conservative social force, this was but a reflection of the wider Muslim social order, in which the heads of families, rather than representatives of the state, were the repositories of social power.

The four legal schools

The system devised by Shafi'i and his successors never attained complete uniformity. Variations, on matters of detail rather than questions of principle, crystallized into four distinctive *madhhabs* or legal schools which disputed among themselves over the method and rules of *fiqh*. The schools were named after the most prominent figures associated with them. The Madinese school was named after Malik ibn Anas, Shafi'i's teacher. The Kufans adopted the name of their most prominent early legist, Abu Hanafi (699–767), a well-to-do merchant of Iranian descent. Shafi'i's pupils, established in Egypt, founded a school which they named after him. The fourth of the Sunni *madhhabs* to have survived into modern times is associated with one of the prominent early traditionists, Ahmad ibn Hanbal (d. 855) who is said to have collected more than 80,000 *hadiths*.

Despite the differences between the three principal schools, they were generally agreed in accepting the system of roots developed by Shafi'i and his followers. For that reason his reputation as the greatest systematizer of early Islamic law makes him more than just the 'founder' of one of the four *madhhabs*. Viewed retrospectively, his historic achievement was to forestall the development of independent regional legal systems based on Madina or Kufa; though the Malikis and Hanafis kept some of the distinctive traditions of their respective schools, they were obliged, after Shafi'i, to accommodate them within an overall framework rooted in the Quran and the Sunna. This supreme intellectual achievement makes Shafi'i one of the great unifiers of Islam.

The Malikis remained the most conservative of the four *madhhabs* and continued to follow the consensus of Madina, which could be justified in Shafi'i's terms because it was the place where the Prophet himself had governed. Thus in questions of marriage they reflected the customs of the northern Arabs: marriages could only be contracted by the parents or guardians of marriage partners, but divorce for the husband was relatively easy. The Hanafi marriage rules by contrast reflected the more complex urban society of Iraq, with the social positions of both husband and wife taken into account in drawing up the marriage contract; for this purpose a detailed hierarchy of the professions was recognized. Generally speaking, the Malikis had a more moralistic view of the law, in which the intentions – good or bad – of a person's actions were taken account of in determining their permissibility. The Hanafis had a more formalistic approach, emphasizing the external conduct of the actor and endorsing the use of legal stratagems (*hiyal*) to get around particular prohibitions – such as the ban on lending at interest. In line with the Kufan tradition, the Hanafi school allowed a greater role for individual reasoning and judicial opinion. The Shafi'is, who followed their master in trying to reconcile the extremes of traditionalism and reasoning, occupied a position midway between the Malikis and the Hanafis.

As well as accommodating the schools of law within a comprehensive system, the process initiated by Shafi'i may be said to have contributed to the unity of Islam in a territorial sense. The Hanafi school became the official doctrine of the 'Abbasid caliphate; for a period, followers of the other *madhhabs* were banned from preaching in the mosques or giving judgements. Without this accommodation of the different schools within a single framework, it is difficult to see how, after the collapse of the caliphal state, the divine law could have avoided falling into the kind of politico-religious fragmentation which produced the wars of religion in Europe. As it was, the political disunity of Islam developed within the context of an underlying legal and religious unity which ignored territorial divisions and in which the use of violence was generally limited to military elites and radical sectarian groups. The pluralism of the Shari'a was sanctioned by a well-attested *hadith*: 'The differences of opinion among the learned within my community are [a sign of] God's Grace.'[21]

The distinctive character of Islam, as compared with that of Christianity, lies less in the fusion of religion and politics (which also occurred

in the West) than in the fact that the division between the religious
and the secular occurs at a different point, between the legal and
political realms. Whereas Christianity inherited a body of secular law
developed under the pagan Romans, Islam developed a system of
religious law more or less independently of the political sphere. The
failure of the caliphal state to realize the Islamic vision of a politically
unified Umma extending throughout the known world had the effect
of placing politics *outside* the purview of religion. Muslim rulers needed
no formal authority, sanctified by religion, comparable to the impressive titles conferred by the papacy upon Christian kings and princes.
Once the royal bodyguards and over-powerful regional governors
(sultans) who inherited the caliphal power had come into their own,
whether they were formally recognized by the caliphs or not was
largely irrelevant, since the caliphs had ceased to have any power. All
they required was the consent of the ʿulama, and in Sunni communities
this was usually forthcoming. At the same time the ʿulama, though
appointed as judges by the rulers, were often extremely reluctant to
compromise the purity of the divine law by serving the establishment.
Far from being integrated (as many Muslims claim), the political and
religious institutions remained distinct. Had they been fused as in
Europe up until the French Revolution, the anarchic division of the
Arab empire into unstable territorial segments controlled by rival
war-lords would have had much more devastating consequences. As
it was, the religious pluralism allowed in the system of *fiqh* prevented
the full mobilization of religious forces in the service of political or
sectarian conflicts. Society functioned more or less independently of
the state, a feature which is still evident in the Muslim world today.

The ʿulama *and the 'closing' of* ijtihad

The relative autonomy of the law, in theory at least if not always in
practice, emerges out of what might be called the professionalization
of the ʿulama. Early discussions on law during the first three centuries of
Islam, were conducted among community elders – merchants, traders,
administrators, artisans – who met in the mosques and market places.
By the fourth Islamic century such informal authority of the 'learned'
had been marginalized in the metropolitan areas, though as Calder
points out, the older, more informal system survived into the twentieth

century in areas 'where literacy, formal education and bureaucratic central control' had not yet taken over.[22] The movement away from mainly oral discussion towards reliance on written texts in the *hadith* literature and books of *fiqh* entailed a narrowing of religious authority 'from a broad spectrum of social classes to a narrow band of suitably educated persons' whose power would be related to their control over the literature.[23] Although judges were appointed from the professional ranks of the *'ulama*, up until the nineteenth century the legal profession was generally free from state regulation. 'Muslim states and governments throughout the centuries had no hand in the training and certification of jurists and jurisconsults whose task it was to formulate the law.'[24] The function of the *'ulama*, moreover, extended far beyond the application of law as such. The role of the *'ulama* in pre-colonial Algeria, as described by Allan Christelow, has much wider application in the pre-modern Muslim world:

Since the ulama are not salaried officials but draw their resources from religious endowments, or from private income, they were not necessarily beholden to government. In their roles as teachers, ritual specialists, and consultants to the community on religious questions, they are apt to become highly sensitive to public concerns and at the same time to gain the trust of the public to articulate their concerns. Having strong classical religious education, they are able to frame these concerns within the established structure of legal discourse. It is critical, then, to understand *shura* (the duty of consultation, enjoined in the Quran) not simply as a sounding of opinion, but as a sounding of learned opinion, in which important public concerns are cast into the form of religious and legal argument.[25]

In attempting to impose self-regulation from within, the different law schools came to rely increasingly on texts passed down from their founders or attributed to them. Hallaq suggests that one reason for this insistence on canonical authority was to exclude the possibility of unqualified persons issuing *fatwas* or legal judgement inconsistent with jurists' consensus that had come into being.[26] Increasing reliance on texts tended to limit the exercise of creative interpretation (*ijtihad*). Radical innovation in ritual or legal matters would tend to upset the consensus of the scholars within each school and there gradually emerged a doctrine after the tenth century that the 'gates of *ijtihad*' had been closed. Henceforth legal decisions would be arrived at according to the principle of *taqlid*, the 'imitation' of earlier masters, with new attempts at *ijtihad* condemned as *bid'a* – reprehensible innovation. Recent scholarship has come to question whether the 'closing of the gates of *ijtihad*' was as widespread as hitherto supposed. *Ijtihad* – a word etymologically related to *jihad*, 'holy war' – implies creative effort in the struggle to fully understand the commands of God. According to the Shafi'ite lawyer Sayf al-Din al-Amidi (d. 1233) it entails 'the total expenditure of effort in the search for an opinion as to any legal rule in such a manner that the individual senses (within himself) an inability to expend further effort'.[27] Wael Hallaq argues that *ijtihad* remained the backbone of the Sunni legal doctrine at least until the sixteenth century, with groups that rejected its exercise (such as the Zahiri school, named after Dawud Ibn Khalaf al-Zahiri who died in 883) excluded from the Sunni consensus and hence doomed to extinction.[28] Nevertheless the fact that the doctrine that the 'the gates of *ijtihad* were closed' gained currency, despite the fact that individual *mujtahids* continued to exercise it, attests a broadly conservative outlook: where innovation does occur, it often presents itself as imitation. Extra-Shari'a legislation was often as much the rule as the exception. 'The caliphs and other secular rulers often had occasion to legislate, but out of deference to the sacred law they called it administration and maintained the fiction that their enactments served only to apply, to supplement and to enforce Islamic law, and were well within the competence assigned to the political authority.'[29]

The mosque and madrasa of Sultan Hasan

Nowhere, perhaps, is the Sunni consensus given a more impressive concrete demonstration than in one of the finest of all Islamic buildings, the great *madrasa* (college) of Sultan Hasan in Cairo, completed in 1363. After the destruction of Baghdad by the Mongols in 1258, Cairo became the unchallenged capital of the Muslim world, a city of about half a million people and the largest in the Old World. The Mamluk rulers, a self-selecting military elite of Turcomans from the Volga region, sought to live down their lowly origins by excelling in works of piety, building and liberally endowing the religious colleges, Quranic schools and hospitals adjoining their tombs. If Chartres cathedral is an emblem of the medieval Christian vision of a hierarchical society pointing ever upward towards heaven, Sultan Hasan is an architectural expression of the Islamic vision in its maturity. Its centre is a vast paved courtyard flanked on each side by four great vaulted enclosures, or *liwans*, which soar to the full height of the walls – some 40 metres (130 feet). In the built-up angles behind each *liwan* are the *madrasas* of the four *madhhabs*, with multiple tiers of lodgings for students. The skilful juxtaposition of voids and solids makes of the sky a ceiling stretching out into infinity, seemingly containing the uncontainable, a brilliant feat of architectural manipulation which creates out of interior space the soaring effect achieved by the exterior of the Gothic cathedral. Here, under the covered *liwans*, the aspiring *'ulama* would congregate around their respective teachers to study the Quran and the *hadiths* and to memorize the complicated and exacting rules of *fiqh*, before setting off to all parts of the Muslim world.

Outside the radical Shi'ite groups, the message of Islam was rarely spread by conscious missionary activity. Rather, it extended itself autonomously along the trade routes by means of the conversion of tribal chieftains who sought social or political advantages in joining the Umma and becoming part of its advanced culture and civilization. Because the *fiqh* operated at a popular cultural level, no central administration was required to mastermind the process. In the more distant reaches of Africa and Asia, wandering merchants or marabouts would attract groups of followers, not least because they enjoyed the cultural prestige conferred by membership of a wider cosmopolitan world. In sub-Saharan Africa, for example, conversion was often a gradual process, in which the local animistic religions were first Islamized and then replaced altogether. Converts usually began by accepting the simple emblems of Muslim culture, such as amulets or costumes which enhanced their prestige locally, before adopting the ritual of prayer and recognizing the categories of the permitted (*halal*) and the forbidden (*haram*) which eventually replaced the local taboos.

In the areas where Muslim culture had taken root, increasing adherence to the rules of *fiqh* gradually squeezed out non-Muslim cultural traditions. Similarly, knowledge of the Quran and the law tended to filter down gradually. Education has always been a pious duty for Muslims, and any merchant or wandering scholar might open a *kuttab* (Quranic School) provided he was reasonably competent in the law, having perhaps read the Quran and studied *fiqh* in one of the cities.

The spreading of the *fiqh* was thus a process which often lasted for generations. In many parts of the world today, including parts of tropical Africa and South East Asia, the process is still far from complete: Islamic worship, law and practice coexist with other religio-cultural forms, of animist or Hindu–Buddhist origin. Religious intolerance of *shirk* (idolatry) is a characteristic of most resurgence movements in Islam. In the outer fringes of the Muslim world such movements represent less a restoration of religious purity than the completion of Islamization.

Although the four schools of *fiqh* coexisted in the great metropolitan cities such as Cairo, in practice they did become normative in specific geographical areas. As the official *madhhab* of the 'Abbasid caliphate, the Hanafi system took root in western Asia, whence it spread, after the conversion of the Mongols, to the Indian subcontinent. Maliki law, though indigenous to Madina, spread westwards into North and Central Africa. Shafi'i law, indigenous to Egypt, also became prominent in Southern Arabia, whence it spread along the monsoon route to East Africa and South East Asia.

The diversity of doctrines within the Shari'a was often compared by Muslim writers to the holes of a fishing net. The metaphor is apt, for the *fiqh* is less a system of law, with a developed apparatus of procedure and enforcement, than a process of socialization and acculturation which progressively transforms human societies in a more or less autonomous manner. To change the metaphor only slightly, the Shari'a may also be compared to the interlaced patterns characteristic of Islamic design which can be extended indefinitely, like wallpaper patterns. In time the process of Islamization takes root, imposing a degree of cultural homogeneity. Observance of the divine law becomes a social factor functioning more or less independently of the state.

Without doubt the Shari'a exercised its greatest influence at the personal and community level. Western critics such as Noel Coulson and Sir Norman Anderson regarded it as unduly idealistic. Coulson saw it as an essentially abstract ideal which can inform, but not govern, the activities of Muslim courts. 'Floating above Muslim society as a disembodied soul, freed from the currents and vicissitudes of time, it represents the eternally valid ideal to which society must aspire.'[30] Anderson saw it as 'divorced from reality', particularly in the realm of criminal procedure, where rigid standards of proof made conviction difficult. As a consequence the administration of justice was never wholly entrusted to the *qadis* and the Shari'a courts over which they presided, but was kept very largely in the hands of the executive and the police.[31] The *qadis* had no power to enforce Shari'a decisions on the rulers, though they could exercise moral persuasion backed by public opinion. The rulers, while formally committed to upholding the Shari'a, were not obligated to submit to the decisions of the *qadis* if such decisions, in public, commercial or criminal matters, went against their interests. However, the impact of the Shari'a on Muslim societies and the way in which social practices that may have pre-dated the coming of Islam were sanctified by inclusion in the *fiqh*, can hardly be in doubt. The Shari'a was particularly important in the realm of personal status and family law, where the provisions regarding marriage, divorce and slavery – with all the problematic consequences they entailed for human rights in general and the rights of women in particular – were seen as having divine sanction. The Shari'a law of succession was also highly influential in preventing wealth from being passed to a single heir, in preference to a multiplicity of claimants.[32] The law of succession, whose 'Islamic' provenance is still the subject of scholarly debate, may arguably have had a negative impact on economic development, by inhibiting the concentration of wealth.

Recently legal scholars working in the West have taken a much more sympathetic view of the Shari'a. By distinguishing between the cardinal principles on which the Shari'a is based, and the received corpus of normative applications operating through the individual decisions of the *faqihs* (jurists) and *muftis* (jurisconsults) Wael Hallaq endorses the modernist *ijtihad* of two 'religious liberalists', Fazlur Rahman and Muhammad Sahrur. Both Rahman, who left or was driven from his post as director of the Islamic Research Academy in Lahore for the more congenial atmosphere of the University of Chicago, and Shahrur, a Syrian engineer, have focused on the contexts of the revealed texts underpinning the Shari'a to argue the case for a 'humanistic law that is suggestively and generally guided, and not literally and textually dictated, by divine intention'.[33] The moral and ethical principles identified in classical legal theory by Abu Hamid al-Ghazali (d. 1111) and following him, the great Andalusian jurist Abu Ishaq al-Shatibi (d. 1388), are essentially human: they are *daruriyyat* (necessities), *hajiyyat* (needs) and *tahsiniyyat* (improvements). Hallaq provides convincing arguments to suggest that, in conjunction with the principle of *maslaha* (public interest) a constant of Maliki jurisprudence, it should be possible to re-formulate a *fiqh* suitable for the present age.

A study which captures the spirit of the Shari'a in a much less abstract and more intimate way is Lawrence Rosen's *The Anthropology of Justice* (Cambridge, 1989). Rosen, a trained anthropologist and lawyer who spent several years observing the procedures of a Shari'a court in Morocco, reaches conclusions that would be hard to extrapolate from written texts. In its actual operations the divine law, in his view, is much more centred on people than legal processes operating in the West. 'Rather than being aimed simply at the invocation of state or religious power, rather than being devoted mainly to the creation of a logically consistent body of legal doctrine, the aim of the Qadi is to put people back in the position of being able to negotiate their own permissible relationships without predetermining just what the outcome of those negotiations ought to be.'[34] Qadi justice is thus directed towards the 'religiously approved goal of encouraging men to contract their own ties within the limits set down by God'.[35] By closely observing the procedures of an actual court, with its bias in favour of oral testimony which is related to 'the belief that face-to-face interaction is necessary for the elaboration of those densely interwoven human ties by which the social order is itself maintained' Rosen succeeds in turning western critiques of the Shari'a on their head. The very absence of generalized legal concepts such as contract or tort around which western judges or scholars refine their conceptual categories liberates justice from the realm of abstraction, allowing it, as it were, to enter the realm of real human beings in real human relationships. Legal 'regularity lies not in the development of a body of doctrine . . . but rather in the fit between the decisions of the Muslim judge and the cultural concepts and social relationships to which they are inextricably tied'.[36] Far from being 'blind', Shari'a justice is knowing: the *Qadi*, like the collector of *hadith*, judges the quality of testimony not just on the basis of its coherence or consistency, but on his knowledge of the witness's reliability: 'When a person regarded as reliable by the court bears witness to a statement it is by the integration of his (social) stature and his word that actions in the world may be transformed into facts that are at once judicially workable and culturally recognizable.'[37]

Divine command versus natural law

Space does not allow more than a brief glance at the actual content of *fiqh*. In the voluminous books compiled by the *faqihs* (specialists in *fiqh*) lists of human actions were compiled and graded according to a scale of moral valuation. There were five main categories according to which almost every activity from prayer to defecation was classified:

1. Obligatory acts (*fard*), omission of which constituted a sin.
2. Forbidden acts (*haram*), commission of which constituted a sin.
3. Recommended acts (*mandub*), where there is merit in doing them but no sin in omission.
4. Undesirable acts (*makruh*), where there is merit is abstaining from them but no sin in commission.
5. Unspecified acts (*mubah*), neither meritorious nor sinful, whether committed or omitted.[38]

In principle, this remarkably comprehensive scheme allows no distinction between religion and morality, law and ethics, crime and sin: all are seen as proceeding directly from the command of God, though there is room for humans to argue about the details. In contrast to Christian theology, which inherited from Plato and the Stoics the concept of the autonomy of morals, mainstream Sunni Islam insisted that God's commands be followed *bi la kayf* – 'without questioning how', leaving to God 'the understanding of his own mystery'.[39] The difference is expressed in Plato's famous Euthyphro dilemma: is an action right because the gods command it, or do the gods command it because it is right? The Mu'tazila, in line with their rationalist view that God is obligated to reward the good, would have answered 'yes' to the second of these questions. For the Hanbalis and Ash'aris, however, whose view would prevail in Sunni counsels up to the present, it was the first question that required an affirmative answer. The idea that God was bound to reward the good compromised his omnipotence. 'Mainstream [Islamic] theology espoused the divine command theory of ethics: an act is right because God commands it – God does not command it because it is right. The latter view was held to be unacceptable because it implied limitations on God's power: He had to conform his will to independent moral standards, thereby undermining the doctrine of divine omnipotence.'[40] The Christian

attitude that God is obligated to reward the good was elaborated by
St Thomas Aquinas and others into a doctrine of natural law. Starting
with Thomas's assertion that it is impossible for the truth of faith to
be contrary to principles known by natural reason, Christian thinking
developed a theory of natural rights that would later evolve into the
modern concept of human rights, deemed by large numbers of people
throughout the world to be no longer chained to their Christian moor-
ings. In the words of the American Declaration of Independence, which
resonate in the Universal Declaration of Human Rights and a host of
other international human rights instruments, the inalienability of the
right to life, liberty and the 'pursuit of happiness' belongs to the
category of self-evident truths, not revealed truths. As John Shepherd
has pointed out, 'Christian theology provided logical space for the
development of moral insights and awareness independently of theology, and it was within this logical space that liberalism emerged and
flourished'. In recent years Muslim lawyers and theologians have
attempted to demonstrate that there are no fundamental incompati-
bilities between Islam and modern secular notions of human rights.
Indeed one authority, Seyed Abd al-Latif, goes on to remark that 'to
the student of the Quran, not one word in the preamble or the objectives
of the Charter and not a single article in the text of the Universal
Declaration of Human Rights will seem unfamiliar. Under a creed
which places man next to God, and brushes aside all distinctions of
race, colour and birth and calls upon mankind to live together as a
family of God ... the Universal Declation of Human Rights must
follow as a basic corollary, or an extension of the Quranic programme.'[41]
Such attitudes are fairly widespread amongst educated, liberal-minded
Muslims but they do not address the ethical difficulties resulting
from the specific character of certain Quranic injunctions, for example
discriminatory provisions against women in inheritance and legal
testimony, and the rights of minorities. To the Westerner familiar with
the post-Enlightenment distinction between law and morality, crime
and sin, the blurring of these distinctions is highly problematic. As
Shepherd points out, the charge that the Shari'a as a whole provides
an example of 'legal moralism' (the term in jurisprudence for the legal
enforcement of morals) does not really stand, because only the second
of the five categories, actions classed as forbidden, are liable to incur
punishment – even if that category includes such matters as sexual acts
between consenting adults not considered punishable under modern

legal systems. Acts classed as undesirable or reprehensible (*makruh*) 'for the doing of which there is no punishment, but for the avoidance of which there is reward' (in heaven) are left to the judgement of God. They may be immoral (and thus sinful) but they are not illegal. Nevertheless the fact that they are both part of the Shari'a's 'seamless weave of religion, law and morality' serves to obscure the distinction between morality and law, leading to the conclusion that 'strictly moral matters that ought not to be subject to legal punishment are nevertheless in practice unjustly penalised', and inverting the properly constituted relationship between ethics and law. In the words of a Muslim critic, 'instead of the ethical values of Islam controlling the law, the legal system submerged the ethical values in the attempt to make every value conform to a legally enforceable rule'.[42]

Marriage and family

During the Prophet's time the women of Arabia had enjoyed a relatively high social status within the prevailing patriarchal system, and the Quranic legislation endeavoured to improve it by granting them rights of inheritance which, though unequal to those of men, did at least assure them economic rights as individuals (rights for which European women had to wait until the nineteenth century). In particular, the *mahr* or bride-price was changed from a payment made to the bride's father to a sum of money or goods given to the woman herself, to be retained by her in the event of her husband's divorcing her. In the religious and social life of early Islam, so far as we know, women prayed along with their menfolk and certainly took an active part in the affairs of the community. We know for a fact that 'Aisha actively campaigned against 'Ali during the 'First Fitna'; her high standing among the earliest Muslim scholars is evident from the large number of *hadiths* traced back to her.

The Quran itself is addressed equally to both sexes. There is a story, recorded in the *hadith* literature, that several of the women in the first Islamic community were ardent feminists. One of them, Nusaiba, who actually took part in Muhammad's battles, asked the Prophet why, in the Quranic utterances, Allah always addressed himself to men rather than women. According to the story God himself recognized the justice of her complaint, and henceforth the revelations were addressed to the faithful of both sexes. (The Quranic locutions are usually *'muslimin wa muslimat'* and *'muminin wa muminat'*.) Despite this, there is undoubted inequality in some of the specific Quranic legislation. Apart from sharing the prejudice, common also to Judaism, that menstruating women are 'impure' or 'polluted', Allah appears to discriminate against them by apportioning to them only half the inheritance of their brothers and by stipulating that, in cases where a male witness to a business transaction is unavailable, two female witnesses may be substituted (2:282). It has been argued, of course, that in a society in which men are obliged to shoulder much greater economic burdens than women, the fact that boys inherit twice as much property as their sisters is not inequitable: the women will keep their property while the men will be obliged to spend theirs on maintaining them. If the Quran is seen as the unalterable, eternally valid Word of God, however, the inescapable conclusion must be that the economic dominance of men in society cannot be altered, because it is sanctioned by divine decree. The doctrine, fundamental to Islam, that the Quran is holy writ must prove an obstacle to feminist aspirations. A similar argument arises in the case of witnesses. Muhammad Asad, following Muhammad 'Abduh, argues that this stipulation 'does not imply any reflection on woman's moral or intellectual capabilities: it is obviously due to the fact that, as a rule, women are less familiar with business procedures than men and, therefore, more liable to commit mistakes in this respect'. While this may have been true for pre-modern times, it can only be regarded as being valid for the future if women continue to be prevented, by men, from familiarizing themselves with business procedures. Again, divine writ appears to insist that women's subordinate economic status is an unalterable fact of existence, rather than the result of time-bound circumstance.

A possibly more important result of these divinely decreed inequalities was that they could be invoked to sanction misogynous attitudes among the faithful generally. Thus Bukhari records a *hadith* which explicitly justifies the denigration of women by reference to the Quran:

He [i.e., the Prophet] went out on the day of the victims and Bairam [i.e., the 'Id al-Adha) to the place of prayer, and passing some women he said: 'O company of women, give alms, for I have seen that many of you will be inhabitants of hell.' 'Why?' said they. Replied he: 'Because you curse much and deny the kindness of husbands. I have not seen – despite your deficiency in intelligence and religion – any sharper than you in captivating the mind of the resolute.' They said: 'What is the defect in our religion and intelligence?' He answered: 'Is not the witness of a woman equal to half the witness of a man? This is the defect in her intelligence. And when she is ceremonially impure [i.e., menstruating], she neither prays nor fasts. This is the defect in her religion.'[43]

Many comparable *hadiths* would be invoked to justify absolute masculine domination.

The misogynism in Islam may perhaps be partly attributed to the absence of outlets for celibacy. Ascetical tendencies are usually strong among the pious: the whole history of western religions illustrates an intimate connection between religious enthusiasm and sexual repression. In Islam, however, celibacy was explicitly discouraged both by the Prophet's own example and by the famous *hadith*, 'There is no monasticism in Islam – the monasticism (*rahbaniya*) of my community is the *jihad*.' A celibate clergy to whom women are forbidden sexually may legitimately relate to them as individuals, including them within the religious life of the community. Partly, no doubt, in response to the needs of its female members, the Roman Catholic Church allowed the cult of a female archetype, the Virgin Mother, to develop freely during the Middle Ages. Female religious orders were also encouraged. Although at the popular level Sayyida Zainab and certain female Sufi saints were thought to have powers of intercession, official Islam allowed no female cults, nor can it be said to have encouraged a specifically feminine approach to the deity. After the Arab conquest of western Asia and North Africa women were to be progressively excluded from the religious and public areas of social life. By Edward Lane's time (in the early nineteenth century) they were forbidden to pray along with the men in the mosques, because 'the Muslims are of the opinion that the presence of females inspires a very different kind of devotion from that which is requisite in a place dedicated to the worship of God'.[44] Few women, even of the upper class, could read or write, and, though they were urged to do their praying at home, very few of them, according to Lane, bothered to do so.[45]

Social practice combined with the reactionary judgements of the *faqihs* to traduce the Quranic vision of sexual bipolarity. The Quranic legislation generally involves an improvement on pre-Islamic custom in the status and rights of women, even though a degree of inequality was sanctioned (for example, in the laws of inheritance). Unfortunately, because they were presented dogmatically and ahistorically as part of an eternal order decreed by God, they could be and were invoked to justify the belief that women were basically inferior to men, spiritually and intellectually. Nevertheless the Quranic vision of sex and pro- creation as the greatest of Allah's miracles did not altogether disappear from the Muslim world-view. Numerous *hadiths* testify to a positively modern attitude towards sex. The contrast with Christian attitudes is striking. The Christian position on marriage was authoritatively laid down by St Paul: 'It is a good thing for a man not to touch a woman; but since sex is always a danger, let each man have his own wife and each woman her own husband.' Celibacy is superior, but if marriage (which is no sin) is embarked on, there must be absolute equality between the sexes:

The husband must give his wife what she has the right to expect, and so too must the wife to the husband. The wife has no rights over her own body; it is the husband who has them. In the same way the husband has no rights over his body; the wife has them. Do not refuse each other except by mutual consent, and then only for an agreed time . . .[46]

The Quran places far more emphasis on the value of marriage and sexuality, but, unlike St Paul, fails to stress the equality of marriage partners:

And [you ought to] marry the single from among you as well as such of your male and female slaves as are fit [for marriage]. If they [whom you intend to marry] are poor, [let this not deter you;] God will grant them sufficiency out of His bounty . . . (24:32)

'Marriage is the half of religion,' states a popular *hadith*, and the Prophet certainly bore out this maxim in his own behaviour. A *hadith* in Bukhari's collection urges the faithful: 'Copulate and procreate! I shall gain glory from your numbers on the Day of Judgement!'[47]

Frustration on the part of either sex is seen as a potential threat to the social order. According to another well-known *hadith*, if a man sees a woman he fancies, he should go at once and make love to his wife. The attitude stresses women's sexuality at the expense of their individuality, and clearly reduces them to the status of sex-objects:

The Prophet saw a woman. He hurried to his house and had intercourse with his wife Zainab, then left the house and said: 'When the woman comes towards you, it is Satan who is approaching you. When one of you sees a woman and is attracted to her, he should hurry to his wife. With her it would be the same as with the other one.'[48]

Commenting on this *hadith*, the traditionist Muslim states that, in comparing her to Satan, the Prophet was referring to the 'irresistible attraction to women God instilled into man's soul', as well as to 'the pleasure man experiences when he looks at the woman and the pleasure he experiences in anything related to her. She resembles Satan in his irresistible power over the individual.'[49]

Several western writers have contrasted Islam's active view of female sexuality with the assumptions of female passivity in the western tradition, up to and including Freud. The Imam Ghazali, the most influential of Islam's medieval theologians, made it clear that a man must satisfy his wife (or wives) in order to prevent the frustration of women from becoming a threat to the social order:

The virtue of the woman is a man's duty. And the man should increase or decrease sexual intercourse with the woman according to her needs so as to secure her virtue.[50]

In his chapter on marriage, Ghazali cited a *hadith* emphasizing the need for skill in love-making:

The Prophet said: 'No one among you should throw himself on his wife like an animal. Before making love there should be a messenger between you and her.' People asked him: 'What sort of messenger?' The Prophet answered: 'Kisses and words.'[51]

A woman, of course, is similarly obliged to satisfy her husband. According to other *hadiths* in Bukhari's collection, a wife who refuses her husband is cursed by the angels till she returns to his bed. A woman must never refuse her husband, even on the saddle of a camel.[52]

Whereas the sexual ideal in Christianity involves a progressive sublimation of the instincts, that in Islam (and Judaism, which it more closely resembles) is a symbol of cosmic harmony:

When a man looks upon his wife [goes another *hadith*] and she upon him, God looks mercifully upon them; when they join hands together their sins disappear in the interstices of their fingers. When he makes love to her the angels encircle the earth. Voluptuousness and desire are as beautiful as the mountains. When the wife becomes pregnant, her reward is fasting, prayer and *jihad*.[53]

However, the Shari'a ideal of love, based on the complementarity of the sexes, contrasts strongly with the reality of human society. Sexual bipolarity is strongly affirmed in the vision; the divine power of sex is a force so dangerous that if allowed to escape from the proper channels it will bring about social chaos. In theory the marriage rules are simple and flexible. In practice, because marriage is an economic institution involving family interests, sexual expression is dampened by economics, and it is mainly women who pay the price.

Decline in female rights

The erosion of the rights granted to women begins with the early schools of law. For example, the Maliki rule that marriage contracts must be signed by parents or guardians contradicts the Quran's individualistic spirit. Other rules are given restrictive interpretations. For instance, the Quran stipulates that the woman's *'idda* period before being allowed to re-marry after divorce should be three menstrual periods (65:4). If she is not menstruating or is irregular in her periods, the interval is three calendar months. Malik, however, insisted that non-menstruating or irregular women should have to wait for twelve months before re-marrying. The Quranic right of divorce by declaration (*talaq*) was similarly abused in favour of men. The Quran demands that the woman should be fully supported by her husband during the *'idda* in accordance with her normal standard of living (65:1-6) – a right which Malik reduces to mere subsistence. Most of the early jurists were agreed that the three pronouncements on the part of the husband which made the divorce irrevocable should be evenly spaced over the waiting period, to allow time for reconciliation. The Quran hints at this in 65:1: '[For though] thou knowest it not, after that [first breach] God may well cause something new to come about.' Yet the Sunni *faqihs*, though officially disapproving of it as an 'innovation' (*bid'a*), came to recognize as legal a form of *talaq* in which the three pronouncements were made simultaneously and irrevocably, allowing the husband to re-marry during the *'idda*. Thus the *'idda*, intended to ensure paternity and allow for reconciliation, became a device whereby men could circumvent the rule restricting the number of wives to four and indulge in multiple polygyny. A man could have four wives legitimately, as well as several others on the *'idda* at one time. This device was much used in Somalia after the abolition of slavery and concubinage.[54] The triple *talaq* also produced some paradoxical results, for, since it was irrevocable, the husband who changed his mind could not take his wife back until she herself had been married to, and divorced from, another man. In Lane's time it was not unusual for a wealthy and irrascible husband to pay a pauper ('generally a very ugly person and one who is blind') or to purchase a slave (often a pre-adolescent boy) to become his wife's husband for one day. In the case of a slave, he would be 'presented' to the wife, which would automatically annul the marriage, since marriage between a woman and her own slave was illegal.[55]

Similar economic and legalistic restrictions were applied to the *khul'*, the Muslim woman's right of divorce at her own behest. According to several traditions the wife of one of the Prophet's Companions came to him and demanded a divorce from her husband on the ground that, despite his irreproachable character and behaviour, she 'disliked him as she would dislike falling into unbelief after having accepted Islam'. The Prophet allowed the divorce, but stipulated that she should return to her husband the garden he had given her as a dower.[56] The early authorities agreed that when a woman initiated a divorce she must, as the contract-breaking party, return the dower to her husband. This right of *khul'* was, however, widely abused. Payment of the dowry was often made in two instalments, the second and larger part being paid only in the event of the man's divorcing his wife. Under this rule, a divorcing wife might be obliged to 'return' property which she had never, in fact, received, since the wife was not allowed to employ the *khul'* unilaterally, but had to abide by the normal provisions of the marriage contract. In the case of a wealthy wife, the husband could make it extremely expensive for her to purchase her freedom. A poor wife would have no chance of acquiring the unpaid part of the dower.

Beyond the Arab world the Islamic marriage rules had to be accommodated to a variety of social structures moulded by economics, custom and other non-religious elements. Thus in western Asia and

North Africa, where the position of women had been traditionally weak, the *fiqh* effectively consolidated their inferior social status. The customary laws of the Berbers, still applied in parts of Morocco and western Algeria, and those of certain Yemeni tribes, continue to deny females the right of inheritance altogether. In parts of West Africa and South East Asia, on the other hand, Islamization produced almost opposite effects. In Northern Nigeria, the practice of *khul'* was assimilated to the customary rule which allowed a women to divorce her husband on returning the bride wealth.[57] Among the Yoruba of Western Nigeria, on the other hand, as in the matriarchal societies of Sumatra and Java, the Shari'a applies exclusively to religious duties, while marriage and inheritance are governed by customary laws. Even where Muslim laws appear to sanction certain institutions, such as polygyny, this can have very different social consequences in countries with different traditions: thus, whereas in Arab countries additional wives and their children would demand to be housed in separate establishments, in Indonesia the second wife of a mainly absent husband might end by becoming an unpaid servant to the first.

Another device by which female property rights were eroded lay in the institution of family *waqfs*. Basically, a *waqf* is a pious endowment such as a mosque, school or public drinking fountain. An adaptation of the Byzantine *pia causa*, it embodied the principle of tribal ownership of property. *Waqfs* were originally institutions for the poor and needy. Endowed by wealthy rulers or merchants, they were at the core of the medieval system of public welfare which exceeded anything outside the Muslim world before the twentieth century. In theory, the property held by a *waqf* had been 'given to God' and was therefore inalienable. The income from it belonged to the poor. However, wealthy families were sometimes able to use the *waqf* system to avoid parcelling up property in accordance with the inheritance laws stipulated in the Shari'a.

Women and the veil

The word *hijab* (veil or barrier) occurs in seven places in the Quran, six of them in Makkan *suras* where the word is generally used to denote the idea of a barrier or obstacle. Most of these references are to spiritual or moral matters, such as the *hijab* separating deity from mortals (42:51) or wrongdoers from the righteous (7:46, 41:5). One verse (17:45) addresses the Makkans who fail to heed the Quranic recitations because God has placed an 'invisible *hijab* between [Muhammad] and those who will not believe in the life to come'. Only one of these usages refers to female seclusion – when Mary, the mother of Jesus 'withdrew from her family to an eastern place and kept herself in seclusion (*hijaban*) from them' (19:16–17). The seventh occasion dating from the Madinese period refers to the need for the Prophet's wives to be behind a *hijab* or screen when his male visitors converse with them or petition them:

And [as for the Prophet's wives] whenever you ask them for anything that you need, ask them from behind a screen; this will but deepen the purity of your hearts and theirs. (33:53)

It has been suggested that the measure became necessary to protect the 'Mothers of the Believers', as they came to be called, from slanders, indignities or the importunities of petitioners. While conservative or scripturalist commentators argue that a provision addressed to Muhammad's wives – the very models of chastity – must apply *a fortiori* to ordinary Muslim women who may be less chaste, liberals or modernists argue that the verse does not refer to Muslim women in general; the same verse goes on to state that the Prophet's wives may not marry after his death – a provision which obviously applies exclusively to them. A passage enjoining female modesty, however, does occur in the same *sura* (33:59) and is clearly directed to Muslim women in general: 'O Prophet! Tell thy wives and thy daughters and the women of the believers to draw their *jilbabs* close round them . . . so that they may be recognized and not molested.'[58] Another enjoins modesty on both men and women.

Tell the believing women to lower their gaze and to be mindful of their chastity, and not to display their charms [in public] beyond what may [decently] be apparent thereof; hence, let them draw their head-coverings over their bosoms. And let them not display [more of] their charms to any but their husbands, or their fathers, or their husbands' fathers, or their sons, or their husbands' sons, or their brothers, or their brothers' sons, or their sisters' sons, or their womenfolk, or those whom they rightfully possess [i.e. slaves] or such male attendants as are beyond all sexual desire, or children that are as yet unaware of women's nakedness; and let them not swing their legs [in walking] so as to draw attention to their hidden charms. (24:30–1)

The words used in these verses – *jilbab* and *khimar* – refer respectively to the cloak and head covering. The modest dress of the Muslim women is contrasted with the immodesty of the women of the time of *jahiliya* who were wont to flaunt their charms (33:33).

These urgings towards modesty do not of themselves imply inferiority; and, although there are discriminatory provisions in the Quran (over inheritance and testimony, to give but two examples), these need not necessarily conflict with the widely held view that the general thrust of Quranic teaching is directed towards improving women's rights and security. Modernists argue that none of the verses on female modesty necessarily leads to the 'veiling' or segregation that became the hallmarks of Islamic urban life from classical times till the modern period. An early commentator, al-Qiffal, regarded the phrase 'beyond what may . . . be apparent' as meaning 'that which a human being may openly show in accordance with prevailing custom'.[59] The Mu'tazili theologian al-Jahiz wrote that in the early period of Islam women mixed freely and unveiled with men; another early authority al-Wahidi says that the scarf (*khimar*) covering head and bosom of Muslim women was required to differentiate them from slaves. This seems entirely plausible in view of the fact that, as the Islamic laws governing slavery developed, female Muslim slaves were under a lesser obligation than freeborn Muslim women to 'hide their nakedness' when at prayer.[60]

Nevertheless, the provisions detailing the permissible degrees of relationship in which women might 'display their charms' had far-reaching social consequences. Though local customs varied, the rules implied a progressive de-sexualization of women in the public sphere leading to the sexual apartheid which came to characterize large segments of mainstream, urban Islamic society. In the company of her *mahrams* – the men to whom she was forbidden in marriage – a woman might appear as a sexual being. In the public domain, or those parts of the household where male visitors were received, she had to be addressed – like the Prophet's wives – through the veil or screen lest a sexual spark be lit, creating a social conflagration. *The Lawful and the Prohibited in Islam*, an influential guide to contemporary Muslim behaviour by the conservative 'alim (scholar) Yusuf al-Qaradawi, originally published in 1960, endorses a commentary on the *hijab* verse (33:53) by the Imam al-Qurtubi. The purification referred to in this verse, says al-Qurtubi,

... means such thoughts as occur to men regarding women and to women regarding men. This will remove any possibility of suspicion and accusation, and will protect [their] honour. This command implies that no one should trust himself to be in privacy with a non-*mahram* woman; the avoidance of such situations is better for one's purity of heart, strength of soul, and perfection of chastity.[61]

Qaradawi goes on to cite a *hadith*, according to which the Prophet is supposed to have warned particularly against *khulwa* (a man and a woman alone together, unchaperoned) between a married woman and one of her male in-laws, since a relative obviously finds it easier than a non-relative to gain access to the women's quarters.

'Beware of entering where women are.' A man from the Ansar asked, 'O Messenger of Allah, what about the in-law?' He replied, 'The in-law is death.'

Qaradawi elucidates by warning of the 'dangers and even destruction' inherent in such privacy. If the unchaperoned couple sin together, 'religion is destroyed'; if her husband divorces her, the wife is ruined. It follows that social relationships are torn apart because of the mutual suspicions of relatives.[62] In such a reading of Muslim tradition female chastity becomes the linchpin of the social order, the bulwark against *fitna* or social strife. It is not so much private virtue that is seen to be at stake, but rather the dream of social harmony encompassing the Islamic ideal.

Sexual apartheid and slavery

It would be wrong to attribute the loss of status to which women were apparently subjected entirely to the conservative or misogynistic interpretations of the Quranic rules, though doubtless such interpretations played their part. The real culprits, in the view of many modern writers, are slavery and concubinage. The custom of veiling, as we have seen, may have originally been adopted to distinguish 'respectable' Muslim women from concubines. In the Arabian heartlands, concubinage, like slavery, existed, but seems to have been limited by the relatively undeveloped state of warfare and the economy. We read in the Prophet's biographies of Bilal the Abyssinian slave (one of the first converts to Islam and inevitably a hero of the Black Muslim movement in the United States) and of Maria the Copt, the Prophet's Egyptian concubine. But these appear to be exceptional figures in the original Muslim community. The conquests of Persian and Byzantine lands brought a vast increase in wealth and, in accordance with the customs of the times, some of this wealth involved the traffic in human beings.

The condition of slaves, like that of women, may well have improved with the coming of Islam, but the institution was not abolished, any more than it was under Christianity at this period. The Quran regards emancipation as a meritorious act (2:177; 90:13). The *hadith* literature commends the kindly treatment of slaves, who should be treated as brothers, especially if they are Muslims. Manumission is recommended as a way of making amends for excessive chastisement, or as expiation for breaking the fast of Ramadan. A well-known *hadith* promises that 'The man who frees a Muslim slave, God will free from hell, limb for limb.' Restrictions were placed on enslavement. It was forbidden to enslave free members of Islamic society, including *dhimmis* (non-Muslims) residing in *dar al-Islam*. Slavery was regarded as legal only for captives acquired in the *jihad* or holy war outside the borders of *dar al-Islam*, or for those born into slavery. Though Arab and Muslim traders became notorious in the supply of African slaves for the American and Caribbean plantations, there are few examples in the annals of Islam of the collective forced labour found in the Western hemisphere. There are some important exceptions: the draining of the swamps of Lower Iraq by slaves imported from East Africa prompted the Khariji Zanj revolt against the 'Abbasids towards the end of the ninth century. Nearly a thousand years later the Omani rulers of Zanzibar used slave labour in the large-scale commercial production of cloves. But by and large slavery in the Islamic heartlands was directed towards two purposes, the military and domestic. Slave-soldiers (Mamluks) imported as boys from Central Asia and trained in the military arts, rose to the highest positions of state without completely losing their servile status. Slaves, especially female slaves, employed as domestics in the wealthier Muslim households not only freed their owners from drudgery. By offering alternative models to the respectable, segregated female behaviour honoured by tradition, they sustained the Islamic patriarchy while simultaneously presenting a counter-cultural alternative.

According to the *hadith*, a twofold reward in heaven is promised to the man who educates his slave-girl, frees her and marries her.[63] The Quran, of course, placed a restriction on the number of wives a man had, but no limit was placed on the number of slave-concubines. There were some inducements towards improving the status of the concubine: if she had a child by her master, she was entitled to the legal status of *umm walad* – mother of the child, which meant that she could not be sold and was freed upon her master's death. In line with the above-cited *hadith*, female slaves who showed an aptitude for study were given musical and even literary educations. Nevertheless, it seems clear from numerous surviving legal texts that the primary purpose of the concubine is not the bearing of children, but the giving of pleasure. For example in the case where a concubine has a child with one of two co-owners and becomes his *umm walad*, the other must be compensated for the loss of the slave's sexual services (*'uqr*).[64] A concubine may be expected to provide work as well as pleasure. But, as the famous Indian law manual, the *fatawa hindiya* has it, one must 'respect the custom by which one gives better clothes to the concubine who provides pleasure alone'.[65]

Islam and capitalism

The *hiyal*, or tricks, by which the *faqihs* managed to find their way round certain inconvenient Shari'a provisions were not confined to questions of family law and inheritance. As Maxime Rodinson has demonstrated, the prohibition of *riba* (lending at interest) was widely evaded by such devices as the double contract of sale or the artificial purchase of merchandise concealing an interest-bearing loan. However, it would be wrong to conclude from this or similar studies that the Shari'a had no impact on the economic life of Muslim societies. Laws, even when honoured in the breach, can still impede the growth of institutions which their absence might allow to develop. The prohibition of *riba* may have been widely evaded in an *ad hoc* way; but the sum of exceptions does not amount to a system.

This raises a question that has been the subject of lively debate among scholars and specialists. Was 'Islam' an obstacle to capitalist development? Marxist writers, including Rodinson and Bryan Turner, are inclined to argue that whatever impeded the emergence of capitalism in the Muslim world cannot be attributed to religious factors.

Rodinson, after reviewing the Prophet's very positive attitude towards trade, points out that in general the *fiqh* 'condemned practices that might disturb the free play of supply and demand'.[66] On the basis of what he admits is rather slender evidence, Rodinson suggests that by the beginning of the period of European intervention, wage labour was already being widely employed as part of a process of petty commodity production – an early stage, according to classical Marxist theory, in the development of capitalist production. Commensurate with this, and with the related process of early capital accumulation, was the development of a 'bourgeois class' – also in line with classical Marxism. However, as Rodinson points out, unlike its European counterpart, 'this bourgeoisie, conscious as it was of itself, of its strength and value, never achieved political power as a class, even though many of its individual members succeeded in occupying the highest appointments in the state'.[67]

Unfortunately, Rodinson, who is as erudite as he is persuasive, does not satisfactorily explain why the Muslim bourgeoisie failed to achieve political power as a class, thereby inaugurating a capitalist revolution along the lines achieved in eighteenth-century Europe. He contents himself with an essentially negative formulation:

If the bourgeoisie did not maintain and develop the strength it possessed in the first centuries AH; if the states dominated by a hierarchy of nobles and soldiers prevented it from exercising sufficient weight in relation to political power; if the town did not succeed in acquiring sufficient domination over the countryside; if manufacturing capital did not develop on the same scale as in Europe or Japan; if primitive accumulation of capital never attained the European level – all this was due to factors quite other than the Muslim religion.[68]

Among the non-religious factors, he suggests the availability of cheap labour from the countryside which gave little incentive to technical innovation, the Eastern tradition of a strong state depending on public works, and the unpredictable waves of invaders from central Asia.

In his study, Rodinson briefly examines, and rejects, Max Weber's thesis that European capitalism developed, out of the formalistic legal thinking in the tradition of Roman law, a collective mentality marked by a 'superior degree of rationality'. Rodinson argues that Weber was mixing cause with effect – his examples of 'rationality' being the result, and not the cause, of capitalist development. He points out, quite correctly, that 'the Quran accords a much larger place to reason than do the sacred books of Judaism and Christianity'.[69] Bryan Turner, in a study devoted to Weber's rather disparate writings on Islam, does rather more justice to the great sociologist, stating:

Weber shows that rational, formal law, autonomous cities, an independent burgher class and political stability were totally absent in Islam . . . Industrialization was not impeded by Islam as the religion of individuals . . . but by the religiously determined structure of the Islamic *states*, their officialdom and their jurisprudence.[70]

However, by a subtle analysis which attempts to demonstrate that the views of Marx and Weber are not in fundamental conflict, Turner concludes that it was socio-political rather than religious factors which prevented the autonomous development of capitalism in the Muslim world. He quotes with approval a statement by Sami Zubaida: 'It was not the attitudes and ideologies inherent in Islam which inhibited the development of a capitalist economy, but the political position of the merchant classes *vis-à-vis* the dominant military–bureaucratic classes in Islamic society.'[71]

Space will not allow a full account of Turner's analysis, which is substantially based on the same historic premises as Rodinson's – namely that the Muslim merchants did not develop autonomous organizations comparable to the powerful European city guilds which classical Marxists regard as a prerequisite of capitalist development. However, in denying the presence of a positive religious factor in this situation, both writers seem to have overlooked the *negative* impact of the Shari'a law in preventing the growth of such autonomous organizations.

The Middle Eastern city

Few things are more pregnant with culture shock for the western visitor than a first encounter with a traditional Muslim city such as the old city or Gamaliya area of Cairo. Instead of orderly boulevards flanked by pavements and rows of buildings, public or private, such as are to be found in any European city from Madrid to Moscow, one is confronted with a twisted labyrinth of lanes and dark alleys, low houses stretching into the distance between closed courtyards with high walls.[72] In the past, before Muslim cities became swamped by immigrants from the countryside, the bustle of the bazaar areas, with their specialized sections of merchandise (cottons, silks, carpets, spices, metal goods and jewellery – the last located centrally for maximum security), contrasted with the silence of the residential areas, often dingy dead-ends with nothing to indicate their function beyond the *mashrabiya* lattice-work windows that project above street-level like the sterns of so many men o' war. The quiet spaciousness and dignity of the traditional houses, with their paved courtyards, trickling fountains and pleasant gardens – designed, according to Lane, to ensure the seclusion of females, but also perfectly adapted to the climate – indicate above all the primacy of family life among middle- and upper-class urban Muslims. The narrowness of the streets outside, inaccessible to wheeled traffic, where pack-animals and humans fight for space, was not the result of bad planning on the part of the Arab conquerors. They were an unintended consequence of a fact of Muslim life: the continuous encroachment on public space by private interests. Thevenot, a Frenchman who visited Cairo in the mid-seventeenth century, was quick to notice the point:

There is not a single fine street in Cairo, but a mass of little ones turning hither and thither, which clearly demonstrates that all the houses were built without design, each person choosing all those places which pleased him to build on, without considering whether he stop up a street or no.[73]

This encroachment of the public domain was not confined to the affluent merchants or *'ulama* who could afford to build houses. An examination of many small workshops or coffee-houses lining the streets would reveal that they had been placed in front of the original buildings – and in the case of the coffee-houses (of which there were more than 1,000 in Lane's Cairo) half the lattice-work structure would be out in the road. The customary right to use public places for private purposes is still a feature of many Muslim cities where the authorities have abandoned attempts at draconian European-style policing. In modern Cairo, many of the streets of the splendid nineteenth-century 'European' city, built by the Khedive Isma'il to impress the royalty of Europe, have reverted to type and are now littered with open-air workshops for making furniture or repairing motor vehicles.

The key to the seemingly anarchic or 'irrational' growth of the Muslim city may lie in a singular fact of the Shari'a law: the absence of the Roman-law concept of 'legal personality'. In Europe the public right is an abstraction which can be upheld by defending it in law as a 'legal person'. Litigation between the public and private interest can therefore – for civil purposes – take the form of an adjudication between two parties. In criminal law one party is always the state, which brings a case against a suspected criminal as though it too were a legal party on a par with the accused. This principle applies not only to the state but to companies and corporations, groups of individuals endowed for the purposes of the law with legal personalities.

The absence of juridical personality in the Muslim law may not have been an oversight: it is certainly consistent with the uncompromising individualism of the Shari'a. Many aspects of Roman–Byzantine law and administration were taken over by the Arabs, including those concerned with municipal organization. The *muhtasib*, for example, a powerful official charged with ensuring equality of measures and other fair dealings, and who eventually accumulated considerable power to enforce public order generally, was the direct successor of the Byzantine official known as the *agoranomos* (market overseer). But in the public sphere the Shari'a seems to have taken no steps to define the interests of the community *vis-à-vis* those of the individual. The principle was taken so far that

> ... stealing from the public treasury was not held subject to the *hadd* punishment for theft, because the illegal act was not committed against a juristic agent independent of the thief who was, along with every other Muslim, considered part-owner of the *mal Allah*, and thus part-owner of what he had stolen.[74]

This absence of a juridical definition of the public sphere had far-reaching consequences. Islamic law did not recognize cities as such, nor did it admit corporate bodies.[75] Whereas in late medieval Europe the cities came to be administered by powerful corporations representing the merchant classes, the Muslim city remained in certain respects a collection of villages in which the group interests of families predominated over class interest. This may have been the 'original sin' of the Muslim bourgeoisie in the Marxist sense: they failed to develop consciousness of themselves as a class, and therefore never acted as one. It therefore seems quite wrong to assume, as do many Marxist writers, that this failure 'must not be misinterpreted or attributed to Islam'.[76]

Legal institutions are not just expressions of social realities, though they may originate as such. In the course of time, by ascribing a certain status in law to individuals or groups, they can mould the identity of individuals, persuading them to act in conformity with certain specific and clearly defined expectations. Class consciousness in most European societies was rooted not just in the economic environment, but in the status ascribed to certain social groups – the aristocracy, the clergy, the city guildsmen, the artisans, as well as the various categories of agriculturalist from yeoman farmers down to free peasants, villeins and serfs. All this took place under a legal order adapted and developed from the Roman law during the late medieval period. In Islamdom, though parallel categories undoubtedly existed in terms of their social and economic functions, the Shari'a denied them formal recognition in public law. As Rosen observes: 'It is not ... that broader social interests are unknown or that specific concepts of social utility are absent from Islamic law as practised in Morocco.' Indeed, he might have added here that the concept of *maslaha* – public interest – has an important role in Maliki *fiqh* and was adopted by reformers in other legal traditions. 'What is missing [he adds] until at least the beginning of western influence, is the institutionalization of the public as an entity whose interests might be assessed like those of a person. In the absence of the idea that corporate entities might constitute jural personalities the social interest enters the law as a localized interpretation of the legal status of particular named persons and their highly personalized acts.'[77] Elsewhere I have suggested that the idea of the public as an entity that can be treated as a person in law is consonant with the absence in Islam of a Church, the mystical institution or 'body of Christ' standing between the medieval Christian and his or her God, through which alone salvation was possible and which in law would become the model for secular institutions such as city corporations or trading companies in which the interest of the group transcended those of its individual members.[78] In a discussion that covers much of the same ground Pervez Hoodbhoy evaluates the role of Islamic law in inhibiting or preventing the emergence of autonomous cities and corporations and of a self-confident bourgeoisie able to withstand the arbitrary power of dynastic government, a prerequisite for the scientific and technological revolution which gave birth to the modern world. 'Asking why the scientific revolution did not occur in Islam is practically equivalent to asking why Islam did not produce a powerful bourgeois class.'[79] After briefly examining Weber's view that the 'theocratic judicial administration has interfered and must necessarily interfere with the operation of a rational economic system',[80] Hoodbhoy concludes that 'in strictly formal and textual terms, Weberians are probably right in arguing that the Islamic Shari'at is hostile to important elements of capitalism, and this did block the emergence of institutional banking along the lines which Europeans were then developing'. However, following Rodinson, Hoodbhoy rejects the Weberian argument that a capitalist revolution in Islam was wholly prevented by the operations of Islamic law, because of the extent to which the rules forbidding interest were systematically violated. Two additional factors, he maintains, are needed to account for the failure of Muslim societies to produce a vigorous, innovative and politically assertive bourgeois class: the existence of an urban ruling class based on a stable system of extraction from the peasantry; and the 'absence of autonomous cities and trade guilds which played such an important role in the development of European capitalism'.[81]

While it is hard to fault Hoodbhoy's analysis of the socio-economic factors inhibiting capitalist development in Islam, he does not relate the absence of corporate institutions such as autonomous cities or trade guilds specifically to the absence of the concept of legal personality in Islamic law. Yet he reaches conclusions that are wholly consistent with this view: given that the Church was 'an all-powerful institution which commanded the total allegiance of its subjects' and which left absolutely no room for dissent, its absence in Islam left a vacuum in terms of a 'central-political religious authority which could resolve or mediate disputes', leading to a process of sectarian fragmentation.[82]

To add a few links to this argument I suggest that in the West the Church, the 'mystical body' of Christ which alone guaranteed salvation, became the archetype in law of a whole raft of secular corporations that succeeded it during the early modern period. The mystic qualities of fictional personhood originating in the Body of Christ were eventually devolved to joint stock companies and public corporations with tradable shares.[83] Western capitalism and the bourgeois revolution that accompanied it has a distinctly Christian underpinning (one that is paradoxically 'Catholic' rather than 'Protestant' in origin, as Weber famously claimed, because its legal foundations are rooted in the idea of the Church as a distinctive body separated from society and infused with divine authority). The legal fiction of group personality taken over from the Church was its legal prerequisite. Group personality creates group identity (witness the company liveries worn by the wealthier merchants and traders in London and other cities in early modern times, to distinguish themselves from the humbler journeymen and artisans). The western corporation commands a special kind of group loyalty that, crucially, transcends the interests and ties of kinship. The burghers not only become a class (which they may arguably constitute in other, non-Christian societies), but become conscious of themselves as separate, distinct and powerful. (Witness Rembrandt's magnificent group portraits of the company Staatsholders, or the *Nightwatch*, perhaps his most famous painting, an icon that does for the city militia what Piero della Francesca's San Sepulchro *Resurrection* does for the Image of Christ.) The corporate group becomes the vehicle for the accumulation of capital. The burghers continually reinvest their money in the company which, crucially, not only transcends the sum of its individual members, but exists for eternity, just like the Church. Whereas Islamic law requires that a merchant's estate be redistributed amongst his kin upon his death (a requirement that may be circumvented only partly by the creation of a family *waqf*) the capital invested in the western corporation may continue to grow independently of an individual's decease. In terms of political economy the Church's gift to modernity was the institutional template adopted by its secular imitators. Hoodbhoy comes close to recognizing the significance of this process in registering a concluding irony: 'Paradoxically, a superior moral position – the right of the individual to interpret doctrine without the aid of priests – appears to have led to a systemic organizational weakness which proved fatal to Islamic political and economic – not to speak of scientific and technological – power in the long run.'[84]

The doctrinaire assumption that each individual is answerable for his actions only to God, implicit in the Shari'a and elaborated through the 'science' of *fiqh*, strongly militated against any public recognition of group interests other than those based on kinship. Thus the individual depended for support on the only social structure which enjoyed unqualified divine – and hence legal – recognition: the family. To this day, in much of the Muslim world, the interests of kinship usually predominate over those of office, profession, class or state. What is denounced as 'corruption' (whether this consists in accepting bribes, taking private commissions on government contracts or 'stealing from the public treasury') may often be described in less moralistic terms as a simple matter of putting one's family first.

Islam and the state

A further consequence of the Shari'a involves the somewhat ambiguous relationship that has always existed – and persists – between Islam and the state. Theoretically the ruler's legitimacy (outside the Shi'ite tradition) depended on his willingness to 'enjoin the good and forbid the evil' in accordance with the Divine Law. In practice Muslim rulers proved unwilling to submit themselves to the Shari'a when it affected their personal interests, and Muslim *qadis* were powerless to enforce judgements against high or powerful state officials. Thus, while in the realm of personal or family matters the Shari'a could be implemented on the basis of doctrines elaborated by the *faqihs*, in matters concerning the relation between the ruler and his subjects, land transactions, and even substantial areas of criminal law, power of decision remained with the rulers, who governed by decree or settled disputes through their own *mazalim* (complaints) courts. Thus state institutions grew up parallel to Islamic ones, leading to a *de facto* separation of the religious and secular spheres which contradicted the theoretical unity of *din wa dunya* (religion and world). However, such a state and its institutions involved at best a qualified recognition on the part of the *'ulama*: it was a necessity to be tolerated rather than a positive, earthly expression of the divine ideal. In time, however, the *'ulama* generally became upholders of the status quo, lending their weight to support established authority. Thus the famous Hanbali jurist Ibn Taimiya (d. 1328) would argue:

God has imposed the duty of enjoining the good and forbidding the evil, and that is possible only with the authority of a chief. Similarly, all the other duties which He has ordered, like the *jihad*, [the administration of] justice, pilgrimage, public prayer, festivals, brotherly help, the application of punishments and so forth can only be observed by means of the power and authority of the leader. It is thus that people say 'the Sultan is the Shadow of God on earth' and 'Sixty years with an unjust imam is better than one night of anarchy.'[85]

Nevertheless, accepting the necessity of government was not the same as according divine–legal recognition to the ruler in the realm of public law; and whereas in occidental polities the divinely appointed sovereignty of the monarch would eventually be appropriated by 'the people', acting through representative institutions, the Muslim state retained its essentially arbitrary character, *de facto* successor to a divinely instituted polity, but not a corporative entity embodied in the person of a monarch or a formalized assembly representing the 'estates' of his realm. The absence of legally recognized institutions, either at state level or at that of much smaller units, largely accounts for the 'informal' style which still governs Muslim politics, and the manner in which biological ties of kinship still remain politically decisive. Even where kinship did not always function directly, as with the *futuwa* guilds or Sufi brotherhoods, kinship became paradigmatic of social organization: lacking formal recognition in law, such groups were bound solely by moral ties comparable to the group loyalties operating within families.[86]

The Shari'a: human-centred, oral-based system

Despite the limitations placed on the Shari'a and the restrictions on its application, it has continued to loom large in the social memory of many Muslims today, who demand that Islamic society should be governed in accordance with the laws instituted by God rather than by laws created by men. Critical observers such as the French Algerian scholar Mohammed Arkoun have characterized this outlook as nostalgic and and ahistorical, the product of a 'social imaginary that is termed "Islamic" but that in fact sacralizes an irreversible operation of political, economic, social and cultural secularization'.[87] Like other Islamic institutions the Shari'a as applied in pre-modern times, and today in some traditional sectors of society, gave primacy to oral procedures. In contrast to courts in the West, personal knowledge of the plaintiffs and defendants is vital to the Shari'a judge's role. As Rosen observes, 'almost all of the evidence that the *qadi* received was oral in nature: physical evidence is rarely adduced in court and even documents seem to speak, as it were, less in the disembodied voice of a neutrally asserted fact than as the preserved tones of witnesses now absent or deceased'.[88]

Rosen contrasts the primacy given to oral testimony in the Moroccan court with the impersonality of evidence in western legal proceedings. 'Where in the West we have increasingly de-emphasized the personal attributes and background of litigants and defendants and sought to refine our legal and technical evaluation of physical evidence, Islamic courts continue to stress the person rather than the single event and thus feel more comfortable with oral than with material testimony.'[89] Until well into this century the legal and religious cultures of Islamdom have been welded to the oral, personalistic modes of interaction that are characteristic of pre-modern societies generally. When Islamist radicals demand the 'restoration' of the Shari'a, the cruel penalties (the beheadings, stonings, and amputations for petty thefts or sexual indiscretions) that outrage western sensibilities have a *shibbolethic* character, attracting headlines and proclaiming their defiance of 'western' concerns over human rights. Yet even these 'medieval barbarities' appear humane and intimately personal when compared with the creaking machinery of 'blind' justice operating in the United States, where citizens able to afford good lawyers escape the death penalty by means of plea bargains, while the poor (who are disproportionately black, and often Muslim) wait, sometimes for years in the cells on death row as their fates are decided by politicians with an eye for the popular vote. Behind the rhetoric and 'social imaginary' of Muslims who demand the Shari'a's 'restoration', lies another, profounder memory which rarely receives its due from western observers: that of a culture in which the social was personalized, despite its often tyrannical or arbitrary systems of government.[90] The appeal of this society, with its 'human-friendly character' under the Law, which covered a complex network of private familial relationships under the all-encompassing aegis of divine compassion, is not in doubt. How much of this 'sacred canopy' can be salvaged in the face of the depersonalizing effects of modernity is another question entirely.

5   Sects and Solidarity

The theologization of conflict

The divisions of Islam, in contrast to those of Christianity, have their origins in politics rather than dogma. This is not to say that dogmatic and theological questions do not form part of these divisions. However, the questions over which they first crystallized were political to the extent that they were primarily concerned with leadership of the community. Having a religious ideology built on the social foundations of tribalism, the Muslims expressed their aspirations first in the terms of group loyalty, and only afterwards in terms of the doctrinal and theological accretions surrounding these loyalties.

The factor of 'asabiya, or group solidarity, thus had a religious as well as a political dimension. During the formative period of Islam, up until about the tenth century AD, the allegiances involved in the early struggles for power in the Muslim community acquired an archetypal significance. For posterity, history became overlaid with meta-history, so much so that the actual events were less important than the accretions of myth and sentiment surrounding them. There is nothing unique to Islam in this process: all the historical religions contain a similar core of fact surrounded by the cloud of meta-history. What distinguishes meta-history from history is significance as distinct from factuality. If religion can be defined as a set of symbolic forms which relate humans to the ultimate conditions of their existence, then a historic religion is one which creates out of certain events a structure of meaning which transcends the immediacy of circumstance and makes them permanently symbolic of the human predicament.

From the first, opposition to the prevailing currents in Islam centred on the person of 'Ali, the Prophet's cousin and husband of his daughter Fatima. Later Shi'ite doctrine maintained that the Prophet explicitly designated him as his successor (at a place called Ghadir Khumm, on their return from the Farewell Pilgrimage). Sunni writers dispute this, saying that the Prophet merely urged his followers to hold 'Ali in high esteem. Although after the Prophet's death some of the Ansar may have favoured the succession of 'Ali, no significant party at the time appears to have backed his claims against Abu Bakr. His comparative youth (he was between 33 and 36) was probably against him in a society in which leadership was usually exercised by older men. However, 'Ali is said to have held himself aloof after Abu Bakr's election, and to have refused to make his homage to the caliph. Fatima is said to have had claims on lands held by her father which Abu Bakr rejected on the ground that 'Prophets have no heirs'.

Nevertheless, in the course of the first three caliphates a number of factors contributed to make 'Ali a leading focus of opposition. Foremost among them was his own uncompromising character. According to several sources, he was a balding, broad, stocky man, with a hairy body and a long beard which became white as he grew older. Having an unrivalled knowledge of the Quran, he was so meticulous in matters of prayer and ritual that many of his contemporaries attributed the burnished surface of his rather prominent forehead – which they likened to the knee-joint of a camel – to the frequency of his prostrations. During the caliphates of Abu Bakr and 'Umar, he evidently kept himself apart, implicitly criticizing their policies by failing to endorse them. He seems to have been an uncompromising, somewhat naive idealist. We are told that he unsuccessfully urged 'Umar to distribute the entire revenues resulting from the conquest, without holding back anything for the public treasury. More significant for future developments was his behaviour in the electoral council, or Shura, convened by the dying 'Umar to choose his successor. According to several traditions, 'Ali was offered the caliphate by his peers, on condition that he would rule according to the Quran and the Sunna, and that he would accept the precedents established by his two predecessors. 'Ali absolutely refused to accept the second condition, presumably because he disapproved of some of Abu Bakr's and 'Umar's acts. 'Uthman was then offered the caliphate on the same terms and accepted.

Under the caliphate of 'Uthman the seeds of dissent germinated. 'Ali attracted to himself dissident elements, including some soldiers who had lost out in the distribution of lands and pious Quran reciters who resented the way in which 'Uthman allowed his Umayyad clansmen to acquire the most important administrative posts. One outspoken critic of 'Uthman's regime was Abu Dharr al-Ghifari, a personality often invoked by left-wing movements in Islam. When 'Uthman sent Abu Dharr into exile, 'Ali insisted on publicly escorting him out of Madina, despite an explicit prohibition from the caliph. When mutinous soldiers from Egypt, joined by rebel contingents from Kufa and Basra, besieged the caliph in his house, 'Ali tried to mediate on their behalf. Although he refused to place himself at their head, his attitude was not entirely discouraging and he may even have agreed with their demands for the caliph's abdication. However, he was unable to prevent the situation getting out of hand and the caliph was murdered.

Although 'Ali denounced the murder as an act of *jahiliya*, his failure to produce the culprits made him unacceptable as caliph to that section of the Umma (including the Syrian troops and 'Uthman's Umayyad clansmen) who remained loyal to the dead caliph's nephew. Moreover, though overwhelmingly supported in Madina as the only leader capable of restoring order, he was soon faced by dissent on both flanks. Two leading Companions, Talha and Zubair, renounced their allegiance to him and, supported by 'Aisha, threatened to cut him off from his Iraqi supporters. Soon after defeating them at the Battle of the Camel (in which Talha and Zubair were killed) 'Ali found himself confronting the Syrian Governor Mu'awiya's army at Siffin. His eventual decision to seek a compromise with Mu'awiya promoted a rebellion of his more militant supporters, mainly from the tribe of Tamim, which included a large number of Quran reciters. During the armistice following the agreement at Siffin, a group of several hundred of these so-called 'seceders' (Kharijis – literally, 'those who went out') left 'Ali's camp at Kufa and established themselves on the bank of the Nahrawan canal near the site of what is now Baghdad. Although 'Ali inflicted a severe defeat on them in July 658, enough of them survived to continue the secessionist movement and one of them, Ibn Muljam, avenged his comrades by assassinating 'Ali three years later, in 661.

The Kharijis

The Kharijis were the first of the radical sects to separate themselves from the mainstream of Islam during its formative era. As with most other sects, their position involved a mixture of political and religious attitudes. Politically, their rejection of both 'Uthman and 'Ali as caliphs drove them to the position that any good Muslim could be the leader of the community, even a former slave, so long as he enjoyed the Umma's whole-hearted confidence. Consciously replicating Muhammad's original movement, Khariji groups made their *hijra* to camps in the desert, whence they made war on the rest of the Muslims, whom they regarded as infidels. In law they observed the Quran and the Sunna with puritanical strictness, considering as an apostate anyone guilty of serious crime. Like other militant groups which came after them, including the Nizari Isma'ilis ('Assassins'), the followers of the Sudanese Mahdi in the nineteenth century, and the extremist Takfir wa'l Hijra group recently active in Egypt, they endeavoured to actualize the Quranic eschatology in their own activity. They were the People of Paradise. All other Muslims, including the 'grave sinners' among them, were the People of Hell, whom they themselves, as instruments of God's justice, were obliged to punish. Today, in surviving Khariji communities, known sinners are still punished by the ultimate religious sanction – denial of the rite of burial.

The Kharijis were extremely puritanical in sexual matters. One of their sects even went so far as to suppress from the Quran as unworthy of God's word the story of the attempted seduction of Joseph (12:23–35), in which a very positive attitude towards human sexuality is displayed. As a major Islamic movement, however, they suffered from a fatal weakness: they never succeeded in developing their group solidarity beyond the primitive tribal stage, making it impossible for them to take control of the metropolitan centres. In Iraq they enjoyed for a time the support of the rural peasantry, who resented the exactions of their Arab conquerors. But they never had much support from the garrisons of the cities, and were eventually destroyed by the armies of the caliphs. Despite these defeats as a major movement, however, Khariji doctrines continued to inspire revolts among oppressed or marginal groups throughout Islamic history. In the ninth century a group of black slaves imported from East Africa to work the saltpetre mines of Lower Iraq revolted and enslaved their masters. Their leader, 'Ali ibn Muhammad, adopted Khariji doctrines to justify killing those who refused to join the rebellion. At one stage in the revolt, which lasted thirteen years, the rebels decapitated all their prisoners and threw the heads into a canal, which floated them down to Basra where relatives were able to identify them.

Though the Azraqis and other sects were suppressed, a modified form of Kharijism survived among the followers of 'Abdullah ibn Ibad. Realizing that a majority of the Muslims would never support them, Ibn Ibad taught a version of the Khariji doctrine which enabled them to compromise, at least temporarily, with the realities of 'infidel' rule. The absolute polarization of the world between the People of Paradise and the People of Hell was replaced by a kind of purgatory – the 'Sphere of Prudent Fear'. The Imam of the People of Paradise was replaced, for the nonce, by a temporary 'Imam for Defence'. The draconian laws which equated such offences as wine-drinking and fornication with apostasy were modified – these matters would be dealt with on the Day of Judgement.

The Ibadis created a flourishing state among the Berbers of Western Algeria. Its capital, Tahert, attracted Khariji settlers from many other parts of the Muslim world. The chronicler Ibn Saghir, who was not a member of the sect, drew an idyllic picture of this Muslim Geneva:

There was not a foreigner who stopped in the city but settled among them and built in their midst, attracted by the plenty there, the equitable conduct of the Imam, his just behaviour towards those under his charge, and the security enjoyed by all in person and property.[1]

Tahert was destroyed by the Fatimid caliphs in the tenth century. Another Khariji revolt, led by the scholar and preacher Abu Yazid, lasted nearly forty years, and almost destroyed Fatimid power in the Maghreb, before the rebels were defeated in a bloody battle at Mahdiya in 946. Though Abu Yazid escaped, he died from his wounds the following year, and his body was brought in triumph to the caliph. 'His corpse,' wrote Ibn Khaldun, 'was flayed and the skin was stuffed with straw and placed in a cage as a plaything for two apes which had been trained for this task.'[2]

The Ibadis were virtually wiped out in the Maghreb, and all that survive are a few communities in the Mzab area and on the island of Jarba. At the opposite end of the Arab world, however, they fared a great deal better. In Oman, Ibadism is still the official creed; while as recently as the 1950s an Ibadi Imam, Ghalib ibn 'Ali, held sway in the traditional stronghold of Nizwa in the Jabal Akhdar. Before his overthrow by the Sultan with the help of British forces in 1954, he played (with some help from the Saudis) the classic role of an Ibadi

leader: guardian of Khariji puritanism against the corrupting foreign influences represented by the Sultan and his British allies. Although a small minority in today's Muslim world, the Khariji attitude of treating Muslim sinners as infidels closely resembles that of some modern fundamentalist groups.

In their first secessionist movement, as in their later revolts and actions, the Kharijis had created a tradition, founded on the Prophet's career, of seeking to realize the Islamic vision through deliberate political action. The activism of the Kharijis expressed itself in classic Khaldunian form – in the social cohesion or *'asabiya* of the tribe with its elected chief. The vision has been described by W. Montgomery Watt as that of the 'charismatic community'. It was clearly ill-suited to the needs of metropolitan societies such as Egypt and Mesopotamia, where tribalism interacted with the more diversified patterns of urban life. A tribal society, with its powerful sense of group cohesion and hostility to innovation might successfully transform itself into a small city-state such as Tahert or even Nizwa; but it could hardly expect to evolve into an urban culture without a radical transformation of its natural allegiances. In a more complex society, based on a higher degree of specialization and the division of labour, the *'asabiya* of the 'charismatic community' was inadequate: the group needed something more durable around which to coalesce.

The centralized polities of Egypt and Mesopotamia also contained the relics of much more ancient cultural traditions which Islam might transform or modify, but could never eliminate. These traditions combined urban populism with a history of divine kingship, both of which were capable of finding expression in Islamic terms. The populist elements re-emerged in the association of normal, 'civilized' social behaviour with the figure of the Arabian Prophet. Elaborated and systematized by the legists, it crystallized into the classical system of *fiqh* examined in the last chapter.

But however popular the figure of the Prophet and universal the norms associated with his utterances, this was hardly an adequate pole for urban group loyalties to revolve around. The very success of the *fiqh* as a normative social system left a vacuum in the consciousness of the masses once the universal system of Islam had become triumphant. Private pietism might find expression in the meticulous observance of ritual, but it did not stimulate the public enthusiasm capable of commanding group loyalties. In most areas of Islamic society the vacuum was largely filled by personal devotion to figures of outstanding piety endowed with charismatic prestige. In the formative period these figures were, *par excellence*, members of the *ahl al-bait*, the Prophet's household – in particular, the tragic figures of 'Ali and his son Husain, the Prophet's martyred grandson. It would be a mistake to suppose that this devotion was peculiar to Shi'ism. However, it was in Shi'ism that it took on its characteristic sectarian form.

The Twelver (Imami) Shi'a

Every day is 'Ashura and
Every place is Karbala

For the Shi'a, literally 'partisans' of 'Ali who make up some 12 per cent of the Muslim community, the tragic débâcle of the House of 'Ali has become a major religious festival. Karbala rivals Makka as a place of pilgrimage. The Day of 'Ashura (the tenth of the month of Muharram, when Husain was killed) is comparable to Yom Kippur or Good Friday in the Jewish and Christian calendars. In the traditional 'Ashura celebrations, processions of flagellants would pass through the streets, flailing the skins off their backs to expiate by their own agonies the sufferings of the Imam Husain and his small band of companions. These funeral processions are not dissimilar from the Good Friday celebrations in many Latin countries where the crucifix is paraded through the streets, followed by an effigy of the Virgin draped in black and accompanied by a brass band with a specially dirgeful timbre. Whether experienced religiously as vicarious suffering, or aesthetically as tragedy, such occasions have a cathartic function. They penetrate the human psyche and its emotional structure, activating and renewing them in the same way that physical exercise activates and renews the body.

In Iran, where Shi'ism is the national cult, the death of Husain is regularly celebrated in *ta'ziya* passion plays and at weekly religious gatherings of families and neighbourhood groups, where professional narrators, known as *rouzeh-khans*, make lingering word-pictures out of every poignant detail of the Karbala tragedy. The long hot trek across the desert by the holy family and its little band of followers;

the cruelty of Ibn Ziyad, the Umayyad commander, who cut them off from their only source of water; the final act of martyrdom by the Imam, as he donned his grandfather's sacred mantle, perfumed himself and mounted his white horse, carrying his youngest child: all this is recounted solemnly and ritualistically, like the passion of Christ in the liturgy.

With his six-month-old son 'Ali Asghar in his arms, the Imam cried out to the enemy that as this innocent babe had defiled none, at least he should be spared and a little water given to him to allay his thirst. But the reply was an arrow shot at the child's neck which pinned it to his father's arm. After returning the cruelly murdered child to its sorrowing mother's arms (who then sang a mournful mother's lament over her dead child) the Imam returned to pay the last of the sacrifice with his own blood. Arrow after arrow followed piercing his body into a sieve until, when the aged Imam fell from his horse his body did not touch the ground but was held off the ground by the arrows that were sticking out of his body. Shamr [one of the Umayyad soldiers] who has earned everlasting shame for himself, after deriding the fallen hero, cut off his head. Ruqaiya, Husain's young daughter, weeps over the death of her father whose head is then brought into her presence whereupon she falls upon it moaning and sobbing until she, too, dies of sorrow, prostrate over the severed head.[3]

At each of these details, noted the observer who recorded this *rouza*,

. . . the audience bursts into loud, unrestrained sobbing, moaning and slapping of the forehead and beating of chests. The words . . . are carefully chosen by the narrator to maximize the sentiments and emotions associated with filial and parental love which are strongly felt by each of the participants.[4]

The event of Karbala, that unhappy episode in Islam's long and some-times bloody history, is thus elevated into an archetype of human suffering, a suffering made tolerable by its incorporation into a wider, and ultimately beneficial, cosmic order.

If Sunni Islam, with its Pharisaic attention to the detailed observance of law and ritual projects, like orthodox Judaism, has a continuous awareness of the sacrality of everyday living, in which eating, defecat-ing, washing and a host of other routine actions are conducted within a framework of divine law linking the individual with the cosmic order, Shi'ism like Roman Catholicism places its distinctive emphasis on the experience of suffering and the problem of evil. Suffering and death are the most difficult issues with which ordinary people, and societies, have to come to terms. Why do people suffer? Why is there evil in the world? Why do the unjust seem to prosper, while the righteous or the weak so often go to the wall? Many sociologists have seen in religious beliefs and customs attempts to resolve these problems symbolically, by means of culturally constituted defence mechanisms. As Clifford Geertz writes:

As a religious problem, the problem of suffering is, paradoxically, not how to avoid suffering but how to suffer, how to make physical pain, personal loss, worldly defeat or the helpless contemplation of others' agony something bearable, supportable – something, as we say, sufferable. The problem of suffering passes easily into the problem of evil, for if suffering is severe enough it usually, though not always, seems morally undeserved as well. [Both problems] raise the uncomfortable suspicion that the world, and perhaps man's life in the world, has no genuine order at all ... And the religious response to this suspicion is in each case the same: the formulation, by means of symbols, of an image of such genuine order of the world which will account for, and even celebrate, the perceived ambiguities, puzzles and paradoxes in human experience.[5]

Shi'a Islam and Christianity, in contrast to Sunni Islam and Judaism, draw upon the historic experience of defeat and martyrdom, elaborating symbolic defences against the realities of suffering. Both movements were born out of failure and frustration. What little is really known about the historic origins of Christianity suggests that it was a Jewish messianic movement related to, though distinct from, the national movement of the Zealots. The failure of Christ's movement, which ended ignominiously in the leader's execution by the Romans, confronted his followers with the choice of either accepting defeat, which would have entailed disintegration of the movement and the betrayal of its founder, or of overcoming defeat by sublimation. The second course was adopted by Christ's disciples, who put it about that Christ was not really dead but would shortly return as Messiah. This gave the movement an added impetus and urgency: preparation for the Second Coming which most early Christians believed to be imminent.

Like the early Christians, the followers of Husain refused to 'face the facts' after the defeat of their leader at Karbala. An even closer parallel with Christianity is suggested by the Shi'ite historians who emphasize the voluntary nature of Husain's sacrifice. Instead of trying to raise military support in the Hejaz, the Prophet's grandson made his way towards Kufa with a tiny band of fifty companions. On the way his sympathizers warned him that the situation was desperate. 'The hearts of the Iraqis were for him but their swords were for the Umayyads.' If he proceeded to Kufa he and his party would certainly be butchered. Husain persisted in his plan, despite these friendly protests, deliberately seeking the martyrdom that he knew must revitalize the cause of the Prophet's House. His decision proved fully justified. In later generations the whole Muslim community – and not just the Shi'ite sectarian militants – would look back with horror at the enormity of Karbala, where the Prophet's surviving grandson, leader of the *ahl al-bait* (literally, 'people of the house'), was massacred along with his pathetic band of followers by Muslim forces of the corrupt and cynical Umayyad caliph, Yazid ibn Mu'awiya.

In early Islam, as in early Christianity, history and meta-history constantly interact. The actual events of history, mythologized and writ large in the popular imagination of a mainly non-literate society, become the source of a new consciousness leading to distinctive social and political affiliations. One can discern in the results a new form of *'asabiya* in which the sense of tribal community, lost in the transition from pastoral to urban society, is regained – albeit in a sublimated form – by means of membership of a religious subculture. During the medieval period the organizations which filled the gap between the individual Muslim, isolated in his aloneness before the awesome Quranic deity, were the Sufi *tariqas*, whose functioning will be investigated in the next chapter. However, during Islam's formative centuries the same function was performed by groups owing allegiance to the *ahl al-bait* and its numerous representatives.

We know that many of 'Ali's earliest supporters were *qaris* – Quran reciters – who were renowned for their piety. Though some of them deserted to the Kharijis because of what they regarded as his weak political leadership, many remained under the Umayyad dictatorship, forming a kind of opposition group critical of its worldly policies. After 'Ali's death and the events of Karbala these pious elements tended to become increasingly attached to the cause of the *ahl al-bait*. In due course they became adherents of various members of the Prophet's family – 'Abbasids, Zaidis, Ja'faris, Isma'ilis, Fatimids or

Nizaris – not so much because there existed an unbroken continuity between the 'founders' and the later generations of followers who came to make up these communities, but rather because all of them represented a religio-political outlook which sought legitimacy by associating itself with one of these august figures.

The first response to the death of Husain was an action, partially religious in character, which helped shape the future direction of Shi'ite religiosity. About 3,000 of the Kufans, led by several prominent *qaris*, sought to avenge him by attacking Ibn Ziyad, the Umayyad governor responsible for the massacre. Rejecting support from the rebel caliph, who at that time controlled much territory in northern and central Arabia, they first visited the grave of Husain, where they gave themselves up to wild expressions of grief, before proceeding to attack an Umayyad force of at least three times their number. A proclamation of these so-called Tawwabin, or Penitents, has survived, which makes it clear that they would restore the caliphate to the Prophet's family or die in the attempt, thereby atoning for the death of his grandson, caused by their desertion. Not surprisingly, the Tawwabin were cut to pieces by the forces of Ibn Ziyad and very few survived. However, a more militant group led by Mukhtar al-Thaqafi espoused the claims of Muhammad ibn al-Hanafiya, a son of 'Ali by 'the Hanafi woman' and therefore no descendant of Muhammad. It was in Mukhtar's propaganda that another characteristically Shi'ite theme (but one that is also present in other sections of the Islamic community) first appeared: the idea of a promised *mahdi* (literally, 'the expected one') or messiah who would bring peace and justice to a world torn by strife and oppression.

Shi'ite eschatology

The idea of the *mahdi* has variously been ascribed to Persian, Jewish and Christian influences, as well as to an independent development in the Arab–Muslim tradition. Probably mahdism assimilated all these influences from the new cosmopolitan society of the Arab empire. Divine kingship had existed among the southern Arabs and Persians before the coming of Islam. In the crisis following Muhammad's death some of the Ansar (whose ancestors migrated from southern Arabia) may have resisted paying homage to Abu Bakr, preferring 'Ali because they believed that Muhammad's prophethood somehow inhered in members of his family. The mixed Arab–Persian population of Kufa, centre of Mukhtar's rebellion, included several Christian–Arab tribes, while the southern Arabs outnumbered the northerners by a ratio of three to two. The Iraqi city was evidently fertile soil for ideas of charismatic leadership. The Persian element included former captives converted to Islam, peasants and other migrants, traders and craftsmen who felt themselves the victims of social and ethnic discrimination. The Persian tradition itself included the 'ancient Indo-Aryan idea of a chosen, God-begotten family transmitting the Glory of God from generation to generation and eventually producing a *saoshyant* or messiah'.[6]

Nevertheless, in contrast to the Tawwabin, Mukhtar's movement was primarily one of political and social protest. This much is apparent from the fact that Husain's surviving son, 'Ali Zain al-'Abidin (the soubriquet means 'ornament of the pious'), who refused to back Mukhtar's movement, was replaced by Muhammad ibn al-Hanafiya, who evidently permitted Mukhtar to use his name in the course of a revolt that was suppressed in 687. The activists wanted a candidate who would be prepared to make an open bid for the caliphate, even if he were not a direct descendant of the Prophet.

The more moderate followers of 'Ali and Husain pursued the quietist line of Zain al-'Abidin, accepting the *de facto* rule of the Umayyads without according it *de jure* recognition. 'Ali Zain al-'Abidin contributed to the specifically religious tradition of Shi'ism. Before his death in 712 or 713 he is said to have nominated his eldest son, Muhammad al-Baqir, as his successor and heir to his spiritual heritage. The more activist Shi'ites, however, transferred their allegiance to his son Abu Hashim. Others, who may have been influenced by the fact that neither Ibn al-Hanafiya nor Abu Hashim was of the Prophet's line, gave their support to Muhammad al-Baqir's younger half-brother Zaid, who also wished to pursue an activist policy aimed at overthrowing the Umayyad caliphate and restoring the Prophet's heritage. Thus, early in the eighth century there were at least three groups of 'Alid loyalists: two of them representing the activist approach of Mukhtar and a 'legitimist' group following the quietist and spiritualizing attitude of Zain al-'Abidin.

The first of these groups to make a serious attempt at political action were the followers of Zaid ibn 'Ali. While Muhammad al-Baqir and his son and heir by designation, Ja'far al-Sadiq, continued to reside peacefully in Madina, eliciting much respect from the pious for their scholarship and devotion to religious duties, but showing little inclination towards rebellion, Zaid insisted that the caliph–imam's duty lay in 'establishing the good and prohibiting the evil', if necessary by force. In so doing he managed to win over some of Baqir's supporters, as well as erstwhile followers of Ibn al-Hanafiya and Abu Hashim. His programme also drew support from the Mu'tazili group of theologians active in Kufa and Basra. As advocates of the doctrine of *qadar*, or free will, it was logical that they should espouse the cause of political action. Zaid, however, also alienated the more militant Shi'ite activists by the concessions he was prepared to make in order to win maximum support for his movement: this involved accepting Abu Bakr and 'Umar (but not the reviled 'Uthman) as legitimate caliphs, despite their 'inferiority' to 'Ali.

Although Zaid's revolt in 740 was a failure, he himself being killed along with many of his followers, his son Yahya continued the struggle in Khurasan, where he won some support from troops loyal to 'Ali, before meeting the same fate as his father in 743. Moreover the movement survived in two remote and widely separated mountainous areas. By the late ninth century a Zaidi state had been established in Tabaristan, south of the Caspian, and another based on Sa'da in the mountains of Yemen. The Zaidi doctrine of the Imamate, developed by their leading theorist Qasim al-Rassi (d. 860), lay somewhere between the Shi'ite and Khariji positions. The true Imam must be a descendant (like Zaid) of 'Ali and Fatima; he must combine mastery of religious knowledge ('ilm) with the political acumen necessary to sustain the rebellion against the authorities. He need not, however, be the son of an Imam, nor need there be an Imam at all if no suitably qualified candidate emerged. Like Kharijism, Zaidism represented an attempt at reconstructing the early Muslim polity on the basis of a very personal relationship and sense of responsibility between the Caliph and his community. Like Kharijism, it was unsuited to a large-scale international society demanding more complex forms of socio-political organization; like Kharijism, it proved highly resilient and durable in mountainous regions remote from the centres of power. The Imamate of Yemen survived, virtually untouched by foreign influences, until well into the twentieth century under a succession of remarkably competent – if sometimes severe – rulers. Although a weak and incompetent Imam proved unable to hold his country together following the death of his father in 1963, the 'royalist' tribesmen emerged the real victors of a seven-year civil war in which the 'republican' side was supported by considerable numbers of Egyptian troops, armaments and aircraft. A revived Imamate, under a 'suitably qualified candidate', though unlikely, does not seem to be beyond the bounds of possibility in the future.

Shi'ite activism proved rather more successful at the second attempt. A series of revolts, beginning in Khurasan but backed overwhelmingly by the pious intellectuals of the major cities, finally brought down the Umayyad caliphate in 750. It was led by Abu Muslim, a former slave of Ibrahim, Imam of the Hashimis, who inherited the 'Alid movement of Mukhtar and Ibn al-Hanafiya. Ibrahim claimed descent from 'Abbas, the Prophet's uncle and a late-comer to Islam. But he had an additional claim to the support of 'Alid loyalists, having acquired the Imamate by designation from Abu Hashim, which allowed him to benefit from the pro-'Alid organization set up by Mukhtar. Many Shi'ite supporters would no doubt have been unhappy about this arrangement had they known about it. Not only were these 'Abbasids (as they came to be known) not descended from the prophet, they were not even descendants of 'Ali, who by now had acquired his own special claims to loyalty. The 'Abbasids could claim, however, that in terms of patrilineal descent (which was all that counted in Muslim society) they stood in the same relation to the Prophet's family as did 'Ali himself. Moreover, in his propaganda Abu Muslim carefully concealed the fact that the rebellion was being undertaken on behalf of the 'Abbasids, announcing only that the Umayyads would be replaced by a member of the *ahl al-bait*. Thus the 'Abbasids succeeded in gaining Shi'ite support that might otherwise have been denied to them.

In the event, the Umayyads got wind of these developments and had the Imam Ibrahim imprisoned and murdered. According to some accounts, the local leader of the movement in Iraq, Abu Salama, did not feel duty bound to Ibrahim's designated successor, his younger brother Abu al-'Abbas, and offered the caliphate instead to Ja'far al-Sadiq, whose claims, of course, were far superior. Ja'far is said to have refused. If true, the story suggests that Ja'far and his supporters were by now irrevocably set upon the course that would eventually separate them from the Muslim community religiously as well as politically.

By refusing the challenge of political power, Ja'far was effectively echoing Christ's statement: 'My Kingdom is not of this world.' It could be argued, of course, that he was merely acting out of caution; but such an attitude would hardly have been worthy of Husain's great-grandson. At all events, after Abu Muslim's movement was successful, political power passed to the family of 'Abbas, who held it for more than a century and, in the purely titular form of the caliphate, for very much longer, until the Mongol irruption of 1258.

'Abbasid absolutism

After their triumph the 'Abbasids – like many revolutionary victors after them – turned on their erstwhile supporters, especially the extremists among them. Generally, the change of government was welcomed by the pious elements. The fact that the new rulers were not from the inner circle of the Prophet's family was less important than the fact that they agreed to rule more strictly in accordance with the Quran and with the Muhammadan norms that were in the process of being developed (as described in the previous chapter). However, like all successful rulers they found it necessary, upon acquiring power, to exchange revolutionary fervour for broad consensus. This they achieved by conceding the principal demands of the former 'pious opposition': equality of opportunity for Arabs and *mawali*; appointment of judges from among the *'ulama*; and, in general, government in accordance with the Quran and the Sunna. At the same time, they were bound to disappoint the activist elements among the Shi'a, whose eschatological hopes had seen in the coming of the 'Abbasids the dawn of a universal age of equality, righteousness and justice. The quietist or 'spiritualizing' elements around the Imam Ja'far al-Sadiq were probably left more or less unmolested – although Shi'ite tradition suggests that the Imam and all his successors in the 'Twelver' line (see p. 434), barring the last, were poisoned by the 'Abbasid caliphs. Ja'far's version of the Imamate and of the expected coming of the *mahdi* does not seem, for the time being, to have disturbed the new emerging social order.

Mahdist ideas had, however, by now become widely disseminated. The demand for universal justice invariably accompanies the collapse of an unpopular government. Popular movements, as many 'moderate' revolutionaries have found to their cost, rarely stop short at demanding a change of rulers. In a religious society the utopian demands of the oppressed tend to be couched in eschatological language. The day of reckoning promised in scripture is deemed to be nigh, when sin will be punished and virtue rewarded. At times of social unrest and economic stress, it is the rich and powerful who are usually thought to be sinful, the poor and oppressed virtuous or at least innocent. Biblical eschatology animated such radical movements as the Anabaptists of Munster and the English Levellers. In the Quran the sociopolitical possibilities of the Last Day are even more apparent than those contained in the Book of Revelation, for it is clear in many passages that the Quraishi rulers will be among the damned. The Umayyads were literally as well as metaphorically kin of the merchant aristocrats who resisted God's message. To save their own skins they had embraced Islam at the last possible moment, and had then proceeded to take over the movement, corrupting it from within, distorting or ignoring its universal message.

In a society in which lines of kinship were all-important, it was natural that mahdist claims should be made on behalf of leaders close to the Prophet's inner family (even though, in many traditions, the expected messiah was identified with the second coming of Jesus). It was from this group, from within the Quraish, that God had chosen His Messenger, with such spectacular results. As pretenders in the line of Muhammad ibn al-Hanafiya, the 'Abbasids to some extent benefited from these eschatological expectations. By contrast, the failure of Zaid's revolt may partly be attributed to the fact that he refused to allow mahdist claims to be made on his behalf. The 'Abbasid caliphs encouraged these expectations by giving themselves grandiloquent titles: al-Saffah ('the Bloodshedder': 750–4); his brother al-Mansur ('the Victorious': 754–75); and, most appropriately, al-Mahdi (775–85), father of al-Rashid ('the Righteous': 786–809). Al-Mahdi, whose full name was Muhammad ibn 'Abdullah, was given his title by his father at a time when a well-known *hadith* was in circulation:

Even if there remains for the world but one single day, God will extend it until He sends a man from the people of my house [*ahl al-bait*], whose name will be the same as mine, and the name of his father will be that of my father. He will fill the earth with equity and justice, just as it is now filled with tyranny and oppression.[7]

Within a generation or so the 'Abbasids had developed the caliphate along absolutist lines, incorporating many of the Sassanid traditions. The imperial style, with the caliph as 'God's Shadow upon Earth', was reinforced by the decision to build a new capital at Baghdad, near the former Sassanid capital at Ctesiphon. At the height of their glory, during the reign of Haroun al-Rashid, the 'Abbasids controlled territory comprising most of western Asia, all Arabia (except for Oman) and the lands south of the Mediterranean. The only fully independent Muslim states were in the Berber Maghreb and in Spain, where an Umayyad prince who escaped the general massacre of his family founded an independent kingdom. Trade flourished and expanded. Ocean-going dhows carried by the monsoons sailed to China in the east, where the emperor granted Muslim merchants special privileges; trading colonies were founded on the East African coast as far south as Mozambique. The unification of the Indian Ocean brought immense prosperity to the empire. The caliphs appropriated much of this wealth in taxes, only to redistribute it again in a somewhat arbitrary manner in which politics mixed with piety and prestige.

The 'Abbasid government combined the traditions of Persian absolutism with some distinctively Islamic features. The remoteness of the caliphs, dramatized by an elaborate court ceremonial drawn directly from Sassanid models, emphasized their elevation above the factional disputes of ordinary men and women. As God's vice-regents upon earth they elicited an adoration which scandalized the pious, savouring as it did of *shirk*, the 'association' of lesser beings with the divinity. The caliph was supported by a dependent bureaucracy which, though aristocratic in origin, disposed of no power of its own. The famous Barmakid family, formerly Buddhist priests at Balkh, near the Oxus, discovered this to their cost when Rashid, jealous of the enormous power they had acquired as state secretaries to successive caliphs, literally destroyed them overnight: one was beheaded, his father and brother died soon afterwards in prison.

At the popular level, however, Islamic egalitarianism contributed to the breakdown of social and ethnic barriers. In an expanding economy extending over a vast area of the globe, the 'Abbasid empire offered an unprecedented range of social and geographical mobility. Moreover this mobility was achieved from a relatively small though sound agricultural base in the Sawad by maximizing the possibilities of trade. It was a society in which birth counted for less than wealth and in which almost any man endowed with sufficient talents 'could make a fortune or reach the highest positions with little regard for his birth'.[8] As an ever-growing proportion of the subject peoples converted, Islam became free from its associations as the religion of the conquering Arabs. New converts became plain Muslims on a par with other believers. They were no longer, as in Umayyad times, required to become the 'clients' of Arab tribes. The Arabic language now became the *lingua franca* of a vast new international society. 'Islam became a badge, not of a ruling class, but of a cosmopolitan, urban-oriented mass'[9] transcending ethnic and social boundaries.

Historically the 'Abbasid caliphate, though short-lived, was no mean achievement. However, it inevitably failed to satisfy the aspirations of the pious and the revolutionary militants who had sought in the overthrow of the Umayyads a chance to restore the Islamic purity of the Madinese community (which by now was coming to acquire the glow of retrospective perfection). Disillusionment had set in quickly. A Shi'ite revolt in the Hejaz in 762, backing the mahdist claims of Muhammad al-Nafs al-Zakiya ('the Pure Soul'), great-grandson of the martyred Husain's elder brother Hasan, won the support of, among many others, the great jurists Malik and Abu Hanifa. After suppressing the revolt the caliph Mansur had Malik flogged, while Abu Hanifa ended his days in prison. Further Shi'ite revolts, always supported in the Hejaz and its Holy Cities, occurred in 786 (when one of the rebel leaders, Idris ibn 'Abdullah, escaped to the Maghreb, where he founded a kingdom based on Fez), and in 814–15. Most of the *'ulama*, however, expressed their attachment to the *ahl al-bait* less politically. If intellectual activity supplies a psychological substitute for action, then perhaps the development of a rational jurisprudence based on Muhammadan tradition provided an avenue for the pious less dangerous than politics. The outcome of this development was, however, a growing 'culture gap' between the intellectual circles around the court and the popular movement led by the traditionists, the *ahl al-hadith*.

Theological debates

The philosophical and intellectual controversies of early Islam originated in the discussions of the pious intellectuals during the Umayyad era. Their point of departure was essentially political: Umayyad supporters argued that their rule, whatever injustices it entailed, had been decreed by God. The opposition countered by insisting that man, not God, is responsible for evil actions. Out of this discussion arose the more general question of determinism versus free will. Is the sinner predestined to sin, because God is omnipotent? Or is he responsible for his own evil acts, which to some extent limits God's power, since He is bound to punish them? Since advocates of both positions enlisted the Quran in their support, the dispute became involved in the argument, referred to in Chapter 3 (see p. 99), about the status of the divine text. The advocates of predestination argued that the Quran was the 'uncreated' speech of God because it refers to certain specific events which God in His omnipotence and omniscience must have willed and known about. The advocates of free will replied that the Quran clearly insists on human responsibility, as implied in the doctrine of the Day of Judgement; the Quran is thus God's speech, 'created' under certain circumstances – a view which implied that God could have created a different Quran should the circumstances have been different.

The advocates of the 'created' Quran emphasized the references to an 'Arabic' Quran which occur in the divine text; they accused their opponents of a form of *shirk* or bi-theism in allowing that an eternal being – the Quran – coexisted with God. The controversy ranged around the interpretation of the Quran as well as its status. An 'uncreated' Quran, being, as it were, an aspect of the Godhead, was absolutely unchangeable. The decrees of a 'created' Quran, on the other hand, were evidently subject to time and place, and might possibly be overruled by a divinely inspired Imam or caliph. The advocates of free will and 'createdness', who eventually came to be known as the Mu'tazilis, emphasized the uncompromising character of God's unity (*tawhid*). Their conception of the deity, influenced by neo-Platonist ideas, was more remote and abstract than that of the *ahl al-hadith*. They believed that anthropomorphic expressions such as 'God's hand' or 'face' must be understood allegorically, and developed a style of defining God by negation: 'He is not a body, not a form, not flesh nor blood, not an individual, not substance nor attribute . . . etc.'[10] Similarly, the expression 'God's speech', referring to the Quran, must be understood figuratively, since speech, a human function, belongs to the category of 'things created'. Eventually the advocates of the 'uncreated' Quran won the day, but not without a struggle.

During the reign of the 'Abbasid caliph al-Mamun (813–33), the

Mu'tazili intellectuals in court favour were allowed to establish a kind of inquisition, known as the *mihna*, before which the leaders of the *ahl al-hadith* were obliged to proclaim their adherence to the doctrine of the 'created' Quran. Many of them refused to do so, including the redoubtable Ahmad ibn Hanbal, despite torture, imprisonment and threats of death. In 849 the policy was abandoned as a failure, and the government stabilized its position towards the *'ulama*, most of whom supported the *ahl al-hadith*, by conceding them supremacy in matters of doctrine. The dogma that 'the Quran is the speech of God, uncreated' became a shibboleth of Sunni orthodoxy, and Mu'tazili theology was confined to the ranks of the Shi'a until resurrected by Sunni reformers in the last century.

Socially, the victory of the doctrine of the 'uncreated' Quran served to strengthen the role of the *'ulama* as the interpreters of the divine word, making them guardians of the *ijma'* of the community in the face of the absolutism of the rulers. This, of course, gave them considerable social and political power. Theoretically, the Quran was available to everyone. In practice it could only be read and understood by those with a sound knowledge of classical Arabic and access to the works of *tafsir*, or scholarly exegesis. Such scholars, who were drawn from all social classes, effectively counterbalanced the influence of the bureaucrats and ministers (*katibs* and *wazirs*) who clustered round the dynastic courts. This influence was often of a conservative nature, making it difficult for the rulers to introduce changes. But it had the positive effect of counteracting the growing inequality and social stratification which always occur when a ruling elite has a monopoly of education.

The polity which resulted from the compromise between the caliphs and the *'ulama* has been called a 'divine nomocracy' rather than a 'theocracy', for it consisted in a society based on the rule of laws decreed by God, rather than a state governed by someone claiming to be His earthly representative.

Culturally, the theological victory of the *'ulama* gave support to the iconophobic tendencies common to Judaism and some eastern churches. Whereas the Umayyads had employed Byzantine artists to embellish their mosques, palaces and hunting lodges with delightful representations of birds, plants and animals, Islamic art in the mainstream Sunni culture was to develop in a wholly abstract direction. Calligraphy alone was permitted to give revelation a visible form. No images of created things were to be allowed to seduce the mind away from the contemplative absorption of the divine word, that powerful solvent of all mental fixations. With its exuberant variety of styles, its contrasting modes of geometrical rigour and melodious rhythm, Arabic calligraphy became a flamboyant elaboration of the text on the visual plane which complemented the music of its recitative upon the ear.

The Ash'arite synthesis

The theological underpinning of Sunni Islam was completed by Abu al-Hasan al-Ash'ari (873–935) who occupies a moderate position comparable to that of Shafi'i in law. Following the *ahl al-hadith*, Ash'ari held to the doctrine of the 'uncreated' Quran and did his utmost to defend God's omnipotence. Originally a Mu'tazili, he converted to the traditionists after having several dreams during the month of Ramadan, during which the Prophet Muhammad appeared to him and urged him to support 'what was related from himself' – i.e., the *hadith*. Ash'ari promptly abandoned the Mu'tazili camp and went to the other extreme, joining the Hanbalis. However, in a subsequent dream the Prophet appeared once more and, looking somewhat displeased, said to Ash'ari: 'I did not tell you to give up rational arguments, but to support the true *hadiths*!'[11]

Thus inspired, Ash'ari developed a theological position which gave philosophical support to the Quran and the Sunna on the basis of rational arguments. Free will, in Ash'ari's system, was reduced to the bare minimum compatible with personal responsibility on the Day of Judgement. God's omnipotence was illustrated in the famous story of the Three Brothers. The First Brother had a high position in paradise, having lived long and done many good works. The Second Brother had died as a child, and found himself in limbo, on the edge of paradise. The Third Brother, a wicked man, had been consigned to hell. In Ash'ari's story, the Second Brother complained to God that by being made to die early he had been deprived of the opportunity to earn himself a place in paradise by good works. To this God replied that He had foreseen that, had the Second Brother been allowed to grow up, he would have become a sinner, thereby ending up even worse off. On hearing this the Third Brother cried out angrily from hell, asking God why He had not cut him off early, before he had committed the sins which brought him there. To this, of course, there was no answer.

Ash'ari's point was similar to Alexander Pope's 'Presume not God to scan!' God's omnipotence and his omnibenevolence cannot be reconciled within the bounds of ordinary logic. By the same argument, the Quran, God's revelation, cannot be subjected to rational explanations. The anthropomorphisms and the eschatology must be taken as they stand, not metaphorically, 'without specifying how' (*bi la kaif*) God, as Creator, may ultimately be responsible for evil in this world, but this detracts neither from His goodness nor from the responsibility of men for their actions. The Ash'aris rationalized God's omnipotence within an atomistic theory of creation, according to which the world was made up of discrete points in space and time whose only connection was the Will of God which created them anew at every moment. Such a world of course implied the possibility of miracles. For, although natural laws were no different from 'God's custom', there was nothing to prevent the Creator from breaching them at will. Accounts of prophetic miracles in the Quran could thus be taken literally, while attention was focused on their purpose within the overall context of the divine message.

The Ash'ari system was 'philosophically anti-philosophical', rather in the manner that Shafi'i's jurisprudence was rationalistically anti-rational. Both thinkers erected impressive intellectual defences in order to uphold the Sunni consensus in favour of the primacy of revelation – the unique and unrepeatable irruption of the divine into human history represented by the Quran and the Prophet's Sunna. The Mu'tazilis and their philosopher successors had fought for the primacy of reason, in the belief that a God who was good could not be other than rational. Though they produced such outstanding thinkers as Farabi, Ibn Sina (Avicenna) and Ibn Rushd (Averroës), the rationalists were never able to acquire a substantial following among the urban *'ulama* – though they were patronized and inspired by the more elitist Shi'ite leaders. For the 'Abbasid caliphs, and thence for the great majority of the rulers who succeeded them, Quranic literalism and *taqlid* (imitation of the established authorities in matters of doctrine and law) were an intellectual price that had to be paid for the continuing loyalty of the urban populations. Freedom in ideas and social equality are not always found to be compatible.

The systematic philosophers like Farabi and Ibn Sina tried hard to limit the cleavage between philosophy and dogma by pursuing their speculations within the framework of *tawhid* (divine unity). However, the attempt to synthesize the remote and abstract God of the philosophers with the all-pervasive and omnipresent deity of the Quran was never successful in the sense of becoming socially acceptable. The philosophers tried to maintain the principle of Quranic infallibility by arguing that it contained one message, to be understood literally, for the masses and another for the philosophical elite who were entitled, by virtue of superior intelligence, to interpret scripture allegorically. Such elitism, however, went against the populist grain of urban Sunni Islam and the systems of the philosophers were confined mainly to the sectarian Shi'a groups, or re-emerged, heavily disguised, as the products of gnosis in the writings of the Higher Sufis.

The Shi'ite 'ulama

There was, however, an alternative to the swamping of rational exegesis by populist sentiment masquerading as the defence of revelation against the attacks of reason. This was the path, chosen by the Shi'a, of enlightened spiritual leadership. Unlike the *ahl al-sunna*, the Shi'a found in the doctrine of the Imamate a device which enabled them to erect a quasi-sacerdotal structure within the framework of Islam. The Shi'ite *'ulama* were not endowed with any formal sacerdotal authority: there are no sacraments in Islam and nothing comparable to the medieval Catholic doctrine that certain rituals are automatically efficacious, even when performed by wicked and corrupt priests. Nevertheless the Shi'ite idea of *nass* (designation) contains a notion of spiritual succession broadly comparable to the Apostolic succession in the Catholic priesthood. This in turn permits a flexibility in the interpretation of scripture on the part of the Imams or their representatives, who are assumed to be in possession of the understanding necessary to reveal the innermost truths contained in them.

The idea of *nass* was closely associated with another aspect of Shi'ism, namely that the Quran contains esoteric meanings that can only be properly interpreted by the Imams of the *ahl al-bait*. The divine text itself states:

He it is who has bestowed upon thee from on high this divine writ, containing messages that are clear in and by themselves – and these are the essences of the divine writ – as well as others that are allegorical . . . (3:7)

For the Shi'a, the esoteric interpretation of the Quran (*tawil*) opened the way for a spiritual elite capable of exercising considerable social power. A modern Shi'ite text explains:

. . . *tawil* or hermeneutic interpretation of the Holy Quran is not concerned simply with the demonstration of words. Rather it is concerned with certain truths and realities that transcend the comprehension of the common run of men; yet it is from these truths and realities that the principles of doctrine and the practical injunctions of the Quran issue forth.

The whole of the Quran possesses the sense of *tawil*, of esoteric meaning, which cannot be comprehended directly through human thought alone. Only the Prophets and the pure among the Saints of God who are free from the dross of human imperfection can contemplate these meanings while living on the present plane of existence. On the Day of Resurrection the *tawil* of the Quran will be revealed to everyone.[12]

In the earliest period of the Shi'a only the 'sinless' Imams of the *ahl al-bait* could provide authoritative interpretation of the scriptures. Even today, Shi'ites of the Twelver (Imami) tradition only accept as authoritative clarifications of the Quran which come from the Prophet himself or members of his family.

The spiritual and intellectual elitism of the Shi'a is projected back on to the authority of the Imams of the *ahl al-bait*, all of whom (apart from 'Ali and Husain) are said to have been poisoned at the behest of the Umayyad or 'Abbasid caliphs. Whatever the truth of these traditions, they illustrate and to some extent serve to justify the deep ambivalence existing in Shi'ite Islam towards the exercise of political power.

The sanctity of the Imams of the Shi'a, together with their spiritual authority, increased with their distance from political power. The main body of the Twelver Shi'a came, in effect, to recognize that exercising political power could only undermine their spiritual authority. They found the solution to the resulting dilemma by announcing that the last of their living Imams, Muhammad al-Muntazar, had finally 'disappeared' in 940, to reappear at the end of the world as the promised *mahdi*, to 'fill the earth with equity and justice as it was filled with oppression and tyranny'. This doctrine of *ghaiba* (occultation) enabled moderate Shi'ites to come to terms with the *de facto* political authority of the 'Abbasids without according them *de jure* recognition. The solution was not radically different from that of the Sunni *'ulama*, who likewise chose *de facto* acceptance of the monarchy as the preferable alternative to anarchy. The difference for the Shi'a, however, was that their *'ulama* came to exercise authority on behalf of the Imam *in absentia* – a fact which, combined with the greater emphasis placed upon the esoteric meanings of the scriptures, endowed them with proportionally greater intellectual and spiritual authority.

The effect of the moderate Shi'ite 'Twelver' compromise became apparent within a decade or so of the last Imam's 'disappearance'. By the mid tenth century the 'Abbasid caliphs' temporal power had effectively disintegrated. Where Shi'ite movements failed to gain out-right control, provincial governors became autonomous and founded hereditary dynasties, or local tribesmen seized power, giving the caliph only nominal allegiance. In 945 a Shi'ite dynasty, the Buyids, actually established itself in Baghdad. However, the leader, who called himself 'Amir al-Umara' ('Commander-in-Chief'), acknowledged the theoretical supremacy of the 'Abbasid caliph and made no sustained effort to force the *'ulama* to adopt Shi'ite theological attitudes or to acknowledge the authority of the 'Hidden Imam' or his representatives. It was to be another five centuries before Twelver Shi'ism established itself as the official doctrine of the Iranian state.

Despite its early compromises with the temporal power Shi'ite Islam has continued to exercise its potential for revolutionary mobilization – or, to be more accurate, to provide the ideological underpinning for revolutionary movements – for more than a millennium, from the early tenth century to the present day. Time and again, the millenarian doctrines associated with the *mahdi* have proved an effective means of mobilizing popular discontent: a pretender who claimed descent from the *ahl al-bait* and proclaimed himself the promised messiah was automatically assured the support of a sizeable section of the community. Not surprisingly, Shi'ism in its radical versions has had a natural attraction for tribal and other solidarity groups seeking to replace the political power.

The Fatimids

Prior to the establishment of Iranian national Shi'ism in the sixteenth century the most successful movement of this kind was that which led to the founding of the Fatimid dynasty in North Africa. Like other more radical Shi'ite groups, the Fatimids were Isma'ilis, followers of Isma'il ibn Ja'far, elder son of the Sixth Imam, who predeceased his father. The Isma'ilis believe that before Isma'il's death Ja'far had already chosen him as his successor by *nass* (explicit designation), and that prior to his own death Isma'il in turn so designated his own son Muhammad. Isma'ilis are sometimes known as 'Seveners', since, according to them, Isma'il ought to have been the Seventh Imam. The 'Twelvers', or Imamis, as the mainstream body of the Shi'a are called, deny this, claiming that Ja'far passed over Isma'il for the succession either because he pre-deceased his father or because he committed the sin of drinking wine. The Seventh Imam of the Twelvers is Ja'far's second son, Musa al-Kazim, who died of poisoning on the orders of Harun al-Rashid in 799.

In the differences between Twelvers and Seveners much more is involved, however, than a mere dispute about the succession. The early Isma'ilis belonged to the extreme 'batinist' persuasion, which placed the most emphasis on the esoteric (*batini*) meanings of the Quran. Their intellectual temperament was elitist and conspiratorial. Aware of the dangers to which they were exposed, they practised *taqiya* or dissimulation, protecting themselves against accusations of disbelief and preserving from the prying eyes of the ignorant the secret knowledge they believed themselves to possess.

For the Imamis the doctrine of the Hidden Imam conveniently disposed of the problem of the Imamate, with its potential for creating political and religious factionalism. However, there would always be those for whom the *de facto* acceptance of existing political authority and an unjust social order would seem to represent a fundamental betrayal of Islam's activist message. The Prophet had transmitted God's Word, around which he had built the first Islamic community. His actions as a statesman and leader had also been inspired, or even controlled, by God. It was but a small step from this to seeing in his person an immanence or manifestation of the deity: a step which the Christians had taken with their belief in incarnation. Those who identified themselves with the dissenting tradition associated with the *ahl al-bait* naturally saw this immanence as descending, by *nass* designation, down the line of the Imams. Indeed the extremists (*ghulat*) among them made the First Imam, 'Ali, the equal, if not the superior, of the Prophet.

The elevation of 'Ali to almost god-like status occurred in gradual stages. The first consisted in placing rather more emphasis upon the *batini* (esoteric) than the *zahiri* (exoteric) interpretation of the Quran. Although the Prophet was assumed to have the special *'ilm* or secret knowledge necessary to understand the secret meanings of the scripture, the fact that as an archetypal figure he featured so largely in Sunni tradition encouraged the exaggerators among the batinists to place more emphasis upon the Imamate of 'Ali and his successors: this was the second stage. The third stage – only achieved by such extremist communities as the 'Alawis (Nusairis) and Druzes of Syria, the 'Ali Ilahis of Iran and the Nizari (Aga Khanid) Isma'ilis or Khojas of India – entailed the elevation of 'Ali and the Imams to a position not far below the deity – a belief regarded with horror by all the Sunnis and most other Shi'ites. However, because these beliefs involve a flexibility of scriptural interpretation denied to the *ahl al-zahir* and the Sunni consensus, they allow for the accommodation of antinomian, revolutionary, rationalist and syncretist tendencies. The Imams or their representatives – following the example of the 'Abbasids – found it possible to activate eschatological expectations by declaring themselves to be the long-awaited *mahdi*. In at least one case they took this a stage further by taking it upon themselves to abrogate the Shari'a, announcing that, spiritually speaking, the Day of Judgement had come.[13] Intellectually they freed themselves from the confines of received knowledge (integral to the doctrine of revelation) to indulge in free-range speculative thinking in philosophy and metaphysics. Thus in spite of their religious isolation, they exercised a considerable influence on Islamic intellectual culture. At the more popular level, they permitted the accommodation within a broad Islamic framework of some of the earlier religious traditions of West Asia and the Indian Subcontinent: in particular the pre-Hellenistic and Hellenistic cults of ancient Syria (among the 'Alawis and Druzes), the gnostic traditions of the Zoroastrians in Iran, and the Hindu–Avatar traditions of Iran and northern India.

Extreme or antinomian religious positions can often be related to socio-economic factors, although the traditions to which they give rise may eventually acquire an autonomous existence. Ideas – whether or not these are expressed religiously – are sometimes like time-bombs waiting to be activated at the right moment. As an influence on medieval Islam, batinism had a somewhat similar function to that of Marxism during the earlier part of the twentieth century, rationalizing revolts and occasionally guiding the actions of the leaders of popular movements and the founders of radical new dynasties. Because such movements occurred within a society in which pastoralism exercised a major influence and the principal social structure was the family based on patrilineal kinship, they were usually described in terms of allegiance to allegedly ancestral figures from the *ahl al-bait* and the Imams descended from them, rather than in terms of a particular set of ideas or the individuals propagating them. Thus schisms, intellectual rivalries or ideological differences were usually presented as disputes about the succession. In this way the group allegiances characteristic of the early Arabian Islam came to inform the much wider urban-based Islamic political culture. In the Christian and post-Christian West we find Arians, Nestorians, Donatists, Manichaeans, Lutherans, Calvinists, and so on down to the Marxists, Leninists and Trotskyists of our own day, all of them adherents of ideological or religious movements labelled with the names of their founders. In contrast, most of the groups formed in the earliest period of Islam (roughly up to the tenth century), including 'Alawis, Fatimids, Isma'ilis, Musta'lis, Taiyibis, Nizaris and so forth, all of whom claimed allegiance to members of the *ahl al-bait*, are defined, as in most segmentary tribal formations, at a point of bifurcation in a common family tree.

The Isma'ili hierarchies

The central tradition among the *ghulas* or *batinis* is the Isma'ili one. Most of the splinter-groups associated with it, including the Qarmatis (long defunct), the Druzes, the Nizaris (Khojas or Aga Khanids) and the Musta'lis (Bohoras), share a common heritage of religious and theosophical ideas which set them apart from the mainstream of Islam. Some of these ideas would later emerge in the teachings of the Sufi masters and so find their way back into the central tradition. The central concept, as in the Quran itself, is that of *tawhid*, the Divine Unity. The *batini* thinkers took the Mu'tazili rejection of any kind of anthropomorphism or 'Association' (*shirk*) to its logical conclusion:

Allah, in His majestic unity, stands totally above and aloof from the chains of cosmic and spiritual entities . . . No attributes derived from sense experience can be attributed to Allah, no efforts of the human imagination, however fertile and far-reaching, can grasp His unique nature; and no analogy, comparison or resemblance can be drawn between Him and His creatures. Indeed, Allah is asserted to be beyond even the categories of being and non-being, of existence and non-existence.[14]

The cosmos comes into being through the Universal Intellect (*'aql al-kull*), representing a final principle of logic, order and reason. This in turn engenders a principle of animation known as the *nafs al-kull* (universal self/soul), which, by informing a combination of elements (the earth, air, fire and water of traditional medieval science), formed the mineral, vegetable and animal orders of the physical world. A contrary motion proceeds back through this hierarchy of compound beings to the *'aql al-kull*. The return to the ultimate source of being which the Sufis sought by the mystics' path was, for the Isma'ilis, primarily intellectual. They saw themselves as a hierarchy of worshippers seeking rational truth on ever higher levels, a hierarchy culminating in the Imam, or, rather, his ancestor 'Ali, representing the *nafs al-kull*, the principle of universal animation which set the whole community in motion.

This system, typically rationalistic and hierarchical, embodied many Ptolemaic and neoplatonic ideas; in due course it managed to accommodate Zoroastrian and Vedic influences as well. While accepting revelation as the core of its epistemology – for the Isma'ilis knowledge was acquired spiritually, by means of gnosis – it was also supra-rational: the cosmos had a miraculous coherence and order, proceeding as it did from the Universal Intellect. Being essentially speculative and antidogmatic, the system proved, like theosophical Sufism, with which it later became intermixed, less hostile to scientific inquiry than the scripturalist mainstream of Sunni Islam. In its own time the *batini* tradition particularly encouraged mathematics as an instrument for freeing the mind from bodily images and attachments, and complex numerological patterns were elaborated around the One. Unlike most modern science, however, it did not proceed from an ontological or metaphysical vacuum: scientific inquiry was a kind of meditation on nature, a fleshing out with facts of underlying assumptions accepted as part of revelation. In such a world-view scientific inquiry becomes a form of *tafsir*, or exegesis, an interpretation or discovery of truths already given.

Modern Muslim writers, such as Sayyid Ahmed Khan and Muhammad Iqbal, who sought to harmonize religious truth with modern scientific discovery, found much to inspire them in the writings of the Ikhwan al-Safa ('Brothers of Purity'), a group of Isma'ili-influenced speculative thinkers writing at Basra in the early tenth century. The early Isma'ilis also exerted considerable influence on the development of Muslim philosophy. The father of Ibn Sina (Avicenna 980–1037) was a convert to Isma'ilism. Another Isma'ili convert, Nasir al-Din al-Tusi (d. 1274), proposed a new model of planetary motion which Copernicus may have learned of through Byzantine and Greek sources. Tusi himself established an astronomical observatory which became the model of the earliest European observatories of Tycho Brahe and Kepler.

The *batini* systems contained some ingenious routes for linking their cosmology with human history. Drawing on Pythagorean, Babylonian and Chaldean traditions, they became fascinated with number analogies, mystic numerals and letters, which they incorporated into a complicated hiero-history of prophetic emanations. Each age had a prophet who was accompanied by an *asas*, or 'silent one', who understood the inner meanings of revelation. (Moses had Aaron, Jesus had Peter, Muhammad had 'Ali, and so forth.) It is not difficult to see how, if the *batini* meaning of the Quran were stressed above the *zahiri*, 'Ali would supplant Muhammad in the minds of the believers.

Sectarian offshoots of the Shi'a, including the Nusairis ('Alawis) of Syria and the Druze community (now divided between Syria, Israel and Lebanon), produced their own distinctive versions of these hierarchies. The Nusairis developed a trinitarian doctrine of emanation, in the persons of Muhammad, 'Ali and Salman al-Farisi. (The last, a Persian freedman and Companion of the Prophet, featured very largely in Shi'ite tradition, partly, no doubt, because he was the first Muslim with whom the *mawali* could identify.)

Central to the extreme Shi'a doctrines, is the role of the Imam, usually traced through the line of Isma'il ibn Ja'far. Two of the most successful Isma'ili movements benefited from the presence of a living Imam able to command powerful group loyalties and to activate them for political and social aims. One of them led to the founding of the Fatimid dynasty which ruled Egypt for nearly two centuries. The other has survived into our own time, in the remarkable community headed by the Aga Khan.

The cult of the sacred person is, in one form or another, as central to Shi'ism as it is to Christianity. Whereas Sunni egalitarianism called upon all men to accept a minimum number of injunctions and symbols derived from the unique and unrepeatable event of the Quranic revelation and the Life of the Prophet, Shi'ism graded men into a hierarchy in accordance with the stage they had reached in the pursuit of spiritual knowledge. In a medieval social system contained within the material limits of a modest agricultural surplus, such a hierarchy represented an ideological complement to the existing social order. Whereas the Sunni ideal of social equality remained largely unrealized, Shi'ite elitism proved, time and again, a potent instrument for effecting social and political change.

The Imam was the microcosm, the perfect man in whom the divine intelligence was manifested. The idea of a hypostatic union between the human and the divine need not necessarily be attributed to Christian influences. It finds expression in much more ancient cultures throughout the world. In the Islamic heartland it formed part of the tradition of Egypt, South Arabia and Persia. As Hodgson has pointed out:

> The infallible Imam as such was not so hard for any Medieval to conceive of. Given an approach to knowledge as a finite quantity of foreordained facts – rather than a process of inquiry within experience – it could seem not impossible that some person, by inheritance or by nature, should possess all of these facts.[15]

The Imamate could be activated either directly by a claimant from the *ahl al-bait*, or indirectly through someone claiming to be his deputy. In either event the source of its political power lay in the network of *da'is* or missionaries acting on his behalf.

Isma'ili antinomianism

The *da'is* were highly trained in the esoteric sciences. Like the Jesuits of the Counter-Reformation, they were taught to sound out their targets carefully before declaring themselves. They rarely indulged in polemics or openly engaged their opponents. Indeed, there is a close parallel between the various *da'i* networks and the esoteric doctrines preached by them. They adopted the practice of *taqiya*, concealment of one's true beliefs, to protect themselves from persecution. In consequence they deemed it prudent to preach not frankly but allusively, according to a kind of 'code'. Such a practice was bound to reinforce the elitist idea that the 'truth' was only known to the innermost members of the movement – i.e., those *da'is* who were closest to the Hidden Imam. Those extreme Shi'ite sects which eventually crystallized into closed communities, such as the 'Alawis and Druzes, developed elaborate rites of initiation to protect these 'secret' truths, endowing them with a mystique which made outsiders suppose that they were too dangerous for general consumption. Opponents of these movements naturally imagined the worst of them. Accusations of paganism and sexual promiscuity were made against Qarmatis, Nusairis and Druzes. More significant was the extent to which the habit of coded communication affected the development of their actual doctrines, and this helps to explain how, paradoxically, the more esoteric traditions espoused by them proved more compatible with intellectual modernization. As Hodgson remarks with his usual penetration, it was natural for them to suppose that

... even the Author of the Universe Himself will adopt an allusive way of speaking on subtle matters, both in revealed books and in the very laws of nature. Now if one is thus persuaded that God may speak in cipher, as it were, it is not absurd to seek for the traces of such a cipher; and if a code is suggested which gives consistent results whenever applied in God's works, there will be a high presumption that it is the right one. This is what the Isma'ilis thought they had in their *tawil*, their system of interpretation which they applied so freely, both to sacred books and to all nature.[16]

The first Isma'ili movement to make a major impact upon Muslim society was started by Hamdan Qarmat in the latter part of the ninth century. He seems to have begun his mission (*da'wa*) in Kufa during the 860s as part of a wider movement against the 'Abbasid caliphate conducted in the name of Muhammad ibn Isma'il. In the tenth century the Qarmatis founded a dynastic state based on Bahrain which achieved notoriety in 969 when its leader occupied Makka and carried off the Black Stone. The Qarmatis are said to have practised a form of communism, in which all personal property, including animals, jewellery and furniture, was pooled. It was even claimed that women were held in common. However, most of these reports came from their enemies and need to be treated cautiously. The Isma'ili writer Nasir i-Khusraw was highly impressed by the level of justice, internal order and social welfare he found in the Bahraini state, although public prayers and fasting had been abolished. The Qarmati state in Bahrain survived until 1077, when it was overrun by beduin tribesmen.

The most far-reaching dynasty created by the Isma'ilis was that of the Fatimids (so-called because they legitimized themselves by claiming descent from 'Ali and Fatima), who established themselves in North Africa in 909 and conquered Egypt sixty years later. North of Fustat, near the site of ancient Memphis, they built themselves a fine new capital of gardens and palaces which they named al-Qahira (Cairo), 'the Victorious One'. At its height, Fatimid power extended from the Atlas mountains to Sind. They ruled in Ifriqiya (Tunisia), Egypt, Syria, the Hejaz, Yemen and Oman at a time when, under its Buyid overlords, the 'Abbasid caliphate was confined to Mesopotamia and the Iranian plateau.

The original base for Fatimid power had been in Qairawan, in what is now Tunisia, where an Isma'ili *da'i*, 'Ubaidallah, proclaimed himself *mahdi* in 909, gaining the support of the Kutama Berbers of western Algeria. Although his claims were rejected by *da'is* loyal to Hamdan Qarmat in Syria and Khurasan, after the conquest of Egypt in 969, during the reign of the fourth Fatimid ruler, al-Mu'izz, most of the *da'is* in Persia, Sind, Syria and Yemen came round to recognition of the new caliphate. Although the Isma'ili venture was to end in failure – they never succeeded in uniting the whole of Islam under a new Fatimid caliphate – they governed successfully as Imam–Caliphs for more than a century before succumbing like their 'Abbasid rivals to the domination of their troops. Their political influence extended a network of *da'is* operating everywhere except Spain and the central 'Abbasid territories. For a time they were recognized in the holy cities of Makka and Madina, which greatly enhanced their prestige, since it gave them control of the Hajj. For one glorious year (1058) Fatimid rule was even proclaimed in Baghdad, when a dissident Turkish general decided to recognize the Cairo caliph. But they never persuaded the Shi'ite Buyids to recognize them as legitimate descendants of 'Ali. Soon afterwards the remaining 'Abbasid lands and most of Syria were overrun by the Seljuk Turks, who remained staunchly Sunni and chose to preserve the formal office of the Baghdad caliphate.

By developing Cairo as an entrepôt between the Mediterranean and the Indian Ocean, building up their sea power and controlling much of the trade between Europe and the Indies, the Fatimids made the Egyptian capital a great centre of culture and learning. They founded al-Azhar (reputedly named after Fatima al-Zahra) as a training centre for their *da'is*. Said to be the world's oldest university, it is still the leading institution of religious learning in the Muslim world, though long since, of course, a bastion of Sunnism. The elegant keel-form arches surmounting the delicate colonnades of al-Azhar's central court-yard are still a reminder of the excellent architectural taste of the Fatimid era.

The decline of the Fatimids began when strife broke out among their Sudanese and Turkish troops, and ended with the Crusader attacks and the rising Seljuk power in the East. In 1171 Salah al-Din al-Ayyubi (known to the West as 'Saladin'), a Kurdish general who had risen in the service of the Seljuks, took power in Syria and Egypt after reconquering Jerusalem from the Franks, and restored the Sunni con-sensus as the most generally accepted doctrine in the Middle East.

The Fatimid legacy

The Isma'ili attempt to win the whole of Dar al-Islam for their Imams resulted, eventually, in failure. But it leaves a legacy in three religious sects which have survived into the present – the Druzes, the Bohoras and the Khojas.

The Druzes are far removed from the mainstream of Islam, having carried their belief in the divine Imamate to the point where they may be said to constitute a separate religion. Named after an Isma'ili *da'i* named Darazi, who taught that the third Fatimid caliph Hakim (r. 996–1021) was in effect the personification of the *'aql al-kull* (the cosmic intellect), Druzism became the ideology of a peasant revolt in what is now Lebanon where most of the community resides. Like other Shi'ites the Druze are allowed to practise *taqiya* (concealment of their true beliefs) to avoid persecution which allowed them to adopt a modified version of the Hanafi *fiqh*, official *madhhab* of the Ottoman Empire. They practise endogamy, insisting on equal treatment for men and women in marriage, and, with rare exceptions, refuse converts.

In a simplified version of the Isma'ili hierarchy, which distinguishes between the enlightened leadership around the Imam and the masses for whom the truth is dangerous, the Druzes are divided into two ranks, the *ʿaqils* ('sages') and *jahils* ('ignorant ones'). The *ʿaqils*, who may include women, are initiated into the inner secrets of the faith after passing a series of rigorous spiritual tests. They are required to live sober, devout lives, supported by the toil of their hands. They must avoid stimulants and participation in raids or feuding. The more respected among them become *shaikhs*, presiding over weddings, funerals and other religious functions. The *jahils* are allowed more personal licence than the *ʿaqils*, but it is assumed that they will be denied spiritual growth. They may, however, have the chance of initiation in a future life, for, like Hindus and some Greek gnostics, the Druzes believe in the transmigration of souls. The *jahils* believe that there is a finite number of souls in the community, and that a dead person's spirit enters the next child to be born. While such popular beliefs clearly reinforce Druze *ʿasabiya*, the *ʿaqils* appear to have a much more sophisticated and developed theology, including emanationist ideas derived from neoplatonism and Vedic sources, and some of the pantheistic doctrines common to Ibn 'Arabi and other Sufi writers.

Like other religious minorities who sought refuge in the Lebanese Mountain, the Druzes acquired feudal overlords who, in return for the protection they offered, were encouraged to adopt the religion of their clients. The most outstanding were the Ma'n family, who under the Amir Fakhr al-Din II (1590–1635) controlled the whole of Mount Lebanon, the Shouf and the Hawran region, as well as much of northern Galilee. Although in the eighteenth century power passed to the Shih-abs, a Sunni family claiming Quraishi descent, some of whose leaders converted to Maronite Christianity, the Druzes continued to provide the Lebanese amir's military underpinning. Since the eighteenth century, the leading Druze overlords have been the Arslans and the Jumblats, a family of Kurdish origin.

Although their power has declined since the seventeenth century the Druze have displayed impressive group allegiance in recent times. When Israel backed the Druzes' historic rivals, the Christian Maronites, during the 1975–84 civil war, Druze militias controlled the central part of Lebanon – the Shouf – pushing back the Maronites and the Israelis, who were reluctant to disarm the Druze for fear of mutiny among Druzes serving in the Israeli armed forces. Uniquely among Arabs living under Israeli rule, Palestinian Druzes are permitted to serve in the army.

The Isma'ilis

The most remarkable relic of medieval Isma'ilism is the Khoja community of India, best known through the person of its Imam, the Aga Khan, who claims descent from Nizar, a Fatimid pretender who died in prison after having been deposed. Like other Isma'ili splinter-groups, including the Musta'lis who survive in India's Bohora community, the Nizari *da'is* abandoned the Fatimid caliphate in its declining years and established an autonomous *da'wa* enabling them to survive, and eventually prosper, as a community. The Nizari Isma'ilis, whose adherents now live in India, Pakistan, Tajikistan, China, Syria, Europe, East Africa and Canada, have become a wealthy religious sect. Their Imam, Aga Khan IV, controls a vast business empire which includes more than seventy industrial enterprises in Asia and Africa, newspapers in East Africa, hotels, supermarkets and stud farms in Europe, not to mention untold investments in international companies. Curiously enough, this eminently respectable trading community was once a byword for political terrorism, and gave the world a term – assassination – which described its principal tactic.

The 'Assassins' attacked the Seljuk armies from their strongholds in Iran and Syria. They specialized in killing the commanders, since this usually caused the Seljuk formations, bound by personal loyalties, to disband. Although their famous last stronghold at Alamut was overrun by the Mongols in the 1250s, the Nizaris survived as an underground movement in Iran and Syria and prospered in Gujerat, where the *da'is* had made a number of converts from among the Hindu merchant castes. The basis of the sect's modern revival was a decision by the Bombay High Court in 1866 to award the tithes of this now wealthy Indian merchant community to the Nizari Imam, Aga Khan I, who had recently arrived from Persia after quarrelling with the Shah. The Aga Khan and his successors used the wealth so acquired not only to amass personal fortunes but to win for the community a 'place in the sun' of the British Empire. The Aga Khan's spiritual authority has enabled him to impose religious and legal obligations on his followers which have allowed them to adjust to modern conditions without loss of religious faith – something which Sunni Islam, with its legalistic and literalistic traditions, has found much harder to achieve. The Isma'ilis have become the world's most prosperous Islamic community outside the oil regions; it is a community, moreover, whose prosperity has been achieved as a result of its own efforts under a succession of astute and capable 'living Imams'.

As well as funding heath and education projects in East Africa, India, Pakistan and Tajikistan, the Aga Khan's organization has been active in conserving the historic fabric of many places threatened with urban development such as the old quarters of Zanzibar and Cairo. The Aga Khan Award for Architecture – one of the largest prizes in the world – encourages architectural innovations that harmonize with Islamic social traditions without slavishly imitating the past.

Another Shi'ite faction which has survived and gained some prominence – as well as notoriety – in recent times is the Nusairi community based on Latakia in Syria. The Nusairis (generally known as 'Alawis) trace their *isnads* back to Ibn Nusair, a notable of Basra who proclaimed himself *bab* ('gate') to the Tenth Imam of the Shi'a, 'Ali Naqi, in 859. During the tenth century his movement gained a following in northern Syria among people thought by some scholars to be of Phoenician descent. The movement also seems to have been influenced by Qarmati ideas circulating in the same area during this period. Like the Druzes, whom they resemble theologically, the 'Alawis are an initiatory sect who keep their secrets closely guarded. Little was known about them until 1863 when one Sulaiman Effendi of Adana converted to Christianity and published one of their texts.

According to 'Alawi belief, manifestations of God occur cyclically in three persons. In the Muslim era this trinity consisted of 'Ali, Muhammad and Salman al-Farisi; previous manifestations included Aristotle, Plato and Socrates. There is an elaborate cosmology relating these manifestations to the planets. Like the Druzes, the 'Alawis believe in the transmigration of souls and think that each human soul will one day return to its primordial state as a star. 'Alawi doctrine evidently contains many traces of pre-Islamic beliefs, including Christianity, neoplatonic Judaism and ancient Syro-Phoenician Sabaism.

A hardy peasant people with a long tradition of self-protection, the 'Alawis proved excellent soldiers, able and willing to counter the growing weight of Sunni-based nationalism in the cities. Under the aegis of the Arab nationalist Ba'ath party a number of 'Alawi families acquired a predominant position in the Syrian armed forces, including the President Hafez al-Asad, who came to power in 1970. 'Alawi dominance, allied to other social, political and economic factors, led to a state of virtual civil war in Syria between 1979 and 1982, culminating in the abortive Muslim Brotherhood rebellion in Hama, suppressed at an estimated cost of 10,000 lives.

Shi'ism and Iran

The most dramatic manifestation of Shi'ite radicalism in modern times occurred within the main body of the Twelvers or Imamis, when the fall of the Pahlavi monarchy in 1979 and its replacement by the militantly 'Islamic' government headed by Ayatollah Khomeini created an upheaval in international relations as drastic as any since the Second World War. Its main lines of development were laid down from the sixteenth century.

About ten per cent of all Muslims are Shi'ites of the Imami (Twelver) faith. Most of them are concentrated in Iran and its peripheral territories – Pakistan and Afghanistan to the east, Turkmenistan and Azerbaijan to the north, Turkey, Iraq, Bahrain and the Saudi province of Hasa to the west. There is also a semi-autonomous Shi'ite community in the strife-torn region of southern Lebanon. The distribution of Shi'ites around the Iranian highlands and in areas, such as Bahrain, once subject to Persian rule is not accidental. Since the sixteenth century Shi'ism has been the religious ideology of the regimes holding power in Iran and such territories as the fortunes of war brought into its orbit.

From the beginning there were elements in the Shi'ite faith which made it particularly appealing to the Persians. The dispossession of 'Ali and his clan from their rightful inheritance by the worldly Umayyads was a cause with which non-Arabs could readily identify. Many of the Persian *mawali* supported the 'Abbasid revolution, which, before it developed into a new, expanded Arab caliphate, represented the claims of Islamic universalism against the tribal *'asabiya* of the Umayyads, whose behaviour so often resembled that of their Quraishi ancestors. The doctrine of the Imamate was well suited to the needs of non-Arabs without direct access to the Quran through oral or written media. Whereas any illiterate beduin could both hear and memorize passages from the divine text, Persian speakers needed to have it transmitted to them through mediators who, in due course, were represented as acting on behalf of the Hidden Imam. Moreover Imamism was able to act as an Islamic bearer of Persian national and cultural values. Whereas Byzantium survived the Muslim conquest for eight centuries, remaining a beacon of hope for defeated Eastern Christianity, Sassanid Persia had been destroyed completely. The Churches survived as protected communities, but Zoroastrianism, though granted scriptural status, all but disappeared. As an 'opposition' movement within Islam, Shi'ism supplied an ideological alternative to a Sunnism which, with its overwhelming emphasis on an Arabic text, represented the official ideology of the conquerors. The Shi'ites could look on their rulers as usurpers without rejecting the broader religious and cultural framework of Islam.

There were also historic figures who symbolized the link between Shi'ism and Persian national identity. As has already been suggested, Salman al-Farisi, the freedman who allegedly instructed the Muslims in digging the *khandaq* (ditch) which saved Madina from the Quraishi cavalry, loomed large in the *batini* tradition partly, one suspects, because of his Persian origin and his unusual standing as one of the earliest non-Arab Companions. (For similar reasons the Abyssinian Bilal has latterly become a cult-figure among some American Black Muslims.) The Fourth Imam, Zain al-'Abidin, also known as Sajjad, was the son of the martyred Husain by the daughter of Yazdigird, last of the Sassanid kings. Thus most of the Imams of the Shi'a had the Persian blood royal running through their veins. Among other things, the messianic expectation of a *mahdi* from this line conveyed the hope of a deliverance of Persia from the Arab conquest (rather as the Jewish messiah was expected to come from the Royal House of David).

There were intellectual factors as well. The potential for rationalization contained in the *batini* tradition seems to have had a particular appeal for thinkers of Persian ancestry. Ibn Sina (Avicenna) was the son of a convert to Isma'ilism, and though he broke with the *batinis* he absorbed much of their method and overall approach. The spiritualizing aspect of Shi'ism, contrasting with the public and formal religiosity of the Arabs, also found some *rapport* with Persian tradition. Like Augustinian Christianity, Shi'ism was profoundly influenced by the Manichaean dichotomy between the material and the spiritual, a dualism entrenched in the distinction between *batini* and *zahiri* interpretations of the Quran. Imami Shi'ism thus eventually became a suitable bearer of Persian cultural values and assumptions within the framework of Islam. The eventual 'Shi'ization' of Iran, however, was not accomplished without compulsion.

The Safavids

The Safavid dynasty which ruled in Iran from 1501 to 1722 was the first in Islamic history to make Shi'ism a state religion. Previously Shi'ite rulers, including the Buyids and Fatimids, had been content to claim a Shi'ite legitimacy for their power, leaving most of their subjects to practise Sunnism. The network of *da'is* emanating from Egypt during the height of Fatimid power seems to have been more concerned with extending Islam in far-reaching territories or attacking their 'Abbasid enemies than with consolidating Isma'ilism in Egypt; this was one reason why Saladin encountered practically no opposition when he assumed full power in Cairo.

The Safavids were originally Sunni Azeris from the highlands of Azerbaijan in north-west Persia. Their eponymous ancestor, Shaikh Safi al-Din Ishaq (d. 1334), had become leader of a local Sufi order, extending his authority among the semi-nomadic Turcoman tribesmen who eventually became the elite corps of the Safavid forces. The movement does not appear to have acquired a Shi'ite character for at least a century. It eventually did so probably in order to distinguish itself from the rising Ottoman power in the West and to enlist the support of Shi'ite elements, not only in Iran, but in Syria and Anatolia as well. The founder of the dynasty, Shah Isma'il I, who seized power in Tabriz in 1501 and extended his sway over what is now Iran during the next decade or so, claimed descent from the Seventh Imam of the Twelvers, Musa al-Kazim, according to a forged genealogy. Shi'ism was proclaimed the state religion, the Shah exercising his authority directly on behalf of the Hidden Imam. The Turcoman tribesmen who upheld Isma'il's power wore special red turbans containing twelve folds commemorating the twelve Imams. Known disparagingly to the Ottomans as Qizilbashis ('Redheads'), they were fanatically devoted to their leader, whom they thought of as Hidden Imam himself.

Without a Shi'ite ideology to distinguish its rulers from the Ottomans, Persia might well have become absorbed by its more powerful Sunni neighbour. The Safavids imported Shi'ite *'ulama* to provide the ideological underpinning for their government. Many of them may have been Isma'ili *da'is* from Syria or Bahrain, who were willing to change their allegiance in order to promote the essentials of the *batini* faith. The Safavid rulers also appointed commissar-type officials known as *sadrs*, whose duty it was to ensure the allegiance of the *'ulama*. Resistance was met with force. The new Shi'ite *'ulama*, backed by the power of the state, were in a strong position to enforce religious conformity. In due course ideological uniformity cemented territorial unity. The modern Iranian nation came into being.

The crucial developments affecting modern Iranian Shi'ism occurred in the period of turmoil following the decline of the Savafids during the eighteenth century. Having come to power, like the 'Abbasids and Fatimids, by exploiting messianic expectations, they found they could consolidate it most effectively by exercising it on behalf of the Hidden Imam. The eschatological hopes, actualized during the revolution, were, as usual, deferred indefinitely once power had been achieved. However, after the Savafids had begun to decline (their zenith had been reached during the reign of 'Abbas the Great from 1587 to 1629), the Shi'ite *'ulama* began to exercise an increasingly independent authority. The long interregnum (1722–79) that followed the end of the dynasty witnessed a vigorous debate between two groups of *'ulama* – the *usulis* and the *akhbaris* – which replicated in many respects the much earlier debates between the *ahl al-kalam* and the *ahl al-hadith* under the 'Abbasids.

The *akhbaris* argued that, in the absence of the Imam, it was not permissible for an *'alim* (scholar) to exercise *ijtihad* (individual interpretation) or reason in determining the law. Instead he must rely exclusively on the traditions (*akhbar*, 'reports' – another term for *hadith*) which the Shi'a derived from the Quran, the Prophet and the Twelve Imams. The *usulis* (from *usul*, 'roots' or 'origins') held that since their authority came from the Hidden Imam, they had the right, even the duty, to exercise individual *ijtihad* on his behalf. There were theological as well as political dimensions to the debate. The *usulis* inherited the rationalism of the Mu'tazilis, which is also prominent in Isma'ili tradition. Man has free will. God's justice is both rational and comprehensible: he is obliged to reward good and punish evil. In other words God Himself is subject to a version of natural law. It follows that knowledge of the divine purpose must be accessible, not only to the Hidden Imam, but to virtuous men using the faculty of reason – i.e., *ijtihad*.

The debate continued into the nineteenth century, with victory eventually going to the *usulis*. They won partly because Iran's rulers never regained the spiritual authority lost to the *'ulama* during the period of Safavid decline. The Qajar Shahs, who held power from 1785 to 1924, never succeeded in establishing a centrally controlled bureaucratic state comparable to the Ottoman Empire after the administrative reforms (*tanzimat*) or to Muhammad 'Ali's Egypt. *Usuli* doctrines conferred more spiritual authority, and hence more social power, upon the *mujtahids* than the doctrines of the *akhbaris*.

The Shi'ite clergy

After their victory the *usulis* were free to develop the characteristic institutions of modern Iranian Shi'ism. Foremost among them was the special position of the *'ulama*. For the *ijma'* of the community, always latent in Sunnism, though usually exercised by the *'ulama*, they substituted the exclusive *ijma'* of the *mujtahids*. The latter, while not organized into a 'Church' on the Catholic model, nevertheless constitute a hierarchy with exclusive access to religious knowledge. Ordinary believers, including the ruler, are supposed to place themselves under the guidance of a *mujtahid* of their own choice, known as a *marja' i taqlid*. The senior *mujtahids*, known as Ayatollahs (from *aya*, 'sign' [of God]), elect their own *marja' i taqlid*, who, in effect, exercises supreme religious authority. Many of the Ayatollahs (including the revolutionary leader Khomeini) belong to the hereditary class of Sayyids, who claim descent from the Prophet.

The *mujtahids* receive a rigorous training in the religious sciences, including the school of *fiqh* traced back to the Imam Ja'far al-Sadiq. Ja'fari *fiqh* reached its full development in the nineteenth century and was eventually accepted by most of the Sunni *'ulama* as a fifth *madhhab* on a par with the Hanbali, Hanafi, Maliki and Shafi'i schools of *fiqh*. Even though the sources of Ja'fari *fiqh* are different, deriving from the teachings of the Imams as well as those of the Prophet, its overall content is generally similar to that of the Sunni *madhhabs*. The best-known Imami Shi'ite legal institution is the *mut'a*, or temporary marriage contract, made for a fixed term of years, months or even days. After the termination of the contract, the woman only has to observe half the *'idda* period of a normal marriage. Even this, however, can be avoided if the couple immediately makes a second contract which remains unconsummated. The custom seems to have existed in Arabia during the time of the Prophet. The fact that it was prohibited by the caliph 'Umar, who is not recognized by the Twelvers, probably accounts for its adoption by them.

Western and some Muslim critics of *mut'a* regard it as a form of legalized prostitution. The fact that a proportion of the *mahr* or dowry paid by the man to the woman is returnable if she terminates the contract prematurely, as is her right, has been used to justify the claim that the woman 'hires' herself to the man for purely sexual purposes. Undoubtedly the institution has been abused in this way. In the past, travellers would be met by professional brokers who, for a fee, would arrange a temporary marriage for the period of their sojourn. The institution's defenders, however, maintain that the Prophet and the Imams allowed it because it provides a morally acceptable and socially regulated alternative to adultery, thereby serving to uphold permanent marriage and family values. An exclusively Twelver institution, *mut'a* is not permitted by the Isma'ilis or any other Shi'ite sect.[17]

Apart from *mut'a*, there are a few ritual practices distinguishing Imami Shi'ism from mainstream Sunni Islam. Although, like the Sunnis, the Shi'a regard the Hajj as one of the 'pillars' of the faith, they are accustomed to making supplementary pilgrimages to the tombs of the Imams – especially those of Husain in Karbala, Fatima in Qom and the Eighth Imam, 'Ali Rida, at Mashhad. In the past, Friday congregational prayers featured much less prominently in Shi'a than in Sunni practice. There was even learned discussion as to whether, in the absence of the Imam, it was necessary or appropriate to hold Friday prayers at all. The use of mosques as rallying points since the Iranian revolution, particularly at Friday prayers, which have been massively attended, is one of many indications of how the revolution has activated latent eschatological expectations. Though Khomeini never made any formal statement to the effect that he was the Hidden Imam, his tumultuous reception on his return from exile, and the fact that since he took over the leadership of the state he has been known to all his supporters as 'the Imam', point to the same conclusion.

Whatever its contributory causes, whether social, economic or political, the outcome of the Iranian revolution has been a direct consequence of the position occupied by the religious leadership in Iran since the eighteenth century. The *mujtahids* were not just a spiritual elite. They disposed of a degree of social, economic and political power which made them a growing force in the land. They had the right to collect and distribute the two religious taxes, the *khums* (a 'fifth', or 20 per cent) on all trading profits, and the *zakat*, normally a wealth tax assessed annually at 2½ per cent. In a decentralized polity the collection and distribution of these taxes made the *mujtahids* the only welfare agency. In addition to acting as tax collectors (which, of course, provided opportunities for illicit self-enrichment), the *mujtahids* and the *mullahs* controlled by them were entitled to a 10 per cent commission on the *waqf* properties they administered – which provided them with a legitimate source of independent wealth. Some of these *waqfs* now constitute very substantial properties: for example, most of the eastern city of Mashhad belongs to the *waqf* that administers the Imam 'Ali Rida's shrine. Another institution which added considerably to the social power of the Shi'ite *'ulama* was *bast* – the right of sanctuary in mosques and other holy places – which included the homes of the *mujtahids*. Two of the Qajar rulers, Muhammad Shah (1834–48) and Nasr al-Din Shah (1858), tried to abolish *bast*, but were defeated by the organized resistance of the *mujtahids*.

In addition to the protection it afforded the Shah's political enemies, *bast* symbolized an important strand in Twelver Shi'ism: the illegitimacy of the state. *Bast* was justified theologically as a refuge from illegal tyranny with the only legitimate authority – the territory under the direct control of the Hidden Imam's representatives. The institution of *bast*, and *mujtahid* independence generally, were strengthened by the fact that after the loss of Iraq in the seventeenth century the principal Shi'ite shrines of Najaf and Karbala were situated in Ottoman territory. Nineteenth-century travellers recorded how Karbala actually afforded a sanctuary to thieves preying on Shi'ite pilgrims. But this situation also enhanced the political independence of the *'ulama*, since the Sunni Ottoman rulers were not averse to an institution which could be used to embarrass their Persian neighbours. As Nikki Keddie has observed, the location of the religious leadership beyond the borders of the state, together with the selection of a senior *mujtahid* as the *marja' i taqlid* for all the others, created in nineteenth-century Iran a form of church–state dichotomy similar to that which prevailed in medieval Christian Europe. The religious organization asserted, and was often able to support, claims superior to those of the merely secular government.

The independence of the Shi'ite *'ulama* in nineteenth-century Iran expressed itself in two ways: against the state itself and against the increasing pressure of European influence in the form of Russian and British imperialism. The two elements came together in the famous tobacco agitation of 1891–2, when Nasr al-Din Shah was forced to revoke a concession granting a British subject a monopoly over the production and sale of tobacco. This highly successful clerical intervention into the affairs of state was not simply one in a long chain of incidents in which the *mujtahids* used their power to veto government decisions. It also represented the beginnings of the continuous political involvement of the clergy which culminated in the Constitutionalist Movement of 1906 and which – after the interruption of seven decades – was to erupt once more in a clergy-led revolution against the Qajars' Pahlavi successors. But this is to look too far ahead. By 1900 the strands of Twelver sectarianism had already become entangled with those of the modernist movement. Before this can be assessed, a further tradition of classical Islam must be examined, that of the Sufi saints and the religious orders which came after them.

1. Yusuf flees the attentions of his Egyptian master's wife. Though not mentioned by name in the Quran, she is known in Islamic tradition as Zulaikha. The story, related in the 12th Sura of the Quran was extremely popular and was elaborated, most famously, in the masterpiece *Yusuf u Zulaikha* by the fifteenth-century Persian poet Jami. From a manuscript of the Bustan of Sa'di completed by the calligrapher Sultan Muhammad Nur. Bukhara *c.*1535.

2. A double page from an early Quran written in the eigth century CE or later. This very early example of the Arabic script contains neither the short-vowel signs nor the diacritical marks that distinguish different consonants from each other.

3. The opening chapter of the Quran (Surat al-Fatiha) and the opening passage of the Surat al-Baqara ('The Cow') in Egyptian Nashki script (c.1510). The Fatiha or Opening, recited during the five daily prayers, is sometimes called the 'Mother of the Book' – the quintessence of Islam.

4. Lithograph showing two of the four liwans of the great courtyard in the mosque–madrasa and tomb complex of Sultan Hasan in Cairo as it appeared to the British artist David Roberts in the nineteenth century.

5. The first ships sail through the newly-opened Suez Canal in 1869. The magnificent feat of engineering, achieved at the cost of several hundred Egyptian lives, enabled Britain to gain the strategic and political hold on Egypt that lasted until the Suez Crisis of 1956.

6. A princely youth offers a wine cup to his Sufi master beneath a tree. Wine is celebrated in Sufi literature as a symbol of spiritual grace despite its formal prohibition in the Quran.

7. Sufi dervishes (mendicants) perform their traditional whirling dance during Ramadan. The dance, a dhikr or remembrance of God, brings the Sufi close to the divine in a ritual that balances spiritual ecstasy with formal discipline.

8. The great pilgrim caravan, a mobile city containing tens of thousands of Muslims, winds its way from Cairo to Makka. The camel in the foreground bears a *mahmal* containing the *kiswa*, the black silken canopy that covers the Ka'ba. Engraving from Sir Richard Burton's 1854 account of the Hajj.

9. Pilgrims wait for sundown on the slopes of Jabal Rahma – the Mount of Mercy – above the plain of 'Arafat. The 'standing' at 'Arafat, climax of the five-day Hajj ceremonies when more than two million pilgrims foregather, prefigures the Day of Judgement.

10. Mohamed Reza Shah Pahlavi, his royal symbols shattered, clings to the coat-tails of imperialism whist cringing before a dragon unleashed by the Ayatollah Khomeini. The left-hand corner shows scenes of tortures inflicted by SAVAK, the Shah's security police. The inset cameos claim for the Islamic revolution the legacies of Seyyed Mahmud Taleqani (d. 1979) – above, with angels and Dr 'Ali Shari'ati (d. 1977).

11. The tomb of the Ayatollah Khomeini, Near Tehran. The writing beneath his portrait says: 'Peace upon you, O Ruhallah!'

12. & 13. Changing times, unchanging garb: Kuwait street markets. Above photographed by Freya Stark in 1937; below by Yves Herman in December 1998. Upper-class women in the Gulf states may still wear the veil in public while showing off the latest designer clothes in the privacy of their homes.

14. Women wearing burqas, the tent-like garments covering the whole body. Faizabad, Afghanistan, May 1998. Since the Taliban took over most of the country, women have been obliged to wear burqas and to give up jobs as teachers, doctors and bureaucrats.

15. Muslim women and girls in Paris demonstrate in favour of the right of female students to wear the hijab in class, 1989. A pupil who refused to remove her headscarf even for physical education classes became both national heroine and pariah. 'France is my freedom, so is my veil!' she proclaimed.

6 *Spiritual Renewal*

Love or justice?

If one could sum up in a phrase the essential difference between the two great western monotheisms, one might say that whereas Christianity is primarily the religion of love, Islam is above all the religion of justice. This does not, of course, mean that Christians are necessarily better at loving than Muslims, or that Muslim society lends itself more successfully to the realization of justice. A pessimistic view of religion would suggest exactly the opposite. The Christian imperative, 'to love one's neighbour as oneself', is far too universal to be given practical application, except at a purely individual level. The admonition to 'love one's enemy' takes little account of the social and political circumstances in which the majority of people find themselves. A very few Christians have found it possible to follow the conclusion of Christ's teaching to the point where they become pacifists. The cruellest and most destructive wars in human history have been waged against each other by nominally Christian states.

Similarly, most Muslim states are ruled by bloody and repressive dictatorships which, far from satisfying the imperative of social justice exemplified by the Prophet's career, seem to be incapable of granting even the most basic human rights to their citizens. Official murder, arbitrary imprisonment and extra-legal government in all its forms can be found in Muslim states from Morocco to Malaysia. The very promise of justice conveyed in the Quranic message seems to militate against its realization: by raising expectations of such a political character, Islam presents its rulers with an impossible challenge. Like Marxist governments, which they resemble in this respect, Muslim rulers find it necessary to pre-empt ideologically inspired attacks upon themselves by appropriating the vocabulary and rhetoric of their potential opponents. 'Islamic' justice, like 'Christian' love, acquires a hollow ring.

Nevertheless, despite this perversion, or rather inversion, of their respective ideals as they are applied or misapplied, in practice, the two watchwords, love and justice, can usefully act as signposts to a wide range of differences between the two religions in terms both of their acknowledged practices and dogmas and of the unconscious prejudices of their adherents. Love is the warmest and most deep-rooted of human emotions. Its intensity is felt in proportion to the paucity of its objects. One loves a parent, a child or a sexual partner more strongly or deeply than a multitude. As the cement of most family and sexual unions, love is essentially exclusive. In order to universalize this emotion, to utilize it in the service of religion, the Christians have had to humanize the deity, investing it with the character of a love-object. 'Jesus loves you,' proclaim the slogans. The relationship is personalized and, like all true love, must be reciprocated. Gentle Jesus, a model of young manhood, inspires an intensely personal kind of love. Alone and naked on the cross, he excites a pity not unmixed with eroticism. However, love of the human person in Jesus is but a stage on the road to the love and awareness of a God 'who so loved the world' that he sent his only son to die in it. The personal and intimate nature of Christian love ensures that the divine is conceptualized in essentially human terms. We cannot love what we cannot understand: the corollary of Christian love is a deity who resists all attempts at de-anthropomorphization.

In contrast, the God of the Quran is approached with awe and veneration rather than love.

Know, then, that God is sublimely exalted, the Ultimate Sovereign, the Ultimate Truth: there is no deity save Him the Sustainer, in bountiful almightiness enthroned! (23:116)

God is described in this passage and elsewhere as 'Malik al-haqq' – 'King of Truth and Justice'. The word *al-haqq*, according to Asad, 'signifies "the Truth" in the absolute, intrinsic sense, eternally and immutably existing beyond the ephemeral, changing phenomena of His creation'. The same word is used, significantly, in connection with the prohibition on killing:

Do not take any human being's life – [the life] which God has declared to be sacred – otherwise than in the pursuit of justice [*ila bi'l haqq*]. (6:151)

Justice and truth, as well as mercy, are thus seen as essential attributes of God. 'God's decrees' are the natural laws instituted by him. Those who disobey them 'sin against themselves': God himself remains unaffected by their foolishness.

Whoever does what is just and right, does so for his own good; and whoever does evil, does so to his own hurt: and never does God do the least wrong to His creatures. (41:46)

The proper approach for a Muslim is to submit to the decrees of God, as represented by the laws of nature and the rules laid down in the Quran and the Prophet's Sunna:

O you who have attained to faith! Pay heed unto God and pay heed unto the Apostle and to those from among you who have been entrusted with authority. (4:59)

As if to underline the identity of the Muslim's submission (*islam*) to God with the working of the natural order, the Quran combines the cosmic imagery of shadows with the prostrations of prayer:

And before God prostrate themselves, willingly or unwillingly, all [things and beings] that are in the heavens and on earth, as do the shadows in the mornings and the evenings. (13:15)

God's 'reward' for the essentially rational and self-interested submission to his decrees by mankind is the altruistic gain of human social harmony:

Say [O Prophet]: 'No reward do I ask of you for this [message] other than [that you should] love your fellow-men.' (42:29)

Love, it would seem, belongs to the human sphere. The all-embracing cosmic deity conveyed in the Quran cannot be apprehended closely enough to elicit the warmth of love in the average human. Yet from the first there were Muslims whose psychic or spiritual needs were unsatisfied by mere obedience to the deity and the dutiful observance of his commandments. They sought a closer and more intimate relationship by means of ascetic practices, arduous spiritual exercises and complicated liturgies. They came to be known as Sufis, after the woollen garments (*suf* = wool) allegedly worn by the earliest exemplars of this movement, as well as by the followers of Jesus whom they particularly admired. Through the work of its saints, its theosophers and, eventually, by means of its organized lodges of lay adherents, the Sufi movement brought an inner spirituality into an Islam which otherwise tended to crystallize into a religion concerned mainly with the outward forms of legal observance and the pursuit of political power. The contemplation of the 'god within' revitalized Islam, replenishing its psychic reserves and fructifying its structures, both legal and intellectual, with a new injection of energy.

The Fundaments of Sufism

The 'God within' is well attested in the Quran:

Now verily it is We who have created man and We know that his innermost self whispers within him: for We are closer to him than his neck-vein. (50:16)

In addition to the general experience of Muhammad's revelation, mystical by definition, the Quran alludes to two particular visionary experiences: the visitation of an angel who appeared 'two bow-lengths away, or even nearer' (53:5–9), and the celebrated Night Journey (Al-Isra, title of the 17th *sura*) in which the Prophet was 'transported' from the Holy Shrine (presumed to be Makka) to the 'furthest shrine' (*al-masjid al-aqsa*) (17:1), assumed to be Jerusalem, now considered the third holiest shrine of Sunni Islam after Makka and Madina. Early Muslim opinion was divided as to whether the Prophet travelled physically or only in spirit. 'Aisha, one of the most important sources of *hadith* reports, maintained emphatically that 'he was transported only in his spirit, while his body did not leave its place'.[1] The mystics of Islam have always rejected the naive view that the Isra was a miraculous occurrence.

Direct experience of the numinous tends to call into question the absolute validity of the visible and material world. The mystic perceives epistemologically what the ascetic feels morally: for this reason the two are usually combined in one person. For the Muslim ascetic, the Quran is also a point of departure:

Know [O men] that the life of this world is but a play and a passing delight, and a beautiful show, and [the cause of] your boastful vying with one another, and [of your] greed for more and more riches and children. (57:20)

Piety and asceticism are intimately bound up with a rejection of the world's 'vanities'. As Louis Massignon, the greatest modern authority on Sufism, put it:

The mystic call is as a rule the result of an inner rebellion of the conscience against social injustices, not only those of others but primarily and particularly against one's own faults: with a desire intensified by inner purification to find God at any price.[2]

Psychologically, the intensity of personal faith, understood in terms of a sense of proximity to God, sustains the mystic–ascetic in his or her decision to withdraw from the world of outward deceptions. The mystic's 'rebellion' is a quietist one, but contains within itself the potential for political action. The sense of proximity to God does not necessarily lead to withdrawal. In certain personalities, and under certain conditions, it becomes converted to revolutionary activism, as we shall see later in this chapter. The transition was exemplified by the Prophet himself in the *hijra* from Makka to Madina. Sufis would often interpret the *hijra* individualistically, as a personal 'migration' from evil. Among the Kharijis, and among the later reformist movements such as the Almohads, the Wahhabis and the Muslim Brothers, the *hijra* retained its two-sided character of personal purification and prelude to a crusade aimed at reforming the whole community. Sometimes this transformation from quietism to activism was stimulated by foreign, particularly European, encroachments on *dar al-Islam*. However, this was not necessarily the case: the transition from a spiritual to an active *jihad* is intrinsic to Islam, as will be shown in the cases of the Berber, West African and Indian reform movements described at the end of this chapter.

In view of the intimate connection between ascetic withdrawal and pious activism, it is not surprising to find that figures associated with opposition movements within Islam figure largely in the Sufi hagiographies. Many Sufi orders traced their chains of mystic teachers back to 'Ali whom the Shi'ites, of course, also regarded as a repository of esoteric knowledge. The Sufi master Abu al-'Qasim Junaid (d. 910) regarded 'Ali as a 'natural mystic' who, however, had been too preoccupied with worldly affairs to develop the higher gnostic disciplines. Other figures from whom they claim spiritual descent include Abu Dharr al-Ghifari and Hasan al-Basri, both of whom are associated with the pious opposition to the Umayyads.

A letter from Hasan al-Basri, who died in 728, has been recorded which contains most of the attitudes later associated with Sufism:

Beware of this world with all wariness; for it is like a snake – smooth to the touch, but its venom is deadly. Turn away from whatsoever delights thee in it ... put off from thee its cares, for that thou hast seen its sudden chances, and knowest for sure that thou shalt be parted from it; endure firmly its hardships, for the ease that shall presently be thine ... Hard is the life of man if he be prudent, dangerous if comfortable, being wary ever of catastrophe, certain of his ultimate fate.[3]

The prophets, according to Hasan, had been sent by God as a warning to men against the dangers and snares of the world:

For this world has neither worth nor weight with God; so slight it is, it weighs not with God so much as a pebble or a single clod of earth; as I am told, God has created nothing more hateful to Him than this world, and from the day He created it He has not looked upon it, so much He hates it. It was offered to our Prophet with all its keys and treasures, and that would not have lessened him in God's sight by so much as the wing of a gnat, but he refused to accept it ...[4]

Disinterested love

Among the earliest Sufi adepts was Rabi'a al-'Adawiya, the famous freedwoman of Basra. In her rejection of marriage, she sought the ultimate mystic's path of union with God:

The contract of marriage is for those who have a phenomenal existence. But in my case there is no such existence, for I have ceased to exist and have passed out of self. I exist in God and am altogether His. I live in the shadow of His command. The marriage contract must be asked from Him, not from me.[5]

Rabi'a sought to approach God with a love that was wholly altruistic, and absolutely free from the self-interest of Quranic morality. Taking a flaming torch in one hand and a jar of water in the other, she dramatized her disinterest, proclaiming:

I am going to light fire in Paradise and to pour water on to Hell, so that both veils may be taken away from those who journey towards God, and their purpose may be sure and they may look towards their Sustainer without any object of hope or motive of fear. What if the hope of Paradise and the fear of Hell did not exist? No one would worship his Sustainer or obey Him.[6]

Explaining her own attempts to love God purely for his own sake, she exclaimed: 'I should be a wretched hireling if I served God from fear.' Her verses on the two kinds of love, the pure and the interested, are much quoted:

> I have loved Thee with two loves, a selfish love and a love that is
>   worthy [of Thee]
> As for the love which is selfish, I occupy myself therein with
>   remembrance of Thee to the exclusion of all others,
> As for that which is worthy of Thee, therein Thou raisest the veil that
>   I may see Thee
> Yet there is no praise in me in this or that
> But the praise is to Thee, whether in that or this.[7]

Disinterested love of God, celebration of poverty and a desire to purify oneself inwardly in order to come closer to the transcendent are the perennial themes of Sufi writing and practice from the earliest times. They inject a warmth into Islam which is lacking in the legalistic observance advocated by the Sunni *ulama* or in the fanatical loyalty of the Shi'ites to the tragic memories of their Imams. Even the ascetic practices of the Sufis have a disinterested quality. In the absence of a doctrine of original sin, writes Michael Gilsenan, an anthropologist who has made a study of Sufism,

. . . salvation is not imperilled by man's inherently sinful nature and his endless need for penance and the renewal of intention . . . Suffering . . . whether just or unjust, of the individual or of the community, is not a dominant mode of purification or redemption or a path to salvation; it has no positive soteriological meaning crystallized in the symbol of the human–divine crucified saviour or the persecuted community in exile . . .[8]

The aim of the ascetic practices of the Sufi masters was not to earn themselves credits in the next world by mortifying the flesh in this, but rather to liberate the spirit for improved communication with the divine. Once this had been achieved, ascetic practices were often relaxed. Many of the Sufi masters married, thereby becoming founders of saintly lineages.

The same author has described the rigours to which a modern Sufi *shaikh* (born in Cairo in 1867) subjected himself in order to 'refine his nature'. The practices are essentially the same as those performed by the earliest Sufi masters:

For three hundred days in the year he fasted; each night he recited twelve thousand times the formula *la ilaha illa allah* (there is no god but God); for six years he repeated as an individual *dhikr* (Sufic exercise) the name of Allah thirty thousand times in a night, and for two years he abstained from sexual intercourse, avoiding even the company of women. Finally, he prayed to the Prophet Muhammad, whom he always held in the highest reverence, for two hours each night. Such a discipline had a severe physical effect – piles, bleeding and excessive thinness. He himself is quoted as saying that his parents and friends became increasingly concerned and others mocked him. At last . . . he came to see that effort of this kind was not sufficient and that truth might be sought within the individual soul without following so demanding a bodily ascetic regime. He then relaxed these practices, but never entirely gave them up, remaining a *zahid* (ascetic) until he died.[9]

Mystical communion

Muslim asceticism doubtless owed something to non-Muslim influences. The Prophet himself may have acquired the habit of nocturnal vigil and prostrations from Christian hermits; and there is no doubt that the earlier Sufi masters drew on the mystical traditions of the Eastern churches. One of the most celebrated of these was Abu Yazid al-Bistami (d. *circa* 875) whose sayings (about 500 of them) have been recorded in oral tradition. His teacher, called Abu 'Ali al-Sindi (possibly an Indian from Sind), was ignorant of Arabic, and in return for instruction in the techniques for achieving mystical communion, Abu Yazid taught him the Quran. While we know little of these techniques, the language through which Abu Yazid sought to express his mystic experience was wholly Quranic. In particular, he adapted and developed the stylistic peculiarity known as *shath* ('roaming' or 'straying'), whereby the pronoun shifts from the third to the first person: in a manner reminiscent of the Quran itself, Abu Yazid addressed his auditors as if he were God, implying a mystical exchange of roles with the divine. The conventionally pious were, unsurprisingly, scandalized by such ecstatic utterances (*shathiyas*) as 'Glory be to Me!', 'How great is My Majesty!'. A lengthy report of his efforts to achieve a state of union with God (*fana*), however, reveals two themes which would recur in the theosophy of Ibn 'Arabi: the annihilation of the subject–object relationship in the supreme mystical encounter, and the related idea of a return to an undifferentiated state of identity with the Absolute:

Then I gazed upon Him with the eye of truth, and said to Him 'Who is this?' He said, 'This is neither I nor other than I. There is no god but I.' Then He changed me out of my identity into His Selfhood, and caused me to pass away from my selfhood through His Selfhood, showing me His Selfhood uniquely; and I gazed upon Him with His Selfhood . . . Then I gazed upon Him with His Light, and knew Him through His Knowledge, and communed with Him with the tongue of His Grace, saying, 'How fares it with me with Thee?' He said, 'I am thine through thee; there is no god but Thou.'[10]

Such statements claiming *fana*, or union with God, were far from acceptable to the pious *'ulama*. Nevertheless, with a few rare exceptions Sufism did not meet with the religious persecution encountered by other *batini* extremists, such as the Qarmatians, whose challenge to the *status quo* had a more overtly political character. From the earliest period men such as Abu 'Abdullah al-Harith al-Muhasibi (781–837) and his famous pupil Junaid sought to combine asceticism and mystic communion with the divine with strict observance of the Shari'a. In his commentary on the sayings of Abu Yazid, Junaid developed a somewhat disingenuous way of explaining away the apparent blasphemies contained in them. If someone said, 'There is no deity save Me so worship Me', he was obviously quoting Quran 21:25. In the same way, when Abu Yazid cried, 'Glory be to me!', he was simply reporting God's speech, not referring to himself.[11]

Junaid, known as the 'paragon of the sober Sufis', laid the foundation of the systematic theosophy which would later find its supreme expression in the work of Ibn 'Arabi. According to the doctrine of *tawhid* or 'Oneness' first enunciated by Junaid, everything, including the human self, pre-existed in God and must eventually return to Him. On the basis of a somewhat idiosyncratic interpretation of two Quranic verses (7:166–7), Junaid elaborated the theory that God made a covenant with mankind at the time when the latter 'did not exist except in so far as it existed in Him'. By adopting the Way of Sufism (*tasawwuf*) a man would 'die to himself' in order to 'live in God'. This dying is the *fana* or self-extinction referred to by Abu Yazid. The new 'life in God' is called *baqa* (subsistence):

By passing away from self the mystic does not cease to exist in the sense of existence as an individual; rather his individuality, which is an inalienable gift from God, is perfected, transmuted and eternalized through God and in God.[12]

By recognizing this double dimension to existence, according to which the adept can live, as it were, simultaneously in a state of union with God and on an earthly plane, Junaid circumvented the obvious difficulties created by those, like Abu Yazid, who claimed to be 'part of God' and therefore, logically speaking, above the law.

The scandal of Hallaj

The victory of 'orthodox' or moderate Sufism over the ecstatic or 'drunken' variety was not achieved without a prolonged struggle. The victors were the moderates from both camps – the Sufi-minded legists and their mystic counterparts, the lawfully minded Sufis. The most celebrated victim of the struggle was al-Husain ibn Mansur (857–922), known as al-Hallaj, or 'the wool-carder'. The life and death of al-Hallaj, martyr, mystic and saint, has been the subject of a massive two-volume study by the French orientalist Louis Massignon, so rather more is known about him in the West than about other equally influential figures.

An Arab speaker from Fars, al-Hallaj first adopted Sufism in Basra, where he became a fervent ascetic. On his first pilgrimage to Makka he remained immobile for a whole year in the courtyard of the Haram, constantly fasting and maintaining a perpetual silence. On returning to Persia he gave up his formal adherence to Sufism, urging his followers to seek the 'God within' by bringing an inner significance to bear upon ritual acts. ('Proceed seven times round the Ka'ba of your heart,' he said.) His enemies among the *ahl al-zahir* accused him, wrongly according to Massignon, of wishing to abolish the 'outer' acts themselves.

After further pilgrimages and a lengthy missionary journey to India, beyond the frontiers of *dar al-Islam*, he settled in Baghdad, where he proclaimed the doctrine of 'unity of witness' (*wahda al-shuhud*), a not uncomplicated theosophy according to which the adept's 'union with God' is to be understood not as a 'unification of substance', but as the result of 'an act of faith and love' in which the Sufi's intention to merge his intelligence, his will and his ego with God is acted upon by divine grace. In announcing that God was witnessing to Himself 'in the heart of his votary', al-Hallaj aroused the suspicions of the *ahl al-zahir* (the exoteric legalists), even though he took care, in his dogmatic theology, not to depart from the framework of Sunni orthodoxy. His claim to be 'the truth' (*al-haqq*) was taken by his enemies to imply a blasphemous identification with the divine. 'If you do not recognize God,' he said, 'at least recognize His signs. I am that sign, I am the creative Truth [*ana al-haqq*] because through the Truth I am a truth eternally . . .'[13]

Al-Hallaj foresaw, and welcomed, his martyrdom. The parallels with Christ are compelling, and were certainly in his mind as he faced imprisonment, trial and execution on the gibbet. Like Jesus he prayed for his enemies while dying:

Here are these Thy worshippers who have come together to kill me, out of zeal for Thee, to approach Thee [by offering a sacrifice] . . . Forgive them! If Thou had revealed to them what Thou hast revealed to me, they would not do what they are doing. And if Thou hadst hid from me what Thou hast hid from them I would not have been put through the trials which I am now undergoing. Praise be to Thee for what thou doest! Praise be to Thee for what Thou willest![14]

His last words as he hung on the gibbet, his hands and feet having been cut off, were, 'All that the ecstatic wants is to be alone with the One.' He was exposed on the gibbet for two days before being decapitated. His body was then sprinkled with oil, set on fire and the ashes thrown into the Tigris from the top of a minaret.

The fate of al-Hallaj was exceptional. His real offence, in the eyes of the authorities, was that he proclaimed in public what the 'sober' Sufis experienced privately. Some of his statements had a distinctly Shi'ite tinge, such as his insistence on the 'inner meanings' of ritual acts. The authorities were afraid that his popularity, which was considerable, would encourage antinomian attitudes among ordinary people, inspiring them to question the formal religiosity of the caliphs and the *zahiri 'ulama* who upheld their authority. 'Sober' Sufis such as Junaid, who had been friendly with al-Hallaj, criticized his outspokenness without questioning the validity of his religious experience.

The synthesis of al-Ghazali

Junaid was the first architect of the compromise between the ecstatics and the theologians that would culminate with the work of Abu Hamid al-Ghazali (1058–1111) in the eleventh century. For the time being the 'drunken' Sufis circulated mystic *hadiths*, such as one according to which the Prophet is supposed to have said: 'I have moments of familiarity [with God] when neither cherubim nor Prophet can contain me.' The 'sober' Sufis sought to maintain the supremacy of the Quran and the Sunna and insisted on reversing this dictum by containing Muhammad the mystic within the figure of Muhammad the Prophet. Whereas the mystic consciousness must remain satisfied with the individual experience of 'union' with God, the Prophetic consciousness, as exemplified by Muhammad's career, implied that moral activism must remain dominant. If God had not commanded the Prophet to 'return to society' after his experiences on Mount Hira, *dar al-Islam* would never have come into being.

While Junaid was a 'sober' Sufi who sought to contain the mystic's ecstasy within the framework of the Shari'a, Ghazali approached the problem from the opposite direction. An *'alim* (scholar) trained in theology and *fiqh*, he aimed to achieve the revitalization of the Shari'a way by re-injecting into it the altruistic love and pietism of the Sufis. In this he succeeded where the misrepresented and misunderstood al-Hallaj had failed. This was largely because his credentials as a *faqih* and a formal theologian were impeccable.

Born at Tus in Khurasan (Persia), Ghazali became a pupil of Juwaini, the foremost theologian of his time. His gifts were such that by the age of 33 he had been appointed professor at the new academy of religious studies at Baghdad, established by Nizam al-Mulk, vizier of the Seljuk Sultan Malikshah, to defend Sunnism against the spread of Isma'ili propaganda. Despite his intellectual success, Ghazali had a restless, self-questioning temperament, which he describes in his autobiography:

From my early youth since I attained the age of puberty . . . until the present time when I am over fifty, I have ever recklessly launched out into the midst of these ocean depths, I have ever bravely embarked on this open sea, throwing aside all craven caution; I have poked into every dark recess, I have made an assault on every problem, I have plunged into every abyss, I have scrutinized the creed of every sect, I have tried to lay bare the innermost doctrines of every community. All this I have done that I might distinguish between true and false, between sound tradition and heretical innovation.[15]

The science of theology (*'ilm al-kalam*), which was the first to engage his attention, failed to satisfy him: while attaining its own aims, the preservation of orthodoxy and its defence against the deviations of the heretics, it did not serve his purpose, which was the search for truth. Seeking enlightenment elsewhere, he turned to 'philosophy', including the natural sciences, which gave him a powerful insight into the marvels of creation. According to Ghazali, no one who had studied anatomy could fail to wonder at the perfection of human and animal organs, and to recognize in them evidence of the Creator's master hand. However, he found himself unable to go along with the natural scientists: in particular, he rejected their denial of the resurrection and the future life. He accepted that there was much truth in Aristotle, whom, like Plato and Socrates, he regarded as a 'theist'. Nevertheless, some of the works of the philosophers contradicted the teachings of Islam and must be counted as heresy or unbelief. As for the theoretical sciences, including mathematics and logic, Ghazali concluded that they served neither to prove nor disprove the existence of God. Anyone who thought Islam could be defended by going against mathematical or logical truth was committing a grievous crime against religion.

Ghazali found politics too worldly a discipline to satisfy him. Ethics, as taught by the philosophers, tended to mix truth with falsehood and was clearly unsuited for popular instruction. Like the philosophers, Ghazali believed that the majority of people had to be protected from potentially harmful ideas. He inveighed against the Isma'ilis or *batinis* and their writings, particularly the *Epistles* of the Ikhwan al-Safa: 'Just as the poor swimmer must be kept from the slippery banks, so must mankind be kept from reading these books.'[16] His most sustained campaign, however, was aimed at the Muslim neoplatonists, particularly Farabi and Ibn Sina (Avicenna). Having mastered their writings so thoroughly that his study of their method and doctrine in *The Intentions of the Philosophers* led to the belief among Latin scholars that 'Algazel' was himself a neoplatonist, he rounded on them in his celebrated *Tahafut al-Falasifa* ('The Collapse [or "Incoherence"] of the Philosophers'), using philosophical arguments to refute a number of propositions put forward by the Muslim neoplatonists. He condemns them for their emanationist belief in the eternity of the world, for the belief that God is simply an intellect having knowledge only of universals, for their rejection of causal necessity and for their denial of the resurrection of the body. The 'natural' sequence of cause and effect – such as fire burning cotton – was not, as the philosophers had argued, an automatic or necessary conjunction of events. Since God is not bound by any order, causal or other, it is merely the effect of God's will, acting directly or indirectly through an angel. God could just as well decide not to let the cotton burn. The miracles mentioned in the Quran (such as Jesus' resurrection of the dead or Moses' transformation of a stick into a serpent) might therefore be understood factually. The resurrection of the body, denied by the philosophers, was similarly possible. The *Tahafut* reaffirmed official Sunni hostility to philosophical rationalism rather in the manner that Ash'ari had restored traditionalism against the theological rationalism of the Mu'tazilis. Once again, urban populism had found its intellectual champion against the subversive elitism of the rationalists, and had succeeded in arming itself with some of the enemy's weapons.

Philosophically speaking, however, Ghazali's was far from being the last word. The same century saw a celebrated rebuttal of Ghazali's *Tahafut* by the Spanish-Arab philosopher Ibn Rushd (Averroës – 1126–98). In *Tahafut al-Tahafut* ('The Collapse of "The Collapse"', better known as 'The Incoherence of "The Incoherence"'), Ibn Rushd tried to restore the balance between scripturalism and philosophy by rehabilitating *tawil*, or allegorical interpretation, a style of hermeneutics widely practised by Sufi and Shi'ite writers, but generally eschewed by the Sunnis. Ibn Rushd's method, however, made it necessary for him to resort to an intellectual double standard far more elitist than anything proposed by Ghazali. According to Ibn Rushd, the Quran's 'ambiguous' passages could only be understood by the philosophers; and he attacked Ghazali and other theologians for sowing the seeds of heresy and discord in Islam by unlawfully revealing secrets of interpretation which should be reserved for those who are fit to comprehend them. The fact that Ibn Rushd, Sunni Islam's last great speculative philosopher, was quite content to hold the office of Grand Qadi of Seville shows how far preservation of the Shari'a, symbolizing the Quran's external (*zahiri*) message, had come to outweigh all other dimensions of the Quranic message in the hearts of the faithful.

Ghazali's search for truth, and the difficulty he experienced in finding it, involved him in a severe moral and psychological crisis. He felt himself to be on the brink of a crumbling sandbank, in constant danger of hell-fire. Satan told him that this was merely a 'passing mood' that would soon disappear. But his sense of chronic unease and imminent personal doom refused to leave him. He became incapable of delivering his lectures. God caused his tongue to dry up, he could hardly swallow or eat a single morsel of food. He became so weak that the physicians gave up hope. The trouble arose from the heart, they said, whence it spread to the constitution. Finally, at the age of 37, Ghazali took the plunge. He gave away his wealth and made provision, by means of a *waqf*, for his family. 'Nowhere in the world,' he would write, 'have I seen better financial arrangements [than in Iraq] to assist a scholar to provide for his children.'[17]

The sanctification of daily living

After a sojourn in Damascus, Ghazali proceeded to Jerusalem. For ten years he lived the life of a Sufi, engaging in ascetic practices, seeking solitude and mystic truth. Ecstasy he experienced only occasionally, though he did not cease to hope for it. 'Things innumerable and unfathomable' were related to him. Like the Sufis, Ghazali came to the conclusion that there were modes of cognition lying beyond the realm of the intellect. The knowledge so acquired could only be communicated by revelation. This realization brought him to believe in the absolute necessity of ritual observance, based on a reaffirmation of the Quran and the Sunna. Ghazali's renewed commitment to the

Shari'a found expression in his most influential work, the *Ihya 'ulum al-din* ('The Revival of the Religious Sciences'), which he wrote after returning to Baghdad on the caliph's orders. In essence, the *Ihya* is a manual for daily living, one which, as W. Montgomery Watt has pointed out, would not be out of place in a monastic order with a very strict rule. The details of vegetative life – eating, sleeping, ablutions, entering the lavatory – as well as the religious offices, including prayer, fasting and supererogatory exercises, must be conducted in such a way as to maintain a consciousness of God's presence at all times. Sin must constantly be avoided, the various organs protected from all varieties of evil: the ear from heresy, slander or obscenity; the tongue from lies, slanders and the 'backbiting . . . [which] is more serious than thirty adulteries', from wrongly discussing theology and metaphysics, from cursing or scoffing at God's creatures; the stomach from unlawful foods and that 'which hardens the heart, impairs the intellect and weakens the memory'; the private parts from everything unlawful, including harmful thoughts; the hands from beating a Muslim, from receiving unlawful wealth, from harming any creature or from writing what may not be uttered; the feet from going to an unlawful place or from hastening to the court of a wicked ruler; the heart from envy, hypocrisy and pride – sins which, according to Ghazali, 'are the most prominent among the *'ulama* of our time'.[18]

Ghazali's work lays down the rule of an earnest, somewhat joyless religiosity, pregnant with *gravitas* and unleavened by humour. He cites a *hadith* according to which 'the man who speaks a word to make his friends laugh is thereby hurled into the pit of hell for seventy years'. He is far removed from the ecstatic vision of the 'drunken' Sufis, even though he fully acknowledges the value of their religious experience. For all his efforts to discover God by following the mystics' path, Ghazali's vision remains firmly tied to orthodoxy or – to be more precise – to ortho*praxy*, correct ritual practice and behaviour. It is this very quality that explains his immense and abiding influence. The *Ihya* became (and probably still remains) the most-quoted religious text after the Quran and the classical *hadith* collections. Its essential spirit, informed by Ghazali's immense intellectual authority, is that of the Sufi orders which came into being within a generation of his death. Indeed, study of the *Ihya* was compulsory for members of many orders up to the twentieth century. It was the bedside reading of Hasan al-Banna, founder of the Muslim Brotherhood (d. 1949).

Although Ghazali himself never founded a Sufi brotherhood, remaining always an *'alim* rather than a Sufi *shaikh*, his influence, both on the brotherhoods and upon Islam itself, proved to be incalculable. By animating the 'outward' framework of legal observance with the 'inward' quality of mystic experience he helped bridge the gap which must always exist between personal virtue and institutionalized religiosity. Both the *'ulama* and the mystically inclined would look to his works for edification and instruction, and both groups would find in them arguments with which to confront the subversive influence of the philosophers and other intellectual elitists such as the *batinis*. Like Shafi'i, he employed his intellectual gifts to endow the piety of the urban classes with intellectual respectability, reaffirming populist values by re-establishing the primacy of the Quran and the Sunna. In one respect his achievement surpasses that of Shafi'i: whereas the great *faqih* brought uniformity to the structure of the Shari'a law, maintaining its cohesiveness in the face of the developing rivalries between the Hanafis and Malikis, Ghazali's work served to re-integrate the whole legal superstructure with the psychic or spiritual infrastructure, re-injecting into the Quran and the Sunna, and into the edifice of law built upon them, the sanctity of the Prophet's mystic consciousness. For this he has been called the greatest Muslim after Muhammad.

Before consideration of the Sufi brotherhoods and their contribution, in both their original and reformed versions, towards the spread of Islam and its renovation, two individuals should be mentioned who, in different ways, brought the development of mystic consciousness to its furthest conclusion. They are Ibn 'Arabi (1165–1240), the theosophist, and Jalal al-Din Rumi (1207–73), the poet of the Mawlawi dervishes. Though neither had an influence on mainstream Islam comparable to Ghazali's, both cultivated the individualistic tradition of 'intoxicated' Sufism to the point where their work transcends the boundaries of Islam and emerges into the realm of universal religious consciousness. For this reason they are almost better known, and more highly regarded, outside the Islamic tradition than within it.

Ibn 'Arabi

Muhyi al-Din ibn al-'Arabi, known to his admirers as the 'Shaikh al-Akbar' ('the Greatest Master') was born in Spain, where he spent the first thirty years of his life. His father was a friend of Ibn Rushd, who was impressed by the depth of Ibn 'Arabi's religious convictions. His 'conversion' to Sufism occurred when he was quite young, in the course of an illness. The experience so changed his life that he subsequently came to regard his earlier years as a period of *jahiliya*, or ignorance. At the age of about 30 he left Spain, travelling first to Tunis and then on to Cairo and Jerusalem before making the pilgrimage to Makka. He spent two years in the Holy City, frequently performing the *'umra*, reading and meditating near the Ka'ba, which he regarded as the meeting point of the invisible (*ghaib*) and visible (*shuhud*) worlds. In 1204 he was persuaded by a group of Anatolian pilgrims to settle at Malatya on the Euphrates. Later, at the age of 65, he went to live in Damascus under the protection of the influential Ibn Zaki family.

Ibn 'Arabi was an immensely prolific writer. In the course of his life he is said to have composed some 846 works. More than 400 works attributed to him have survived, most of which are believed to be genuine. The best known are the massive *Futuhat al-Makkiya* ('The Makkan Revelations'), a veritable Sufi encyclopedia built round his visions of the Holy City; the *Fusus al-Hikam* ('The Essentials of Wisdom'), which he claimed the Prophet actually dictated to him in a dream; and the *Turjuman al-Ashwaq* ('Interpreter of Desires'), a collection of love poems addressed to the daughter (whom he eventually married) of a Persian resident in Makka, to which he appended his own commentary.

Ibn 'Arabi combined mystical insight with vast erudition. Not only was he perfectly familiar with the writings and teachings of Sunni theologians, *'ulama* and philosophers, but he was also widely read in the literature of the Isma'ilis and Mu'tazilis. In some respects his learning imposes an obstacle for scholars, since he never developed a systematic frame of reference, instead borrowing eclectically from the different vocabularies of his authors. In the main, however, he took over the legacy of the Muslim neoplatonists, including Farabi, Ibn Sina and his father's friend Ibn Rushd, and reissued it as the product rather of mystic intuition than of reason. In this respect his position is similar to that of Ghazali, who also placed intuitive revelation (*kashf*) and the knowledge deriving from it (gnosis or *ma'rifa*) above intellectual reasoning. However, whereas Ghazali's mystic meditations led him back to a strict re-affirmation of the Quran and the Sunna, Ibn 'Arabi's brought him close to the attitude of identity with God for which al-Hallaj was martyred. Though scarcely more cautious in his statements than al-Hallaj or Bistami (he claimed to be 'the Seal of the Saints', a 'perfect manifestation' of the 'Spirit of Muhammad'), he lived in a more tolerant age and, probably more important, enjoyed the protection of powerful interests.

Ibn 'Arabi's theosophy embodied many of the assumptions of the Muslim neoplatonists. God is pure being (in philosophical terms, a necessary existent), free from all other attributes. This was a view the Muslim philosophers had developed from their understanding of Aristotle, neoplatonism and the ideas of the Mu'tazilis. (A certain confusion about Aristotle's real ideas resulted from the fact that an Arabic collection of neoplatonist writings, including fragments of Plotinus' *Enneads*, was thought to be a 'Theology' by Aristotle; even Ibn Rushd, whose great commentary on Aristotle re-introduced that philosopher to the West, was ignorant of Greek.) Like Farabi, Ibn Sina and other Muslim neoplatonists, Ibn 'Arabi rejected the Aristotelian dualism of God and matter, the Unmoved Mover and his creation, adopting instead the emanationist view of reality as a continuum or 'unity of being' (*wahda al-wujud*) made up of different grades. He tried to avoid the pantheistic implications of this view by making a distinction between the 'hidden' aspect of the divine, which cannot be known or described, and the aspect of lordship (*rububiya*), through which God enters into a relationship with the world as its creator. The divine, in its uniqueness, manifests itself through a series of *logoi*, or prophetic epiphanies, starting with Adam and culminating with Muhammad. Ultimately, the creation belongs to the same reality as God, having originally existed as a series of archetypes in the divine mind, whose highest manifestation is the Adamic *logos*, or 'perfect man'.

Ibn 'Arabi conceived of human consciousness as existing along the scale of a similar continuum, characterized by 'light'. Just as the stream of being proceeds by a process of emanation, from the Absolute Indivisible One through the various 'intellects' down to the lowest animate or inanimate creatures, so the light of consciousness flows down the hierarchy of human intelligences. Subject and object merge in the

same continuum. Any disjunction between them is illusory, as is
the difference between the One and the many, the first and the last,
the eternal and the temporal, the necessary and the contingent. Within
such a system, in which the observer perceives himself as being part of
the observed, the categories of thought and being are indistinguishable.
Man (or microcosm) is patterned on to the universe (or macrocosm).
The result is a mystical humanism in which man is the 'microcosmic
being' through which God contemplates himself, God's *khalifa* (vice-
regent) on earth.

Divinity and humanity are thus not two distinctive natures, but
rather 'two aspects which find expression at every level of creation',
divinity corresponding to the hidden aspect of reality (*al-batin*), humanity to the external (*al-zahir*). The relation between God and his creation
is that of a mirror to the image:

Try ... to see the body of the mirror as well as looking at the form that it
reflects: thou wilt never see it at the same time ... God, then, is the mirror in
which thou seest thyself as thou art, His mirror in which He contemplates His
names.[19]

In Ibn 'Arabi's system, God is the only Reality: all things pre-exist
as ideas in the knowledge of God from which they emanate and
to which they must ultimately return. His argument suggestively
combines the metaphysical idealism of the neoplatonists with the
theology of *tawhid* adopted from the Mu'tazilis. Like previous
exponents of Sufi theosophy, Ibn 'Arabi arrives at a fusion of theology
and philosophy by way of mystic illumination: human reason alone,
he maintains, is far too limited to guide the seeker towards real understanding of the 'unity of being' running throughout creation. Such
unity must be felt before it can be grasped intellectually. Ibn 'Arabi
constructed what has been called 'the most imposing monument of
mystical speculation ever seen'.[20] If the language through which it was
articulated sounds arcane to modern ears, the reality it sought to
express seems to conform both with the fundamental world-view of
the Quran and with the conviction which underlies much modern
scientific research, that there must be a unifying principle in nature.

Rumi

Jalal al-Din Rumi, the greatest mystic poet of Persia and possibly of all Islam, was born into a family of 'ulama in Khurasan in 1207. At the age of 12, during the Mongol invasion, he and his family settled at Konya in Turkey, then usually known as Rum (Rome) from its Byzantine associations. He was initiated into Sufism by one Burhan al-Din, a former pupil of his father's, under whose tutelage he passed up the various rungs in the Sufi ladder of spiritual awareness. On Burhan al-Din's death in 1240 Rumi himself became a Sufi *shaikh*. He soon acquired a number of *mūrids* or followers, who were attracted by his extraordinary eloquence and personality. In 1244, however, there occurred a strange transformation in the Master* which greatly disconcerted his followers. A wandering holy man – who came to be known as Shams al-Din of Tabriz – appeared in Konya, and Rumi, despite his growing reputation as a Sufi *shaikh*, seems to have fallen completely under his spell. For Rumi the dervish represented the 'Complete Being' or 'Perfect Man' (*al-insan al-kamil*), the true image of the 'Divine Beloved' which he had long been seeking. Ignoring his own disciples, the Master became a pupil once more. The dervish persuaded him to discard his books and devote himself to him. Twice the *mūrids* and Rumi's family drove the dervish away in order to reclaim their Master. Eventually they murdered him in secret. (His coffin is thought to have been found during recent repairs to the mosque in Konya.) Though the loss of Shams brought Mawlana to the brink of madness, he devoted more and more of his time to declaiming poetry, listening to music and dancing. In 1249 he announced that Shams al-Din had reappeared in the person of one his *mūrids*, a handsome but illiterate goldsmith named Salah al-Din, whom Rumi appointed his deputy. Salah al-Din died in 1258; his successor as deputy, Husam al-Din Hasan, became the inspiration behind Rumi's greatest poem, the *Mathnawi* ('Epic'). On Rumi's own death in 1273 he became head of the order.

Rumi's literary output was staggering. In addition to the *Mathnawi*, which consists of six books of about 25,000 rhyming couplets, he composed some 2,500 mystical odes and at least 1,600 *ruba'is* or *ruba'iyat*

---

* *Mawlana*, literally, 'Our Master': hence the name of Rumi's order, the Mawlawiya, usually anglicized in its Turkish form, Mevlevi.

(quatrains). Virtually the whole of the *Mathnawi* was dictated to Husam al-Din in the decade and a half before Rumi's death. Mawlana recited the verses whenever and wherever they occurred to him – dancing, in the bath, standing, sitting, walking, by day or by night. Husam repeated the verses back to him before making any necessary corrections. Although the structure is apparently formless, with anecdotes, animal fables and materials drawn from the Bible, the Quran and Persian folklore irrationally juxtaposed and sometimes unexpectedly interrupted, there is an underlying thematic coherence. What Ibn 'Arabi ratiocinates through metaphysical speculation, Rumi, the 'drunken' Sufi driven to express his ecstasy in poetry, conveys by shifting images and Aesop-like morality tales. The unity of God, perceived throughout the natural order, is constantly and paradoxically proclaimed in the discursive and fragmentary utterances of the poet. The result is not wholly unlike a re-rendering of the Quran itself: indeed the *Mathnawi* has been called both 'the Sufi Quran' and 'the Quran in Persian'.

No doubt the *Mathnawi*'s emotional intensity derives in part from the poet's own vulnerable personality: his longing for love is sublimated into a kind of cosmic yearning. The Love Object, though divine and therefore unknowable, yields a very human kind of love. In the Quran a remote and inaccessible deity addresses man through the mouth of his Prophet. In the *Mathnawi* it is the voice of the human soul, bewailing its earthly exile, which cries out, seeking reunification with its creator. The poem's famous opening lines establish a theme which constantly recurs:

> Listen to the reed, how it tells a tale complaining of separations –
> Saying, 'Ever since I was parted from the reed-bed, my lament hath
> caused men and women to moan;
> I want a bosom torn by severance, that I may unfold [to such a one]
> the pain of love-desire.
> Everyone who is left far from his source wishes back the time when
> he was united with it.'[21]

The divine source from which man comes and to which he yearns to return is often linked to the ocean in Sufi imagery. The individual is a drop of water temporarily detached from the sea, to become part of it again when life is extinguished. The same image is suggested by

Sigmund Freud's expression 'oceanic consciousness', a state of mind whose origins, he suggests, derive from the time when the infant has not yet acquired a sense of its own identity or separateness. In Rumi's poem the dyadic relationship refers not just to the individual *vis-à-vis* the mass, but to the outward or phenomenal forms ('accidents') on the one hand and creative energy ('substance') on the other. In the following passage they are symbolized respectively by the foam at the top of the waves and the sea or ocean itself:

> The grief of the dead is not on account of death; it is because they
>   dwelt upon the phenomenal forms of existence
> And never perceived that all this foam is moved and fed by the sea
> When the sea has cast the foam-flakes on the shore, go to the
>   graveyard and behold them!
> Say to them: 'Where is your swirling onrush now?' and hear them
>   answer mutely, 'Ask this question of the sea, not of us!'
> How should the foam fly without the wave? How should the dust rise
>   to the zenith without the wind?
> Since you have seen the dust, perceive the wind; since you have seen
>   the foam, perceive the ocean . . .[22]

Man himself is a vehicle of the divine consciousness, an intelligence which emerges through the ascending hierarchy of created forms:

> First he appeared in the world of inorganic things
> Thence he passed into the vegetable state and lived
> The plant-life many a year, nor called to mind
> What he had been; then he passed from the vegetable state
> To animal existence, once more
> Remembering not the vegetable state,
> Save only when moved towards it in spring,
> The season of sweet herbs,
> Like babies which seek the mother's breast unconsciously;
> Or like the excessive inclination the young Sufi novice feels towards
>   his Sheikh,
> Drawn by [his] Universal Intelligence . . .*[23]

---

* The Logos with whom the Perfect Master is identified.

Thus Rumi suggests that the intelligence which manifests itself in humanity is a spiritual dimension which inheres in the very structure of the universe that gave rise to it. As the passage cited above indicates, the idea of spiritual evolution has an important social ramification: the spiritual attraction the young Sufi feels for his master becomes the cement of the Sufi *tariqa** or brotherhood. For it was this 'divine' intelligence, manifested in saintly charisma and transmitted down the generations, which converted the individual spiritual athleticism of the *shaikhs* into human associations capable of wielding social power and exercising political authority.

The Sufi tariqas

It may not be coincidental that the first Sufi order or *tariqa*, the Qadiriya, was founded within a generation of Ghazali's death in 1111. Towards the end of his life he had abandoned teaching for the second time and returned to his native Tus. Here he established a *khanqa* or hermitage, where young disciples were trained in a monastic atmosphere. Ghazali did not, however, become the founder of any Sufi *tariqa*. The credit for being the first of these is usually given to 'Abd al-Qadir Jilani (1077–1166), Ghazali's younger contemporary and, like him, of Persian ancestry.

A story is told about the special Sufi quality of 'purity', or disinterestedness, for which Jilani became famous. Like Ghazali, he had been sent off as a very young man to study in Baghdad. Before he set out, his mother had given him all his inheritance in the form of eighty gold coins sewn into his coat. On the way, the caravan in which he was travelling was set upon by bandits. Jilani, who seemed fairly impoverished, was almost ignored. However, as they were about to leave, one of the bandits asked him casually if he had any money – whereupon Jilani, without hesitation, showed him where his coins were hidden. Astonished at such honesty, the bandit took Jilani to the chief of the gang. The young scholar explained to him that if he had begun his search for truth by telling a lie, he could not have expected to get very far. The robber chief was so impressed, we are told,

---

* Literally 'path' or 'way'. In popular usage the word came to signify the organization as well as its theoretical basis (see pp. 244ff.).

that he abandoned his predatory ways and adopted a life of piety – becoming the first of many converts allegedly made by the saint.

After a time spent studying philosophy and Hanbali law, Jilani became the disciple of the Sufi Shaikh al-Dabbas (d. 1131). In 1127 he began preaching publicly, proclaiming his desire to 'close the gates of Hell and open the gates of Paradise for all mankind'. The main thrust of his teaching was an attack on worldliness and a Christ-like emphasis on charity. For many Sufis, including Jilani, Jesus was the symbol of pure human altruism: they revered, and sometimes practised, his injunction to appease aggression by 'turning the other cheek'. Jilani's popularity was such that a *ribat* or monastery was built for him outside the city. Many Jews and Christians are said to have been converted to Islam as a result of his ministry. In later generations many miracles would be attributed to him.

It is unlikely that Jilani intended to 'found' a religious order, apart from training his immediate spiritual disciples. However, after his death his sons carried on his work, and eventually branches of the Qadiriya order were founded from West Africa to South East Asia. Two other important early traditions, which in due course bifurcated into distinct brotherhoods, were the Suhrawardiya and the Rifa'iya. The former was founded by the nephew of a Sufi master, Abu al-Najib al-Suhrawardi, who had studied with Ahmad al-Ghazali, brother of the famous Abu Hamid and a renowned Sufi master. The nephew, 'Umar (d. 1234), was befriended by the caliph al-Nasr, who built a *ribat* for him. In many respects the Suhrawardiya remained an aristocratic order, patronized by the elite. However, towards the end of the fourteenth century it gave rise to a more populist order, the Khalwatiya ('seclusionists'), which became highly influential in the Ottoman Empire when one of its members, the 'Sufi' Bayazid, became Sultan (1481–1511).

The Rifa'iya order was founded by Ahmad ibn 'Ali al-Rifa'i, a holy man who spent all his life at his home in the marshes of Basra, except for one pilgrimage to Makka. His followers became famous for the spectacular frenzies in which they indulged, during which they would eat live poisonous snakes, enter blazing ovens, ride upon lions or other dangerous animals, or perform comparable feats, including acts of self-mutilation. According to Ibn Battuta, who visited some Rifa'i dervishes in Khurasan, they would 'place iron rings in their hands, necks and ears and even their male members so that they are unable to indulge in sexual intercourse'. The original aim of these exercises, of course, was to signify the victory of the spirit over the flesh and to mark the latter's temporary annihilation in 'Absolute Reality'. By the nineteenth century, however, as Lane suggested, many of these feats had been reduced to mere conjuring and other forms of charlatanry designed to impress the credulous.[24]

The Rifa'iya in due course gave rise to two important Egyptian orders, the Badawiya and the Dasuqiya. Sayyid Ahmad Badawi (b. 1199) has become an Egyptian national hero for rousing his followers to fight the Crusader invasion of Louis IX in the thirteenth century. His shrine at Tanta in the Delta is widely venerated and his *maulid* (anniversary) is one of the most popular festivals in the whole of Egypt. Ibrahim al-Dasuqi (d. 1288) was originally admitted into the Suhrawardiya, Rifa'iya and Badawiya (membership of the *tariqas* was rarely, if ever, exclusive), but eventually founded his own independent *tariqa*, the Dasuqiya. Another order which became prominent in Egypt was the Shadhiliya, founded by Abu al-Hasan al-Shadhili (d. 1258).

The orders and Muslim society

As they evolved, the *tariqas* developed into social structures through which an individual master's holiness or charisma was transmitted to posterity. Like other groupings in Islamic society, such as the *futuwa* trade-guilds to which they were sometimes linked structurally, they were relatively informal associations. Their popularity in urban society was largely due to 'the almost complete absence of corporal life or institutions'.[25] In the Shari'a vision nothing stood between the individual and the totality of the Umma except the family, to which the individual was tied not only by blood, but by a whole series of legally enforceable duties. In urban society the orders constituted a form of solidarity which made up for the lack of alternative groupings outside the family. Reinforced by initiation ceremonies and group practices such as *i'tiraf* (public confession), a *tariqa* conferred a close sense of brotherhood upon its members. In cities it was not uncommon for an individual to belong to several *tariqas*, though in country districts village organization was often interlocked with membership of one particular *tariqa*.

The role of the brotherhoods in spreading Islam in the peripheral areas among nomads and peasants, pagans and the adherents of more advanced religious cultures, can hardly be underestimated, and will be considered in the last section of this chapter. In general, however, it can be said that the Sufi *tariqas* performed a function of mediation between the divine and human worlds such as the Sunni *'ulama*, with their uncompromising scripturalism, were prevented from exercising in any formal manner. A *faqih*, a *mufti* or a *qadi* could decide upon questions of law which, as we have seen, theoretically included all spheres of human activity. He was less likely to be disposed, by temperament or training, to provide a model for social behaviour, or inducements to more active forms of devotional activity. The religious duties enjoined by the law were few, simple and austere, being largely confined to prayer and the observance of Ramadan and major festivals such as the 'Id al-Fitr. The Sufi *tariqas* supplied the ground for a much richer and more colourful liturgical growth, based on the devotional practices of the early adepts.

The *tariqa* itself is, strictly speaking, a 'theoretical and sound method of guidance'[26] devised by a Sufi *shaikh* and transmitted through his followers. The organization through which a *tariqa* extends itself in Muslim society is properly referred to as a *ta'ifa*; in non-specialist usage, however, the word *tariqa* is usually taken to mean both the rule and the order. The brotherhoods themselves, writes Michael Gilsenan,

... became as multi-faceted as the worlds of which they were so integral and representative a part – now military, now pietistic, now devoted to scholarly and theoretical pursuits, now to ecstasies and the intoxication of the senses; now the province of the religious and social elite, now of the illiterate and deprived masses; dedicated to the highest mysteries of the few, and to the exoteric simplicities of the many.[27]

The structure of the tariqa

We should be wary of making facile generalizations about the social organization or internal functioning of the *tariqas*. Nevertheless a certain structure is common to most, if not all, the pre-modern Islamic brotherhoods. Full membership is usually confined to males (as much because of existing social custom as by any formal rubric). The members, known as *mūrids* (aspirants), *faqirs* or dervishes (mendicants), are bound together by an oath of allegiance (*bay'a*) to their Guide (*shaikh*, *murshid* or *pir*), who heads a hierarchy of ranks within the order and is connected by a chain (*silsila*) of inherited sanctity (*baraka*) or kinship to the founding Saint. The *silsilas*, modelled on those originally devised to authenticate *hadith* reports, usually extend back, via the founders of the earliest orders, through such early masters as Hasan al-Basri, Junaid and Abu Yazid to members of the Prophet's household and ultimately to the Prophet himself. The Sufi *tariqas* thus legitimized religious authority in the same manner as the sectarian groups. The idiom of kinship, so ubiquitous in the social sphere, was extended to the religious, the lines of blood and *baraka* frequently overlapping. The main difference between the sects and the orders was that the latter, in their earliest phase of development, renounced even implicitly political aims (though later the *shaikhs*, like the *'ulama*, would assume an important political role as guardians of Islamic tradition). In fact, they re-channelled much of the spiritual energy formerly animating the sectarian groups: their rise to influence coincided with the overthrow of Shi'ite governments in Baghdad (1055) and Egypt (1171) and their replacement with Sunni regimes by the Seljuks. The *tariqas* took over from the Shi'a the *bay'a* or oath of allegiance originally given to a member of the House of 'Ali or his representative. The idea of *baraka* being transmitted either genetically or spiritually from master to pupil down the ranks of the orders bears a close similarity to the Shi'ite idea of *nass* (designation).

   In their proliferation, which was accelerated in the Central Islamic lands after the Mongol conquest brought many learned refugees into the countryside, the *tariqas* accommodated both 'orthodox' and 'hetero-dox' attitudes. Safi al-Din (d. 1334), progenitor of the Safavid dynasty, began his career as a Sufi *pir* by studying with a *shaikh* of the Suhrawardi order. However, after his descendant Shah Isma'il (d. 1524) had made Shi'ism the Iranian state religion, the Shi'ite *'ulama* became avid per-secutors of the Sufi orders, partly, no doubt, because they realized that the *pirs* were capable of exercising a similar socio-religious power to themselves. The Bektashi order in Anatolia, though closely associated with the Ottoman state until the abolition of the Janissary Corps in 1826, showed such reverence for the House of 'Ali that they may be regarded as crypto-Shi'ites, many of their adherents being drawn from the so-called Alevi community. At the opposite end of the spectrum one finds the militantly Sunni Naqshbandi order, which includes both

Abu Bakr and Ja'far al-Sadiq in its *silsila*. The Naqshbandiya has always been closely associated with 'official' Islam, having no separate organization of *zawiyas* or convents and holding its *dhikr* ceremonies in public mosques. In the nineteenth century Naqshbandi *shaikhs* were instrumental in winning recognition of the Ja'fari (Shi'ite) *madhhab* as a school of *fiqh* on a par with the four Sunni schools.

From about the twelfth to the nineteenth centuries Sufism in all its varieties became so widespread and pervasive as to be virtually co-extensive with Islam. The orders had become both bastions of orthodoxy and refuges of dissent. Saladin, restorer of Jerusalem and arch-suppressor of Shi'ite sectarianism in Egypt, welcomed the Asiatic Sufis there and founded several convents or *zawiyas*. His example was followed by the Mamluk sultans and their amirs: many of the magnificent buildings with which they endowed the city of Cairo were Sufi foundations. By the end of the fifteenth century the orders were well represented at the centre of state power. Hundreds of Sufi dervishes took part in the attack on Constantinople in 1483 which finally delivered the last outpost of Byzantium into the hands of the Ottomans; while in Egypt thirty-two years later the last independent Mamluk sultan, Qansuh al-Ghuri, faced the armies of the Ottoman conqueror, Selim the Grim, flanked by dervishes of the Badawi, Qadiri and Rifa'i orders grouped round their *shaikhs* and their banners.

The cult of saints

The triumph of the brotherhoods as popular movements was not achieved without strong and continuous opposition from the *'ulama*. From the time of al-Hallaj, official Islam had found the claims of the Sufi masters hard to swallow. At the heart of their objections was the challenge which the Sufi *shaikhs* offered to the spiritual hegemony of the *'ulama*. From the time of Shafi'i onwards, the Sunni doctrine held that revelation had been a 'once-and-for-all-time' occurrence, never to be repeated. Only those well versed in the scriptures were competent to dispense spiritual guidance, which could only consist in interpret-ations of the divine text or rulings based on the Sunna. Sufi pietism cut across this essentially legalistic and formal version of Islam. The veneration of the *mūrids* for their *shaikhs* not only challenged the social power of the *'ulama*, but questioned the very basis of the Shari'a as representing 'power of the law over life and thought'.[28] The *pirs* themselves represented a 'natural' religious aristocracy, *walis* ('friends') of God preselected by the Almighty on account of their spiritual purity. The absolutist claims of the *shaikhs* obviously called into question the book-learning, often arduously achieved, of the official *'ulama*. Most of the leading *shaikhs* claimed to have received their vocations, or confirmations of them, directly from God or the Prophet in dreams or visions. Like the Prophet himself, they were not thought of as men going out into the world with the aim of founding *tariqas*: they were believed to be acting under direct divine guidance. The vocational or confirmatory visions are not only found in stories about the foundation of new *tariqas*; they also appear in accounts of disputes following the death of a *shaikh*, when one or more of the *mūrids* might have a vision confirming one of their number in the succession.

In addition to these visions, and the absolute claims to religious authority sustained by them, there were other challenges with which the official authorities had to contend. Miraculous claims were constantly made on behalf of the saints. They were credited with thaumaturgic powers, and the belief that their *baraka* retained its potency after death, lingering around their tombs like some beneficent radioactivity, gave rise to the saint cults which flourished mainly in mountainous, rural and desert areas far from the disapproving eyes of the *'ulama*. Saint-worship has generally diminished in recent times, having succumbed to the combined onslaught of official Islam and secular governments capable of extending their authority into formerly marginal areas. But it is still possible in most Arab and Muslim countries to find country-folk, especially women, praying at the tomb of some long-forgotten local saint, usually a crumbling edifice containing a sarcophagus draped with fading green banners embroidered with Quranic inscriptions. In their heyday the orders provided an outlet for female devotion denied by official Islam, which tended to uphold the essentially male supremacist values of desert and city. Women were enrolled into the orders as associate members and were even sometimes permitted to preside over groups of female *mūrids*. It was customary for them to visit the tombs of saints on Fridays and other holy days while the menfolk attended congregational prayers at the mosques.

As well as being reputedly able to cure physical ailments, the saints tended to create a miraculous ambience around their persons. Virtually anything they did could acquire a miraculous character in the eyes of their followers. Michael Gilsenan collected a number of stories about a modern Cairene saint, Shaikh Salama ibn Hasan Salama (1867–1940), founder of the Hamidiya branch of the Shadhili order. They range from supernatural interventions (such as the occasion when the Shaikh eliminated the writing from the ledger of an English clerk who had offended him) down to such mundane but agreeable occurrences as the unexpected discovery of a sum of money or the catching of a fast bus. Other pieces of good fortune attributed to the saint included avoidance of disaster (missing a train which later crashed or a service-taxi which drove into the Nile) and the rescue of a *mūrid* from the path of an oncoming train. (This incident, occurring after the Shaikh's death, was attributed to his intervention from beyond the grave.) Significantly the Shaikh, despite his lack of formal scholarly training, is said to have effortlessly defeated the *'ulama* on their own territory, answering correctly the subtle doctrinal questions they put to him, or posing to the Shaikh al-Islam (as the Rector of al-Azhar University, the chief theological dignitary of Sunni Islam, is known) theological questions to which he could find no answer. As Gilsenan sees it, these 'miracles' (*karamas* – literally, 'acts of divine grace') are part of the wider 'universe of explanation' by means of which the *mūrids*, many of whom are illiterate and all of whom are poor, come to terms with their world. The Shaikh 'is a means that a mysterious, transcendent, predestinating God is assumed to use in the regulation of all things'.[29] A 'symbolic representation of a total order of things', he becomes, in other words, a personalized channel of communication with the divine: 'Linking men with their concepts of the Divine plan, he restates it and guarantees its mysterious outworkings. From him they can obtain baraka and through him they intercede for assistance in mundane affairs.'[30]

As has already been intimated, the idea of inherited *baraka* suggests itself inevitably in societies (such as those which predominate in the Muslim world) which set considerable store by patrilineal descent. As in Shī'ism, the lines of biological and spiritual inheritance often overlap, but not necessarily so. While mystic power, or *baraka*, may be transmitted through the blood-line, by means of designation, by visionary appointment, or by a combination of all three, it usually suffers some diminution of potency – not least because a portion of it is bound up in the personality of the original founder. However, both the decline in the leadership's real charismatic power and that in the *baraka* associated with the tomb of a departed saint serve, in different ways, to institutionalize the saint's following. From having been a relatively informal gathering of disciples, brought together and animated by the master's living presence, the *tariqa* develops its own institutional dynamic: one which must sometimes be replenished by occasional injections of authentic 'living' *baraka* from new divinely inspired leaders if the institution is to last.

A notable example of *baraka*-exploitation, corresponding to Max Weber's famous concept of the 'routinization of charisma', is provided by the Kazeruniya order which became the 'Lloyd's' of medieval Islam. Though actually founded in the fourteenth century the *tariqa* associated itself with Abu Ishaq of Kazerun near Shiraz (d. 1033), a saint of Iran whose *baraka* was thought specially effective against the dangers of sea-travel in the Indian Ocean. Agents of the brotherhood could be found in many major sea-ports on the monsoon route, including Calicut, Malabar and Chuan-Chow in China. Intending travellers would make a vow promising to pay a certain sum of money to the brotherhood if they reached their destination safely, with a premium for surviving a specially hazardous passage. A promissory note was passed from the agent to the brotherhood, which disposed of an elaborate organization for collecting the exact amount pledged. The funds were employed to finance the brotherhood's wide-ranging charitable activities.

The Sufi lodges

The characteristic institutions of the brotherhoods were the convents or hostels known by various names in different regions: *khanqas* (hospices) mainly in areas of Persian influence; *ribats* (frontier posts) in marginal areas of the Mashriq and Maghreb; *zawiyas* ('corners') mainly in North Africa; *khalwas* ('retreats') in western Asia; *tekkes* (centres) in Turkish-speaking areas. Trimingham has characterized the evolution of these institutions, within the context of the orders as a whole, in three stages. The first he calls the *khanqa* stage, during which the master and his pupils moved around fairly informally from one district to another. There were few regulations; the lodges and convents were relatively unspecialized and undifferentiated. As in the case of Jilani, the master and his pupils were sometimes housed at the expense of a friendly ruler. *Ribats* were originally fortified dwellings built to defend the faithful in predominantly non-Muslim areas. They often became centres of teaching and religious propaganda, and were sometimes built, and endowed, as *waqfs* around the tombs of fallen *mujahids*. The term *ribat* was adopted by Sufi adepts to describe the place where they waged the 'spiritual *jihad*' against worldly passions.

During the *khanqa* stage the *shaikh* was essentially a spiritual guide. Internal discipline was relatively democratic: the brothers sought permission from their companions rather than from the *shaikh* if they wished to be absent. A list of rules dating from the eleventh century urges cleanliness, both private and common devotions, Quranic recitation, theological and devotional exercises (*wird*) and ministering to the needs of the poor. The inmates are discouraged from gossiping or selfishness. The *khanqa* was an association of people prepared to live a common Islamic life, rather than a guidance centre for instilling a distinct Islamic religious discipline. Anyone could be admitted to a *khanqa* provided he could satisfy the *khadim* (steward) that he had studied under a recognized *shaikh*. The *khanqas* were also used as inns for ordinary wayfarers.

Trimingham describes the second phase in the development of Sufi organization as the *tariqa* stage. Occurring mainly during the primacy of the Sunni Seljuks during the thirteenth century, the *tariqa* stage involved the formalization and transmission of distinctive mystical doctrines, rules and methods. For the individual, whereas the *khanqa* stage involved the replication of the primary act of 'Islam' or Self-surrender to God, the *tariqa* stage implied submission to a specific rule, such as the Qadiri, Suhrawardi or Rifa'i, as outlined above. This period saw the development of *silsilas* legitimizing the order by referring it back to a suitably august holy personage (and ultimately, of course, to the Prophet himself). The imposition of a disciplined rule on otherwise wayward religious impulses can be described, using Weberian terms, as the 'routinization of mysticism'. The individualistic experience of the wandering dervish who moves from *pir* to *pir* or *khanqa* to *khanqa* is channelled into larger cooperative organizations. The characteristic Sufi ritual known as the *dhikr* ('remembrance') is developed at this stage, with the aim of inducing a state of collective ecstasy. Dervishes who remained outside the *tariqa* institution were known as *malamatis* and *qalandaris*. *Malamatis* rejected all outward show of religiosity, including prayers and the supererogatory exercises (*tarawih*) associated with Ramadan. *Qalandaris* exhibited more extravagantly antinomian attitudes, shaving their heads and placing iron rings in their hands, ears and penises, like the Rifa'iya. Some took their contempt for official Islamic *mores* so far as to invite accusations of immorality and debauchery.

The third and final phase in Trimingham's classification is the *ta'ifa* (denomination) stage. This occurred primarily during the fifteenth century, during the founding period of the Ottoman Empire. The *ta'ifa* stage develops more authoritarian patterns. The *mūrid* must surrender to a person – the *shaikh* of the order – so there is a consequent narrowing in the focus of mysticism. A favourite image of the early Sufis, the adept's 'corpse' being washed by his *shaikh*, is given a formal, institutionalized meaning. The *shaikh* becomes the doctor of souls, the teacher who alone can give correct guidance to the *mūrid*. He is 'the calm light in the veiling darkness, the shade of the verdant tree in the desert', the 'spiritual father completely possessing the *mūrid* who will do nothing save by his opinion or guidance in all affairs and will only leave him to obtain his daily bread'.[31] It is at the *ta'ifa* stage that the orders become deeply implicated in the cult of saints.

The *zawiyas, tekkes* and *khanqas* associated with the final stage of Sufic development were often built around the tomb of the founding saint. The North African *zawiya*, for example, is usually a complex of buildings, including a small mosque, a Quran school, a large room for *dhikrs* and *hadhras* (religious occasions) and dwellings for the *shaikh* and his family, as well as rooms for affiliates, pilgrims and travellers. Just how prevalent these institutions were throughout the Maghreb may be gathered from the instances of the word Sidi (from Sayyid, as saints are called in North African parlance) in Maghrebi place-names. A few orders practised celibacy but generally this was discouraged. In Turkish *tekkes*, for example, married dervishes had their own dwellings, but were obliged to sleep in the convent once or twice a week. *Mūrids* usually kept their wives and children in neighbouring villages, only the *shaikh* being entitled to house his family in the *khanqa* or *zawiya*. The latter was often endowed as a *waqf* by the founding saint's family or some of his wealthier followers. Not infrequently, however, they were self-supporting, having their own flocks and areas of cultivation.

Spiritual hierarchies

The organization of the *tariqas* was hierarchical, and, as they developed, increasingly complex. The hierarchy was built around the concept of ascending gradations of spiritual illumination. Sufis used the word *tauba* (repentance) to indicate their 'conversion' to Sufism, their resolve to abandon the worldly life and devote themselves to the service of God. Two key terms from the early Muslim experience are taken over and given internalized, spiritualized application. The act of joining a *tariqa* is described as making one's *hijra* – that is, forswearing evil ('Makka') and espousing the good life ('Madina'); while the spiritual struggle against 'the world, the flesh and the devil' is described as *jihad*. The term *mujahada* (a collateral form of *jihad*) is taken, in Sufi terminology, to mean the 'earnest striving after the mystical life'. A *hadith* of the Prophet places this 'striving of self' (*mujahadat al-nafs*) above the 'lesser' *jihad* against infidelity.[32] Thereafter (according to an early text dating from the eleventh century), the Sufi progresses through various stations (*maqams*) in his search for God. These range from *khalwa* (withdrawal), through *murakaba* (constant 'God-consciousness'), leading to 'satisfaction' (*rida*) and freedom (*hurriya*) from material considerations, to the final states of gnosis (*ma'rifa*), love (*mahabba*) and a 'yearning' (*shauq*) to be constantly with God.

The Sufi who decided to climb this arduous spiritual ladder had, during the latter phase of the movement, to join one of the recognized *tariqas*. Aspiring Sufis usually served a three-year novitiate. The first was devoted to 'service of the people', the second to 'service of God' and the final year to 'watching over his own heart'. Communal service included doing household chores. Among the Mawlawis the domestic aspect of the novitiate lasted almost three years: 1,001 days of unbroken service were required, the last year being spent in the kitchens. The initial ceremony of initiation was presided over by the chief cook. Khalwatis, on the other hand, were expected to go into retreat from the first, reporting on their visions to the *shaikh*. After completing the novitiate, the aspiring Sufi usually underwent a ceremony of investiture. Initially this included the adoption of the characteristic woollen garb worn by the early ascetics. From about the eleventh century this was gradually replaced by a patched garment known as the *muraqqa'* or *khirqa*. The *khirqa* was the outward sign that the *mūrid* had made his oath of fealty (*bay'a*) to the *shaikh*. In some Turkish and eastern orders the *khirqa* was supplemented by distinctive trousers, waistbands and headgear. After completing the appropriate initiation rituals, the novice or affiliate (someone merely taking a 'short course' in Sufi studies) was presented with a certificate (*ijaza*) containing his name, that of his *shaikh*, and the *silsila* of his order. By the fourteenth century, *ijazas* were easy to come by. Ibn Battuta, himself no Sufi, collected them as traveller's trophies. In the nineteenth century, when modern forms of transport had greatly increased the number of pilgrims from Africa, and the Far East, the revived orders made Makka a centre of recruitment, and many pilgrims were to be seen returning from the Hajj sporting tubular cases containing their *ijazas* round their necks.

The *shaikh* who is head of the *ta'ifa* often claims descent from the original founder. By analogy with the political organization of Islam, he is usually known as the Saint's *khalifa* or deputy. Ordinary members are usually divided into regular *murids*, who have dedicated their lives to the order, and lay affiliates. Outsiders usually refer to the former as *faqirs* ('poor ones') in Arabic, or its Persian equivalent, *darwish* ('mendicant') from which the anglicized 'dervish' is derived. The formal offices within an order do not necessarily correspond to the hierarchy of spiritual states outlined above; they are concerned exclusively with the order's 'external relations' with the outside world. Only the *shaikh* himself combines seniority within the organization with assumed spiritual superiority.

Sufi ritual

The central feature of Sufi ritual is the *dhikr* or remembrance. The Quranic basis for it is found in the verses urging believers to 'remember God with increasing remembrance and extol His limitless glory from morn to evening' (33:41). According to a modern Sufi writer, Frithjof Schuon, ' "the remembrance of God" is at the same time a forgetting of self; conversely the ego is a kind of crystallization of forgetfulness of God'.[33] Repetition of the divine names, an essential part of most *dhikr* ceremonies, is supposed to result in a 'knowledge of God' by way of contemplation. The *dhikr* usually begins and ends with a repetition of the divine name, a type of religious activity also found in the 'Jesus prayers' of Eastern Christianity and in Buddhism. In Islam it is often linked to the *tahlil* formula (*la ilaha il-la allah*: 'There is no deity but God'), which is pronounced rhythmically, accompanied by controlled breathing. The technique seems to have been handed down from the earliest masters: according to a *hadith* of Abu Yazid al-Bistami, 'for gnostics, worship is the observance of breaths'. Breath control is an important part of other religious disciplines, including Yoga, and may be employed to induce unusual psychic states by limiting the supply of oxygen to the brain. Controlled ecstasy may also be induced by certain physical movements. Among the orders these range from the gentle turning from right to left with which the Qadiris accompany the *tahlil* formula, a technique attributed to 'Abd al-Qadir al-Jilani himself, to the spinning of the Mawlawiya or 'Whirling Dervishes', who have performed their famous dance in several European cities. The eleventh-century mystic Ahmad al-Ghazali described the significance of these movements:

The dancing is a reference to the circling of the spirit round the cycle of existing things, on account of receiving the effects of the unveilings and revelations; and this is the state of the gnostic. The whirling is a reference to the spirit's standing with Allah in its inner nature and being, the circling of its look and thought, and its penetrating the ranks of existing things . . .[34]

The dance of the Mawlawiya produces a disciplined ecstasy apparent to anyone who watches it. Rumi's intoxicated energy survives in the dance of his order, but it is harnessed into a brilliantly choreographed display that achieves a delicate balance between symmetrical precision and spontaneous movement. The dance, perfected over seven centuries, has none of the self-conscious theatricality of classical or modern ballet. The viewer is a vicarious participant in the action, not a member of an audience; the dancers seem oblivious to the presence of observers – so much so that the viewer enters to some degree into the interiority of their experience.

All communal *dhikrs*, though differing in form and style, seek to achieve a submergence of the individual into the communal identity and, by means of such temporary loss of ego-consciousness, a sense of the 'unity of the beyond and the within'. Ontologically speaking, the inner state at which the adept arrives may not differ from that achieved by means of yogic exercises: what makes it characteristically

Islamic is the liturgical and communal context in which it happens. The sense of human brotherhood and physical solidarity to which Islam gives tangible manifestation in the Hajj and the ritual discipline of congregational prayer remains an essential element in the mystic communion of the *dhikr*. The pressure towards social conformity forces the *mūrid* to purge his search for a higher consciousness of any anti-nomian or individualistic elements. Before he can approach God, he must first attend to his fellow beings, subsuming his identity within that of a group which represents, in microcosm, the whole Islamic community.

In its liturgical meaning also the *dhikr* remains a characteristically Muslim activity. The ritual's dominant purpose is the 'saturation' of self in Allah. Gilsenan points out in connection with the Hamidiya Shadhiliya that the names of God employed in their *dhikr* are those which focus above all on his transcendence and power:

No plea is addressed to the Almighty; there is no supplication, no imploring of His grace . . . the concentration is on the Absoluteness of God, His Transcendent, Eternal Being, *not* His attributes such as those of Mercy and Compassion. No action of God is expected, or requested, in the *dhikr*. No material blessings will follow. From this point of view, the *dhikr* is non-instrumental in character.[35]

The *dhikr*'s character is non-contingent, its spirit the disinterested search for the divine in the tradition of Rabi'a al-'Adawiya and Ibn 'Arabi. This is not to say, however, that such states of 'being' are achieved without a certain amount of psychological manipulation, which can degenerate into 'mystical mechanization'. The constant attacks on popular Sufism mounted by 'official' Islam in modern times owe much to the general disrepute into which it was brought by undisciplined *dhikrs* and the more primitive forms of saint-worship.

Reform, renewal and the spread of Islam

Apart from contributing towards the creation of group identities within the loosely textured societies of the Muslim cities, the most signal historic contribution of the Sufi orders was towards the spread of Islam in the peripheral regions. In this respect the *tariqas* inherited earlier traditions of Isma'ili *da'wa*, evangelizing distant tribes and communities in mountainous and tropical regions. Where the *da'is* had proclaimed the divine government of their Imam, the Sufi dervishes cultivated the veneration of saints. Both movements centred on the cult of personality rather than on the proclamation of scripture. A Sunnism based mainly on the upholding of legal norms enshrined in an Arabic text could hardly be expected to penetrate the cultures of non-Arab illiterates far removed from the cosmopolitan world of the great Islamic cities. Yet, in the long term, official Islam was to benefit from the very practices which orthodoxy condemned. The wilder extravagances of the intoxicated dervishes, which earned such disapproval from grave city gentlemen learned in *fiqh*, took on a different colouring in societies familiar with shamanism or witch-doctors. The easy-going tolerance of wandering marabouts, equipped with prayer-mats and magical formulae borrowed or adapted from scraps of Islamic lore, was well suited to the winning of converts in peripheral regions, for, while the symbols of religious power were familiar and hence reassuring, the dervishes nevertheless carried with them the cultural prestige of the greater Muslim society. Islamization was mostly a gradual process, occurring over generations. In contrast to the official *'ulama*, the dervishes were free to bend the rules to suit the customs and habits of different peoples. Only after a period of 'cultural Islamization' had passed were partly converted peoples suitably prepared to take on the full burden of Shari'a conformity. This was particularly the case with animists in non-Arab regions, where a long process of acculturation was required before they were even in a condition comparable to the *jahiliya* of the pre-Islamic Arabs. The Shari'a accommodated and legitimized many pre-Islamic Arab customs, which made its observance less burdensome to Arabs than to other peoples.

In many parts of the Islamic world, notably Indonesia and West Africa, two of the most populous Muslim regions, Islamization was far from complete when European colonial power intervened in the process, delaying it in some places and accelerating it in others. Whether or not the European presence acted as a catalysing force, the final stage in cultural Islamization took the classic form of a *jihad* against pagan 'backsliding'. The model of a polytheism resulting from the degeneration and fragmentation of an atavistic monotheism served, as in Muhammad's original movement, to legitimize a variety of local campaigns to impose reforms on different societies, bringing them more closely into line with Shari'a norms. In some instances the *tariqas* themselves provided the institutional framework through which reform was enacted. In others the reform of Islam embraced a frontal attack on all varieties of Sufism. Such differences were, however, more apparent than real. All the reform movements sought, in different ways, a 'return' to a purer Islam closer to Shari'a norms. To this extent all of them, whether or not explicitly opposed to certain Sufi practices, come within the scope of the neo-Sufic revival.

The spread of Islam in the peripheral regions occurred almost imperceptibly. Any attempt to describe it is bound to be over-schematic if tedious repetition and detail are to be avoided. Conversion was never the exclusive preserve of the Sufi orders. In trading centres resident Muslim immigrants observed the law and attended the local mosque in a conventional manner owing little or nothing to Sufi organization or practice. Nevertheless, members of the orders with their impressive spiritual lineages were sometimes credited with bringing the 'truth' to these metropolitan outposts of the faith. At the same time there is little doubt that the loose, relatively informal structures of both official and unofficial Islam allowed syncretist tendencies to develop in areas which were either remote from the literary culture of the cities or which came within the orbit of non-Muslim high cultures. The former category applies particularly to the spread of Islam in the Maghreb, Black Africa and Central Asia; the latter to its development in southern Asia and the Far East.

The Maghreb and Black Africa

The process of Islamization can be a highly complex one, involving as it does the gradual adoption of Islamic norms and outlook by people of widely differing cultures. In parts of West Africa the initiative came mainly from above. Muslim traders and marabouts who journeyed south of the Maghreb into what are now Mauritania, Mali and Nigeria, and into the riverine states of Senegal and the Volta, carried with them an aura of cultural prestige that commended them to the rulers of territories. A king who protected Muslims or even converted to Islam became part of the international community, giving him considerable advantages over non-Muslim rivals. Literacy (in Arabic), the expansion of trade and even the opportunity to dispossess his non-Muslim neighbours by launching a *jihad* against them provided the inducements which made Islam an attractive 'royal cult' for many West African princelings. A successful *jihad* need not necessarily lead to mass conversions: subject peoples might more usefully furnish slaves and booty whilst remaining *kafirs* without any rights. The cultural prestige associated with Islam was often expressed in terms of admiration for its superior magic. A green turban received from the Sharif of Makka during attendance at the Hajj was a more impressive symbol of authority than any local tribal fetish. In the 'royal' Islam of West Africa, Islamic practices often coexisted with pagan cults. An *'alim* who visited the court of Askiya Dawud (1549–83), ruler of Songhay on the Upper Niger, who had the reputation of a scholar and patron of Islamic learning, was scandalized to find the rituals of divine kingship being observed, and dared to tell the ruler to his face that he must be 'mad, corrupt or possessed'. Askiya's reply showed how far this nominally Muslim ruler felt compelled to go along with his people's traditions: 'I am not mad myself,' he told the scholar, 'but I rule over mad, impious and arrogant folk. It is for this reason that I play the madman myself and pretend to be possessed by a demon in order to frighten them and prevent them from harming the Muslims.'[36]

The success of Islam in propagating itself, particularly in its Sufic and maraboutic versions, in regions where a direct assault by conquest was impracticable was largely due to what I. M. Lewis calls 'its truly catholic recognition of the multiplicity of mystical power': '. . . in the voluminous Quranic store-house of angels, jinns and devils, whose number is legion, many of these traditional powers find a hospitable home; and passages from the Quran are cited to justify their existence as real phenomena'.[37] So long as Allah's lofty pre-eminence was not compromised, many local cults could be accommodated within the realm of *al-ghaib*, the 'unseen' or 'hidden' world. The supreme deities which exist in many pagan traditions could be assimilated to Allah. Lesser local deities could be Islamicized or explained away as vernacular terms for God's attributes, or as the jinns or spirits of Quranic folklore. Ancestor cults could be accommodated to Islam by tagging local kinship groups on to Sufi *silsilas* or Arab lineages. By such methods the Somali cattle-herders, originally evangelized under Qadiri auspices, acquired Quraishi ancestry. This 'canonization' of ancestors as Sufi saints conferred inherited *baraka* upon the Somali clans, providing them with the prestige of an Arabian spiritual ancestry. Elsewhere, for example, in the Central High Atlas, special 'saintly' lineages, traced back to 'Ali and the Prophet through one or other of the many Sufi *silsilas*, provided a kind of theocratic 'constitutional' framework through which a fissiparous tribal society achieved a basic minimum of cooperation. The leaders of saintly families, who usually resided in the vicinity of the tombs of their holy ancestors, would undertake the supervision of tribal elections, arbitrate in inter-tribal disputes and generally help guarantee the complex seasonal arrangements governing the movement of people between the high mountain pastures and the desert's edge. The function of such saintly families was virtually identical to that of the Quraish, hereditary guardians of the Ka'ba, during the time of the Prophet.

In Islam, syncretism in ritual is much more difficult to justify than syncretism in theology. Whereas every kind of religious belief can be accommodated within the framework of Islamic concepts merely by the adoption of Islamic terminology or symbols, the outward recognition of these symbols in formal religious observance is a matter on which orthodoxy is severe and uncompromising. One may privately think of Allah as Waq or Soko; one cannot, however, perform rituals such as prostration or 'dusting' oneself before the king in accordance with local traditions without inviting accusations of *shirk* – polytheism, or the 'association' of lesser beings with God. In Africa syncretism of belief inevitably spilled over into the corruption of ritual. Rain-making ceremonies were accompanied by Muslim prayers; Sufi *dhikr* came to be held not merely in 'remembrance' of Allah, but also to appease pagan goddesses credited with malevolent powers.[38] Such practices as the *zar* cults (exorcism ceremonies) or the ingestion of *baraka* by physical means (including copulation with a holy man, or drinking his vomit) are part of a pattern of diffusion in the peripheral and marginal regions of the Muslim world, where the absence of the literate class of urban scholars left spiritual power, untempered by learning, in the hands of those who were free to exercise it in any manner they found congenial or appropriate. Wherever conditions allowed, however, they provided the pretext for reformers who sought to purify Islam by bringing local practice more closely into line with Shari'a norms.

Jihad *movements and reformed* tariqas

Broadly speaking, these reformist movements fall into two categories: the *jihad* and mahdist movements which sought to recreate a purified Islamic society *in toto*, rebuilding, as it were, the Madinese caliphate on new foundations; and the reformed *tariqas*, which sought to regenerate existing polities by bringing the Sufi orders more closely into line with Shari'a norms. One should not, however, make too much of this distinction. All the reform movements represent a common ambition to restore or impose stricter Shari'a practice and ritual in accordance with the models established by the Prophet and the earliest Muslim community. They also represent, in varying degrees, the desire to restore the pristine Islamic state in the face of real or perceived threats of pagan backsliding and non-Muslim rule. The forms taken by such movements varied considerably, occurring as they did in many different social and cultural milieus. But their inspiration was usually scriptural and charismatic.

Generally the *jihad* and mahdist movements led to the founding of new states on Khaldunian lines, based on a combination of religious authority and tribal 'asabiya. They occurred mainly in peripheral and undeveloped regions, far from the great cities, where pastoralism in one form or another remained the predominant mode of agricultural production. The reformed *tariqas* operated both in arid regions, on the basis of tribal organization, and in more highly centralized agrarian states. The flexibility of *tariqa* organization enabled reformers to seek their objectives by more variable means than the classic sequence of *hijra* followed by *jihad*. Under certain conditions, a reformed *tariqa* might transform itself into a *jihad* movement, creating a state on the basis of *tariqa* organization. But whereas *jihad* and mahdist movements in general were radical, utopian and aggressive, neo-*tariqas* were more inclined to be compromising, pragmatic and defensive.

The model of the *jihad* movement, despite the occasional use of mahdist eschatology, was the secessionism of the early Kharijis, who made a Manichaean division of the world into two camps, the true Muslims, or 'People of Paradise', and the 'People of Hell', comprising everyone else, including pagans, non-Muslims and any Muslims who refused to join their camp. The model of the reformed *tariqas* was initially the piety and asceticism of the early Sufi masters. In each case the Quranic vision, interacting with the real world, was subtly different. The mahdist or *jihad* leader tended to imitate the armed Prophet of Madina, doing battle against God's enemies under divine inspiration. The neo-*tariqa* leader was generally more influenced by the Makkan phase of the Prophet's career, when, in the face of the prevailing infidelity and corruption of the Holy City, he gathered around himself a group of followers committed to reforming themselves by observing a common religious discipline, leaving aside, for the present, the wider question of transforming society.

Ibn Tumart and the Almohad empire

An early and far-reaching movement in the *jihad* tradition was the Mahdiya of Ibn Tumart (d. 1130), which overthrew the Almoravid empire in Spain and the Maghreb and led to the foundation of the most durable and civilized of all the Berber states. Ibn Tumart was born in a settled Berber village in the anti-Atlas, and like many reformers spent a period studying in the East before returning to his homeland. The story that he met Ghazali in Baghdad is probably untrue; in Baghdad, however, he was strongly influenced by the Ash'ari school of theology which, in contrast to the Maliki school prevailing in the Maghreb, allowed the figurative interpretation of the Quran. The Maliki *'ulama* of Spain and the Maghreb had been among the most conspicuous targets for Ghazali's attacks, and it is reported that the Almoravid rulers had, at their behest, ordered all copies of the *Ihya* to be destroyed.

On returning to the Maghreb, Ibn Tumart began preaching the uncompromising unity of the divine (*tawhid*) according to Ash'ari tenets. His followers (like the Druzes and later the Wahhabis) described themselves as Muwahhidun ('unitarians'), from which the Spanish 'Almohad' derives. The Berber preacher took a stern line on sexual segregation, women's dress, the consumption of alcohol, music and dancing: the puritanical austerity of his doctrine is still in evidence in North Africa to this day. The most original project he sponsored was the translation of the Quran into the Berber tongue. His attacks on the life-style of the Almoravid amirs brought him increasing political trouble. Consciously emulating the Muhammadan and Khariji models, he eventually made the *hijra* to his native district in the anti-Atlas, accompanied only by a few followers. Here he made many converts among the local Berber tribes and, having received their *bay'a* (homage) proclaimed himself Mahdi or 'Imam of the Age'. Though he died shortly after his first major (and far from successful) encounter with the Almoravid armies, his successor, 'Abd al-Mumin, eventually overthrew them and proclaimed himself caliph, transforming what had been an ideological movement into a dynastic state. Under a survey commissioned by 'Abd al-Mumin in 1159, all non-Almohad Muslims were classified as infidels and made liable to forfeit their property. At the height of their empire the Almohads controlled territory stretching from Cyrenaica to the Atlantic and from Mali to Valencia. Three of the greatest philosophers, Ibn Tufail (d. 1185), Ibn Rushd (Averroës) (d. 1198) and the Jew Ibn Maimun (Maimonides) (d. 1204), flourished under their rule. The Ash'ari doctrines held by Ibn Tumart enabled the Almohad rulers to harmonize the Arab and Berber elements in their culture and to maintain intellectual double standards: strict adherence to the Shari'a for the masses, free intellectual speculation for the enlightened few. The contrast was well illustrated by Ibn Rushd himself, who, in addition to being the most enlightened and rationalistic philosopher produced by medieval Islam, was grand *qadi* charged with administration of the Shari'a.

From about the middle of the thirteenth century the Almohad empire began to suffer the classic symptoms of Khaldunian decline. The moral and psychic energy which had sustained it became diffused once more, leading to a collapse of the empire into a number of competing Berber kingdoms. The disintegration of central power saw a corresponding rise in the influence and authority of the *tariqas* and *zawiyas*. By the time a new imperial power had succeeded in reunifying the Maghreb, the *tariqa* habit and maraboutism had become so ingrained that even the rulers claiming to carry the Prophet's blood in their veins were incapable of governing without the support of one or other of the leading orders.

Dan Fodio and the empire of Sokoto

Whereas the Almohad movement sought to revitalize and purify the already Islamicized society of the Maghreb, the *jihad* of Shehu Usumanu Dan Fodio (in Arabic, 'Uthman ibn Fudiy) (1754–1817) took place in a mixed society of 'court Muslims' and pagans. While representing itself as an attack on the 'corruption' of Islam by the rulers of Hausaland, it also contained a proselytizing dimension, for by attacking the syncretic practices of 'royal' Islam and paganism it brought into the Umma many people without previous attachment to the faith.

The towns of the Sahel, the 'shore' of arid and cultivable land south of the Sahara, had been infiltrated by Muslim settlers and pastoralists from Umayyad times. However, the cities and townships witnessed a growing tension between the class of urban 'ulama and their rulers who, as already indicated, were prone to mixing formal adherence to Islam with court rituals of pagan origin. The tension between the 'ulama and their rulers was further complicated by the influx of pastoral peoples from the north, a movement which in the eighteenth century gave rise to a series of *jihads*, the most celebrated and far-reaching of which was Dan Fodio's. Fulani cattle-herders, light-skinned Muslim tribesmen moving southwards from Mali in search of pasture, were the main bearers of this sub-Saharan version of the Khaldunian cycle. In 1725 Ibrahim Musa, a Fulani 'alim, proclaimed the *jihad* and founded the state of Futa Jallon in the highlands where the Senegal and Gambia rivers have their source. The movement spread to Futa Toro on the coast (modern Guinea), where an independent imamate was formed which lasted till the French conquest.

Dan Fodio was born in 1754 into a family of urban Fulani scholars, in the independent Hausa kingdom of Gobir. He spent much of his early life moving from one town to another, in order to study with different scholars. Influenced by the Berber theologian Muhammad al-Maghili, he argued that syncretic practices were more outrageous in the sight of Allah than outright paganism, because, whereas pagans were backward people who knew no better, the 'mixers' (including, of course, the court Muslims) were in a position to corrupt Islam by leading good Muslims astray. The Shehu's attacks were clearly aimed at, among others, the King of Gobir, who responded by forbidding his followers to wear turbans or veils. In the classic Muhammadan manner, in 1804 Dan Fodio made his *hijra* to beyond the borders of the kingdom.

The emigrants began raiding. Other Hausa rulers began to persecute their Muslim subjects. A number of Fulani shaikhs, Qadiri Sufis and 'ulama from Futa Toro joined the *jihad*; other Fulani, backed by the Tuareg, joined the enemy. By 1807 Dan Fodio had overrun Kano, Zaria and other Hausa city states. In 1808 Alkalawa, capital of Gobir, fell to the *mujahidun*. The conflict cut across ethnic and kinship ties, local antagonisms and group loyalties. After the fall of Alkalawa Dan Fodio devolved much of his authority to his son, Muhammad Belo, who became first Sultan of Sokoto, the most powerful Muslim emirate in what eventually became the British colony of Nigeria. A descendant of Dan Fodio, Sir Ahmadu Belo, Sardauna of Sokoto, was regional premier of Northern Nigeria until his assassination in the military coup of 1966 which overthrew the Federal Government.

Arabian Wahhabism

The syncretic accretions which *mujaddids* ('renovators') such as Ibn Tumart or Dan Fodio found so objectionable were the inevitable result of the penetration of Islam into non-Arab cultures where local Berber or African custom ran against the current of Islamization. It is not without significance that both leaders drew their inspiration from the 'Abbasid rather than the Madinese caliphate. The period of formative Islam which had most relevance for their situation was that of assimi-lation and growth in the pluralistic society of the ninth and tenth centuries, rather than the purely Arab Islam of the Prophet's era. Ibn Tumart, while strictly adhering to Shari'a norms based on the Quran and the Sunna, was almost Mu'tazili in his condemnation of literalistic and anthropomorphic interpretations of scripture. This was not simply due to his hostility to the Maliki *faqihs* who held sway in the Maghreb: non-Arabs, however 'fundamentalist' their disposition, can only be expected to accept Islam on terms which recognize that all speech, including the 'divine', has a contingent character – an attitude of mind which lends itself naturally to allegorical interpretation. For this, if for no other reason, it seems wrong to dismiss his theology as being of merely 'minor importance'.[39]

Similarly, 'Uthman Dan Fodio was 'fundamentalist' only in the most general sense of the term. Regardless of his explicit statements, he sought, not to restore a pristine Islam that had never existed in Africa, but to introduce the metropolitan Islam which represented the highest culture of which he was aware. The legal sources quoted in Fulani literature are mostly late 'Abbasid. With so many pagan practices around which could be condemned as *shirk*, the African had no need to identify this sin in terms of 'innovative' practices.

The culture of the Arabian Peninsula being predominantly Arab, the *jihad* of the Wahhabis had a subtly different character from that proclaimed by the Berber and West African innovators. Whereas the latter sought to employ Islam, as the 'Abbasid caliphs had done, as a way of integrating their societies into the high culture of the Fertile Crescent, the Arabs of Najd had a different, almost opposite objective. For them, Islam affirmed their distinctive identities as Arabs. It was no accident, therefore, that the ideology through which they sought to reaffirm this identity in the face of the cosmopolitan culture of Iraq and the Hejaz was a version of pristine Islam derived from their ideas about the Madinese caliphate, one which laid particular stress on strict adherence to the divine text's linguistic integrity.

Muhammad ibn 'Abd al-Wahhab (1703–92) shared with his model, the medieval Hanbali theologian Ibn Taimiya (d. 1328) an uncompromising hostility to what both men saw as the contamination of Islam by non-Muslim innovations or practices borrowed from Christianity or introduced by the Sufi *tariqas*. Reacting against popular Egyptian practices such as the celebration of the Prophet Muhammad's birthday, Ibn Taimiya had insisted on redrawing the boundaries around Muslim life: not even the most trifling resemblance must be allowed to exist between Muslims and non-Muslims. All Muslim life must begin from a point where 'a perfect dissimiliarity with the non-Muslims has been achieved'.[40] Ibn Taimiya spent much of his time in prison. His first incarceration occurred after a quarrel in his native Damascus with a Christian whom he accused of insulting the Prophet's memory. Indicted by his enemies for anthropomorphism, he replied by accusing them of antinomianism and hashish-taking. A brilliant polemicist, he wrote pamphlets attacking both the monism of Ibn 'Arabi and the spiritualizing *tawil* of Ibn Tumart. He made himself unpopular with the 'ulama of his day by his condemnation of legal innovations such as the triple *talaq* (repudiation) by which Sunni husbands could instantly divorce their wives without undergoing a process of reconciliation, as well as numerous other *hiyal* ('tricks') by which the spirit, if not the letter, of the law was violated. Rejecting both *tawil* (esoteric interpretation) and *tasbih* (anthropomorphism) he shared Ibn Hanbal's belief that God could only be described as 'He has described Himself in His Book and as the Prophet has described Him in the Sunna' (which is to say in those texts that are fully accessible only to Arabs). Ibn Taimiya was considered a *mujtahid mutlaq* (having the right of absolute or unrestricted *ijtihad*) by his contemporaries. He apparently held to the principle that every rule must be derived from the Quran and the Sunna, although he allowed limited applications of *ijma'* and *qiyas*.[41] This approach was conservative but far from rigid: the plurality of the material on which legal decisions were based allowed for considerable variation.

Ibn 'Abd al-Wahhab went further than Ibn Taimiya in his rejection of borrowings by equating Sufi practices with those of the pagan idolators, seeing in his own age a *jahiliyya* or period of ignorance even worse than that which prevailed before Muhammad. This was a discourse that would be revived during the latter half of the twentieth century by Sayyid Qutb and others, who equated *jahiliyya* with the 'westernizing' tendencies of modern governments.

The idolators of our own time are worse in their idolatry than the ancients because the ancients were worshipping God in times of affliction and associating others with Him in times of prosperity, but the idolators of our own time are always guilty of associating others with God whether in prosperity or affliction.[42]

The Hanbali *madhhab* to which both Ibn Taimiya and Ibn 'Abd al-Wahhab subscribed had remained, despite Ahmad ibn Hanbal's official rehabilitation under the 'Abbasids, something of an opposition movement within the wider culture of the Mashriq. Though eventually recognized as one of the four Sunni *madhhabs*, they never constituted a school of *fiqh* comparable to the other three. In line with his general repugnance for human reasoning in law, Ibn Hanbal rejected *qiyas* unless absolutely necessary. For him the Quran and Sunna were not so much the sources of law, as the law itself. Although he was capable of the subtlest juridical reasoning, he eschewed any formal rational-ization of legal methodology, believing that legal decisions must be arrived at by continually referring back to these sources (as distinct from reference to a body of *fiqh* derived from them).

In theory Wahhabism allowed that anything not explicitly forbidden in the Quran or the Sunna was permissible. In practice, during militant phases of the movement, attacks on ritual innovations such as tomb-worship tended to spill over into attacks on practices not explicitly sanctioned by the Prophet. Ibn Hanbal himself is said to have abstained from eating water-melons because of the lack of any *hadith* on the subject. The original Wahhabis banned music, dancing, poetry, silk, gold, all ornaments and jewellery because of *hadiths* condemning them. Their twentieth-century imitators, among both the Ikhwan and more recent religious opponents of the Saudi monarchy, have attacked tobacco-smoking, the telephone, radio and television as 'innovations' unsanctioned in scripture.

Nevertheless, the flexibility implicit in these doctrines has allowed the Saudi rulers to push through reforms with the minimum of opposition from the *'ulama* (whose most influential elements, the al-Shaikh, are descendants of Ibn 'Abd al-Wahhab). Telephone, radio and television were introduced – once it had been proved that they could be used to transmit the Word of God. A host of other innovations have followed, including the abolition of slavery (though this is sanctioned in the Quran) and the introduction of female education (something which misogynistic *hadiths* could be cited to oppose). In short, Wahhabism has not proved an insuperable obstacle to development in what has become one of the world's most rapidly changing Muslim societies, although, as was seen in the opening chapter of this book, it can still supply the ideological ground for an attack on such innovations as would-be reformers, radicals or revolutionaries deem to be corrupt and un-Islamic.

Naqshbandi reformism

The reformed *tariqas* and *jihad* movements which specifically addressed themselves to the situation created by European colonial conquest in the nineteenth century will be referred to in the following chapter. No account of the heritage of Sufism in pre-colonial times would be remotely adequate, however, without reference to the oldest and longest-established reformist tradition, the Naqshbandiya. This medieval order, which became immensely influential in Central Asia and the Indian Subcontinent, faced many of the dilemmas encountered by reformist movements in the twentieth century. Its responses to the challenge of non-Muslim power as well as to the predicament of Muslims living in predominantly non-Muslim cultural and religious milieu, ranged from the rejectionist *jihad* to a spiritualizing doctrine permitting total collaboration with infidels on the political front. The range of the Naqshbandiya's responses from the fifteenth to the nineteenth centuries corresponded more or less accurately to the responses of *dar al-Islam* as a whole when presented with the even more formidable challenge of non-Muslim power in the nineteenth and twentieth.

The Naqshbandi order, which includes 'Ali, Abu Bakr, Salman al-Farisi, Ja'far al-Sadiq and Abu Yazid al-Bistami in its *silsilas*, derives from the *tariqa* of Abu Yaqub al-Hamadhani (d. 1140), but takes its name from that of a later *shaikh*, a Tajik mystic named Baha al-Din al-Naqshbandi (d. 1389). The early Naqshbandi masters were closely linked with the *malamatis* (literally, 'blameworthy ones'), who rejected all outward show of religiosity, concentrating upon the inner life while engaged in the affairs of the world. One of the order's most distinctive rituals is the 'silent *dhikr*' (*dhikr khafi*) practised alongside the spoken *dhikr*. Naqshbandis say that 'Ali used to read the Quran out loud, while Abu Bakr did so silently. Two Naqshbandi sayings express the order's outlook: 'The exterior is for the world, the interior for God'; and 'Solitude within society'. Like practical Christians, Naqshbandis believe that piety may better be expressed by social activity than by withdrawal from the world – an attitude which separates religious from political commitments, accounting for the order's success in adapting itself to varied political environments, collaborating with worldly powers when necessary, but resisting them by force where circumstances made this seem desirable.

Since the order reserved the 'interior' or mystical life for God, it remained firmly committed to outward Shari'a observance where this was the norm. 'There is no *tariqa* outside the Shari'a' is another Naqshbandi maxim. Hence it had little difficulty in adapting to existing social or religious patterns. It was above all the order of the *'ulama*. In the Ottoman empire Naqshbandi *shaikhs* often doubled as the imams of public mosques, where the *mūrids* held their *dhikrs*. Although at the height of its influence in Turkey the order controlled a widespread network of *tekkes* (there were more than 50 in Istanbul during the 1880s), separate *zawiya* organizations were never considered essential. Under adverse conditions, however, Naqshbandis do not even consider it necessary to hold regular meetings between the *shaikh* and his *mūrids*: once the *bayʿa*, or oath of allegiance, has been sworn, an esoteric connection is supposed to have been established which transcends physical separation. The *mūrid* is given a set of *wirds* or daily recitations to make, if necessary in private. Similarly, in the Naqshbandi *silsilas* there are chronological gaps which were presumably bridged by purely spiritual initiations via dreams or visions – for example, the initiation of Abu Yazid al-Bistami (d. 879) by Ja'far al-Sadiq (d. 765). The three regions where the Naqshbandiya have flourished most successfully are Anatolia, Central Asia and the Indian Subcontinent.

Western and Central Asia

In the nineteenth century the order enjoyed official Ottoman patronage after the suppression of the Bektashi order, which had distinct Shi'ite leanings. It was in the forefront of opposition to the Tanzimat reforms which sought to modernize and strengthen the Ottoman state bureaucracy in the face of the empire's growing subservience to the European powers. In 1925, after the abolition of the caliphate, two Naqshbandi *shaikhs*, Sa'id and 'Abdullah, led a Kurdish-backed rebellion against Ataturk's secularizing policies. After Ataturk had abolished the *tariqas* they continued to thrive underground. Recently the order has seen a revival in the so-called 'Nur Sect', or 'Followers of Light', founded by Sa'id Nursi (1873–1960), a Kurdish *shaikh* from eastern Turkey. The Nur group has published a number of popular works on science and technology. After forming an alliance with the National Salvation Party led by Necmettin Erbakan, which stood for a fundamental reversal of secularism and a re-Islamization of Turkish life, the group switched its allegiance to the Justice Party, which was much more closely identified with Turkish nationalism.

In Central Asia the success of the Naqshbandiya among Turkic tribes was evidenced by the popularity as a place of pilgrimage of Baha al-Din's mausoleum near Bukhara. From the fifteenth century, Tartar tribesmen had grafted Naqshbandi *silsilas* on to their lineages, which facilitated the spread of the order west into Anatolia and south into India. Members of the order were largely responsible for proselytizing among the Uzbeks, who brought it as far east as Xinjiang (Chinese Turkestan). Outside Persia, where a Naqshbandi sub-group led by the self-styled *mahdi* Nurbakhsh (1393–1465) converted to Shi'ism, the leaders of the independent states which arose in the wake of the Mongol conquest favoured the order, honouring its *shaikhs* by building mausoleums for them and *khanqas* for their dervishes. With important centres at Samarkand, Merv, Tashkent and Bukhara, from the eighteenth century the order played a leading part in resisting the Russian advance. In the Caucasus the Khalidiya branch of the order founded by Mawlana Khalid al-Baghdadi (d. 1827) was the mainspring of resistance to Tsarist attacks, from the time of Shaikh Mansur at the end of the eighteenth century to the final capture in 1859 of the Daghestani leader Imam Shamil after a series of campaigns lasting three decades. Though Shaikh Shamil's campaign, one of most prolonged and celebrated instances of Muslim resistance to European imperialism, ended in defeat, Naqshbandis were active in a subsequent uprising in 1877, and provided the leadership for the short-lived Imamate of Daghestan and Chechnya during the interregnum between the collapse of the Tsarist empire and the establishment of Soviet rule. After the disintegration of the latter the same networks of *mūrids* or *moolvis* (as the Russians came to call members of the orders) have sustained the military campaign against Russia prompted by Moscow's refusal to grant the Chechens full independence.[43] In Central Asia the Naqshbandiya order organized the Andijan revolt of 1898; after the Bolshevik revolution it supplied most of the leaders of the Basmachi revolt which the Soviets only finally succeeded in putting down in 1932.

For all its tradition of militancy in Central Asia and the Caucasus, the Naqshbandi order survived during seven decades of Soviet rule precisely because it was well adapted to undertake 'underground' Islamic activity. Whereas the Qadiriya, the other leading order active in the Soviet Union, was liable to attract attention by its ecstatic rituals, the Naqshbandiya offered a form of private religious activity which successfully escaped official attention. As a whole the *tariqas* offered a 'parallel religion' to the official Islam backed by the Soviet authorities, with its carefully chosen, party-approved *mullahs* and licensed mosques. Since only the chosen few were given exit visas to attend the Hajj, local pilgrimages to saintly tombs were encouraged by the 'alternative' religious leadership as a way of keeping religion alive. Although Russian spokesmen are inclined to blame 'fundamentalist infiltration' funded by Iran or Saudi Arabia for revival of Islamic activity in Transcaucasia or the former Soviet Central Asian republics, there is an abundance of evidence that the revival is based on the re-activation of indigenous Sufi networks that were dormant, but not destroyed, during the Soviet period.[44]

South Asia

The Naqshbandiya's reformist influence and activities have been most extensive in the Indian Subcontinent. Here, as in Africa, the gradual proselytizing undertaken by other Sufi orders had led to the development of forms of religious syncretism in which Islamic practices had become intermixed with local Hindu cults and beliefs. Hinduism, however, is far removed from African paganism. Though 'polytheistic' in the sense of recognizing a multiplicity of forms through which the divine may manifest itself, it belongs to the tradition of an advanced and ancient civilization upheld by a literate and highly cultivated caste of Brahmins whose knowledge of the world and its arts was in no manner inferior to that of their Muslim conquerors. In terms of the prevailing values underpinning the two systems, a clash was inevitable. Whereas the thrust of Islam is towards social equality and religious conformity, that of Hinduism is towards social hierarchy and 'spiritual anarchism'.[45] Whereas the logic of Islam, as of other western monotheisms, propels it towards an intolerant rejection of alternative formulations of religious truth, the trend in Hinduism has been towards a universal acceptance of other faiths within a hierarchical order which links, however tenuously, the rarified speculations of the intellectuals with the *bakhti* devotionalism of the masses.

Despite this fundamental incompatibility between Islamic and Hindu world-views, the Mughal ruler Akbar (1556–1605) made a serious effort to harmonize relations between his Muslim and Hindu subjects by according to the latter a degree of toleration that placed them on a level of equality with the dominant Muslims. Proclaiming his own right as an absolute *mujtahid*, he set about changing those aspects of the Shari'a which conflicted with the rights of his Hindu subjects. Thus Hindus were exempted from paying the *jizya* tax which symbolized their status as *dhimmis*; disabilities impeding their employment in the army and bureaucracy were removed. More controversially, Akbar forbade Hindu girls from converting to Islam in order to marry Muslim men, thereby extending to Hindu families the same protection enjoyed by Muslim families against their daughters marrying out of the faith. In an effort to further standardize social practice, Akbar forbade Muslims to marry their first cousins and discouraged child-marriage among Hindus. He opposed slavery and tried to abolish *sati* – the practice whereby high-caste Hindu widows were burnt along with their dead husbands – and gave permission for them to re-marry, like Muslim widows. Eventually he and his entourage became vegetarians, partly, no doubt, in order to discourage cow-slaughter and so avoid offence to Hindus.

In extending a religious toleration that increased the power of the state by strengthening the allegiance of his non-Muslim subjects, Akbar was drawing upon several traditions within Indian Islam. Under Hindu rulers the Indus and Ganges regions had long been a haven for religious refugees, including Jacobite Christians, Jews, Zoroastrians and Isma'ilis, who enjoyed relative freedom from persecution within the Brahmanic caste-system. After the Muslim conquest forcible conversion was rare, as was active proselytizing. Lower- or out-caste Hindus tended to be naturally drawn to Islam, since conversion enabled them to escape their degraded status and acquire education and employment in government service. Inter-marriage between Muslim men and Hindu women had further encouraged natural conversion, though it also brought Hindu cultural influences into Muslim families. Of those who undertook conversions, the Sufi *pirs* were by far the most successful. Acquiring reputations as individual holy men, they were closer to the illiterate classes than the *'ulama* and fitted inconspicuously into local traditions. More decisively, they were tolerantly prepared to accept non-Muslims as probationary disciples, gradually absorbing them into Islam by personal precept.

This contact between the two religious traditions produced not only syncretic developments at a popular level, but a theosophical synthesis at the highest. Kabir (1440–1518), an outstanding popular teacher and poet, rejected the rituals of both religions, proclaiming a universalist theism that transcended both of them. His disciple Guru Nanak (1469–1539), under the combined influence of Kabir's ideas and Sufic and Hindu theosophy, launched the Sikh movement in the Punjab, which, from being a strict if eclectic monotheism, developed into a separate religious community affirming a predominantly counter-Islamic group identity.

The Emperor Akbar patronized both Sikh *gurus* and Sufi *pirs*, especially those of the Indian Chishti order, who were notable for their universalist tendencies. But court ritual departed increasingly from Indian Sunni tradition. In 1581 he promulgated his famous 'Divine Faith' (*Din Illahi*), a monotheism based on reason and asceticism. Imitation (*taqlid*), the unreasoned following of traditional exegesis and *fiqh*, was condemned. Quranic concepts such as devils, jinns and angels were given rationalist interpretations. Sensuality, lust, misappropriation and deceit were prohibited. The Sufi virtues of piety, devotion, gentleness and 'yearning for God' were extolled. The cult, which amounted to an aristocratic court *tariqa* with the Emperor as its *shaikh*, combined Ibn 'Arabi's mystic doctrines with courtly flattery. Despite his lack of formal education, Akbar seems to have had a genuine concern for the disinterested pursuit of religious and philosophical truth and an intelligent awareness of his duty as head of a multi-religious empire. He was a man far ahead of his time.

Inevitably there were both Muslims and Hindus who found Akbar's reforms intolerable and sought to retreat into their separate traditions. The Shari'a norms often ran directly counter to the pluralistic traditions embedded in Indian society. A Muslim ruler could, like Akbar, achieve a certain balance by abandoning the Shari'a's claim to universality, reducing it to one form of religious observance among others. But by so doing he reduced his Hindu and Muslim subjects to a common level, depriving the latter of their special sense of historic mission as the final and most faithful bearers of God's messages to mankind. No rarefied theosophical speculation, no spiritual despotism, however morally earnest or enlightened, could compensate for the sense of betrayal felt by ordinary Muslims at the cultural fusion implied by Akbar's reforms. Given the traditions into which the Shari'a had crystallized by the sixteenth century, the reaction that followed was inevitable.

The Naqshbandi order became the spearhead of this reaction. A relative late-comer to India, it had gained a foothold at court during the latter years of Akbar's reign, through the influence of one of its *shaikhs*, Khawaja Baqi-billah. It gathered momentum during the reign of Akbar's successor, Jahangir (1605–27), under the leadership of Baqi-billah's disciple Shaikh Ahmed Sirhindi. At the beginning of his career Sirhindi showed signs of a mystical megalomania not unlike that of Akbar, claiming to have surpassed Abu Bakr himself in gnosis and to have elevated the 'reality of Muhammad' to the 'stage of Abraham'. However, the extravagance of Sirhindi's claims earned him a reprimand from Baqi-billah – and a salutory spell in prison from the Emperor. On his release the *shaikh* appeared somewhat chastened, and set about formulating a role for India's Muslims leading to communalism and ultimately to separatism.

Sirhindi's campaign had ideological and social dimensions. As a Naqshbandi reformer, or *mujaddid*, he attacked those esoteric aspects of Sufism which he saw as facilitating the mixing of Islam and Hinduism at both aristocratic and popular levels. Thus he condemned Ibn 'Arabi's ontological monism (*wahda al-wujud*, 'unity of being') or, rather, the versions of it transmitted by Indian commentators who believed, plausibly enough, that it could be harmonized with Hindu pantheism. The idea that God alone is existent makes physical objects into mere 'flashes' or 'appearances' which can be worshipped as manifestations of the divine will. In Sirhindi's view, if such syncretic possibilities remained unchecked, Indian Islam must inevitably dissolve into the polymorphous structures of Hindu religion. The *tariqas*, which were largely responsible for popularizing Ibn 'Arabi's doctrines, would have to be firmly subordinated to the Shari'a – in line with the Naqshbandiya's well-known principles. Like Ghazali, Sirhindi believed that the mystic experience must be made to conform with the *zahir*, or outward forms, of Islam if they were not to become contaminated by heterodoxy or disintegrate into personal whimsicality. The alternative theosophy he proposed has been described as 'phenomenological monism' (*wahda al-shuhud* or 'unity of witness'), a doctrine which, while seemingly little different from Ibn 'Arabi's, preserves an absolute and unbridgeable distinction between the Creator and his creations. Reality is not (as in Ibn 'Arabi) the mirror through which God contemplates himself: rather, it is his reflection, which must never be confused with the original. This distinction, however subtle, opened the way for a complete re-affirmation of the Shari'a: the *'ulama* must be supreme, both in the sphere of outward observance and in that of profound inner speculation.

The supremacy of the *'ulama* over the *pirs* had fundamental consequences for the community: Islam and *kufr* (disbelief), which in the Indian context meant Hinduism, were rigidly, irreconcilably opposed to each other. The honour and security of Islam were dependent upon the humiliation of the unbelievers. Whoever held infidels in affection and esteem or kept company with them, dishonoured his own religion. A good Muslim was expected to avoid contact with non-believers even in daily business.[46]

The influence of Sirhindi and his successors has been incalculable. As Ahmed remarks, it checked the process of Indian Islam's disintegration into syncretic heresies, and gave it 'the rigid and conservative stamp' it bears today. The intellectual leaders of modern Muslim India, including Sayyid Ahmed Khan, Muhammad Iqbal and Abu l-'Ala al-Maududi were all, in various ways, indebted to Sirhindi.

The immediate result of Sirhindi's campaign was, however, to push the community towards communalism. By insisting on the irreconcilable character of the two faiths, that the Muslims must at all costs preserve themselves from contamination by Hinduism, he abandoned

Islamic universalism for Shari'a particularism. With Muslims a numerical minority, this was to prove a disastrous ideological base for a
multi-confessional empire. When Sirhindi's teaching had finally borne
fruit, becoming official policy during the reign of Aurangzeb (1658–
1707), it provoked numerous Hindu revolts, bringing Muslim power to
the verge of extinction, thus opening the way to European intervention
and, ultimately, to colonial rule.

Shah Wali Ullah

Sirhindi's intellectual successor, Shah Wali Ullah of Delhi (1703–62),
was another Naqshbandi *shaikh* who continued the work of bringing
Sufism firmly into line with the Shari'a. The son of a Naqshbandi
mujaddid, he retained a qualified admiration for Ibn 'Arabi. Wali Ullah
was a contemporary of Muhammad ibn 'Abd al-Wahhab, and there
are definite similarities between them. Both sought to discard the
superstructure of the *fiqh* and to return directly to the Quran and the
Sunna as advocated by Ibn Taimiya. Both stressed the need for constant
ijtihad. However, whereas Ibn 'Abd al-Wahhab's fundamentalism,
applied in the relatively homogeneous environment of Arabian Islam,
led to a Khariji-style division of the world into 'us' against 'them',
identifying all who failed to conform to Wahhabi tenets as 'infidels'
liable to attack, Wali Ullah's occurred in a world where non-Muslims
were numerous and powerful. So, while maintaining the momentum
of the Naqshbandi campaign against syncretism, he took a much
broader view of Islamic allegiance. In theosophy he sought to reconcile
Sirhindi's phenomenological monism with the ontological monism of
Ibn 'Arabi; in theology he tried to blur the distinction between the
Mu'tazili and Ash'ari positions; in Shari'a, he sought to harmonize the
differences between the four *madhhabs*, taking the majority Hanafi view
(diametrically opposed to the narrow puritanism of the Wahhabis) that
anyone who had once professed themselves a Muslim remained one,
whatever their sins or failings. Confusing the two movements, the
British described Shah Wali Ullah and his supporters as 'Wahhabis'.

As an Indian, Shah Wali Ullah had to develop a much more sophisticated and less literalistic understanding of the scriptural imperatives
than that of his Arabian counterpart. Whereas for the Najdi '*alim*, *ijtihad*
meant determining the law by referring back to sources in his own
language and formed in the same cultural milieu, for the Indian it
involved a striving to discover the Shari'a's underlying purpose and

intentions. Najdi fundamentalism involved a restoration, pure and simple, of the supposed conditions of the Madinese caliphate – a restoration which still seemed feasible in the eighteenth century, since in the Arabian heartland things had changed relatively little since the days of the Prophet, while the *jahiliya* which the Wahhabis discerned around them corresponded closely to the descriptions in the Quran and *hadiths*. In the crumbling feudalism of the Mughal decline in India, fundamentalism meant a search beyond the letter of the Shari'a to its spirit – an attitude of mind that led, not only to the reactionary conservatism of thinkers like Abu l-'Ala al-Maududi, but to the progressive modernism of Sayyid Ahmed Khan and Muhammad Iqbal, and to those other modernists who saw, and continue to see, in *ijtihad* Islam's necessary response to growth and change in human society.

The seeming paradox that both progressive and reactionary modernist movements in Islam draw upon the 'fundamentalism' of Ibn Taimiya is grasped more clearly if the different environments of his two leading apostles, Ibn 'Abd al-Wahhab and Shah Wali Ullah, are taken into account. The latter's position is only deceptively similar to the former's. In spirit, as in doctrine, Wali Ullah is closer to the Berber 'fundamentalism' of Ibn Tumart. Like Ibn Tumart, Wali Ullah opposed the *'ulama* of his day, recognizing that their knowledge of Arabic gave them a monopoly of access to the scriptures and hence of religious authority and social power (making them, in the Indian context, 'Muslim Brahmins'). Again like Ibn Tumart, Wali Ullah took the radical step, against the opposition of the *'ulama*, of translating the Quran into the vernacular tongue – in his case Persian, the language of the average educated Indian Muslim. In 1743 he founded his own school for the study of the Quran and *hadiths*. Two of his sons furthered his religious propaganda by making translations of the Quran into Urdu, the demotic language of Indian's Muslims.

With the collapse of Muslim power and the growing encroachment of the British and the Hindu Marathas, Wali Ullah's Naqshbandi reformism developed into militancy, culminating in the *jihad* launched against the Sikhs by Sayyid Ahmed Barelvi in 1831. This was a crucial development for Indian Islam, for it anticipated the end of communalism: Barelvi's attempted *hijra* from infidel British rule to the *dar al-Islam* he tried to create on the Afghan frontier foreshadowed the massive and bloody *hijra* in which half a million people were to die in 1948.

Barelvi was a disciple of Wali Ullah's son and successor, Abdul Aziz. Like his predecessors, he militated against Hindu accretions in certain ritual practices, while showing considerable tolerance towards different religious and theological currents within the Islamic fold. Under Barelvi's leadership, however, the reform movement moved away from its institutional connections with the Naqshbandiya, merging its own *tariqa* with those of the other leading Indian orders – the Qadiris and the Chishtis – and subsuming them all within renovated Shari'a orthodoxy which Barelvi called the Tariqa-i-Muhammadiya, the Way of Muhammad. This movement, a forerunner of such twentieth-century reform movements as the Muhammadiya movement of Indonesia, founded in 1907, or the Muslim Brotherhood of Egypt, founded in 1928, combined Sufic discipline with Shari'a norms, making, as it were, the Sunna itself into a *tariqa*. In a non-Arab milieu where the majority of people had no access to the scriptures, the *tariqa* structure, with its authoritarian leadership and organized self-discipline, provided the means by which Shari'a orthodoxy protected itself against the continued encroachments of Hindu society. In 1826, following the hallowed path from 'Makka' to 'Madina', Barelvi tried to emigrate to a region along the North-West Frontier where he could found an Islamic state on liberated territory. Unfortunately this region, though inhabited by Muslims, was under Sikh control. Barelvi's *jihad* against the Sikhs was a dismal failure: the Pathan tribesmen on whose support he depended proved unreliable, especially when Barelvi tried to impose Islamic taxes on them, and deserted in large numbers. He was finally defeated and killed by the Sikhs at Balakot in 1831. The Tariqa-i-Muhammadiya, however, remained a militant Islamic movement in India, and its supporters played a leading part in the great rebellion of 1857. Thereafter they remained a thorn in the side of the British Raj, not being finally suppressed until the 1880s.

China and the Pacific

In the Far East, the Naqshbandi order, expanded by pilgrims returning from the Hajj, played a prominent part in stimulating resistance to the Dutch in Acheh (Northern Sumatra) and contributed to Muslim militancy in the Southern Philippines. In China it was instrumental in creating the so-called 'New Sect', a movement which led to an unprecedented assertion of Muslim identity in a country where the community had long become assimilated, culturally and politically.

Though scholars are still in dispute about many of the details surrounding the New Sect, their original Naqshbandi provenance is not in doubt.

Islam was originally established in China by Arab, Persian and Indian traders. As early as the eighth century there were Muslim communities with their own *qadis* in Canton and Chuan-Chow (named Zeitun by the Muslims). In addition to these coastal communities, subsequent centuries saw a substantial influx of Muslim immigrants from Central Asia, including bureaucrats and soldiers imported by the Mongol Yuan dynasty (1279–1368). The social and political pressures on Chinese Muslims led to a superficial acculturation. Having become ethnically Chinese (through intermarriage with Chinese women), the Muslims adopted the Chinese language and Chinese dress. Mosques were built in the style of pagodas, the muezzin making the call to prayer inside the courtyard. Knowledge of Arabic was confined to the imams or 'akhunds', although as with other non-Arabs, the use of Arabic greetings became a Muslim shibboleth. Nevertheless, observance of ritual and dietary laws ensured that the Chinese Muslims retained a separate identity as a religious community. The Hui, as they came to be known, were regarded as foreigners by the majority of Han Chinese. The situation persists to this day, Muslims being recognized as a national minority with their own 'autonomous region' in Ning-Hsia (Kansu), though they are widely distributed elsewhere. Before the emergence of the New Sect the Hui attitude was summed up in the phrase, 'Muslims indoors, Chinese outdoors'.

The Islamic revival in China dates from the late eighteenth century, when a number of Naqshbandi *shaikhs* led a *jihad* against the Chinese Emperor from Khokand (Uzbekistan) and found support among the Muslims in Xinjiang. In response to the sinicizing policies of the Manchu emperors in the nineteenth century, the Chinese Muslims became increasingly assertive of their identity. The New Sect appeared after the return from the Hajj of Ma Ming Hsin, a *shaikh* of the Jahriya branch of the Naqshbandiya, which traces its spiritual descent from 'Ali and practises the vocal *dhikr*, increasing group self-consciousness and solidarity. The New Sect and its affiliated branches appear to have been behind every Muslim rebellion in China down to the present century, including two major revolts which shook the Manchu empire. The first, led by Ma Hua Lung, lasted from 1862 to 1877 and affected most of Kansu and Shensi provinces; the second, led by Tu Wen Hsin, who took the Muslim name Sultan Suleiman, established a Muslim state which ruled half the province of Yunan. One of the leaders of the Yunan rebellion, Ma Te-hsin, was the first scholar to translate the Quran into Chinese.[47]

Conclusion

The record of the Naqshbandiya, combining inner spirituality with an outward, political, posture ranging from acquiescence to militancy, according to circumstances, should warn us against characterizing Sufism as a purely mystical or quietist dimension of Islam. The *tariqa* organization, whether built into a kinship system or acting as a kinship surrogate, could be transformed from contemplative to militant activity without change to the structure. The ties of allegiance between a *shaikh* and his *mūrids*, based on rigorous discipline and absolute obedience, could cement group loyalties as firmly as the '*asabiya* of the tribesfolk. The group's ideology – whether focused on extreme Shari'a rectitude like that of the Wahhabi Ikhwan, or tending towards Mahdism as in the movements of Ibn Tumart and Muhammad Ahmad in the Sudan, almost invariably had a Khariji aspect, in that nominal or cultural Muslims tended to be anathematized as infidels. The revolutionary potential of such movements sprang from the underlying psychological processes. The individual Sufi's rejection of the 'world' is a necessary prelude to his attempt to transform it, while the sense of brotherhood and comradeship fostered by the common ritual lends him the courage to wage the *jihad*. Indeed, the personal or 'inner' *jihad* against evil furnishes the preparation for the external *jihad* which aims to destroy evil in the world.

The revitalizing force of Islamic spirituality is something that will always find political expression when the occasion demands it. Like all other central Islamic traditions, its legitimacy derives from the Muhammadan paradigm. The examples contained in this chapter should have made it clear that this latent militancy can be directed against any social or political order perceived as threatening the well-being of the community. From the eighteenth century, however, the danger to Islamdom appeared to be coming increasingly from Europe, which, because of its overwhelming economic power and military superiority, demanded a much more radical response than a spiritual renewal or reaffirmation of Islamic militancy. Before the Muslims could hope to fight off the European threat with any chance of success they would have to undergo an intellectual revolution that would enable them to re-state the message of Islam in modern terms. This was the problem that would exercise the most fertile Muslim minds from the mid nineteenth century, when the hegemony of western civilization seemed most assured.

7 Challenge from the West

The casual visitor to modern Cairo will at first sight see little to distinguish it from other cities which have succumbed to the utilitarian banalities of the twentieth century. Apart from the river Nile, whose gleaming surface cuts a shimmering swathe through the geometrical patterning of blocks and tenements, it is a noisy, dirty, smelly place, a cacophanous confusion of pedestrians and automobiles, where the sensible tourist usually remains in the cool of a hotel lobby, only venturing out in an air-conditioned bus to visit the dozen or so sights recommended by the tour operators. One of the places on the tourist agenda is the bazaar area known as the Khan al-Khalili: a covered *suq* or traditional Arab market, where enterprising shopkeepers offer hand-crafted souvenirs for several times the price they fetch a few streets away. The customary bargaining rituals, according to which buyers and sellers arrive at an agreed and fair price, depend, of course, on a common knowledge of the market – something the tourist cannot hope to acquire in three days. The foreigner who wants to pick up a good bargain must take along an Egyptian companion.

Visitors who are not easily put off by the importunities of shop-keepers and who keep calm in the face of endless demands for *bakshish* from small children may soon begin to notice some interesting para-doxes. In the older quarters of the city around the Khan al-Khalili, where most of the men still wear the *galabiya* and women always cover their heads if not their faces, the attitude people display towards foreigners conveys a confusing mixture of friendliness and hostility. At one moment you can be inundated with offers of tea and coffee, and plied with friendly questions about your national origins and family situation; at the next you sense an undertone of menace as someone collides with you in a way that is obviously not accidental, or explodes into fury if you take a perfectly innocuous photograph. The one response that seems to be lacking is the normal urban indifference of the Western city: it seems impossible, if you are a foreigner, to avoid being noticed. This applies especially to females. European women invariably complain about being molested – sometimes in a manner so crude that indignation must give way to Rabelaisian laughter. Yet to be treated like a whore seems extraordinary in a society that sets such store by the chastity of women and the hospitality accorded to strangers. Sometimes, of course, the behaviour of foreign women invites the approaches of which they frequently complain. I myself once watched, with fascinated embarrassment, as a tall young woman, possibly American, bra-less and clad in a sleeveless shirt, wearing shorts which exposed the upper portions of her thighs, purchased some mangoes from a stallholder, a dignified young peasant clad in the traditional *galabiya*. This woman – I reflected – is sexually assaulting the man, though she may not realize it. Her garb was a systematic violation of all the sartorial codes governing male–female relations in traditional Islamic society. Only the extreme boorishness of superpower arrogance could produce such a display as this. The mango-seller remained resentfully polite – this was Maadi, a residential suburb much patronized by foreign families, and it would be more than his livelihood was worth to create a fuss here. But in less affluent parts of the city this woman would have encountered the outright hostility her appearance unwittingly invited.

Such extreme gaucherie is, however, still the exception, even in countries like Egypt that have come under increasing American political and cultural influence. If European women find themselves molested, it is not because of the behaviour of a few of their ignorant or foolish peers, but rather because they are seen to conform to stereotypes derived mainly from cinema and advertising, stereotypes full of potent images of European female sexuality. Even where local laws forbid female display in advertising and severely censor movies available for cinema and television, young men returning from the fleshpots of London or Paris, and the growing business of smuggling 'blue' videotapes for private consumption, ensure that the stereotypes retain their sharpness. The response among the unsophisticated, who know little of European customs and habits, is an almost equal mixture of attraction and repulsion: fascination at the sexual opportunities supposedly on offer, repulsion at the thought that such delectable temptations have so obviously been planted by the devil.

Encounters of this kind, multiplied a thousandfold, are the raw data which make up the tortuous and often agonized discourse of relations between Muslim societies and the West, a discourse that has ebbed and flowed over the past century with the flux and reflux of Western political and cultural hegemony. Because of its intimate and personal character, the arena of sexuality is one of its most emotive battle-grounds. Few things have traditionally more incensed the defenders of *dar al-Islam* than the thought that the corruption and promiscuity they perceive in European society may spread to their own, undermining and ultimately destroying the cherished family values which hold them together. But there are many other areas of mutual incomprehension and conflict. Militarily, politically, economically and culturally dominant, the West has come to pose first a challenge and finally a threat to the Islamic world. Since the end of the eighteenth century the problem of the dominant West, whether perceived as Christian, secular or atheist, has been the major preoccupation of thinkers and activists, and indeed of all those Muslims who have tried to work out the relevance of the Quranic message for their generation. The West – like its women – has been a simultaneous source of attraction and repulsion: admiration for its institutions and for the technical prowess that has enabled so many of its citizens to enjoy undreamed-of freedoms and opportunities; disgust at its vulgarity, its seeming callousness and spiritual emptiness, combined with a deep sense of unease that Allah, whose Way has been shown for all mankind in the Holy Quran and the Sunna, should have permitted infidels to violate all but the innermost chambers of the House of Islam. Unlike Christianity, which experienced persecution during the first three and a half centuries of its existence and learned to survive, even to flourish, under non-Christian governments, Islam is a religion 'programmed for victory'. Broadcast to the world on the triumphant wings of the Arab conquest, its formative period occurred at a time when its political hegemony seemed assured. The experience of defeat and failure *vis-à-vis* non-Muslims (if we except the temporary set-back of the Battle of Uhud) was something for which no Prophetic precedents were available: even the Imams of the Prophet's House, whose Christ-like betrayals and sufferings nurtured the Shï'ite faith, had been persecuted by nominally Muslim rulers.

The burden of history

Muslim defeat at the hands of Christian powers had occurred long before the nineteenth century, when most of *dar al-Islam* came under European domination. Sicily and Spain had been lost to the West, while from the sixteenth century the Russian state began to expand over Muslim lands in Central Asia and the Caucasus. Arguably, a more serious threat to Islamic civilization came from the Mongol invaders, who finally destroyed the 'Abbasid caliphate and disrupted the eastern trade routes. But in the West neither the Mamluk state in Egypt nor the Ottoman Empire based in Anatolia, which finally took Constantinople in 1453, was able to arrest the long process of Islamic decline *vis-à-vis* the Christian powers, which reached its nadir during the first quarter of the twentieth century. There were economic and political reasons for this decline, some of which have a religious dimension. In Western Asia the destruction of Baghdad by the Mongols facilitated the development of the Sufi *tariqas*, fostering a spiritualizing and anti-rationalist approach to Islam in what had once been the centre of the empire. During the same period in Europe the hegemony of the Church was coming under increasing pressure from the forces of humanistic rationalism which culminated in Protestantism and the Enlightenment. In the Islamic heartlands the conservatism of the *'ulama*, epitomized by their reluctance to permit the introduction of print (see pp. 358–61 below), helped sustain a climate hostile to technical innovation. At a time when Europeans were transforming their economies by means of such revolutionary devices as heavy-wheeled ploughs and horseshoes, substantially increasing the agricultural surplus available for investment, Middle Eastern societies were exhibiting a lack of mechanical inventiveness within a much more conservative 'policy of provision'. Agriculture, always more limited because of the aridity of the region, declined as insecure rulers devoted less and less energy to such vital areas of investment as irrigation. Whereas in the West the Roman law which came back into use after a long period of eclipse from the thirteenth century upheld the legal status of corporate groups such as urban guilds and private companies, fostering the development of a vigorous, ambitious and self-confident bourgeoisie, in the Muslim world the social, cultural and political environment impeded the emergence of independent, expanding centres of power within society. Later, after the voyages of discovery, the wealth of the Americas flowed into the treasuries of European monarchs and their armouries.

Inevitably the rise of a dynamic Western Europe in conflict with a stagnating Muslim world created a situation in which most of *dar al-Islam* came under Europe's economic and political domination. According to a famous, if apocryphal, irony, it was one of the greatest Arab seafarers, Ibn Majid, who piloted Vasco da Gama's squadron in the Indian Ocean, after the latter had rounded the Cape of Good Hope in 1498, thereby ending the Muslim monopoly over the monsoon trade routes which had contributed so much to the wealth of Baghdad and later of Cairo. After capturing Hormuz in 1508 the Portuguese were strong enough to impose restrictions on traders from the Gulf to the Malabar coast.

In India the British expanded their influence following the death of Aurangzeb and the weakening of the Mughal empire in the Maratha wars. By 1818 their hegemony extended, by either conquest or treaty, over most of the Subcontinent, except for the Indus valley. In 1857, after the collapse of the 'Mutiny' led by Indians still loyal to him, the British deposed the last Mughal ruler. Nineteen years later the British Prime Minister Benjamin Disraeli provided Queen Victoria with a new title, 'Empress of India', thereby making members of one of the world's largest Muslim communities nominal subjects of a female Christian ruler. British naval power, expanding westwards from India, took in the varied shaikhdoms of the Persian Gulf, where local rulers were obliged to sign treaties for the suppression of slavery and 'piracy'; in 1839 the British occupied the Port of Aden in southern Yemen in order to create a coaling station for future fleets.

In the Far East the Dutch replaced the Portuguese as the leading colonial power following the founding of Batavia (Djakarta) in 1619. After the Javanese War of 1825–30 they instituted increasingly direct forms of colonial rule both in Indonesia and in the Malaysian archipelago which they opened up, in competition with the British, for the production of cash crops for the European market. As in tropical Africa, the improved communications led to an expansion of Islamic activity and increasing Shari'a orthodoxy which militated against both foreign rule and local Hinduistic syncretism.

The Russians began displacing Muslim peasants from the Volga basin from the sixteenth century. By 1813 they had taken over most of the Caucasus; by the 1870s they had conquered most of Turkestan, leaving a handful of autonomous sultanates, including Bukhara, surrounded by Russian territory. In their wars with the Ottoman Empire they broke the Turkish monopoly in the Black Sea, annexing territory around the Sea of Azov. In the 1870s they would have gained complete control of the Dardanelles, had other European powers not intervened on behalf of the Sultan.

At the western end of the Muslim world, France began its expansion into the Maghreb by occupying Algiers in 1830 and gradually extending its control over the Sahara. In 1881 it occupied Tunisia, establishing a protectorate there. By 1912 the Sultan of Morocco, the only independent ruler left in the Maghreb, was too weak to resist French 'help' in asserting his authority over the 'lands of insolence' in exchange for protected status. Spain responded to this move by occupying a different part of Morocco allotted to it under a treaty in 1904. In 1911 Italy decided to conquer the remaining Ottoman territories west of Egypt. Following the defeat of the Ottoman Empire in the First World War, Britain, which already had a protectorate in Egypt, established Mandates in Palestine (with specific provision for Jewish colonization), Transjordan and Iraq. France likewise administered mandated territories in Syria and Lebanon. By 1920 the only independent Muslim states remaining were Turkey, Persia, Afghanistan, Central Arabia (Najd), the Hejaz and northern Yemen. The rest of *dar al-Islam* was either under direct colonial rule or under some form of internationally recognized European 'protection'. Everywhere the Europeans established two new principles: the freezing of boundaries and the freezing of dynasties. They insisted on demarcating or making permanent territorial boundaries which had been hitherto non-existent or constantly shifting. Henceforth it was to be clear which government would be held responsible for which piece of territory. At the same time they insisted on the principle of dynastic succession (though not necessarily according to the European system of primogeniture): legitimacy of succession would prevent the disruptive disputes that inevitably followed the departure of a traditional ruler. The effect of both these changes was to increase imperialist control. In order to control the marginal lands for which they were now being held responsible, the newly legitimized dynastic rulers were often obliged to accept European help. With the Khaldunian 'merry-go-round' halted, the Muslim countries were even less well equipped than before to resist

European encroachments by throwing up new and vigorous military leaderships.

Effects of European hegemony

In the Middle Eastern heartlands, European power at first showed itself indirectly, by stimulating the governments of Egypt and the Ottoman Empire to enact the reforms that would enable them to ward off foreign domination. However, the economic measures which accompanied such reforms helped draw these countries into the net of an imperialist system which, in Egypt's case, brought about the very threat it had been intended to avoid – British military intervention. Throughout the region the growing economic influence of local Christian, Jewish and foreign-protected minorities allied to the Europeans inhibited the development of strong national bourgeoisies capable of resisting foreign hegemony. The protected status of *dhimmis* under the Shari'a, constitutionally endorsed by the Ottoman *millet* system, according to which Christians and Jews enjoyed autonomy within the empire in the spheres of family law and education, became the Trojan Horse by means of which foreign cultural and economic influence penetrated the region, undermining the relatively homogeneous social system that had always coexisted with military rule and religious plurality.

In 1798 Bonaparte's brief and ill-fated expedition to Egypt brought about the collapse of the Mamluk system which was replaced from 1805 by the new-style patrimonial autocracy of Muhammad 'Ali, an Ottoman soldier from Albania who ruled independently of the Ottoman sultan except in name. Having destroyed the last vestiges of Mamluk power by massacring most of their *amirs*, he took direct control over the lands they had enjoyed as tax farmers of the Ottoman sultan, converting the whole of Egypt into one vast personal estate. The new model Egyptian army, led by the Turkish–Mamluk officer class, enabled Muhammad (Mehmet) 'Ali and his successors Sa'id (1848–63) and Isma'il (1863–79) to occupy Syria and the Hejaz for a limited period and to conquer the Nilotic Sudan as far as the Equator. The achievements of his dynasty included the building of the Suez Canal (completed in 1869), the expansion of agriculture through the construction of new irrigation canals, the progressive control of the

Nile's annual flooding by the construction of dams and barrages, and the building upon land thus reclaimed of the new, 'Paris-style' Cairo, a city of fine villas and broad boulevards thoroughly fit for Europeans. These successes, however impressive, only served in the end to accelerate the country's integration into a world economic system dominated by the West. If the francophile Isma'il's dream of 'making Egypt part of Europe' was indeed realized, it was at the price of making it a European colony. In the short term, Muhammad 'Ali's policy of turning over vast tracts of land to the production of long-staple cotton for the mills of Lancashire yielded new, unprecedented wealth, some of which even filtered down to the wretched *fallah*, who ate meat and bought himself a Nubian concubine. In the long term it proved disastrous, as the collapse of cotton prices following the end of the American Civil War led to bankruptcy and British financial, administrative and, from 1882, military control.

The Ottoman Empire itself scarcely fared better. Faced with the loss of its Christian Balkan provinces, where the nationalist mood had been fanned by western influence throughout the nineteenth century, Sultan Abdul Mejid (1839–61) enacted a series of reforms collectively known as the Tanzimat (literally, 'regulations'). They built upon changes already imposed by his predecessor Mahmud (1808–39), including the wearing of the fez, a truncated, cone-shaped red felt hat, in place of the turbans and other miscellaneous headgear that had hitherto distinguished *'ulama* from dervishes, merchants from *amirs*, *dhimmis* from Muslims. The Tanzimat gave legal force to the sartorial equality already enjoined on Ottoman citizens. Individuals of all faiths were now to be treated equally before the law. This was a change of doubtful popularity, since Muslims resented losing their superior status, while native-born *dhimmis* had long learned to turn their notionally inferior status to economic and political advantage. Local Christians and Jews, as well as members of other minorities, looked to their foreign co-religionists for protection. Europeans were exempted from these changes, being entitled under the Capitulations previously signed with various European governments, to have their cases judged before their own consular courts. Thus the Tanzimat, in the name of legal rationalization, abandoned one of the cardinal practices of the Shari'a and accelerated that community of interest between the religious minorities and foreign powers which led, among other disastrous events, to the Crimean War (1854–6) and the massacres of Syrian and

Lebanese Christians in the 1860s. Plans to establish a secular university foundered on the opposition of the *'ulama*; the foreign missionary schools and colleges originally established to serve the needs of the local *dhimmis* and foreign communities became increasingly popular with the Muslim upper and middle classes. With missionary schools the main source of modern education, modernization became equated with western cultural penetration and upper-class privilege, both of which were identified in the eyes of the pious populists with a 'Christian' offensive against Islam.

Muslim responses

The encroachments of Christian power into *dar al-Islam* met with a variety of responses, both military and ideological. Briefly they may be characterized as the archaic, the reformist, the modernist and the neo-traditionalist. The archaic response, exemplified by the revolts of 'Abd al-Qadir, the Mahdi Muhammad Ahmad, Dipa Negra and many others, usually occurred in regions far from the metropolitan centres where the classic *hijra–jihad* scenario could be enacted. Modernism may be defined as the response of those who basically accepted the new order introduced by the Europeans and sought to reform or rationalize Islamic thought and institutions in order to bring them into line with the new reality – the point of departure being that present reality. Reformism was more the attitude of those who sought to strengthen Islam by internal reforms, in order to enable it to assert itself more effectively against what they still regarded as an alien and hostile civilization – here the point of departure was the idea of Islam. Whereas the modernist sought to clothe modernity in Islamic dress by proving that the Quran properly understood was no barrier to progress, the reformist sought to provide the Islam he knew and loved with modern clothes, believing that those aspects of modern or Western reality which seemed incompatible with Islamic teaching and practice must be discarded. The neo-traditionalist, like the reformist, aimed to be discriminating about what he accepted and what he rejected of modern western civilization. But, unlike the reformist who looked to the example of the earliest generation of Muslims in order to pare down the inherited body of Islamic lore and practice to an irreducible core of positive teaching and legislation, the neo-traditionalist reaffirmed the later accretions in the face of what he saw as the reformist's modernist backsliding. Naturally, these are fairly loosely defined categories representing positions which often overlapped: my labels are interpretative rather than strictly descriptive. I have, however, tried to avoid using the term 'fundamentalist'. Most of the movements or responses in question, except for the ultra-modernist, which verges on the secular, are 'fundamentalist' in the sense that each seeks to assert what it regards as the essentials – making the term too generalized to be useful. In another sense, 'fundamentalism', being a term borrowed from Biblical literalist movements within Christianity, is inappropriate because literalism or rejection of *tawil* is not necessarily a common feature of the Islamic movements under consideration.

Archaic responses

We have already seen how in West Africa and the Indian Subcontinent Sufi *tariqa* organization provided the basis for *jihads* against syncretic tendencies of assimilation into non-Islamic cultures. The transformation of an erstwhile quietist *tariqa* into a fighting organization was even more spectacular when anti-Islamic forces were perceived as coming from the Christian enemy, or nominally Muslim infidels controlled by them. During the nineteenth century the modernized government of Ottoman Egypt, as well as the more immediate threats posed by Britain, France, Russia and Holland, sparked off a number of *jihad* movements inspired by the new activist Sufism, especially in the peripheral regions of Africa and the Far East. One such movement, led by 'Abd al-Qadir (1808–83) a *shaikh* of the Qadiriya, followed the French conquest of Algiers in 1830. 'Abd al-Qadir established a state in Western Algeria which the French were forced to recognize, giving him time to organize his government on classic Madinese lines, securing regular revenues by collecting *zakat*, administering justice according to the Shari'a and appointing salaried deputies (*khalifas*). However, in 1839 the agreement broke down after the French had attacked 'Abd al-Qadir's territory and he resumed the *jihad*. The French, who enjoyed Ottoman support, replied with a ruthless scorched-earth strategy, and in 1847 'Abd al-Qadir was finally defeated, captured and driven into exile.

Several other archaic movements in North Africa were led by

self-styled Mahdis. All were regionally limited, enabling the French to suppress them bit by bit. The most formidable and celebrated *mahdiya*, however, occurred in the Nilotic Sudan, where Muhammad Ahmad, a *shaikh* of the Sammaniya branch of the Khalwatiya, proclaimed himself Mahdi in 1881, the year before the British occupation of Egypt. The support he enjoyed from the Baqqara tribe and the settled inhabitants of the Upper Nile was prompted mainly by resentment at the Egyptian administration – in particular its heavy taxation, its attempts to suppress the slave trade and its policy of employing European governors such as the Englishmen Sir Samuel Baker and General 'Chinese' Gordon. An early proclamation of the Mahdi blamed the 'Turks' (i.e., the Egyptians, still nominally subjects of the Ottoman Sultan) for introducing non-Shari'a laws and levying the *jizya* (poll-tax) on Muslims:

Verily these Turks thought that theirs was the kingdom and the command was in their hands. They transgressed the command of God's messengers and of His prophets and of him who commanded them to imitate them. They judged by other than God's revelation and altered the Shari'a of our Lord Muhammad, Messenger of God.[1]

Muhammad Ahmad had begun his career by acquiring an exceptional reputation for piety and asceticism at Aba Island in the White Nile. His decision to declare himself Mahdi may have been prompted, as in Ibn Tumart's case, by the urging of his chief disciple, 'Abdullahi. Both men were no doubt aware of the Mahdist expectations surrounding the end of the thirteenth *hijra* century (November 1882) among the Sudanese tribes. To his close associates, however, Muhammad Ahmad confided the secret that the mahdiship had been conferred upon him by the Prophet in a vision. In the classic manner he made the *hijra* (to Jabal Qadir in the Juba mountains) before launching his *jihad* against the 'Turks' at El Obeid, which surrendered in January 1883. Thereafter the mahdists (who called themselves the Ansar) found themselves in direct confrontation with the British, who had taken control of Egypt and its dependencies after the collapse of Colonel 'Urabi's nationalist movement in September 1882. An expeditionary force of 8,000 men under Hicks Pasha, a retired Indian Army officer, was ambushed and annihilated at Sheikhan (Hicks himself was killed, and there were only 250 survivors). The following year Gordon, instead of sticking to his instructions to evacuate the garrison at Khartoum, tried to 'smash up' the Mahdi with extra money and Indian troops. The rest of the story is well known. In October 1884 the Mahdi left El Obeid, besieging first Omdurman, which fell in January 1885, and then Khartoum. The relief expedition from Egypt came too late for General Gordon, who died a Christian martyr's death, leaving the Victorian public with a thirst for revenge. On Friday 30 January 1885, the Mahdi made his triumphal entry into Khartoum in time to lead the noon-day prayer in the congregational mosque. Six months later he was dead, probably from typhus, though rumour had it (as with the Prophet's untimely death soon after his greatest victory) that he had been poisoned by one of his concubines.

Having challenged – and humiliated – British power in a strategic and increasingly sensitive region of Africa, the mahdist state was doomed. Like the first Islamic state, it would have needed to expand continuously in order to maintain its momentum and prevent internal collapse. In the late nineteenth century the British were powerful enough to contain it within the relatively poor region of its origin. The agriculture of the Gezira was insufficient to support the military machine, even though peasant cultivators were expropriated to make room for Baqqara tribesmen. The population declined drastically and popular discontent with unruly military governors grew apace. In 1898 the Khalifa's forces were almost completely destroyed at Omdurman, the Mahdi's tomb was desecrated and all but one of his offspring massacred.

The failure of 'Abd al-Qadir and the Mahdiya pointed to the futility of the archaic response. European power had proved too overwhelming to resist directly: the *hijra–jihad* scenario was no longer practicable in a world of machine-guns, soon to be supplemented by mechanized transport and air-power. Similar revolts in the peripheral areas, such as the *jihad* against the Dutch in Java led by Dipa Negra, were doomed unless they came to terms with the realities of European power. Thus the Sanusiya in Cyrenaica maintained their network of beduin-based *zawiyas* by recognizing Ottoman authority, paying taxes to Turkish officials and refraining from any overt acts against the Sultan. Although they disliked the Turks, they recognized them as being the only independent Muslim power capable of withstanding the pressure from Europe. When the Italians invaded in 1911, the beduin continued their resistance under Sanusi auspices. Despite Italian attempts to destroy it, the order maintained sufficient authority to provide the main source of resistance to the Fascist occupation. The victorious allies duly rewarded the order by establishing a Sanusi monarchy in Libya in 1945.

In the Caucasus the Imam Shamil waged a heroic campaign against the Russians from 1834 to 1859 under the spiritual authority of his *murshid* and father-in-law, Sayyid Jamal al-Din al-Ghazi-Ghumuqi, *shaikh* of the Khalidiyya branch of the Naqshbandiyya. Although the Islamic state he governed in strict accordance with the Shari'a proved unable to resist eventual incorporation into the Tsarist empire, Shamil's memory remained alive among the peoples of Daghestan and Chechnya, who mounted successive revolts against Russian and Soviet rule in 1863, 1877–8, 1917–19, during the Second World War and in 1994–6, when the war in Chechnya posed a severe crisis for the Yeltsin presidency.[2] Renewed fighting in the region as the latest edition of this book went to press was blamed on Islamist or 'Wahhabi' militants, some of them from the Arab world, who were said to be challenging the 1996 settlement in order to create an 'Islamic republic' in Daghestan and Chechnya. A more plausible explanation was the survival of Sufi networks and allegiances after more than seven decades of Soviet rule.

Another reformed *tariqa* which survived into recent times was that founded among the Swat Pathans of India's North-West Frontier by a Naqshbandi *shaikh*, the Akhund Abdul Ghafur, in the 1870s. The Akhund avoided encroaching on British territory, which persuaded the latter to recognize his government. Such restraint was, however, relatively rare. In general, the European presence and growing cultural and economic influence had the effect of activating the political dynamic latent in *tariqa* organization: 'The colonizing European presence is the one crucial variable determining the conversion of peaceful religious organizations into militant "nationalist" ones.'[3]

The failure of the Ottoman caliphate

Given the realities of European power, the archaic responses were obviously inadequate. Yet the effort to modernize and revive the metropolitan Sunni polities on the traditional basis was to prove equally futile. The nineteenth century saw one military disaster after another for the Muslims. The collapse of the Indian 'Mutiny' in 1857 ended any hope of achieving a reversal of British power by armed revolt. The failure of Colonel 'Urabi's movement in Egypt in 1882 yielded a similar conclusion. Thereafter Muslim aspirations focused on a revival of pan-Islamic power under Ottoman leadership. This mood was astutely exploited by Sultan 'Abdul Hamid II who recognized in 'Islam' the only source of prestige and authority capable of holding his crumbling empire together. To compensate for the loss of his territories to Christian rulers, he revived the ancient title of caliph, persuading the European powers that this gave him a quasi-papal spiritual authority over Muslims everywhere. This claim, which was linked to Ottoman occupancy of the Hejaz and guardianship of the Holy Cities, met with some approval from the more traditional classes, who needed a figurehead around which to rally in order to resist European encroachments. Its most tangible benefit was the construction of the Hejaz railway from Damascus to Madina, ostensibly to facilitate the pilgrimage, which was paid for by subscribers from all over the Muslim world. Its true purpose, however, was to enable the Sultan to increase his military grasp over the Peninsula.

However, the revived caliphate proved no more able to revitalize a demoralized Umma than the Mahdiya, or the other 'archaic' rebellions. 'Abdul Hamid's call for a *jihad* against Britain and France in 1914, following his decision to join in the war on the side of Germany and Austria, proved a dismal failure. The British and French had no difficulty in finding *'ulama* to counter the *jihad* declaration with *fatwas* urging loyalty to the colonial governments. The British successfully played the 'Arab card' against the Ottomans by encouraging the Sharif of Makka to rebel against his Turkish overlords in the hope of establishing a revived Islamic empire under a Quraishi caliphate. Though the Sharif's action merely succeeded in paving the way for his more astute rival, 'Abd al-'Aziz Al Sa'ud (Ibn Saud), his sons Faisal and Abdullah eventually acquired puppet kingdoms in Iraq and Transjordan. After the defeat of the Ottoman Empire in 1918, the Khilafat Movement, a popular agitation of Indian Muslims backed by the Mahatma Gandhi, campaigned for peace terms that would allow the Sultan-Caliph to retain control over the Holy Cities. In the event, however, the movement was outflanked by the actions of the Turks themselves, under their military commander, Mustafa Kemal (later known as Ataturk). Having saved Constantinople from a British landing on the Dardanelles, Ataturk managed to keep the bulk of the Ottoman armies intact, preventing an allied invasion of the Anatolian heartland. Backed by a new National Assembly, he accepted the loss of the Arab provinces, while repulsing and eventually overturning the attempt by Greece to occupy the mainly Greek-inhabited Aegean littoral. In so doing he established a state based on the idea of Turkish nationhood rather than on Islam. The Turkish nation, which was deemed to have existed long before the coming of Islam, was to embody the people, as in Britain, France, Italy or Germany. In 1922 the last Ottoman sultan was sent into exile; in 1924 the caliphate was formally abolished. The Sharif of Makka's announcement that he was now caliph met with practically no support, and was in any case soon overtaken by 'Abd al-'Aziz's conquest of the Hejaz. Henceforth the destinies of the Muslim peoples were to be entrusted to national governments arising from the rubble of the Ottoman collapse or under the auspices of the colonial powers.

The nationalist thinkers who influenced these developments remain for the most part outside the scope of this study. There was, however, a specifically Islamic contribution which helped pave the way for the emergence of secular nationalism and the traditionalist reaction provoked by it.

Intellectual modernism: Sayyid Ahmed Khan

The first of the modernist thinkers to have a substantial impact upon the Muslim world at large was Sir Sayyid Ahmed Khan (1817–98), founder of the Muhammadan Anglo-Oriental College at Aligarh in India, where European arts and sciences were taught, in English, alongside traditional Islamic studies. The aim was to produce an educated elite of Muslims able to compete successfully with Hindus for jobs in the Indian administration. A Sayyid of Persian ancestry whose family had enjoyed close connections with the Mughal court, Ahmed Khan's experience of the 'Mutiny' had convinced him that the 'archaic' struggle against foreign rule was hopeless. The only hope for survival lay in modernizing Islamic institutions by progressive educational policies in the context of loyalty to Britain. In fact Ahmed Khan's analysis of the causes of the 'Mutiny' – a century of exploitation and misrule by the East India Company – was fairly close to that of the British reformers in India who persuaded the government to transfer responsibility for the subcontinent's affairs to the British parliament.

Ahmed Khan's decision to collaborate with Britain led him towards addictive anglophilia. In 1868 he adopted a 'Western' life-style. On a journey to England the following year he attended Dickens's last public reading, met Thomas Carlyle and visited Cambridge, which became the model for Aligarh, a seminary for producing Indian Muslim gentlemen. British rule in India, he once told the Viceroy, Lord Lytton, was 'the most wonderful phenomenon the world has ever seen', loyalty to which sprang 'not from servile submission to foreign rule, but from genuine appreciation of the blessings of good government'.[4] Ahmed Khan's loyalism was consistent and was duly rewarded. In 1887, the year he advised Muslims not to join the National Congress, he became a member of the Viceregal Legislative Council; the following year he became a Knight Commander of the Star of India.

Ahmed Khan's emotional attachment to Britain was of a piece with his liberal and rationalizing religious outlook. Seeking to reconcile the contradictions between Islam as traditionally understood and the modern sciences he so much admired, he set about reinterpreting the Quran, drawing heavily on both the reformism of Shah Wali Ullah and the speculative rationalism of the Mu'tazilis and Ikhwan al-Safa. Comparing the nineteenth century with the ninth century, when Islamic thinkers first grappled with the challenge of Greek philosophy, he wrote:

Today we are as before in need of a modern *'ilm al-kalam* by which we should either refute the doctrines of the modern world or undermine their foundations, or show that they are in conformity with the articles of Islamic faith.[5]

In interpreting the divine text, Ahmed Khan accepts the right of unrestricted personal *ijtihad*, based on an accurate understanding of the Arabic idiom of the Prophet's time. Individual passages may be understood literally or symbolically: like the classical philosophers he accepts the principle that different levels of understanding might be achieved by the masses and the educated elite. Thus he argues that the punishment stories were related, as in the Old Testament, not as historical verities, but as morality tales using a popular legendary framework. Angels are 'properties' of things or conceptualizations of the divine moral support which encourages man in his endeavours; jinns are projections of evil desires. A fundamental distinction has to be made between details of revelation (*furu'*) referring to specific historical situations and the general principles (*usul*) underlying them. In principle God's laws are identical with the laws of nature: as the Final Cause or Creator, his laws, which he maintains as the disciplines of creation and existence, determine the causal relationships governing all material and non-material things. All human morality and social ethics derive from these natural laws. Thus in principle the Shari'a is rooted in natural law; in practice it reflects the ideas and attitudes of the first generation of Muslims. In questioning the Sunna as an infallible source of law comparable to the Quran, Ahmed Khan criticized the methodology of the early *hadith* collectors, including Bukhari and Muslim, in terms similar to those subsequently employed by western orientalists such as Ignaz Goldziher and Joseph Schacht. In confronting the arguments of western missionaries, notably the orientalist scholar Sir William Muir (1819–1905), with whom he was personally acquainted, Sayyid Ahmed severely restricted the authority of the *hadith* literature as sources for the life of the Prophet, thereby widening the gap between the Quran, as 'recited revelation' and 'unrecited revelation' (i.e. *sunna*). In distinguishing between revealed and non-revealed materials in the corpus of *hadith* literature he came to a far-reaching conclusion. Only when the content is unequivocally religious, is a text (other than the Quran) to be taken as revelation. On the basis of this reasoning he declared several traditional Muslim institutions, including polygamy, slavery and concubinage, to be forbidden. All laws were accordingly subject to change according to circumstances. The only exceptions were the *'ibadas*, religious duties, which were absolutely perfect and immutable. This attitude had important political implications: so long as the British guaranteed Muslims the right to perform their religious duties, namely the 'five pillars', rebellion against their government would be illegal.

Ahmed Khan's modernism inevitably incensed the more traditionalist *'ulama*, whom he tried to placate by placing them in charge of Islamic studies at Aligarh. In one respect, therefore, his attempt to bridge the gap between science and religion resulted in failure, for by making concessions to the traditionalists he introduced into his system of education the very dualism against which he militated in his writings. His dilemma was the same as that which faced most of the reformers who came after him. The gap between scientific and religious truth could only be bridged by abandoning literalistic interpretations of the divine texts, or even, in the case of *hadiths*, by challenging their authenticity, thus leaving much of the law open to changes which, in the circumstances, facilitated western domination and cultural penetration.

Pan-Islamic activism: Jamal al-Din al-Afghani

The most outspoken and vigorous attack on Ahmed Khan's ideas came from outside India and from an unexpected quarter: Sayyid Jamal al-Din al-Afghani was, despite his name, a Persian Shi'ite, born at Asabad near Hamadan in 1838 or 1839. A passionate advocate of the need for the Umma to unite in the face of the European threat represented especially by Britain, he concealed his origins in order to avoid arousing the hostility of his Sunni auditors. A man of action before he was a thinker, Afghani was a born intriguer and polemicist. An extreme ascetic, he once threatened to castrate himself when the Ottoman Sultan urged him to marry. Following a traditional education in Iran, he went to Afghanistan, where he claimed to be a Turk, concealing his Shi'ite origins. Here he urged the military ruler of Qandahar, Azam Khan, to make an alliance with the Russians against the British. However, after Azam was ousted by his half-brother, Afghani was obliged to leave for Istanbul, where he joined a group of Tanzimat reformers in urging the Muslims to emulate the 'civilized' nations of the West. Having been appointed to the reformist Council of Education he scandalized the *'ulama* by giving a public lecture in which he equated prophecy with philosophy, describing prophecy as a 'craft': although generally consistent with the Mu'tazili outlook of the Shi'i *'ulama* in Iran (where it is still taught today), this was regarded as heretical by the Sunnis. In 1871 he was expelled and went on to Cairo, where his attacks on the Khedive Isma'il and his British patrons made him popular in nationalist circles. It was in this period that he found his leading disciple, Muhammad 'Abduh, with whom he had a relationship similar to that of a Sufi *pir* and his *mūrid*. A supporter of Colonel 'Urabi's nationalist movement, Afghani was expelled in 1879 for his inflammatory speeches. Several of his followers, however, participated in 'Urabi's government before its overthrow by the British in 1882.

From Egypt Afghani went to Hyderabad in India, where he associated chiefly with the followers of Ahmed Khan. In 1881 he made his celebrated attack on Ahmed Khan, in a pamphlet entitled *Refutation of the Materialists*, in which he accused Sayyid Ahmed and his like, who included materialists from Democritus to Darwin, of opening the 'gates of bestiality', thereby inviting the 'perpetration of shameful deeds and offensive acts'. In this pamphlet Afghani deliberately misrepresented Ahmed Khan's ideas: the latter did not, as he claimed, deny transcendence. The true motive for his attack was political rather than religious. He sought to present Ahmed Khan's collaboration with the British Raj as resulting from religious turpitude, in order to discredit the reformer who was gaining ground with the Indian 'ulama. Two years later, in a rejoinder to a lecture by Ernest Renan attacking Islam for being hostile to science, Afghani strongly criticized the 'Muslim religion', as currently practised, for stifling free thought and progress – which shows that he had not shed his liberal ideas.

In Paris, where 'Abduh joined him in 1884, Afghani published a periodical in Arabic, *Al-'Urwa al-Wuthqa* ('The Strongest Link'), which attacked the British and supported 'Abdul Hamid's pan-Islamic pretensions while outlining his essentially liberal and reformist attitudes. In 1885 he went to Tehran, but failed to persuade Nasr al-Din Shah to enlist further Russian support against the British. He then spent two years in St Petersburg intriguing against the British before returning again to Persia, where he agitated against the sale of concessions to foreigners. After getting wind of the Shah's plans to expel him, he took sanctuary in a shrine near Tehran. The Shah was forced into violating *bast* before Afghani would consent to remove himself, first to Iraq and then to London, where he continued to agitate against the concessions in speeches, pamphlets and messages addressed to the Shi'ite leaders. His propaganda was a significant factor in the Tobacco Boycott of 1891. In 1892 he returned to Istanbul at the invitation of 'Abdul Hamid, where he surrounded himself with a somewhat heterodox group of pan-Islamists. In 1896 one of his acolytes, Mirza Reza, shot and killed Nasr al-Din Shah in Tehran. The Sultan refused Iranian demands for Afghani's extradition, although three of his Persian associates were sent back and duly hanged for their complicity. The following year Afghani died, from cancer of the chin.

The apparent contradictions in Afghani's thinking and the seeming duplicity of his actions are largely explicable in terms of his overriding concern to unite the Umma against the West. He was shrewd enough to see Britain as a greater threat to Islamdom than Russia, because of its more advanced economic system and its active political involvement in Egypt and India. While sharing many of the ideas of Ahmed Khan and the Tanzimat reformers, he turned against them viciously once he perceived the dangerous fissures their doctrines and activities opened up beneath the surface. He failed to realize that the reforms he believed in could not be won without a severe internal struggle in which unity must be the first casualty. The 'Islam' he sought to defend was a civilization, a faith and an allegiance, rather than a carefully formulated religious doctrine. He wanted simultaneously to close the gates against the West and replace the crumbling medieval edifice behind the city walls with a bright new building on classical foundations. Such a double objective was far beyond the capacity of the demoralized leadership of his day, and he died an embittered and disappointed man. But his vision remained, for all who sought a change for the better in the Muslim world, whether through a return to the roots of faith, through governmental reform, or a combination of both. He is therefore claimed as an intellectual progenitor by nationalists, pan-Islamists, by the reformist Salafiya movement and by many of today's 'fundamentalists', though strictly speaking, he belongs to none of them.

Salafi reformism: Muhammad ʿAbduh

The chief exponent of Afghani's ideas, Muhammad ʿAbduh (1849–1905) was a man with a very different temperament. Born into a peasant family in Egypt his attachment to his country of origin brought him, like Ahmed Khan, to collaborate with the British, rejecting Afghani's pan-Islamic militancy. Early in his career he had come under the influence of a Sufi *shaikh* who had freed him from the 'poison of ignorance' and the 'bonds of literalism'. This influence later merged with his reading of European authors, especially Tolstoy and Herbert Spencer, with whom he was personally acquainted, to create a broad-minded liberalism not far removed from that of Ahmed Khan. Lord Cromer, the British Consul General in Cairo and effective ruler of Egypt from 1883 to 1907, regarded ʿAbduh as an 'agnostic' – a reflection of the extent to which he identified 'Islam' exclusively with the traditionalism current in his day. While ʿAbduh never went so far as Ahmed Khan in adopting a European life-style, he visited Europe whenever possible in order to replenish himself spiritually.

During his collaboration with Afghani on *Al-'Urwa al-Wuthqa*, 'Abduh tended to justify Islam in its social rather than its theological aspects. Like Ibn Khaldun and Ibn Rushd, he saw it as an essential ingredient of social happiness. His main concern was to interpret it in a manner that would release its liberating spirit, enabling Muslims to take their place scientifically and culturally alongside the nations of Europe. For this the political problem would have to be shelved: Afghani's attempts to rouse the Muslims to action through their rulers were doomed to failure and would only provoke the wrath of European powers. In 1888, after the collapse of *Al-'Urwa al-Wuthqa*, 'Abduh returned to Egypt – a momentous decision which implied his accept-ance of the reality of British power. Thereafter he concentrated his efforts on legal reform and education. He entered the legal service and rose to become first a judge and eventually the Mufti of Egypt in charge of the whole system of Shari'a law. In his legal rulings he adapted from the Maliki school, in which he had been trained, the principle of *maslaha* (public interest) allowing the law to be changed according to modern requirements: 'If a ruling has become the cause of harm which it did not cause before, then we must change it according to the prevailing conditions.'[6]

Another principle adopted by 'Abduh, previously employed by the Indian reformer Shah Wali Ullah, was *talfiq* (literally, 'piecing together'), whereby rulings could be given by systematically compar-ing the views of the four *madhhabs*, and going behind them to the Quran, *hadith* and principles of the *salaf al-salih* (pious forebears). In his official capacity as Mufti of Egypt 'Abduh was bound to give rulings according to the Ottoman Hanafi code. His influence as a reformer derived from the private *fatwas* he gave on demand, and from his miscellaneous writings, especially in *Risalat al-tawhid* ('The Theology of Unity') his most popular work, and from his lectures which were collected and published in the periodical *al-Manar* ('The Lighthouse') by his disciple Rashid Rida from 1897 to 1935. Rashid Rida, a Syrian Naqshbandi who, unlike 'Abduh, never visited Europe or learned its languages and was therefore much less influenced by foreign ideas, emphasized the Salafi aspect of 'Abduh's work, making it more acceptable to conservatives or fundamentalists than it would otherwise have been.

In his theology 'Abduh followed Afghani, trying to maintain a balance between reason and revelation. He could not accept the possibility of a contradiction between God's spoken truth in the Quran and his Truth as revealed in nature. He did not, however, go so far as the Mu'tazilis in subjecting God's power to the principle of justice. Instead he side-stepped the issue by assimilating ethics to aesthetics:

Voluntary actions may also be distinguished as beautiful or ugly according to the idea of their utility or harmfulness. [This distinction] can be discovered by human reason and the senses without the aid of revelation.[7]

The purpose of revelation was therefore not, as the traditionalists maintained, to arbitrarily endow certain acts with the character of good or bad, 'but to help fallible reason by defining some of the good and bad acts on the basis of the utility principle'.[8]

'Abduh's ideas were consistent with his position as a man attempting to reconcile the conflicts of his time. Like Afghani he saw that the overwhelming power of the West lay in the vastly superior scientific knowledge at its disposal. The Muslims must free themselves from *taqlid* ('imitation') of traditional authority if they were to benefit from this power and to acquire the capacity to resist those who were using it against them. This could be achieved without sacrificing the basic truths of Islam, since the rational truth of science and the truth of revelation must, in the final analysis, be identical.

This belief that the truths of religion and science could be harmonized, integral to the whole modernist viewpoint, was naive in one aspect, since it was based on the essentially medieval premise that science, like scripture itself, is a finite body of knowledge awaiting revelation, rather than a dynamic process of discovery subject to continual revision. In Egypt, as in India, the establishment of non-religious institutions of learning, encouraged by 'Abduh, opened the floodgates to secular forces which threatened Islam's intellectual foundations.

A similar conflict had, of course, occurred in the Christian West, especially during the latter part of the nineteenth century. Like 'Abduh and some of his followers, Christian thinkers had tried to maintain the absolute authority of revelation by discovering in scripture intimations of scientific phenomena or laws subsequently revealed by experiment. In the West, however, this process of accommodation between the scientific and religious outlooks had been going on for centuries, and had been leading towards conclusions very different from any that most Muslims were as yet prepared to accept. Liberal theologians from Schleiermacher in the eighteenth century to Tillich in the twentieth have developed a subjective or existentialist view of revelation which centres on its meaning for man, culturally, historically and personally, while leaving science to discover the objective laws governing the universe. Such a theology, however, implies the dethroning of revelation from the category of absolute to that of relative truth – and, ultimately, to that of a particular mode of discourse within a culturally determined symbolic framework.

Elements of this approach can be inferred from the writings of Ahmed Khan, Afghani and 'Abduh, all of whom were especially aware of Islam's historic importance as a source of culture and civilization. As competent Muslim scholars, they had no need to borrow the exegetical tools of Western analysis if they wished to give their scripture a symbolic interpretation: the whole *batini* tradition, from the writings of the Ikhwan al-Safa to the theosophy of Ibn 'Arabi can be adapted to his purpose, not to mention the work of Mu'tazili exegetes such as Zamakhshari.

Their problem was twofold: firstly, in Islam the divine is believed to have manifested itself primarily in the form of a text, so that any scientific or linguistic analysis which casts doubt on that text's integrity must threaten the central citadel of faith – hence the furore caused by the publication in 1926 of a book on pre-Islamic poetry by the Egyptian writer Taha Husain which cast doubt on the authenticity of one of the main sources of Quran and *hadith* interpretation.

The second, related, problem facing the modernists was that the Quran and such portions of *hadith* as must be salvaged to maintain the Quran's authenticity contain a core of positive legislation which, though rooted within the culture of a particular time and place – seventh-century Arabia – cannot be given a relativistic or symbolic interpretation without abandoning the cultural and social norms it sanctifies. A Westernized, philosophically inclined elite can honour Quranic prohibitions in the breach, drinking alcohol, failing to observe Ramadan, indulging in unlicensed sex and disregarding those aspects of Islamic law and practice that it finds uncongenial without necessarily rejecting the higher religious truths enshrined in the divine text; but in the absence of a socially embedded tradition of natural law it is always vulnerable to the charge that it is failing in its duty of 'enjoining the good and forbidding the evil'. Muslim religiosity has both politically radical and socially conservative consequences. It is radical because it is prepared to challenge authority when those in power are seen to be departing from Islamic norms of behaviour. It is conservative because, in the last analysis, the social rituals embodying these norms cannot be abandoned without inviting the accusation of infidelity. The history of reform since the time of 'Abduh shows a tendency to slide from liberalism to traditionalism as the conservatives demonstrate a greater capacity in times of crisis to mobilize mass support.

The swing from liberalism back to traditionalism has been shown most clearly in two regions sharing prolonged exposure to Western influences – the Arab East, including Egypt, and the Indian subcontinent. Iran, with its distinctive Shi'ite national tradition, is in many respects a special case; while landlocked Afghanistan, still largely tribal, is only now experiencing the kind of upheaval that Egypt and Turkey underwent a century or more ago. In the peripheral regions of Africa and the Far East, traditional forms of Islam may be reasserting themselves, but here Islam is often a badge of racial or ethnic identity, and demands for an Islamic state or stricter observance of ritual may have nationalist or particularist overtones.

Egypt and the Arab world

In Egypt the reformist liberalism represented by 'Abduh opened the way for a secular nationalism which sought to relegate religion to the sphere of private belief, enabling a new, Western-educated elite to take control of the country's affairs and to create a national state on the European model. The religious establishment, always subservient to political power in Sunni countries, capitulated to this development. The Islamic reaction was led by the more conservative reformers, notably 'Abduh's disciple Rashid Rida and his spiritual heir Hasan al-Banna, founder of the Muslim Brotherhood.

   'Abduh's return to Egypt in 1888 and his quarrel with Afghani over the pan-Islamic question showed that he had begun to recognize that henceforth the future of Islam must lie within the geographical frontiers upheld by the colonial powers and recognized in international law. The term *watan* ('homeland'), a word without pedigree in classical

Islamic political thought, appears with increasing frequency in his writings as the unifying factor around which Islamic activity should coalesce. The collapse of the Ottoman Empire little more than a decade after his death proved him right. Two of his close associates, Ahmad Lutfi al-Sayyid and Sa'ad Zaghloul became the intellectual and political leaders of modern Egyptian nationalism. Lutfi al-'Sayyid argued that, since three millennia of ancient history had endowed the Egyptian personality with a 'pharaonic core', no amount of borrowing from the West would threaten its identity. Zaghloul led the agitation which resulted in Egypt's becoming a constitutional monarchy under indirect British control in 1922.

Although it failed to satisfy the demands of the nationalists, Egypt's limited independence represented the first victory of the Arab national state over the Umma. Article 1 of the 1923 Constitution (adapted from the Belgian Constitution) declared the country to be a 'sovereign state, free and independent'. Submission to any Islamic super-state was precluded by insisting that this sovereignty was 'indivisible and inalienable'. Article 3 granted all Egyptians equal rights, duties and equality before the law regardless of race, language or religion, thereby abolishing the old Shari'a distinction between Muslims, *dhimmis* and unbelievers. Article 12 declared that 'freedom of conscience is absolute', implicitly contradicting the Shari'a, which prescribes the death penalty for apostates, though Article 13 added the proviso that 'the state protects the free exercise of all religions and creeds in conformity with the usages established in Egypt'. Article 23 recognized that 'all powers emanate from the nation', whilst Articles 24 to 28 gave parliament full power of legislation unhindered by any reference to Islamic law. Clauses dealing explicitly with religion were limited to Article 149, declaring Islam to be the religion of the state, while Article 153 entitled the state – through the person of the King – to appoint religious leaders and to control other religious institutions through a ministry of *waqfs*. Thus in Egypt, as in Turkey, a secular state had come into being, embodying the idea of the nation. Similar constitutions, effectively placing Islam on a similar footing to the churches in Western countries, were established in most other Muslim states when they came to independence after the colonialist retreat.

The creation of the national state made it possible for an emerging native elite to aspire to the Westernized life-style adopted by the European and *dhimmi* upper classes. However, this only widened the gap between the traditional classes, both rural and urban, who wore traditional costume, punctiliously observed Ramadan and other Muslim festivals, and the westernized elites, who wore European dress and often took to such habits as drinking alcohol and attending mixed social gatherings.

In Egypt this situation persisted even after an intermediate class, consisting mainly of native-born army officers, technicians and government employees, came to power in 1952, setting a trend that would be imitated in those Arab states most closely exposed to Western cultural influences. Though the traditional classes, activated by the Muslim Brotherhood, had played their part in bringing Gamal 'Abd al-Nasir (Nasser) and his Free Officers to power, the new nationalist elite soon discarded their former supporters, governing the country instead by a combination of police methods and bureaucratic controls. Nasser and other Arab military rulers who followed his path effectively coopted the religious establishment, which found in 'Abduh's use of *ijtihad* and *maslaha* the instruments by which they could produce *fatwas* legitimizing almost anything their masters cared to ask for – reforms that often offended the traditional classes by changing the status of women, or limiting private property or the jurisdiction of the religious courts. With the official *'ulama* playing second fiddle to reforming officers and bureaucrats, the opposition among the traditional classes turned increasingly to the radical alternatives offered by the Muslim Brotherhood and its affiliates.

Activist Reformism: The Muslim Brotherhood

The Society of Muslim Brothers, founded by Hasan al-Banna in 1928, became one of the main sources of political radicalism in Egypt once Sa'ad Zaghloul's party, the Wafd, had become too closely identified with the colonial interest. (The Communist Party enjoyed a certain amount of support among the small industrialized proletariat and partly westernized intelligentsia, but its appeal was too limited to compete seriously with that of the Brotherhood.) A schoolteacher by training, Banna had begun preaching his reformed doctrines in mosques, schools, and private homes away from the watchful eyes of the authorities. Theologically, Banna's views were fairly close to those of 'Abduh and his Salafi disciple, Rashid Rida. He attacked the *taqlid* of the official *'ulama*, insisting that only the Quran and the best-attested *hadiths* should be the sources of the Shari'a. Some of his followers were considerably more radical, challenging even the canonical *hadith* collection of Bukhari and Muslim: they were fond of quoting an anti-*hadith hadith* according to which the Prophet is supposed to have said: 'Take from me only the Quran.' They were defensive about the *hadd* (Quranic) punishments, using the classic modernist argument that the thief should have his hand amputated only when the perfectly just Islamic society, in which there was no want, had been realized.

Where Banna and his followers differed from Rida and 'Abduh was in their determination to create the Islamic society by positive social, political and in some cases military action. While endorsing most of 'Abduh's modernist positions, they utterly rejected his acceptance of the colonial reality. In this respect their political position was closer to Afghani's, though like Afghani they often found themselves making compromises with the existing political power. Both Banna and his successor Hasan al-Hudaibi claimed at various times that Egypt's existing constitutional framework could be adapted to satisfy the requirements of an Islamic state. Islam was an ideal to be worked for, comparable to the ideals of the French and Russian Revolutions: within its framework, development was not only possible, but also desirable and necessary. The Shari'a, however, must reign supreme: its *de facto* replacement by imported European codes had symbolized the rejection of 'God's law', destroying the essence of Muslim society.

At first, Banna aimed to build his Muslim polity within the framework of Egypt. A combination of neo-Sufi *tariqa* and political party, the Brotherhood attracted members from all social groups, including civil servants and students, urban labourers and peasants, artisans and merchants. Members were arranged into units called 'families', families into 'clans', clans into 'groups' and groups into 'battalions'. Brothers met for prayer, including nocturnal vigils. Much stress was placed on athletics for the young – in order to keep their minds off sex. Members were enjoined to observe religious duties assiduously, and to avoid the evils of gambling, drinking, usury and fornication. Stress was placed on the 'Islamization' of home and family, and loyalty to Brotherhood leaders. Each 'family' was collectively responsible for its members' actions. Banna once described his Brotherhood as 'a Salafiya message, a Sunni way, a Sufi truth, a political organization, an athletic group, a cultural-educational union, an economic company and a social idea'.[9] In his own estimation, however, the reformist aspect, tinged with Sufism, seems to have been paramount. In 1943, convinced of British plots to kill him, he wrote a 'farewell message' in which he stated:

My Brothers, you are not a benevolent society, nor a political party, nor a local organization having political purposes. Rather you are a new soul in the heart of this nation to give it light by means of the Quran . . . to destroy the darkness of materialism through knowing God.[10]

Despite this disclaimer, the size of the Brotherhood made it a force to be reckoned with. It was alternately wooed by the Palace, which saw in its support a means of improving its image in the Arab world, especially during the mounting struggle for Palestine after the Arab revolt of 1936; and by the left, which sought its support in industrial and political strikes. Its momentum grew even greater with the swell of anti-British feeling after the Anglo-Egyptian treaty of 1936. Throughout this period Banna deftly maintained his independence, earning the hostility of the left and the suspicion of the establishment. In 1948 a group of Brotherhood volunteers fought in the Palestine War, alongside the Egyptian army, where they came into contact with the Free Officers, the nationalist group in the Egyptian army which was to overthrow the monarchy in 1952. After the widespread disturbances following Egypt's defeat in the war the government dissolved the Brotherhood. In December 1948 Nuqrashi Pasha, the Prime Minister, was assassinated by a Brotherhood member. Banna repudiated the murder, arguing that since its dissolution the Brotherhood could no longer be held responsible for the actions of individual members. The following February, however, he himself was assassinated, with, it is thought, the complicity of the incoming premier. In the trials of Nuqrashi's assassins, the prosecution failed in its bid to prove that the whole Brotherhood was implicated in the murder: while accepting that the Brotherhood had been involved in 'murder and destruction', the court rejected prosecution claims of a 'revolutionary conspiracy' and passed relatively lenient sentences on the accused.

The dissolution of the organization led to the emigration of many Brothers, who spread its message to Palestine, Transjordan, Syria and even Pakistan. Hudaibi, the new leader, cultivated a respectable image, repudiating the Brotherhood's terrorist wing, the so-called 'secret organization'. 'There is no secrecy in the service of God,' he said, 'no terrorism in religion.'[11] In 1951, when Nahhas Pasha, the Wafdist Prime Minister, unilaterally abrogated the Anglo-Egyptian Treaty, the Brotherhood came out in open support of the government, calling for a *jihad* against the British, while members were trained and armed by sympathizers in the army. The massacre by the British army of more than a dozen auxiliary policemen at Ismailiya in January 1952 brought matters to a head. The following day, 'Black Saturday', much of Cairo went up in flames. The role of the Brotherhood in the disturbances was evident from the symbolic character of the targets selected – foreign clubs and hotels, bars, cinemas and restaurants: establishments where foreigners and Muslims they regarded as *kafirs* or renegades congregated. In July the Free Officers led by Nasser placed General Nagib, an army officer acceptable to the Brotherhood, at the head of a junta which forced King Farouk to abdicate and disbanded all political parties. In the 'honeymoon period' after the revolution, the Brotherhood was offered three government posts, but Hudaibi declined. He disagreed with the Revolutionary Command Council (RCC)'s policy of agrarian reform and may have feared that the Brotherhood's image would be tarnished by the responsibilities of office. Nasser and Nagib made a much publicized visit to the tomb of Hasan al-Banna.

The honeymoon, however, was not to last. The RCC, still trying to remove the British from the canal zone by negotiation, accused the Brotherhood of secretly acquiescing in the British presence. Hudaibi countered by accusing the government of backing dissidents in his organization. In 1953 the RCC declared the Brotherhood a political organization and therefore subject to the law abolishing political parties. Hudaibi was accused of blocking the land reforms and of aiming to 'overthrow the present form of government under cover of religion'. The Communists welcomed the Brotherhood in the common struggle against Nasser, whom they regarded as an 'Anglo-American stooge' after his negotiation of the Anglo-Egyptian agreement. Sayyid Qutb, the Brotherhood's leading intellectual, took charge of liaison with the Communists. The 'secret apparatus' was revived and planned Nasser's assassination. The attempt was made in November 1954. Its failure provided Nasser with the opportunity of crushing the organization completely. In a series of show trials, backed by confessions extracted under torture, the whole leadership was implicated in the plot. Seven were sentenced to death, including Hudaibi and Nasser's would-be-assassin, Mahmud 'Abd al-Latif. Hudaibi's sentence was, however, commuted on grounds of age and health. The hangings produced a shocked reaction in Egypt, and were greeted with angry demonstrations in Jordan, Syria and Pakistan.

After the débâcle of 1954, the Brotherhood remained quiescent for a decade, with most of its 4,000 activists either in prison or in foreign exile. The nadir of its fortunes was reached in 1965 when, following the discovery of an alleged plot to overthrow him, Nasser arrested another 1,000 members and placed 365 of them on trial. Several were executed, including the activist leader, Sayyid Qutb, who had only been released from jail the previous year. There seems to have been a Saudi connection, with King Faisal playing the 'Islamic card' against Nasser, with whom he was contesting the leadership of the Arabs in Yemen and elsewhere. Faisal and his ally King Husain of Jordan began giving succour to Nasser's enemies in the Brotherhood, providing them with influential university posts or even coopting them into government. Nasser's catastrophic defeat in the June 1967 war against Israel further discredited his brand of secular nationalism, despite the well-orchestrated pleas from the Egyptian masses that he should not resign. Israel's unilateral annexation of Jerusalem, followed by the burning of the al-Aqsa Mosque, Islam's third-holiest shrine, in 1969 inflamed religious feelings everywhere. Pan-Islamic sentiments were further exacerbated by the Jewish state's creeping annexation of the Occupied West Bank, and by the tacit support its policies received from the West, particularly the United States.

Sayyid Qutb: Revolutionary Ideologue

Although Banna is revered by supporters of a revitalized Islam as the Muslim Brotherhood's founder, it is Sayyid Qutb (1906–66) who became the movement's most influential theorist and the leading ideologue of the Islamic Revolution in Egypt and countries far beyond its borders. Though two of his key ideas, the concept of *jahiliya* as applied to the present and the establishment of *hakimiya* – divine sovereignty on earth – as the aim and purpose of Islam were adapted from the Indo-Pakistani writer Abu'l 'Ala Maududi, it was Qutb and his followers who took these concepts as models for revolutionary action. Qutb's execution in 1966 on charges of terrorism and sedition after a blatantly political trial and the brutal tortures to which he and his colleagues were previously subjected at the hands of the police has given him the status of a *shahid* or martyr, adding to his stature and popularity as a man prepared to sacrifice his life for 'authentic' Islam.

Born near the city of Asyut in Upper Egypt into an educated, nationalist family, he was a gifted child. He is said to have memorized the whole of the Quran by the age of ten. He went on to receive a modern education at the Dar al-'Ulum, the Western-style academy in Cairo where 'Abduh had taught. He was delicate, small of stature and being of partly Indian extraction was very dark skinned, which may have exposed him to racism in America. A critical factor which distinguishes Qutb from his more conservative predecessors, including Banna and Maududi, is the extent of his exposure to Western cultural influences. As Yvonne Haddad suggests

His life experiences as well as his death became a perfect illustration of one of the processes through which a revolutionary passes from enchantment with the West to the helplessness and marginality that it may inspire in those who find its values and norms not only foreign but inadequate, [till they] finally . . . return to the roots where reintegration, conversion and a new vibrant identity cohere, and the new human being becomes part of the revolutionary movement aimed at changing the world and bringing in a new ethical moral order based on freedom, brotherhood and justice for all.[12]

Qutb's rejection of the West was not that of the conservative concerned with preserving his culture's traditions against foreign encroachments, but rather that of the 'born-again Muslim' who having adopted or absorbed many modern influences makes a show of discarding them in his search for personal identity and cultural authenticity. During the 1930s when he began working as an inspector for the Ministry of Education he published poetry, stories, articles and works of literary criticism. (He was later to renounce all these works, and regretted ever having written them.) The poet 'Abbas Mahmud al-'Aqqad – an admirer of William Hazlitt and the English romantic poets – was one of his mentors, as was the writer Taha Husain, a senior adviser at the ministry. The critical change in the direction of his life occurred between 1948 and 1951 when Qutb was sent by the ministry to study American methods of education. He studied in Washington DC, at the University of Northern Colorado (where he received his MA) and at Stanford University. He returned to Egypt with an uncompromising hatred for the West and all its works. He was outraged by universal support in America for Israel, which at that time was struggling to establish itself in the face of Arab hostility. His writings hint that other, more personal, experiences may have riled him. He was appalled by the racism and sexual permissiveness, as well as the pro-Zionism, he encountered in America. In one of his works he warns against the contamination of Islam by modern culture, with its inducements to indulgence and desire, citing the example of a church in the United States where he saw people dancing with coloured lights to the 'sexually arousing' music and lyrics of 'Baby, It's Cold Outside'. One suspects that he may have been attracted, as well as repelled, by what he saw. The puritan is often an inverted sensualist: who knows what slights or rejections the intelligent and highly educated but small and dark-skinned Egyptian may have been exposed to in 1950s America?

Despite Qutb's wholesale rejection of the West, several scholars have detected unacknowledged western influences in his later, more radical, writings. Shahrough Akhavi shows how Qutb constantly refers to Islam's primary texts, the Quran and *hadith* (prophetic traditions) ahistorically, while reinterpreting them in novel ways in order to claim Islamic origins for concepts like democracy and social justice largely derived from western, but unacknowledged, intellectual sources.[13] On the face of it his language is absolutely uncompromising and unequivocal. Qutb calls on his fellow Muslims to reject the West and Westernizing governments, such as those, including Egypt, which have introduced non-Islamic legal systems, because they are being ruled by 'other than what God sent down' (i.e. the Quran). There can only be one law, and that is the Shari'a. God has prohibited Muslims from receiving guidance from any source save the Quran. In contrast to all other systems or ideologies, the Islamic concept or vision (*tasawwur*)

... is a divine [one] that proceeds from God in all its particularities and its essentials. It is received by 'man' in its perfect condition. He is not to complement it from his own [resources] or delete any of it; rather he is to appropriate it and implement all its essentials in his life.[14]

In his commentary on the verses of the Quran condemning 'those who do not judge according to what God sent down' as 'unbelievers ... oppressors ... sinners' (5:44, 45, 47) (verses whose context clearly applies to Jews and Christians), Qutb departed from centuries of

commentaries by changing the meaning of the verb *yahkumu* from
'judge' to 'rule', thereby implicitly sanctioning collective action against
the government that fails to rule in accordance with true Islam.[15]
However, it is far from clear what Qutb's version of Islam amounts to
as he places far less emphasis on the Islamic state he theoretically
wishes to see in power than on the *jahili* state he deplores. Like other
Islamists, including Maududi, he holds a naive view about human
nature, believing that, once individuals have been converted to the
truth of Islam, a community of true believers will come into being in
which 'there is no need of earthly laws, regulations, and devices of
enforcement'.[16]

In contrast to his vague ideas about the nature of the true Islamic
state, his critique of the status quo is comprehensive and devastating,
leading to the conclusion that, whatever the circumstances, the true
Islamic society must be rebuilt from scratch:

> Today we are in the midst of a *jahiliya* similar to or even worse than the *jahiliya*
> that was 'squeezed out' by Islam. Everything about us is *jahiliya:* the concepts
> (*tasawwurat*) of mankind and their beliefs, their customs and traditions, the
> sources of their culture, their arts and literature, and their laws and regulations.
> [This is true] to such an extent that much of what we consider to be Islamic
> culture and Islamic sources, and Islamic philosophy and Islamic thought . . . is
> nevertheless the product of that *jahiliya*.[17]

Qutb goes on to state that the *jahiliya* which is based on the unacceptable
'sovereignty of man over man, and which deviates thereby from existential being (*al-wujud al-kawni*) . . . that *jahiliya* was not represented
by mere theory'. Instead it was represented by what he calls a 'dynamic
concrescence', embracing a whole complex of *jahili* values, understandings, sentiments, traditions and customs capable of mobilizing society,
consciously or otherwise, to 'serve its existence and to defend its being'.
It follows that 'any attempt to destroy that *jahiliya* and to restore
mankind to God once more must be undertaken by a dynamic social
movement even more powerful than the modern *jahiliya*.'

Qutb believed that the creation of such a powerful dynamic force
required the creation of a new elite among Muslim youth that would
fight the new *jahiliya* as the Prophet had fought the old one. Like the
Prophet and his Companions, this elite must choose when to withdraw
from the *jahiliya* and when to seek contact with it. This is far removed

from the idea of 'defending' Islamic society from the 'West'. Since contemporary society is so thoroughly permeated by *jahiliya* such a project has ceased to be practicable. Nor does it offer a coherent programme for political action. The issue of how the Shari'a should be applied under modern conditions, of how to salvage the divinely instituted authority of the Shari'a from the centuries of *jahili* accretions is never really addressed. In the final analysis Qutb's idea of true Islam seems almost Kirkegaardian in its individualism: his 'true Muslim' is one who makes an existential choice, a 'leap of faith' for Islam. Departing radically from traditional exegetical methods (including those of Maududi) Qutb suggests that the truth of the Quran, the evidence of its divine provenance, ultimately resides in its aesthetic qualities. His encounter with European romanticism was assimilated, not rejected, drawing him towards the conclusion of revelation-as-art.

Thus Qutb joins many thinkers who argue that in the field of religion, as in the communicative sciences generally, it is consciousness and not knowledge upon which truth, or reality, or Being, is to be grounded. In particular, Qutb is to be associated with those who have argued or intimated that the aesthetic is the appropriate form of discourse on religious, social and historical matters. An important difference is to be found in the fact that Qutb is not referring to the role of the artist as an interpreter of the cultural consciousness of a particular era. Qutb writes rather of the role of revelation which conveys, by means of a divine art, a transcendent religious consciousness ... [T]he teaching of the Quran is not merely meant to affect the emotional attitudes of Muslims towards Islam, it is also meant to convince them that external social experience is to be brought into conformity with the aesthetically defined inner experience of truth.[18]

It follows from this that, while being formally committed to the social project of rebuilding an authentic Islamic society free from contamination by centuries of *jahiliya*, the born-again Muslim must either engage in an internal migration (*hijra*) from the *jahili* world surrounding him, or bear personal witness against a corrupt and oppressive political system through armed struggle, if necessary at the cost of his life. Qutb authenticated his vision, as Binder points out, by embracing the act of martyrdom, the 'ultimate affirmation'. His ideas set the agenda for Islamic radicals, not just in Egypt but throughout the Sunni Muslim world and were a significant influence on the Islamic revolution in Iran (see below).

Qutb's Bequest: The Assassination of Sadat

After Nasser's death in 1970 his successor, Anwar Sadat, sought to present a more positive Islamic image for his regime by frequently having himself televised at prayer and by peppering his monologues with Quranic references. He cautiously encouraged the growing Islamic mood by releasing all Brotherhood prisoners and promising to bring Egyptian law more closely into line with the Shari'a. After his 'corrective coup' against former Vice-President 'Ali Sabri and other leftists in the leadership in 1971, Sadat actually encouraged the formation of Islamic committees in the universities, in order to counter leftist influence. By the late seventies most of the student committees had come under the control of the Brotherhood and its affiliates.

After expelling his Soviet military advisers in 1972 and winning a partial victory over Israel the following year, Sadat opened the doors of the Egyptian economy to the West, hoping to attract a massive injection of foreign capital. The effects of this policy, both economic and cultural, served to strengthen support for the Brotherhood and its affiliates. Culturally, the relatively straight-laced puritanism of the Nasserist era gave way to a new permissiveness in which Alexandria and Cairo once more became the leading Middle Eastern 'fleshpots', attracting thousands of visitors from Saudi Arabia and the Gulf. Economically, the *infitah* exacerbated social divisions, as rents rocketed, food prices rose sharply and local manufacturing capacity was decimated by cheap foreign imports. Inevitably the extremist groups among the Brotherhood's affiliates became the most active opponents of the *infitah* and the Westernizing influences unleashed by it. In 1974 a small band calling itself the Islamic Liberation Group mounted an armed attack on the Military Academy at Heliopolis in which 11 people were killed and 27 injured. Another group, known as Takfir wa'l Hijra* played a leading part in the sacking of dozens of nightclubs along Cairo's Pyramids Road during the food riots in January 1977. Six months later the same group kidnapped and assassinated the former Minister for

---

* *Takfir* means 'declaration of infidelity': the group's name thus carried Khariji overtones – first denounce one's fellow-Muslims as infidels, then make the *hijra* separating oneself from them.

Waqfs, Shaikh Muhammad Dhahabi, when the government refused to release 60 of their comrades. Four hundred and ten of the group's members were arrested and 23 executed, including the group's leader Shukri Ahmad Mustafa. Other extremist militant groups included the Mukafaratiya ('Denouncers of the Kafirs'), the Jund Allah ('God's Soldiers') and the Jama'a al-Jihad ('Jihad Society'). Altogether membership of the extremist groups was said to exceed 4,000.

Sadat's response to these developments was to encourage the moderate Brotherhood leaders, isolating the militants. Two leading exiles, 'Umar Talmasani and Sa'id Ramadan, were allowed to return to Egypt, Talmasani to take over the editorship of the Brotherhood's principal organ *Al-Da'wa*, Sa'id Ramadan to lead a group of nine Brotherhood-affiliated deputies in the Egyptian parliament. (The Brotherhood was not permitted to campaign openly in the parliamentary elections, but no one can have been in much doubt as to who its representatives were.) For a period this strategy succeeded. Sadat's policy of making peace with Israel, launched after his spectacular visit to Jerusalem in November 1977, was popular with the Egyptian *fallahin* who had provided most of the cannon fodder for successive Arab wars against Israel. Despite considerable outrage provoked by his visits to Jerusalem, where he was televised worshipping in the al-Aqsa Mosque (implying *de facto* recognition of Israel's sovereignty), Sadat obtained the support of the *'ulama* of al-Azhar university, and even, tacitly, that of moderate Brotherhood leaders, for his policies.

The failure of the Camp David agreement to provide a settlement acceptable to the Palestinians, as well as the increasingly deleterious effects of Sadat's economic policies (which, like those of the Khedive Isma'il, seemed to involve wholesale capitulation to Western interests without yielding any proportional benefits, save to a small minority of speculators and profiteers), eventually drove even the Brotherhood moderates into more open opposition alongside Sadat's Nasserist and left-wing critics. In September 1981, reportedly under pressure from Israeli premier Menachem Begin, who warned him that Israel would not withdraw from Sinai so long as open criticism of Camp David was tolerated in Egypt, Sadat rounded on the opposition, arresting more than 1,500 dissidents, mostly Islamic militants. The army was purged of 200 officers thought to be too friendly to the Brotherhood, all independent mosques and religious societies were closed down and all preachers were obliged to register with the Ministry of Waqfs.

Just over one month later, Sadat was assassinated while reviewing a military parade to mark the anniversary of the October 1973 war. The chief assassin, Lieutenant Khaled Islambouli, was the brother of one of the Takfir wa'l Hijra suspects arrested on 3 September.

Throughout most of its career the Muslim Brotherhood has been a fluid mass movement, rather than a well-structured political organiz- ation. This has been the source of both strength and weakness. Its mass character and relatively inchoate structure has enabled it to survive successive waves of persecution. At the same time, lack of firm organiz- ation and effective political leadership have made it virtually imposs- ible for it to commit itself to a coherent set of policies capable of being translated into action. As a result it has usually succumbed to the twin perils facing any loosely organized radical movement: a tacit compromise with the status quo on the one hand, precipitating a reactive extremism on the other. Doctrinally its attitudes have generally been in line with the reformist approach of Muhammad 'Abduh and Rashid Rida, casting aside the dead weight of *taqlid* and *fiqh* and benefiting from the liberating impact of *maslaha* and *ijtihad* to create an up-to-date Islam suited to modern conditions. In practice, however, both its membership, consisting largely of urban petit bourgeois and rural immigrants, and the symbols around which it coalesces, give the Brotherhood a more positively traditional character. Since reformism has been coopted, not only by secularists in power but by the official *'ulama* whose task it is to legitimize their actions, the Brotherhood has become emotionally, if not always intellectually, traditionalist.

The Brotherhood in Syria and Sudan

Throughout the 1970s and early 1980s the Muslim Brotherhood remained the principal vehicle for Sunni political activism, not only in Egypt but also in Syria, where it enjoyed the support of the Iraqi and Jordanian governments. The domination of the Regional Command of the Ba'ath Party by a group of 'Alawi sectarians led by Hafiz al-Asad had given some plausibility to the accusation that Syria had fallen into the hands of an "Alawi dictatorship'. While there was no evidence that Nusairi religious ideas had penetrated the thinking of the Ba'ath Party ideologists, sectarian *'asabiya* was undoubtedly the true source of their political power.

The Arab Nationalism of the Ba'ath Party, like that adopted by Nasser after he discarded the Brotherhood in 1954, represented the ascendancy of the Arab 'nation' over the Islamic Umma, though it was felt that the two concepts could be harmonized. Nasser's initial efforts – notably unsuccessful – were directed towards creating unity at state level in order to give expression to an aspiration, strongly felt during the 1950s and 1960s, that the Arabs constituted a nation (*qawm*) on the basis of common language and culture. This theory had been latent in the thinking of the reformers: Rashid Rida, for example, had sought to revive, in theory at least, the idea of an Arab Caliphate, though he never found a suitable candidate for this office. It was also an unstated assumption in the ideology of the Muslim Brotherhood: Banna, among others, had regarded the transfer of power to non-Arabs after the first four 'Rightly Guided' caliphs as the true reason for the decline of Islam.[19] Only Arabs, because of their language, could taste the real Islam. For the majority of Arabs, Islamic and Arab identities merged imperceptibly: the two were not, as in Turkey, in opposition, particularly if the cultural and 'civilizational' aspect of Islam, as distinct from its religious or legal content, were emphasized.

While the Egyptian Copts, who saw themselves as true descendants of the ancient Egyptians, could take refuge in 'Pharaonic nationalism', for Syrian Christian Arabs the problem of nationality was more delicate. Even before the demise of the Ottoman Empire many of them had suspected that the Arab 'nation' might exclude them. Those who, unlike the Lebanese Maronites, wished to dispense with foreign 'protection' tended to give 'Arabism' a more secular character or even sought in Marxism a way out of their difficulties. One of the most influential Arab nationalist writers was Michel 'Aflaq (1910–89), co-founder and ideologist of the Ba'ath Party. Born into a Greek Orthodox family, he had lived for a time in Paris before returning to Syria in 1936. His étatist brand of socialism bore the hallmarks of the Popular Front. For 'Aflaq, as for the Turkish ideologist Ziya Gokalp, the nation pre-dated Islam: however, whereas for the Turks this assumption led logically to a complete separation of religion and politics, for 'Aflaq and other Arab nationalists 'Islam' was the supreme embodiment of 'Arabism'. In 1943 'Aflaq wrote:

Europe is as fearful of Islam today as she has been in the past. She now knows that the strength of Islam (which in the past expressed that of the Arabs) has been reborn and has appeared in a new form: in Arab nationalism.[20]

For this reason, he concluded, Europe befriended 'traditional' Islam, with its 'superficial worship, vague and colourless values', in order to Europeanize it.[21]

'Aflaq's Ba'athist ideology (the word *ba'th*, 'rebirth', appears in Quranic verses about the resurrection) appealed across the sectarian divisions of Syrian and Iraqi society in the name of an 'Arab' common denominator able to include Sunnis and Shi'ites, Isma'ilis and Druzes and the various Christian communities. The major grouping excluded by the Ba'athist ideology was the non-Arab Kurds, concentrated mainly in the mountains of northern Iraq, but also settled in Syria. The universalist and egalitarian appeal of Ba'athism made it attractive to army officers who came to power in Syria and Iraq during the early 1960s, while its organizational structure, modelled on the one-party socialist states of Eastern Europe, made it a suitable vehicle for extending the power of the state, and the welfare patronage at its disposal, throughout society.

Formerly impoverished outsiders compared with the Sunni who dominated the cities, the 'Alawis (Nusairis) had risen to power through the political and military committees of the Ba'ath Party, maintaining their own cohesion while dividing that of their opponents. This was not so much a pre-planned policy of 'entryism' as the result of ordinary politicking, in which individuals greedy for power tended to recruit supporters from their own families and communities and pack them into influential committees. Paradoxically, a party such as the Ba'ath which is formally committed to secular aims and does not recognize *a priori*, sectarian or other group allegiances, is probably more vulnerable to this form of manipulation than a formation which assumes the existence of alternative group loyalties. In Syria, as in most Arab countries, the army plays a decisive role in political life, and the disproportionate number of 'Alawi officers has become a powerful source of Sunni resentment. In June 1979 Brotherhood militants, aided by the duty officer at the Aleppo military academy, massacred sixty cadets, all of them 'Alawis. Subsequent reprisals by the regime for this and other acts of terror committed by the Brotherhood or its affiliates (membership of which is now a capital offence) included the massacre of 400 prisoners at Palmyra in 1980 and the virtual destruction in February 1982 of the city of Hama, a traditional Brotherhood stronghold where there had been a rebellion. The onslaught on Hama resulted in the loss of an estimated 10,000 lives.

Another major centre of the Muslim Brotherhood's activity has been the Sudan, where, since independence in 1954, it has campaigned for the adoption of a permanent constitution based on the Quran and the Sunna. During the 1960s, however, this demand was frustrated by the traditional political parties connected with the *tariqas*, as well as by leftists and Nasserists entrenched in the universities and trades unions. An attempt by the progressive young leader of the Umma Party, Sayyid Sadiq al-Mahdi, who was also heir-apparent to the leadership of the Ansar, to forge a reformist alliance of Islamic forces was frustrated by Colonel Ja'far Numeiri's Communist-backed coup in 1969. However, after the Communists themselves tried to oust Numeiri in 1971, he removed the leftists from his government and gave their posts to leaders with *tariqa* connections. A new constitution adopted in 1973 proclaimed that 'Islamic law and custom shall be the main sources of legislation'. Islamization was carried a stage further when, in 1977, Numeiri set up a commission for the revision of Sudanese laws, to bring them more closely into line with the Shari'a. This opened the way for government participation by the moderate wing of the Brotherhood led by Dr Hasan al-Turabi, who in 1978 accepted the post of Attorney-general. Relying on the principle of *maslaha*, Dr Turabi allowed members of the Brotherhood to stand as candidates for the Sudan Socialist Union, the only official party allowed by Numeiri. By the autumn of 1980 they had gained a number of seats in the new People's Assembly.

Turabi's compromise with the military government was not, however, to the taste of the Brotherhood's more militant members, or to the progressive wing of the Umma Party led by Sayyid Sadiq al-Mahdi. Sayyid Sadiq, an Oxford-educated scholar who briefly held the premiership in 1968, was impatient at the extent to which the current Islamization programme compromised with – and sanctified – out-dated social customs. He believed very strongly, in line with his family's mahdist tradition, that each generation must interpret the Quran anew in accordance with the needs of the age.

Since the military coup which brought General 'Umar al-Bashir to power in 1989 Hasan al-Turabi, through the National Islamic Front (NIF) which he heads, has been the effective power behind the throne. While he professes to believe that 'an Islamic order of government is essentially a form of representative democracy',[22] the fact remains that the Sudan's programme of Islamization has been taking place on the back of a highly authoritarian military regime. In contrast to Egypt, the Front enjoys considerable support from the urban middle class and takes, at least formally, a progressivist attitude towards women in the workforce. Women are 'among the most active and visible organisers' of the NIF.[23] Nevertheless, in the view of its critics, Islamization has led to a programme of cultural genocide against non-Muslim peoples such as the Dinkas and the Nuers who can be readily identified with the pre-Islamic pagans. It has also led to a prolongation of the civil war with the predominantly Christian south. Far from being a source of reintegration for a society alienated from itself by imported secular or western influences, the Brotherhood's ideology has proved much more divisive than the variegated mystical traditions of Sudanese Islam it is seeking to replace. For all his protestations that 'Islamic thought – like all thought – only flourishes in a social environment of freedom and public consultation',[24] Turabi's support for military dictatorship demonstrates that, when his ideological and personal interests converge, he prefers not to put this theory to the test of public opinion.

Indo-Pakistan

If Egypt, with its proximity to Europe, became the intellectual power-house of Western Islam, India, subject to Hindu, Persian and Anglo-Saxon influences, became in the late nineteenth and early twentieth centuries a source of religious and intellectual vitality of equal importance for the Muslim world. As in the West, the growing impact of modernization and occidental influence produced an evolution from progressive liberalism to reactive traditionalism. However, in Indo-Pakistan, as in some other non-Arab regions, the process took on a much more combative and urgent character. Faced with the spectre of Hindu domination, whether appearing in the guise of religious orthodoxy or that of a secular modernism imposed by an elite of pandits and technocrats, a substantial number of Indian Muslims made their *hijra* to Pakistan, converting *dar al-harb* into *dar al-Islam*, where their leaders fiercely debated the ideal Islamic state. Their vision was, however, markedly different from that of the Arab reformers. The Islamic state envisaged by their most articulate spokesman, Abu l 'Ala Maududi, was not so much an ideal Medanese polity reinterpreted to suit the conditions of the twentieth century as a recreation of an idealized Muslim society as it was deemed to have existed in India before its destruction by the British Raj. This way of thinking bore some resemblance to that of the ultra-orthodox Ashkenazi Jews who settled in Israel only to preserve the garb and social customs of the eighteenth-century Polish Diaspora.

Speculative Modernism: Muhammad Iqbal

The seminal thinker of modern Indian Islam is unquestionably Muhammad Iqbal (1875–1938), poet, mystic, philosopher and intellectual founder of Pakistan. More learned and subtle in his thinking than Muhammad 'Abduh, he combined the mystical rationalism of the Persian tradition in which he was reared with an understanding of Western modes of thought unsurpassed by any Muslim writer before or since. Whereas Ahmed Khan had exhibited in his career an overwhelming desire to be accepted as an 'Anglo-Indian gentleman', Iqbal, like his Hindu contemporary Tagore, belonged to a generation for which such a position could be more or less taken for granted. Each was free to explore, from a position of intellectual if not of social equality, the *Zeitgeist* of his particular community, and to present it in terms which Europeans could understand.

After a traditional Islamic education Iqbal came under Western influence first at Lahore and then at Cambridge, where he studied from 1905 to 1908 before going on to complete a doctorate in Persian metaphysics at Munich. His earliest poems were written in Urdu, but following his sojourn in Germany he became more romantic and mystical, writing increasingly in Persian. The Quran, he believed, reflected an essentially dynamic outlook, one which was linked directly to the principle of *ijtihad* in the Shari'a, fixing the position of man within an evolving cosmos. Aziz Ahmed has summarized this aspect of Iqbal's thought:

The movement of the individual self is directly related to the principle of movement in the universe, from chaos towards a pattern of order. Universe as well as life are involved in a process of continuous becoming; and man, who stands at the peak of evolution, can maintain, in himself and in the society to which he belongs, the momentum of this primeval movement by ever-new conquest of the forces of nature.[25]

Iqbal's mystical humanism reflected his reading of Bergson and Nietzsche, as well as ideas developed from the traditions of Islamic neoplatonism. Nietzsche's 'superman' and Ibn 'Arabi's 'Perfect Man', Bergson's '*élan vital*' and Rumi's evolutionary spiral, merge in his thinking, along with perceptions drawn from Hegel, Whitehead, Russell and Einstein. The work of modern metaphysicians, mathematicians and physicists has not only destroyed the self-subsistent materialism of classical physics: it also serves to refute the Ash'ari view of time as absolute and ultimately indivisible. Thus the 'unseen world' (*al-ghaib*) referred to in the Quran is 'not something foreign to the world of matter, but permeates it through and through'. While the Prophethood of Muhammad is located in history, his Message is only 'final' in the sense that it is eternally valid, its aim being 'to awaken in man the higher consciousness of his manifold relations with the universe'.[26] Prophecy is a special mode of mystic consciousness, a 'mode of economizing individual thought and choice by providing ready-made judgements, choices and ways of action' – a mode of understanding appropriate to the childhood of the human race:

With the birth of reason and the critical faculty, however, life, in its own interest, inhibits the formation and growth of non-rational modes of consciousness . . . The Prophet of Islam seems to stand between the ancient and modern world. In so far as the source of his revelation is concerned he belongs to the ancient world; in so far as the spirit of his revelation is concerned he belongs to the modern world . . . The birth of Islam . . . is the birth of inductive intellect. In Islam prophecy reaches its perfection in discovering the need of its own abolition.[27]

Theologically, Iqbal affirms the dominance of free will without having recourse to Mu'tazilite rationalism: only as an 'ever-growing ego can [man] belong to the meaning of the universe'. There are no pleasure-giving and pain-giving acts, only ego-sustaining and ego-dissolving ones. Resurrection is therefore not an external event, but the 'consummation of a life process within the ego'.[28] Heaven and Hell are states, not localities: Heaven the 'joy of triumph over the forces of disintegration', Hell a 'corrective experience which may make a hardened ego once more sensitive to the living breeze of Divine Grace'.[29]

Using Bergson's distinction between 'time' and 'duration', Iqbal frees the Quranic ideal from its historic setting. The ideal Islamic state has never been fully realized, and should not be confused with the government of the Orthodox Caliphs, as is done by most Muslim revivalists. It is still dormant in the conscience of man. Political activity should therefore not be directed towards the restoration of an idealized Islamic past but towards a future in which the concept of Caliphate or 'vice-regency' is equated with the service of humanity:

In this ideal state man's vice-regency of God would fulfil itself and honour its trust, by acknowledging that the ownership of all land vests in God and by accepting that man's duty is to produce wealth for the benefit of all humanity.[30]

This ideal is not incompatible with socialism. Marxism, however, gets bogged down in the negative side of the *tahlil* formula ('There is no god . . .') while failing to emerge into the creative and positive one ('. . . but Allah'): 'The religion of that God-ignoring prophet [Karl Marx] is based on the equality of all stomachs.' Communism therefore has much in common with western imperialism. 'Both are dynamic and restless. Both ignore God and betray man. One does this by revolution, the other by exploitation. Between these two millstones, humanity is ground to dust.'[31]

Iqbal came to the conclusion that, as a step towards the realization of the ideal Islamic state, the Muslims of India must have a state of their own:

The religious order of Islam is organically related to the social order which it has created. The rejection of the one will inevitably involve the rejection of the other. Therefore the construction of a polity on Indian national lines, if it means a displacement of the Islamic principles of solidarity, is simply unthinkable to a Muslim . . . The principle of European democracy cannot be applied to India without recognizing the facts of communal groups . . . I would like to see the Punjab, North-Western Frontier Province, Sind and Baluchistan amalgamated into a single state . . . the formation of a consolidated North-West Indian Muslim state appears to me to be the final destiny of the Muslims at least of North-West India.

Iqbal, who died in 1938, did not live to see the bloody birth-pangs of Pakistan. It was left to Muhammad 'Ali Jinna, leader of the Muslim League, to act as its midwife. Iqbal had foreseen that a Muslim state dominated by upper-class Westernized Muslims like Jinna would not of itself satisfy the ideal of Islamic government; but he believed that if Islamic law were properly applied 'at least the right of subsistence' would be secured to the Muslim masses: 'For Islam the acceptance of social democracy in some suitable form and consistent with the legal principles of Islam is not a revolution but a return to the original purity of Islam.'[32]

If Iqbal's political thought became the main inspiration of the Pakistan movement, it was left to his disciples to work out what a 'return to the original purity of Islam' meant in practical terms. Few Indian Muslims shared his breadth of culture. The liberalism of his outlook commended itself to the anglicized upper classes, while his charismatic reputation, enhanced by his fame as a poet, made him the popular idol of the masses. But, as with 'Abduh, none of his successors was strong enough to maintain both positions at once. At first the liberals established a parliamentary oligarchy which paid lip-service to Islamic principles – an Indian version of British Toryism which complemented the upper-class Fabianism of Nehru and his daughter in India. When this foundered it was replaced by a Western-oriented dictatorship of the Punjabi officer class under Brigadier-General Muhammad Ayub Khan. Disillusioned with the empty rhetoric of a cosmetic Islamic state which fell far short of Iqbal's ideals, opposition generally ran through more secular channels. The Awami League in the East and Zulfikar Ali Bhutto's Pakistani People's Party in the West became the principal forces of organized political activity both before and after the crisis over Bangladesh.

Having been coopted by a discredited upper class, reformist Islam in Pakistan never developed into a mass movement comparable to the Muslim Brotherhood in Egypt. This was partly because, in the Indian environment, survival rather than planning the future had become the principal issue facing the Muslim communities. Distributed throughout the Subcontinent in a variety of mainly urban settlements, there was in reality no common consciousness or consensus of experience upon which progressive reformers could build. After Pakistan's traumatic birth in 1947, the problem of its relations with India and the difficulty of keeping its two halves together were rather more pressing issues than problematic debates about the content of an Islamic constitution. Apart from the political question, there was no way in which a Salafi movement, involving a return to first principles, could develop a popular character in a society where even the literature had no direct access to the Quran and the Sunna. In such an environment, Islamic religiosity crystallized around the formal symbols of Indian Muslim identity – a Pharisaic observance of ritual, dress and social custom, combined with a deep distrust, not just of the West which had ceased to be the burning issue, but of modernity as such, in all its forms. Unlike the Arab world, where (outside the Arabian Peninsula) even the most reactionary *faqihs* had been painfully educated into accepting most of the cardinal points of the modernist rubric, the Indian *'ulama* had retained all the defensive inwardness of the ghetto, fearful that any loosening of the gates of *ijtihad* would lead to an inrush of Western and Hindu influences, destroying both their religion and their distinct-ive identity. The parallels with attitudes to be found in the East European Jewish communities are compelling.

Systematic Neo-traditionalism: Sayyid Abu l 'Ala Maududi

The man who tried to bridge the gap between the ultra-traditionalist *'ulama* and the liberal elite was Sayyid Abu l 'Ala Maududi (1903–79), described by Wilfred Cantwell-Smith as 'much the most systematic thinker of modern Islam'.[33] Maududi's thought is rigid and conservative; but it aspires to be both comprehensive and self-contained. His basic premise is that Islam is entirely self-sufficient and does not need to explain itself in terms other than its own. He is not interested in harmonizing his Islamic ideology with other systems. For Maududi, Islam is perfect and needs no justification. Instead he endeavours to expound, by an idiosyncratic combination of *ijtihad* and literalist exegesis, the Islamic dogma as he sees it, covering every field of human activity from politics to the sexual life. He interlards his exposition with polemics attacking a West which he finds morally repulsive and, fundamentally, incomprehensible. Largely ignorant of Western high cultural and intellectual traditions, his views are mostly picked up, second hand, from articles in newspapers about various social problems. He never applies the same canons of criticism to contemporary Muslim societies: the perfection of 'Islam' is forever compared with the actual imperfections of Western society: like is not compared with like.

Maududi articulates the narrow outlook of the traditionalist Muslim middle class in India and elsewhere, a class which feels its identity and values increasingly threatened by western economic and cultural encroachments. He defends these values by moving in to the attack: the West is morally decadent and corrupt and must be resisted. There is no necessity for an agonizing reappraisal of Islam in the light of modern reality. All that needs to be done is to modernize the *fiqh* to suit new situations. The only real difference between Maududi and the traditionalist *'ulama* is that, whereas they tend to be out of touch with reality, concerning themselves with arcane and usually irrelevant questions, Maududi has the courage to confront modernity with the whole of the traditional Shari'a edifice. In his hands 'Islam' becomes much more than a succession of hair-splitting legal judgements emanating from an archaic social system. It is a full-blown 'ideology' offering answers to every human and social problem. It is mainly for this reason that, despite his rigidity, Maududi is widely admired by Muslim radicals from Egypt to Malaysia. He is one of the very few non-Arab writers on Islam to have been widely translated into Arabic. Along with Sayyid Qutb, he is the most widely read theoretician among young Sunni activists. The strength of his system is that particular aspects (such as his insistence on traditional *purdah* for women) can be discarded without damage to the structure of the whole.

Theoretically Maududi's system is more radical than the way he applies it in practice. With Ahmed Khan, he holds the view that Islam is 'the natural religion of man, the religion that is not associated with any person, people, period or place'.[34] But, whereas this attitude led Ahmed Khan and other modernists towards an acceptance of religious pluralism, Maududi insists uncompromisingly that the Shari'a must be applied to the whole human race:

The Quran does not claim that Islam is the true compendium of rites and rituals, and metaphysical beliefs and concepts, or that it is the proper form of religious (as the word religion is nowadays understood in Western terminology) attitude of thought and action for the individual. Nor does it say that Islam is the true way of life for the people of Arabia, or for the people of any particular country or for the people preceding any particular age (say the Industrial Revolution). No! Very explicitly, for the entire human race, there is only one way of life which is Right in the eyes of God and that is al-Islam.[35]

'Not a single injunction of [the Quran] can be suspected as having been addressed to a particular people,' insists Maududi.[36] Like the traditionalist *'ulama*, Maududi regards all six canonical *hadith* collections and the Quran (which he interprets in a very literalistic manner) as the supreme sources of the Shari'a. He also accepts much of the dogma contained in the four schools of *fiqh*: 'the differences that appear in the four schools are but the natural outcome of the fact that truth is many-sided'.[37]

While he accepts *ijtihad* and *qiyas* as flexible elements in the Shari'a, he has little use for them in practice, at least in the areas of social and family life. His traditionalism is most evident in his general attitude to women, and, in particular, in his defence of *purdah*, the complete veiling and segregation of women as practised in India. He attacks all the modernists who claim that the Quran and *hadiths* are free from *purdah* injunctions: 'The most one could differ in the matter was whether the hands and the face were to be covered or left uncovered.'[38] He concludes, with impeccable logic, that women should be completely covered outside the home (where they should always remain, except when absolutely necessary) because the face is the most attractive part of the human body. If the object of the Shari'a is – as it must be – to 'curb indecency and obscenity, then nothing can be more unreasonable than to close all the minor ways to indecency [i.e., by covering the other parts of the body] but to fling the main gate wide open'.[39] Similarly, birth control is condemned by the Shari'a in all but the most exceptional circumstances because it involves a 'rebellion against the laws of nature'.[40] He rejects the view that the world is becoming over-populated, arguing instead that pressure of population leads to economic development. Men should not be deterred from breeding by the 'phantom of scarcity'.

Like Iqbal's, Maududi's doctrine of *khilafa* – man's 'vice-regency' – is thus in no way taken to mean that because the world's resources are finite, humans should exercise caution and moderation in exploiting them. On the contrary, though sovereignty over the universe and over the whole world belongs to God, we have the right, even the duty, to exploit them for the benefit of humanity. Private wealth and property are permissible, provided they are employed in the service of 'virtue and public welfare', through payment of *zakat* and other religious taxes. The evils of capitalism result from the moral shortcomings of the rich who refuse to recognize the needs of the poor; they are not caused by the system of private ownership as such. Thus, while Maududi claims that Islam, unlike other systems of East and West, is uniquely placed to solve man's economic problems, his remedies (apart from the prohibition of *riba*, which he interprets to mean lending at interest regardless of profit) do not differ substantially from the welfare capitalism of New Dealers and social democrats.

Maududi's primary aim is to present 'Islam' as an absolute and self-sufficient ideology, completely distinct from and opposed to both the Western way of life and its Eastern socialist equivalents. 'The fact . . . is that Islam and Western civilization are poles apart in their objectives as well as in their principles of social organization.'[41] Western humanism he often characterizes as 'man-worship', a form of *shirk* which he contrasts with Islamic *tawhid* (God's unity). Like 'Abduh (and unlike Iqbal), he holds the essentially medieval view that 'science' consists of a 'systematized body of knowledge',[42] whose discoveries can be appropriated for the benefit of Islam without causing an epistemological upheaval that must lead to a radical revaluation of Islam's intellectual premises as understood by the traditionalists – a revaluation that must affect all traditional formulations of the Shari'a.

As well as being an ideologist, Maududi was the creator and leader of a militant Islamic organization, the Jamaat-i-Islami. He originally opposed the creation of Pakistan because he feared the liberalism of its founders and the British-trained administrators who would be required to run it.

All persons who have been trained for running the affairs of a secular state . . . are totally unfitted for an Islamic state which requires human beings of a very different character for its citizens, voters, councillors, office-bearers . . . It requires men who have the fear of God in their hearts; who feel a sense of responsibility towards God; who prefer the next life to the present; in whose eyes moral gain or loss is much more important than worldly success or failure . . .[43]

Abandoning his revolutionary programme for the conversion of the whole of India to Islam, as a first stage in the conversion of the whole of humanity, he accepted the reality of Pakistan, opting for a gradualist approach towards the Islamization of its law and constitution, though he had previously condemned the Muslim League for taking a similar line. He accepted that the *fiqh* would have to be modernized in certain areas of constitutional, international and criminal law, and accepted Pakistan as a *de facto* national state. Thereafter his efforts were concentrated on making Pakistan a 'theo-democracy' based on the Shari'a which would enforce, among other things, the abolition of interest-bearing banks, sexual segregation and veiling of women, and the *hadd* penalties for theft, adultery and other crimes. He admitted that his Islamic state would bear a certain resemblance to Communist and Fascist states, being based on an all-embracing ideology. However, he vigorously denied that its implementation would lead to human rights abuses. Pakistani non-Muslims would enjoy the rights Islam accords to minorities. He accepted the rulings of the medieval *faqihs* regarding the rights and disabilities of *dhimmis*: they would have the 'same freedom of conscience, expression and opinion' as Muslims and would be subject to the same penalties for theft and other crimes. They would be debarred from holding certain key offices in the Islamic state, but not otherwise discriminated against.[44]

The Jamaat-i-Islami became the spearhead of the movement to transform Pakistan from a Muslim homeland into an Islamic state. In the Constituent Assembly's discussions on the Constitution in 1951, Maududi, who had been jailed for his oppositional activities, joined hands with the traditionalist 'ulama in outlining 22 Basic Principles of an Islamic state. They included the demand that all existing laws contrary to the Quran and the Sunna should be gradually phased out, and that the state should be based on 'the principles and ideas of Islamic ideology'.[45]

The *dhimmi* question came to the fore in the anti-Qadiyani agitation in 1953. The Qadiyanis, a faction of the Ahmedi sect, were followers of Ghulam Ahmed of Qadiyan, who had advanced claims to prophethood in the late nineteenth century. Though many of his followers, who shared a modernist outlook, interpreted these claims metaphorically, Maududi and the traditionalist 'ulama believed that the Qadiyanis had formed themselves into a separate Umma by designating non-Qadiyanis as *kafirs*, by prohibiting intermarriage with other Muslims, and by praying separately from them. Under the Raj they had been treated as Muslims: indeed, the support they received from the British was the real source of resentment against them, since Ghulam Ahmed's claims were scarcely more blasphemous than those advanced by Muhammad Ahmad and other African *mahdis*. There was also a strictly political motive in the agitation: Muhammad Zafrullah Khan, the Foreign Minister, was a Qadiyani, as were other influential figures. The attack on the sect was thus directed at individuals in the government as well as at the easy-going liberalism of the secularists who were prepared to take a broad view of the question: 'Who is a

Muslim?' The agitation led to serious rioting in the Punjab which was only quelled after the imposition of martial law. The report produced by Mr Justice Munir in the aftermath of these disturbances squarely faced the issue that had been fudged in the discussions over the Constitution: an 'Islamic State' as defined by the Maududists and the *'ulama* was incompatible with democracy in the modern sense of the term. A 'lack of bold and clear thinking, the inability to understand and take decisions', had brought about 'a confusion which will persist . . . until our leaders have a clear concept of the goal and of the means to reach it . . . Opposing principles, if left to themselves, can only produce confusion and disorder, and the application of a neutralizing agency to them can only produce a dead result.' The report concluded:

. . . as long as we rely on the hammer when a file is needed and press Islam into service to solve situations it was never intended to solve, frustration and disappointment must dog our steps. The sublime faith called Islam will live, even if our leaders are not there to enforce it. It lives in the individual, in his soul and outlook, in all his relations with God and man, from the cradle to the grave, and our politicians should understand that if Divine Commands cannot make or keep a man a Musalman, their statements will not.[46]

Maududi was sentenced to death for his part in the Qadiyani agitation, but the sentence was commuted to 14 years' imprisonment, of which he served only two. Disregarding Munir's advice, in 1956 the Constituent Assembly approved the first Pakistan Constitution – a document which persisted in trying to square the circle of having an Islamic Constitution in a multi-confessional state. The Jamaat-i-Islami declared itself satisfied with the lip service paid to Islam in this document, hoping to achieve its real implementation by political pressure and agitation. In fact the political anarchy resulting from the electoral collapse of the Muslim League led to the imposition of martial law in 1958, sweeping away the Constitution. 'Islamic' was dropped from the name of the Republic. Ayub Khan, who established a presidential cabinet in 1962, left the traditionalist *'ulama* to their own devices, though he incurred their hostility by introducing a reformed Family Law which restricted divorce and polygamy in accordance with a liberal Hanafi ruling. The Jamaat-i-Islami played a prominent part in the agitation which brought about the downfall of Ayub's government in 1969; but it made a poor showing in the elections the following year, winning only eight seats from a field of 488 candidates. It continued to agitate over the Qadiyani question, eventually pressuring the government of Mr Bhutto into declaring the Qadiyanis a non-Muslim minority.

The Jamaat also played its part in bringing about the downfall of Bhutto in 1977; and, though Maududi had once declared military rule of any kind to be 'un-Islamic', he enthusiastically supported General Zia ul Haqq during the early months of his rule. With the Jamaat's backing, Zia made Islamization the ideological cornerstone of his government: *hadd* penalties, including flogging and amputation, were introduced for alcohol consumption, *zina* (illicit sex), *qazf* (false accusations of *zina*) and theft. Though amputations were rare, public floggings became a popular spectator sport, this punishment being inflicted for 'hoarding and profiteering' as well as for *hadd* offences. Shari'a benches empowered to revise existing laws and sentences were introduced in each of the four provincial High Courts: 'Islam' was thus being permitted to challenge the existing legal and constitutional system.

Unlike the Muslim Brotherhood in Egypt the Jamaat-i-Islami never developed into a mass movement. Its Sufi style methods of recruitment, with members pledging allegiance to the organization rather than to Pakistan and its constitution, has made it vulnerable to accusations of disloyalty and lack of patriotism. Although the Jamaat is actively involved in educational and social welfare projects, its cult-like reputation has led to accusations of brainwashing, diminishing its electoral appeal. Its insistence on ideological purity based on Maududi's somewhat rigid interpretations of Islamic legal tradition has tended to alienate more pragmatic members of the middle class, while its efforts to promote a more equitable relationship between peasants and their landlords who still dispose of vast quantities of electoral patronage have brought it up against Pakistan's traditional 'feudal' order. Although it initially supported General Zia ul Haqq's 'Islamization' policies the Jamaat tended to distance itself from them when the government became unpopular. In the latter years of his regime, prior to his death in an air-crash in 1989, Zia turned away from the Maududists towards the moderate reform movement led by Maulana Abdul Hasan al-Nadwi of Lucknow. An admirer of both Iqbal and Banna, Nadwi followed 'Abduh in recognizing the need for the separation of religious and political spheres. Stressing the importance of education, he criticized the Maududist preoccupation with the political struggle, which he believed could only foment strife among

Muslims. These predictions, alas, have proved all too accurate. In recent years Pakistan has seen increasing violence between Sunni and Shi'i militants, as well as a continuing undercurrent of violence between native Pakistani Punjabis and the Muhajirs (migrants from India during Partition and their descendants). There have been several well-publicized sectarian massacres as well as much less publicized instances of 'sectarian cleansing' of Shi'i vilages in the Northern Areas by Sunni militants. Part of the instability is doubtless due to the influx of militant Mujahidun and their weaponry from Afghanistan, along with the narcotics which invariably give rise to gangsterism. But, given the presence of a substantial Shi'i minority along with Pakistan's different ethnic communities, Islamization must inevitably lead to sectarian polarization, not least because its Sunni versions will be seen to impinge on the authority of Shi'i religious leaders and the autonomy of Shi'i communities. In the light of the conflicts that had already erupted, the announcement by Prime Minister Nawaz Sharif in 1998 that the country would henceforth be governed in accordance with Shari'a law boded ill for future peace. Given the scale of potential sectarian and social conflicts Sharif's move threatened to unleash and the growing danger of war with India over Kashmir, the suspension of democracy by the army in the summer of 1999 was greeted with indifference, if not relief, by a majority of people.

The Islamic revolution in Iran

The origins and cause of the Iranian revolution can only be dealt with briefly here. To summarize a complex situation crudely, the Shah of Iran was brought down by a combination of economic and political factors, mostly of his own making. Unlike the Ottoman dominions and Egypt, which had long been exposed to Western influences, Iran remained comparatively isolated until the end of the nineteenth century. (Before the opening of the Suez Canal in 1869, Iran lay 11,000 miles from Western Europe by the sea-route which carried most of the trade.) The Qajar Shahs who eventually inherited Safavid power ruled over a loosely structured polity in which the Shi'ite *ulama* disposed of considerable social power. In the 1890s they succeeded, partly under Afghani's inspiration, in mobilizing a vigorous and successful national protest against the tobacco monopoly granted by the Shah to an Englishman, Major Talbot. The Tobacco Agitation proved to be the dress rehearsal for the full-blown, but remarkably peaceful Constitutional Revolution of 1905–6, when a section of the 'ulama united with the business community to force the Shah into granting a Constituent Assembly that would protect them from unfair foreign competition. The 'ulama who backed the revolution argued that, in the absence of the Twelfth Imam, it was important to impose constitutional checks on the arbitrary power of rulers similar to those in force in Europe. Their opponents, led by Shaikh Fazlollah Nuri, insisted that the true constitution was the Quran and the Sunna, and that European constitutional ideas were basically inimical to Islam. Nuri managed to introduce an amendment into the constitution ensuring that no laws were passed by the Majlis (assembly) till approved by a board of 'ulama.[47] The fact that a significant section of the 'ulama were in favour of constitutional reform indicates a degree of political sophistication among the Shi'ite clergy and a willingness to embrace modernity that would re-surface after the collapse of the Pahlevi regime in 1978–9.

The National Assembly was successfully defended against an attempted counter-revolution by Muhammad 'Ali Shah in 1908; but the divisions inevitable in this fragile coalition between liberal modernists and the more traditionalist 'ulama opened the way for the Anglo-Russian intervention – a situation complicated by the establishment of a Soviet republic in Gilan after the Bolshevik Revolution. The conflict was shelved – but not resolved – by the rise to power of Reza Khan, who, like Mustafa Kemal in Turkey, came up through the ranks of the army. At first Reza's modernizing nationalism enjoyed the support of some of the 'ulama and the conservative reformers in the Majlis. However, once he had achieved absolute power, taking the crown and title of Shah in 1926, he instituted draconian changes which struck at the roots of the old pluralistic, tribal society. Not only was a new centralized bureaucracy created, but ethnic solidarities were broken up by the manipulation of tribal animosities. Traditional costumes were banned and European dress, including the wide-brimmed felt hat, was forcibly introduced. Though officially registered *mullahs* were exempted from the latter rule, the new hats were specifically designed to interfere with the rule of prayer. Women's emancipation was imposed by force: the veil was outlawed, as was the traditional *chador* covering women from head to foot. Government employees, from ministers to road-sweepers, were ordered to parade their wives in public, though women were still denied the right to vote. Like his Qajar predecessors, the Shah made some generous concessions to foreign companies. Thus, under an agreement signed in 1933 with the Anglo-Iranian oil company and intended to last until 1991, Iran was to receive only between 10 and 20 per cent of its oil revenues. Like Ataturk (whom he greatly admired), Shah Reza created a new, Western-educated intelligentsia to run his bureaucracy. Unlike Ataturk, however, he never tried to consolidate his government by means of a nationally organized modern political party and took to governing increasingly by means of military and police repression.

In 1941 the British and Russians, fearing a pro-Axis coup by army officers, deposed Shah Reza and placed his son, Muhammad Reza, on the throne. The weak and vacillating young monarch was almost unseated in 1952, when he was forced to appoint Muhammad Mossadeq, a popular nationalist leader, as his Prime Minister. Mossadeq, supported by the Communist Tudeh Party, which was active among the oil workers, nationalized the Anglo-Iranian Oil Company; however, the following year he was overthrown in a military coup engineered by Britain and the United States on behalf of the young Shah. From 1953 the Shah, backed by the army, ruled in a manner very similar to that of his father. Many areas of the economy were modernized, new roads and factories were built and the army, equipped with the latest US weaponry, became the second most powerful local force in the region. (The most powerful, that of Israel, provided the Shah with military advisers and experts in counter-insurgency.)

The rise of OPEC during the 1960s and early 1970s emboldened the Shah to push for higher oil prices, and for a period the higher revenues made the country appear very wealthy – at least on paper. In social terms, however, Iran presented a very different picture. Partial land reforms in the countryside, the exploding development of the cities and rural migration created a restless class of deracinated peasants who eked out a miserable livelihood in the shanty-towns surrounding Tehran and other conurbations. Though oil and other factory workers benefited from the rise in oil revenues, the economic infrastructure was inadequate to permit much of the new wealth to filter down into the community. Galloping inflation and a massive rise in urban rents ensured that only a minority of the Westernized middle class, particularly those with foreign connections, enjoyed the fruits of the country's exports. Corruption in court circles became an open scandal, as it became known that the Shah and his family had siphoned off millions of dollars into foreign bank accounts, and had appropriated much of the national product through such institutions as the Pahlavi Foundation – ostensibly a charitable organization – which owned a controlling interest in a chain of mines, hotels, factories and agribusinesses. Like his father, who had made himself the country's largest land-owner and employer, the Shah turned a considerable slice of Iran's economy into a personal fiefdom.

No doubt many people benefited from the Shah's reforms: considerable improvements were made in health and education under the so-called 'White Revolution' launched in 1963, in which some 1.6 million peasant families obtained land. However, agricultural stagnation, rising rents and general inflation meant that by the mid 1970s more and more people felt themselves to be worse off. This was especially the case in great cities like Tehran, where between 1967 and 1977 (the decade of the oil boom) the proportion of urban families living in one room actually increased, from 36 per cent to 43 per cent.[48]

The Shah finally sealed his fate by sheer political ineptitude. Belatedly, in 1975, he tried to broaden his power-base by creating a single political party, the Rastakhiz or 'Resurgence' Party, on the East European totalitarian model. Two areas of society previously untouched by the regime – the *bazaari* merchants and the religious establishment – were suddenly encroached upon. The Party took over all the ministries and public media. Branches were opened in the bazaars and donations forced out of small businessmen: suddenly, instead of tolerating indifference or passive opposition, the regime was demanding active support. The *'ulama* were explicitly attacked. The Shah was declared to be a 'spiritual leader'; the *mullahs* were denounced as medieval 'black reactionaries'. The religious calendar was abolished and a royalist calendar (dating from the supposed foundation of the ancient Iranian monarchy) was substituted. By means of the Party, the state encroached upon the autonomy of the *waqfs* (from which the Shi'ite *'ulama* derived most of their livelihoods), in what was clearly seen as a first move against the independence of the religious establishment. The 1967 Family Protection Law – which had raised the minimum age of marriage for girls to 18, contrary to the Shari'a – was, for the first time, rigidly enforced. Girls who expressed their opposition to the regime by wearing the traditional *chador* were banned from universities and government offices.

This attack on the religious establishment might have succeeded if the Shah had not simultaneously alienated the secular middle-class groups. In 1977, however, he launched a massive 'anti-profiteering' campaign, blaming them for the high rate of inflation. A number of leading industrialists were arrested. Naturally this infuriated the business community, whose members were perfectly aware of the goings-on at court, and the wealthier among them followed the Pahlavi example of transferring their capital abroad. The smaller *bazaari* businessmen, who had always had close ties with the *'ulama*, had already been alienated by the Shah's campaign against the religious establishment. The final element in the formidable coalition the Shah was ranging against himself was the industrial proletariat itself. Premier Amouzegar sparked off a whole chain of strikes in the oil and manufacturing industries by carrying out deflationary measures which included the cutting of bonuses.

The events leading immediately to the Shah's downfall in 1979 (the burning of an Abadan cinema, repeated cycles of demonstrations, shootings and mourning processions) are well documented and need not be repeated here. The important fact is that the monarch succeeded in alienating every significant group in the country – the 'Westernized' business community, the salaried middle class, the *bazaari* merchants, the factory workers, the service workers and the armies of unemployed, under-employed and semi-employed *mustazafin* (*les misérables*) who lived in the shanty-towns, as well as a section of the rural population. The question that concerns us here is how and why 'Islam' came to play its decisive ideological role in the revolution.

Shi'ism and revolution

Basically, three aspects of Iranian Shi'ism contributed to the triumph of the revolution: the revisionist neo-Shi'ite ideology of the intellectuals and left-wing activists; the traditional religious hierarchy of Qom and Najaf (Iraq), led by the impressive, charismatic and uncompromising figure of Ayatollah Khomeini; and the popular Shi'ism of the 'Hosseini-yat' – the culture of *rouzehs* and passion plays, imported from the villages into the shanty-towns and other districts inhabited by the *mustazafin*.

Shi'ite modernism is a comparatively recent development compared with the reformed Sunnism of 'Abduh and his followers. One reason for this was the backwardness of Iran in the nineteenth century compared with Egypt and India. Another, paradoxically, is that the 'High Shi'ism' represented by the seminaries of Qom and Najaf was philo-sophically and legally more adaptable than the *fiqh* dispensed by the traditionalist *'ulama* in Sunni countries. The victory of the *usulis* over the *akhbaris* in the nineteenth century and the principle that only a living *mujtahid* may interpret the law made it possible to introduce many aspects of modernization without encountering opposition from the *'ulama*. It was partly for this reason and partly because of their independent social power that a large section of the Iranian *'ulama*, unique among Muslim clergy, were able to join hands successfully with the liberal constitutionalists in 1905–9. Nevertheless, the stresses between the *'ulama* and the government remained, becoming more acute as a new technocratic elite, trained in Western ways and adopting many Western mannerisms, established a commanding position in society. To the social resentment of those who felt themselves excluded from the benefits of the oil wealth was added the opposition of those *'ulama*, led by Khomeini, who considered that Shaikh Nuri had been right in predicting that 'constitutionalism would be a meaningless trick allowing more, not less, European domination'.[49]

Shi'ite Neo-traditionalism: Sayyid Ruhallah Khomeini

Khomeini, a Sayyid from Arak who, like many *mujtahids*, had studied and taught at the famous Fayzieh *madrasa* (college) in Qom, first came to political prominence in 1962–3, during the protests against the Shah's 'White Revolution' – a programme which partially broke up the large estates, distributing land to the peasants, nationalized forests, denationalized state-owned factories, extended the vote to women and established a rural literacy corps. The reforms were evidently aimed at creating support for the Shah among the entrepreneurial middle class and the peasantry without antagonizing too many big land-owners. The Shah organized a national referendum which, according to the government, demonstrated 99.9 per cent 'approval' for the programme. The opposition, which included an alliance of *bazaari* merchants, clergy, public employees and Mossadeq's former sup-porters in the National Front, responded by organizing a wave of public demonstrations during the month of Muharram (June 1963) which left many hundreds of dead in Tehran, Qom, Isfahan, Shiraz, Mashhad and Tabriz. As with the Constitutional Revolution and Mos-sadeq's movement, the opposition was made up of widely disparate elements. Khomeini maximized its appeal, however, by concentrating on the government's misdeeds rather than on the specifics of his own programme. In only one of his proclamations, for example, did he join with the traditionalist *ulama* in opposing the franchise for women; on the other hand he vigorously denounced the Shah's regime for 'living off corruption, rigging elections, violating the constitutional laws, stifling the press and political parties, destroying the independence of the universities, neglecting the economic needs of merchants, workers and peasants, undermining the country's Islamic beliefs', and generally capitulating to the West.[50]

For his part in the agitation Khomeini was deported, first to Turkey and thence to the Shi'ite centre at Najaf in Iraq. Here he was to prove much more dangerous than when he was inside the country. Whereas the clergy who remained in Iran could be virtually silenced, expressing their opposition only in Delphic ambiguities, the Iraqis, who had their own quarrels with the Shah over the Kurdish question and over navigation in the disputed Shatt al-'Arab, were not averse to allowing Khomeini a political voice so long as he refrained from attacking the regime in Baghdad. From Najaf, Khomeini openly denounced the Shah, comparing him to Yazid, murderer of Husain, and urging the faithful to overthrow his satanic regime. At the same time he set forth, in a series of lectures to religious students, a radical programme for Islamic government entitled Velayet-i Faqih ('the Jurist's Trusteeship'), in which he argued that the government should be entrusted directly to the *ulama*:

Islam is the religion of militant individuals who are committed to truth and justice. It is the religion of those who desire freedom and independence. It is the school of those who struggle against imperialism . . .[51]

Present Islam to the people in its true form so that our youth does not picture the akhunds (mullahs) as sitting in some corner of Najaf or Qom, studying the questions of menstruation or childbirth, instead of concerning themselves with politics, and draw the conclusion that religion must be separate from politics. This slogan of the separation of religion and politics and the demand that Islamic scholars should not intervene in social and political affairs have been formulated and propagated by the imperialists; it is only the irreligious who repeat them. Were religion and politics separate at the time of the Prophet (peace and blessing be upon him)? Did there exist, on one side, a group of clerics, and opposite it, a group of politicians and leaders?[52]

In the lectures, which contain polemical attacks on the 'imperialists, the oppressive and treacherous rulers, the Jews, Christians and materialists', Khomeini reverts to Nuri's argument that Islamic government is constitutional, not in the sense of being subject to laws decreed by a majority of the people, but because 'the rulers are subject to . . . conditions . . . set forth in the Noble Quran and the Sunna'.[53] Islam knows not monarchy: 'There is not the slightest trace of vast palaces, opulent buildings, servants and retainers, private equerries . . . and all the other appurtenances of monarchy that consume as much as half of the national budget.'[54] Above all, the ruler who adheres to Islam as well as being of a high personal moral standard must necessarily submit to the *faqih*, asking him about the laws and ordinances of Islam in order to carry them out. This being the case, the true rulers are the *faqihs* themselves, and rulership ought officially to be theirs – entrusted to them, rather than to those who are simply obliged to follow them on account of their own ignorance of the law.[55]

Khomeini's message, delivered to theology students in Najaf, was unambiguous. To a classic, Afghani-style appeal to the faithful to defend Islam against imperialist attacks, Khomeini added the specific corollary that the *faqihs* – that is to say the clerical establishment – must be entrusted with the full responsibility of government. His doctrine was simultaneously revolutionary and ultra-conservative, calling for militant activism, yet demanding that the religious establishment, of which he himself was an important member, had the right, even the duty, to govern the state. This was indeed a radical departure, not only from his previous positions (in 1941, for example, he had stated: 'We do not say that government must be in the hands of the *faqih*; rather we say that government must be in accordance with God's law . . . with the *supervision* [emphasis added] of the religious leaders'[56]), but from the whole Shi'ite tradition of *de facto* acceptance of political authority which had grown up since Safavid times.

If Khomeini's real position had been fully known and understood, it is doubtful if he would ever have acquired a following massive enough to bring down the Pahlavi monarchy. But, in addition to his role of religious firebrand, Khomeini was a highly astute politician. In his public pronouncements he carefully avoided reference to the *velayet-i faqih*, confining himself, as in 1963, to generalized attacks on US and Israeli imperialism, violations of the constitution, discrepancies of wealth, palace corruption, the waste of national resources on luxuries and weaponry and the evils of SAVAK, the Shah's secret police, whom Khomeini's followers accused of murdering his son Mustafa in 1977. Indeed, up to the time he came to power in 1979, Khomeini continued to argue for a restoration of the 1906 Constitution. A traditionalist *mullah* masquerading as a new Afghani, he might have been convincing to the impoverished folk of the shanty-town if they had known about him, and he had his supporters within the religious establishment, most of them former pupils from Qom. These included Ayatollah Hossein Montazeri, a teacher of *fiqh* at Qom; Ayatollah Muhammad Beheshti, an astute political operator who managed to get SAVAK to approve his being placed in charge of the government-financed mosque in Hamburg; Ayatollah Morteza Motahari, the most intellectual and liberal-minded of Khomeini's followers; Hojjat al-Islam Akbar Rafsanjani; and Hojjat al-Islam Ali Khamenei: all would play leading parts in the Islamic Revolution. But in itself Khomeini's message cannot have had much appeal for the most active opponents of the Shah's regime – the liberals of Mossadeq's old National Front, remnants of the Communist Tudeh party, and the 'new left' movements, inspired by similar developments among Palestinian and Latin American youth, that had mushroomed in the wake of SAVAK repression.

The task of bringing the nationalists, modernizers, leftists and miscellaneous radicals into the ranks of Khomeini's followers fell to the Islamic leftists led by Sadeq Ghotbzadeh and Abu'l Hasan Bani Sadr, acting under the inspiration of the guru of the Shi'ite modernists, Dr 'Ali Shari'ati. Without Shari'ati's immense reputation among the Iranian youth, and without the crucial support lent to Khomeini by Ghotbzadeh, Bani Sadr and the leftist guerrillas in the first weeks of the revolution, it is doubtful whether the coalition of disparate elements that brought down the Shah would ever have come together.

Shi'ite Speculative Modernism: 'Ali Shari'ati

Born in 1933 in a village in Khurasan, Shari'ati received his early education from his father, Aqa Muhammad Taqi Shari'ati, a free-lance *mujtahid* who, though not a trained *mullah*, founded in Mashhad the Centre for the Propagation of Islamic Truth, an institution devoted to modernist Quranic exegesis. After learning Arabic, Shari'ati trained as a teacher. He gave an early indication of his socialist leanings by translating a biography of Abu Dharr al-Ghifari (subtitled 'The God-Worshipping Socialist') by the Egyptian novelist 'Abd al-Hamid al-

Sahar. The book described how, after the Prophet's death, Abu Dharr denounced the first three caliphs, supported 'Ali and, after the latter's defeat, withdrew into the desert in order to keep alive the radical Islamic tradition of supporting the poor against the worldliness of the rich.[57] After graduating from Mashhad University in 1960 Shari'ati won a state scholarship to Paris, where he obtained a doctorate in sociology and Islamic studies. This was the heyday of student radicalism and the beginning of the Third World movement heralded by the Cuban and Algerian revolutions. Shari'ati attended lectures by Louis Massignon as well as popular Marxist professors, and undertook translations of Sartre, Camus, Guevara, Giap and, notably, Fanon. While translating Fanon Shari'ati wrote the French West Indian writer several letters complaining about his hostility to religion. The 'Wretched of the Earth', Shari'ati believed, could not resist Western imperialism unless they regained their cultural identity, which was closely bound up with religion.

Shari'ati's sojourn in Paris coincided with an upsurge in the activity of the Liberation Movement, the Islamic-orientated wing of Mossadeq's National Front led by Mehdi Bazargan, an engineer, and Hojjat-al-Islam (later Ayatollah) Mahmud Taleqani, a leading religious supporter of Mossadeq who had been forced into retirement after the Shah's coup. The Liberation Movement's Paris branch, with its affiliated Islamic Students' Society, was presided over by Ghotbzadeh and Bani Sadr. Shari'ati joined the Front, editing and writing for its various publications and rapidly becoming the most influential voice among the oppositionists. In 1965 he returned to Iran with his wife and two children. After spending six months in jail for his opposition activities he was allowed to return to his native Khurasan, where he taught in an elementary school and, for a time, at Mashhad University. His classes were suspended, however, when the authorities decided they were becoming too popular, and in 1967 he moved to Tehran, where he began teaching history and sociology at the famous Hosseiniya-i-Ershad, a religious foundation supported by veterans of the Liberation Movement. Bazargan taught thermodynamics there, and Motahari (Khomeini's ex-pupil) and Taleqani taught theology.

Shari'ati became immensely popular. His claim to be developing a new 'Islamic sociology' attracted both secular and religious students. Notes and tapes of his lectures were soon circulating, not only in Tehran but also in the provinces. The Islamic terminology of his discourse not only protected him from official repression, but also made his message more accessible to students from traditional family backgrounds. In 1973, however, SAVAK finally moved against him, closing down the Hosseiniya, arresting Shari'ati and banning his works. He remained nearly three years in prison until a petition from the Algerian Government secured his release. After being kept in home detention for two years he was allowed to leave for England, where he died suddenly in 1977, aged 44. Shari'ati's supporters claim he was murdered by SAVAK, but the British coroner reported a massive heart attack as the cause of death.

Those of Shari'ati's writings so far available in English are somewhat sketchy and eclectic, exhibiting an idiosyncratic approach to Islam and a general, if superficial, familiarity with Left Bank politicial writing. In one of his better-known works, *Marxism and Other Western Fallacies*, he takes on Marx and Sartre, both of whom are condemned for their misunderstanding and rejection, presented as typically Western, of religion. There is no consideration of the ideas of Weber, Durkheim, Kierkegaard, William James or other important Western writers on religion. Shari'ati's approach was intuitive rather than scholarly. He gives no references to the authorities he cites and at times appears to misrepresent them. His attitude towards Marxism seems to have more to do with its popular appeal for the student left than with its value as a methodology or style of analysis. Nevertheless his grounding in Islamic intellectual traditions gave him a base from which to evaluate Western culture and society in terms which Westerners and, more importantly, the partly Westernized youth of Iran, could understand.

In line with his own political commitment, much of Shari'ati's writing presents an activist approach. Islam, he claims, 'is the first school of thought that recognizes the masses as the basis, the fundamental and conscious factor, in determining history and society'. In support of this proposition he cites the favourite modernist verse from the Quran:

Verily God does not change the state of a people until they change the state of their own selves. (13:11)

Unlike most religious writers, he refrains from accusing Marxists of *kufr* (disbelief):

Examine carefully how the Quran uses the word *kafir*. The word is only used to describe those who refuse to take action. It is never used to describe those who reject metaphysics or refuse to accept the existence of God, the soul or the resurrection.[58]

Shari'ati's quarrel with Marxism is two-fold. Sociologically, he claims, Marx failed to distinguish between the forms of ownership, class relations and the tools of production on the one hand, and the structure of domination between rulers and ruled on the other. This failure had its outcome in Leninist and Stalinist industrialism. By assuming that the superstructure of domination arose out of relations of production, the Communists thought that public ownership of the means of production would put an end to the dehumanizing exploitation of capitalism. Actually, all they succeeded in doing was to create a different version of bourgeois society: '. . . the difference between Marxism and the western bourgeoisie [*sic*] is that [the latter] promotes a bourgeois *class* and [the former] a bourgeois *society*'. Here Shari'ati's critique of Soviet and Chinese communism is in line with that of other 'new left' critics; he follows Fanon in arguing that the Third World countries can never recover the self-confidence necessary to modernize their societies until they have first 'returned to their roots' in the popular culture:

When the intention is to deny the West, to resist it, Marxism is considered the most effective weapon against it; whereas it is seldom realized that Marxism itself is utterly a product of the history, social organization and cultural outlook of this same West. This is not simply because its founders and leading figures are all Western, but rather, to employ a Marxist analysis, the ideology itself must be accounted a mere superstructure resting on the social infrastructure of the bourgeois industrial system of production in the modern West.[59]

Marxist models, Shari'ati argues, are not simply inappropriate for Islamic societies – though, in common with other critics, he recognizes how unsuccessful Marxist ideas and parties have been in Muslim countries – they are contradictory and wrong in themselves. By denying the autonomous and absolute character of human values they reduce men and women to creatures of production. Whereas Marx's philosophy takes human beings out of the realm of necessity and into history, his sociology puts them back into the mechanistic world of nature. The philosophy is therefore clearly at odds with the sociology: the language in which Marx condemns capitalism is loaded with values derived from western humanism – values whose autonomy he denies: 'Assuming a mystical tone, he speaks of humanity as self-aware, truthful, proud, free, knowing, endowed with moral virtues . . .'[60] In a sense, therefore, Marxists are really idealists masquerading as materialists. Having established the non-material basis of ethical values, Shari'ati goes on to attribute them to the divine in man, a 'bi-dimensional being', a 'compound of mud and the divine spirit'. This dualism is internal to man, not part of nature. Its uniqueness to man is symbolized by the Quranic story of the angels prostrating themselves before Adam. Humanity's role as God's vice-regent is a function of human free will. The human being's relation to the divinely ordained laws of the universe is analogous to that of the agriculturalist who has the 'freedom' to cultivate trees and plants in accordance with the pre-existing laws of nature. The prophets 'have discovered the divine norms existing in society and nature and, through the exercise of their will in conformity with these norms, they have perfected their mission and attained their goal' of building new societies, civilizations and histories. In Shari'ati, voluntarism is vindicated and attributed directly to the divine in humanity acting in conjunction with revelation.[61]

The radical political implications of this doctrine become most explicit when Shari'ati identifies 'God' with 'the People'. Two classes, the rulers and the ruled, have stood opposed throughout history: 'In the classless society, Allah stands in the same rank as *al nas* [the people] in such a fashion that whenever in the Quran social matters are mentioned Allah and *al nas* are virtually synonymous.'[62] In the same way, the statement that 'property belongs to God' means that capital belongs to the people as a whole. These are the principles that Abel son of Adam, 'Ali, Abu Dharr, Salman al-Farisi and the Imam Husain stood for against Cain, Mu'awiya and the Umayyad dictators. They represent *tawhid* (unity) against *tawlid* (production) and *shirk* – that is, the disintegrative forces of class and nationalism, the 'world-view that regards the universe as a discordant assemblage full of disunity, contradiction and heterogeneity, possessing a variety of independent and clashing poles, conflicting tendencies, variegated and unconnected desires, purposes and wills'. Islam, the religion of *tawhid*, finds its ideal society in the Umma, whose social system is based on equity, justice and common ownership – that is, the classless society. Its perfect representative is the 'theomorphic man' in whom the spirit of God has overcome the half of his being that relates to *iblis* (Satan), to clay or sediment.

[This] ideal man passes through the very midst of nature and comes to understand God; he seeks out mankind and thus attains God. He does not bypass nature and turn his back on mankind. He holds the sword of Caesar in his hand and he has the heart of Jesus in his breast. He thinks with the brain of Socrates and loves God with the heart of Hallaj . . . Ideal man has three aspects: truth, goodness and beauty – in other words, knowledge, ethics and art. He is a theomorphic being exiled on earth: with the combined wealth of love and knowledge, he rules over all beings. In front of him the angels prostrate themselves. He is the great rebel of the world.[63]

Shari'ati's mystical humanism owes something to Marx and to Sartre, but rather more to the Shi'ite philosophical tradition of Ibn Sina, Mulla Sadra and High Sufism. His 'theomorphic man' is a blend of Camus's *homme revolté* and Ibn 'Arabi's 'Perfect Man'. Shari'ati is versatile enough in Quranic exegesis to recognize that 'the language of religions, particularly the language of the Semitic religions in whose prophets we believe, is a symbolic language'. It is a 'multi-faceted language, each aspect of which addresses itself to a particular generation and class of men'.[64] The *ayas* (signs) of the Quran are allegorical; the signs of God revealed in nature, however, contain 'positive scientific worth'; they are not mere 'illusions or veils covering the face of truth'. Unlike Ibn 'Arabi, Shari'ati is a phenomenological rather than an ontological monist. He regards the Quranic view of nature as being 'closer to the approach of modern science than to that of ancient mysticism'. In a passage reminiscent of Iqbal he argues that Einstein points the way to an 'invisible and unknowable essence that sometimes shows itself in the form of matter, and sometimes in the form of energy'. Science can render knowable the *zahir* or outer manifestations of reality. The 'unseen' reality (*al-ghaib*) is hidden because it is unknowable: the Quranic division of the world into *shahada* and *ghaib* 'is an epistemological one, not an ontological one'.[65]

Shari'ati's approach offers radical possibilities, not only of action, but of interpretation, with consequent implications for religious leadership:

We have to clarify that we want the Islam of Abu Dharr, not that of the royal palace; of justice and true leadership, not that of the caliphs, class stratification and aristocratic privileges; of freedom, progress and awareness, not of captivity, stagnation and silence. We want the Islam of the fighters, not that of *ruhani* [spiritual leaders]; the Islam of the ʿAli family, not that of the Safavi family.[66]

It would be the intellectuals rather than the traditional clergy who would bring about this return to the radical Islam of ʿAli and Abu Dharr, Shariʿati explained in a pamphlet which, coincidentally or not, bears the same title as Lenin's famous call to action: *What is to be Done?* They, rather than the *mullahs*, would be the genuine exponents of the 'dynamic revolutionary Islam'.[67]

Understandably the ʿulama, even those who worked in the progressive establishment at the Hosseiniya, found this aspect of Shariʿati's message highly objectionable. In 1968 Ayatollah Motahari, one of Khomeini's closest disciples, resigned from the Hosseiniya in protest against Shariʿati's anti-clerical lectures. The more conservative ʿulama found his views even more offensive, issuing statements condemning his theological 'errors'. Khomeini, however, demonstrated his characteristic political astuteness by refusing to condemn Shariʿati. Moreover, without referring to him by name he continued to use phrases borrowed from Shariʿati, such as *mustazafin* ('the wretched'), 'the rubbish of history' and 'religion is not the opium of the masses', thereby creating the impression that he substantially agreed with Shariʿati's views.[68] The young intelligentsia who idolized Shariʿati concluded that Khomeini was much more liberal in outlook than they would have done had they carefully read the Najaf lectures. By tacitly supporting Shariʿati, Khomeini established the basis for the combined leadership of the Shiʿite ʿulama and the 'Shiʿite PhDs' which placed itself at the head of the anti-Shah movement and which fell apart almost as soon as power had been achieved.[69]

Popular Eschatology and the 'Karbala Paradigm'

The Islam of Khomeini and Shariʿati, the populist and the revolutionary, could never have established itself without a combination of military force and popular mass support. The military arm of the revolution was supplied by the guerrilla movements, which were broadly divided into two groups – the Marxist Fedayeen and the Islamic Mujahidun. The Fedayeen were mostly the children of the secular-minded Westernized middle classes. The Mujahidun, with many fewer women, were mostly the sons of the 'religious' classes – merchants, bazaar traders and clergy.[70] Shariʿati's influence was greater among the Mujahidun, although by the mid 1970s part of the latter's leadership had veered towards Marxism. In political terms the military activities of the guerrillas were less effective than the repression they provoked. Like the urban guerrillas in certain Latin American countries, they presented a challenge which converted an authoritarian government into an outright military dictatorship. The repressive measures employed by SAVAK did much to discredit the Shah's regime at home and abroad. Executions – often illegal – and the use of torture, assassination and other acts of state terrorism helped to undermine support for the Shah among the traditional and Westernized middle classes, while the publicity these atrocities received in the US adversely affected his image there, contributing to his downfall. After Jimmy Carter's presidential victory in 1976, on a platform that included a general commitment to human rights, the Shah came under pressure from his closest ally to modify his repressive policies at a stage when discontent could only have been met by the further use of force. As with Louis XVI in 1789, political liberalization at this juncture was probably the worst possible course of action the Shah could have taken in his own interest.

If the guerrillas made their contribution to the fall of the Shah by helping to discredit his regime, the *mustazafin* of the densely crowded tenements and shanty-towns finally brought him down. Here the Islamic frame of reference developed by Shari'ati and Khomeini was to prove decisive. Both thinkers, unlike the more traditionally minded clergy, were prepared to exploit the popular Shi'ism of the masses. The revolutionary or "Alid' Shi'ism which Shari'ati had contrasted with the institutionalized or 'Safavid' Shi'ism of the official clergy may have been pitched at radically minded intellectuals, but it could also be harmonized with the popular religious culture of the illiterate rural immigrants who sought to reproduce, in their new and unfamiliar urban environment, the traditions and customs of their villages.

The 'villagization' of urban culture is a phenomenon that has been observed by many sociologists and is easily understood. The familiar religious festivals help to mitigate urban anomie, often taking on a more strenuous character in compensating for feelings of insecurity experienced in the new environment. In Egypt and North Africa this popular religious feeling is expressed in Sufi *dhikrs, hadras* and *zar* cults, as well as in the more orthodox festivals such as the 'Id al-Adha and the Prophet's birthday. In Iran, with its special tradition of folk Shi'ism, mass piety is focused upon the rituals and *rouzehs* associated with the martyrdom of Husain at Karbala, along with the messianic expectations implicit in the doctrine of the Imamate. During the months leading up to the revolution, the 'Karbala paradigm' – to borrow a phrase from the anthropologist Michael Fischer – was fully exploited by Khomeini, both before and after his return from exile in Paris in January 1979. At about the same time, the Mujahidun and Shari'ati's followers helped to fan popular messianic expectations by putting it about that Khomeini was, in effect, the expected Imam (a blasphemy of which the traditional leadership would never have been guilty). Although Khomeini never explicitly referred to himself as the expected Twelfth Imam, the fact that he allowed himself to be called 'Imam' by his enthusiastic supporters amounted to deliberate exploitation of this concept.

At the popular *rouzehs* in the shanty-towns and poorer districts of Tehran the Shah had often been compared to Yazid, murderer of Husain and arch-tyrant of Shi'a mythology. The Muharram mourning ceremonies had once before been exploited by the opposition, during the protests against the 'White Revolution' in 1963. In November 1978, following a day of serious rioting caused by the shooting of several student demonstrators in Tehran, the Shah imposed a military government under General Azheri. The opposition called for a general strike and there were three days of disturbances in Tehran and other major cities. In December General Azheri banned the traditional 'Ashura marches commemorating the Karbala massacre. A senior *ayatollah*, the liberal, Shari'atmadari, replied that no one needed permission to take part in a religious procession. From Paris, where he had gone after his expulsion from Najaf the previous October, Ayatollah Khomeini proclaimed that torrents of blood might be spilled at 'Ashura, but the Blood of Husain would triumph over the Sword of Yazid. Good Muslim soldiers should desert if ordered to fire on their brothers and sisters. On the eve of 'Ashura (9 December) the senior *ayatollah*, Mahmud Taleqani, marched at the head of a procession in Tehran numbering about half a million people; on 'Ashura itself (10 December) some two million people shouting 'Death to the Shah!' gathered near the Shahyar monument, built by the Shah with money extorted from the *bazaari* merchants to celebrate 2,500 years of monarchy. On 28 December the Shah tried his last gamble and appointed Dr Shapur Bakhtiar, a member of the secular nationalist party, the National Front, Prime Minister. Bakhtiar persuaded the Shah to 'go on holiday', thereby

probably forestalling a military coup. Khomeini condemned the Bakhtiar government, and the Prime Minister was expelled by his colleagues
in the National Front. On 19 January, the traditional Arba'in or Fortieth
Day after the Death of Husain, Khomeini called for a massive demonstration against the Bakhtiar government which was attended by more
than a million people in Tehran alone. On 1 February, after Bakhtiar
had realized that resistance was hopeless, he rescinded his orders to
the troops to close the airport, and Khomeini returned to a welcoming
crowd of some two million ecstatic people. As Shari'atmadari observed
somewhat caustically, 'No one ever expected the Hidden Imam to
return in a Jumbo Jet.'[71]

Thus, by uniting a disparate group of political forces around Khomeini, the Islamic Revolution actualized the latent eschatological expectations of Imami Shi'ism and activated the 'Karbala paradigm' for
political ends. Never since the Second World War had there been such
a massive popular movement as that which brought down the Shah's
regime.

8 *After Word (1999)*

A clash of civilizations?

More than two decades after the proclamation of an Islamic revolution in Iran the Islamist political fervour afflicting the Muslim world shows little sign of abating. In Algeria the civil war between Islamists and the government has devastated the country at the cost of more than 70,000 lives. In Egypt, where the government, unlike Algeria, still appears to have the upper hand, the estimated casualty rate is much lower – about one tenth of the Algerian figure – but the cost has been prodigious, with tourism, the country's largest foreign currency earner devastated and the country's ancient Christian minority increasingly fearful for its future. In the Palestinian Authority Islamist militants have adopted the 'rejectionist' position abandoned by the PLO since 1988, threatening to undermine the Oslo peace process – in ironic collusion with Jewish fundamentalists who also believe themselves to be acting on divine instructions. In Afghanistan the Taliban, a Pashtun-based movement that originated among Sunni religious students in the country's rural madrasas and the refugee camps of Pakistan, have taken control of most of the country, with devastating consequences for the Shi'i and non-Pashtun populations and for women of all ethnic or religious backgrounds. With Islamists already entrenched in Iran and Sudan and the possibility of their coming to power in Algeria, alarm bells began ringing on both sides of the Atlantic. Was a revitalized 'fundamentalist' Islam the new menace that would replace communism as the principal challenge to the secular, liberal, democratic values of the West?

This view, put forward among others by Samuel Huntington, the influential Harvard political scientist,[1] and Willy Claes, former secretary-general of NATO, was based on the premise that the difference between 'Islamic' and 'Western' civilizations and value systems was

as fundamental in terms of economic management and social organization as that which formerly divided the Eastern and Western blocks. It
was disputed by many leading scholars and journalists who argued that,
despite its rhetorical excesses, the Islamist movement was not so much
a 'threat' to the West or the regimes supported by it, as a reflection of a
crisis – or series of crises – internal to the Islamic world, or between
countries some of which are Muslim. A significant refutation of the
Huntington/Claes scenario was occurring in the Balkans as this essay
went to press, with NATO forces engaged in a war against an Orthodox
Christian power in the defence of the territorial and human rights of a
population containing a significant number of European Muslims. On
closer inspection, the crises afflicting the Muslim world reveal themselves to be little different from those afflicting non-Islamic nations.

The political dimension

In theory Islam is an inherently political religion. As well as being the
bearer of divine revelation, the Prophet Muhammad founded a polity
or 'state' which his successors the caliphs transformed into an empire
stretching from the Atlantic to the Indus valley. Although the empire
rapidly lost its political cohesion as rival claimants fought each other for
the leadership, the elaboration of the laws derived from the Quran and
the *hadiths* by the *'ulama* came to supply the unchallenged, and unchal-
lengeable, rules of daily social life. After the first disputes resulting in
the split between Sunni and Shi'a the Muslim ruler's legitimacy came to
depend less on his lineage than his role as protector of the *umma* and
preserver of the Shari'a in accordance with the Quranic injunction to
'enjoin the good and forbid the evil'. Despite many regional variations,
the application of the Shari'a over the course of fifteen centuries produced a remarkably homogeneous international order, bound by
common customs and ways of doing things, which contrasted strikingly
with the group solidarity or tribalism (*'asabiya*) operating at the level of
power politics. Islamic identity *vis-à-vis* the rest of the world became a
matter of practice as much as belief, orthopraxy as distinct from orthodoxy. Whereas the Christian road to salvation was determined mainly
by doctrine and sacraments, Muslims lived in a world of ethical precision
where rules were specified, together with the means of enforcing them.

However, although comprehensive in theory, the system was never complete. In theory the rulers (sultans or emirs) ruled according to the Shari'a with 'ulama support. In practice the 'ulama were often forced to acquiesce in the loss of their legal monopoly. Islamic law was supplemented by local customary laws and the decrees of rulers in substantial areas of commerce, taxation, public and criminal law. Moreover since the *qadis* were appointed by the rulers, they were powerless to enforce decisions that went against those rulers' interests. A *de facto* separation of politics and religion came into existence. But it was not formally acknowledged by the 'ulama who continued to uphold the principle that sovereignty belonged to God alone. A major consequence has been the continuance of 'Islam' as a political factor: for so long as the principle has continued to exist that Islam is a 'total way of life' that makes no distinction between God and Caesar, people have sought to realize the Islamic ideal through political action – or, to express the same idea more cynically, they have tried to achieve political power by exploiting Islam's rich symbolic repertoire.

What little we know of the Madinese Caliphate suggests that power politics, assassination, war and plunder played the part they had always done in Arabian history – only now they were focused on a more ambitious end: the aggrandizement of the Umma, a supra-tribal community bound by a common allegiance to God, his Prophet and the Caliphs. It is the actual success of this venture, as much as the utopian promise conveyed by it, that has worked on the imagination of Muslims down to the present. For the social disciplines taught by the Quran and the Sunna, sustained by the idea of a universal, supra-tribal deity, provided the ideological cement which served to unite segmentary formations, enabling them to control much larger territories and eventually to enjoy the benefits of a city-based civilization.

Islam is an urban religion conceived in a pastoral milieu. It is the ideology that accompanies the perennial movement of herdsmen into the settled regions, facilitating their integration into the more cosmopolitan world of the city. However, in encouraging the movement from the periphery to the centre and breaking down the communal allegiances that have kept the tribesfolk apart from each other, Islam also serves to erode urban solidarity. By proclaiming uncompromisingly that the allegiance of man is due to God alone, it inhibits the development of that distinctively urban patriotism which, rooted in the structures of the Church in Europe, accompanied the formation of social classes and enabled corporate and class allegiance to transcend the biological ties of kinship. The impact of Islam upon society was therefore paradoxical: while proclaiming its hostility to kinship solidarity, it also militated against the emergence of alternative sources of allegiance. Neither city nor monarchy, nation nor 'people' – or their representatives – were endowed with the kind of legitimacy that could enable them to alter the divine law or introduce new laws that could bind the community unconditionally. The decrees of amirs and sultans, the enactments of legislative assemblies, were powerless to introduce social changes which flouted the Shari'a or went against the grain of communal feeling. Power inevitably acquired an arbitrary character – though up till the present century, when the available means of control multiplied, this arbitrary power was less than dictatorial, being conditional upon the duty of upholding the Shari'a, 'enjoining the good and forbidding the evil'.

The failure of Islam's original utopian mission of creating a single united polity bound by the Shari'a was implicitly recognized by Ibn Khaldun, who made an important distinction between the ideal Islamic state (*khilafa*) and the existing dynastic state (*mulk*) based on kinship solidarity (*'asabiya*). Since by his time the Caliphate had ceased to exist, he devoted his analysis almost exclusively to *mulk*, which he considered necessary both for social well-being and for Islamic *da'wa*. Unlike more idealistic thinkers, he recognized *'asabiya* as a fact of life, and therefore as a potential source of good. Ibn Khaldun's pragmatism was admired by reformers like Muhammad 'Abduh and the Maghrebi nationalist 'Allal al-Fasi, founder of the Moroccan Istiqlal party, both of whom came to accept the *watan*, or territorial homeland, as the basis for Muslim allegiance within the broader ethnic and geographical diversity of *dar al-Islam*. Not insignificantly, Ibn Khaldun was vigorously condemned by the more idealistic reformers, including Rashid Rida and Maududi, who saw in his acceptance of *'asabiya* an argument for compromising with the sin of nationalism.

Theoretically, allegiance to the *watan*, or national state, is incompatible with the supreme loyalty due to the Islamic Umma: it is particularist where Islam is universal; its sovereignty belongs to the monarch or people, where in Islam sovereignty belongs to God alone. The *watan* creates arbitrary frontiers around itself, whereas the Umma exists wherever there are Muslims to engage in communal prayer and to observe the Shari'a. In fact, however, Islam has never failed to accommodate itself to the realities of power – an *ad hoc* process for which thinkers like al-Mawardi and Ibn Khaldun supplied theoretical justification.

Dynamics of reform

The principal intellectual forebears of the modern fundamentalist or 'Islamist' political movements which would challenge governments from the Maghreb to Malaysia during the latter decades of the twentieth century, were to be found in the Middle East and South Asia, with increasing cross-fertilization between the two regions. From the eighteenth-century CE Islamic reformers such as Shah Wali Ullah in India and Muhammad ibn 'Abd al-Wahhab in Arabia had prepared the ground for a modernist movement by seeking to purge Islamic belief and ritual from the accretions and innovations acquired over the centuries, particularly the cults surrounding the Sufi *walis* or 'saints', living and dead. An Islam pruned of its medieval accretions was better able to confront the challenge of foreign power than a local cult bounded by the intercessionary power of a saint or saintly family. The movements of resistance to European rule during the nineteenth century and early twentieth century were led or inspired by such renovators (*mujaddids*), most of them members of Sufi orders, who sought to emulate the Prophet Muhammad's example by purifying the religion of their day and waging war on corruption and infidelity.

Both modernists like Sayyid Ahmed Khan and reformers like Muhammad 'Abduh were inspired by the same example. Their problem was not, as 'Abduh's patron Lord Cromer would argue, that 'reformed Islam is no longer Islam'; but rather that there was no institutional hierarchy comparable to a Christian priesthood through which theological and legal reforms could be effected. The absence of a church which makes Islam the supreme example of a lay religion in which each believer is spiritually equal to all the others may have facilitated the spread of ideals and values that in pre-modern times were unique in their egalitarianism and their universalist appeal. But paradoxically the absence of a powerful and educated ecclesiastical body, against which the state could contest its authority, added to the problems the contemporary Islamic world is experiencing in adjusting to modern realities. In the western tradition it was churchmen, from Schleiermacher to Tillich, who formulated the theologies that would make it possible for Christians to find a destiny in a secular world from which the deity was progressively retreating, enabling them to find a niche for the divine in the human psyche, in the subjectivity of 'absolute dependence' or the Ground of Being. Islam does not lack the spiritual or intellectual resources for such a project. The work of modernists and reformers from Ahmed Khan and 'Abduh to present-day intellectuals such as Nasr Abu Zaid and Abdul Karim Soroush testifies to the ways in which a new hermeneutic combining modern methods of critical analysis with the classical exegetical techniques is contributing to the task of regeneration, offering 'signposts on the road' for a faith which combines an ethic of personal responsibility with a public commitment to social justice.

Compared to the western churches, however, the institutional structures through which reform and modernization might have been effected in Islamdom became atrophied and inward-looking. If the purpose of theology is to provide a whole account of human destiny by means of the re-expression of tradition in terms of contemporary culture, by reconciling received tradition with modern circumstance, the Sunni religious establishment with some exceptions proved inadequate to the task. Rejecting modernism in favour of the safer, more congenial work of preserving the tradition and the cultural attitudes enshrined therein, they turned their backs on the critical changes in scientific thought and technology that came to define modernity. The conservatism of the *ulama* establishment included, crucially, resistance to the introduction of print, and its corollary, the mass extension of literacy, the prerequisite for the successive cultural and scientific revolutions that took hold in Europe. As a consequence, the reformist spirit took hold of society *outside* the institutional structures under *ulama* control. Whereas in Europe, for example, the Jesuits were at the forefront of educational reform, the *ulama* in both Egypt and Ottoman Turkey preferred to acquiesce in the introduction of secular education outside their control, rather than embracing the new learning as their forebears in Islam's classical age had done in the course of their first encounters with Hellenism. Instead of occurring as a result of organic changes from within the religious tradition (a possibility that was certainly present in the eighteenth century, as Peter Gran has shown),[2] Islam's 'protestant reformation' was forced upon the Muslim world from the outside through the perceived agencies of Western economic, political and military power. Given the accelerating pace of change in the nineteenth and twentieth centuries this development might seem to have been inevitable. But not all religiously sanctioned traditions faced with the threat of European hegemony responded in an ostrich-like manner. Brahmanical and Japanese scholars embraced the new knowledge in sufficiently significant numbers to influence or legitimize the process of change. The results are clear to see. Since defeating Russia in 1905, Japan has been the world's leading non-Western industrial power. Yet the amount of foreign capital invested in Japan in 1913 (approximately $1,000 million at 1968 values) was the same as that invested in Egypt (compared with $1,750 million for India, and $1,100 million for China).[3]

Not all the backwardness afflicting the Muslim world *vis-à-vis* modernity is attributable to cultural factors. Geography also played its part: Egypt's proximity to Europe made it much more vulnerable than Japan to European economic exploitation and military control. Nevertheless, on several crucial indices including literacy (male and female) and scientific knowledge, the developmental gap between the Muslim world and the West persisted for internal cultural reasons, while the Japanese were rapidly closing the gap. The Japanese example challenges the assumption that modernization necessarily leads to westernization and consequent loss of cultural identity. By the 1870s, at the beginning of the Meiji Restoration, Japan already enjoyed high levels of literacy, despite the difficulties of learning the ideographic script with its frequent duality of meanings (Japanese words written in Chinese characters.) The educational authorities under the Meiji mandated universal elementary schooling, for girls as well as boys, predicated on the assumption that mothers would need to help children with their homework. At first the programme met with fierce resistance. Schools were burned down as poor peasant families feared the loss of children's earnings. Despite initial resistance, female education took off. In 1890 only 30 per cent of eligible girls attended school. By 1910 the figure was 97.4 per cent.[4]

Resistance of the 'ulama

Literacy is the key to development and in most of Islamdom this was inhibited by the conservatism of the 'ulama who resisted the introduction of print. Print technology lay at the heart of the cultural revolution that created modernity in the West. Without it, the Italian Renaissance would not have spread and become permanent for the whole of Europe. The emergence of modern capitalism would have been inconceivable along with its consequence, democracy, whose expansion in Europe and America is directly associated with the hegemony of substantial and continuously enlarging literate elites. Among the most important consequences of print was the transformation of the religious life of the West. Print technology was integral to the Reformation. Lutheranism was 'the child of the printed book'. Print was responsible for the spread of Renaissance humanism with 750,000 copies of Erasmus's books, excluding his translation of the New Testament, sold during his lifetime (1469–1536). It was equally important for the Catholic counter-reformation, and for the scientific revolution generated by both. (It should not be forgotten that, despite the trial of Galileo before the papal Inquisition in 1632 on charges of heresy arising from his advocacy of the Copernican cosmology, Descartes, the father of modern rationalism and pioneer of the scientific method, was the product of a Jesuit education, and remained a Roman Catholic for the whole of his life.)

Rather than embracing print technology as the churches had done in western Europe, the *'ulama* were generally resistant. As early as 1493 Jewish refugees from Spain established presses in Istanbul printing Bibles and secular books, but they were ignored by the *'ulama*. A single press established by Muslims in the Ottoman capital aroused so much opposition that it had to be closed down. As Francis Robinson suggests, the roots of this resistance were theological as much as cultural. For Muslims the Quran was the very Word of God in language, more central to Islamic theology than the Bible is for Christians or the Torah is for Jews. Preference was always given to oral recitation, with aspirants to leadership learning all of it – or as much of it as possible – by heart. The written Quran, while celebrating the Divine Word calligraphically, was primarily an aid to memory and correct oral transmission. In the 1920s the Egyptian standard edition was produced, not from variant manuscript versions, but from a study of the different traditions of recitation, of which there are fourteen.[5] The theology of the oral word was central to a person-centred idea of knowledge, where the reliability of the transmitter was considered as significant as the knowledge transmitted. In the science of *hadith*, the *isnads* or chains of transmission took precedence over content. It was known, significantly, as *'ilm al-rijal* 'the science of men'. Transmission of book learning, in Islamic tradition, took on a similar form. The publication of a new book would take place orally, usually in a public mosque, with the copyist reading the text back to the author. Like the rehearsal for a stage performance, the author might make several additions or emendations before giving permission, in the form of an *ijaza* or licence, for the work to be 'transmitted from him'. If the work entered the curriculum of the madrasa the same process would be followed: the pupil would commit the text to memory, along with explanatory materials, before receiving an *ijaza* to teach that text.[6] As Robinson points out 'person to person transmission was at the heart of Islamic knowledge. The best way of getting at the truth was to listen to the author himself.' In pre-modern times scholars such as Nasr-i Khusraw and Ibn 'Arabi travelled all over the Islamic world in search of knowledge obtainable from others. 'When a scholar could not get knowledge from an author in person, he strove to get it from a scholar whose *isnad* or chain of transmission from the original author, was thought to be the most reliable.'[7]

Decline of the 'ulama

In the Ottoman Empire and later in Egypt, the 'ulama would eventually succumb to change. But it was not of their own making. It came in response to external pressures effected through the agency of an increasingly secular state. As guardians of the tradition the Ottoman 'ulama had been a powerful estate within society. After studying in their madrasas, they received their *ijazas* (diplomas) showing they had completed their religious education. Their names were inscribed in official ledgers. As members of the ruling military (*askeri*) class they were exempt from taxation. But they were more independent than other *askeris* as their personal estates were exempt from confiscation. Their autonomy was strengthened by means of the wealth they amassed through the administration of charitable trusts (*awqaf*). As functionaries, teachers, *faqihs* and judges they comprised a majority of the educated population of the empire.

Even before the reforms known as the Tanzimat, introduced under Western pressure between 1839 and 1876, the Ottoman Sultan had succeeded in bringing the 'ulama under state control. The Sheikh al-Islam, their leader, was given an official residence near the Palace, while the leading legal authority, the Chief Mufti, was put in charge of a government department. By introducing these and other reforms, including the abolition of the Janissary guards and the introduction of secular education for the new-style secular bureaucrats, Mahmud

II (r. 1808–39) opened the way to the separation of religion and state which became a distinctive feature under his successors. Unaware of the danger to their autonomy, the *'ulama* effectively collaborated in their demise. According to historian Uriel Heyd, 'the leading *ulama* . . . were not farsighted enough to realize that the Westernizing reforms supported by them would eventually destroy the Islamic character of Ottoman state and society'.[8]

The traditional Islamic education remained largely unchanged and available to a diminishing number of people. By the mid 1840s only the exceptional student of independent means, unusual ability and strong motivation could be expected to embark on the study of Islam. At the primary level the *'ulama* continued to resist the introduction of change. For example, the study of maps was banned because they were thought to constitute 'drawing', forbidden by Islam. The map, so vital to the development of modern national consciousness, developed as a secular icon, outside the spiritual frame. The same situation prevailed, with modifications, in Egypt, where the *'ulama* were more concerned with preserving the tradition than opening it up to embrace the new learning. In both countries *'ulama* conservatism led to the development of an unintegrated, parallel culture. So long as the madrasas held a monopoly on the traditional religious sciences (*'ilm*) the new schools were free to teach the modern secular sciences. But reforming the oral-based system of religious instruction was taboo. Thus Muhammad 'Abduh's efforts to reform Islamic education at al-Azhar, the foremost academy of Sunni Islam, by reorganizing the curriculum, were persistently frustrated by both teachers and students.[9]

The *'ulama in India*

The main exception to the ostrich-like refusal of the *'ulama* to embrace reform came from India. Unlike their counterparts in the Islamic West the Indian *'ulama* adopted the new technology of print from the 1820s. By the end of the century thousands of Muslim religious texts and tracts were being printed in Urdu, the demotic language of India's Muslims. According to Robinson, the decisive reason for the abandonment by the Indian *'ulama* of twelve centuries of oral tradition was the advent of British rule. Without the power of an Islamic government to support them, they feared that the Muslims, the vast majority of whom were converts from Hinduism, would revert to Hindu practices.

To this end they instituted a programme of printing, publication and translation of the Islamic classics from Arabic and Persian into the vernacular. From the first they urged caution, advising readers not to consult any books without reference to qualified scholars. But there was no going back on the path thus opened up in the direction of 'Islamic protestantism'. 'For Muslim Protestants the route to survival was scriptural knowledge, knowledge of the Quran and the traditions, and how to be a Muslim. Print was central to broadcasting this knowledge and making it available.'[10] This Islamic reformation had a paradoxical relationship with the British colonial authority. While benefiting from the infrastructure constructed by the British, particularly the railways, for the distribution of their literature, the Indian reformers, who based themselves mainly in the northern city of Deoband, where they founded a flourishing academy in 1867, eschewed all contact with the British-run *kafir* state. Having created systems operating outside the state, their idea of independence ultimately consisted in the rule of the 'ulama. Like other 'ulama, they opposed the idea of Pakistan once they realized that it would be ruled by secular-minded Muslims. They thought they would have a better chance of exercising power within a secular India, where they hoped – quite unrealistically – to be granted judicial autonomy.[11]

The politicization of Islam

As indicated above, the decline of the 'ulama as the guardians of Islamic tradition was accompanied by the rise of a parallel tradition of secular learning imported wholesale from the West. Whereas Christian clergy were for the most part the 'objective' agents of secularization, charged with the task of redefining the religious tradition of the West in the context of the new cosmologies and 'maps of reality' emerging from the revolution in scientific thought, their Muslim counterparts avoided the painful and challenging task of accommodation. They tacitly accepted change so long as they were permitted to maintain their control over a much restricted domain. While comprehensive in theory, the Shiri'a was for the most part limited (outside the Arabian peninsula) to matters of ritual and personal status. (Even in Wahhabite Arabia, the demands of an increasingly complex economy meant that in all-important areas of civil and commercial law, the Shiri'a was supplemented more and more by administrative decrees.) With the 'ulama turning their backs on change, the task of reintegrating the knowledge and culture imported from the West within the frame of Islamic tradition, or of finding a discourse in which the 'eternal message' of Islam could be expressed and understood in terms of contemporary reality, increasingly fell to the religious autodidacts. From the time of Ahmed Khan to the present, the pioneers of Islamic resurgence (including Hasan al-Banna, Maududi, Sayyid Qutb and most of their followers) have tended to be members of the laity – that is to say, men educated outside the madrasas and other institutions of learning under *'ulama* control. This process has accelerated during the post-colonial era, when the newly independent governments invested massively in secondary and higher education. Newly literate youth, the beneficiaries of secular schools and colleges, encounter Islamic tradition without the benefit of the long apprenticeship which characterized the *'ulama* class in the past. Freed from the traditional patterns of learning which are seen as having been compromised by state control, the Islamist youth are inclined to interpret Islam in a political or ideological fashion.[12] For example, the Jama'a al-Islamiya, the group to which Khalid al-Islambouli who assassinated the Egyptian President Anwar al-Sadat in 1981 belonged, which became the main force in student politics during the late 1970s and 1980s, began in the mid-1970s in the city of Minya with a reading group of nine people who studied the works of Ibn Taimiya, Maududi, Sayyid Qutb and others.[13] Although a prominent cleric Sheikh 'Umar Abd al-Rahman, a Shari'a professor trained at the University of al-Azhar, subsequently arrested and imprisoned in the United States for his part in the bombing of the New York World Trade Center in 1994, became the group's religious adviser and *éminence*, it was the teachings of Sayyid Qutb that provided the movement with focus and direction.[14]

Islam and terrorism

With the involvement of Islamist activists in conflicts in different political theatres, the impression of Islam as a 'violent' religion has been gaining ground in the media. This in turn has led to accusations of 'Islamophobia'. Muslim critics and their sympathizers argue that the media give a distorted impression by placing a disproportionate emphasis on acts of violence committed in the name of Islam and by operating a 'double standard'. Acts of violence committed by terrorists from religious backgrounds other than Islamic or Jewish are usually described in non-religious terms: for example, the messianic apocalypticism that erupted with disastrous results at Waco, Texas in 1993 was never described as 'Christian', though its prophet David Koresh was steeped in the Old and New Testaments and nearly all his followers were recruited from Seventh Day Adventist Churches. In the Northern Ireland conflict atrocities are attributed to 'republicans' or 'loyalists' rather than to 'catholics' or 'protestants', although the religious affiliations of the various paramilitary groups are universally known and understood.[15]

Terrorism, of course, is notoriously difficult to define objectively, since one person's terrorist is another's freedom fighter. Defined by Augustus Richard Norton as the 'deliberate and random uses of violence for political ends against protected [i.e. non-combatant] groups', it has historic roots in the Middle East, but is far from being exclusive to one confession. Arguably, the first modern act of political terrorism in the region was the bombing of the King David hotel in Jerusalem by Irgun Zvai Leumi led by Menachem Begin; the assassinations of Lord Moyne, the British minister, and Count Bernadotte, the UN mediator, by Jewish extremists long preceded that of Anwar Sadat by their Muslim counterparts. The Sabra and Chatilla massacres, connived at if not actively encouraged by the Israeli army, and the Israeli bombings of Palestinian camps in Lebanon (where the victims of cluster bombs were rarely seen on television) have cost many more non-combatant lives than atrocities committed by Palestinians. Nevertheless, Norton's observation that 'phrases such as "Islamic terrorism" significantly misrepresent the religious roots of violence committed by Muslims' does not entirely dispose of the problem. There *is* a religious dimension to much modern terrorism and it is not just related to the VIP treatment martyrs expect in paradise. The Manichaean division of the world between the People of God and the rest (pagans, infidels, gentiles) is a form of absolutism which dehumanizes the 'other' as ruthlessly as the secular ideologies of nationalism and class conflict; but, while Nazism and communism had recourse to anthropological and sociological theories to sanction mass murder, the new generation of revolutionary terrorists finds its justification in religious texts. God assisted Joshua in the slaughter of the Canaanites – a lesson not lost on Baruch Goldstein, responsible for the massacre of Arab worshippers in Hebron in 1994. Muhammad expelled or massacred the Jewish tribes of Madina and waged the *jihad* against the Makkan polytheists. Though his campaigns may have been moderate by the standards of the day, the precedents remain, enshrined in the Quran and still usable by those modern Islamist ideologues who push aside centuries of qualifying hermeneutics with a dismissive sweep of the hand.

Palestinian fighters in the Israeli-occupied territories of the West Bank and Gaza, adopting the nomenclature of the medieval Isma'ili 'assassins', refer to themselves as *fidaiyin* – those who sacrifice (themselves). For the Israelis and their Western backers they are 'terrorists'. The Afghans and their Muslim supporters who fought against Soviet occupation in Afghanistan (with money and arms supplied by the West) were known almost universally as *mujahidun* – 'holy warriors' (more literally, 'those who struggle in the Path of God'). For the Russians and the Afghan government supported by them they, too, were terrorists. All such groups, of course, claim a religious and ethical justification for their acts. The Shi'i Hizbollah who have inflicted several costly defeats on the Israelis and their allies in the Israeli-protected zone of Southern Lebanon regard themselves as honourable defenders of Islam against its western enemies, notably the United States. In an Open Letter released to the press in 1985 the Hizbollah proclaimed: 'Each of us is a combat soldier when the call of *jihad* demands it and each of us undertakes his task in the battle in accordance with his lawful assignment within the framework of action under the guardianship of the leading *faqih*.'[16]

Although at least one of the Quranic verses urging the Muslims to fight their enemies explicitly states that the *jihad* is defensive ('And fight in God's cause against those who wage war against you, but do not commit aggression – for, verily, God does not love aggressors' – 2:190), the classical legal theories were formulated in the ninth century CE during the period of rapid expansion before the Islamic empire broke up. *Jihad* (meaning 'effort' or 'struggle') may be applied to the moral effort against evil (sometimes known as the 'greater *jihad*'), or to the military struggle against the enemies of Islam (the 'lesser *jihad*'). In the latter case it is a collective obligation for Muslims (*fard kifaya*) which may be fulfilled if a sufficient number of people take part. If this does not happen, the whole of the *umma* is deemed to be in error. Incorporating the customs of pre-Islamic warfare, as well as ideas adapted from the Byzantines, the doctrine allows for an element of chivalry, with safeguards for women and children, the old and the sick. Commenting on the limited nature of the wars conducted by the Prophet of Islam P. J. Stewart has written: 'If Islamic rules were followed today, much of modern warfare would be impossible, and terrorism would be unthinkable. There would be no attacks on civilians, no retaliation against innocent parties, no taking hostage of non-combatants, no incendiary devices.'[17]

It remains true, however, that under the classical theories the polytheists are faced with the choice of conversion or death. Those unbelievers who belong to the Peoples of the Book (initially Christians and Jews, later extended to Zoroastrians, Hindus and others) are granted protection on payment of the *jizya* and other taxes. The doctrine presupposes a united *umma* under a single caliph. In Shi'i jurisprudence the expansionist *jihad* cannot be waged in the absence of the Imam. A defensive *jihad*, however, is permissible – as in the first Gulf war (1980–8), when Iran was attacked by Iraq, or in Lebanon, where attacks by the Lebanese Hizbollah against the United States and Israel were presented as the defence of Muslim territory against foreign aggression.

The re-interpretation of the doctrine of *jihad* to justify assassinations or acts of terrorism under modern conditions is a logical consequence of the theories of Maududi and Qutb who applied the concept of *jahiliya* to contemporary circumstances. An important legal precedent was established by Ibn Taimiya, who declared the Mongol rulers of Syria unbelievers, despite their formal conversion to Islam in which they pronounced the profession of faith. Following Ibn Taimiya the Wahhabis of Arabia waged *jihad* against their Shi'i and Hijazi enemies from the mid eighteenth to the early twentieth centuries, until the Saudi dynasty they brought to power was obliged, after the conquest of Makka, to adopt a more ecumenical approach. Sayyid Qutb's definition of *jahiliya* as applying to contemporary regimes was given practical application by an Egyptian engineer, Muhammad 'Abdul Salam Faraj, Khalid Islambouli's mentor. In a pamphlet entitled the Absent Duty (*al-farida al-ghaiba*), quoted at the trial of the Egyptian president's assassins in 1982, Faraj argued that the Egyptian government was an infidel government because of its refusal to introduce the Shari'a law outside the restricted areas of personal status and inheritance.[18] It was an individual duty for each Muslim to rise in armed rebellion against this infidel regime in order to replace it with the rule of Islam.[19] Despite the constraints implicit in the classical doctrine of *jihad*, the ideology thus formulated, legitimating violence against the state, extends to violence against innocent civilians. Thus a disciple of Sayyid Qutb, Tal'at Fuad Qasim, a leader of the Jama'a

Islamiya, the group responsible for many acts of violence in Egypt, regards attacks on tourists as legitimate because tourism is a source of corruption and attacks on it harm the state.

First, many tourist activities are forbidden, so this source of income for the state is forbidden. Striking against such a major source of income will be a major blow against the state ... Second, tourism in its present form is an abomination: it is a means by which prostitution and AIDS are spread by Jewish women tourists, and it is a source of all manner of depravities, not to mention being a means of collecting information on the Islamic movement. For these reasons we believe that tourism is an abomination that must be destroyed. And it is one of our strategies for destroying the government.[20]

The paranoid character of this statement, with its explicit anti-Semitism, exposes the degree to which the modern concept of *jihad*, influenced by Qutbist ideas, has evolved from its roots in classical legal theory, assimilating, consciously or otherwise, fascist ideas about racial or ethnic 'purity'. In November 1997 more than 60 European tourists, including several British men, women and children, were massacred at the Temple of Hatshesput near Luxor in an atrocity that made headlines all over the world. British tabloid newspapers linked the massacre to Shaikh 'Umar Abd al-Rahman currently serving a life sentence in the United States for his part in the World Trade Center bombing in 1994. The reason for including Shaikh 'Umar in the story was a statement from the Jama'a Islamiya blaming Egyptian police for the Luxor casualties, stating that their objective had been to take foreign hostages for use as bargaining chips for the release of Shaikh 'Umar. Condemnations of the massacre by the Iranian government, Shaikh Ahmad Yasin, the leader of the Palestinian Hamas and by the Lebanese Hizbollah were widely ignored in the Western media, creating the impression that such actions meet with more approval in the Muslim world than is actually the case. The cumulative effect of headlines such as 'Islamic terrorists strike again' is to create the impression that the religion, if not inherently violent, is somehow responsible for violent actions committed in its name.

The impression is deliberately reinforced by Islamist militants who appropriate the rhetoric of Islam in furtherance of aims that, on closer inspection, often turn out to have local rather than global causes. Thus the same Shaikh Ahmad Yasin, while condemning the Luxor massacre, bears ultimate responsibility for the suicide bombings committed in Israel by members of Hamas. There are indeed Muslims who engage in acts of violence and destruction, just as there are Jews, Christians, Sikhs, Hindus and members of other faiths, or no faith at all, who engage in terrorism. But, where commentators usually make it clear that in most traditions extremists come from small, unrepresentative minorities, or (like the Hindu Tamil Tigers) have specific local agendas, Muslims tend to be tarred with the terrorist brush in a more generalized way. Given the record of human rights violations by many Muslim governments, who routinely torture their Islamist opponents or those suspected of sympathizing with them, acts of violence committed by Islamist rebels often have a reciprocal character, with the rebels engaged in what is in effect a 'blood-feud' with the authorities. Despite the publicity given to terrorist spectaculars and the attention given to individuals such as 'Carlos the Jackal' or the former Sa'udi 'godfather' 'Usama bin Laden, in the calculus of terror the balance still lies with the state. From the Palestinian camps in Lebanon to the hills of Kurdistan and marshes of Southern Iraq the victims of atrocities committed by legally constituted governments (including those of Israel and the United States) vastly outnumber the victims of rebel activity.

Islam and democracy – a burgeoning debate

The designation of any government as 'infidel' opens the way to the 'vanguardist' politics advocated by Sayyid Qutb and his intellectual heirs, who include the Algerian Islamic Salvation Front (FIS) leader 'Ali Belhaj. Belhaj, the Egyptian Jama'a Islamiya and such groups as the Hizb al-Tahrir and the Muhajirun (active amongst Muslim students on campuses in Britain) reject democracy as alien to Islamic traditions. 'As for us, the people of the Sunna, we believe that justice [*haq*] only comes from the decisive proofs of the Shari'a and not from a multitude of demagogic actors and voices. Those who followed the Prophet were a very small number, while those who followed idols were a multitude' argues Belhaj.[21] Following the victory of the FIS in the first round of the Algerian elections in June 1991 the same leader was quoted as saying: 'It's a victory for Islam, not for democracy.'[21] It was statements such as these that helped generate public support for the military coup forestalling the second round of the general elections in

December that would have given the FIS a clear majority at the polls.

Islamist rejection of democracy, however, is neither absolute nor universal. A number of Islamist intellectuals have responded to the often cruel and tyrannical treatment meted out to the Islamist opposition in the Middle East and North Africa by 'domesticating' or authenticating democracy and human rights within an Islamic frame of reference. Distinguishing between the roots (*usul*) of Islam and its branches (*furu'*) writers sharing this approach apply this distinction to 'values' and 'techniques'. The values are fundamental and cannot be negotiated. But techniques are themselves regarded as morally neutral (*mubah*). Thus modern democratic systems may embody the values of *shura* (consultation) as enjoined by the Prophet. The technique or method by which consultation is achieved is left open. The style of reasoning is often teleological: God did not grant the Prophet a son, thereby barring hereditary rule, enjoining instead *shura*. After his death God left the details of political organization for the Muslim community to define for themselves, in accordance with their varying needs and aspirations.[22] Another fundamental value addressed in the debate is that of pluralism, a degree of which is implicit in the oft-cited *hadith*: 'Differences between the learned of my community are a blessing.' Yet there are limits to pluralism just as there are limits to the application of human reason in questioning the commands of God. The discourse on democracy and human rights is limited by the legal moralism implicit in most understandings of Shari'a. Acts are good or bad because God so commands them; God does not command them *because* they are good. As Gudrun Krämer, who has surveyed the literature, points out, ideals of unity epitomized in the theology of *tawhid*, consensus and harmonious balancing of groups and interests remain paramount. 'Unity is contrasted with strife, conflict and anarchy and consensus with the abomination of *fitna*.' Limits are therefore set to legitimate pluralism, a theme which emerges quite clearly in the debate about freedoms of thought, creed, speech and association. At the same time it is accepted that God created people different and that differences of opinion (*ikhtilaf*) are natural, and beneficial to humankind and the Muslim community, provided they remain within the limits of faith and common decency. Krämer concludes that, despite these obvious limitations

the present Muslim/Islamist discourse on Islam and democracy [*shura*] has not only adopted and declared as Islamic, or compatible with Islam, core elements of modern democratic political organisation such as elections, representation, parliamentary rule or the separation of powers. It has also incorporated, on one level at least, key values such as freedom, equality, individual responsibility and accountability – even though a close analysis of Islamist positions on human rights, women, non-Muslims, freethinkers, agnostics and atheists will reveal that the general principles ('no compulsion in religion', 'freedom of thought', equality and so forth) are in most cases confined to the framework of Islam.[23]

The ideologization of Islam

Although the politicization or 'ideologization' of Islam is a worldwide phenomenom, there are few indications that 'Islamization' whether imposed from above by the state or from below in response to populist pressures, amounts to a coherent political programme. While all Islamists would agree that the prerequisite for an 'Islamic' state involves the 'restoration' of Islamic law in its entirety, there is no consensus about the means to be employed or even the ultimate shape that such a project would take. Mohammed Arkoun, one of the most astute of the commentators on contemporary Islamism, argues that religious consciousness among Muslims has been 'demythologized not by historicizing religious knowledge but through the ideological manipulation of popular belief and of the richest parts of the tradition'. He sees this manipulation as an aspect of the 'social imaginary' which tends to preclude objective analysis or reflection about the past, masking the inevitable processes of modernization and secularization:

Forced to forswear colonial domination, the West has since the 1960s launched a search for a new expression of modernity, while the Muslim world has, quite to the contrary, turned away from these opportunities and proposed instead an 'Islamic' model which is beyond all scientific investigation. This notion constitutes the triumph of a social imaginary that is termed 'Islamic' but that in fact sacralizes an irreversible operation of political, economic, social and cultural secularization. Analysts have barely noticed this new role of Islam used at the collective level as an instrument of disguising behaviours, institutions and cultural and scientific activities inspired by the very Western model that has been ideologically rejected.[24]

Writing in a similar vein the Islamic scholar Aziz al-Azmeh deplores the anti-Enlightenment character of much modern Islamist thought, which he sees as having been informed by ideas of social Darwinism incorporated into the discourse of Afghani and 'Abduh through the influence of Herbert Spencer, along with ideas derived from the medieval Islamic natural philosophy with which Afghani was familiar. According to this discourse, 'Islam' and 'the West' are unique historical subjects, each of which is 'self-enclosed, impenetrable in its essence, and is a substance presupposed by history rather than being its product'.

Al-Azmeh sees in the 'transcendental narcissism of the invariant historical subject' a parallel with the European fascist ideologies that are ultimately derived from Jacobinism:

The secret of Islam as a political category lies therein, that the image of the total state is reproduced under the guise of reaffirming a pre-existing identity endowed with an ontological privilege, an identity which is but the nominal node for the interpellation, by nominal association, of a host of tokens . . . And what this Islam devolves to is the mirror images of the modernist state which originated with the Jacobins, was routinized and historicized in the Napoleonic state, and exported worldwide . . . The modernism of this proposed state is the fundamental feature of this supposedly pre-modern creature of postmodernism.[25]

In pursuing their political project today's Islamists 'are wilfully confusing Islamic law with the requirements of Islamist ideology' by refusing to recognize the extent to which the law responded to changing circumstances.

In theoretical terms, Muslim jurists, though not the Shi'a, have adopted a highly sceptical view of the finality of their judgements; hence the readiness to recognise views that may be contradictory. It is recognised – though this recognition is not shared by Islamist ideologues – that it is against natural justice and natural law (which accords with divine will) to foist ordinances of relevance to the seventh century upon the twentieth.[26]

Critics of the 'legal moralism' implicit in the post-Ash'arite era in Sunni legal tradition might disagree with al-Azmeh's statement that Muslim jurists were influenced by considerations of natural justice. But, significantly, it is the Shi'i exception that proves the rule. Having preserved the character of a separate 'estate' within society relinquished by their Sunni counterparts, the Shi'i *ulama* were forced to address the implications of Shari'a state after 1979.

The 'Islamic' Republic of Iran

Contrary to the view widely held in the West Khomeini did not impose a fully 'Islamic' system of government in Iran (comparable, for example, to Saudi Arabia, where the government rules in accordance with the Shari'a, supplemented by royal decree). The 1979 Constitution is really a hybrid of Islamic and western liberal concepts. As Sami Zubaida points out, there is a 'contradictory duality of sovereignties'. Article 6 refers to the 'sovereignty of the popular will' in line with democratic national states, but the principle of *velayet-i faqih* gave sweeping powers to Khomeini as 'chief jurisconsult' or trustee. The Constitution is the keystone of a range of institutions, including the *majlis-i shura* (consultative assembly), composed of elected members under the supervision of a Council of Guardians. Though the Shari'a is supposed to be the basis for all law and legislation, many of the civil codes from the previous regime were retained: there were three court systems, the *madani* (civil) courts, the Shari'a courts and the 'revolutionary courts', which handed out often arbitrary punishments by the *komitehs* or revolutionary guards. Islamization was introduced in a number of areas. Women were forced to wear 'Islamic' clothing and removed from certain professions, including the law, interest-bearing loans were forbidden and education was altered to include Islamic doctrines.[27] In practice, the Council of Guardians proved an embarrassment by vetoing as contrary to the Shari'a various measures voted by the Majlis, including a major land reform. In January 1988 Khomeini ruled decisively in favour of the Majlis, arguing that the power of the Islamic state was comparable to that enjoyed by the Prophet Muhammad and took precedence over Shari'a, even by forbidding such basic pillars of the faith as prayers, fasting and *hajj*. Now that the Islamic state had been won, religious obligations were 'secondary' to government decrees. By giving the state priority over Islamic law from within the religious tradition Khomeini ironically initiated a process that could open the way to a *de facto* secular regime in which the power of the clergy as a separate estate was effectively neutralized.[28]

The reduced status of the Shi'i hierarchy became apparent on Khomeini's death in June 1989 with the election by the Guardianship Council of the then President, 'Ali Khamenei, as Khomeini's successor to the position of Wali Faqih, supreme jurisconsult. As Khamenei was only

Hojjat-al-Islam at the time (i.e. a middle-ranking cleric), the choice in effect negated the revolution's most significant achievement, which had been to place government under the moral and juridical authority of the supreme spiritual leadership – known in Shi'i terminology as the *marja'iyya* (after the highest clerical rank, the *marja' al-taqlid*, source of imitation, of whom there are several). The succession was legitimized by an amendment to the constitution which sanctioned the eventual separation of the *marja'iyya* as theological authority from the *velaya* (guardianship or legal authority), by allowing any *faqih* with 'scholastic qualifications for issuing religious decrees' to assume the leadership. The result was a divorce between political and religious functions at the highest level in blatant contradiction to Khomeini's doctrine. Since then Iran has witnessed an increasingly open conflict between the spiritual authority of the senior clergy and the politico-religious leadership exercised by the clerics actually in power. In January 1995, in an open letter to the authorities, Ayatollah Ruhani declared that life in Iran had become 'unbearable' for those who adhered to true Islamic principles. He felt he 'could not remain a spectator while Islam is violated daily' and the 'true religious leaders' were silenced in a country claiming to be an Islamic republic. He claimed that his home had been attacked by armed criminals who threatened to kill him unless he pledged allegiance to Khamenei. In July the same year his residence was raided again and his son was arrested. Other senior clerics, or their spokesmen, articulated similar views. Seyyed Mohammad Qomi, a son of Ayatollah Seyyed Hasan Qomi-Tabatabai, asserted that state and religion were incompatible, and must be separated. Since governments were bound to commit immoral acts, it was counter to the interests of religion that they be run by clerics. The experience of Iran since 1979 had done damage to Islam and its religious leaders. 'Terrorism, torture, bombing, explosions and hostage taking', which had no place in Islam were now identified with it. The rule of the clerics had only brought disgrace to Islam.[29]

'Abdul-Karim Soroush

The same critique has been articulated even more forcefully by one of Iran's leading intellectuals, the philosopher 'Abdul-Karim Soroush, a professor at Tehran University. Adopting a view of religion in line

with Western phenomenology, Soroush argues that religion, unlike
ideology, cannot be cast in any one shape, but bears interpretations
that vary in accordance with time and circumstance. In themselves,
God and his revelation are eternal, perfect and immutable. But 'religion,
or revelation for that matter, [in itself] is silent'. In order to enter the
realm of humanity a religion becomes involved with human language
and human understanding, and this is a realm in which everything is
relative and subject to criticism. There are no absolutes.[30] Soroush
draws on the Sufi conceptions of the 'constrictions' and 'dilations' of
the mystic's heart to diagnose the alternations of closure and openness
in Islamic societies towards the larger contexts of human knowledge,
with particular reference to philosophy and the natural and social
sciences. Like the liberal theologies within the Christian tradition the
kalam-i jadid with which he is associated strives to provide a credible
response to modernity and secularity, distinguishing between the
religious ideals of Islam and its current practitioners, the *usul* (roots
or 'fundamentals') and the *furu'*, which are its branches. As Soroush
sees it the legal methodology of the past cannot by itself provide
rulings for situations which arise within a modern Islamic society.
Soroush distinguishes between *fiqh-i sunnati* ('traditional *fiqh'*) and
fiqh-i puya ('dynamic *fiqh'*). ' "Traditional *fiqh"* is in a kind of retreat,
fearful of contamination by foreign non-Islamic thoughts and values,
while "dynamic *fiqh"* is forward-looking,' and concerns itself with
addressing questions about the relevance of religion in the broader
context of modern living. Religion is richer, more comprehensive
and more humane than mere ideology. It can generate weapons,
instruments and ideals, but of itself transcends all of these things. It
is like the very air we breathe: essential for human beings in all times
and places, but without any one particular form. Imposing a fixed
interpretation on religion – any religion – makes it rigid, superficial,
dogmatic and one-dimensional. Khomeini's movement, according to
Soroush, will not bear the appropriate fruits unless his followers
nurture 'a new understanding of the faith'.[31]

Soroush has been physically attacked on several occasions and has
been subjected to harassment and intimidation by militants, such as
the Ansar-i-Hizbollah, assumed to have links with Khamenei and the
right-wing elements associated with the Society of Combatant Clergy
(JRM) in the Majlis (parliament). In May 1996, in an open letter to the
then President Rafsanjani, Soroush accused the Ansar-i-Hizbollah of

'fostering barbarism' with the 'covert support of various authorities'. Recent developments, however, indicate that Soroush is far from being isolated and that the political tide is moving in his direction. In April 1996 elections to the Majlis produced a setback for the JRM and advanced the cause of its more liberal challengers, the Servants of Iran's Construction. An even more decisive shift in public opinion was demonstrated a year later, in May 1997, with the unexpected election of Seyyed Mohammed Khatami to the presidency with a massive majority (more than 20 million votes to 7.2 million) over his rival, the Speaker of the Majlis, 'Ali Akbar Nateq-Nouri, who had the support of the conservative establishment. A former Minister of Culture, noted for his patronage of the film industry (which now boasts such internationally recognized talents as 'Abbas Kiarostami), Khatami was supported by a broad coalition of forces, including industrialists, urban professionals, university students, educated women and technocrats. The right-wing elements surrounding Khamenei, however, are far from having yielded their collective grip on power. A number of leading intellectuals have been murdered in mysterious circumstances, it is thought by elements in the security services sympathetic to the 'hard line' of Khamenei and the JRM. As this essay went to press the former Mayor of Tehran Gholamhossein Karbaschi had been convicted of corruption and faced a prison term after what was widely reported as being a political show-trial mounted by his conservative opponents. The Ayatollah Mohajerani, Minister of Culture under Khatami faced attempts by conservative MPs to impeach him for allowing an explosion of 'irresponsible' press freedom. The culture wars between the two wings of the Islamist movement whose brief moment of unity in 1979 had brought down the regime of the Shah, were far from being resolved. It was to the revolution's credit, however, and to the constitutional principles it sanctified, that the struggle was generally conducted along constitutional lines – a contest for power between different branches of government rather than outright civil war, as in Algeria. In contrast to most Arab regimes which relied on military force rather than moral authority to sustain themselves in power, the Shi'i *'ulama* were grappling with modern realities. Their very divisions proclaimed an important message to the Islamists elsewhere. Contrary to the dreams of the ideologues, Islam has no single 'solution' for the problems of politics. There are no Islamic models for modern government and administration.

The Rushdie affair

The unresolved contest between a relatively liberal government aiming to end Iran's international isolation in order to encourage much-needed foreign investment and the Khomeinist clergy with its supporters among the poorer sections of society is epitomized by the Rushdie affair. The scandal brought the regime a degree of international notoriety surpassing its other acts of terrorism (including the murder of the Shah's last prime minister Shahpur Bakhtiar) or crimes against its citizens committed domestically. Salman Rushdie, a naturalized British author who had been born in Bombay and educated at Rugby School and Cambridge, had won international acclaim with his second novel, *Midnight's Children*, which won the prestigious Booker Prize for fiction in 1984. His fourth novel, *The Satanic Verses*, was published in November 1988 to massive publicity on both sides of the Atlantic, as his publishers Viking-Penguin sought to recoup a reputed advance of $650,000 paid to the author under a two-book contract. The title – from the story of the *gharaniq* mentioned in Tabari (see pp. 43–4 above) – which could be seen as casting doubt on the authenticity of the Quranic revelation, alerted pious Muslims living in the West to the novel's potentially transgressive character. The characters satirized in the novel include Khomeini, the bearded and turbanned Imam-in-exile who plots the overthrow of the evil Empress of Desh from a rented flat in London's Kensington and the Prophetess Ayesha who leads her followers to a watery death in the Arabian Sea after promising them that they will walk, dry shod, to Makka. The latter episode was based on a real incident at Hawkes Bay near Karachi in Pakistan in February 1983, when thirty-eight people, all of them Shi'ites, entered the sea in the expectation that a path would open enabling them to walk, via Basra, to the holy city of Karbala in Iraq. Eighteen women and children, who had been placed in trunks that were locked and put into the sea, were drowned. The movement was inspired by one Naseema Fatima, daugher of the expedition's leader, who claimed to be acting on instructions from the Hidden Imam. In the novel Rushdie purges the incident of its sectarian character: the Prophetess Ayesha (named after Muhammad's youngest wife, the daughter of Abu Bakr, a revered figure in the Sunni tradition who is often reviled by the Shi'a) leads her doom-bound followers in the direction of Makka rather than Karbala. It is not clear what purpose the novelist had in 'Sunnifying' this episode: was he trying to tease the Sunnis by associating an example of Shi'a credulity with the religious mainstream? Or was he trying to suggest that religious credulity is not a monopoly of the Shi'a? Or perhaps he was merely suggesting, in a general sense, that the psychic orientation of India's Muslims lies westward in the direction of Arabia. 'Islam', writes the Asian-American critic Gayatri Chakravorty Spivak, 'has its head turned away from the subcontinent, across the Arabian sea.'[32]

The passages Muslims of nearly all persuasions found most offensive, however, concerned an episode that occurs in the dream or fantasy of one of the principal characters, a Bombay immigrant named Gibreel Farishta, in the course of a psychotic breakdown that ends in his suicide. The psycho-drama is written in a style that might be described as comic picaresque, combining the magical realism of Gunter Grass's *The Tin Drum* and Mikhail Bulgakov's *The Master and Marguerita* with the urbane Englishness with which Evelyn Waugh describes his own hallucinatory experiences in *The Ordeal of Gilbert Pinfold*. In Gibreel's dreams, which are linked to his 'archangelic other self' as revelator of the Quran, the Prophet Mahound (the name by which Crusading demonologists knew Muhammad), the faithless Jahilites of the city of Makka patronize a brothel called The Curtain, where prostitutes act out the part of Mahound's wives in a series of scenes that appear to be loosely inspired by Jean Genet's play, *Le Balcon*. The characters at the centre of this section of the novel are Salman (identifiable with Rushdie himself but also with the Prophet's Persian companion, Salman al-Farisi or Salman-i Pak, Salman the Pure as he is known in the Persian-Urdu tradition) and the renegade poet Baal, an unreconstructed pagan, who takes refuge in the brothel, where he pretends to be a eunuch. Like Rushdie himself, Baal is endowed with a certain uncanny prescience: 'A poet's work,' he says, 'is to name the unnameable, to point at frauds, to take sides, start arguments, shape the world and stop it from going to sleep. And, if rivers of blood flow from the cuts his verses inflict, then they will nourish him.'[33] At least twenty-two people were to die in the campaign of protests that followed the book's publication – nineteen of them in the Indian subcontinent, two in Belgium and one in Japan.

The protests began in the northern English cities of Bradford, Bolton and Dewsbury, where there are sizeable Muslim communities. But the campaign rapidly became internationalized as the Jamaat-i-Islami and other Islamist organizations put themselves at the head of the protest. The first protesters, mainly from the Barelwi communities of India and Pakistan who hold the Prophet's person in particular veneration, holding *dhikr* ceremonies in his honour in a manner that recalls the Real Presence of the Roman Catholic Mass, seemed genuinely astonished and outraged at the alleged 'insult' to the memory of the Prophet perpetrated by Rushdie, his publishers and their supporters in the literary establishment and press in Britain. The Jamaatis and others who jumped on the anti-Rushdie bandwagon once it had started to roll had the more overtly political objective of using the protest to highlight Muslim grievances and to raise the public profile of British Muslims whom they sought to influence or control. Given the close links between the Muslims in Britain and their kin in South Asia, the demonstrations in the more highly charged politico-religious atmosphere of India and Pakistan inevitably took a violent turn, and it was after the first fatalities in Islamabad, Pakistan, that the Ayatollah Khomeini issued the famous *fatwa* declaring Rushdie an apostate whose blood must be shed (*ma'dhur al-dam*). Exceeding his powers as a *mujtahid* – an interpreter, but not an executor of the law – Khomeini called on all zealous Muslims to execute Rushdie and his publishers 'quickly, wherever they find them, so that no one will dare to insult Islam again. Whoever is killed in this path will be regarded as a martyr . . .' Immediately after the *fatwa* was issued, the Fifth of June Foundation, one of many Islamic charitable trusts established after the revolution offered a reward of 20 million *tumans* (about three million US dollars) to any Iranian who would 'punish the mercenary [Rushdie] for his arrogance'. Non-Iranians would get the equivalent of one million dollars. Despite efforts by the Iranian government and other European governments, including the British government, to improve relations, the *fatwa* remained a symbolic and practical obstacle to any détente between Iran and the western democracies. Although in law a *fatwa* may die with the person who issued it, Khomeini's death in 1989 merely led 'Ali Khamanei, his successor as the chief faqih, to reaffirm it on successive anniversaries; while, despite the diplomatic efforts of the British and sympathetic officials in the Iranian government, the 'contract' on Rushdie's life issued by religious foundations under Islamist control remained in force. A statement by Rushdie in September 1998 to the effect that his ordeal was over proved premature. Though the Khatami government had reached agreement with the British Foreign Office to 'let sleeping *fatwas* lie', as it were, the Fifth of

June Foundation immediately challenged the government by announcing that the bounty on Rushdie's head had been increased.[34]

Attacks on Islamic humanism

Rushdie was far from being the only Muslim intellectual targeted for alleged blasphemy or for offending the sensitivities of believers, whether conservatives or radicals. Inside Iran dozens of intellectuals have been executed or assassinated by militants suspected of being connected with the security services. The anti-intellectual polemics have thuggish overtones. In 1995 the female signatories to a petition by a group of 134 Iranian writers demanding greater intellectual freedom were attacked by officials of the regime as prostitutes; the men were described as drug users, homosexuals and perverts.

In Bangladesh the feminist writer, Taslima Nasrin, was forced into exile to avoid charges of blasphemy and defamation of the faith after drawing attention in her novel *Shame* to atrocities committed against Hindus in the wake of the Ayodhya riots in India. In Sudan the Islamic humanist scholar Mahmud Muhammad Taha, founder of the Republican Brotherhood, was hanged in 1985 during the last months of the Nimeiri regime after being convicted for apostasy. Taha had argued that the Quran contained two messages aimed at different audiences: the Makka *suras* embodied a higher or secondary level of religious understanding comparable to Sufi ideas of gnosis or *irfan* (the so-called Second Message of Islam), while the Madinese *suras* were aimed at the lower or primary level of those who were not yet sufficiently spiritually advanced to attain to the secondary level of understanding. All the aspects of Quranic doctrine such as *jihad*, slavery, capitalism, gender inequality and segregation, the veil, polygyny and the rules regarding divorce, that are either problematic for modernist interpretations or incompatible with progressivist ideas belong to this primary-level message which is seen as incompatible with universalist aims of the Second Message.[35]

In Egypt artists and intellectuals have been regularly attacked by preachers whose iconoclastic sermons are circulated on audio and video casettes. In June 1992 Farag Foda, the prominent Egyptian writer, was gunned down in Cairo. According to Egyptian police the same assassin was responsible for stabbing Naguib Mahfouz, Egypt's best-known novelist and the first Arab writer to have won the Nobel Prize for Literature. Foda had incurred the wrath of clerics in the University of al-Azhar for defending the principles of secularism and denouncing the infiltration of al-Azhar by members of the Muslim Brotherhood. No prominent cleric was prepared to make an unequivocal denunciation of his murder: indeed Shaikh Muhammad al-Ghazali, a member of al-Azhar's influential Islamic Research Academy who appeared as a defence witness in the trial of Foda's assassins, declared that anyone who objected to the full implementation of the Shari'a was *ipso facto* a non-Muslim and apostate. Anyone killing such a person was not liable for punishment, as they would be executing a legitimate Quranic punishment under Islamic law. Mahfouz, whose novel the *Children of Gebalawi* (*Awlad Haritna*) can be read as a humanist fable that questions the existence of God, has long been a target of extremists. Cartoons in Islamist publications showed him entering the jaws of hell carrying copies of his books. Other prominent victims of official or populist censorship include Alaa Hamed sentenced in December 1991 to eight years' imprisonment by an Emergency State Security Court for his novel *Distance in a Man's Mind*, which the court considered a threat to 'national unity' and 'social peace' and Dr Nasr Abu Zaid, an assistant professor of Arabic at Cairo University.

Abu Zaid aroused the fury of both Islamists and traditionalists for his lectures and writings on the historicity of the Quran. Many of his insights derived from modern critical theory. Abu Zaid saw the piecemeal revelation by which the Quran came down to Muhammad as 'an act of communication which naturally includes a speaker, which is God in this case, a recipient, which is Arabic, and a channel which is the Holy Spirit'.[36] The historicity of the Quran, he insisted, did not mean that the text was an entirely human product. But the historical text was nevertheless subject to human understanding and interpretation, whereas God's words existed in a dimension beyond their reach.

The Mu'tazilites [he argued] drew from the Quranic text on the assumption that it was a created action and not the eternal verbal utterance of God. In other words, the relation between the signifier and the signified exists only by human convention; there is nothing divine in this relationship. They endeavoured to build a bridge between the divine word and human reason. That is why they maintained that the divine word was a fact which adjusted itself to human language in order to ensure well-being for mankind. They insisted that language was the product of man and that the divine word respected the rules and forms of human language.[37]

The anti-Mu'tazilites held a different view of language in general and God's speech in particular. Language, according to them, is not a human product but rather a divine gift to man. Therefore if the referent does not exist in the real 'seen' world, it must have existence in unseen reality. Abu Zaid concluded that a socio-historical analysis was needed for a true understanding of the Quran based on modern linguistic methods. Up to now, only the philological approach had been acceptable. Socio-historical analysis had been rejected, not only in textual interpretation, but throughout the domain of Islamic scholarship where even today, very few Muslims accepted the notion of the 'createdness' or non-eternity of the Quran. If the Quran was not eternal, it must have been created in a certain historical context leaving room for the reinterpretation of religious law. God's word had to be understood according to the spirit, not according to the letter. The final consequence was that public authorities were entitled to the primary role in the interpretation and application of the law.[38]

In the propaganda campaign against Abu Zaid legal proceedings were begun which could have ended in his wife being obliged to divorce him in accordance with Shari'a rules forbidding Muslim women to marry non-believers. Hounded by the militants, Abu Zaid and his wife chose exile together. The Abu Zaid affair has echoes of the earlier campaign against Taha Husain, the Azhar-trained scholar and writer whose literary-critical writings on the Quran and pre-Islamic poetry earned him the wrath of the orthodox during the 1920s. Abu Zaid himself, however, pointed to a crucial difference. Taha Husain was accused of apostasy by people from outside the university, at that time a bastion of liberalism, and the university defended him. Abu Zaid was accused of apostasy inside the university, where the Islamists dominate the student's unions. 'Taha Husain was never called a *kafir* (unbeliever). What's most telling is how the conception of apostasy has now been transplanted into the university.'[39]

Civil war in Algeria

In Algeria the army's cancellation of the second round of the national elections after the Islamic Salvation Front (FIS) won the first round in December 1991 led to an increasingly bloody civil war that came to resemble, in its barbarity and carelessness for the lives of non-combatants, the campaign fought by the French against Algerian nationalists nearly two generations earlier. The civil war, which to date is said to have cost more than 70,000 lives, greatly exacerbated the culture wars between the Islamists and their opponents, with musicians, poets, playwrights, novelists and journalists under sustained attack from the Islamists. During the brief period of FIS rule at the municipal level in 1991, gyms and mixed swimming areas were banned, cafés serving alcohol were closed down and the FIS launched a wholesale attack against *rai*, the hybrid of Arab music and western rock popular among Maghrebi immigrants in France and politically disaffected Algerian youth. In September 1994 Cheb Hasni, a popular *rai* singer, was murdered in France after Islamist militants had called for the death sentence for singers they considered 'vulgar'. Scores of writers and journalists critical of the Islamist movement have been murdered, including the award-winning novelist and editor, Tahar Djaout, who was shot in the head outside his home in 1994 and died in a coma. 'Hit lists' containing the names of journalists were circulated in mosques around the country. One Islamist tract seen by western journalists in 1994 listed thirty Francophone journalists 'sentenced to death'. Nine had already been murdered. Audio cassettes containing explicit calls by militant preachers to assassinate anyone suspected of collaborating with the authorities were circulated. Many journalists, artists and writers either moved abroad, or decided to write under assumed names. Though the armed groups rarely claimed responsibility for the murders of writers and artists, threats to writers and their families were commonplace. Tahar Djaout had no illusions about the risks he was running in publishing *Ruptures*, an explicitly anti-Islamist weekly: 'Silence is also death,' he wrote in one of his last published pieces. 'If you speak, you die. If you keep quiet, you die. So speak and die.'[40]

The pressure on intellectual freedom in Algeria was as strong from the government as from the militants, with journalists restricted to reporting only government versions of violent events on the inside pages, and all Islamist publications banned and scores of preachers arrested and imprisoned for sermons deemed to be inciting or defamatory towards state institutions. Analysts such as Hugh Roberts placed the blame for the vice in which Algeria's liberal culture was being crushed squarely on the state. 'Between 1989 and 1992 the majority of Islamists demonstrated comprehensively their willingness to operate within the framework of the pluralist constitution. They have only resorted to guerrilla violence since this option was abruptly and brutally denied them, on no good grounds whatever, with the lunatic decision to ban FIS in spring 1992.'[41] In 1999 constitutional sanity began to be restored. In a relatively orderly campaign the Foreign Minister 'Abd al-'Aziz Bouteflika was elected President to succeed President Zeroual. Although most of those Islamist parties that were not actually banned boycotted the election or disputed its results, the size of the turn-out indicated that after a brutal decade of bloodletting the majority of Algerian citizens were prepared to acquiesce in a form of government that fell far short of an Islamic state.

The general climate of religious intolerance in which intellectuals are under increasing attack cannot be simply explained by the argument that Islamist groups are driven to extremes by government repression and brutality. Several Egyptian commentators place the blame for the puritanism and rigidity infecting the country's public culture – for example, the increasing pressure on women to wear the veil – on foreign influences, notably that of conservative Saudi Arabia and, in a different sense, that of revolutionary Iran. In Saudi Arabia and the Gulf states Egyptian expatriate workers and their families were subjected to a climate of intolerance that denies the positive fruits of Enlightenment culture (the works of Freud, Marx and many western philosophers and social scientists are banned in Saudi Arabia) while emphasizing the rigidly doctrinaire version of Islam proclaimed by Muhammad Ibn 'Abd al-Wahhab, to the exclusion of many works by Islamic philosophers and mystics.

Mohammed Arkoun believes that the roots of such populist attitudes are embedded in a theology grown rigid through more than ten centuries of scholastic repetition and community devotion. 'The concept of tolerance is a modern achievement that cannot be dissociated from the philosophical critique of truth.' 'It is unfortunate that philosophical critique of sacred texts – which has been applied to the Hebrew Bible and the New Testament without engendering negative consequences for the notion of revelation – continues to be rejected by Muslim scholarly opinion.' Until the texts of the Muslim canon – the Quran and the collections of *hadith*, currently deployed as cultural and political icons by both governments and Islamist opposition groups – have been subjected, like their western counterparts, to scholarly scrutiny and re-assessment, intellectuals will find no place in which to preach the Enlightenment gospel.[42]

Cultural schizophrenia

The crisis in Muslim cultural attitudes epitomized by the attacks on Salman Rushdie and other Muslim intellectuals reveals a complex of anxieties that is close to the heart of the relationship between Islamic tradition and modernity. Whereas in the West modernity is usually perceived as having emerged out of developments within the Judaeo-Christian cultural tradition, in much of the Muslim world modernity with both its conveniences and displacements is seen as having been imposed, borrowed or adopted from 'outside'. At heart the Islamist project is not so much anti-modernist as a manifestation of a desire to enjoy modernity on one's own cultural terms. This, however, raises some fundamental difficulties. First, despite appearances, there is no consensus about how Islam should define itself in cultural terms. Second, one may, on a temporary basis, enjoy the fruits of modernity without adhering to its fundamental premises. In the long term, however, such a project risks cultural schizophrenia and marginalization.

In his remarkably penetrating essay, *Cultural Schizophrenia*, the Iranian philosopher Daryush Shayegan analyses the complex cultural attitudes displayed by Muslims who find themselves living in a world whose cultural and spiritual references have changed without a reciprocal shift having occurred from within.

There is a void which I cannot fill in the content of my representations, trailing far behind the industrial productions which surround me on all sides. This yawning gap is not just a difference in mode of life, but a change in my mode of perception. My thought has been sheltered from the great shocks of history. In the West, revolutions caused by scientific and technical upheavals produced paradigm shifts which moulded consciousness to the imperatives of each new way of looking. This has not occurred in my case. My consciousness is still rooted in a world of enchantment. It is true that, as a result of continual bombardment, I am susceptible to the irresistible attraction of new things; but their genealogy and archaeology remain unknown to me. New ideas strike me with full force, stamp their imprints on my mind leaving indelible traces, but hardly manage to alter the content of a memory which refers stubbornly to its own genealogy. I know that times have changed, that the world has been transformed, that history unceasingly shapes new modes of production and new social relations; but the content of this history was formed in my absence.[43]

Shayegan describes the paradigm shift in Western consciousness that occurred at the dawn of modernity as 'a *lowering of the gaze*. . . a change of focus from primary contemplation of smudged, distant horizons to sharp scrutiny of the most immediately accessible concrete things'. He concludes that 'scientific observation, interest in the specific and particular, the quantitative measurement of objects, found a place in human consciousness only when the lure of metaphysical temptations started to fade'.[44] Shayegan's *lowering of the gaze* or paradigm shift in perception corresponds to Descartes's definition of intuition as 'the indubitable conception of a clear and attentive mind which proceeds solely from the light of reason'.[45] The Islamic intuition, particularly in the expressions it found in the Isma'ili and other Shi'i versions, allowed for a God of Reason who refrained from daily intervention in human affairs, although the Shi'i eschatologies, like those in the Judaeo-Christian traditions, always contained the latent potentiality for human action perceived as occurring under divine auspices. The Quran having been 'sent down' as the standard or criterion (*furqan*) according to which human reason should be exercised, the Mu'tazilites and their heirs in the Shi'i communities believed that God had left it for human beings to order the world in accordance with human reason, altering the law to suit the requirements of the day. However, the populist reaction against the Mu'tazila which culminated in the victory of the Ash'arites drove Mu'tazili rationalism out of mainstream Sunni orthodoxy. Although Mu'tazilism remained alive in the Shi'i traditions, the failure of the enlightened Fatimid caliphate with the consequent reduction of Isma'ilism to sectarian status, and the limitation of the Shi'i Twelver tradition mainly to Iran and its adjacent regions, created an anti-rationalist climate hostile to the reception of modern scientific thought.

Islam and modern science

The late Professor Mohammed Abdus Salaam, joint winner of the 1979 Nobel Prize for Physics (the only Muslim scientist to have been so honoured), has stated: 'There is no question, but today, of all civilizations on this planet, science is weakest in the lands of Islam. The danger of this weakness cannot be over-emphasized since honourable survival of a society depends directly on its strength in science and technology in the condition of the present age.'[46] The hostility of modern Muslim governments towards science is manifested by the paucity of papers published in scientific journals. According to the 1988 Science Citations Index, Pakistan had 4 publications, compared with India's 90: with 102 million, Pakistan's population is approximately one-seventh the size of India's. An even greater imbalance in scientific output exists between Israel and the Arab countries, with Arab output (based on an overall population of 100 million) a mere one per cent of Israel's (population 4.5 million). As Pervez Hoodbhoy, a leading Pakistani physicist points out, the Arab deficit cannot be attributed to lack of material resources. Between 1967 and 1976 Arab GNP increased from $25 billion to $140 billion without a proportional increase in scientific output. The anti-scientific climate among some of the wealthier oil-producing states is exemplified by the views expressed by the Saudi delegates to a high-level conference held in Kuwait in 1983. The Saudis held that pure science tends to produce 'Mu'tazilite tendencies' potentially subversive of belief.[47]

Hoodbhoy sees the Islamization programme introduced under the Zia regime in Pakistan as having been particularly hostile to scientific and rational education. The list of religious directives included: imposition of the *chadar* (veil) for female students, organization of afternoon prayers during school hours, compulsory Arabic from the sixth grade, Quranic recitation as a matriculation requirement, an alteration of the definition of literacy to mean religious knowledge, the elevation of *maktab* (Quranic) schools to status of regular schools, recognition of *madrasa* (traditional Islamic) certificates as equivalent to master's degrees, the grant of twenty extra marks for applicants to engineering universities who have memorized the Quran, the introduction of religious knowledge as a criterion for selecting teachers of science and non-science subjects, and the revision of conventional subjects to emphasize 'Islamic values'.[48]

Similar measures are likely to be imposed wherever Muslim governments find it expedient to succumb to Islamist pressures. Pursued in isolation, such measures might be regarded as laudable attempts at cultural and religious defence against the encroachments of modern 'materialism'. In the context of a global economy they make Muslims more vulnerable than peoples from other developing societies to foreign exploitation. In contrast to India whose Brahmanical leaders adopted the ideologies of social democracy and industrial protectionism in order to build an impressive manufacturing capacity, Pakistan pursued an open-door policy towards foreign imports, discouraging the indigenization of technology and forestalling any increase in the 'tiny number of highly skilled scientists and engineers'. Whereas India now has between 70,000 and 80,000 PhDs in natural sciences and engineering, Pakistan has only 1,000.[49] The combined effect of scientific backwardness and attacks on the intellectual freedoms necessary for cultural creativity does not just lead to cultural and economic impoverishment. As the Pakistani example illustrates, internal repression has the effect of emphasizing consumption at the expense of production. The paradoxical long-term effect of the Islamist project would be to turn *dar al-Islam* into a macro-version of Saudi Arabia where, in the absence of a vigorous indigenous culture, people consume the tritest products of Hollywood in the privacy of their homes, while observing the strictest Islamic proprieties on the streets.[50]

Islamism and materialism

As several commentators have pointed out, many of the Islamists (such as 'Abd al Salam Faraj, the architect of Sadat's assassination) have been drawn from the ranks of applied scientists, such as engineers, who seek in holy texts the same rigour and absence of ambiguity they expect to find in technical manuals. Martha Munday observes that 'men of sustained legal training, be it in the tradition of Islamic *fiqh* or in that of modern civil law, are not prominent in the leadership of the religious reform movements of most Arab lands today'. The literalism they apply to the interpretation of texts, she suggests, 'requires a radical reduction of the corpus and its presentation in a form that never admits discussion of textual authority. The text of instruction take the form of a manual of procedure; the law that of a list of injunctions.'[51] This is very far removed from the original spirit of *ijtihad*, which was based on recognition that texts could never yield absolute certainty in the search for truth. For the Arab scientist, Munday suggests, the quest for certainty in law compensates for the absence of certainty in science and for the fact that the Arab scientist or technician is powerless to influence scientific discussions.

To the local university come men licensed by a professional certification obtained from abroad – from a university of the core – and tied for life to the distant sources of the scientific truths in which they deal. Yet so long as such scientists remain at home they become virtually barred from any serious role in the certification of scientific truth. Irremediably the discourse of 'hard' science is produced elsewhere. What answer for self-respect? . . . A tradition of legal idealism is pressed to provide another model for the producton of truth. The search opens for an unchanging indigenous criterion begging no certification from outside, for a criterion that can overrule by moral force the shifting truths of the committees of specialists.[52]

Despite their jeremiads attacking the materialism of the West (which they wholly misinterpret, because, unlike the Japanese, they are blind to its cultural diversities), fundamentalists in the world of Islam, as in the United States, are in a profound sense materialistic. They make admirable technicians, bringing to their work the ethical disciplines they apply in daily living. Scientific inquiry, however, is predicated on uncertainty, the posture of 'epistemological doubt', an attitude at odds with the certainties, including material rewards, they seek in religion. As the Islamic scholar and novelist Daniel Easterman has explained, the scandal the post-Enlightenment West holds for much of the Muslim world is that knowledge acquired through doubt has proved more powerful in creating material prosperity than revealed knowledge or divine guidance. This would be fine if Islamic societies eschewed material prosperity in the cause of spirituality. But, as Easterman points out, this is rarely if ever the case, since Islamists generally subscribe to what might be called the Argument from Manifest Success, whereby the truth of Islam was demonstrated through its historic achievements:

Much modern Muslim writing tries to play down the triumph of the West by emphasizing the dark side of the European and North American experience, the inner angst of a bankrupt civilization on the verge of collapse. The problem is that Islam itself is peculiarly vulnerable on this score. There is very little point in sneering at the material success of others if at the same time one measures one's own achievements by precisely the same criteria: the unprecedented triumph of Muslim arms, the glories of the Abbasid, Andalusian or Mughal empires, the scientfic advances of the Islamic Middle Ages . . .[53]

Modernity has been described by one of its foremost analysts as involving the 'institutionalisation of doubt'.[54] With social change increasingly driven by advances in technology, the idea that revealed knowledge can contain more than moral guidance risks absurdity. At one end of the Islamic spectrum the French surgeon and spiritualist Maurice Bucaille – in a book that is widely distributed by Islamic *da'wa* (missionary) organizations – argues on the basis of partial and eclectic interpretations of Quranic verses that much modern scientific knowledge, from biology to cosmology, is contained in the divine text, waiting, as it were, to be 'discovered'. The problem with this approach – apart from the way it concretizes the language – is that scientific paradigms change, as new hypotheses establish themselves, leaving the Bucaillists with egg on their faces. Hoodbhoy the theoretical physicist observes that 'in Bucaille's book there is not a single prediction of any physical fact which is unknown up to now, but which could be tested against observation and experiment in the future'.[55] At the other end of the spectrum lies the cultural schizophrenia that makes Saudi Arabia, an intellectually underdeveloped country despite its wealth, the first and only Muslim country to have sent an astronaut into space. Yet in Saudi Arabia, in common with other Muslim countries, the pre-Copernican Ptolemaic cosmology still receives official sanction. In an article that became notorious in progressive circles, the President of Madina University and former chief Mufti Shaikh 'Abd al-'Aziz ibn Baz, winner of the 1982 King Faisal International Award for Services to Islam, insisted on the basis of his interpretation of Quranic cosmology, that the earth is the centre of the universe, with the sun, stars and moon moving around it. In an earlier version of the same tract dissenters were threatened with a *fatwa* declaring them unbelievers.[56] A less egregious example of cultural schizophrenia is a daily occurrence on flights by Pakistan International Airlines, where the flight attendant announces 'In a few minutes *insha'llah* [according to the will of God] we shall be landing at such-and-such . . .' Whether she is aware of it or not the flight attendant is endorsing the Ash'arite theory of causality, according to which God intervenes continuously to move or transform matter. It is not certain if PIA has been directly influenced by the Institute of Policy Studies, a Maududist think-tank in Islamabad entrusted with the task of making scientific text-books more 'Islamic', but the announcement is consistent with its recommendations. These include the rubric that effects must not be directly related to physical causes because this will lead to atheism. Thus it is un-Islamic to teach that mixing of hydrogen and oxygen automatically produces water. According to the Islamic way, 'when atoms of hydrogen approach atoms of oxygen, then by the will of God oxygen is produced'.[57]

If taken seriously, PIA's pious etiquette challenges modernity at its epistemological heart. As Giddens has so ably explained, the institutionalization of doubt that characterizes modernity is balanced by faith or trust in abstract systems. Security on an air journey does not depend on the passenger's mastery of the technical paraphernalia that make it possible, nor even exclusively on the pilot's skills, but rather on a formidable range of integrated systems from radar, to air-traffic control, to mechanics, engineers and designers. It is not so much 'materialism' or 'man-worship', the favourite targets of Islamist polemicists, that threatens to undermine the faith of Islam as understood in the majority traditions, but rather that trust in abstract systems which compensates for the absence of divinity in the daily consciousness of post-industrial humanity. The processes of modernity are universal and inherently globalizing.[58] They are driven by the ever-expanding search for markets. Unlike the religious traditions they are threatening and transforming everywhere, the processes of modernity are goal-less. They are no longer the adjunct of Western imperialism, though anti-imperialists, who include many Muslims, are inclined to see them as such. The gradual decline of European and Western hegemony, as Giddens points out, has as its other side the expansion of modern institutions worldwide. 'The declining grip of the West over the rest of the world is not a result of the diminishing impact of the institutions which first arose there but, on the contrary, as a result of their global spread.'[59] Foremost among these institutions is the nation state. Despite the widespread nostalgia for the pan-Islamic *umma*, it is the nation state that commands the allegiance, not just of government supporters, but of the Islamists themselves, however reluctant they may be to admit it. In the Muslim heartlands, as Roy points out, modernization has already occurred, but it has not been absorbed within a commonly recognized and accepted conceptual framework. It has happened 'through rural exodus, emigration, consumption, the change in family behaviour [a lower birthrate] but also through the cinema, music, clothing, satellite antennas, that is, through the globalization of culture'.[60]

Victory of the nation over the ulama

Following the abolition of the caliphate in 1924 the legitimacy of the territorial governments established after decolonization was always open to challenge on Islamic grounds. The new national states were in most cases imposed on societies where the culture of public institutions was weak and where ties of kinship prevailed over allegiances to corporate bodies. In most Middle Eastern countries and many others beyond the Muslim heartlands, the ruling institutions fell victim to manipulation by factions based on kinship, regional or sectarian loyalties. Even when the army took power, as the only corporate group possessing internal cohesion, the elite corps buttressing the leadership were often drawn from a particular family, sect or tribe. In the period following de-colonization the new elites legitimized themselves by appealing to nationalist goals. Their failure to 'deliver the goods' either economically or militarily (especially in the case of the states confronting Israel) led to an erosion of their popular bases and the rise of movements pledged to 'restore' Islamic forms of government after years of *jahiliya* rule.

Despite the failure of nationalist regimes and the apparent popularity of their Islamist opponents, it is highly questionable whether the Islamist movement is leading towards an erosion of territorial boundaries or the undermining of the state. The Iranian revolution, hailed in 1979 as an Islamist victory, has failed to break out of the Shi'ite sectarian enclave in which it occurred. The failure of the Iraqi Shi'ites to rise up against Saddam Husain between 1980 and 1988, despite his murder of their leaders, proved that in Iraq at least national allegiances were stronger than sectarian or religious ones. The overwhelming majority of Iraqi Shi'ites fought loyally for Iraq during the First Gulf War. However much pressure it may have been subjected to, this majority (and Arab Shi'ites make up about sixty per cent of the Iraqi population) has shown no interest in a war against the Iraqi state. The same inference must be drawn on Iran's failure to intervene after Operation Desert Storm when Saddam Husain attacked the holy Shi'ite cities of Najaf and Kerbala in 1991. The interests of the Iranian state took precedence over religious solidarity or the protection of the holiest shrines of the Shi'a.

Iran is exceptional in having Shi'ism as the state religion and, because of the way in which the clergy were institutionalized under a flexible and ultimately rationalist Mu'tazilite theology, a faction of them have succeeded in maintaining power under modern state conditions although, as we have seen, a degree of pluralism is built into their system and they are very far from speaking with a single voice. In Sunni countries where the Islamist movement is largely driven by lay enthusiasts, the lack of leadership implicit in the absence of hierarchy has given the state the upper hand. Where Islamists have succeeded in gaining or influencing power, as in Sudan and in Pakistan, it has been on the backs of the military who remain the ultimate arbiters and sources of power. In other theatres, as these Islamist movements have gained ground with mass support from the newly urbanized poor (the *mustadhafin* or 'wretched ones' from whom Khomeini drew his support in Iran), the message has effectively gone down-market, with more naive and literal interpretations of tradition coming to the fore. Olivier Roy describes these movements as 'neo-fundamentalist' as distinct from Islamist, but 'neo-traditionalist' might be more appropriate. The 'pure' traditionalist may observe rules or conventions, adhering to received interpretations of the tradition, without question, unaware of alternative choices. The 'neo-traditionalist' makes a conscious effort to assert the received interpretations in the face of opposition or hostility, while rejecting (unlike the Islamist) the 'ideologization of Islam' which inevitably entails some modernist infiltrations. The slide from Islamism, which seemed to threaten international stability by holding out the prospect of an alternative to western consumer capitalism, to a neo-traditionalism similar to Saudi Arabia's is part of a pattern discernible throughout the Muslim world. Roy sees the 'failure' of political Islam to live up to its earlier expectations as being due to a fundamental flaw in Islamist political philosophy. In the theories of Maududi and other Islamist writers, responsibility for government is placed in the hands of 'the men who bind and loose' (*ahl al-aqd wa'l hall*). These are supposed to be good Muslims, as it were, by definition. In this theory political institutions function only as a result of the virtue of those who run them; but virtue can become widespread only if society is already 'Islamic'. Thus Islamist political theory is caught in what might be called a virtuous circle or logical cul-de-sac. Rather than offering a radically new political vision for a Muslim world beset by tyrannical, corrupt and incompetent regimes, Islamism is proving incapable of unifying the Muslim world, or even changing the regional balance of power. The result, as Roy sees it, is reduced to little more than a bid for political power justified in Islamic terms. Despite a formal commitment to the solidarity of the Islamic *umma* and even in the case of movements such as the Hizb al-Tahrir (Islamic Liberation Party) to a restored Caliphate, the Muslim national state remains the only plausible object of political ambitions. 'From Casablanca to Tashkent, the Islamists have moulded themselves into the framework of existing states, adopting their modes of exercising power, their strategic demands, their nationalism . . .'[61] Although committed to the elimination of corruption, Roy argues that in the event of succeeding to power the Islamists will face exactly the same alternatives that face the present regimes, as well as most other Third World governments: a tired and corrupt state socialism offset by a black market, or a liberal neoconservatism constrained to follow the prescriptions of the International Monetary Fund, with occasional pious gestures in the direction of 'Islamic banks'. The much-vaunted 'restoration of the Shari'a' simply means that Islamization will target personal law and penal law, as has happened in Pakistan.

The Taliban

A prime example of the slide from Islamism to neotraditionalisms in the context of a struggle for power within the Muslim nation state is offered by the Taliban movement in Afghanistan. Fostered in the refugee camps of Pakistan during the *jihad* against the Soviet-backed government, and in the network of rural *madrasas* in Afghanistan that became the foci of anti-Soviet resistance, the Taliban came to world attention in 1996 with the capture of Kabul. They scandalized international opinion by ordering women out of schools and colleges, offices and factories and back into their homes, forcing them to wear the stifling tent-like *burqa* in public places. In the formerly cosmopolitan city, where women had been a majority of the student body and had been free to mix socially with men for the better part of four decades, music and dancing were forbidden, and television sets destroyed. Violently sectarian in their religious outlook, the Taliban regard the Shi'a as infidels (in stark contrast to most Islamists who tend to be ecumenically minded, minimizing sectarian differences). They were responsible for the massacre of between two and five thousand members of the Shi'ite Hazara community after the capture of Mazar-e Sharif in August 1998. They brought Iran to the brink of intervention by murdering nine of the Islamic Republic's diplomats. Originally funded by Saudi Arabia, Pakistan intelligence and covertly supported by the CIA, the Taliban are among the world's largest exporters of heroin, upon which the funding of their movement now increasingly depends. Based exclusively on the Pashtun tribes that predominate in the southern part of the country and in Western Pakistan, the rise of the Taliban (who at the time of writing controlled four-fifths of the country and had just withdrawn from peace negotiations with their enemies in the north) represent in effect a form of Pashtun nationalism in the guise of Hanafi Sunni ultra-orthodoxy. As indicated by their nomenclature (*talib* means student – i.e. of a traditional *madrasa*), their original education was strictly traditionalist, comprising a version of Hanafi *fiqh* strongly influenced by the nineteenth-century reformism of the Indian Deobandi school. Teachers and students at the private *madrasas*, where most of them were educated, were not accepted at the State Faculty of Theology, founded in 1951, where modernist influences would have been strong. On visiting the *madrasas* that formed the cradle of the movement in 1984, including one in Panjway, the home town of their leader, the *Amir al-Mu'minin* Mullah Omar, Olivier Roy found none of the usual Islamist propaganda in the shape of tracts by Maududi or Qutb. The books he saw 'were very traditional, solely pertaining to religion, and never to politics, economics or other such topics'.[62] The Taliban represent, in what might be called a modified version of the Khaldunian paradigm, a regional ethnic movement that overcomes local allegiances based on tribal segmentation by presenting itself in universalist terms. Although they are all members of local Pashtun tribes, tribal affiliation did not play a part in recruitment to the *madrasas*, where 'a religious and pedagogical hierarchy replaced their familial and tribal connections . . . But paradoxically the way the Taliban have been able to supersede tribal segmentation points towards not a new universal Islamic identity, but an unstated but prevalent Pashtun identity.'[63]

Despite their anti-western rhetoric, their public executions and their attacks on women, which have outraged world opinion, the Taliban's bid for recognition as the legally constituted government of Afghanistan has received support from oil interests in the United States and, paradoxically, from the US Drugs Enforcement Agency who subscribe to the implausible belief that the Taliban will cease exporting opiates to *dar al-harb* once they are firmly established in power.[64]

Islam and feminism

The Taliban takeover of Kabul drew the attention of the world's media to the whole question of the role of women in Islamic societies and their rights as human beings. The first Taliban decrees announced after each major takeover required women to curtail their movements in public, to dress 'decently' (interpreted as a requirement to don the stifling *burqa*), and only to appear in public accompanied by a close family relation (*mahram*). Girls' schools were closed and female work outside the home forbidden. In Herat and Kabul the public baths – essential for female hygiene in traditional Islamic cities – were closed. In their assaults on Afghanistan's rich and variegated urban culture, the Taliban have rightly been seen as agents of 'villagization'. In November 1995 UNICEF announced that it was suspending assistance to education programmes in those parts of Afghanistan where girls were excluded from education, citing its commitment to the principles of the UN Convention on the Rights of the Child, to which Afghanistan is a signatory. Taliban spokesmen stated that they did not feel bound by UN human rights instruments, recognizing only the Shari'a. Constantly needled by other international agencies and NGOs who threatened to follow UNICEF's lead (without necessarily implementing it, for fear of making things worse), the Taliban responded by asking why no mention had been made of human rights' violations against women under the Rabbani government, still officially recognized at the UN. 'Abductions, forced marriages, rape and trafficking in little boys and girls were universally acknowledged, but the international community chose not to make an issue of these violations.'[65] Taliban spokesmen privately indicated to concerned observers that restrictions on women were partly intended to protect them from their own young warriors, citing the previous conquest of Kabul by the Muhajidun. 'Young immature Mujahidun who had grown up on the battlefield under the influence of conservative leaders marvelled at the unveiled Afghan women newsreaders on TV, concluded they must be promiscuous, and – Kalashnikovs at the ready – waylaid the ladies at the studio gate, saying "Tonight you are mine".'[66]

The almost universal outrage that greeted the Taliban's restrictions on women raises complex issues about how the Shari'a is interpreted, confirming that there is no single position on women commanding universal acceptance. Iranian spokesmen condemned the Taliban for bringing the Shari'a into disrepute. The Islamic republic, of course, has its own anti-Taliban agenda following the massacre of the Hazaras and the murder of nine Iranian diplomats which brought the country to the brink of military intervention in 1998.[67] Compared with the Taliban view, the Islamic republic's attitude to women is positively liberal. Moreover, it has evolved since the revolution, exposing the gap between the regime's Islamic rhetoric and the political realities. In opposition and exile Khomeini had opposed the female franchise introduced by the Shah and denounced the Family Protection Laws introduced in 1967 and 1976 which limited the rights of men in divorce cases, improved the rights of women and raised the age of marriage to 18. Khomeini declared that divorces obtained according to these laws would not be recognized and marriages subsequently contracted would be punished as adulterous. Yet *chador*-clad women were among the most active participants in the revolution: the rhetoric of the time stressed that 'true Islam' fully protected female rights, while granting them a dignity and status denied by Western 'sexploitation', which reduced them to the condition of prostitutes. After coming to power with much female support the clergy were in no position to remove the female franchise. Islamic legal practice was restored to the extent that the age of marriage for girls was lowered to 13, and in some cases 9, the official age of maturity. However most of the provisions of the Shah's laws protecting the rights of women in marriage were retained. A new family law passed in 1992 represents, in the view of the anthropologist Homa Hoodfar, 'one of the most advanced marriage laws in the Middle East (after Tunisia and Turkey) without deviating from any of the major conventional assumptions of Islamic law'.[68] At the same time, under clerical pressure, female employment in the public sector has been decreasing at a rate of 2 per cent per year, and women are prevented by law from occupying certain senior offices of state. In May 1998 conservatives introduced two parliamentary bills widely regarded as anti-feminist, that would outlaw press coverage of domestic violence, stifle criticism of laws affecting women and segregate medical services. While there was no certainty that the bills would succeed, their introduction demonstrates that in Iran, more than any other Middle Eastern country, the highly contentious issue of women's rights is being debated on the basis of contested interpretations of Islamic law, within the forum of an elected assembly. This may not be a fully fledged democracy in accordance with western models, but such open and public debate would be unthinkable in a conservative society such as Saudi Arabia's, where women are still forbidden to drive motor vehicles.

Islamists argue that on matters relating to the status of women Muslims are committed to forms of segregation that differ widely from 'Western' notions of equality. Some of these forms are retained symbolically through the custom of veiling, even when economic conditions dictate that women participate in the workforce. Male–female separation in public has become one of the Islamist shibboleths, and in this respect Muslim practice differs from the social conservatism governing male–female relations in, say, India or Japan. The significance of such symbolic gestures, however, is questionable. Is the 'veiled' Malaysian female aeronautical engineer treated better or worse than her Japanese counterpart? And would any difference in the treatment she receives be attributable to religious factors?

As Deniz Kandyoti has argued, economic changes consequent on globalization have tended to increase social inequalities, 'dislocating local communities and producing massive migratory movements and the influx of women into the labour force'.[69] Everywhere women are exposed to encounters with men outside their *mahram* groups, the range of consanguinity traditionally permitted under Islamic law. While men may view women as being more capable than they were in the past, they may also feel threatened by them. The educated and economically independent woman, especially if she is unmarried, may be seen to compromise a man's honour and hence his status among other men. As the anthropologist Michael Gilsenan has observed in the context of Lebanon, *sharaf*, 'the honour of person and family which is particularly identified with control of women's sexuality, is crucial to the public, social identity of men'.[70]

The cultural nationalism prevailing throughout the Islamic world has meant that 'Islam' has provided the only legitimate discourse or forum within which women's rights can be discussed. Many young Muslim women who seek to distance themselves from the cultural symbolism associated with western dress have adopted the 'indigenous feminist' approach, donning the *hijab* (veil) or *chador/chadar* as it is known in Iran and Pakistan to differentiate themselves from the elite bourgeois women of earlier generations who threw off the veil as a gesture of emancipation or under instructions from reforming governments. Wearing the 'veil' may facilitate access to public spaces previously reserved for men without threatening their 'honour'. At the same time the woman preserves her own dignity and sense of honour: 'Through the *hijab* a woman affirms that her submission to God outweighs her submission to man.'[71] The veil is not necessarily a symbol of 'patriarchal oppression', although it may be such in places like Afghanistan. Increasingly Muslim feminists, veiled or unveiled, are seeking to address the substantive issues affecting women's rights in the Islamic world: high fertility, low rates of employment and low literacy, all of them factors linked to the low status of women everywhere. At the same time there remain textual obstacles to complete equality under the Islamic rubric, for example the Quranic rule stating that in certain legal transactions a woman's testimony is only worth half that of a man. Thus in Pakistan women seeking to bring charges of rape are legally disadvantaged in comparison with the men they accuse by the Quranic rules on testimony.

Conclusion

The battle to 'save Islam' from the destructive power of modernity has been lost. Despite appearances to the contrary, the God of exoteric Sunni Islam who manifests himself primarily through the unalterable structures of the Law, is moribund, if not yet dead. As Muslims encounter an increasingly pluralistic world the unreflecting orthopraxy that governed everyday activity and social relations comes under increasing challenge. The days when 'the average Muslim repeats rituals by rote and accepts without thinking an inherited tradition'[72] are long past. As Anita Weiss, an anthopologist working among women in Lahore, Pakistan has noted, 'The combination of the new international division of labour and global telecommunications revolution is having a more penetrating effect on social norms within Muslim society than any external force ever had.'[73] Globalization and modern communications technology make awareness of pluralism and its corollary, religious choice, a permanent fact of life. A Muslim identity that consciously asserts itself through a selective application of the Law in certain areas, for example in the legislation of male–female relations, or by making a shibboleth out of the Quranic penalty of amputation for theft, faces pressures from humanitarian concerns on the outside and the forces of dissolution from within. The crisis of modern Islam is less a crisis of spirituality than a crisis of authority: who has the power to alter the Law, to see that new interpretations consonant with the needs of the modern world will gain acceptance? In the absence of uncontested religious authority in the Islamic mainstream, every attempt to reform the law or to harmonize it with modern legislation risks falling victim to populist sloganizing: 'Tampering with the Law is contrary to the rule of God!'

The challenge for Islam today is to find forms of Islamic expression and reassertion in the face of globalization that can restore dignity and meaning to a Muslim world fractured by the impact of modernization. The solutions, I believe, are to be found in those Islamic traditions that resisted the encroachments of populist orthopraxy in the past, notably the spiritual disciplines of Sufism and the forward-looking orientations of modern Shi'ism. The distinguished American scholar Peter von Sivers links the rise of the modern Islamist movement with the decline of the Sufi orders. Without mysticism, von Sivers argues, the contemporary Islamists are caught in two intellectual dilemmas. Modernists, adapting the ideas of the European Enlightenment, began with demands for a 'rational' religion. They ended by turning against religion altogether. A similar narrowness of focus, he suggests, is shared with the Islamists, who, reacting against the modernists, are caught in the same 'all-or-nothing' attitudes. Von Sivers believes that, without the revival of mysticism allowing for a degree of pluralism in society, the Islamists will never be able to accommodate all believing Muslims.[74] William Chittick, another major American scholar, regards Sufism, the 'vision of union and oneness' as the 'heart and soul of Islam'. If 'the understanding of the inner domains of Islamic experience is lost . . . nothing is left but legal nit-picking and theological bickering'. The modernism to which today's Islamists are heirs is beginning to look frayed, not least in Iran. 'Nowadays,' Chittick observes, 'the dissolution of Western cultural identity and an awareness of the ideological roots of ideas such as progress and development have left the modernists looking naive and sterile.'[75]

A similar point of view is put forward by P. J. Stewart, who believes that Islam may well become the world's majority religion, overtaking Christianity in the next century. The argument he advances is highly original. According to recent research, religiosity, like other endowments, may be genetically transmitted. In Christianity and Buddhism, Stewart argues, the religiously gifted condemn their genes to extinction by the practice of celibacy. In Islam there is no celibacy, and the Sufi orders, which in the past acted as a kind of spiritual yeast in society, may be the carriers and preservers of a vital genetic component. At present the secularists or Islamic reformists and the Islamists or 'theopoliticals' as Stewart calls them, are locked in a debate that deliberately excludes Sufism. Yet the future of Islam must lie in a renovated mystical orientation where depth of religious feeling can be yoked to

metaphorical understandings of the Quran and the Prophetic traditions.[76]

There are signs that this is already happening. Islamism has been
checked, if not defeated, in Central Asia, where Muslim populations
benefiting from the universal literacy bequeathed by the Soviets are
turning to Sufism rather than political Islam. Despite the clamour of
media-grabbing organizations such as Hizb al-Tahrir and its offshoot
the Muhajirun, one of the fastest growing Islamic movements in the
West (and worldwide) is the pietistic Tablighi Jamaat, a strictly non-
political organization whose spiritual roots lie in the reformed Sufism
of the Naqshbandi order in India.[77] There are many other indications
of a positive and fruitful future for Islam in the West, where (despite
a pronounced media bias towards reporting episodes of 'Islamic violence') the climate of free association, freedom of expression and
religious freedom fosters the development of the spiritual as distinct
from the legalistic Islamic traditions. Paradoxically, the very absence
of a body of classical legal doctrine concerning the role of Muslim
minorities in the non-Muslim world (*dar al-harb*) must facilitate the
development of new forms of religious expression uncontaminated
by the narrow legalism of the *faqihs* and the brutal and increasingly
sterile confrontations between the Islamists and their government
opponents. The presence of an increasingly well-educated diaspora
raised in the Western democracies, able to assert itself culturally
through the media and politically through the democratic process can
only increase the attractions of democratic solutions in the Islamic
heartlands. The scandal of the Algerian suspension of democracy, with
the terrible cost in human life that followed, is a lesson that does not
have to be repeated.

The vocabulary of Islam and its symbols will continue to exercise a
powerful attraction over people's minds so long as there are large
bodies of believers who remained unintegrated in the political process.
The Quran's attacks on social injustice and the abuse of wealth, combined with the Prophet's activist example, can always be invoked to
mobilize opposition to Muslim governments perceived as corrupt or
unjust, especially those which fail to equip themselves with convincing
Islamic credentials. To that extent Islam seems set to remain on the
political agenda for many decades. Freed from the rigidity which makes
so much Islamist activity seem culturally sterile (when compared, for
example, with sophisticated variants of the Hindu-Buddhist tra-

ditions), Islam could prove a highly suitable faith for the next century of the common era, and one with an important message. For beyond the admonitions to the faithful to create the good society by observing the Law, there is a message addressed to the whole of humanity. It is a message that proclaims the Eternal Transcendent, and man's special responsibility as guardian of this planet. It is a message which calls on men and women to show gratitude for the world's bounty, to use it wisely and distribute it equitably. It is a message phrased in the language and imagery of a pastoral people who understood that survival depended upon submission to the natural laws governing their environment, and upon rules of hospitality demanding an even sharing of limited resources. In a world increasingly riven by the gap between rich and poor nations, and in growing danger of environmental catastrophe, this message has an urgent relevance. It is one we ignore at our peril.

References

All Quranic quotations are from The Message of the Qur'ān, *translated and explained by Muhammad Asad (Gibraltar, 1980). Asad follows the text of the recension of Hafs ibn Sulayman al-Asadi as it appears in the so-called 'Royal Egyptian' edition published in Cairo in 1337 H.*

1 Introductory: Pilgrimage to Makka

1. Muhammad Asad, *The Road to Mecca* (Tangier, 1974), p. 357
2. Hafiz Wahba, *Arabian Days* (London, 1964), p. 129
3. BBC Summary of World Broadcasts ME/7129/A/1f
4. *Guardian* (14 Sept. 1982)
5. *International Herald Tribune* (20 July 1990)
6. *Independent* (11–13 July 1990, 6 Oct. 1990); BBC Monitoring Reports (4, 11–13 July 1990)
7. Michael Wolfe, *The Hadj – A Pilgrimage to Mecca* (London, 1994), pp. 163–4
8. Ibid., p. 174
9. *Encyclopaedia of Islam*, 2nd edn (Leiden, 1955), entry under 'Ka'ba'
10. Genesis 21:13
11. Asad, *The Road to Mecca*, p. 355, cf. Genesis 21:12–21
12. *Encyclopaedia of Islam*, 2nd edn (Leiden, 1955), entry under 'Ka'ba'
13. A. Guillaume, *The Life of Muhammad*, translation of Ishaq, *Sirat Rasul Allah* (Oxford, 1955), pp. 35–6
14. Guillaume, op. cit., pp. 46–7
15. ibid., p. 52
16. Al-Azraqi, Abu al-Wahd Akhbar Makka (ed. Wüstenfeld), vol. 1 (Leipzig, 1858; rpr. 1964), pp. 108–9; cited in F. E. Peters, *Muhammad and the Origins of Islam* (Albany, NY, 1994)
17. 'Ali Shari'ati, *Hajj*, trans. Ali A. Behzadnia and Najla Denny (Houston, Texas, 1980), p. 41
17. Shari'ati, *Hajj*, p. 41
18. *Time* (16 July 1990); *International Herald Tribune* (20 July 1990)
19. Shari'ati, *Hajj*, p. 69

ADDITIONAL WORKS CONSULTED

Ezzedine Guellouz, *Mecca, the Muslim Pilgrimage* (Tunis, 1979)

Mohammed A. R. Khan, 'On the meteoritic origin of the Black Stone of the Ka'bah', *Popular Astronomy*, 46, no. 7 (Aug.–Sept. 1938)

Encyclopaedia of Islam, 1st edn (Leiden, 1913), entries under 'Ka'ba', 'Mahmal', 'Mecca', "Umra'

Encyclopaedia of Islam, 2nd edn (Leiden, 1955), articles under 'Hadjdj', 'Hanif', 'Hidjaz Railway', 'Ibrahim', 'Id al-'Adha', 'Isma'il'

Z. Badawi and Z. Sardar, *Hajj Studies* (London and Jedda, 1979), vol. 1

Russel King, 'The pilgrimage to Mecca: some geographical and historical aspects', *Erdkunde*, 26 (Feb. 1964), pp. 1231–43

A. S. Tritton, 'A pilgrimage from Morocco', *Islamic Studies*, Karachi, 5, no. 1 (March 1966)

Abdullah 'Ankawi, 'The pilgrimage to Mecca in Mamluk times', *Arabian Studies*, London, 1 (1974), pp. 116–66

Richard Burton, *Personal Narrative of a Pilgrimage to Al-Madinah and Meccah* (London, 1855–6; facsimile reprint of 1893 edn, Dover Publications, New York, 1964)

The Autobiography of Malcolm X (Harmondsworth, 1970)

Movement Studies 1978 (film), directed by Mick Czaki for the Hajj Research Centre, Jeddah

Mimar: Architecture in Development, Singapore, 4 (April–June 1982)

2 *Muhammad the Model*

1. Ira Lapidus, *A History of the Islamic Peoples* (Cambridge, 1993), p. 20

2. Norman Cohn, *Cosmos, Chaos and the World to Come: The Ancient Roots of Apocalyptic faith* (London and New Haven, 1993), p. 96

3. N. H. S. Nyberg, *Die Religionen des Alten Iran* (Leipzig, 1938) in Mary Boyce, 'Zoroastrianism' in J. Hinnells (ed.), *A Handbook of Living Religions* (London, 19), p. 175

4. Maxime Rodinson, *Mohammed* (Harmondsworth, 1973), p. 77

5. C. G. Jung, *Psychology and Religion* (Yale and Oxford, 1938), p. 99

6. Muhammad Asad, *The Message of the Qur'ān* (Gibraltar, 1980), p. 814, n. 14

7. John Burton, 'These are the High-flying Cranes', *Journal of Semitic Studies*, 15 (Jan. 1970), pp. 246 ff; other refs in Malise Ruthven, *A Satanic Affair: Salman Rushdie and the Wrath of Islam* (London, 1991), pp. 38–9

8. Guillaume, op. cit. p. 232

9. ibid., p. 233

10. See Muhammad Asad, *The Message of the Qur'ān* (Gibraltar, 1980), n. 218 at Quran 2:229

11. F. Donner, *Early Islamic Conquests* (Cambridge, Mass., 1982), p. 9

12. Quoted in Muhammad Asad, *The Principles of State and Government in Islam* (Gibraltar, 1980), p. 32

ADDITIONAL WORKS CONSULTED

Ernest Gellner, *Muslim Society* (Cambridge, 1981)

W. M. Watt, *Muhammad at Mecca* (Oxford, 1953)

W. M. Watt, *Muhammad at Medina* (Oxford, 1956)

Charles Issawi, *The Arab World's Legacy* (Princeton, 1981)

Ibn Khaldun, *The Muqaddimah*, trans. F. Rosenthal, 3 vols. (Princeton, 1967)

Muhammad Zafrulla Khan, *Muhammad, Seal of the Prophets* (London, 1980)

Tor Andrae, *Mohammed: The Man and his Faith* (London, 1936)

J. S. Trimingham, *Christianity among the Arabs of Pre-Islamic Times* (London and Beirut, 1979)

3 *The Quranic World-view*

1. Thomas Carlyle, *On Heroes and Hero Worship* (orig. pub. as *Heroes, Hero-worship and the Heroic in History*, 1841), edn with *Sartor Resartus* (London, 1914), p. 299

2. Quoted in Helmut Gaetje, *The Qur'ān and Its Exegesis*, trans. A. T. Welch (London, 1976), p. 201

3. ibid., p. 199

4. ibid., p. 58

5. Quoted in Gaetje, p. 56

6. Quoted in Gaetje, pp. 121 ff.

7. Jonathan Raban, *Arabia Through the Looking-Glass* (London, 1979), p. 19

8. Toshihiko Izutsu, *God and Man in the Koran: Semantics of the Koranic Weltanschauung* (Tokyo, 1964), p. 13

9. Izutsu, *God and Man*, p. 95

10. Muhammad Asad, *The Message of the Qur'ān* (Gibraltar, 1980), n. 2 at Quran 1:2

11. Izutsu, *God and Man*, p. 120

12. e.g., Quran 23:80, 85

13. Izutsu, *God and Man*, p. 151

14. cf. Quran 2:70, 75

15. Al-A'sha al-Akbar, *Diwan*, ed. Muhammad Hussein (Cairo, 1950), 33:32–4

16. Quoted in Izutsu, *God and Man*, p. 174

17. Asad, *Message*, p. iv

18. A. J. Arberry, *The Koran Interpreted* (London, 1955), vol. 2, p. 322

19. A. Yusuf Ali, *The Holy Qur'ān – Text, Translation and Commentary* (Leicester, 1978), p. 1679

20. *The Diwans of Abid ibn al Abras of Asad and Amir ibn al Tufail*, etc., ed. and trans. Sir Charles Lyall (Cambridge, 1913 and 1980), p. 31

21. *The Times*, 2 April 1976
22. Asad, *Message*, n. 106 at Quran 20:120
23. Genesis 3:16–17
24. Mohammed Iqbal, *Six Lectures on the Reconstruction of Religious Thought in Islam* (Lahore, 1930), p. 117
25. cf. Quran 8:12
26. *Diwan al Hamasa*, 713:4, quoted in Izutsu, *God and Man*, p. 237
27. cf. Quran 2:257
28. cf. Izutsu, *God and Man*, pp. 57–8
29. *Sahih* of al Tirmidhi (Cairo, 1950), II, p. 157, cited in Izutsu, *God and Man*, p. 55
30. *Diwan al Hamasa*, 762:1, quoted in Izutsu, *God and Man*, p. 206
31. cf. Toshihiko Izutsu, *The Structure of Ethical Terms in the Koran* (Tokyo, 1959), p. 218
32. Genesis 20:30–8
33. e.g. in Michael Fischer, *Iran: From Religious Dispute to Revolution* (Cambridge, Mass., 1980), p. 72
34. Exodus 14; Quran 7:136ff.
35. Asad, *Message*, n. 7 at Quran 17:5
36. Asad, *Message*, n. 15 at Quran 32:17
37. Yusuf Ali, *Holy Qur'ān*, n. 5240 at Quran 56:35
38. Jalal al-Din al-Suyuti, *Kitab al Anwar* (Tunis, n.d.), p. 26, quoted in Abdelwahab Bouhdiba, *La Sexualité en Islam* (Paris, 1979), p. 94; cf. English tr. by Alan Sheridan, *Sexuality in Islam* (London, 1985), p. 75
39. Suyuti, *Kitab*, p. 38, quoted in Bouhdiba, *Sexualité*, p. 98; Sheridan, p. 78

ADDITIONAL WORKS CONSULTED

Patricia Crone and Michael Cook, *Hagarism* (Cambridge, 1977)
John Wansbrough, *Koranic Studies: Sources and Methods of Scriptural Interpretation* (Oxford, 1977)
Richard Bell (ed.), *The Qur'ān*, 2 vols. (Edinburgh, 1937, 1939)
Richard Bell, *Introduction to the Qur'ān* (1953), ed. and rev. W. M. Watt (Edinburgh, 1978)
Kenneth Cragg, *The Event of the Koran* (London, 1972)
Encyclopaedia of Islam, 2nd edn (Leiden, 1955), article under 'Al-Kur'ān'

4 *Law and Disorder*

1. Sayyid 'Uwais, *Letters to the Imam al-Shafi'i* (Cairo, n.d.)
2. ibid.
3. J. Schacht, *Origins of Muhammadan Jurisprudence* (Oxford, 1950), 1959 edn, p. 140
4. Wael B. Hallaq, *A History of Islamic Legal Theories* (Cambridge, 1997), p. 3

5. Norman Calder, *Studies in Early Muslim Jurisprudence* (Oxford, 1993), p. 167

6. ibid., p. 194

7. Hallaq, *History*, p. 30

8. ibid., p.4

9. M. G. S. Hodgson, *The Venture of Islam* (3 vols, Chicago, 1974), i, p. 327

10. Hallaq, *History*, p.209

11. Al-Zubaidi (d. 1790), *Taj al-'Arus*, cited in Chibli Mallat, *The Renewal of Islamic Law* (Cambridge, 1993), p. 3

12. Aziz al-Azmeh, 'Islamic Legal Theory and the Appropriation of Reality', in Aziz al-Azmeh (ed.), *Islamic Law: Social and Historical Contexts* (London, 1988), p. 250

13. Norman Calder, 'Legal Thought and Jurisprudence', in John Esposito (ed.), *The Oxford Encyclopedia of the Modern Islamic World* (4 vols., New York, 1995), ii, p. 450

14. ibid.

15. Calder, *Studies*, p. 219

16. ibid., p. 212

17. Quoted in Schacht, *Origins*, p. 135

18. Calder, *Studies*, p. 230

19. Muhammad b. Isa al-Tirmidhi, *Sahih*, cited in Muhammad Asad, *The Principles of State and Government in Islam* (Gibraltar, 1980), p. 38

20. Hallaq, *History*, p. 20

21. Jalal al-Din al-Suyuti, *al-Jami 'al-Saghir*, cited in Asad, *Principles*, pp. 48, 106

22. Calder, *Studies*, p. 183

23. ibid., pp. 184–5

24. Hallaq, *History*, p. 208

25. Allan Christelow, 'The Transformation of the Muslim court system in Colonial Algeria: Reflections on the Concept of Autonomy', in al-Azmeh, *Islamic Law*, p. 218.

26. ibid., p. 209

27. Sayf al-Din al-Amidi, *al-Ihkam fi usul al-ahkam* (Cairo, 1914), vol. 4, p. 218 cited in Bernard Weiss, 'Interpretation in Islamic Law: The Theory of Ijtihad', *American Journal of Comparative Law* 26 (1978), p. 207

28. Hallaq, *History*, pp. 32, 33; Wael B. Hallaq, 'Was the Gate of Ijtihad Closed?' in Ian Edge (ed.), *Islamic Law and Legal Theory* (Aldershot, 1996), pp. 287–385

29. J. N. D. Anderson, 'Law as a Social Force in Islamic Culture and History', in Edge, *Islamic Law*, p. 526

30. N. Coulson, *A History of Islamic Law* (Edinburgh, 1964), p. 2.

31. Edge, *Islamic Law*, p. 494

32. ibid., p. 497

33. Hallaq, *History*, p. 254

34. Lawrence Rosen, *The Anthropology of Justice – Law as Culture in Islamic Society* (Cambridge, 1989), p. 17

35. ibid., p. 38
36. ibid., p. 18
37. ibid., p. 23
38. Abu Muhammad ibn 'Ali ibn Hazm, *Al-Muhalla* (Cairo, 1347 H), vol. 1,
pp. 62–4, quoted in Asad, *Principles*, pp. 13–14. Ibn Hazm's classification, the
three permissible categories *mandub*, *makruh* and *mutlaq*, are treated as
subdivisions of *mubah*, 'allowed' acts, commission or omission of which do
not constitute sins
39. Aziz al-Azmeh, cited in Ian Netton, *Allah Transcendent* (London, 1994),
p. 26
40. John Shepherd, 'Islamic Ethics and the Ethics of Liberalism: The Logic of
a Creative Synthesis', in Theodore Gabriel (ed.), *Contemporary Islamic Issues*
(New Delhi, forthcoming)
41. A. B. K. Brohi, 'The Nature of Islamic Law and the Concept of Human
Rights', in International Commission of Jurists et al., *Human Rights in Islam*
(Geneva, 1982), p. 54
42. Kemal Faruqi, 'Legal Implications for Today of *Al-ahkam al-khamsa* (The
Five Values)', in Richard G. Hovannisian (ed.), *Ethics in Islam* (Malibu, 1995),
p. 69
43. Muhammad ibn Isma'il al-Bukhari, *Sahih* (Cairo, 1312 H), vol. 4, p. 91,
cited in Bouhdiba, *La Sexualité en Islam* (Paris 1979), p. 144; see also A.
Guillaume, *The Traditions of Islam* (Oxford, 1924), pp. 125–6
44. Edward Lane, *An Account of the Manners and Customs of the Modern
Egyptians* (London, 1836; facsimile of 1860 edn, Dover Pubs., New York,
1973), p. 82
45. ibid., pp. 63, 82
46. I. Corinthians 7 *et seq.*
47. A. Bouhdiba, *La Sexualité en Islam* (Paris, 1979), pp. 112, 113. English
translation by Alan Sheridan (London, 1985), p. 90
48. Muhammad ibn Isa al Tirmidhi, *Sunan* (Madina, n.d.), vol. II, p. 413,
Bab. 9, *hadith* 1167, quoted in F. Mernissi, *Beyond the Veil* (Cambridge, Mass.,
1975), p. 11
49. Muslim ibn al Hajjaj, *Al Jami al Sahih*, vol. III (Book of Marriage), p. 130,
quoted in Mernissi, *Beyond the Veil*, p. 11
50. Abu Hamid al Ghazali, *Ihya 'ulum al din* (Cairo, n.d.), p. 50
51. ibid.
52. Aini, *'Umdat al qari shar'ih al-Bukhari* (Istanbul, 1308 H), vol. 9, p. 484,
quoted in Bouhdiba, *Sexualité*, p. 111
53. Masud al-Qanawi, *Sharh lamiat ibn al-Wardi* (Cairo, 1310 H), p. 14, quoted
in Bouhdiba, *Sexualité*, p. 110
54. Nawal el Saadawi, *The Hidden Face of Eve* (London, 1980), p. 206
55. Lane, *Manners and Customs*, pp. 180–1
56. Muhammad Asad, *The Message of the Qur'ān* (Gibraltar, 1980), n. 218 at
Quran 2:229

57. Coulson, *Islamic Law*, p. 138

58. cf. Bouhdiba, *Sexualité*, pp. 139–40

59. Asad, *Message*, n. 36 at Quran 24:31

60. *Encyclopaedia of Islam*, 2nd edn. (Leiden, 1955), entry under 'Abd (vol. 1, p. 27)

61. Yusuf al-Qaradawi, *The Lawful and the Prohibited in Islam*, tr. Kamal al-Helbawi *et al.* (Indianapolis, n.d.), p. 150

62. ibid., p. 151

63. *Encyclopaedia of Islam*, vol. 1, p. 26

64. ibid., p. 28

65. Bouhdiba, *Sexuality* (tr. Sheridan), p. 106

66. Maxime Rodinson, *Islam and Capitalism* (Harmondsworth, 1977), p. 34

67. ibid., p. 55

68. ibid., p. 57

69. ibid., p. 91

70. Bryan S. Turner, *Weber and Islam* (London, 1974), p. 13

71. ibid., p. 173; Sami Zubaida, 'Economic and Political Activism in Islam', *Economy and Society*, 1 (1972), p. 324

72. X. de Planhol in *Cambridge History of Islam* (4 vols., Cambridge, 1970), iiB, p. 453

73. ibid., p. 456, citing J. de Thevenot, *Relation d'un voyage fait au Levant* (Paris, 1664), p. 239

74. G. von Grunebaum in *Cambridge History of Islam*, iiB, p. 491

75. J. Schacht in ibid., p. 563

76. C. Cahen in ibid., p. 520

77. Rosen, *Justice*, p. 49

78. Malise Ruthven, *Islam: A Very Short Introduction* (Oxford, 1997), p. 90

79. Pervez Hoodhboy, *Islam and Science: Religious Orthodoxy and the Battle for Rationality* (Kuala Lumpur, 1992), p. 126

80. Max Weber, *Economy and Society* (New York, 1968), vol. 2, p. 823, cited in Hoodhboy, *Science*, p. 127

81. Hoodbhoy, *Science*, p. 129

82. ibid., p. 132

83. The argument that follows is partly based on Otto von Gierke, *Political Theories of the Middle Ages*, tr. F. W. Maitland (Cambridge, 1900), including Maitland's Introduction; and Ernest H. Kantorowicz, *The King's Two Bodies – A Study in Medieval Political Theory* (Princeton, NJ, 1957)

84. Hoodhboy, *Science*, p. 132

85. Ibn Taymiyya, *Siyasa Sharī'a* ('Le Traité de droit publique d'Ibn Taymiyya'), tr. H. Laoust (Beirut, 1948), p. 172

86. I am grateful to Jim Piscatori for his help in this section

87. Mohammed Arkoun, *Rethinking Islam: Common Questions, Uncommon Answers*, ed. and tr. Robert D. Lee (Boulder, 1994), p. 13

88. Rosen, *Justice*, p. 21

89. ibid., p. 89

90. ibid., p. 53

5 Sects and Solidarity

1. Ibn Saghir, *Actes du XIVième Congrès des Orientalistes*, trans. A. de Motylinski (Paris, 1908), pt 3, p. 68, quoted in Charles-André Julien, *History of North Africa* (London, 1970), p. 28

2. Julien, *History*, p. 62

3. Gustav Thaiss in N. R. Keddie (ed.), *Scholars, Saints and Sufis* (Berkeley, 1972), p. 356

4. ibid.

5. Clifford Geertz, *The Interpretation of Cultures* (London, 1975), p. 104

6. Bernard Lewis, *Origins of Ismailism* (Oxford, 1940), p. 25

7. Abu Daud, *Sunan al Mustafa* (Cairo, n.d.), vol. II, p. 135, cited in S. H. M. Jafri, *Origins and Early Development of Shi'a Islam* (London, 1979), p. 268

8. M. G. S. Hodgson, *The Venture of Islam* (3 vols., Chicago, 1974), i, p. 304

9. ibid., p. 305

10. W. M. Watt, *The Formative Period of Islamic Thought* (Edinburgh, 1973), pp. 246–7

11. W. M. Watt, *Free Will and Predestination in Early Islam* (London, 1948), p. 139

12. Sayyid Muhammad Husain Tabataba'i, *Shi'ite Islam*, trans. S. H. Nasr (Houston, 1979), p. 99

13. For a comprehensive account of the 'resurrection of Alamut' (1164) see Christian Jambet, *La grande résurrection d'Alamût: Les formes de la liberté dans le shi'isme ismaélien* (Paris, 1990)

14. A. Esmail and A. Nanji in S. H. Nasr (ed.), *Isma'ili Contributions to Culture* (Tehran, 1977), p. 244

15. M. G. S. Hodgson, *The Order of Assassins* (The Hague, 1955), p. 19

16. ibid., p. 5, n. 11

17. See *Mahjubah: The Magazine for Muslim Women*, Tehran, 1, no. 8 (October 1981), pp. 52–6; Tabataba'i in *Shi'ite Islam*, pp. 227–30; N. Coulson, *A History of Islamic Law* (Edinburgh, 1964), pp. 110, 111

ADDITIONAL WORKS CONSULTED

David Bryer, 'Origins of the Druze Religion', *Der Islam*, 52, no. 1 (Feb. 1975)

J. C. Wilkinson, 'The Ibadi Imama', *Bulletin of the School of Oriental and African Studies*, 39, no. 3 (1976)

Encyclopaedia of Islam, 1st edn (Leiden, 1913), entries under 'Kharidjites', 'Al-Husayn B. 'Ali B. Abi Talib', 'Karbala', 'Shi'a'

Encyclopaedia of Islam, 2nd edn (Leiden, 1955), entries under 'Alamut', 'Duruz'; 'Isma'iliyya', 'Karmati'

M. G. S. Hodgson, 'How Did the Early Shi'a Become Sectarian?', *Journal of the American Oriental Society*, 75 (1955)

John Townsend, *Oman: The Making of a Modern State* (London, 1977)

6 Spiritual Renewal

1. Muhammad Asad, *The Message of the Qur'ān* (Gibraltar, 1980), p. 996
2. *Encyclopaedia of Islam*, 1st edn (Leiden, 1913), entry under 'Tasawwuf'
3. A. J. Arberry, *Sufism* (London, 1968), p. 33
4. ibid., p. 34
5. ibid., p. 42
6. *Encyclopaedia of Islam*, 1st edn, entry under 'Rabia al Adawiya'
7. Margaret Smith, *Rabi'a the Mystic and Her Fellow-Saints in Islam* (Cambridge, 1928), pp. 102–3
8. Michael Gilsenan, *Saint and Sufi in Modern Egypt* (Oxford, 1973), p. 137
9. ibid., p. 14
10. A. J. Arberry, *Revelation and Reason in Islam* (London, 1957), p. 99
11. ibid., p. 98
12. Arberry, *Sufism*, p. 58
13. ibid., p. 60
14. Louis Massignon, *La Passion d'Hallaj* (2 vols, Paris, 1922), i, p. 303
15. W. M. Watt, *The Faith and Practice of Al Ghazali* (London, 1953), p. 20
16. ibid., p. 56
17. ibid., p. 60
18. ibid., pp. 133–40 *passim*
19. Ibn 'Arabi, *The Wisdom of the Prophets* ('Fusus al-Hikam'), trans. Titus Burckhardt and Angela Culme-Seymour (Aldsworth, 1975), p. 24
20. R. A. Nicholson, *Rumi, Poet and Mystic* (London, 1950), p. 24
21. Jalal al Din Rumi, *Mathnawi*, trans. R. A. Nicholson (6 vols., London, 1929–37), i, 1–5
22. ibid., vi, 1454–60
23. ibid., iv, 3637ff.
24. Edward Lane, *An Account of the Manners and Customs of the Modern Egyptians* (London, 1836; facsimile edn, Dover Pubs., New York, 1973), p. 241
25. E. E. Evans-Pritchard, *The Sanusi of Cyrenaica* (Oxford, 1949), p. 2
26. Louis Massignon in *Encyclopaedia of Islam*, 1st edition, entry under 'Tasawwuf'
27. Gilsenan, *Saint and Sufi*, p. 5
28. J. Spencer Trimingham, *The Sufi Orders in Islam* (Oxford, 1971), p. 241
29. Gilsenan, *Saint and Sufi*, p. 33
30. ibid., p. 43

31. ibid., p. 72

32. Arberry, *Sufism*, p. 75

33. Frithjof Schuon, *Understanding Islam*, trans. D. M. Matheson (London, 1976), p. 123

34. Trimingham, *The Sufi Orders*, p. 195

35. Gilsenan, *Saint and Sufi*, p. 168

36. I. M. Lewis, *Islam in Tropical Africa* (Oxford, 1966), p. 311

37. ibid., p. 60

38. cf. Vincent Crapanzano in N. R. Keddie (ed.), *Scholars, Saints and Sufis* (Berkeley, 1972), p. 342

39. J. F. P. Hopkins in *Encyclopaedia of Islam*, 2nd edn (Leiden, 1955), entry under 'Ibn Tumart'

40. Muhammad Umar Memon, *Ibn Taimiya's Struggle against Popular Religion* (The Hague, 1976), p. 78

41. Benjamin Jokisch, 'Ijtihad in Ibn Taymiyya's Fatawa', in R. Gleave and E. Kermeli (eds.), *Islamic Law: Theory and Practice* (London, 1997), pp. 119–21

42. Muhammad B. 'Abd al-Wahhab in *Majmu'at al-rasail wa'l masail al-najdiyya* (Cairo, 1928), pp. 74–5, trans. Elizabeth Sirriyeh in E. Sirriyeh, *Sufis and Anti-Sufis – The Defence. Rethinking and Rejection of Sufism in the Modern World* (Richmond, Surrey, 1999), p. 24

43. Hamid Algar, 'Naqshbandiyah' in John Esposito (ed.), *Oxford Encyclopedia of the Modern Islamic World*, vol. 3, p. 228

44. e.g. Alexei V. Malashenko, 'Religious and Political Change in the Soviet Moslem Regions', in V. Naumkin (ed.), *State, Religion and Society in Central Asia* (Reading, 1993), pp. 162–75

45. Aziz Ahmed, *Islamic Culture in the Indian Environment* (Oxford, 1964), p. 75

46. ibid., p. 185

47. Raphael Israeli, *Muslims in China: A Study in Cultural Confrontation* (London and Malmö, 1978)

ADDITIONAL WORKS CONSULTED

Hamid Algar, 'The Naqshbandi Order' (unpublished typescript kindly lent to me by Professor Albert Hourani)

M. Molé, *Les Mystiques musulmans* (Paris, 1965)

Albert Hourani, *The Emergence of the Modern Middle East* (London, 1981), ch. 5

A. J. Arberry, *The Doctrine of the Sufis*, translation of Abu Bakr al-Kalabadhki, *Kitab al-Ta'aruf li-mathab ahl al-tasawuf* (Cambridge, 1935, 1977)

Majid Fakhry, *A History of Islamic Philosophy* (London and New York, 1983)

7 Challenge from the West

1. P. M. Holt, *The Mahdist State in the Sudan* (Oxford, 1958), p. 34

2. Moshe Gammer, *Muslim Resistance to the Tsar: Shamil and the Conquest of Chechnia and Daghestan* (London, 1994). *Guardian*, 9 August 1999

3. A. S. Ahmed, *Millennium and Charisma among the Pathans* (London, 1976), p. 9

4. Aziz Ahmed, *Islamic Modernism in India and Pakistan 1857–1954* (London, 1967), p. 33

5. *Encyclopaedia of Islam*, 2nd edn (Leiden, 1955), entry under 'Ahmed Khan'

6. Zaki Badawi, *The Reformers of Egypt – a Critique of Al-Afghani, 'Abduh and Ridha* (London, 1976), p. 46, citing *Tafsir al Manar*, IV, p. 350

7. Muhammad 'Abduh, *Risalat al-tawhid* (Cairo, 1346 H), pp. 73–80, cited in Nadav Safran, *Egypt in Search of Political Community* (Cambridge, Mass., 1961), p. 67

8. ibid.

9. Richard Mitchell, *The Society of Muslim Brothers* (London, 1969), p. 14

10. ibid., p. 29

11. ibid., p. 88

12. Yvonne Haddad in John Esposito (ed.), *Voices of Resurgent Islam* (Oxford, 1983), p. 67

13. Shahrough Akhavi in Esposito (ed.), *Oxford Encyclopedia*, iii, p. 402

14. Haddad in Esposito, *Voices*, p. 74

15. Akhavi, loc. cit.

16. Leonard Binder, *Islamic Liberalism: A Critique of Development Ideologies* (Chicago, 1988), p. 177

17. Sayyid Qutb, *Ma'alim fi'l tariq*, cited in Binder, *Liberalism*, p. 179

18. Binder, *Liberalism*, p. 195

19. ibid., p. 210

20. Quoted in Hisham Sharabi, *Nationalism and Revolution in the Arab World* (New York, 1966), p. 112

21. ibid.

22. Hasan al-Turabi in Esposito, *Voices*, p. 244

23. Sondra Hale in Joel Beinin and Joe Stork (eds), *Political Islam: Essays from the Middle East Report* (London, 1997), p. 243

24. ibid., p. 241

25. Ahmed, *Islamic Modernism*, pp. 142–3

26. Muhammad Iqbal, *Six Lectures on the Reconstruction of Religious Thought in Islam* (Lahore, 1930), pp. 11, 12

27. ibid., p. 176

28. ibid., p. 165

29. ibid., p. 170

30. Ahmed, *Islamic Modernism*, p. 159

31. ibid.

32. From Iqbal's letters to Jinna quoted in Ahmed, *Islamic Modernism*, pp. 160, 162

33. W. Cantwell-Smith, *Islam in Modern History* (Princeton, 1957), p. 234

34. Sayyid Abul 'Ala Maududi, *Towards Understanding Islam* (London, 1980), p. 20

35. Maududi, *The Religion of Truth* (Lahore, 1967), pp. 3, 4

36. Maududi, *Towards Understanding*, p. 81

37. ibid., p. 104

38. Maududi, *Purdah and the Status of Woman in Islam* (Lahore, 1979), p. 20

39. ibid., pp. 197, 198

40. Maududi, *Birth Control* (Lahore, 1978), p. 73

41. Maududi, *Purdah*, p. 23

42. Maududi, *The Religion of Truth*, p. 23

43. Maududi, *The Process of Islamic Revolution* (Lahore, 1979), pp. 15, 16

44. Maududi, *The Islamic Law and Constitution* (Lahore, 1977), pp. 270f.

45. ibid., pp. 316–18

46. Munir Report (1954), p. 229, cited in Ahmed, *Islamic Modernism*, p. 242

47. See Michael Fischer, *Iran from Religious Dispute to Revolution* (Cambridge, Mass., 1980), pp. 149–50

48. Ervand Abrahamian, *Iran Between Two Revolutions* (Princeton, 1982), p. 447

49. Fischer, *Iran*, p. 151

50. Abrahamian, *Iran*, p. 425

51. Ayatullah Ruh Allah Khumayni, *Islam and Revolution*, selection of speeches and writings trans. and ed. H. Algar (Berkeley, 1981), p. 38

52. ibid., p. 28

53. ibid., p. 55

54. ibid., p. 57

55. ibid., p. 60

56. ibid., p. 170

57. Abrahamian, *Iran*, p. 465

58. Quoted in Abrahamian, *Iran*, p. 465

59. 'Ali Shari'ati, *Marxism and other Western Fallacies*, trans. H. Algar (Berkeley, 1980), p. 49

60. ibid., p. 23

61. 'Ali Shari'ati, *On the Sociology of Islam*, trans. H. Algar (Berkeley, 1979), p. 116

62. ibid.

63. ibid., pp. 123–4

64. ibid., p. 71

65. ibid., p. 84

66. Abrahamian, *Iran*, p. 470

67. ibid., p. 471

68. ibid., p. 479

69. cf. Ernest Gellner, *Muslim Society* (Cambridge, 1981), p. 43

70. Abrahamian, *Iran*, p. 492

71. See M. H. Heikal, *The Return of the Ayatollah* (London, 1981), p. 177

ADDITIONAL WORKS CONSULTED

Albert Hourani, *Arabic Thought in the Liberal Age 1798–1939* (Oxford, 1962)

Middle East Journal, Washington DC, 37, no. 1 (1983), articles by Mangol
   Bayat, Yvonne Haddad, Bassam Tibi

Edward Mortimer, *Faith and Power: The Politics of Islam* (London, 1982)

E. I. J. Rosenthal, *Islam in the Modern National State* (Cambridge, 1965)

Hamid Enayat, *Modern Islamic Political Thought* (London, 1982)

V. S. Naipaul, *Among the Believers: An Islamic Journey* (London, 1981)

Michael Gilsenan, *Recognizing Islam: An Anthropologist's Introduction* (London,
   1982)

Mohammed Ayoob (ed.), *The Politics of Islamic Reassertion* (London, 1981)

H. A. R. Gibb, *Modern Trends in Islam* (Chicago, 1950)

Janet L. Abu Lughud, *Cairo: 1,001 Years of the City Victorious* (Princeton, 1971)

J. Piscatori (ed.), *Islam in the Political Process* (Cambridge, 1983)

John L. Esposito (ed.), *Islam and Development* (Syracuse, New York, 1980)

G. H. Blake and R. I. Lawless (eds.), *The Changing Middle Eastern City*
   (London and New York, 1980)

8 *After Word (1999)*

1. Samuel Huntington, 'The Clash of Civilizations', *Foreign Affairs*, Summer
1993

2. Peter Gran, *The Islamic Roots of Capitalism* (Syracuse, 1998)

3. Charles Issawi, *The Arab World's Legacy* (Princeton, 1981), p. 309

4. David Landes, *The Wealth and Poverty of Nations* (London, 1998) p. 419

5. Francis Robinson, 'Technology and Religious Change: Islam and the
Impact of Print', *Modern Asian Studies*, 27, 1 (1993), p. 237

6. ibid., p. 230

7. ibid., p. 237

8. Cited by Richard L. Chambers in N. Keddie (ed.), *Scholars, Saints and Sufis*
(Berkeley, 1972), p. 35

9. Daniel Cercelius in Kaddie, *Scholars*, pp. 193–4

10. Robinson, 20

11. ibid., 20

12. Dale Eickelman in John Esposito (ed.), *Oxford Encyclopedia of the Modern
Islamic World* (4 vols., Oxford, 1995), iii, p. 342

13. Interview with Tal'at Fuad Qasim in Joel Beinin and Joe Stork (eds.),

Political Islam – Essays from Middle East Report (London/New York, 1997), p. 315

14. ibid., p. 317

15. *Islamophobia* (Runnymede Trust, London, 1997), ch. 5

16. Augustus Richard Norton in Esposito (ed.), *Oxford Encyclopedia of the Modern Islamic World*, iv, p. 207

17. P. J. Stewart, *Unfolding Islam* (Reading, 1993), p. XX

18. A translation of al-Faraj's famous tract, *al-farida al-ghaiba* (variously translated as 'The Hidden Imperative', 'The Missing Precept' or 'The Neglected Duty') and the official *'ulama* riposte are discussed at length in Johannes J. G. Jansen, *The Neglected Duty: The Creed of Sadat's Assassins and Islamic Resurgence in the Middle East* (New York, 1986); see also Gilles Kepel, *The Prophet and Pharaoh: Muslim Extremism in Egypt*, trans. Jon Rothschild (London, 1985)

19. Rudolph Peters in Esposito (ed.), *Encyclopedia*, ii, pp. 372–3

20. Tal'at Fuad Qasim interview with Hisham Mubarak in Beinin and Stork, *Political Islam*, p. 321

21. François Burgat and William Dowell, *The Islamic Movement in North Africa* (Austin, Texas, 1993), p. 1995

22. Gudrun Krämer, 'Techniques and Values – Debates on Islam and Democracy', in Gema Martin Munoz (ed.), *Islam, Modernism and the West. Cultural and Political Relations at the End of the Millennium* (London/New York, 1999), pp. 174–90

23. ibid., pp. 186–7

24. Mohammed Arkoun, *Rethinking Islam – Common Questions, Uncommon Answers*, trans. and ed. Robert D. Lee (Boulder\Oxford, 1994), p. 13

25. Aziz al-Azmeh, *Islams and Modernities* (London, 1993), p. 31

26. ibid., p. 12

27. Sami Zubaida, *Islam: The People and the State* (London, 1993). The same points are made in Zubaida's article 'Is Iran an Islamic State?', in Stork and Beinin, *Political Islam*, pp. 103–19

28. Zubaida, in Stork and Beinin, p. 107. The text of the letter to President Khamenei, reproduced in BBC Summary of World Broadcasts, part 4, 8 January 1988, is cited in Fred Halliday, 'The Politics of Islamic Fundamentalism', in Akbar S. Ahmed and Hastings Donnan (eds.), *Islam, Globalization and Postmodernity* (London, 1994), p. 100

29. *Middle East International*, no. 507 (20.1.95), pp. 13–14

30. Don Cupitt, 'Face to Faith: Humanity and Hope', *Guardian*, 22 November 1997

31. John Cooper in John Cooper et al., *Islam and Modernity – Muslim Intellectuals Respond* (London, 1998), pp. 38–54

32. Gayatri Chakravorty Spivak, 'Reading The Satanic Verses', *Public Culture*, Fall 1989, p. 82

33. Salman Rushdie, *The Satanic Verses* (London, 1988), p. 97

34. On the Rushdie affair, see M. Ruthven, *A Satanic Affair: Salman Rushdie and the Wrath of Islam* (London, 1990, 1991); Michael M. J. Fischer and Mehdi Abedi, *Debating Muslims: Cultural Dialogues in Postmodernity and Tradition* (Madison, Wisconsin, 1990), pp. 383–442. Gilles Kepel, *Allah in the West: Islamic Movements in America and Europe*, trans. Susan Milner (Cambridge, 1997) pp. 81–148. The entry in the *Oxford Encyclopedia* is unreliable.

35. Mohamed Mahmoud in John Cooper *et al.*, *Islam and Modernity – Muslim Intellectuals Respond* (London, 1998), pp. 105–17

36. Nasr Hamid Abu Zaid in Cooper *et al.*, p. 195

37. ibid., p. 194

38. ibid., p. 198

39. 'Silencing Is at the Heart of My Case', Nasr Hamid Abu Zaid interview with Elliott Cola and Ayman Bakr in Beinin and Stork, p. 332

40. *Guardian*, 7 November 1994

41. *Index on Censorship*, 4 May 1994

42. Mohammed Arkoun, *Rethinking Islam*, p. 35

43. Daryush Shayegan, *Cultural Schizophrenia: Islamic Societies Confronting the West*, trans. John Howe (London, 1992), p. 6

44. ibid., p. 34

45. 'Regulae Rule Four', cited in John Cottingham (trans. & ed.), *René Descartes: Meditations on First Philosophy*, revised edn. (Cambridge, 1996), p. xxiii

46. quoted in Pervez Hoodbhoy, *Islam and Science: Religious Orthodoxy and the Battle for Rationality* (Kuala Lumpur, 1992), p. 28

47. ibid., p. 29

48. ibid., p. 37

49. ibid., p. 35

50. Olivier Roy, *The Failure of Political Islam* (London, 1994)

51. Martha Munday in Aziz al-Azmeh (ed.), *Islamic Law*, p. 22

52. ibid., p. 21

53. Daniel Easterman *New Jerusalems: Reflections on Islam, Fundamentalism and the Rushdie Affair* (London, 1993), p. 37

54. Anthony Giddens, *The Consequences of Modernity* (Cambridge, 1990), p. 176

55. Hoodhboy, *Islam and Science* p. 68

56. ibid., p. 48

57. ibid., p. 54

58. Giddens, *Consequences*, p. 177

59. ibid., p. 52

60. Roy, *Failure*, p. 23

61. ibid., p. 194

62. Olivier Roy, 'Has Islamism a Future in Afghanistan?' in William Maley (ed.), *Fundamentalism Reborn? Afghanistan and the Taliban* (London, 1998), p. 205, n. 3

63. ibid., p. 209
64. Richard Mackenzie, 'The United States and the Taliban', in Maley, op. cit., p. 96
65. Nancy Hatch Dupree, 'Afghan Women under the Taliban', in Maley, op. cit., p. 147
66. Dupree, op. cit., p. 150
67. *Guardian*, 14.9.98; *Observer*, 6.9.98
68. Homa Hoodfar, 'Devices and Desires: Population Policy and Gender Roles in the Islamic Republic', in Beinin and Stork, *Political Islam*, pp. 220–33
69. Deniz Kandyoti, 'Women, Islam and the State', in Beinin and Stork, p. 186
70. Michael Gilsenan, *Lords of the Lebanese Marches – Violence and Narrative in an Arab Society* (London, 1996)
71. Burgat and Dowell, p. 106
72. Paul Walker, *Sijistani*, p. 55
73. Anita Weiss in Akbar S. Ahmed and Hastings Donnan (eds), *Islam: Globalization and Post-Modernity* (London, 1994), p. 128
74. P. von Sivers, 'Islam in the Middle East and North Africa', in Esposito (ed.), *Oxford Encyclopedia of the Modern Islamic World*, ii, p. 260
75. William C. Chittick, 'Sufi Thought and Practice', in ibid., iii, pp. 102–9
76. Stewart, *Unfolding Islam*, p. 220–22
77. John King, 'Tablighi Jama'at and the Deobandi Mosques in Britain' in Peter B. Clarke (ed.), *New Trends and Developments in the World of Islam* (London, 1998), pp. 75–92

Suggestions for Further Reading

Quran

'Ali, 'Abdallah Yusuf (tr.), *The Holy Quran* (with commentary) (Leicester, 1979)

Arberry, A. J., *The Koran Interpreted* (Oxford, 1990)

Asad, Muhammad, *The Message of the Qur'ān* (Gibraltar, 1980)

Bell, Richard, *Introduction to the Qur'an* (1953), ed. and rev. W. M. Watt (Edinburgh, 1978)

Burton, John, *The Collection of the Qur'an* (Cambridge, 1977)

Gatje, Helmut, *The Qur'an and Its Exegesis*, tr. and ed. A. T. Welch (Berkeley, 1976)

Izutsu, Tohishiko, *The Structure of Ethical Terms in the Koran* (Tokyo, 1959)
    God and Man in the Koran: Semantics of the Koranic Weltanschauung (Tokyo, 1964)

Wansburgh, John, *Quranic Studies: Sources and Methods of Scriptural Interpretation* (Oxford, 1977)

Welch, A. T., art. 'al-Kuran' in *Encyclopaedia of Islam*, new edn., vol. 5, pp. 401–31, (Leiden, 1981)

Hadith

Abu Dawud, *Sunan Abu Dawud*, tr. A. Hasan, 3 vols. (Lahore, 1984)

Brown, Daniel, W., *Rethinking Tradition in Modern Islamic Thought* (Cambridge, 1996)

Al-Bukhari, *Sahih al-Bukhari*, tr. Muhammad Muhsin Khan, 9 vols (Chicago, 1979/Lahore, 1979)

Goldziher, I., *Muslim Studies*, tr. and ed. S. M. Stern (London, 1971)

Muslim ibn Hajaj, *Sahih Muslim*, tr. A. H. Siddiqi, 4 vols. (Lahore, 1973–5)

Schacht, J., *The Origins of Muhammadan Jurisprudence* (Oxford, 1950)

Muhammad

Armstrong, Karen, *Muhammad: A Western Attempt to Understand Islam* (London, 1991)

Cook, Michael, *Muhammad* (Oxford, 1983)

Guillaume, A. (tr.), *The Life of Muhammad: A Translation of Ibn Ishaq's Sirat Rasul Allah* (Karachi/London, 1955)

Lings, M., *Muhammad: His Life Based on the Earliest Sources* (London/New York, 1983)

Peters, F. E., *Muhammad and the Origins of Islam* (Albany, NY, 1994)

Rodinson, M., *Mohamed* (Harmondsworth, 1971)

Schimmel, Annemarie, *And Muhamad is His Messenger – The Veneration of the Prophet in Islamic Piety* (London/Chapel Hill, 1985)

Watt, W. M., *Muhammad at Mecca* (Oxford, 1953)
    Muhammad at Medina (Oxford, 1956)

Law

Anderson, Norman, *Law Reform in the Muslim World* (London, 1976)

Al-Azmeh, Aziz (ed.), *Islamic Law: Social and Historical Contexts* (London, 1988)

Calder, Norman, *Studies in Early Muslim Jurisprudence* (Oxford, 1993)

Coulson, N. J., *A History of Islamic Law* (Edinburgh, 1964)

Edge, Ian (ed.), *Islamic Law and Legal Theory* (Aldershot, 1996)

Hallaq, Wael B., *A History of Islamic Legal Theories – An Introduction to Sunni Usal al-Fiqh* (Cambridge, 1997)

Mallat, Chibli, *The Renewal of Islamic Law* (Cambridge, 1993)

Al-Qaradawi, Yusuf, *The Lawful and the Prohibited in Islam*, tr. Helbawy *et al.* (Indianapolis, 1985)

Rosen, Lawrence, *The Anthropology of Justice – Law as Culture in Islamic Society* (Cambridge, 1989)

Schacht, Joseph, *An Introduction to Islamic Law* (Oxford, 1964)

History

Cambridge History of Islam, 4 vols. Cambridge, 1970)

Cook, Michael and Crone, Patricia, *Hagarism: The Making of the Islamic World* (Cambridge, 1977)

Crone, Patricia and Hinds, Martin, *God's Caliph. Religious Authority in the First Centuries of Islam* (Cambridge, 1986)

Donner, Fred, *Early Islamic Conquests* (Cambridge, MA, 1982)

Hodgson, Marshall G. S., *The Venture of Islam: Conscience and History in a World Civilization*, 3 vols. (Chicago 1974)

Hourani, Albert, *A History of the Arab Peoples* (London, 1991)

Ibn Khaldun, *The Muqadimmah: An Introduction to History*, tr. F. Rosenthal, 3 vols. (New York, 1958); ed. and abridged by N. Dawood (London, 1978)

Kennedy, Hugh, *The Prophet and the Age of the Caliphates* (London/New York, 1986)

Lapidus, Ira, *A History of the Islamic Peoples* (Cambridge, 1993)

Anthropology

Ahmed, Akbar S., *Millennium and Charisma among the Pathans* (London, 1976)

Coon, Carleton S., *Caravan: The Story of the Middle East*, rev. edn. (New York 1961)

Eickelman, Dale F., *The Middle East: An Anthropological Approach* (Englewood Cliffs, NJ, 1981/1989)

Geertz, Clifford, *Islam Observed* (New Haven, CT, 1968)

Gellner, Ernest, *Muslim Society* (Cambridge, 1983)

Gilsenan, Michael, *Recognizing Islam* (London, 1982)

General and reference

Ahmed, Akbar S., *Living Islam – From Samarkand to Stornoway* (London, 1993)

Clarke, Peter (ed.), *The World's Religions: Islam* (London, 1988)

Denny, Frederick Mathewson, *An Introduction to Islam* (New York, 1985)
    Enclyclopaedia of Islam, new edn., 6 vols. (Leiden, 1961 – incomplete)

Esposito, John (ed.), *The Oxford Encyclopedia of the Modern Islamic World*, 4 vols. (New York/Oxford, 1994)

Gibb, H. A. R. and Kramers, J. H. (eds.), *The Shorter Encyclopedia of Islam* (Leiden, 1961)

Glassé, Cyril, *The Encyclopedia of Islam* (London, 1990)

Hughes, T. P. A., *Dictionary of Islam* (1896 – available in photo reprint)

Rahman, Fazlur, *Islam* (Chicago, 1979)

Rippin, Andrew, *Muslims: Their Relgious Beliefs and Practices.* I: *The Formative Period* (London, 1990), II: *The Contemporary Period* (London, 1993)

Ruthven, Malise, *Islam: A Very Short Introduction* (Oxford, 1997)

Said, Edward, *Orientalism* (London, 1978)

Waines, David, *An Introduction to Islam* (Cambridge, 1995)

Shi'ism and philosophy

Daftary, Farhad, *The Isma'ilis: Their History and Doctrines* (Cambridge, 1990)
    (ed.) *Medieval Isma'ili History and Thought* (Cambridge, 1996)
    A Short History of the Ismailis (Edinburgh, 1998)
Fakhry, Majid, *A History of Islamic Philosophy* (London/New York, 1983)
Halm, Heinz, *Shi'ism* (Edinburgh, 1991)
Nasir, Khusraw, *Knowledge and Liberation: A Treatise on Philosophical Theology*,
    tr. and ed. Faquir M. Hunzai (London, 1998)
Nasr, Seyyed Hossein *et al.*, *Expectation of the Millennium: Shi'ism in History*
    (Albany, NY, 1989)
Momen, Moojan, *An Introduction to Shi'i Islam* (New Haven, 1985)
Netton, I. R., *Allah Transcendent* (London, 1994)
    *Muslim Neoplatonism. An Introduction to the Thought of the Brethren of
    Purity* (London, 1982)
Richard, Yann, *Shi'ite Islam*, tr. Antonia Nevill (Oxford, 1995)
Walker, Paul E., *Abu Ya'qub al-Sijistani: Intellectual Missionary* (London, 1996)

Sufism

Arberry, A. J. (tr.), *The Doctrine of the Sufis* (Cambridge, 1935/1977)
Attar, Farid ud-Din, *The Conference of Birds*, tr. Afkham Darbandi and Dick
    Davis (London, 1984)
Baldick, Julian, *Mystical Islam: An Introduction to Sufism* (London, 1989)
Chodkiewicz, Michel, *Seal of the Saints: Prophethood and Sainthood in the
    Doctrine of Ibn 'Arabi* (Cambridge, 1993)
Evans-Pritchard, E. E., *The Sanusi of Cyrenaica* (Oxford, 1949)
Gilsenan, Michael, *Saint and Sufi in Modern Egypt* (Oxford, 1972)
Keddie, N. R. (ed.), *Scholars, Saints and Sufis: Muslim Religious Institutions
    Since 1500* (Berkeley, 1972)
Massignon, L., *The Passion of al-Hallaj* (Princeton, 1982)
Ridgeon, Lloyd, *'Aziz Nasafi* (London, 1998)
Rumi, Jalal al Din, *Mathnawi*, tr. R. A. Nicholson, 6 vols. (1929–37)
Schuon, Frithjof, *Understanding Islam*, tr. D. M. Matheson (London, 1976)
Trimingham, J. S., *The Sufi Orders in Islam* (Oxford, 1971)

Reform, modern Islamic politics and contemporary Islam

Ahmed, Akbar and Donnan, Hastings (eds.), *Islam, Globalization and
    Postmodernity* (London, 1994)
Al-Azmeh, 'Aziz, *Islams and Modernities* (London, 1993)

Beinin, Joel and Stork, Joe (eds.), *Political Islam: Essays from Middle East Report* (London, 1997)

Binder, Leonard, *Islamic Liberalism: A Critique of Development Ideologies* (Chicago, 1988)

Burgat, François and Dowell, William, *The Islamic Movement in North Africa* (Austin, 1993)

Choueiri, Youssef M., *Islamic Fundamentalism* (Boston, 1990)

Clarke, Peter (ed.), *New Trends and Developments in the World of Islam* (London, 1998)

Cooper, John *et al.* (eds), *Islam and Modernity: Muslim Intellectuals Respond* (London, 1998)

Eickelman, Dale F., and Piscatori, James, *Muslim Politics* (Princeton, 1996)

Enayat, Hamid, *Modern Islamic Political Thought* (London, 1982)

Esposito, John L. (ed.) *Voices of Resurgent Islam* (Oxford, 1983)
    The Islamic Threat: Myth or Reality? (London, 1994)

Gellner, Ernest, *Postmodernism, Reason and Religion* (London, 1992)

Hourani, Albert, *Arabic Thought in the Liberal Age* (Oxford, 1969)

Hussein, Mir Zohair, *Global Islamic Politics* (London/New York, 1995)

Kepel, Gilles, *The Prophet and Pharaoh: Muslim Extremism in Egypt*, tr. Jon Rothschild (London, 1985)

Mayer, Ann Elizabeth, *Islam and Human Rights: Tradition and Politics* (Boulder, 1991)

Mitchell, Richard, *The Society of Muslim Brothers* (London, 1969)

Mortimer, Edward, *Faith and Power: The Politics of Islam* (London, 1982)

Rahnema, Ali, *Pioneers of Islamic Revival* (London/Atlantic Highlands, NJ, 1994)

Roy, Olivier, *The Failure of Political Islam* (London, 1994)

Sivan, Emmanuel, *Radical Islam: Medieval Theology and Modern Politics* (New Haven, 1985)

Zubaida, Sami, *Islam, the People and the State: Essays on Political Ideas and Movements in the Middle East* (London, 1993)

Sexuality and Gender

Ahmed, Leila, *Women and Gender in Islam: Historical Roots of a Modern Debate* (New Haven, 1992)

Beck, Lois and Keddie, Nikki R. (eds.), *Women in the Muslim World* (Cambridge, MA, 1978)

Bouhdiba, Abdalwahab, *Sexuality in Islam*, tr. Alan Sheridan (London, 1985)

Haeri, Shahla, *Law of Desire: Temporary Marriage in Shīʿi Iran* (Syracuse, NY, 1989)

Kandiyoti, Deniz (ed.), *Women, Islam and the State* (Philadelphia, 1991)

   Beyond the Veil: Male–Female Dynamics in Modern Muslim Society
(London, 1985)

Mernissi, Fatima, *Women and Islam: An Historical and Theological Enquiry*, tr.
Mary Jo Lakeland (Oxford, 1991)

Zuhur, Sherifa, *Revealing Reveiling: Islamist Gender Ideology in Contemporary
Egypt* (Albany, NY, 1992)

Glossary

'ABD: 'Servant' or 'slave'; commonly used as a name when coupled with one of the names of Allah. See also *'Ibada*.

AHL AL-BAIT: 'People of the household', specifically used of the Prophet's household.

AHL AL-HADITH: 'People of the tradition', or traditionalists, for whom the Prophet's example was supreme, even as against Quranic injunction. See also *Hadith*.

AHL AL-KALAM: 'People of debate'; rationalists who upheld the supremacy of the Quran rather than that of the *hadith*.

AHL AL-KITAB: 'People of the book'; originally referred to Muslims, Jews and Christians but came to include Zoroastrians and other groups possessing sacred texts.

AHL AL-SUNNA: 'People of the Sunna' (Sunnis); those who uphold customs based on the practice and authority of the Prophet and his companions, as distinct from the Shi'ites and Kharijis. See also *Sunna*.

AL: Clan or 'House', as in Al 'Imran (3rd Sura of Quran), Al Sa'ud, etc. Not to be confused with *al*, the definite article.

'ALAWI: Member of extremist (*ghulu*) Nusairi sect in N.W. Syria which venerates 'Ali.

'ALID: Descendant of 'Ali, cousin and son-in-law of the Prophet.

'ALIM: See *'Ulama*.

AMIR: 'Commander'; originally military commander but subsequently applied to rulers and members of their families. *Amir al-Muimin* ('Commander of the Faithful'): a title held by caliphs and some sultans.

ANSAR: 'Helpers' of Muhammad native to Madina, as distinct from the Muhajirun who accompanied him from Makka.

'ASABIYA: 'Tribal or group solidarity'; a term used by philosopher Ibn Khaldun in his theory on state formation in North Africa.

'ASHURA: The 'tenth' of the month Muharram, when Shi'ite rituals are held commemorating the death of the Prophet's grandson Husain.

AYA: 'Sign' or 'miracle'; used for verses of the Quran.

BAB: 'Gate'; term applied to representatives of the Shi'ites' Hidden Imams.

BARAKA: 'Sanctity' or 'blessing' vested in and available from holy people, places or objects.

BAST: Twelver Shi'ite institution of sanctuary in mosques and other holy places.

BATIN: 'Inner', 'esoteric' or 'hidden' meaning of a religious text, especially the Quran.

BAY'A: 'Contract' or oath of allegiance binding members of an Islamic sect or Sufi *tariqa* to their spiritual guide.

BID'A: 'Innovation', as distinct from custom and law legitimized by the Shari'a.

CHADOR (Pers.): Traditional Iranian garment covering women from head to foot. See also *Hijab*.

DA'I: 'Propagandist' or missionary, especially in Shi'ite Isma'ili movements. See also *Da'wa*.

DAR AL-HARB: The 'realm of war' or those lands not under Muslim rule, where, under certain circumstances, a war or *jihad* can be sanctioned against unbelievers.

DAR AL-ISLAM: 'Realm of Islam'; originally those lands under Muslim rule, later applying to lands where Muslim institutions were established.

DA'WA: 'Propaganda' or mission.

DERVISH (Pers.): 'Mendicant'; member of a Sufi *tariqa*.

DHIKR: 'Mentioning' or 'remembering'; specifically used for Sufi rituals designed to increase consciousness of God which include the repetition of his name(s).

DHIMMI: Non-Muslim peoples afforded security of life and property (*dhimma*) under the Shari'a on payment of a poll tax (*jizya*).

DIN: 'Religion', 'belief', as opposed to *dunya*, 'worldly existence'.

FALLAH (pl. *fallahin*): Peasant farmer.

FANA: The 'extinction' of individual consciousness, and thus union with God, in Sufism.

FAQIH: Exponent of *fiqh*.

FAQIR: 'Pauper'; term applied to ordinary member of Sufi *tariqa*.

FATWA: Legal decision of a *mufti*.

FEDAYEEN (sing. *fidai*): Soldiers prepared to sacrifice their lives in the cause of Islam. Now used for guerrilla fighters.

FIQH: 'Understanding' (of Shari'a); the system of jurisprudence based on the *usul al-fiqh*.

FITNA: 'Temptation' or 'trial'; the name given to the civil wars which broke out within the expanding Muslim empire during the first 200 years after Muhammad's death.

FUTUWA: Young men's clubs, sometimes similar to guilds.

GHAIB: 'Unseen' and 'transcendent'; hence *al-ghaiba*, the 'occultation' of the Hidden Imams in Shi'ite doctrine.

GHULU: 'Exaggeration'; the over-emphasis of one aspect of doctrine to the point where the whole edifice of the Sunna is undermined. Hence, *ghulas* or extremists.

HADD (pl. *hudud*): 'Boundaries'; divine statutes and punishments contained within the body of the Shari'a.

HADITH (pl. *ahadith*): 'Tradition' or report of a saying or action of the Prophet. One of four roots of Islamic law. See also *Shari'a*, *Usul al-fiqh*.

HADRA: 'Presence' [of God]; Sufi ceremony.

HAJJ: The annual pilgrimage to Makka. One of the five duties (*rukns*) of Islam, required of every believer once in his life if possible.

HALAL: That which is 'permissible', particularly foods which comply with Islamic dietary rules.

HANAFI: Referring to the Sunni legal *madhhab* ascribed to Abu Hanifa.

HANBALI: Referring to the Sunni legal *madhhab* ascribed to Ahmad ibn Hanbal.

HANIF: 'True believer'; a term used to describe those Arabs who were monotheists before the revelation of the Quran.

HARAM: A sanctuary; 'that which is forbidden' by the Shari'a.

HIJAB: 'Screen'; veil traditionally worn by Muslim women in public; always covers the head, but not necessarily the face and hands.

HIJRA: 'Emigration' of Muhammad from Makka to Madina in 622 CE, the base year of the Muslim calendar.

HIYAL (sing. *hila*): 'Artifices' or 'tricks'; legal methods to circumvent general prohibitions.

'IBADA: Religious worship.

'ID AL-ADHA: 'The festival of the sacrifice' on the last day of the Hajj.

'ID AL-FITR: 'The festival of breaking the fast' at the end of Ramadan.

'IDDA: Legally prescribed 'period' during which a woman may not remarry after having been widowed or divorced.

IHRAM: 'State of ritual consecration' during Hajj, when pilgrims wear white garments. See also *Haram*.

I'JAZ: An elliptical quality of beduin speech.

IJMA': Consensus of the Muslim community or scholars as a basis for a legal decision. Shi'ites interpret it as a consensus of Imams.

IJTIHAD: Individual judgement to establish a legal ruling by creative interpretation of the existing body of law. See also *Mujtahid*.

IKHWAN: The 'Brothers', soldiers of 'Abd al-Aziz, founder of the Saudi dynasty, and adherents of the Hanbali reformer 'Abd al-Wahhab.

IKHWAN AL-MUSLIMIN: Muslim Brotherhood, a society founded in 1928 by Hasan al-Banna; originally aimed at re-establishing a Muslim polity in Egypt.

IKHWAN AL-SAFA: 'Brothers of Purity', a group of Isma'ili-influenced thinkers based in Basra in the tenth century.

'ILM: 'Knowledge'; in particular religious knowledge of *'ulama*.

IMAM: 'One who stands in front' to lead the *salat*, hence the leader of the Muslim community. In Shi'ite tradition, 'Ali and those of his descendants considered to be the spiritual successors of Muhammad.

IMAN: 'Faith' or religious conviction.

INFITAH: The 'opening up' of the Egyptian economy to the West in 1972, in the hope of attracting foreign capital.

INSAN: 'Human being', from the root meaning 'to be companionable, agreeable or genial'.

ISLAM: 'Self-surrender' or 'submission'; reconciliation to the will of God as revealed to Muhammad. See also *Muslim.*

ISNAD: 'Support'; chain of authorities transmitting a *hadith,* thus guaranteeing its validity.

JA'FARI: Referring to the sole Shi'ite *madhhab* ascribed to the Imam Ja'far al-Sadiq.

JAHL: 'Ignorance', hence *jahiliya,* 'period of ignorance', or pre-Islamic times.

JIHAD: War against unbelievers in accordance with Shari'a. Also applied to an individual's struggle against baser impulses.

JIZYA: Poll tax levied on *dhimmis* in a Muslim-ruled society.

KA'BA: Cubic building in Makka containing the Black Stone, believed by Muslims to be a fragment of the original temple of Abraham. Focus of prayer (*salat*) and the Hajj. See also *Qibla.*

KAFIR: 'Disbeliever', or infidel who has rejected the message of the Quran.

KAHIN: Traditional shamanistic soothsayer in Arabia at the time of Muhammad.

KALAM: 'Debate' on matters of Muslim theology and cosmology. See also *Ahl al-kalam.*

KATIB: 'Writer', specifically secretary in government office.

KHALIFA: Caliph, the 'deputy' of God on earth. In the Quran applied to Adam, and hence to all humanity in relation to the rest of creation; specifically applied to the early successors of the Prophet as leaders of the Islamic state or *khilafa,* and to the successors of founders of Islamic states or Sufi *tariqas.*

KHANQA (Pers.): Sufi hospice, mainly in areas of Persian influence.

KHARIJIS (Arabic pl. 'Khawarij'): 'Those who go out'; members of a group of puritanical Muslim sects during Umayyad and early 'Abbasid times.

KHUL': 'Renunciation', or divorce initiated by the wife, according to the Shari'a.

KHUMS: 'Fifth'; a tax of one fifth of all trading profits, payable to *mujtahids* in Shi'ite areas.

KISWA: Black 'clothing' or covering of the Ka'ba, renewed annually.

KITAB: 'The book', or religious scriptures. *Umm al-kitab* ('Mother of scripture'): divine *ur*-text of which the Quran is part.

KUFR: 'Disbelief', an ungrateful rejection of Islam. See also *Kafir.*

KUTTAB: School at which the Quran is taught.

MADHHAB: 'Adopted policy'; specifically applied to five recognized systems of *fiqh* (jurisprudence).

MADRASA: 'College', especially for religious studies.

MAGHRIB: 'Sunset', hence the prayer or *salat* at sunset; also Muslim 'occident', i.e., NW Africa, Morocco, for which the French transliteration 'Maghreb' is commonly used.

MAHDI: 'Awaited One'; a Messiah and reformist leader who aims to restore the original purity of the Islamic faith and polity. In Shi'ite tradition the Twelfth Imam.

MAHR: Dowry given to a woman on marriage and retained by her if she is divorced by her husband.

MAKRUH: Acts designated as 'distasteful' or 'undesirable' under Islamic law; there is merit in abstaining from them, but no sin in committing them.

MALIKI: Referring to the Sunni legal *madhhab* ascribed to Malik ibn Anas.

MA'RUF: 'Known'; term used in the Quran for familiar and approved custom; hence, generally, 'the good'.

MASHRIQ: 'Sunrise'; Levant.

MASLAHA: That which is 'beneficial'; term used for the principle of public interest in the Maliki *madhhab*, adopted by modern legal reformers.

MAULID: 'Birthday'; festival celebrating the anniversary of a religious figure.

MAWALI (sing. *Mawla*): 'Associates' or 'clients'; status at first given to non-Arab converts to Islam.

MILLET: Non-Muslim religious community within the *dar al-Islam*.

MUBAH: Acts 'allowed' under Islamic law, commission or omission of which are not sins.

MUFTI: Expert on the Shari'a qualified to give rulings (*fatwas*) upon questions of law.

MUHAJIRIN: Those who emigrated from Makka to Madina with Muhammad. See also *Hijra*.

MUJAHID (pl. *Mujahidun*): Soldier fighting a holy war or *jihad*.

MUJTAHID: Religious scholars sanctioned to make individual interpretations to determine points of law, especially among Shi'a.

MULK: 'Dominion' or existing Muslim state as distinct from the ideal Islamic state (*khilafa*).

MUNKAR: 'Unknown'; term used in Quran for wrongful action as distinct from *ma'ruf*: hence evil generally.

MUQRI: 'Reciter' of the Quran.

MURID: 'Aspirant', or follower of a Sufi master.

MURSHID: Sufi master.

MUSLIM: One who has submitted to God; a follower of the religion revealed to and established by Muhammad. See also *Islam*.

MUSTAZAFIN: The wretched, *les misérables*; impoverished inhabitants of Iranian shanty towns.

MUT'A: Shi'ite legal institution of temporary marriage contract.

MU'TAWWIF: Guide caring for pilgrims in Makka. See also *Tawaf*.

MU'TAZILIS: 'Those who stand aloof'; theologians belonging to the rationalist school which introduced speculative dogmatism into Islam.

MUWAHHID (pl. *Muwahhidin*): 'Unitarian'; one who believes in God's unity (*tawhid*). Term used by Wahhabis and Druzes (among others) to describe their beliefs.

NASS: Designation of a successor, in particular a spiritual successor in the Shi'ite tradition.

PIR (Pers.): Sufi master.

QADI: Judge administering Shari'a.

QARI: 'Reciter', particularly of the Quran.

QIBLA: Direction of the Ka'ba to which Muslims turn while praying, hence the recess in a mosque which shows it.

QIYAS: 'Analogy'; the principle in jurisprudence used to deal with new situations not mentioned in the Quran or Sunna.

QURAN (Koran): 'Discourse' or 'recitation', the immutable body of revelations received by Muhammad.

RA'I: 'Opinion' or personal judgement of *faqihs* in interpreting Quranic rules.

RIBA: 'Usury', as prohibited in the Quran.

RIBAT: Sufi hospice.

RIDA: 'Satisfaction'; stage through which a Sufi progresses in his search for God.

RISALA (pl. *rasail*): 'Report' or 'epistle'.

ROUZEH (Pers.): Recital of the martyrdom of Husain, the Prophet's grandson, performed at religious gatherings in Iran. *Rouzeh-khan*: professional narrator.

RUKN (pl. *arkan*): 'Pillar'; one of the five religious duties prescribed for Muslims: Hajj, *salat*, *sawm*, *shahada* and *zakat*.

SADAQA: Voluntary contribution of alms.

SALAF: 'Predecessors'; appellation of the first generation of Muslims. *Salafi*: term describing the twentieth-century reform movement inspired by them.

SALAT: Ritual worship performed five times daily, one of the 'five pillars' (*rukns*) of Islam.

SAWM: Annual fast and daylight abstinence during the month of Ramadan, one of the *rukns* of Islam.

SAYYID: Descendant of 'Ali's son Husain. *Sidi* (local usage in the Maghreb) is applied to members of saintly lineages.

SHAHADA: Profession of faith whereby a Muslim declares his acceptance of God and his Prophet; one of the *rukns* of Islam.

SHAIKH: 'Elder'; head of a tribe or Sufi master.

SHARI'A: 'The path to a water-hole'; a name given to the sacred law of Islam which governs all aspects of a Muslim's life. It is elaborated through the discipline of *fiqh*.

SHATH: 'Roaming' or 'straying', whereby a mystic addresses his audience as though he were God.

SHI'A: 'Party' of 'Ali, comprising those groups of Muslims who uphold the rights of 'Ali and his descendants to leadership of the Umma.

SHIRK: 'Association' of partners to the divinity; idolatry.

SILSILA: 'Chain' of inherited sanctity (*baraka*) or kinship connecting the leaders of Sufi orders to their founders.

SUFI: Follower of Sufism (Arabic *tasawwuf*), the Islamic mystic path, from *suf* ('wool') garments worn by early adepts.

SUNNA: Custom sanctioned by tradition, particularly that of the Prophet enshrined in *hadith*.

SUNNI: See *Ahl al-Sunna*.

SURA: Chapter of the Quran.

SULTAN: 'Authority' or 'power'; actual holder of power, as distinct from the *khalifa*; later common term for sovereign.

TAFSIR: 'Commentary' on the Quran.

TAHLIL: Prayer – *la ilaha illa allah*, 'there is no deity but God' – particularly used in Sufi rituals.

TA'IFA: Organization of a Sufi order, as distinct from its spiritual path.

TALAQ: Declaration of divorce by the husband according to the Shari'a.

TANZIMAT: Administrative decrees; reforms instituted by the nineteenth-century Ottoman sultans.

TAQIYA: Dissimulation of one's beliefs in the face of danger, especially among Shi'ites.

TAQLID: 'Imitation', or the basing of legal decisions on the existing judgements of the four Sunni *madhhabs*.

TARIQA: 'Path' of mystical and spiritual guidance; a term which also came to be applied to the organization through which a *tariqa* extends itself in Muslim society.

TASAWWUF: See *Sufi*.

TAWAF: Ritual circumambulation of the Ka'ba by a pilgrim during the Hajj or 'Umra.

TAWHID: 'Unity' of God. Central theological concept of Islam.

TAWIL: Esoteric or allegorical interpretation of the Quran, predominant among Shi'ites.

TA'ZIYA: Shi'ite passion plays depicting the death of Husain.

TEKKES (Turk.): Sufi centres in Turkish-speaking areas.

'ULAMA (sing. *'alim*): 'Learned men', in particular the guardians of legal and religious traditions.

UMMA: Community of believers, in particular the community of all Muslims.

'UMRA: Lesser pilgrimage to Makka which can be performed at any time of the year.

USUL AL-FIQH: 'Roots' or foundations of jurisprudence. In the Sunni *madhhabs* they comprise: the Quran, the Sunna, *ijma'* (consensus) and *qiyas* (analogical deduction). See also *Fiqh*.

WAHY: 'Inspiration' or 'revelation' of the Quran.

WALI: 'One who is near God'; a saint in popular Sufism.

WAQF (pl. *awqaf*): Pious endowment of income originally for a charitable purpose; sometimes used as a means of circumventing the Shari'a's inheritance laws.

WATAN: 'Homeland' or 'nation', a concept borrowed from Western nationalism.

WAZIR: Administrator or bureaucrat appointed by the ruler.

WIRD: Private prayer in addition to the *salat*.

ZAHIR: 'Manifest' aspects of God, as distinct from the hidden or *batin*; hence literal or exoteric meaning of Quran or *hadith*.

ZAKAT: 'Purity'; term used for a tax of fixed proportion of income and capital (normally 2½ per cent) payable annually for charitable purposes; one of the *rukns* of Islam.

ZAR: Exorcism ceremonies.

ZAWIYA: 'Corner'; building for Sufi activities.

ZINA: Sexual relations outside marriage, including both adultery and fornication, prohibited in the Quran.

Genealogical Tables

The family of the Prophet

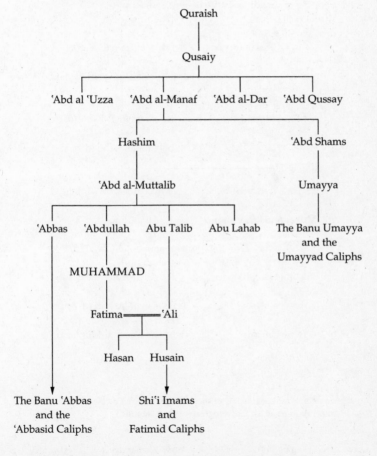

The Shiʻi Imams

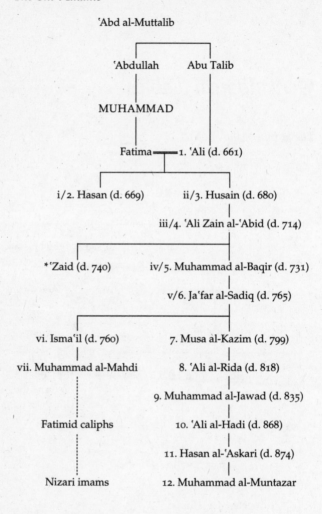

'Abd al-Muttalib

'Abdullah   Abu Talib

MUHAMMAD

Fatima —— 1. 'Ali (d. 661)

i/2. Hasan (d. 669)   ii/3. Husain (d. 680)

iii/4. 'Ali Zain al-'Abid (d. 714)

*'Zaid (d. 740)   iv/5. Muhammad al-Baqir (d. 731)

v/6. Ja'far al-Sadiq (d. 765)

vi. Isma'il (d. 760)   7. Musa al-Kazim (d. 799)

vii. Muhammad al-Mahdi   8. 'Ali al-Rida (d. 818)

9. Muhammad al-Jawad (d. 835)

Fatimid caliphs   10. 'Ali al-Hadi (d. 868)

11. Hasan al-'Askari (d. 874)

Nizari imams   12. Muhammad al-Muntazar

Arabic numerals indicate the line of succession recognized by the 'Twelver' Shiʻis
Roman numerals indicate the line recognized by the Ismaʻilis

* recognized as *imam* by the Zaidis

Source: Albert Hourani, *A History of the Arab Peoples* (Cambridge, MA., 1991), p. 486
Adapted from J. L. Bacharach, *A Middle East Studies Handbook* (Seattle, 1984), p. 21

A Chronology

c. 570–622 Muhammad in Makka

622–32 Muhammad in Madina

632–4 Caliphate of Abu Bakr. Muslims triumph in wars of apostasy. Arabia unified

634–44 Caliphate of 'Umar. Most of Fertile Crescent, Egypt and much of Iran conquered. Expansion into North Africa

644–56 Caliphate of 'Uthman. Conquests continue northward, eastward and westward
Text of the Quran collected and standardized

660, 668, 717 Arabs fail to capture Constantinople

656–61 First *fitna* or civil war during caliphate of 'Ali

661 Murder of 'Ali. Establishment of Umayyad caliphate by Mu'awiya in Damascus

680 Second *fitna*. Mu'awiya's succession by his son Yazid provokes rebellion by Husain b. 'Ali. 'Martyrdom' of Husain and followers at Karbala

685–705 Reign of 'Abdul Malik, builder of Dome of the Rock in Jerusalem

687–91 Kharijis prevail in much of Arabia

692 'Rebel' caliph Ibn al-Zubayr, though widely recognized, defeated and killed by Umayyad force at Makka

711 Arabs advance into Spain

712–13 Arabs conquer Transoxania (Bukhara and Samarkand)

728 Death of Hasan al-Basri, early Sufi master

732 Battle of Poitiers: Charles Martel checks Arab advance into France

744–50 Third *fitna*. Weakened by internal dissent, Umayyad dynasty overthrown by 'Abbasids (749)

756 Umayyad rule established in Spain

765 Death of Ja'far al-Sadiq, sixth Imam of the Shi'a. Movement divided between Isma'ilis, Ithna'asharis ('Twelvers') and Zaidis

767 Death of Abu Hanifa (b. 699), founder of the Hanafi legal school

795 Death of Malik b. Anas (b. 713), founder of the Maliki school

786–809 Reign of Haroun al-Rashid, model caliph of Islam's 'golden age'

801 Death of Rabi'a of Basra, mystic and poet

813–33 Caliphate of al-Mamun. Ascendancy of Mu'tazili ('rationalist') school of theologians

820   Death of al-Shafi'i (b. 767), founder of the Shafi'i school

847–61 Caliphate of al-Mutawakkil, who reverses pro-Mu'tazili policy

861–945 Breakup of 'Abbasid empire as provinces become independent till caliphal government loses territorial power completely

855   Death of Ahmad Ibn Hanbal (b. 780), founder of Hanbali school

870   Death of al-Bukhari (b. 810), hadith collector

873   Death of Muslim (b. hadith collector. 'Disappearance' of 12th Imam of the Shi'a, Muhammad al-Muntazar (the 'Awaited One')

874   Death of Abu Yazid al-Bistami, first of the 'drunken' Sufis

873–940 Lesser ghayba or Absence during which Imam of the Twelver Shi'a is represented by Four wakils (deputies)

909   Creation of first Isma'ili Fatimid state in Ifriqiya (present-day Tunisia)

922   Execution of al-Hallaj for heresy, a martyr for later Sufis

929–61 Umayyad ruler 'Abdul Rahman III establishes Umayyad caliphate at Cordoba (Spain)

935   Death of al-Ash'ari, theologian who reconciles dogmas of the ahl al-hadith with philosophical methods of the Mu'tazila

940   Beginning of the Greater ghayba (absence or occultation) when Twelvers lose contact with their Imam

945   Shi'i Buyids take Baghdad, making caliph a virtual prisoner

969–1171 Fatimid (Isma'ili) caliphate in Egypt

998–1030 Mahmud of Ghazna (in present-day Afghanistan) invades Northern India

1037–1220 Seljuk Turks, starting in Central Iran and moving westwards, restore Sunni orthodoxy in the heartlands

1071   Seljuks defeat Byzantines at Battle of Manzikert, opening Anatolia to Turkish settlement

1056–1147 Almoravid dynasty, originating in sub-Saharan Africa, halts a Christian advance in Spain

1090–1118 Nizari Isma'ili uprisings against Sunni caliphate

1091   Seljuks make Baghdad their capital

1096–1291 Crusaders hold parts of Syria and Palestine

1099   Crusaders take Jerusalem

1111   Death of al-Ghazali (b. 1058), Sunni mystic and jurist

1130   Death of Ibn Tumart, founder of Almohad dynasty in Spain

1187   Saladin (Salah al-Din al-Ayyubi) expels Crusaders from Jerusalem

1198   Death of Ibn Rushd (Averroes), philosopher (b. 1126)

1205–87 Rise of Delhi Sultanate in India

1220–31 Mongol raids in Transoxania and Eastern Iran cause massive destruction of cities

1225   Almohads abandon Spain. Muslim presence reduced to small kingdom of Granada (1232–1592)

1227   Death of Chingiz Khan

1240   Death of Ibn 'Arabi (b. 1165), Sufi theosopher

1256 Fall of Alamut, last Isma'ili stronghold south of Caspian

1258 Destruction of Baghdad by Mongols

1260 Mamluks (military slaves) who succeed the Ayyubids in Egypt defeat the hitherto invincible Mongols at the Battle of 'Ayn Jalut in Syria

c. 1300 Emergence of Ottoman (Osmanli) dynasty in Bithynia on the Byzantine frontier in Western Anatolia

1326 Ottomans capture Bursa, their first real capital

1362 Ottomans capture Adrianople (Edirne) in Balkans

c. 1378 Emergence of Timur Lang ('Tamerlane') a Turk who rose in the Mongol service in Transoxania to conquer much of Central and Western Asia

1389 Ottomans defeat Serbs, assisted by Albanians, Bulgarians, Bosnians and Hungarians, at Kosovo in central Serbia

1405 Death of Timur

1406 Death of Ibn Khaldun (b. 1326) philosopher and 'father of sociology'

1453 Mehmed 'The Conqueror' (1451–81) captures Constantinople and subdues Byzantine empire

1498 Vasco da Gama rounds Cape of Good Hope, ending Muslim monopoly of Indian Ocean trade

1501 Rise of Safavid power in Iran. Twelver Shi'ism becomes the state religion

1517 Ottomans conquer Egypt and Syria

1520 Ottomans conquer Rhodes

1526 Battle of Panipat (India) enables Babur, a Timurid prince to become founder of the Mughal Empire; Battle of Mohacs makes Catholic Hungarians tributaries of Ottomans

1529 Ottomans besiege Vienna

1552 Kazan Khanate annexed by Moscow

1556–1605 Reign of Akbar, third Mughal emperor, who fosters Hindu–Muslim cultural and religious rapprochement

1625 Death of Ahmed Sirhindi, anti-Akbarist reformer

1658–1707 Aurangzeb, last of the major Mughal emperors, reverses Akbar's universalist policies

1682–99 Ottomans lose Hungary and Belgrade in war with Austria and Poland.

1718 Peace of Passarowitz consolidates Ottoman losses to Habsburgs

1739 Delhi sacked by Iranian monarch Nadir Shah, ending effective Mughal power

1757 Wahhabis take al-Hasa in Eastern Arabia. British victory at Plassey opens India to British expansion

1762 Death of Shah Wali Allah, Sufi reformer in Sirhindi tradition

1774 Treaty of Kuchuk Kaynarji. Following defeat by Russia, Ottomans lose Crimea. Tsar recognized as protector of Orthodox Christians in Ottoman lands

1779 Qajar dynasty established in Iran

1789–1807 First Westernizing Ottoman reforms under Selim III

1798   Bonaparte lands in Egypt, defeats the Mamluks at the Battle of the
       Pyramids, generates interest in European culture

1805–48   Muhammad 'Ali begins process of modernization in Egypt. 1820
       begins conquest of Sudan

1806   Wahhabis sack Shi'ite shrines of Najaf and Karbala

1815–17   Serbian revolt against Ottomans

1818   Britain becomes paramount power in India

1821–30   Greek War of Independence

1830   French occupation of Algeria begins. Khartoum founded as British–
       Egyptian outpost on Upper Nile

1832–48   European powers save Ottoman sultan from invasion by Egyptian
       Viceroy, Muhammad (Mehmed) 'Ali

c. 1839–61   Sultan Abdul Majid initiates Tanzimat reforms

1857   Failure of Indian 'Mutiny' leads to abolition of the East India Company,
       opening way for incorporation of India into British Empire

1859   Defeat of Imam Shamil in Caucasus followed by Russian annexation of
       Chechnya and Daghestan

1867   Foundation of the academy of Deoband in Northern India by a group
       of the reformers, who eschew all contact with the British-run *kafir* state

1868   Russian annexation of Kazakhstan completed. Amirate of Bukhara
       becomes Russian protectorate

1869   Opening of Suez Canal

1875   Collapse of Egytian finances. Suez Canal sold to British

1876   First Ottoman constitution promulgated after palace revolution

1876–1909   Sultan Abdul Hamid suspends constitution, enacting major
       reforms in education, transportation and communications through
       dictatorial rule

1881   French protectorate in Tunisia

1882   Occupation of Egypt after 'Urabi revolt, partly inspired by al-Afghani.
       Sir Evelyn Baring (later Lord Cromer) effective power behind the throne

1885   General 'Chinese' Gordon killed in Khartoum during Mahdist revolt
       against British-backed Egyptian rule

1889   Return of Muhammad 'Abduh, al-Afghani's disciple to Egypt; decides
       to collaborate with the British
       Military students in Istanbul found first 'Young Turk' revolutionary
       organization, Society of Union and Progress

1897   Death of Sayyid Jamal al-Din al-Afghani (b. 1838), pan-Islamic reformer
       and activist

1898   Defeat of the Mahdist movement under an Anglo-Egyptian force under
       General Kitchener at the Battle of Omdurman
       Death of Sir Sayyid Ahmed Khan (b. 1817), Islamic modernist reformer
       and founder of Aligarh College (1875)

1905   Death of Muhammad 'Abduh (b. 1849), founder of the modern *salafiyya*
       reform movement

1906   Muslim League founded in India

1906–8   Constitutional Revolution in Iran

1908   Young Turk revolution forces Sultan to restore constitution and reconvene parliament

1909   Separate Muslim and Hindu provincial electorates in India

1911–13   Italy takes Tripoli from Ottomans

1912   French protectorate in Morocco

1914–18   Defeat of Ottoman Empire in First World War. Egypt formally declared British Protectorate

1916–18   British-backed Arab revolt against Turkish rule under leadership of Sharif Husain of Makka, his son Faisal and T. E. Lawrence

1917   Balfour Declaration opens the way for increased European Jewish settlement in Palestine

1917–20   Russian Revolution and civil war leads to Soviet–Muslim conflicts in Central Asia. Muslims of Kazakhstan, Azerbaijan and the Caucasus struggle for regional independence. Overthrow of Autonomous Republic of Turkestan by Russian forces (1918) precipitates Basmachi revolt. Bukhara and Khiva absorbed into Soviet state. Some leading Muslim *'jadidists'* (renovators) join the Communist Party

1919   San Remo Conference. League of Nations Mandates awarded to Britain in former Ottoman territories of Palestine, Transjordan and Iraq and to France in Syria and Lebanon
Faisal b. Husain expelled by French from Damascus and established on throne of Iraq. His younger brother 'Abdullah established on throne of Transjordan
Egyptian leader Sa'ad Zaghloul leads delegation (*wafd*) demanding independence for Egypt. His deportation sparks nationalist 'revolution'

1919–22   Turkish War of Independence: Mustafa Kemal (Ataturk) rallies nationalist forces to defeat Greek invaders and resist European dismemberment of Anatolia

1922   Ottoman Sultanate abolished. Egypt granted formal independence, but British retain control over defence, foreign policy, Sudan and the Suez Canal

1923   Treaty of Lausanne ensures Turkey's territorial integrity

1924   Soviet Central Asia reorganized under socialist republics of Uzbekistan, Turkmenistan, Kazakhstan and Kirgizia
Ottoman Caliphate abolished. Turkish Sharï'a courts replaced by civil courts
Khilafat movement in India blames British for abolition. Ibn Saud conquers Hijaz, expelling the Sherif Husain and establishing neo-Wahhabi kingdom

1926   Lebanon enlarged and detached from Syria under French auspices

1928   Hasan al-Banna, Egyptian schoolteacher, founds the Muslim Brotherhood

1932   Iraq granted independence and admitted to League of Nations

1935   Death of Rashid Rida (b. 1865), Islamic reformer and leader of the *salafiyya* movement

1936   Palestinian revolt against British rule in Palestine and the increase in Jewish immigration provoked by Nazi rule in Germany. Muhammad'Ali Jinnah assumes leadership of Muslim League, ending Muslim backing for Congress

New Soviet Constitution organizes Muslim Central Asia into six Union Soviet Socialist Republics (Uzbekistan, Azerbaijan, Kazakhstan, Turkmenistan, Tajikistan and Kirgizia) and eight Autonomous Soviet Socialist Republics including Tataristan, Bashkiria, Daghestan and other Caucasian units under communist control

1938   Death of Muhammad Iqbal, poet, philosopher and progenitor of Pakistan

1940–7   Muslim League adopts idea of separate Muslim state for Indian Muslims

1941   British suppress pro-Axis revolt by Iraqi army officers

1942   British force Egyptian King Farouk to replace pro-Axis prime minister with one more amenable to the Allied cause

1943   Beginning of Zionist terror campaign against British in Palestine

1945   Arab League founded under Egyptian General Secretariat

1946   Transjordan, Lebanon and Syria recognized as independent. Widespread Hindu–Muslim rioting in India

1947   Indian independence. Creation of Pakistan out of Muslim majority areas, excepting Kashmir

1948   British end mandate in Palestine. Arab armies routed following proclamation of Israel. Palestinian exodus creates massive refugee problem. Amir 'Abdullah of Transjordan annexes East Jerusalem (including the Old City) along with the West Bank

Egyptian government bans the Muslim Brotherhood. Latter responds by assassinating Prime Minister Muhammad Nuqrashi

1949   Hasan al-Banna assassinated by Egyptian security agents in retaliation for the murder of Nuqrashi

1952   Egyptian monarchy overthrown by Arab nationalist army officers led by Gamal 'Abd al-Nasser with support from the Muslim Brotherhood

1956   Nasser nationalizes the Suez Canal, provoking Anglo-French military intervention in secret collusion with Israel

1958   Pro-British Iraqi monarchy overthrown in bloody *coup d'état* masterminded by General 'Abd al-Karim Kassem

1963   Execution in Egypt of Sayyid Qutb, writer and Muslim Brotherhood's most militant ideologist

Iraq's President Kassem overthrown in coup by Ba'athist military officers under 'Abd al-Salam 'Arif

1965   Palestinian Liberation Organization (PLO) founded

1967 The Six Day War leaves the whole of Sinai peninsula, the West Bank (including the Old City of Jerusalem) and the Syrian Golan Heights under Israeli military control

Yasser'Arafat (Abu Amar), commander of al-Fatah, the largest guerrilla organization, becomes leader of the PLO

1968 President'Abdul Rahman'Arif (brother and successor to'Abdul Salam) overthrown by General Ahmad Hassan al-Bakr. Real power held by Saddam Hussein al-Takriti

1969 Pro-British Sanusi monarchy in Libya overthrown in Nasser-style *coup d'état* led by 27-year-old Colonel Mu'ammar Qadhafy

Organization of the Islamic Conference (OIC) established to promote Islamic solidarity and foster political, economic, social and cultural cooperation among Muslim states

1970 Hafez al-Asad, an air force general from the 'Alawi (Nusairi) minority takes power in Syria at the head of the Ba'ath party

Civil war in Jordan between the army and Palestinian guerrillas ('Black September')

Anwar Sadat succeeds to the Egyptian presidency following the death of 'Abd al-Nasser

1972 Bangladesh, formerly East Pakistan, wins independence with Indian army help

1973 October (Ramadan/Yom Kippur) War: Egypt establishes a bridgehead on the East Bank of the Suez Canal – the first major success of Arab arms against Israel

Organization of Petroleum Exporting Countries (OPEC) under leadership of Iran and Saudi Arabia imposes a four-fold increase in the price of crude oil, leading to massive 'petrodollar' surpluses for investment in industrialized economies and support for Islamist movements (as well as a world-wide economic recession)

1975 Lebanese civil war provoked in part by presence of militant Palestinian refugees and Israeli reprisals against them

1977 Beginning of negotiations between Egypt and Israel

Zia ul-Haqq, Pakistani general, assumes presidency and imposes martial law. Former President Zulfiqar'Ali Bhutto executed. Zia initiates Islamization programme

Death of 'Ali Shari'ati (b. 1933), Islamist philosopher, in Southampton, Britain

1978–9 Growing unrest in Iran against dictatorship of Shah Muhammad Reza Pahlavi

1979 Ayatollah Khomeini returns from exile in Europe to establish the Islamic Republic in Iran. Fifty-two US diplomats taken hostage and held for 444 days

Camp David peace accords between Egypt and Israel begin the peace process between Arabs and Israelis

Death of Abu'l 'Ala Maududi (b. 1909), Indo-Pakistani ideologue and founder of the Jamaati-i-Islami

President Zia ul Haqq introduces Hudood ordinance, prescribing Quranic penalties for certain categories of theft, sexual misconduct and drinking.

Soviet invasion of Afghanistan in support of ailing communist regime, as well as Western training and armaments for the *mujahidun* (holy warriors) creates a well-trained cadre of Islamist militants

1980–8   Iran–Iraq war, provoked by Iraqi attack on Iran, becomes the longest-lasting international conflict of the twentieth century, leading to the loss of at least half a million lives on the Iranian side and massive economic dislocation

1981   Assassination of Anwar al-Sadat by Islamist extremists

1982   Israeli invasion of Lebanon and expulsion of PLO to Tunisia

Up to 10,000 people killed in government reprisals after failed Muslim Brotherhood rebellion in Syrian city of Hama

1987   Beginning of the *intifada* – a massive, popular uprising of Palestinians against Israeli occupation, spearheaded by stone-throwing children

1988   Shaikh Ahmad Yasin, head of the Islamic Centre in Gaza and a member of the Muslim Brotherhood, founds Hamas, the Islamic Resistance Movement

Ayatollah Khomeini, Iran's religious leader, 'swallows poison' and accepts a cease-fire with Iraq

Death of President Zia ul-Haqq of Pakistan in suspicious air-crash

Publication of *The Satanic Verses* by British Muslim author Salman Rushdie

Muhammad Mahmud Taha, leader of the Republican Brotherhood and a reformer with Sufi leanings, hanged for 'apostasy'

1989   *Fatwa* pronounced by Ayatollah Khomeini against Rushdie in February, with million-dollar bounties for his killers, severely delays the prospect of détente between Iran and the West, despite the presence of pragmatists in the government. On his death in June Khomeini was succeeded as supreme religious leader by 'Ali Khamenei. 'Ali Akbar Hashemi Rafshanjani, widely regarded as a pragmatist, becomes President of the Islamic Republic

In Algeria the Islamic Salvation Front (FIS) wins 55 per cent of the vote in the regional elections

1990   Invasion of Kuwait by Iraqi leader Saddam Husain

1991   Operation Desert Storm, led by the United States with military support from Britian, France, Italy, Saudi Arabia, Egypt, Syria and Pakistan, expels Iraqi troops from Kuwait. Shi'ite revolt in Iraqi cities of Najaf and Karbala brutally suppressed

Disbanding of Soviet Union after failed anti-Gorbachev coup leads to independence for the former Soviet Republics of Central Asia (under the leadership of ex-members of the Soviet *nomenklatura*). In Tajikistan rivalry between the ex-communist leadership and Islamist opposition leads to a bitter and costly civil war

In Algeria the FIS wins 49 per cent of the vote in the first round of the general elections. The army intervenes to prevent an almost certain victory for the FIS in the second round, provoking an eight-year civil war said to have cost at least 70,000 lives

1992　Farag Foda, the prominent Egyptian humanist and writer, gunned down in Cairo

'No-fly zones' established in Northern and Southern Iraq to prevent Iraqi attacks on Kurdish and Shĭi populations. UN sanctions imposed on Iraq lead to significant hardship among vulnerable groups, especially children

1994　Cheb Hasni, a popular *rai* singer, murdered in France. Tahar Djaout, award-winning novelist and editor, shot outside his home in Algiers

1995　Bangladeshi author Taslima Nasreen publishes *Laja* (Shame) a novel which attacks communalism and in particular the treatment of the Hindu minority during the 1972 War of Independence. Banned for supposedly inciting unrest and 'misunderstanding among the communities', a price of £1,700 is put on her head and she flees the country

More than 7,000 Muslim massacred at Srebrenica in Bosnia after UN fails to protect enclave from Bosnian Serb attack

1996　Taliban movement based on *madrasa*-educated students in rural Afghanistan, capture Kabul. Their programme of pacification bears harshly on women and minorities

1997　More than 60 European tourists, including several Britons, massacred near Luxor by Islamists

Muhammad Khatami, former minister of culture, elected President of Iran in an unexpected landslide victory

1998　Taliban fighters murder between two and five thousand members of the Shĭite Hazara community after the capture of Mazar-e Sharif

1999　In Algeria 'Abdul 'Aziz Bouteflika, former foreign minister, elected President on a programme of reconciliation

Pro-democracy demonstrations in Iran suppressed by police and street gangs under conservative control

NATO bombing campaign forces Serbs to relinquish Kosovo, reversing 'ethnic cleansing' of mainly Muslim Albanians

Russia bombs Chechnya on pretext of suppressing 'Islamic terrorism'

2000　(February) Russians occupy Grozni, the capital of Chechnya

In Pakistan General Pervez Musharrat overthrows democratically elected government of Nawaz Sharif

Index